THE MOZI

The Mozi

A Complete Translation

Translated and Annotated by

Ian Johnston

Columbia University Press   New York

ISBN: The Chinese University Press 978–962–996–270–8

Published for North America, Canada, Mexico and Latin America by:
   Columbia University Press
   Publishers Since 1893
   New York   Chichester, West Sussex

Published for the rest of the world by:
   The Chinese University Press
   The Chinese University of Hong Kong
   Sha Tin, N.T., Hong Kong
   Fax: +852 2603 6692
        +852 2603 7355
   E-mail: cup@cuhk.edu.hk
   Web site: www.chineseupress.com·

Library of Congress Cataloging-in-Publication Data
Mo, Di, fl. 400 B.C.
   [Mozi. English]
   The Mozi: a complete translation / translated and annotated by Ian Johnston.
      p. cm.— (Translations from the Asian Classics)
   Includes bibliographical references and index.
   ISBN 978-0-231-15240-2 (cloth: alk. paper)
   I. Johnston, Ian, 1939– II. Title. III. Series.

   B128.M77E5 2010
   181'.115—dc22

                    2009042408

References to Internet Web sites (URLs) were accurate at the time of writing. Neither the author nor Columbia University Press is responsible for URLs that may have expired or changed since the manuscript was prepared.

c 10 9 8 7 6 5 4

To

王亞春

Teacher and Friend

Contents

Preface

Several factors have dissuaded translators from attempting a complete English version of the *Mozi*. These include a perception of the work as one of low literary value and rather uninteresting content, and of Mo Zi himself as a not particularly significant figure in early Chinese philosophy. There are also the recognised difficulties in two of the five sections of the work, those on "dialectics" and defence, due to textual degradation and problems of arrangement. A great deal of work has, however, been done on these chapters since Forke produced his almost complete German translation of the *Mozi* more than eighty years ago. Further, whilst the style of the core essays may be, to a degree, formulaic and repetitive, this is likely to have been for a purpose and should not be allowed to deflect attention from what is, in fact, a content of undoubted philosophical substance, and methods of presentation and argumentation which were quite novel in the context of the more common compilations of gnomic utterances and edifying anecdotes.

Fortunately things have changed in recent times. There is now an increasing awareness of how significant Mo Zi was as a philosopher, and how important the school of Mohism was in the dynamic of pre-Han philosophy. Also, among what might be called the second wave of Chinese studies on the *Mozi*, there was a move away from the focus of the first, text-critical wave to more content-oriented studies. There have been several fairly recent detailed studies, in both Chinese and English, of the two difficult sections referred to above. Also, scattered over the past eighty years, there have been three partial English translations, those of Mei (1929), Watson (1963), and Ivanhoe (2001). Details of these and other relevant works are given in the Introduction and in the Bibliography.

One might say, then, that circumstances were propitious for the attempt at a complete translation. In fact, I came to such an attempt via a somewhat circuitous route, beginning with an interest in the so-called School of Names (Mingjia 名家) and then moving on to a consideration of the interaction between the prominent members of this school, particularly

Hui Shi and Gongsun Long, and the Later Mohists. It soon became clear that a proper understanding of the Later Mohists was dependent upon a detailed knowledge of the "core" doctrines of the earlier Mohists. The attempt to achieve this consolidated my own recognition of the intrinsic interest of Mohist philosophy and the importance of Mohism as a school, and has resulted in the present work.

Having decided to go ahead with a translation of the complete work, the next step was to decide on a format, particularly with respect to the inclusion of the Chinese text. This presented something of a problem given that I foresaw at least two distinct groups of potential readers. First, there would be those whose interest lay solely in the philosophical content. For such people the Chinese text might be seen as an unnecessary component, making the work unduly long and possibly acting as a diversion. Footnotes relating largely to textual issues would compound the problem. Second, there would be those interested in the work as an example of early Chinese philosophical literature and who were proficient in both languages. This group might also be interested in how the translation was arrived at, and the areas of particular difficulty, both textual and interpretative. I decided on a compromise in an effort to satisfy both groups. Therefore the full Chinese text is included but hopefully set out in such a way that the English translation can be conveniently read without reference to the Chinese. Also, the footnotes have been kept brief with reference being made to sources which provide more detailed information on the whys and wherefores of a particular textual emendation or interpretation. An exception is made in the two difficult sections referred to previously where a commentary has been added. In the "dialectical" chapters especially, this could be useful to both groups of readers insofar as interpretative issues are considered as well as textual problems.

Of course, in a work such as this, there are inevitably compromises and shortcomings, although my hope is that, as a result of multiple revisions, particularly those giving attention to the very helpful comments and criticisms of the several readers from The Chinese University Press of Hong Kong and Columbia University Press, most of the shortcomings, at least, have been eliminated. Some of the compromises do, however, remain, dictated for the most part by a perceived need to keep the work within reasonable limits of length. First, there is a relative lack of attention to modern studies of a secondary nature, both Chinese and non-Chinese. In my view, to do justice to such scholarship would require considerable expansion of what is already a very long work and in some respects would detract from the clear presentation of the original work. In fact, I think Mei's solution was the best one, providing a volume of translation with a fairly brief introduction and a separate volume devoted to Mohist thought more generally. However, I have, in the Introduction, aimed to refer to at least the more important secondary studies but their treatment is far from exhaustive. Second, there is the issue of the footnotes, which I have endeavoured to restrict as far as possible whilst still attempting to achieve the two aims of providing information about people, places, and other works being referred to, and considering textual emendations and variations in interpretation by different commentators. As one reader pointed out with respect to the latter, more attention could have been given to the reasons why a particular emendation or interpretation was chosen over other alternatives. Attention to such matters would, I think, have led to an "overload" of footnotes. The compromise has been to give references to commentaries in which the particular issue is discussed in greater detail. Third, I would have liked to retain the commentary which I originally had in the "core" doctrines section which was a place where analytical studies could be referred to. Again, constraints of space resulted in this being excised despite the encouragement of some readers to retain it. Lastly, in this brief *mea culpa* section, I should say I regret the lack of references to Japanese literature. For several reasons, which I shall not elaborate on here, they have not been included.

Something should also be said about certain important and recurring terms, some of which I have rendered in ways which modern scholars might find exceptionable. Many of the terminological issues have been addressed, albeit briefly, either in the Introduction or the notes and comments, but I shall add a few remarks here. For the terms *yi* 義 and *ren* 仁 I have retained the rather old-fashioned English equivalents of "righteousness" and "benevolence" (Hansen speaks of the former as prudish and religious), although in certain places *yi* is rendered differently where the context clearly demands it. I accept that there are objections to these renderings but remain unconvinced that any of the proposed alternatives are unequivocally better. In addition, if the old terms are retained, there should be no doubt about which Chinese terms are being translated. Two other important pairs, which may also be seen as a pair of pairs, are *ai* 愛/*wu* 惡 and *li* 利/*hai* 害. I have retained "love" for the first despite the arguments for a less romantic and emotionally charged term for *ai*, and something that does not carry the Confucian pejorative connotations of "benefit" for *li* (for example, Hansen's "utility"). *Hou* 厚

and *bo* 薄 presented some difficulty, particularly in the "Daqu" (*Mozi* 44). I have opted for "thick" and "thin" based on the suggestion of one of the readers, these being terms which now see some use in philosophical writing in English, but there are many places where a different rendering is called for, especially when *hou* is used alone. There are also difficulties with *jian* 兼 and *bie* 別. For reasons which are considered elsewhere, I have stayed with "universal" for the former and "partial" or "discriminatory" for the latter. One of the values of the "dialectical" chapters is that these and other terms are defined in them or form part of other definitions or explanations.

Clearly no work of this sort comes to completion without considerable assistance from a number of people. It gives me particular pleasure to acknowledge such help, both general with respect to my Chinese studies over the past four decades and specific in relation to this work. In the first group I must start with Wang Yachun 王亞春, to whom this book is dedicated and who was my teacher for more than twenty years before I moved from Sydney to my present rather remote abode in 1999. It was she who gave me my first copies of the *Mozi* which she brought back from Beijing after we had enjoyed several discussions on the importance of the philosopher. It is a great regret that I did not have her continuing help and instruction as I was preparing the translation. For my formal teaching I am indebted to Phillip Lee, now at the University of New South Wales, and to the late A. R. Davis and the members of his excellent department at Sydney University where I was a part-time student for over a decade. For me the Department of Oriental Studies (later East Asian Studies) represented everything that was good about an academic department and I shall always be very appreciative of the teaching I received there and the opportunity to slip away intermittently from my very demanding "other life" and immerse myself in the somewhat esoteric world of ancient Chinese literature. Two members of the department whom I would like to mention specifically are the late Agnes Stefanowska and Mabel Lee, the former particularly in that, amongst other things, she supervised my Ph.D. thesis on Gu Yanwu who was, of course, a fundamental influence on the Qing scholars who "resuscitated" the *Mozi* and began the series of studies which have made the present translation possible. More recently, I owe a considerable debt of gratitude to Geoffrey Lloyd for his criticism and encouragement with regard to my studies of the Later Mohists and who, with Christopher Cullen and Susan Bennett, organised a most stimulating and productive (at least for me!) workshop on my translations of the "dialectical chapters" and related Mingjia texts at the Needham Research Institute in the summer of 2002. I am also grateful to Chung-ying Cheng and Gu Linyu of the *Journal of Chinese Philosophy* for publishing some of this material and for their helpful suggestions in preparing the manuscripts. Mention has already been made of the readers from the two presses, The Chinese University Press of Hong Kong and Columbia University Press, who made numerous suggestions and criticisms, attention to which has greatly improved the work. They, of course, remain anonymous but not so the actual editors, Steven Luk, Tse Wai-keung, and Jennifer Crewe to whom I am especially grateful. In working on the defence chapters I am grateful for the help of Ian McGaw, Christa Springer, and Maria Flutsch in comparing Forke's translation of this difficult material with my own. Further thanks are given to Maria for her collaboration in preparing a bibliography of Japanese materials which, for a number of reasons, was not used. Finally, I would like to thank two friends, Barry Hill and Susan Collis, who have contributed very greatly to the finished work. Neither reads Chinese so their assurances that the inclusion of the Chinese text did not detract from the value of the work to someone wishing to read the translation only has given me much (and much needed) encouragement. The former's comments on literary issues have been especially valuable whilst the same may be said for the latter's views on philosophical matters, although in view of her position, she has been unable to avoid constant exposure to my own engagement with this challenging text and has, in fact, made countless valuable criticisms and suggestions at all stages of what has been a very protracted project.

To all these people, and to others unnamed, go my heartfelt thanks. My hope is that despite its deficiencies, recognised and as yet unrecognised, this work will prove to be of interest and value both to scholars of Chinese and to students of philosophy more generally; and will play some part in establishing Master Mo Zi and the school he engendered in their proper place of prominence in early Chinese philosophy and Chinese intellectual history.

Ian Johnston
Cloudy Bay

Introduction

The *Mozi* is unquestionably one of the most important books in the history of Chinese philosophy. It embodied the first and, at least in the pre-Han period, the most serious challenge to the increasing dominance of Confucianism. It did this by presenting a coherent body of doctrine articulated in a strikingly systematic way. This body of doctrine, contained in the curious triadic arrangement of what might be called the "core" chapters of the work (Chapters 8–38), purportedly offers a definitive cure for the significant social ills of the time. But more than that, the ideas advanced have an enduring relevance going beyond the confines of a particular culture or epoch. Apart from these "core" chapters, there are two specialised sections widely thought to be later than the "core" chapters in composition, which are of critical importance to an understanding of Mohism — the so-called "dialectical" chapters (Chapters 40–45) and the chapters on the defence of cities (Chapters 52–71). The "dialectical" chapters cover a remarkable range of topics including not only logic and disputation, but language more generally, ethics, epistemology and science. The chapters on defence describe a wide variety of specific techniques as well as general principles pertaining to the organisation of the defence of a city. These chapters are a most valuable source of information on this topic at a time when skill in warfare was particularly important and when the Mohists were justly renowned for their abilities in such matters. The two other sections of the work are the epitomes (Chapters 1–7), as Durrant has called them, which touch on various issues of Mohist doctrine in a brief and unsystematic way, and the dialogues (Chapters 46–50) which deal not only with doctrinal issues, but also with aspects of the Mohist engagement in defence as well as their opposition to Confucianism. Not only are these dialogues presented in a lively and engaging fashion, but they are also one of the few sources of historical information on Master Mo and the Mohist movement as a whole.

   Despite this richness of content, the *Mozi* has been a sadly neglected work, both in China itself over two millennia, and in the West since early

Chinese philosophy first became a subject of significant interest in the 19th century. In China, then, there was no tradition of study and commentary, no revivifying Neo-Mohism, and very poor preservation of the text itself, at least until pioneering efforts of rediscovery by men such as Bi Yuan and the Wangs, father and son, beginning in the 18th century. In the West, the neglect of the *Mozi* has been in part a reflection of the Chinese neglect, in part due to the difficulties of the time-ravaged text, and in part due to a false perception of the work as pedestrian and devoid of style in composition and lacking in interest in regard to content. Whilst there have been numerous translations and studies of other major philosophical works from the same period, there has never been a complete translation of the *Mozi* into any Western language, although Forke's 1922 German translation comes close, omitting only some parts of the chapters on defence. Other partial translations and some of the matters alluded to are discussed further in Section VII below.

The primary purpose of the present work is to redress this neglect by providing an English translation of the complete work with accompanying Chinese text, together with notes and commentary of sufficient detail to enable the translation to be read in conjunction with the Chinese text — that is, to bring as much clarity as possible to passages of textual and interpretative uncertainty and to indicate the different views on these passages. Such commentary is particularly relevant in the two specialised areas of dialectics and defence where textual issues and variations in interpretation are especially intrusive. In this brief introduction, before returning to issues relating to the book and the doctrines contained therein, an outline will be given of what is thought to be known about Mo Zi himself and the school he engendered.

I. Mo Zi — The Man

His significance notwithstanding,[1] Master Mo Zi, as he is recurringly referred to in the work bearing his name, remains a shadowy and

---

1. Mo Zi's importance is becoming increasingly recognised amongst Western scholars. For example, Hansen (1992), in the opening to his chapter on Mo Zi, writes: "He is *the most important* philosopher in the early half of the classical period. Analysing his thought carefully gives us a more accurate view of the direction of philosophical thought in China.... Writing argumentative essays and engaging in philosophical reflection both start with Mo Zi. He distinguishes between traditional mores and morality proper. He

mysterious figure. In fact, the most basic details of his life are shrouded in uncertainty. Even the usual historical sources are disappointing, as exemplified by the extremely brief and rather offhand piece about him in the *Shi Ji* 史記,[2] particularly when compared with the whole or part chapters devoted to other philosophers of the period. I shall summarise what is known, or thought to be known, about such matters as when and where he was born, his family and social background, his education, how he spent his life, and when and where he died. It should be stressed that on all aspects there is uncertainty. Indeed, there is even uncertainty and contention about his name. The most common view on this is that Mo was his family name and Di his given name, Zi being his title as "Master" or "Philosopher". Other views are that Mo was a descriptive term applied either to the individual or to the school, and refers to either a countenance blackened by the sun or the colour of a carpenter's string, such things as might characterise an artisan, or to the branding or tattooing suffered by convicts.[3]

Returning to the matters listed, the consensus is that, like Confucius, he was a native of the state of Lu. The main support for this view comes from internal evidence provided by the *Mozi* itself. In fact, Zhang Chunyi, in examining his reported travels to other states, concludes that his base, at least, was in Lu. Evidence for the other two possible states of origin (Song and Chu) is, by comparison, very flimsy. All that can be said is that he seems to have spent some time in both and probably held office in the former.

There is also no clear and direct evidence from which to determine the dates of his birth and death. Estimates are based, first, on "internal"

---

formulates a unique version of utilitarianism and argues for that theory and for an explicit political theory. He offers an interesting version of a state of nature justification for social organization. He works out a coherent pragmatic epistemology and both an operational and a historical theory of language. *And* he gives arguments!" (p. 95, italics are the author's).

2. This occurs at the end of *Shi Ji* 74 and reads: "蓋墨翟，宋之大夫，善守禦，為節用。或曰並孔子時，或曰在其後。" — "Regarding Mo Di, he was a great officer of Song. He was skilled in defensive measures and practised moderation in use. Some say he lived at the same time as Confucius, some say he was later." (*Shi Ji* 74, vol. 7, p. 2350). One of the most detailed and informative statements on Mo Zi and Mohism in early writings is that in the *Zhuangzi* 33 which is reproduced in full in Section VI of this introduction.

3. On this, see Hsiao (1979), note 1, p. 214.

evidence from the *Mozi*, predominantly the dialogue chapters (46–50), in which he is reported to have had dealings with several historical figures, most notably the rulers of states for whom dates are relatively well established. Secondly, there is evidence from other works; those in which he is mentioned and those in which he is not mentioned. Both sources of evidence are open to doubt, depending, in the first instance, on the reliability of the report of the supposed meeting, and, in the second instance, on the vagaries of reference in early Chinese works. There is, however, broad agreement that his life occupied the major part of the 5th century BC. Several different specific dates have been given by scholars as follows: 468–376 (Sun Yirang); 500/490–425/416 (Hu Shi); 479–381 (Qian Mu); 473–390 (Feng Youlan); 490–403 (Fang Shouchu). The variation is obviously quite slight and all agree in taking him to have lived a long life. One thing that does seem clear is his relationship to the major exponents of Confucianism. He must have lived after Confucius himself (551–479 BC) since much of his reported teaching concerns Confucian doctrines, or at least their later elaborations. And he must have lived prior to Mencius (372–289 BC) who clearly articulated his opposition to Mo Zi. On the same grounds, he seems to have been prior to Xun Qing who also expresses the Ru (Confucian) opposition to Mohism. It is, however, possible that Mo Zi's life may have overlapped to some extent with either Confucius (*vide* the *Shi Ji*) or Mencius.

On Mo Zi's background and education there is, once again, an unfortunate paucity of definite information. There is the widespread view, certainly in the West, that he came from the artisan class, but the actual evidence for this is slight as enumerated below:

1. There is the questionable evidence of his name considered above.
2. There is his documented involvement with technical matters and the making of devices, including those for the defence of cities. This alone does not, however, establish that his background was that of an artisan.
3. There is the oft referred-to rejection by King Hui of Chu,[4] taken to be on the basis of his low social standing.
4. There is the supposed pedestrian and unadorned nature of the writing in the *Mozi*, that is, the lack of the style that would

---

4. See *Mozi* 47.3.

distinguish a man of the educated class. Thus, A. C. Graham writes: "The notoriously graceless style of early Mohist writing, ponderous, humourless, repetitive, suggests the solemn self-educated man who writes only for practical purposes and has no opportunity to polish his style as an adviser to princes."[5]

Against these points must be set two important facts. First, whatever may be said about the literary style of the *Mozi* as a work, Master Mo himself appears to have been conversant with Confucian doctrines and with the other significant literature available at the time (e.g. the "Five Classics") if we can accept the reports of how he presented and defended his arguments in the "core" doctrines chapters particularly. This must betoken a considerable level of education. Second, he was almost certainly given high office by at least one ruler and does appear to have followed the life of an itinerant scholar characteristic of members of the educated class at that time. With respect to his supposed origins from the artisan class, there is speculation that "... he was a craftsman, skilled in the use of tools."[6] Some have ventured more specific suggestions — for example, that he was a wheelwright, or a carpenter and carriage-maker (Fang Shouchu). Feng Youlan describes him as a craftsman who rose to the rank of *shi* (officer, knight-errant). Whether he actually practised a trade, and if so what trade, are in fact unknown. There is some evidence that he acted as an adviser to rulers — the most notable example is his role in Song — and also that he travelled to Chu, presumably for the purpose of proselytising. There is also the internal evidence of the *Mozi* that he was engaged in placing disciples in official positions.[7]

On how Master Mo actually spent his life, there is again very little information. Hsiao writes: "As for the events of his life, we know next to nothing, because of the lack of documentary evidence."[8] What little is known is gleaned in major part from the dialogue chapters of the *Mozi* itself and in minor part from the few reports in other early works which give any attention to his activities as opposed to his teachings. Given the prominence of the school, the most plausible account of his life is that it

---

5. Graham (1989), p. 34.
6. Hsiao (1979), p. 215.
7. The somewhat different positions taken on Mo Zi's origins in the excerpts from the *Han Feizi* and the *Zhuangzi* given below should also be noted.
8. Hsiao (1979), p. 215.

was passed in travelling and teaching, with perhaps occasional periods in some official position in a particular state. There is also the suggestion that he spent some time in prison, perhaps reflecting the vagaries of the life of the itinerant adviser dispensing political or military advice in such turbulent times. About the end of his life, nothing is known. When, where, and how he died all remain shrouded in mystery.

II. The Mohist School

There does seem to be general agreement that Confucianism and Mohism were the two main — and to a significant degree contending — schools during the two centuries prior to the Qin hegemony. On this point, Feng Youlan (Fung Yu-lan) begins his account of Master Mo and his school as follows: "Mo Zi is one of the most important figures in Chinese history, a man whose name was constantly linked with that of Confucius from the Warring States period down to the beginning of the Han dynasty."[9] What evidence we have also suggests that the followers of Master Mo were a relatively well-organised sect or school with an established leader or leaders and an orderly transmission of authority. There is also evidence that there were separate schools of Mohism, but this comes from just two short passages in pre-Han writings. It can be seen also that these two passages, quoted below, are not entirely consistent in what they say. The first, from the *Zhuangzi*,[10] is as follows:

> The disciples of Hsiang-li Ch'in, the followers of Wu Hou, and the Mohists of the south such as K'u Huo, Chi Ch'ih, Teng Ling-tzu, and their like all recite the Mohist canon, and yet they quarrel and disagree in their interpretation, calling each other "Mohist factionalists". In their discussions of hard and white, difference and sameness; in their disquisitions on the incompatibility of odd and even they exchange volleys of refutation. They regard the Grand Master of their sect as a sage, each sect trying to make its Grand Master the recognized head of the school in hopes that his authority will be acknowledged by later ages, but down to the present the dispute remains unresolved.

9. Fung Yu-lan (1952), p. 76.
10. *Zhuangzi* 33, translation after Watson (1968), pp. 366–367. For the original text see Guo (1961), vol. 4, p. 1079.

The second excerpt, from the *Han Feizi*,[11] reads:

> Thus, since the death of its founder, the Confucian school has split into eight factions, and the Mohist school into three. Their doctrines and practices are different or even contradictory, yet each claims to represent the true teaching of Confucius and Mo Zi. But since we cannot call Confucius and Mo Zi back to life, who is to decide which of the present versions of the doctrine is the right one?

A number of modern scholars, following particularly Yu Yue, have attempted to link the supposed separate schools to specific components of Mohist doctrine as contained in the *Mozi*. But such attempts must be viewed with circumspection given the lack of any detailed evidence about the schools — how separate they actually were and whether whatever separation did exist was based on doctrinal disparity or merely contingent factors such as geography or the effectiveness of a particular leader in attracting followers. The main evidence for doctrinal differences as the foundation of the separation of the schools comes from the passage in the *Zhuangzi* quoted above. Two issues in relation to this are, firstly, what the "canons" were, and, secondly, that the topics mentioned in the passage are only to be found in the "dialectical" or "logic" chapters and not in the "core" doctrines chapters. On the first point, there are several distinct views advanced by noted students of the *Mozi* as below:

1. That the "canons" are the "dialectical" chapters (*Mozi* 40–45) in their entirety — Sun Yirang.
2. That the "canons" are only the two *Jing* of the "dialectical" chapters (*Mozi* 40, 42) — Liang Qichao.
3. That the "canons" are the "core" doctrine chapters (*Mozi* 8–38) — Hu Shi.

That the specific topics mentioned in the *Zhuangzi* do not appear in the "core" doctrines chapters undoubtedly presents problems for those who take the third position. Despite the paucity of hard evidence, several theories about the apparent division into schools have been advanced.

First, there is the theory that the three components of each of the triads of "core" doctrines represent the three putative schools. This view is most forcibly advanced by Graham in a short monograph published in 1985. His

---

11. *Han Feizi* 19.2 (Fu & Lai [1997], p. 734).

theory is based on detailed textual analysis and involves some textual re-arrangement with regard to the sequence of chapters in certain triads. In short, he postulates three groups of chapters which he terms the H, Y, and J series. The H series he takes to be addressed to princes and ministers of state, the Y series to fellow thinkers, and the J series to be the work of the Southern Mohists and addressed to both audiences. Graham writes: "The Mohism of Y may be the pure doctrine diluted by H out of political expediency, but it may just as well be a pushing of Mohist principles to their logical conclusion by later extremists who have lost hope of winning political influence."[12]

Interesting though this and similar speculations may be, they must be viewed against the background of relative doctrinal uniformity of the components of the triads and the absence within any triad of evidence of fundamental doctrinal dispute. With respect to each of the triads of the ten "core" doctrines, the basic concept being presented (e.g. universal love, condemnation of offensive warfare, rejection of Fate) is the same, although the arguments adduced to support the central thesis may vary within a triad, as may the emphasis.

A second theoretical possibility, raised for example by Mei, is that the putative three schools were divided by their focus on the "core" doctrines, on the issues of the "dialectical" chapters, and on defensive military strategies respectively. There is, however, no actual evidence to support this view. Moreover, the "dialectical" or "logic" chapters are clearly in part directed at providing supporting arguments for points of possible contention in the "core" doctrines which may have come under close scrutiny as a result of the deliberations of the School of Names in particular.

Another issue is who the followers of Mohism actually were — that is, who they were individually, what range of social backgrounds they came from, and how they organised themselves into a cohesive group. As with other aspects of Mohism, it is very difficult to get any significant information on these matters. In fact, the names are the most easily discovered, both from the *Mozi* itself and from other works. Sun Yirang has compiled a list with a moderate amount of detail which is reproduced in summarising tabular form by Mei.[13] In the latter's tabulation, 36 definite

---

12. Graham (1985), p. 28.
13. Sun Yirang's list is found in vol. 15 of Yan Lingfeng (1975), pp. 989–1017. For Mei's list see Mei (1934), pp. 174–175.

and 3 possible Mohists are listed, divided into disciples (19), Neo-Mohists (9), Elder Masters (4), and "Miscellaneous Mohists" (4). Forke also provides a list, divided more simply into disciples and Later Mohists, comprising 34 names, all of which appear on the other lists.[14] In broad terms, the references to these men take one of four forms: (i) Engaged in debate with Mo Zi. (ii) Taking up official positions organised by Mo Zi. (iii) Involved in defensive measures. (iv) Identified as Mohists in other works — for example, Yi Zhi in the *Mencius*. Of course, there is overlap. There is also disappointingly little information on them as individuals, as mentioned above.

On the question of background, Graham suggests that we should think of the Mohist movement "… as a confluence of merchants, craftsmen and déclassé nobles, briefly emerging as a power in the cities as the feudal order disintegrates, but soon to be thrust back by the new bureaucratized Empire into the station which it has pleased Heaven to decree for them."[15] However, just as is the case with Mo Zi's own background, there is little in the way of solid evidence to support any particular viewpoint. In reality, we know next to nothing about the type of men who were attracted to, and active in, the Mohist movement over the two centuries or so of its flourishing.

In summary, then, it seems reasonable to regard Mohism as a well-defined movement continuing after Mo Zi's own death into the early part of the Western Han period. It seems also to have been a movement which attracted loyal adherents organised into a relatively rigid hierarchical structure, and to have constituted the main opposition to Confucianism during these years. The details of how the Mohists were divided into separate schools and what basis underlay any such division are few and insubstantial. That Mohism did not survive as a movement or school beyond the early part of the Western Han is well attested. Why this was so will be considered further below.

III. *Mozi* — The Book

There are three important aspects to be considered in relation to the book: (i) The authorship of the text. (ii) The history of the text. (iii) The structure of the work as it is presently available.

---

14. See Forke (1922), pp. 76–81.
15. See Graham (1978), p. 10.

First, on authorship, a current view is that summarised by Fraser as follows: "... the *Mozi* is not a single composition or work, in the modern sense, but an anthology of diverse writings probably composed at different times by different writers or editors. No part of the anthology purports to be from the hand of Mo Di himself."[16] Regrettably, no specific individuals can be identified as contributors to the work which must, then, be accepted as a composite text compiled by an unknown number of anonymous authors and editors over a period of time extending from the later part of the 5th century BC to the early part of the 3rd century BC, or possibly even later in the case of some parts of the defence chapters.

Second, on the history of the text, of particular value are the writings of Sun Yirang and Wu Yujiang in Chinese, and the work of Durrant in English which takes into account Japanese studies.[17] What can be said at the outset is that there is broad agreement amongst scholars, Chinese, Japanese and Western, that what we now have is a substantial part of a genuine pre-Han text, albeit one with textual difficulties which are of particular significance in certain sections. Thus Lowe, in his recent study, states: "In the preceding outline of the history of the MT (i.e. *Mozi*) text, we have seen that a collection of very similar texts all titled *Mozi* has been passed on from the Han dynasty to the present without, so far as we can tell, any break in the continuity of the transmission."[18] If we look at the sequence in a little more detail, the first record of the work is, as with many pre-Han texts, in the *Han Shu* 漢書, "Yiwen zhi" 藝文志 where it is described as a work in 71 *pian* 篇.[19] Ban Gu's statement is likely to be consistent with, and possibly dependent on, the records of Liu Xiang and Liu Xin.[20] The next known record is found in Gao You's commentary on the *Lü Shi Chunqiu* 呂氏春秋 (ca AD 210) which contains the following

16. See Fraser (2002). For a brief but informative general discussion of the authorship of pre-Han texts see Lau (1963), appendix 1, pp. 90–103.

17. The three works are as follows: Sun Yirang (1894), Wu Yujiang (1993), and Durrant (1975).

18. Lowe (1992), p. 55.

19. *Han Shu* 30, vol. 6, p. 1738.

20. See Durrant (1975), pp. 47–48.

statement: "Mo Zi, surnamed Di, was a man of Lu and wrote a book in 72 *pian*."[21] The view advanced by Sun Yirang (and widely accepted) is that the additional *pian* 篇 is the table of contents.

Subsequently, things became a little confusing with the introduction of *juan* 卷 in place of *pian* 篇, the work generally being spoken of as one of 15 (or 16 — the addition again being the table of contents) *juan*. Such references also include mention of an abridged version which is no longer available. What there is not, and this reflects the extent of the decline of interest in Mohist philosophy from the Qin period on, is any commentary on the work. All we have is a preface to a commentary by Lu Sheng on the "dialectical" chapters which is preserved in the *Jin Shu* 晉書 (ca AD 300) and a possible commentary to the three-volume abridged *Mozi* by Yue Tai which may have been pre-Tang.[22] It also appears that during these centuries — i.e. from Han to Song — 18 of the original 71 *pian* were lost. The most common view on this, and it should be stressed that the evidence is relatively scanty, is that 10 chapters were lost prior to Song and 8 chapters thereafter. Certainly the Ming editions, which will be considered further below, have only 53 chapters (*pian*) although these are arranged in 15 sections (*juan*) as in modern editions. There are, however, 8 chapters present in title only. When, precisely, the text for these chapters was lost is not clear, just as it is not clear when the other 10 chapters, now lacking titles, were lost.

The earliest surviving texts are the four from the Ming dynasty. Two of these are still generally available as follows:

1. The Daoist Patrology (道藏 DZ) text dating from 1445 which is not only available in current editions of that work but also in Yan Lingfeng's 嚴靈峰 compilation of Mohist writing.[23]
2. The Tang Yaochen 唐堯臣 text which dates from 1554 and is preserved in the *Sibu Congkan* 四部叢刊 (SBCK) and in Yan Lingfeng's compilation.

---

21. Cited by Durrant (1975), p. 48.
22. Lu Sheng's preface is to be found in the *Jin Shu* 94, vol. 8, pp. 2433–2434. For discussion of the three-volume version see Durrant (1975), p. 55 and p. 57 et seq.
23. See Yan Lingfeng (1975).

The other two, rare texts are as follows:[24]

3. The Wu Kuan 吳寬 text
4. The Zhi Cheng 芝城 text

It is these texts, particularly the first two, that were used by Qing scholars in their rediscovery of, and detailed textual work on, the *Mozi*. All four texts were consulted by Wu Yujiang in the preparation of his outstanding "present-day" edition.

Turning to the Qing period, it is worth quoting Wang Niansun's words:[25]

Nevertheless, because this book has no corrected text, it contains deletions and errors and is difficult to read. Likewise, because there is no corrected text, ancient characters have not yet been changed and it can be put alongside the *Shuo Wen* for mutual verification.

These comments reflect the nature of the interest which such students of the *Mozi* had in the work. As proponents of the "evidential research" or *kaozheng xue* 考證學 movement, this interest was far more philological or linguistic than philosophical or historical. Nonetheless, the text was revised by a succession of notable scholars, resulting in the relatively reliable and accurate text which we have today. It is, I think, worth mentioning some of the major contributors individually.

(i) Bi Yuan 畢沅 (1730–1797) is the man to whom credit must go for the preparation of the first "modern" edition of the *Mozi* and so of the initiation of the resurgence of interest in the long-forgotten work. Lowe has accurately described it as "... a relatively reliable edition of the text that has served as the foundation for all later textual criticism."[26] While Bi Yuan's official career was marked by more than the usual vicissitudes of official life — and he was posthumously deprived of reputation and property on the grounds of alleged financial impropriety — his scholarly

---

24. See Lowe's (1992) comments on these two texts (pp. 52–53). The first is named after its compiler, the Ming scholar Wu Kuan (see Goodrich and Fang [1976], vol. 2, pp. 1487–1489) whilst the latter is named after the place of its printing in 1552.
25. The translation follows Durrant (1975) who also gives the original text (p. 46).
26. Lowe (1992), p. 54.

endeavours were significant and his help to young scholars noteworthy. His edition of the *Mozi* appeared in 1783 and was prepared with the help of Lu Wenchao 盧文弨 (1717–1796) and Sun Xingyan 孫星衍 (1753–1818), the latter for a time acting as his secretary.

(ii) Wang Niansun 王念孫 (1744–1832) is described by Knoblock as a man who "… had a profound grasp of etymology and phonetics because of his work on the *Guangya* 廣雅 dictionary and an encyclopaedic acquaintance with the major works of philosophy."[27] Like the other noted mid-Qing students of the *Mozi*, his interest was primarily in etymological, phonetic and linguistic issues. His *Mozi Zazhi* 墨子雜志 is included in Yan Lingfeng's *Mozi Jicheng* referred to above. It was part of his extensive textual study of various classics published as the *Dushu Zazhi* 讀書雜志 between 1812 and 1831.

(iii) Wang Yinzhi 王引之 (1766–1834) was one of Wang Niansun's sons and a noted scholar in his own right. He continued his father's work in philology and, in fact, collaborated directly with his father in part. Wang Yinzhi's two most notable works in the field were his *Jingyi Shuwen* 經義述聞, first printed in 1797, and his *Jingzhuan Shici* 經傳釋詞, printed in 1819. It is the former, which consists of annotations and emendations of various passages in twelve ancient texts, that is relevant here.

(iv) Yu Yue 俞樾 (1821–1907) was a scholar of wide-ranging interests and also a noted poet. In his official positions, his strong interest in education was well represented and he also became well-known in Japan. He published two works on early philosophy, primarily as a philologist and textual critic. These were his *Qunjing Pingyi* 群經平議 published in 1867 and his *Zhuzi Pingyi* 諸子平議 published in 1870. According to Tu Lien-che, the former is modelled after Wang Yinzhi's *Jingyi Shuwen* and the latter after Wang Niansun's *Dushu Zazhi*.[28]

(v) Sun Yirang 孫詒讓 (1848–1908) was one of the most prominent of late Qing scholars and a noted collector of rare books and manuscripts. It was after 1877, when his father was appointed Lieutenant-Governor at Nanjing, that he is thought to have begun his work on the *Mozi*. Three hundred copies of his annotated and emended text were published in 1894 with a revised and enlarged second edition following in 1907. Tu Lien-che writes: "He collated the very confused text of the *Mozi*, provided it with

---

27. Knoblock (1988–1994), vol. 1, p. 118.
28. Hummel (1970), p. 945.

interpretations from earlier scholars, and pointed out the inauthenticity of several chapters. The appendix consists of a biographical sketch of Mo Di, a chronological chart of his life, an account of his school and his disciples, a study of statements attributed to him by other authors, references to his school in ancient literature, and a bibliography of the school."[29] All in all, this is an absolutely invaluable work for students of the *Mozi*. Also of value are Sun's study notes, published as *Zhayi* 札迻 in 1894. Much of his later life was devoted to education in his local area. In 1905, he was offered the Chair of Classics at the newly-established Yanjing (Peking) University, but declined.

Apart from these scholars and their studies, there were several editions of the complete or partial text published during the last years of the 19th and early years of the 20th centuries. I shall simply list, in chronological order, the more complete editions published prior to Zhang Chunyi's 張純一 *Mozi Jijie* 墨子集解, first published in 1931, which I take to mark the start of the "present-day" publications. These were the editions by Su Shixue 蘇時學 (1864), Wang Shunan 王樹枏 with Wu Rulun 吳汝綸 (1888) and the latter alone in 1908, Wang Kaiyun 王闓運 (1905), Cao Yaoxiang 曹耀湘 (1907), Zhang Huiyan 張惠言 (1909), and Yin Tongyang 尹同陽 (1919).

Although the labours of these and other scholars were absolutely critical in bringing the *Mozi* back into some sort of focus, it would be erroneous to think that this represented more than a narrow scholarly interest. To put things into perspective, I shall include a quotation from Faber's preface to his translation of a distillation of Mohist thought from 1897.[30]

It is somewhat surprising that the doctrine of Micius (Mo Zi) has for centuries, so to speak, vanished in China. Mencius being promoted to the standard classics and everywhere committed to memory, his pernicious criticism naturally so worked on the masses of the Chinese that no one cares to look at such an arch-heretic who — according to Mencius — does not recognize a father. For this reason the works of Micius are very scarce. I sought for more than ten years in all China without finding a copy. Dr. Legge accidentally found a copy once with a peddler, which I had copied. This is the edition by Peh Yun (Bi

29. See Hummel (1975), p. 678.
30. Faber (1877), p. 4.

Yuan). There is a Japanese edition in 6 volumes, but without any explanation. In a large Taoist collection there are two editions of Micius with commentary, but they have never come under my observation. This collection is also very scarce. A complete copy was to be had some years ago in North China for 200 Taels.

Third, on the structure of the book, as indicated above, it seems probable that the presently available text is an accurate reflection of the original work as catalogued in the *Han Shu*, the only significant changes over the succeeding two millennia being the loss of 18 of the original 71 chapters leaving the 53 chapters of the present text, and the unfortunate but inevitable degradation of the text of such a neglected work. The 53 chapters (*pian* 篇) are arranged in 15 books (*juan* 卷) as indicated in Table 1 below.

Amplifying slightly the summary in the table, for Books 2–9, five of the ten "core" doctrines have a book to themselves whilst the three extant chapters on moderation *jie* 節 (in use and in funerals) are grouped together in Book 6, the single chapters "Percipient Ghosts" and "Against Music" are combined in Book 8, and Book 9 includes the three chapters "Against Fate" as well as the single chapter "Against the Confucians". In Book 11 the inclusion of the first dialogue ("Geng Zhu") with the two "dialectical" chapters ("Daqu" and "Xiaoqu") is somewhat anomalous. Finally, in the case of the defence chapters, the division is between Book 14 which

Table 1: The Arrangement of the *Mozi* into Books and Chapters

Books	Chapters	Content
1	1–7	Short essays, late in composition and of questionable authenticity
2–9	8–39	The triads of the 10 "core" doctrines (7 missing) plus 1 remaining (of 2) chapter "Against the Confucians"
10	40–43	The 2 Canons (經上，經下) and 2 Explanations (經説上，經説下)
11	44–46	The 2 "Choosings" (大取 and 小取) The first dialogue (耕柱)
12–13	47–50	The remaining 4 dialogues
14–15	52–71	The 11 extant defence chapters

contains the seven chapters on specific defensive measures and Book 15 which contains four chapters (68–71) of a more general nature which are quite possibly later additions.

With regard to "present-day" editions of the *Mozi*, the division into *juan* 卷 (books) is preserved by some editors (Wu Yujiang, Zhou Caizhu, and Qi Ruiduan), but not by others (Li Yushu, the *Mozi Baihua Jinyi*, Li Shenglong). What is generally accepted is the "functional" division into five sections based on subject matter, a division which may have originated with Liang Qichao and Hu Shi. This division, which to some degree cuts across the traditional division into *juan*, is as follows:

1. Epitomes[31]: Although these seven short texts form the opening section of the *Mozi* as it now stands, they are quite possibly the latest component in composition.[32] According to Durrant, they are "linguistically separate" from the remainder of the text.[33] In content they are something of a miscellany. Mei describes the first three as "utterly spurious" whilst Hu Shi suggests that the final four may comprise fragments of otherwise lost material.

2. Core Doctrines: Of the ten presumed triads embodying the statements of the fundamental doctrines of Mohism, six are complete and four are incomplete, missing one ("Moderation in Use") or two ("Moderation in Funerals", "Percipient Ghosts", "Condemning Music") members of the triad. The final chapter, "Against the Confucians", is supposedly one of two remaining from the original. It is clearly different in form and subject matter from the other chapters in this section. It might, in fact, be more appropriately linked with the Dialogues, or it might be considered as a summary of the anti-Confucian position expressed in the preceding chapters of the section. However, not all the stated doctrines are in opposition to Confucian views. The division into triads, already considered in relation to division of Mohism into schools (Section II above), has given rise to a considerable amount of speculation. I do not intend to elaborate on this issue here except to say that there are several distinct points of view. One is that there

---

31. This is Durrant's term as mentioned above and is adopted by Lowe (1992), p. 56. It is probably as good a collective term as any.

32. See Lau (1963), pp. 98–99 and Fraser (2002).

33. Durrant (1975), p. 15.

are no substantial differences between the three members of each triad — one commentator has likened them to three sets of notes by different people taken at the same lecture.[34] Another, most completely developed by Graham and discussed above, is that they represent the positions of three different wings or schools of Mohism.[35] A third is that summarised by Fraser as follows: "… we can tentatively conclude that the three versions of each doctrinal essay is primarily chronological: In each triad, the 'upper' essay appears to be of earlier date than the 'middle' essay, which in turn seems earlier than the 'lower' one. In addition, in at least four triads and perhaps more, the division also relates to the essays' origin: The 'upper', 'middle', and 'lower' essays were probably composed by different writers or editors." A fourth possibility, raised by Maeder, is that not all the "core doctrines" were presented in triadic form — i.e. some of the "missing" chapters may never have actually existed.[36]

3. Dialectical chapters: These are also termed the Logic chapters. They are universally accepted as being very difficult due to textual degradation. As mentioned earlier, they cover, in the case of the Canons and Explanations (C & E), a wide range of material. Thus, Tan Jiefu in his rearrangement of the C & E on the basis of subject matter identifies 12 categories.[37] The "Daqu" (*Mozi* 44) presents particular problems but is noteworthy for containing arguments specifically in defence of the original Mohist doctrines. The "Xiaoqu" (*Mozi* 45) is the least damaged of the six chapters and constitutes a very clear statement of Mohist views on the processes

---

34. See Lowe (1992), p. 57.
35. See Graham (1985).
36. For those interested in the question of the triadic arrangement of these "core doctrine" chapters, the following are useful recent sources of information and expressions of different views: Maspero (1928), Fang Shouchu (1957), Durrant (1975, 1977–1978), Graham (1985), Lowe (1992), Maeder (1992), and Fraser (2002) from whose supplement to "Mohism" entitled "Significance and Chronology of the Triads" the above quotation is taken.
37. Tan Jiefu (1981) in his *Mojing Fenlei Yizhu* 墨經分類譯注. The categories are: 名言 (Dicta), 自然 (Nature), 數學 (Mathematics), 力學 (Mechanics), 光學 (Optics), 認識 (Cognition), 辯術 (Argumentation), 辯學 (Dialectics), 政法 (Government), 經濟 (Economics), 教學 (Education), and 倫理 (Ethics).

of reasoning and argument. There is widespread, but not universal agreement that these chapters are the work of "Later Mohists" for whom Hu Shi gives estimated dates of 325–250 BC. Two notable dissenters to this view are Bi Yuan and Liang Qichao. Western opinion on these chapters has been dominated by Graham's very detailed study published in 1978 although Geaney has recently challenged some aspects of Graham's analysis.[38] It must also be recognised that there is a number of specific and very detailed Chinese studies on these chapters and that the views expressed by the relevant scholars, both Chinese and Western, are far from uniform. I shall return briefly to this issue in the introductory comments to the translations of these chapters.

4. Dialogues: There are five of these which have been likened to the Confucian "Analects" by several commentators. They are of particular interest for two reasons. First, they provide a lively alternative statement of the "core" doctrines and are undoubtedly the most readable of the five sections of the *Mozi*. Second, they provide almost all the internal evidence on the details of Mo Zi's life. The most common view is that they are the work of the first generation of Mo Zi's disciples. Fraser has suggested that they date from the middle to late part of the 4th century BC.[39]

5. Defence chapters: These, of which eleven are extant, are like the dialectical chapters insofar as they are bedevilled by textual difficulties. They are also of uncertain origin. Particularly in the first seven of these chapters, the focus is on specific defence methods in keeping with Mo Zi's known interest in defensive techniques and his staunch opposition to offensive war whilst the final four chapters may be of later composition, as noted above. Further discussion of textual integrity, and specific studies, including suggestions for reconstruction, is deferred to the introduction to the translations of these chapters.

IV. The "Core" Doctrines

(i) Exalting Worthiness (*Shang Xian* 尚賢): All three essays in this opening triad are extant. The first begins with a listing of the three

---

38. See Geaney (1999).
39. Fraser (2002), p. 2.

important objectives for a state: to be rich, populous and well ordered. The fact that the opposite of all three obtain in his own time is attributed by Mo Zi to a failure to exalt or honour worthiness and to make use of ability. The principle is simple. If a state has many worthy and good officers (*xianliang zhishi* 賢良之士), men who are virtuous, discriminating in discussion and well-versed in principles, then its order will be "thick" (*hou* 厚) whereas, if it has few, then its order will be "thin" (*bo* 薄). So the basic requirement is to maximise the number of worthy and good officers and the way to do this is to enrich them, ennoble them, respect them, and praise them. It is no different in principle from finding and establishing good archers or charioteers. In this endeavour the key element is *yi* 義 (righteousness, rightness, right action). This is the fundamental criterion of worthiness. Such things as kinship, existing wealth and nobility and close association must be ignored. The authority for Mo Zi's position is provided by the ancient sage kings. For them it didn't matter what a person's background was — if he was worthy (righteous) he was advanced and if he was not worthy he was not advanced, regardless of other considerations. Well-known examples of the former are given. Once in place, such worthy men must be given appropriate rank, salary and executive power so the people will honour and respect them. Further, everyone should realise that nobody is permanently guaranteed high position and nobody is permanently condemned to lowliness. And, finally, the rewarding of worthiness does not represent a recognition of its inherent value — it is because such a policy works in practice.

The second essay starts from the conclusion of the first. Those responsible for ruling who desire stability must see to it that "exalting worthiness" is the foundation of government. It must always be the case that the noble and wise (i.e. the worthy) govern the foolish and base. The sage kings knew this, hence their focus on "exalting worthiness and utilising ability". And this worked in practice, avoiding factionalism and favouritism. Those who are worthy can be counted on to be diligent in the performance of their duties but their positions must be consolidated by the "three foundations" — rank, emolument, and executive power — which give them recognisable status and enable them to function effectively. Ability is also of critical importance and must be set alongside worthiness as a criterion for advancement. As is commonly the case, Mo Zi looks to the ancient sage kings for authority in these matters, providing examples of worthy people who were elevated, but this time adding examples of unworthy people who were punished from among the well-known examples of antiquity. Ultimately, however, Heaven is the model insofar as it doesn't discriminate between rich and poor, noble and base, far and near, and close and distant relatives. Finally, Mo Zi makes the point that the rulers in his own age, in trying to rule without virtue and righteousness, rely on intimidation and force, but this will never work. The basis of successful government must always be the exaltation of worthiness, a principle sanctioned by the ancient sage kings.

The relatively short third essay begins with the same opening statement of the objectives for a successful state as the first essay — to be rich, populous and well ordered — and the same method for achieving this is proposed. It is to establish an administration of loyal and trustworthy officers by rewarding and honouring the good ones and censuring and demoting the bad ones. This was the way of the sage kings. According to Mo Zi, the rulers of his own time pay lip service to the principle of "exalting worthiness" but don't practise it, which makes it clear, in his view, that they understand only small matters and not great matters. The principles they would effectively apply in finding good archers and charioteers, or butchers and tailors are ignored when it comes to finding men to govern. Instead, reliance is placed on existing wealth and nobility, kinship, and fine appearance. Once again, the examples of the ancient sage kings are brought forward, citing situations in which they promoted men solely on the basis of their worthiness. This is all documented in ancient writings, as is the way of worthiness itself: to use one's strength to help people, one's wealth to distribute to people, and one's understanding of the Way to teach people. The then current practice of advancing people on the grounds of kinship, existing wealth and nobility, and fine appearance meant that rewards went to those without merit and punishments were inflicted on those without fault. In addition, the ordinary people became lazy, undisciplined and self-serving. To bring about satisfactory government in their states, the rulers of the time would have to return to the ways of the ancient sage kings, a central component of which is the principle of "exalting worthiness". It is a principle of benefit to all levels, Heaven, ghosts and ordinary people, and is the very foundation of government.

So, although there might be some doubt about the most appropriate translation of the title, there can be no doubt about the central argument which is advanced with typical Mohist clarity. Exalting or valuing worthiness and utilising ability are the very foundations of government. That is, if the primary objective of the political and social administration is to bring about a well ordered and maximally prosperous society, which it patently is, then the administrative apparatus must be in the hands of those who are worthy and capable. What Mo Zi objects to is the employment of people on any other grounds — specifically, kinship, social position (signalled by pre-existing rank and nobility) or physical beauty. This is seen as a fundamental causal component of the perceived decay of social stability in the late Zhou.

Mo Zi offers a threefold support for his central argument which falls within the framework of his general criteria of validation. The three components are:

1. The argument from commonsense: This needs no elaboration.
2. The argument from analogy: This is put in very simple form. If someone wants a well made garment, then a skilled tailor must be utilised, and likewise for the work of a butcher. Obviously this is directed more to the utilisation of ability than to the valuing of worthiness.
3. The argument from historical precedent. Here he presents examples of those who have risen from humble backgrounds or unlikely circumstances to be instrumental in bringing about a well ordered state. In addition, examples of enlightened rulers who are prepared to make use of such people are adduced.

There are several important secondary considerations. The first concerns the meaning of *xian* 賢 and the criteria by which to judge it. Writing in regard to the usage in *Lun Yu* I.7, Legge says: "Written in full, it (*xian* 賢) is composed of the characters for a minister, loyal, and a precious shell. It conveys the ideas of talents and worth in the concrete, but it is not easy to render it uniformly by any one term of another language."[40] There is an overlap with virtue but this does not seem to be an entirely satisfactory rendering. In one statement, Mo Zi has his focus clearly on the diligent application to one's duties and their effective prosecution, laying himself open to Xun Zi's criticism as Hsiao points out.[41] Elsewhere, however, there is a clear identification with *yi* 義 (righteousness) as a basic criterion, although there are again issues of definition.

The second concerns the treatment of such people, that is, the recognition of their worthiness. Here Mo Zi is quite clear. They must be

---

40. Legge (1960), vol. 1, p. 141.
41. See Hsiao (1979), p. 254.

fittingly rewarded in terms of salary and rank, and their decrees must be implemented. This is not so much for the purpose of attracting those who are worthy to the administration, but to ensure that those being administered respect, fear and obey them. The third point concerns the reversibility of status once conferred. History is replete with examples of the corrupting effects of power and its appurtenances. Mo Zi's solution to this potential problem is that all appointments should be open to revocation. This must, in turn, depend on the supreme mundane ruler being and remaining a true judge of worthiness and ability, and someone who will be effective and decisive in dismissing those who no longer meet the criteria.

It is important to realise that this doctrine of Mo Zi's was by no means revolutionary — indeed, he himself was at pains to identify historical precedents. It was not, then, some novel form of class struggle. He was entirely content to maintain the existing hierarchical social structure. His aim was simply to facilitate upward and downward mobility at all levels of administration within it. In this, Mo Zi was not very distant from the evolving Confucian position. Li Shenglong, for example, has drawn attention to three quotations from the Confucian sequence as follows:[42]

1. *Lun Yu*: "Value worthiness, disregard beauty."
2. *Mencius*: "A prince advances the worthy because he has no alternative. But this will cause the lowly to overstep the honourable and the distant to overstep the [near] relatives, so can he be other than cautious?"
3. *Xunzi*: "Although they be the descendants of kings and dukes, or knights and grand officers, if they are incapable of devotedly observing the requirements of ritual and moral principles, they should be relegated to the position of commoners. Although they be the descendants of commoners, if they accumulate study and culture, rectify their character and conduct, and are capable of devotedly observing the requirements of ritual principles and justice, they should be brought to the ranks of prime minister, knight or grand officer."

---

42. Li Shenglong (1996), p. 8. The three references are, respectively, *Lun Yu* I.7, *Mencius* IB.7(3), and *Xunzi* 9.1. The translation of the first is not without difficulty. That of the last follows Knoblock (1988–1994), vol. 2, p. 94. Both *Xunzi* 9 and 12 in particular contain several examples of the similarities in the positions taken by Mo Zi and Xun Zi.

Thus it could be said that Confucius recognised the value of *xian* 賢. Mencius acknowledged that it should be identified and rewarded, albeit with some unease. Xun Zi embraced a position on the subject that was almost identical with that of Mo Zi, what difference there was lying in the precise criteria of "worthiness".

(ii) Exalting Unity (*Shang Tong* 尚同): As with the previous triad, there are issues with the translation of the title. Thus, Lowe writes: "There is some debate among Sinologists over precisely how *shang tong* (literally 'upwardly identifying') comes to mean 'identification with the superior' ..." In my view, the structure is similar to that of the previous title with *shang* 尚 being used in the sense of *chongshang* 崇尚 (to esteem, value) and *tong* 同 like *xian* 賢 being an abstract noun, i.e. "unity" or "uniformity". Again such issues are of little consequence insofar as the argument is entirely clear and very similar in the three components of the triad which are all extant. The key point is well summarised by Li Shenglong: "尚同的涵義，就是統一天下的是非標準，以便統一天下的行動。(The meaning of 'exalting unity' is, in fact, to unify the world's standards of right and wrong as a means of effectively bringing unity to the world's conduct.)"[43]

The first essay, which is the shortest, as is most commonly the case, begins with the characterisation of the "state of nature" existing in very ancient times — people were like birds and beasts, everyone for themselves, one person one principle, and contention everywhere. The world then was in disorder, lacking any effective rule. The solution for this obviously undesirable situation was for the most worthy and able man (*xian* 賢, *ke* 可) to be established as the Son of Heaven and for him to establish in turn an administrative hierarchy consisting of the Three Dukes, feudal lords, princes and government leaders. At each level, the person selected to be in charge should be the one most worthy and able, and should establish the standards of right and wrong at that level. Further, not only should there be unity of principles within each level but also across the levels with the ultimate mortal standard being the Son of Heaven and the ultimate standard overall, Heaven itself.

The second essay opens like the first with consideration of the "state of nature" without any unity of moral principles so there was only disorder and the absence of any mutual assistance. The characteristics of the man

---

43. Li Shenglong (1996), p. 8.

selected as the Son of Heaven to rectify this situation are more extensively
listed. He must be worthy and good, sagacious and wise, skilled in
discussion, and clever. But one such man alone is not enough, hence the
need for the hierarchy as outlined in the first essay to establish unity of
principles. At each level of the hierarchy, the man selected must be the
most benevolent and his *modus operandi* must be to institute rewards and
punishments based on the unified standards of right and wrong, good and
bad. In this essay, there is a more detailed statement about Heaven as the
ultimate standard including a recognition of Heaven's ability to bestow
rewards and inflict punishments in the form of natural disasters and
conditions favourable to agriculture and animal husbandry or otherwise.
Moreover, Heaven must be propitiated by timely and well conducted
sacrifices. The rest of the essay is taken up with a comparison of ancient
(that is, after the establishment of the hierarchical system) and modern
conditions, unfavourable to the latter. In the past, leaders established order
by promoting benefits and eliminating harms which resulted in making
states rich, populous and peaceful. In the present, when there is neglect of
unity of principles, leaders operate on the basis of nepotism whilst inferiors
are recalcitrant and prone to form cliques. The success of the ancient sage
kings was due to their selection of people who embraced "exalting unity"
and implemented unification of principles which they did through a system
of appropriate rewards and punishments based on the unified standards.
Ancient texts such as the *Odes* bear witness to this and help establish it as
the foundation of government.

The third essay begins by stating the basic objectives of government
— to work out what brings order to ordinary people and do it, and to work
out what brings disorder to ordinary people and avoid it. This can only be
done by understanding the *qing* 情 (feelings, conditions) of the people as
the basis for correctly applying rewards and punishments. The question
posed is how this is to be done. There is then mention of the "state of
nature" as in the other two essays and its characterisation as a time of
contention, before proposing the same solution: that is, the establishment
of a Son of Heaven with a hierarchy of leaders at the various levels beneath
him. The sequence is then considered in the order family, state, Son of
Heaven and Heaven, with a focus on the contrast between "love and
benefit" (*ai* 愛, *li* 利) and "hate and harm" (*wu* 惡, *hai* 害). The final step
is unity of principles with Heaven. Again, support for this concept is
derived from the authority of the ancient sage kings. This was not an idea
originating with Mo Zi but dates back to the exemplary rulers. In the final

statement, the point is made that there is no use establishing unity of principles if this is not based on a deep love for the people; without this it won't work.

In summary, then, the argument of all three essays is that for a well functioning society, there must be a unification of standards or morality brought about by establishing a bureaucratic hierarchy in the central kingdom with the Son of Heaven and the "Three Dukes" (*San Gong*) at the top. For distant, and presumably dependent, states, there should be the establishment of feudal lords and appropriate underlings. All selections for these posts are to be based on the criteria of *xian* 賢 and *ke* 可, the latter being understood as *neng* 能 — that is, on worthiness and ability. There is the idea of "conforming upward" (*xiangshang tongyi* 向上統一) in that the standard (*yi* 義) comes from above whereas the conforming comes from below.

What is being opposed here is a society in which there is a multiplicity of standards or viewpoints—in particular, ethical standards. Such a society would be *ipso facto* fragmented and would function badly. So, again, taking the overall objective of Mo Zi's programme as being the establishment of a stable, peaceful and well administered society, this objective is to be achieved by ensuring that there is a unity or uniformity of standards. Schwartz, among others, has drawn attention to the parallel with Hobbes, writing: "… Mo Zi's image of a 'state of nature' as a state of atomized individuals in all-out conflict with each other seems to lead, by a logic similar to that of Hobbes, to the notion that only by the concentration of an undivided authority or 'sovereignty' in one ruler can conflicts among individuals or even groups be overcome."[44]

When it comes to the actual means of ensuring such a unity of standards, Mo Zi describes a five-tier structure: village; district; state; Son of Heaven; Heaven. Within the lowest three levels, unity is to be maintained by a system of reporting notable examples of good or bad conduct to those in charge at that particular level. There is then

---

44. The passage from Hobbes which Schwartz (1985) quotes in relation to this is: "The only way to erect such a Common Power … is to conferre all their power and strength upon one man or upon one Assembly of men, that may reduce all their Wills by plurality of voices unto one Will." (note 19, p. 436) Schwartz is, of course, by no means the only person to draw a parallel between Mo Zi and Hobbes. For a specific study of this point see also Jenner (1982).

implementation of rewards or punishments accordingly, not only to encourage proper conduct but also to encourage reporting of deviations. Mo Zi is less convincing in marshalling his arguments in support of "exalting unity" than he is in the case of "exalting worthiness". The argument from common sense doesn't really apply here. Nor does the argument from analogy. He is forced to fall back on the argument from historical precedent, but even this is somewhat forced and less than persuasive.

One obvious difficulty with an arrangement of this sort involves the highest human level — the supreme ruler (Son of Heaven, emperor). Who selects him and who ensures that he maintains a conformity with the accepted standard? In Mo Zi's structure, this can only be Heaven. Heaven can manifest its displeasure through visitations of a harmful nature — floods, drought etc. — just as it can make known its approval by natural events of a beneficial nature. More difficult to understand, however, is how Heaven actually effects or influences the appointment of the right person in the first place. There have been some recent attempts to argue that the popular will, rather than the will of Heaven, was instrumental in establishing the Son of Heaven. Hsiao, in considering these arguments, writes: "If we abandon such fanciful hypotheses and confine ourselves to the overall character of Mo Zi's thought to draw our inference, that then will be that instituting a Son of Heaven must have expressed the will of Heaven, not that it was an act of popular selection."[45] There does, however, seem to be some place for feedback from below upward in Mo Zi's system.

Another problem in such a system, and one not specifically addressed by Mo Zi, is that there are inherent dangers in encouraging the reporting of good and bad actions and basing rewards and punishments on reports. Ideally, such reports must be without bias or self-interest on the part of those making them, and must be treated equitably and objectively by those receiving them. The dangers inherent in such a system are only too well demonstrated in China's recent history and are a significant danger in any totalitarian or quasi-totalitarian system. Whilst Mohism might fall short of totalitarianism, it is certainly a system in which power is concentrated in the hands of the leaders at the various levels.

---

45. See Hsiao (1979), pp. 241–242. The specific commentators mentioned who suggest that the people may have had a role in selection are Fang Shouchu 方授楚 and Yang Youjiong 楊幼炯.

Finally, as with the previous "core" doctrine, the divergence of Mohism from the two main, organised opposing philosophies — Confucianism and Legalism — is not very great. It is probably most simply stated by saying that the essential difference depends on where the ultimate moral authority lies. For Confucianism, it is in the family, as Schwartz for example argues.[46] In Legalism, it lies with the despotic ruler. In Mohism, it is with Heaven and the ghosts and spirits.

(iii) Universal Love (*Jian Ai* 兼愛): This is the cornerstone of Mohism. Li Shenglong writes, in reference to several accounts of Mohism in early works: "這些都説明了兼愛是墨子思想的核心之核心。(These [studies] make it clear that 'universal love' is the very core of Mohist thought.)"[47] One of the late Qing commentators, Zhang Huiyan wrote: "Universal love is the basic element of Mohism.... Reverence for Heaven, proving the existence of spirits, valuing uniformity, and economy of expenditure are its branches. Anti-fatalism, anti-music, and simplicity in funerals are merely other issues upon which circumstances provoked him to take such stands."[48] Universal love (*jian ai* 兼愛) must, however, be recognised as an abbreviation of the full statement — *jian xiang ai, jiao xiang li* 兼相愛， 交相利 (universal mutual love, interaction for mutual benefit). With respect to the usual translation of *jian ai* 兼愛, there are objections to both components of the term. Thus "impartial" and "inclusive" have been used for *jian* 兼 whilst "care" has been preferred to "love" for *ai* 愛 to escape the religious, romantic and emotional connotations of the latter.[49] I have retained "universal love" for the following reasons. First, it is sanctioned by long use dating from Legge's translation of the *jian ai* 兼愛 triad in his *Mencius*. Second, it captures the idea of extending the love one feels towards oneself, or a child feels for its parents, to others within and beyond the family. Third, it is important that this feeling be, in fact, universal.

---

46. See Schwartz (1985), pp. 142–143.
47. Li Shenglong (1996), p. 5.
48. Quoted by Hsiao (1979), pp. 225–226 who describes Zhang's view as "most perceptive and accurate". The translation is by Mote with minor changes. The original may be found in the MZJC, Zhang Huiyan (1909), p. 90. It is interesting to note that Zhang does not follow the titles of the ten doctrines exactly, nor does he include them all.
49. Thus, Ivanhoe (2001), in his recent translation of some of the "core" doctrines chapters, uses "impartial caring" whilst Fraser (2002), in his survey of the "core" doctrines, uses "inclusive care".

"Impartial" fails to convey the scope although it does provide a good contrast to *bie* 別 which Mo Zi stresses as the opposite to *jian* 兼. Fourth, "love" seems more appropriate as the opposite of "hate", "abhor" or "dislike" (*wu* 惡) which is the term used as its opposite in the *Mozi*. And fifth, the religious connotations of term like "universal love" are by no means inappropriate to a doctrine like Mohism. Finally, on this point, I refer both to Graham who writes: "He calls it *jian ai* 兼愛, which we can hardly avoid translating as 'loving everyone' or 'universal love' ..."[50] and also to the *Dictionnaire Ricci* which has for 兼愛: "L'amour universel; l'amour qui assimile les autres à soi-même sans distinction ..."

Difficulties of terminology and translation notwithstanding, the arguments presented by Mo Zi in the three components of the triad are quite clear. The first essay is very brief. It begins with the unexceptionable claim that to bring order to a disordered world there must be an understanding of the cause(s) of the disorder. At a fundamental level, this is lack of "mutual love" (*xiang ai* 相愛), something which should inform all relationships. If people could learn to love others like they love themselves then they would no longer be able to disadvantage others to gain advantage for themselves. This applies at all levels of society from families through communities to states, and even to collections of states.

In the second essay, there is a more elaborate formulation of this basic argument beginning with the recurring claim that those who are benevolent (*ren* 仁) conduct their affairs with the objectives of promoting what benefits the world and eliminating what harms it. For the purposes of the argument, what harm the world are states attacking each other, great houses usurping each other, lack of kindness and loyalty between rulers and ministers, lack of love and filiality between fathers and sons, and lack of concord and harmony between older and younger brothers. Lack of mutual love, or loving oneself to the exclusion of others, is at the root of all these problems. Their solution, then, is clear — everyone must love others

---

50. See Graham (1978), p. 12. Lowe (1992) also writes: "The term used in the MT for love, *ai*, does not admit any other translation, but ... it is clear that 'love' is to be understood as something radically different from the romantic sentiments the term may call to mind for English speakers. Mo Zi's 'love' seems to be an expanded awareness of others as really no different from oneself." (p. 93)

as they love themselves. The practical objection is raised that this is very difficult to do, as indeed it is. Mo Zi counters by claiming that people don't do it because they don't recognise its benefits (which lie in the reciprocity it generates) and they don't understand the reasoning behind it. If they did, then they could and would do it despite the acknowledged difficulty. The remainder of the essay is devoted to two groups of examples. The first comprises cases of people doing difficult things if the ruler wants them to, whilst the second comprises instances of ancient sage kings who have effectively practised the method.

The third essay begins with the same opening claim as the second — those who are benevolent seek to promote the world's benefits and eliminate the world's harms. The perceived harms are again listed in very similar form. The focus then turns to the comparison between "universal" or "generalised" (*jian* 兼) and "discriminating" or "partial" (*bie* 別). If people are "universal" rather than "discriminating", then they will regard others as they regard themselves. So, if "universal" is established, there is great benefit to the world whilst conversely, if "discriminating" is established, there is great harm to the world. Three objections are raised and dealt with. The first is that "universal" cannot be put into practice — people simply can't or won't embrace it. Mo Zi counters by raising several hypothetical situations in which the implications of the conduct of those who are "universal" are compared with those who are "discriminating" (rulers, officers). The advantage clearly lies with the former. Further, there are the examples of the ancient sage kings who did practise "universality" — Wen, Yu, Tang, and Wu (in that order). The second objection is that "universal" is damaging to filial conduct, which is Mencius' objection (IIIB.9). Mo Zi argues that far from being harmful to filial conduct, universal love is actually beneficial. By regarding others' parents like one's own, there will be reciprocal regard by others of one's own parents which will work to the general benefit of all parents including one's own. The third objection is that it is not possible to change people's ways to make them do something which is difficult. Mo Zi counters with the same examples used in the second essay (Duke Wen of Jin, King Ling of Chu, and King Gou Jian of Yue) showing that people can change their ways at the ruler's behest. So it is possible to make people embrace "universal mutual love, reciprocal mutual benefit" by a system of rewards and punishments, thus eliminating the world's harms.

As many commentators have pointed out, the basic argument adduced in support of establishing such a principle is expediency or, more generally, the utilitarian argument.[51] If such a principle is put into practice, it will prove to be of benefit to everyone from ruler to humble peasant. Mo Zi supports his position by considering several hypothetical situations in which it is obvious that a "universal" person is going to conduct himself better than a "partial" person, by showing that "universal love" actually benefits the people that might seem to be disadvantaged by it, by reference to the ancient sage kings who practised it, and by providing examples of how the people's ways can be changed. In effect, he sets up three pairs of terms — love/hate (*ai* 愛 / *wu* 惡), benefit/harm (*li* 利 / *hai* 害), and universal/partial (discriminating) (*jian* 兼 / *bie* 別) — and argues in favour of the first in each case, and for their necessary interconnection. That is, if the first of each of the three pairs is put into practice, everyone will find this to be to their advantage, and order will reign in the world. His argument is, then, quite simple. Mutual or reciprocal love is clearly the foundation of the most harmonious relationships between small numbers of closely connected people — this stands in no need of further proof. If this is generalised, or universalised, the same benefits will accrue in all relationships and this will be proven by results. The sage kings provide examples of lack of discrimination or partiality which is of benefit to the world, whilst other rulers provide evidence that people's conduct can be modified, even in ways that work to the disadvantage of those affected.

Of particular importance is the relationship of this key Mohist doctrine to Confucianism. It is impossible not to recognise a close coincidence, a point made many centuries ago by Han Yu[52] and reiterated by numerous commentators since. Hsiao equates Mo Zi's *ai* 愛 with Confucius' *ren* 仁, advancing the following four arguments:[53]

1. Identity of Semantic Denotation: He writes: "The two terms, *ren* and *ai*, have the same semantic denotation", and refers to the *Lun Yu* XII.22 which has the following exchange between Confucius and Fan Chi 樊遲："樊遲問仁。子曰，愛人。" Hsiao concludes:

---

51. The matter of Mo Zi's utilitarianism (or consequentialism) has been the subject of several recent studies — for example, Ahern (1976), Vorenkamp (1992), Soles (1999) and Duda (2001). The issue will be raised again in relation to the triad on "Heaven's Intention" but will not be discussed in detail.

52. For Han Yu's essay see Section VII below.

53. Hsiao (1979), pp. 230–231. On this point see also Lai (1993), especially pp. 131–133.

"Since *ren* and *ai* have the same definition, it is scarcely possible that they should have conflicting philosophical implications."

2. The equation of "overflowing love" (*fan ai* 泛愛) with "universal love" (*jian ai* 兼愛).[54] He also mentions the "golden rule" — *jisuo buyu, wushi yuren* 己所不欲，勿施於人.[55]

3. No instances of any attacks on Confucianism in respect to "universal love" despite the clear and strong attacks in relation to other of the "core" doctrines and the general opposition to Confucianism.

4. Mencius' Attack. Hsiao takes the vehemence of Mencius' attack on Mo Zi with respect to the concept of "universal love" to be a manifestation of a desire to distance Confucianism from what, in effect, was a similar doctrine, and therefore a dangerous challenge from the point of view of attracting followers.

There is no doubt that there is a rather close correspondence between Mohism and Confucianism on what was the keystone of Mo Zi's doctrinal edifice. There is no doubt too that Mencius' attack was vigorous, unfair and influential. Li Shenglong has, I think rightly, suggested that the distinction lies in precisely how *ai* 愛 is understood. For Mencius, it was an innate component of human nature; for Mo Zi, it was more than a part of human nature — it was also "within the domain of economics", taking this term in its broadest sense.[56]

(iv) Condemning Offensive Warfare (Fei Gong 非功): In this triad of essays, all extant, what Mo Zi is condemning is not warfare generally, but the waging of offensive war. Defensive warfare he accepts as necessary — indeed, he is a specialist in its techniques. But it is not only offensive warfare that he condemns. He also includes acts of aggression more generally. On the other hand, he does acknowledge some justifiable instances of offensive warfare. In addition, as alluded to above, he himself was actively engaged in defensive war both at a theoretical and at a practical level, as the chapters of Part V make abundantly clear. These essays, on a topic which might be taken as an extension or exemplification of "universal love", are notable for the relatively sharp division in the type

---

54. *Lun Yu* I.6 has: "子曰：弟子入則孝，出則弟，謹而信，泛愛眾，而親仁，…."
55. See, for example, *Lun Yu* XII.2 and XV.23.
56. Li Shenglong (1996), pp. 6–7.

of argument presented in the three components of the triad. But the basic contention remains clearly in focus. Offensive warfare, with a few notable exceptions, is not to be countenanced.

In the first essay, the aim is to show that to conduct offensive war is to act contrary to righteousness, it being assumed here that to act righteously is universally acknowledged as a moral imperative. The argument, then, is ethical and proceeds by what might be called a logical approach. Mo Zi does this in two ways. First, he considers a series of small scale acts of aggression such as stealing another's produce or animals. These are all, by general consent, deemed unrighteous and are, in the ordinary conduct of society, punished accordingly. By analogy, offensive war is just a large scale example of the same thing, therefore it too must be unrighteous. Second, there is the specific case of killing a person. Again, by general consent, this does not accord with righteousness, is morally wrong, and is punished by society. Killing ten people is, arguably, ten times as wrong and so on. How then is the large scale killing in offensive war not an extreme case of this morally wrong act? Not to recognise these two arguments is, according to Mo Zi, to be morally blind or, at the very least, morally confused.

In the second essay, the argument is historical. That is, if one examines the historical evidence on offensive war, the net result is always a loss. Of course, the vanquished suffers the more substantial loss, but the victor also loses. And the latter's loss is both present, in terms of people and materials, and future, in terms of the subsequent engagements which will inevitably occur if policies of offensive war are pursued. This is quite apart from the intangible moral loss which must affect the aggressor. In the third essay, the argument is generally utilitarian and is seen from the three perspectives; those of Heaven, the spirits, and the people. All three suffer loss when offensive warfare is carried out. Heaven loses the people it cherishes. The spirits lose people who would be expected to carry out the sacrifices due to them. The people lose in obvious ways — their lives and their livelihoods.

Mo Zi attempts to deal with two rather obvious objections. The first is that a number of states do appear to have benefited from a policy of offensive war, at least on balance — Chu, Yue, Qin and Qi are examples. This, according to Mo Zi, is all a matter of numbers. Against the very small number of states that appear to have benefited must be set the much larger number of states which clearly have not. He uses the analogy of a doctor who employs a particular medicine. If it works in say four of ten thousand people, it is successful in a very limited sense, but overall it must be judged a failure. The second objection concerns certain offensive military campaigns conducted by ancient kings — specifically, Yu against the Miao, Tang against Jie, and King Wu against Zhou. This, according to Mo Zi, is a question of definition. What he is condemning is *gong* 攻 — offensive war. What the exemplary ancient kings perpetrated (and what Mo Zi condones) was *zhu* 誅 — punishment. These campaigns were obviously and incontestably righteous by virtue of the conduct of the rulers "punished".

This is another of the Mohist "core" doctrines where there is no significant divergence from Confucianism, at least at the root. Admittedly, Confucius nowhere specifically articulates an opposition to offensive war which was, it would seem, a less significant problem at his earlier time. But there is certainly nothing to suggest that he condoned it as an instrument of policy, although he does appear to acknowledge the need for warfare, presumably of a defensive kind.[57] Of considerable interest is Mencius' detailed discussion with Song Keng (a noted pacifist) as the latter was on his way to try to prevent war between Chu and Qin.[58] Here Mencius recognises two limbs of the anti-war argument — that it is unethical and that it is unprofitable. He strongly counsels Song Keng to focus on the first limb, which brings out, perhaps, the crux of the difference between the two schools on this matter.

(v) Moderation in Use (*Jie Yong* 節用): There are only two extant chapters covering this fundamental component of Mo Zi's political and social theory. *Jie Yong* 節用 is probably best rendered "moderation (or economy) in use" since materials rather than money are primarily what are being considered although both Mei and Watson use "Economy of Expenditure". Li Shenglong expands slightly the statement of the basic issue as follows: "節用就是要節省財用。(moderation in use is just to be sparing in the use of wealth/property)."[59] Of course, the issue of the title is a minor one. The substance of the argument is perfectly clear and it is this. A society is best served by exercising moderation or economy in the use of the materials required to make the necessities for that society.

The first of the two extant essays on this topic is very brief. Its starting

---

57. *Lun Yu* XIII.29.
58. *Mencius* VIB.4.
59. Li Shenglong (1996), p. 10.

premise is that, if a sage governs a state, then he can double that state's benefits. He does this not by attacking other states and appropriating their land, people and resources but by doing away with the wasteful use of the resources in his own state. Specific examples refer to clothing, houses, weapons, and means of transport (carts and boats). These should all be made with a strict focus on function and complete avoidance of anything unnecessary, any embellishment or ornamentation. Whilst this may be relatively easy, doubling the state's population may be more difficult. The latter can be achieved, however, by avoiding certain important factors which lead to a reduction in population. These are, particularly, burdening the people with onerous labour, inflicting heavy tax imposts, and engaging in wasteful military campaigns, all of which will be harmful to the well-being of the people, reduce the rate of childbirth, and cause disease and death.

The second essay is only slightly longer. Again, ancient exemplars (enlightened rulers and sage kings) are the starting point. They invariably loved the people and brought them great benefit, and they did this, in part, by establishing rules for moderation in use. The fundamental principle was that artisans should do the work they are trained for and they should make only enough of whatever product they are making and no more, and again the focus should be on function. The bulk of the essay is taken up with the documentation of the criteria for making specific things: food and drink, clothing, weapons and armour, carts and boats, materials for funerals and mourning, and housing. If, in the making of any of these things, something doesn't add to their basic use or benefit then it should not be done. Moreover, they are to be made, or in the case of food and drink, produced, only to these requirements and only in sufficient quantities to ensure that all members of the populace have a sufficiency of all of them. Construction or production, as the case may be, is then to stop. In addition, Mo Zi explicitly and strongly opposes any attempts to acquire unusual or exotic things, either by making them or by importing them. To each according to need and no more. Thus, dwellings should be sufficient to give protection against the elements and no more. Food and drink should be enough to maintain the health and strength of the body and no more, and so on.

As mentioned at the outset, this is a fundamental aspect of Mohist theory. Put another way, in all things, practical utility is to be valued, useless ornamentation, elaboration or excess beyond requirements is not. Two of the "core" doctrines still to be considered — *Jie Zang* 節葬 (Moderation in Funerals) and *Fei Yue* 非樂 (Condemnation of Music) —

are, in reality, extensions of this basic principle as applied to the specific things indicated. As for "moderation in use", Mo Zi's argument takes two familiar forms. The first is the appeal to common sense — if everyone is adequately provided for, then surely this establishes the best circumstances for a well functioning society. The second is the appeal to the example of the sage kings as people who themselves eschewed unnecessary elaboration and, according to Mo Zi, actually laid down specific instructions for the provision of basic requirements — as he himself is attempting to do. Further, although Mo Zi does not actually make this point, it would be difficult to achieve the ultimate goal of a society whose members all manifested "universal love" if the society was not one in which all the people's needs were being adequately met.

This "core" doctrine is another instance where the Mohist and Confucian positions are not far apart. Thus, Schwartz writes: "In the three chapters on 'frugality' or 'economy', we are reminded at first of the *Analects*. The people are impoverished by corvée labour, by the exaction of taxes in kind, by being dragged off to useless wars, and by the unconscionable luxuries of the powerful."[60] Mencius does not mention this particular doctrine in his criticisms of Mo Zi although he does deal with one of the extensions — *Jie Sang* 節喪 (Moderation in Funerals — *vide infra*). Xun Zi is, however, openly and specifically critical, particularly in his chapter entitled "Enriching the Kingdom" where he writes, with reference to Mo Zi as a cause of "social anarchy": "... with his 'Moderation in Expenditures' [he] causes poverty throughout the world." However, earlier in the same chapter, in considering ways to make a kingdom self-sufficient, he has written: "Moderate the use of goods, let the people make a generous living, and be good at storing up the harvest surplus. Moderate the use of goods by means of ritual principles, and let the people make a generous living through the exercise of government."[61]

In recent times, Hsiao has criticised Mo Zi's doctrine of *Jie Yong* 節用 (Moderation in Use) on three grounds.[62] First, that it is a denial of human

---

60. See Schwartz (1985), p. 151.
61. The first quotation is from *Xunzi* 10.8 and the second from *Xunzi* 10.2. In both cases the translation follows Knoblock (1988–1994), vol. 2, p. 128 and p. 121 respectively. In both instances the phrase 節用 is used — see the *Xunzi Xinzhu* 荀子新注 (1979), pp. 148 and 140. "Social anarchy" is Knoblock's translation of 亂.
62. Hsiao (1979), pp. 257–265.

nature — which it undoubtedly is, unless of course human nature can be modified by teachings such as those of Mo Zi. Second, it is contrary to the principles of ruling, which might be the point of divergence from Confucianism. Put most simply, the maintenance of a ruling elite (which Mo Zi himself accepts as necessary) might well require outward manifestations of elite status, the preparation of which would transgress the principles of "moderation of use". The third is the perceived negativity of a policy which concentrates on reducing consumption rather than increasing production. The consequences of the latter can, however, prove ultimately very damaging as our modern age is revealing. I shall leave the final word to Li Shenglong: "墨子的節用主張，對當時乃至後世都是有 積極意義的。(Mo Zi's position on moderation in use had a positive significance not only in relation to his own time but also for later generations)."[63]

(vi) Moderation in Funerals (*Jie Zang* 節葬): There is only one essay on this topic which is, in effect, a special case of the argument for moderation in use. In arguing for moderation in funerals, Mo Zi is actually targeting two things: elaborate funerals (*hou zang* 厚葬) and prolonged mourning (*jiu sang* 久喪), both being seen as detrimental to the state as a whole and to the individuals in the state. Mo Zi bases his argument on what he terms the "three benefits" (*san li* 三利) which are, from the state's point of view, increasing the wealth of its people, increasing the number of its people, and creating order and dispelling disorder.

First, elaborate funerals decrease wealth by excessive use of materials for coffins and burial garments, by the preparation of a large burial mound, and by the burial of materials, particularly valuables, with the dead. Prolonged mourning also decreases wealth by interfering with the productivity of those in mourning. The Mohists' specification of the conditions for burial and their recommendation of reduced mourning periods would clearly obviate these perceived problems. Second, elaborate funerals will decrease the numbers of people if the practice of burying the living with the dead is followed. Of much more significance in this respect are the effects of prolonged mourning. This, according to Mo Zi, will make people weak and ill, and will have an adverse effect on the birth rate. Again, these problems would be resolved by Mohist measures. Third, the combination of elaborate funerals and prolonged mourning, particularly

---

63. See Li Shenglong (1996), p. 10.

the latter, is likely to lead to increased disorder. Elaborate funerals, by reducing resources within family units, may lead to discord. Prolonged mourning, by causing ill-health and a prolonged preoccupation with mourning, must inevitably interfere with the efficiency of those responsible for administration and those engaged in production of various sorts.

Mo Zi also considers two other aspects of moderation in funerals in relation to two of the other "core" doctrines. First, do the practices of elaborate funerals and prolonged mourning reduce the incidence of large states attacking small states? Mo Zi's answer is no — the stronger a small state is in terms of manpower, and the richer it is in terms of materials, the less susceptible it is to attack, and the converse. So these practices, by weakening small states further, make them likely targets for attack. Second, do the practices of elaborate funerals and prolonged mourning bring blessings from Heaven and the ghosts and spirits? Again, Mo Zi answers no. If the people are poor, it is more difficult for them to provide equipment and materials for sacrifices. If the people are few, there may not be enough people to actually carry out the sacrifices. If the people are in disorder, ceremonies may be neglected altogether or carried out at the wrong times. As elsewhere, Mo Zi also invokes the authority of the sage kings to support his argument from basic principles. In fact, he attempts to trace his own recommendations as to how funerals should be conducted back to the sage kings. There is, however, the problem of going against what has become a custom. Mo Zi deals with this by citing customs which have been, or are being maintained despite being obviously detrimental, or even barbarous.

There is no doubt that this "core" doctrine is a point of direct opposition with the Confucians. Confucius' own attitude is made quite explicit in his exchange with Zai Wo whose position is somewhat akin to that of Mo Zi on prolonged mourning. Having grudgingly accepted Zai Wo's right to do as he thinks fit, Confucius says, on Zai Wo's departure, "Yu (Zai Wo) is not benevolent."[64] Mencius, in recording the exchange with Yi Zhi, makes the point that, whilst Mo Zi's recommendations might be acceptable in theory, when it comes to practice, people will not adhere to them because of the way they are.[65]

---

64. *Lun Yu* XVII.21.
65. *Mencius* IIIA.5. On this particular passage see Shun (1991).

(vii) Heaven's Intention/Purpose (*Tian Zhi* 天志): This is arguably one of the two most important of Mo Zi's "core" doctrines along with "universal love". It is, moreover, clearly linked with universal love. Indeed, Heaven's intention is to implement universal love in the worldly or lowest realm. Heaven is the more important of the twofold system (along with ghosts and spirits in the middle realm) of supramundane surveillance and supervision of this lowest realm. Universal love is then expressed in right and good conduct which is essential to the other components of Mo Zi's doctrinal system. The title of the triad is *Tian Zhi* 天志 which is usually rendered in English as the "Will of Heaven". Much more commonly in the essays, Mo Zi speaks of *tian zhi yi* 天之意 or *tian yi* 天意. As Mo Zi describes it, this indicates both a formulation by Heaven of a specific intention or purpose *vis-à-vis* mortals and the capacity to actively intervene in mortal affairs, giving a description of the particular role which Heaven plays in them. This is a range of meaning which "purpose" or "intention" seems to cover better than "will".

The first essay opens with the recurring claim that officers and gentlemen understand only small matters and not great matters, the latter referring to Heaven's purpose. Heaven, according to Mo Zi, is clear in respect to what it desires and what it abhors — righteousness and non-righteousness respectively. It is, moreover, capable of bringing about compliance with what it desires by rewards (life, wealth, order) and discouraging non-compliance with punishments (death, poverty, disorder). Heaven is the apex of an hierarchical system for effecting righteousness (*yi* 義) through successive correction (*zheng* 正) of the levels of society. Mo Zi recognised the following sequence: Heaven>Son of Heaven>Three Dukes and the feudal lords>generals and great officers>ordinary officers> ordinary people. The Son of Heaven is, then, the highest mortal and must implement Heaven's purpose by practising "universal mutual love" and "exchange of mutual benefit". Rulers who did comply were Yu, Tang, Wen and Wu and they were rewarded with possession of all under Heaven, continuation of their lineage, and perpetual praise down the ages. Rulers who did not comply were Jie, Zhou, You and Li and they were punished by loss of all under Heaven, cessation of their line, and being forever reviled. In the case of ordinary people, Heaven is identified as completely understanding them and completely possessing them, the evidence for this being that it provides food for everyone and visits misfortune or punishment on those who harm innocent people. As a result of all this, compliance with Heaven's intention results in rule by righteousness, and opposition to Heaven's intention results in rule by force. Mo Zi characterises the two types of rule by the absence or presence of components of his recurring list of aggressive and exploitative actions. The essay ends with a brief statement that Heaven's purpose is Mo Zi's key standard by which he measures human actions, and is comparable in this respect to a carpenter's square or a wheelwright's compasses.

The second essay opens with a detailed consideration of righteousness and its origin. Righteousness must originate, Mo Zi argues, from those who are noble and wise as it is the pinnacle of nobility and wisdom, and Heaven must be its ultimate source. As in the previous essay, Mo Zi questions the ability of people to recognise the position of Heaven at the apex of his hierarchical structure. But it must be the apex for three reasons: (i) Heaven is capable of rewarding and punishing the ruler who is the highest mortal member of the structure. (ii) The ruler acknowledges this by sacrificing to Heaven and making requests of it — it is never vice-versa. (iii) Heaven is recorded as the pinnacle in ancient texts. Now righteousness (*yi* 義) is linked with benevolence (*ren* 仁) and, to achieve these desirable qualities, there must be compliance with Heaven's purpose. Compliance is defined as the pursuit of what Heaven desires — here identified as helping and teaching others, distributing wealth, loyalty, kindness, compassion and filial conduct — and avoidance of what Heaven abhors, which comprises the opposite of these things as manifest in the list of aggressive and exploitative actions previously referred to. Being benevolent and righteous, and therefore complying with Heaven's purpose, is to manifest this purpose which is to establish universal love and benefit. Mo Zi raises the question of how we know Heaven's love for people is profound (*hou* 厚). He gives six reasons ranging from the creation of heavenly bodies for light to the provision of wood, metal, and birds and beasts for their respective purposes. People should recognise Heaven's beneficence but they don't. Again, the groups of good and evil rulers are cited, the former being characterised as those who were "universal" (*jian* 兼) and the latter as those who were "discriminating" or "partial" (*bie* 別). As in all three essays, Mo Zi concludes with the statement that Heaven's intention is his standard, expanding a little on this point compared to the first essay by spelling out that what complies with this standard is good and what does not is bad, seen in terms of government.

The third essay begins in the usual way by identifying the problems of the world as stemming from lack of what is the topic under discussion — here Heaven's purpose and its implementation, specifically on the part of officers and gentlemen. There must be knowledge of what Heaven desires and what it abhors. The former is righteousness, achieved by being correct, and the latter is non-righteousness. The same pyramid of rectification as in the first essay is given. Again, the first component, Heaven to Son of Heaven or ruler, is seen as the one which people fail to recognise. But this should be clear from the fact that Heaven is capable of rewarding and punishing the ruler, as the ancient sages realised. Further, righteousness comes from the noble and wise and Heaven is the apogee of nobility and wisdom. The key component of compliance with Heaven's purpose is again identified as universal love for people. Heaven demonstrates its own universal love by the provision of food and by punishing those who kill the innocent. That is, Heaven rewards virtue and punishes vice, and again the two groups of early rulers are brought forward as evidence. So compliance with Heaven's purpose is universality, reflected in government by righteousness and avoidance of the acts of aggression and exploitation previously listed. Non-compliance with Heaven's purpose is "discrimination", reflected in government by force and the occurrence of the various forms of aggression and exploitation. The last sections of this essay give the most extended treatment of the concept of Heaven's purpose as a standard, specifically here evaluating officers and gentlemen in terms of this list of aggressive and exploitative actions. There is notable overlap, in terms of examples, with the final part of *Mozi* 17 "Condemning Offensive Warfare".

Thus, in summary, Heaven is the supreme arbiter and controller of human affairs. It is seen as a supramundane agent with a clearly defined intention or purpose for the mortal realm which it can implement by being omniscient and by regulating human actions through a system of rewards and punishments. The key component of Heaven's intention is to bring people to the practice of universal mutual love and exchange of mutual benefit. This will result in benevolent and righteous behaviour through all levels of society and avoidance of acts of aggression and exploitation, whether at a national, family or individual level, which are inimical to the establishment and preservation of a righteous and well ordered society.[66]

---

66. The precise role of Heaven in controlling the conduct and affairs of mortals is a central issue in the debate on whether Mo Zi is a utilitarian or a divine command theorist. That is, does Heaven actually direct people towards right actions or, at least, establish what constitutes right action or is it simply a standard by which the benefits of actions can be established — see the references in note 51 above.

Although the role of Heaven in the affairs of men does not seem to have been one of the points of contention in the doctrinal conflict between Mohists and Confucians, there was clearly a difference in the concept of Heaven held by the two schools. Thus, while the Mohists, as outlined above, saw Heaven as overseeing and intervening in the affairs of the people in ways to direct them to conform to its putative intentions, this was not the case with Confucians. Certainly, however, for the latter, Heaven was again the supreme power (*Lun Yu* III.13/2), but it was beyond men's knowledge and was something about which Confucius did not discourse. Moreover, it was seen as producing virtue in a person rather than rewarding existing virtue (子曰：天生德於予 — *Lun Yu* VII.22). Hsiao, in fact, goes so far as to say: "... as we examine Mo Zi's view of Heaven, we find its fundamental import to be diametrically opposed to Mencius' view, for it binds man's acceptance to that which Heaven has approved."[67] Nevertheless, these differences do not appear in later writers as points of active doctrinal dispute.

(viii) Percipient Ghosts (*Ming Gui* 明鬼): There is only one surviving chapter on ghosts and spirits which are an integral part of Mo Zi's philosophical scheme. For example, the important interrelationship of this doctrine with other Mohist "core" doctrines has been well brought out in the recent study by Wong and Loy particularly in regard to Mo Zi's opposition to offensive warfare.[68] A belief in the existence of ghosts and spirits is also closely related to the concept of reward and punishment as the components of a supernatural structure monitoring and controlling human conduct. Before considering the content of the remaining essay, something should be said about the meaning of the title *Ming Gui* 明鬼. It is generally taken, in Western writings, to mean "explaining" or "clarifying" ghosts. However, examination of the content of the chapter, particularly in places where *ming* 明 is used, suggests that the meaning is really "clear-seeing" or "all-seeing", taken as being an attribute of the putative entities. The critical point about ghosts and spirits is that they are observers of all human actions, however and wherever they may occur. This is particularly brought out in the opening sentence of 31.17 which reads: "Therefore, the awareness of ghosts and spirits is such that it is not possible to do something in the darkest places, whether in wide marshes, in

---

67. Hsiao (1979), p. 246.
68. Wong & Loy (2004).

mountains and forests, or in deep ravines, but that their awareness will certainly know about it." Perhaps *ming* 明 in the title is serving double duty — Mo Zi is "explaining" ghosts (and spirits) and these ghosts (and spirits) are themselves "all-seeing".

The essay itself starts from the premise that the principles of the sage kings of the Three Dynasties have been lost and, as a consequence, the world is in disorder, and that an important cause of this is a loss of belief in the existence of ghosts and spirits and their capacity to reward worthiness and punish wickedness. The form of the essay is a series of claims by non-believers on the existence of ghosts and spirits and Mo Zi's counters to these claims. The first way to establish whether ghosts and spirits exist or not is through the eyes and ears of the ordinary people. If people have seen or heard ghosts and spirits, then they exist whereas, if they have not, then such entities do not exist. Non-believers say that while there may be many examples of ordinary people seeing or hearing ghosts and spirits, they cannot be relied upon. Mo Zi's response is to give a series of five well-documented examples of instances where many people have seen and heard ghosts and spirits — ghosts of wrongly punished officials appearing to exact retribution from those who punished them, ghosts who have appeared to offer encouragement or themselves inflict punishment, and ghosts who have intervened in human disputes. However, the non-believers repeat their claim that the ordinary people are unreliable. Mo Zi counters by turning to the ancient sage kings, citing documented examples of how their conduct manifested their belief in ghosts and spirits. His conclusion is that there is overwhelming evidence that ghosts and spirits can and do reward worthiness and punish wickedness, and can detect both worthiness and wickedness whenever and wherever they occur.

Not only can they do these things, but their power is such that it cannot be resisted. He gives the examples of Jie and Zhou and their being overthrown by Tang and King Wu respectively. They were overthrown because they abused Heaven and insulted the ghosts above, and inflicted calamity and suffering on the people below. Despite their power and strength, they were brought down, thus demonstrating that supramundane forces will reward the deserving however lowly, and will punish transgressors however powerful. On the specific issue of ghosts, Mo Zi's argument here is somewhat weakened by conflating Heaven and ghosts as the agents of these rewards and punishments. Non-believers then take a different tack, claiming that a belief in ghosts doesn't accord with benefiting parents and is harmful to filial conduct. In responding to this,

Mo Zi gives a summary of who or what ghosts are — ghosts of Heaven, ghosts and spirits of the mountains and rivers, and the ghosts of people who have died. In the case of family members who have died, sacrifices and ceremonies will provide sustenance for them and, even if they don't actually exist, such ceremonies will bring people together, so creating social unity and harmony. However, the non-believers claim that such ceremonies are just a waste of materials and serve no purpose. To counter this claim, Mo Zi turns again to the writings of the sage kings and the recorded conduct of filial sons. Having met each of the claims of the non-believers, Mo Zi concludes that, if the aim is to promote the world's benefits and eliminate its harms, there must be an acceptance of the existence of ghosts and spirits, and a recognition of them as all-seeing (*ming* 明).

Thus, most of the chapter is devoted to examining evidence for the existence of ghosts and spirits regardless of what form they actually take.[69] In presenting this evidence, Mo Zi gives a clear account of what he takes to be the significant objections to a belief in ghosts and spirits. There are, in essence, three lines of evidence supporting their existence. The first is the direct evidence of the senses of ordinary people. Ask around any village or town and you will find people who claim to have had direct experience of ghosts or spirits. And, if the reports of ordinary people are deemed insufficiently reliable, there are similar reports emanating from the ruling classes. This constitutes the second line of evidence. Of the five examples cited, four concern condign punishment delivered by the ghost of an unjustly treated person whilst, in the fifth example, the visitation brings reward. The third line of evidence is from the sage kings. The three early dynasties, Xia, Shang and Zhou are considered and, in each case, the notably good early rulers of these dynasties are identified as conducting themselves and initiating practices such that there is a clear indication of their acceptance of the existence of ghosts and spirits. As several commentators have pointed out, this is not a proof that ghosts and spirits exist or even that these early kings had a deep conviction about their existence. In effect, as presented by Mo Zi, it seems like an early form of Pascal's wager.

The real crux of Mo Zi's argument is his examination of the different consequences which follow belief and non-belief in the existence of ghosts

---

69. On this matter see the study by Birdwhistell (1984).

and spirits. After beginning the chapter by attributing the ills of the world, which he lists specifically, to a loss of belief in ghosts and spirits, and then examining the evidence considered above, Mo Zi returns in the final sections of the chapter to the positive and beneficial consequences of a belief in ghosts and spirits. The perceived ills will be resolved. There are three aspects to the good consequences of an acceptance of the existence of ghosts and spirits. First, people will conduct themselves well if they believe they are under constant scrutiny by all-seeing beings capable of delivering rewards and punishments. Second, sacrifices and offerings of food and drink will be directly sustaining to the ghosts of departed relatives. Third, even if, as Mo Zi allows is possible, ghosts and spirits don't actually exist, the gathering of people to carry out the services for them will foster social cohesion and harmony.

Mohists and Confucians were alike in accepting the existence of ghosts and spirits and according them due respect as manifested in the appropriate ceremonies and sacrifices directed to them. As with Heaven, the difference between the schools lies largely in the concept held of ghosts and spirits, and particularly of the role they are seen as playing in human affairs. Whilst for the Mohists they were the other limb of the supra-mundane surveillance system which monitored and corrected human conduct, for the Confucians, it could be argued, they were more remote and inscrutable. In the *Li Ji* there is the statement: "The Master said: 'The way of Xia was to honour Fate, serve ghosts and respect spirits but keep distant from them'."[70] This attitude is also seen in *Lun Yu* VI.20 ("… 敬鬼神而遠之，可謂知矣。" "… respecting ghosts and spirits but keeping distant from them may be called knowledge/wisdom"). The differences between Mohists and Confucians in where the purpose and value of sacrifices to ghosts lay is well brought out by comparing Mo Zi's essay with *Xunzi* 19.11, both passages citing the ancient sage kings as authorities and examples. Finally, on the issue of evidence for the existence of ghosts and spirits, the *Xunzi* has: "As a general rule, when men think there are ghosts, the confirmation of it is certain to be an occasion when they are startled or confused."[71] These differences notwithstanding, as in the case of Heaven, the matter of ghosts and spirits was not, apparently, an issue of doctrinal

---

70. *Li Ji*, "Biao Ji" 32 (《禮記‧表記》), SSJZS, vol. 5, p. 915.
71. *Xunzi* 21.8, Knoblock (1988–1994), vol. 3, p. 109.

dispute between the schools, a point made quite clearly by Han Yu in his essay (*vide infra*).

(ix) Condemnation of Music (*Fei Yue* 非樂): This is, in effect, an extension of the "Moderation in Use" argument, as mentioned above. As with the previous topic, only one essay remains. There are no issues with the title, and the arguments advanced are clear and straightforward. Mo Zi begins with a simple definition of a benevolent (*ren* 仁) person in terms of his actions, which are entirely aimed at bringing benefit and eliminating harm in the world. No consideration is to be given to what might please the senses or comfort the body. In particular, the benevolent person does nothing which might be detrimental to the provision of materials for the people's needs.

The crux of Mo Zi's argument is, then, that music is only to please the senses, and does not bring benefit to the world but harms it by the wasteful use of human resources and materials for what is non-essential. It is not that Mo Zi is unaware of the fact that music does bring pleasure; the important point is that it doesn't bring actual benefit. Mo Zi again turns to the example of the sage kings. What they made were things that did bring benefit, like boats and carts. Musical instruments and performances are not in this category. Mo Zi's argument proceeds with an enumeration of what he calls the "three hardships" (*san huan* 三患) which are hunger, cold and fatigue. Not only does music do nothing to alleviate these hardships, but it also wastefully uses human and material resources which might otherwise be used to do this. Apart from the "three hardships", the same argument applies to other problems, most notably various acts of aggression and domination, and the establishment of order from disorder. Music, according to Mo Zi, does nothing to stop the one or facilitate the other. Not only does music have no value in dealing with these social problems but, because its satisfactory performance requires the participation of men and women in their prime, it takes such people away from their duties of sowing and planting in the first case, and spinning and weaving in the second case. And it is not only the people performing the music that will be diverted from their important duties; it is the listeners too. Again Mo Zi cites early examples, this time of people who displayed an excessive devotion to music, to the detriment of society. Insects, birds and animals are naturally provided for. People, however, must work to provide what is necessary for a well functioning society and music deflects people from this fundamental work at all levels of society. Finally, support can be found in ancient writings in which music and dance are condemned.

In summary, then, music deflects materials from their proper use in meeting the basic needs of the people. The making of musical instruments takes people away from their fundamental tasks which Mo Zi considers under four categories: ruling, administering, farming and weaving. Listening to music does the same. There is also the matter of the class of musicians themselves. They are seen as contributing nothing to the general benefit. On the contrary, they are parasitic insofar as they need to be supported by the labours of other people. The chapter concludes with several examples from earlier writings, the texts of which are unfortunately no longer extant.

The weaknesses in Mo Zi's position against music are not hard to see. First, and most simply, there is the quantitative issue. The actual "wastage" of necessary materials, and the inappropriate deployment of manpower are likely to be very small in comparison, say, to the situation with funerals and mourning. Second, and more important, is the unquantifiable benefit of music to the human spirit, not least in conditions of hardship and difficulty such as Mo Zi mentions. It is these weaknesses, particularly the latter, that Xun Zi seizes upon, devoting a considerable part of his Book 20 to the subject, targeting Mo Zi in particular. Having considered what he sees as the very significant benefits of music, he writes:

> One would have expected that Mo Zi, who condemns music, would have met with some kind of punishment. But all the enlightened kings had already died, and there was no one to put things aright. Stupid fools study him and thereby endanger their own existence. But the gentleman makes clear and brilliant his music and therewith his inner power.[72]

Book 5 of the *Lü Shi Chunqiu* is also devoted to music, extolling its merits and taking a clearly anti-Mohist position — although Mo Zi himself is not mentioned. Here, as in the *Xunzi*, music is not seen as being merely for the pleasure of the senses, but as having a deeper significance. It is a significance, moreover, that was perceived by Mo Zi's own foremost authorities — the ancient sage kings.[73]

(x) Against Fate (*Fei Ming* 非命): There are three extant essays on this topic with relative uniformity of both length and content. The first essay,

---

72. *Xunzi* 20.3. Translation after Knoblock (1988–1994), vol. 3, p. 84.
73. *Lü Shi Chunqiu* Book 5/2 – 5/5. See, particularly, 5/4.4. On this, see also Cook (2002).

which is atypically the longest, starts with a reiteration of the fundamental objectives in administering a state — to make it rich, populous and well ordered. These objectives had been achieved in ancient times, according to Mo Zi, whereas now the very opposite obtained — states were poor, under-populated and in disorder. Fatalists, he claims, attribute these misfortunes to Fate, believing that such things as wealth and poverty, being populous or otherwise, and longevity and early death are determined by Fate. In examining a theory such as the existence of Fate (or, indeed, any theory) criteria are needed. For the purposes of this essay, the three criteria (*biao* 表) are its foundation (*ben* 本) which is to be found in the ancient sage kings; its source or origin (*yuan* 原) which is the eyes and ears of the ordinary people; and its application or use (*yong* 用) which is in its benefit to the ordinary people of the state. The major part of the rest of the essay is devoted to a consideration of the foundation of Fatalism. Thus, in ancient times, the disorder wrought by Jie and Zhou was rectified by Tang and King Wu respectively. The restoration of order was not a matter of Fate; it was due to the endeavours of the exemplary rulers. This is borne out by the ancient writings. Nowhere in them is it said that goodness cannot be rewarded and badness punished, or that being respectful is not beneficial and being evil is not harmful. In any state there is the need for a righteous man at the helm. Then the deities and spiritual beings will receive their due sacrifices and the ordinary people will be benefited. This is why the sage kings established rewards and punishments. But Fatalists claim that rewards and punishments are determined by Fate and are not linked to prior conduct. Such a belief, Mo Zi argues, will adversely affect the functioning of the state at all levels. There will be no incentive for rulers to be righteous, ministers to be loyal, fathers to be compassionate, sons to be filial, older brothers to be caring, and younger brothers to be respectful. The concept of Fate is simply a crutch for evil and indolent people, allowing them to avoid responsibility for their actions and the consequences which ensue. Belief in such a concept does, then, lead to administrators not administering properly, and the ordinary people not fulfilling their functions. It brings no benefit to Heaven, to ghosts and spirits, or to the people themselves. Disorder is the result and this is a great harm for the world.

The second essay is the shortest of the three and begins with another statement about standards or criteria (*yi* 義, *fa* 法) of which the same three in name are again identified — the foundation (*ben* 本), origin or source (*yuan* 原), and application or use (*yong* 用). There is some variation in how these criteria are understood insofar as the foundation here is taken to be in the intentions of Heaven and ghosts, and the origin/source in the eyes and ears of the people. Since some believe in Fate and some do not, how can the issue be resolved? Considering the eyes and ears of the masses, has anyone ever seen or heard Fate? The answer is no. If the same question is posed with respect to feudal lords, or the sage kings themselves, the answer is still no. Whether a state enjoys peace or is threatened by danger, whether it is well ordered or in disorder depends on the government of the ruler and not on Fate. Those who believe in Fate do claim that its recognition dates from the Three Dynasties. That may be so, but, if it is, Mo Zi claims, its origin may be traced to the evil rulers and indolent people of that time. What happened was that the rulers of ancient times who conducted themselves badly and came to grief (e.g. Jie and Zhou) attributed their downfall to Fate and this was duly documented by the sage kings. There are, moreover, other passages in the ancient literature denying the existence of Fate.

The third essay also starts with the need to establish criteria (*fa* 法) to evaluate a doctrine. Here, however, examination (*kao* 考) is substituted for foundation (*ben* 本), although what is examined is again the affairs of the ancient sage kings. The sage kings sought filial sons and worthy and virtuous men so they established rewards for goodness and punishments for evil. It was this that allowed them to provide food for the hungry, clothes for the cold, rest for the weary, and to bring order to the disorder wrought by their evil predecessors. It had nothing to do with Fate. The rulers who believed in Fate were Jie, Zhou, You and Li, who used it as an explanation of their misfortunes. That is, the ancient evil kings created the idea of Fate, and the ordinary people, who were poor and unfortunate, perpetuated it. The problem was recognised by the ancient sage kings who documented it in their writings, examples of which are provided. For a society to function well, people at all levels must believe that goodness and diligence will be rewarded whilst badness and indolence will be punished. It is the same for kings, dukes and high officers running the state, for farmers in their agricultural work, and for women in their spinning and weaving. If people accept personal responsibility for their actions and are responsive to incentives and disincentives, then the state will be well ordered and rich and will have enough material wealth to sustain itself. Conversely, if people believe in Fate, then at all levels they will be remiss in their duties and the state will be disordered, poor, and inadequate in terms of material wealth. In conclusion, according to Mo Zi, Fate must be rejected as being a concept created by the ancient evil kings and perpetuated by the poor and unfortunate. It is not something the benevolent person speaks of.

As can be seen, Mo Zi's argument against Fatalism is very simple. To a significant extent, the simplicity is a result of Mo Zi's failure to provide, in any of the essays, a clear exposition of what Fate actually is or might be. The discussion is really only in terms of what a belief in Fate is presumed to entail. There is no semblance of any argument about determinism and free-will more generally, although the existence of the latter is certainly implied in Mo Zi's social prescription.

What are clearly articulated are Mo Zi's three criteria or standards for evaluating a doctrine or belief. To make such an evaluation, there must be an examination of the doctrine's basis or foundation (*ben* 本), its source or origin (*yuan* 原), and its use or application (*yong* 用). Although there are some minor variations within the triad as to how these criteria are to be applied, fundamentally, the foundation is discovered in the deeds of the ancient sage kings. The source is to be found in direct experience, whether that of the masses or of the feudal lords. The use or application is manifest in the conduct of government directed at the well-being of the populace.

The key, and most readily acceptable, component of Mo Zi's argument against Fatalism is that in actual practice it is detrimental to the functioning of society at all levels. An acceptance that the outcome of one's actions is predetermined by Fate is seen as sapping people's resolve to act worthily and diligently in whatever activity they are engaged in. Conversely, the belief that meritorious conduct and diligent application will be rewarded, either directly by a good immediate outcome, or through the intervention of Heaven or ghosts and spirits, is seen as encouraging diligence and good conduct. In relation to this, Mo Zi traces the belief in Fate to those whose evil conduct and lack of diligence has resulted in a bad outcome, and who endeavour to exculpate themselves by invoking some outside agency rather than acknowledging their own shortcomings. What Mo Zi does not claim, in this context, is that evil rulers attribute their own bad conduct to Fate.

Much less convincing is Mo Zi's application of the second criterion — direct observation. Nobody, he claims, either among ordinary people or among the feudal lords, has ever directly seen or heard Fate, as they have, for example, directly experienced ghosts and spirits. Without defining what Fate actually is, it is difficult to see how this test can be applicable. One does not, of course, directly see or hear a concept in a way that confirms its physical existence, and it is as a concept that Fate is spoken about in these chapters. The third criterion, use, is, in effect, identical with the first. A rejection of Fatalism is likely to foster good government. The paradigmatic good rulers of ancient times are clear examples of this. Conversely, a belief in Fate is likely to result in indifferent or bad functioning, and the evil kings exemplify this.

Ultimately, then, Mo Zi's argument comes down to practicalities. People who believe in Fate are prone to attribute any outcome of their actions to Fate which thus absolves them from any personal responsibility for the consequences of their actions, or for their circumstances. Conversely, a rejection of Fate, coupled with a belief in the capacity of Heaven or ghosts and spirits to reward good conduct and punish bad conduct, is likely to lead to people conducting themselves well and performing their allotted functions diligently. This will, of course, lead to a good society. Hsiao makes the point quite strongly that none of this is really opposed to the fundamentals of Confucianism, writing: "Thus, in relation to the thoughts of Confucius, Mencius, and Hsün Tzu, it would appear that to attack the Confucians using Mo Tzu's anti-fatalism is virtually to fire without a target."[74]

V. Mohist Responses to Other Pre-Han Philosophers

References to other philosophers and schools are very few in the *Mozi*. For the most part Mo Zi is concerned with presenting his own doctrines and arguing for their acceptance. Thus, in the 23 extant chapters on the 10 "core" doctrines, there is no reference to any other philosopher. Of course, this is not altogether surprising given Mo Zi's position in the chronology of early Chinese philosophy, although the unknown range of contributors and the time span of their contributions must be taken into account. What comments and criticisms there are in the work are to be found in the single extant chapter "Against the Confucians" (*Mozi* 39) and two of the five dialogue chapters (*Mozi* 46–50). There are several places in the dialectical chapters (*Mozi* 40–45) where Confucians are briefly referred to, but these are neither very informative nor free of textual uncertainty. What is clear from the dialectical chapters is that their author or authors, whoever they may have been, were engaging with the ideas of other schools, most importantly where these concerned criticisms of Mohist doctrines. Notable

74. Hsiao (1979), p. 250.

in this regard are some of the ideas associated with the School of Names (Mingjia 名家), and especially with Gongsun Long and Hui Shi, although no-one is mentioned by name or indicated by school. I have elsewhere presented analysis of the interrelationship between the Later Mohists (putative authors of the dialectical chapters) and Gongsun Long.[75] Here I shall confine myself to a brief consideration of the three chapters referred to above — "Against the Confucians" (*Mozi* 39), and the dialogues "Geng Zhu" (*Mozi* 46) and "Gongmeng" (*Mozi* 48).

In the specific chapter directed against Confucianism, a somewhat arbitrary division may be made into four parts. The initial sections (39.1–39.3) speak of "Confucians" and attack their doctrines. First, there is the concept of gradations in "treating relatives as relatives", particularly as these bear on funeral and mourning practices. Mo Zi's stated view is that the Confucians are inconsistent in their gradations and hypocritical in their mourning. Second, there is an attack on the belief in Fate, to which, it is claimed, Confucians attribute almost everything — life expectancy, wealth/poverty, peace/danger, order/disorder, success/failure, reward/punishment and good fortune/bad fortune. As presented in the chapters on Fate, Mo Zi's claims are that such a belief undermines personal endeavour and is generally detrimental to the conduct of government and to the functioning of society as a whole. The second group (39.4–39.8) is again directed against Confucians as a school, but focuses on their conduct rather than their doctrines. Some of this criticism is couched in rather strong terms. Mo Zi is particularly virulent about what he sees as their hypocritical and self-serving conduct in relation to funerals, notably their parasitic attachment to the funerals of the rich and prominent for personal gain. In milder terms, he attacks their commitment to ancient forms of speech and dress and their claim to be followers rather than creators. Do these things mean, he asks, that the ancients whom they follow, but who themselves followed no more ancient model, and those who made important and beneficial discoveries, were not themselves worthy and benevolent? The two other points of criticism are what they identify as gentlemanly conduct in battle, which Mo Zi argues works against a favourable outcome, and their claim to be like a bell, responding only when struck. The latter, according to Mo Zi, is likely to result in important failures in their role as advisers to rulers, and also to adversely affect their

---

75. Johnston (2004).

own families. The third group of exchanges are the two involving Yan Zi, supposedly a Mohist and possibly the author of the *Yanzi Chunqiu* (39.9– 39.10). In both these sections, Yan Zi is, after a little persuasion, openly critical of Confucius himself. In the final group (39.11–39.13), there are three brief anecdotes directly critical of Confucius. The charges against him are that his own conduct is not consistent with his doctrines, and that his political advice has, on occasion, led to marked disorder.

Of the two relevant dialogues, in the first ("Geng Zhu" — *Mozi* 46), certain Confucian positions are articulated by people who are taken to have been followers of Confucianism (Wu Ma Zi, a follower of Zi Xia, Gong Meng Zi), allowing Mo Zi to present his own views on the subject. These are expositions rather than arguments. In one section only is there actual mention of Confucius, and this is of interest insofar as Mo Zi defends rather than attacks Confucius while at the same time putting forward his own views. In 46.10 Mo Zi comments on an exchange between Zi Gao, Duke of She and Confucius in which the latter is asked what it is that constitutes government. According to Mo Zi, Confucius gives the wrong answer, but he excuses him on the grounds that the question was wrongly framed.

The second dialogue in question ("Gongmeng" — *Mozi* 48) is the more important in the present context. Of the 24 sections of this dialogue, the first 12 are Mo Zi's responses to a series of questions put by Gongmeng who, although there is some uncertainty on this point, is thought to have been a Confucian. There is only one mention of Confucius and none of Confucians as a school in these exchanges. Again, the questions give Mo Zi a chance to express his own ideas, both on doctrines (condemnation of Fate, condemnation of music, moderation in funerals) and on conduct more generally. In 48.13 Mo Zi questions an unnamed Confucian, asking him, "Why make music?" The Confucian is unable to come up with a suitable reply. There are two other important sections in this dialogue and both involve Cheng Zi who is said to have been a student of both Mohism and Confucianism. In the first (48.14), Mo Zi claims that, "The Way of Confucianism has four principles which are enough to destroy the world." These are: (i) Failure to accept the existence of ghosts and spirits. (ii) The practices of elaborate funerals and prolonged mourning (which may be taken as two principles). (iii) A belief in the importance of music. In the second (48.15), Cheng Zi presents Mo Zi with the interesting question, "You are not a Confucian so why do you praise Confucius?" Mo Zi's reply is essentially that some things are just right and are not matters of doctrinal variation, although he doesn't specify what he has in mind. He concludes with a question of his own, "Why should I never praise Confucius?"

VI. Pre-Han Responses to Mohism

Although Mohism did not survive long as a school or movement, it was clearly a philosophical force to be reckoned with during its heyday. As such, it engaged to a greater or lesser extent with the various other philosophical, political and social movements of the time. In particular, it is probable that the Mohist movement constituted the main opposition to Confucianism in the two centuries immediately prior to the Han dynasty. In general, Mohism was an object of criticism for other schools, albeit on differing bases and with differing degrees of vehemence. Mixed in with this criticism, there was, however, some admiration and respect, both explicit, as is seen, for example, in the *Zhuangzi*, and implicit, as is seen in doctrinal overlap in the otherwise overtly critical *Xunzi*. In this section, I shall briefly consider some of the more notable recorded responses, both in the eponymously titled works of particular philosophers of the period and in compilations.

(i) *Mencius*: There are only three references to Mo Zi in the *Mencius*.[76] Of these, two are very similar and are openly critical of Mohism in an historically important way. The first, I shall quote *in extenso* as follows:

> ... the words of Yang Chu and Mo Ti fill the Empire. The teachings current in the Empire are those of either the school of Yang or the school of Mo. Yang advocates everyone for himself, which amounts to a denial of one's prince. Mo advocates love without discrimination, which amounts to a denial of one's father. To ignore one's father on the one hand, and one's prince on the other is to be no different from the beasts.... If the way of Yang and Mo does not subside and the way of Confucius is not proclaimed, the people will be deceived by heresies and the path of morality will be blocked. When the path of morality is blocked, then we show animals the way to devour men, and sooner or later it will come to men devouring men. Therefore, I am

---

76. *Mencius* IIIA.5(1–3); IIIB.9(9–10); VIIA.26(2). Shun's (1991) article on the first of these passage has already been mentioned.

apprehensive. I wish to safeguard the way of the former sages against the onslaughts of Yang and Mo and to banish excessive views. Then advocates of heresies will not be able to rise. For what arises in the mind will interfere with policy, and what shows itself in policy will interfere with practice.[77]

The second reference is more brief and also links Mo Zi with Yang Zhu, although their doctrines are quite opposed. What connects them is their perceived threat to Confucianism. In both of these references the only Mohist doctrine mentioned is "universal love". The third reference is an exchange (through an intermediary) between Mencius and Yi Zhi, described as a Mohist, on the simplicity or otherwise of funerals. Mencius' criticism of Yi Zhi is that, whilst he espouses Mohist doctrines in theory, in the case of the funerals for his parents, he fails to put the relevant doctrine into practice. Here Mencius does, indeed, put his finger on a weakness of Mohism — it puts demands on people which arguably require actions contrary to human nature and so are impossible to meet consistently. On "universal love", which Mencius calls *ai wu cha deng* 愛 無差等 (love without difference of degree), his criticism is again that this is contrary to human nature.

(ii) *Xunzi*: There are 11 references to Mo Zi or to Mohism more generally in the *Xunzi*.[78] Of these, the relatively detailed attack on Mohist doctrines in 10.8 is clearly the most important. It is too long to quote in full, but in essence Xun Zi's criticism begins by claiming that the teachings of Mo Zi focus too narrowly on the world as suffering from the hardship of inadequate supplies. This is not real, says Xun Zi. It is "... a hardship private to Mo Zi's exaggerated reckoning."[79] The real problem, according to Xun Zi, is "social anarchy" as Knoblock translates it — the actual words are "天下之公患，亂傷之也。"[80] This is, of course, also Mo Zi's primary focus. How can order be re-established in a now disordered world? But in Xun Zi's view, Mo Zi is exacerbating the problem. He is a cause rather

---

77. *Mencius* IIIB.9 — translation after Lau (1970), pp. 114–115.
78. The following references are to Knoblock (1988–1994): 6.4, vol. 1, p. 223; 8.3, vol. 2, pp. 71–72; 8.10, vol. 2, pp. 79–80; 10.8, vol. 2, pp. 127–129; 11.5b, vol. 2, pp. 157–158; 17.12, vol. 3, p. 22; 19.1d, vol. 3, pp. 56–57; 20.1–3, vol. 3, pp. 80–84; 21.4, vol. 3, p. 102; 25.14, vol. 3, p. 176; 25.17, vol. 3, p. 177. Translations are after Knoblock.
79. Knoblock (1988–1994), vol. 2, p. 127.
80. See Liang Qixiong (1983), p. 126.

than a cure. And he is causative particularly through his doctrines of "Condemning Music" and "Moderation in Use".

With respect to the remaining references, there is firstly the linking of Mo Zi with Song Xing in *Xunzi* 6 ("Against the Philosophers"). Both are accused of ignoring "gradations of rank and status" — again an unfair accusation. Indeed, Mo Zi is particularly concerned with the importance of these factors and their general recognition. In this reference, there is, however, also an example of grudging admiration. Speaking of both men, Xun Zi says: "Nonetheless, some of what they advocate has a rational basis, and their statements have perfect logic ..." In *Xunzi* 8.3, as an example of what constitutes the superiority of the "gentleman", the refutation of the doctrines of Mo Zi and Shen Dao is included. The comments in 8.10 are interesting in that they reveal Xun Zi as recognising, at least to a degree, the similarities of Confucianism and Mohism insofar as he acknowledges that there is very little difference between the Mohists and the "vulgar" Ru (*su ru* 俗儒). In *Xunzi* 11.5, Mo Zi is described as advocating the way of the manual labourer, this being a pejorative term, whilst in 21.4 ("Dispelling Blindness"), in a list of supposedly "blind" philosophers, Mo Zi's particular form of blindness is characterised thus: "Mo Zi was blinded by utility and was insensitive to the value of good form."[81]

Mo Zi comes in for particular criticism in the chapters on ritual and music. In the former, there is the statement: "Hence, Ru practices will cause a man to fulfil both ritual and desires, whereas Mohist practices will cause him to lose both." In the latter, there is a detailed analysis of the various perceived benefits of music punctuated at intervals with the recurring comment: "Yet Mo Zi condemns it. How can this be endured?" One particularly pertinent quotation is as below:

> Mozi says: "Music was something the sage kings condemned; so the Ru err in making music." The gentleman considers that this is not true. Music was enjoyed by the sage kings; it can make the hearts of the people good; it deeply stirs men; and it alters their manners and changes their customs. Thus, the Ancient Kings guided the people with ritual and music, and the people became harmonious and friendly.

---

81. The Chinese for this is: "墨子蔽於用而不知文" — see Liang Qixiong (1983), p. 290.

Finally, the short verse in *Xunzi* 25.17 advances the view that Mohist methods only come to the fore in times of chaos.

> An age that lacks a True King
> will impoverish worthy and virtuous men.
> Violently cruel men will eat grass- and grain-fed animals,
> the humane only dregs and husks.
> Ritual and music are destroyed, ceasing to be used.
> Sages go into hiding and secrete themselves,
> so the methods of Mo Di are put into practice.

(iii) *Zhuangzi*: Mo Zi is referred to, or actually discussed, in 10 of the 33 chapters of the *Zhuangzi*. With one notable exception (*vide infra*), the references are critical of Mo Zi and his movement. In Zhuang Zi's considerations, Mo Zi is variably linked with other philosophers — with Confucius several times; with Yang Zhu several times (as in the *Mencius*); and with a wider group including not only Confucius and Yang Zhu, but also others, particularly members of the School of Names (Mingjia).

Considering Confucius first, one important reference is that in which Zhuang Zi attempts to identify the source of philosophical movements, mentioning specifically Confucius and Mo Zi. Speaking of the disorder which results from each person pursuing his own interest — a matter of particular concern for Mo Zi in chapters 11–13 of the *Mozi* — Zhuang Zi writes:

> As a result, there was great consternation in the world, and the Confucians and Mohists all came forward, creating for the first time the rules of ethical behaviour. But what would they say of those men who nowadays make wives of their daughters?[82]

In terms of criticism, Zhuang Zi writes:

> When the Way relies on little accomplishments and words rely on vain show, then we have the rights and wrongs of the Confucians and the Mohists. What one calls right the other calls wrong; what one calls wrong the other calls right. But if we want to right their wrongs and wrong their rights, then the best thing to use is clarity.[83]

---

82. *Zhuangzi* 14. Translation after Watson (1968), p. 165 — see also his note on the problematic final sentence.

83. *Zhuangzi* 2. Translation after Watson (1968), p. 39.

A similar general criticism applied to Mo Zi linked with Yang Zhu is to be found in *Zhuangzi* 12.[84] The most detailed consideration of Mo Zi and the Mohist school is, however, to be found in *Zhuangzi* 33. Not only is this chapter a rare source of information about the later division of Mohism into discrete schools (see Section II above), but there is also an unusually favourable and sympathetic evaluation of the philosopher himself. Of note are the critical reference to the three core doctrines most inimical to human nature,[85] the reference to Mo Zi's reliance on the ancient sage kings as authorities, and the concluding complimentary remarks. This passage is given in full below:

> Not to be extravagant towards later ages, not to be wasteful of the ten thousand things, and not to glory in countless rules but to use string and ink to discipline oneself and prepare against the urgent matters of the age — the Way and the methods of the ancients lay in these things. Mo Di and Qin Guli heard of their practices and delighted in them but they carried them to excess and went to extremes in following them. They created "Condemning Music" and what they called "Moderation in Use". In life there was to be no singing and in death no mourning garments. [They believed in] overflowing love, universal benefit and no aggression and their way was without anger. They also loved study and broad learning and in this were not extraordinary. But they were not the same as the former kings insofar as they reviled the rites and music of the ancients. The Yellow Emperor had the *Xianchi* [music]; Yao had the *Dazhang*; Shun had the *Dashao*; Yu had the *Daxia*; Tang had the *Dahuo*; King Wen had the music of *Biyong* whilst King Wu and the Duke of Zhou created the *Wu* [music]. In the funeral rites of the ancients there were rules for the noble and the base, and superiors and inferiors had grades. The Son of Heaven had inner and outer coffins of seven layers, feudal lords of five layers, grand masters of three layers, and officers of two layers. Only Mo Zi had no singing in life and no funeral garments in death, and a coffin of paulownia wood with no outer coffin, taking this to be the rule and pattern. To use this to teach people is, I fear, not to love people; to use this as one's own practice

---

84. See Watson (1968), p. 141.
85. The three are "Condemning Music," "Moderation in Use," and "Moderation in Funerals" — the three most directly opposed to Confucian doctrines.

is certainly not to love oneself. This is not to overthrow the Way of Mo Zi. Nevertheless, he condemns singing when there is singing, he condemns weeping when there is weeping, and he condemns music when there is music — is this really human? His is a life of labour and a death of parsimony. It is a way of great abstemiousness. It causes people sorrow and sadness and, what is more, it is difficult to practise. I am afraid his Way cannot be regarded as that of a sage. It runs contrary to the hearts of all under Heaven and cannot be borne by them. Even if Mo Zi himself was able to bear it, how could the rest of the world do so? It is set apart from the world and is far removed from the [way of] kings.

Mo Zi advanced his doctrines, saying: "In former times, when Yu controlled the flood waters by clearing the courses of the Yangtze and Yellow Rivers and opening up connections with the four barbarians and the Nine Regions, there were three hundred well-known rivers, three thousand branch rivers, and countless small streams He personally carried a basket and wielded a shovel to join and mix the world's waterways until there was no down left on his calves and no hair on his shins. The teeming rains washed him and the whirling winds blew upon him as he established the myriad states. Yu was a great sage and this was how he gave form to all under Heaven." This caused the Mohists of later ages for the most part to use furs and coarse cloth as clothing and to wear clogs and sandals on their feet. Day and night they did not rest and took their suffering to extremes, saying: "If we cannot be like this we are not following the way of Yu and are not worthy of the name 'Mohists'."

The disciples of Xiangli Qin, the followers of Wu Hou, and the Southern Mohists such as Ku Huo, Yi Chi and Deng Lingzi all recited the Mohist Canons but were contentious, hypocritical and disparate, calling each other "separatist" Mohists. They used the "hard and white" and "sameness and difference" debates to express their opposition and used the discussion of the "incompatibility of odd and even" to respond to each other. They each took their own Master to be a sage and wanted him to be the overall leader, hoping to achieve the succession to later generations, but up to now the matter is unresolved. Mo Di and Qin Guli were right in their ideas but wrong in their practices. The effect on the later generation Mohists was that they subjected themselves to hardship so that they left "no down on their calves and no hair on their shins" in outdoing each other and that is all.

This may be better than disorder but it is worse than good order. Nevertheless, Mo Zi was genuine in his love for the world but he failed to achieve what he sought. Yet, although withered and worn, he never gave up. Truly he was an officer of ability![86]

(iv) *Han Feizi*: There are two significant references in the *Han Feizi*. In the first, Mo Zi is listed with several philosophers. Among them are Hui Shi of the School of Names and Song Xing who is now particularly known for his stand against aggression, a reflection, perhaps, of Mohist influence. About the group, Han Fei says: "... they were like the painter of the whip. And their theories, being roundabout, profound, magnificent and exaggerating, were not practical."[87] There is also reference in this passage to Mo Zi's construction of a wooden kite, attesting to his activities as a craftsman. Later in the same chapter (in the commentary), there is an interesting comment on Mo Zi's apparent deficiencies in literary style — a criticism that has, of course, persisted to the present time. The remarks, made by Tian Jiu 田鳩 during a discussion with the King of Chu, read:

> The teachings of Mo Zi convey the principles of the early kings and theorise the words of the saintly men and thereby propagate ideas among people. If he made his phrasing eloquent, people might, it was feared, harbour the literature but forget the utility, that is to say, he might injure the utility with the literature. That would be doing exactly the same thing as the man of Chu trading his pearls and the Earl of Jin marrying out his daughter. Therefore, the sayings of Mo Zi were mostly not eloquent.[88]

In the second reference,[89] the Mohists are linked with the Confucians in a discussion which begins by giving an account of the later divisions of the two schools considered above with respect to Mohism (Section II). The main point that Han Fei is intent on making is that both schools rely heavily on the authority of the ancient sage kings to support their rival doctrines. But the ways of the sage kings cannot be known with any certainty, which is why, according to Han Fei, the issues between the Mohists and the Confucians cannot be decisively resolved. As an example, he gives an

---

86. *Zhuangzi* 33 — GQF, vol. 4, pp. 1073–1081.
87. *Han Feizi* XI.1. Translation after Liao (1959), vol. 2, p. 27.
88. *Han Feizi* XI.1. Translation after Liao (1959), vol. 2, pp. 33–34.
89. See the *Han Feizi* XIX.2, Liao (1959), vol. 2, p. 298 et seq.

account of their opposing positions on funerals and mourning, contrasting Mohist frugality with Confucian excess. But who is to say which is right?

In summary, the few references in the *Han Feizi* suggest some points of relatively close similarity between Mohism and Legalism and some areas of marked divergence. Of the former, one might mention the concept of a centralised controlling bureaucracy which is responsible for determining moral codes — although here the two schools rely on different authorities — as well as the use of *fa* 法 or standards, and the implementation of a system of rewards and punishments to ensure adherence to the imposed standards. Of the latter, one might mention the quite different attitudes to aggressive militarism and to the authority of ancient sages and kings.

(v) *Lü Shi Chunqiu*: In this work there are twenty specific references to Mo Di or members of his school.[90] In examining these, several points emerge. The first and most prominent is undoubtedly the recurring mention of Mohism in conjunction with Confucianism which gives the strong impression that these were the two dominant philosophical movements of the Warring States period and were relatively equal in importance then, however differently they were treated by history subsequently. Second, on the issue of Mo Di's own background, there are two statements identifying him as an officer or knight (*shi* 士), and bracketing him with Confucius in this regard. Thus, in 24/5.3 it states: "Confucius, Mo Di, and Ning Yue, all of them scholar-knights who wore the clothes of commoners, reflected on the state of the world." Third, there is little of a specific nature about Mohist doctrines. Both Mo Di and Confucius are seen as being committed to benevolence and righteousness (*ren* 仁 and *yi* 義), although in 17/7.1 where the things that particular philosophers valued (*gui* 貴) are listed, Mo Di is associated with "universality" (*jian* 兼) whereas Confucius is associated with "benevolence" (*ren* 仁). In fact, numerically the most frequent reference to Mohist teaching concerns defence, although several of these instances relate to his disciples or later members of the school. In one such reference, involving Meng Sheng, the following general statement about rewards and punishments (integral to Mohist political philosophy) is found:

---

90. Using the numbering given by Knoblock and Riegel (2000) these are: 1/5.5; 2/4.3; 4/3. 2; 12/5.2; 13/3.5; 13/7.1; 14/3.3; 15/1.4; 15/3.1; 15/5.2; 15/7.5; 16/7.1; 17/7.1; 18/7.3; 19/2.3; 19/3.4; 21/5.2; 22/3.1; 24/5.3; 26/2.5. The translations of the excerpts follow Knoblock and Riegel.

The Mohists believe that those who do not obey the leader do not understand the teachings. Severe punishments and generous rewards are insufficient to make people reach this state. In the present age, many advocate stern punishments and generous rewards, but in earlier ages such people were those who mistook faultfinding for careful examination. (19/3.4)

Finally, mention is made of two other sections. The first is Book 5 which is devoted almost entirely to music, but contains no reference to Mo Zi. The second is 13/4 which, as Knoblock and Riegel point out, is strongly tinged with Mohist views.

(vi) *Huainanzi*: In this work there are fewer and generally less substantial references than in the *Lü Shi Chunqiu*.[91] The pattern is, however, closely similar in the two works. Indeed, in two instances, what is reported is identical. Again, there is a preponderance of references linking Mohism with Confucianism or, in one instance, comparing the two founders of their respective movements. There is also one reference linking Mo Di with Yang Zhu as in the *Mencius*. There is, as would be expected, reference to Mo Di's military expertise; for example, the recurring story of his meeting with Gongshu Pan in relation to the defence of Song. Finally, there is the statement (in 21/7) that Mo Zi studied Confucian methods but found them wanting. Specific mention is made of elaborate funerals as being wasteful of material and impoverishing the people, and of prolonged mourning as harming the living and damaging the conduct of affairs.

VII. Han Yu's Essay

I have included this brief essay here for two reasons. First, it shows that Mohism was not entirely moribund even many centuries after its apparent demise. Second, it points up the areas of convergence between Mohism and Confucianism at a time when discussion was no longer bound by a perceived need to establish doctrinal superiority.

Confucians ridicule Mohists because of [their] "Exalting Unity", "Universal Love", "Exalting Worthiness", and "Percipient Ghosts".

---

91. I have located 11 references as follows (the page numbers refer to the *Xinyi Huainanzi* ed. Xiong Lihui (1997): 9/16, p. 437; 11/12, p. 535; 12/4, p. 584; 12/18, p. 641; 13/7, p. 672; 16/11, p. 846; 17/14, p. 942; 19/3, p. 1039; 19/4, p. 1043; 20/10, p. 1115; 21/7, p. 1178.

Confucius was in awe of great men so, when he was living in a country, he did not condemn its great officers. But when the *Spring and Autumn Annals* ridicules opinionated ministers, is this not "exalting unity"! When Confucius [speaks of] "overflowing with love", "cleaving to the benevolent", and "widely conferring benefits and helping everyone" as being sage-like, is this not "universal love"! Confucius valued the worthy insofar as he divided his disciples into four classes to advance and praise them and [said the gentleman] dislikes the thought of his name not being preserved after death. Is this not "exalting worthiness"! Confucius sacrificed [to the spirits] as if they were present and ridiculed those who sacrificed as if they were not really sacrificing. He said: "When I sacrifice, I shall receive blessing." Is this not "recognising ghosts"! Confucians and Mohists were equal in the approval of Yao and Shun just as they were equal in their condemnation of Jie and Zhou. They were alike in [their teaching of] cultivating the self and rectifying the mind to bring order to the world's states. How were they not both pleased with this? I think that the disputes arose amongst their later students, each wishing to advance the theories of their own teacher. There are not "two teachers" in terms of their basic doctrines. Confucius certainly made use of Mo Zi and vice-versa. If they had not made use of each other, there would not have been Kong and Mo.[92]

VIII. The Translation

There are very few translations of the *Mozi* into Western languages and only one that is almost complete — that of Forke into German, published in 1922. There are two main reasons for this paucity, both touched upon in the earlier sections. The first is the extraordinary and sustained lack of interest in Mo Zi, his sect and his book, which extended from the Han period to the mid-Qing period. The second is that two of the five sections present considerable difficulty, not only for translators, but also for Chinese scholars themselves. These difficulties are due primarily to the state of the text of the two sections, but also to some degree to the subject matter and method of its presentation.

---

92. The essay is to be found in the *Chang Li Xiansheng Wenji* 昌黎先生文集, Sanmin Shuju, Taipei, 1999, vol. 1, pp. 34–37. The specific references to the *Lun Yu* are as follows: I.6; VI.28; I.7; XV.19; III.12.

Prior to the publication of Forke's work, there were several partial translations which, in chronological order, were: (i) The translation of the three chapters on universal love in his work on the *Mencius* by Legge in 1861. (ii) The publication of some sections translated into German by Faber in 1877. (iii) A translation of the chapter on moderation in funerals by De Groot in 1894. (iv) A work on Mo Zi with numerous passages translated into French by David in 1907.[93] Shortly after Forke's translation appeared, Y-P Mei produced two complementary books on Mo Zi. One was a translation of what he called the "ethical and political works" and the other was a general study of the philosopher and his philosophy.[94] The translated material included all of Parts I, II and IV, but completely omitted Parts III and V. Mei was somewhat critical of Forke's endeavours with these singularly difficult sections — "... and the German version of the Logic chapters as well as of these last chapters (i.e. the military chapters) not infrequently misses the original."[95] — perhaps unjustly under the circumstances. After a lapse of more than three decades, two partial translations were published. The first was by Burton Watson into English, published in 1963, and including at least one example of each of the ten triads of the "core" doctrine chapters,[96] together with the chapter "Condemning Confucianism". The other partial translation was by Schmidt-Glintzer into German, appearing in 1975 and including most of the first two Parts (chapters 1–39).[97] Most recently, in a compendium of early Chinese philosophy, Ivanhoe has included complete or partial English translations of eight chapters from Part Two, all but one of which were included in Watson's earlier work.[98] Two English translations of the difficult sections on "dialectics" and defence are those of A. C. Graham in the first case and R. D. S. Yates in the second case. These are considered more fully in the introductions to the respective Parts.

---

93. For details, see Mei (1934), p. 60.
94. Mei (1929) and (1934).
95. See Mei (1934), p. 57.
96. Watson (1963). There are two chapters on "Exalting Worthiness," "Moderation in Use," and "Heaven's Intention."
97. Schmidt-Glintzer (1975).
98. Ivanhoe (2001), pp. 55–110.

The present translation, particularly of Parts I, II, and IV, is based primarily on five modern editions as follows:

1. Wu Yujiang 吳毓江, *Mozi Jiaozhu* 墨子校注, first published in 1943 and reprinted in two volumes in 1993. It contains a very detailed commentary and a substantial appendix of considerable value (vol. 2, pp. 1001–1094).

2. Li Yushu 李漁叔, *Mozi Jinzhu Jinyi* 墨子今註今譯. Published in 1974 as a single volume which omits the *Canons* and *Explanations* and the defence chapters. The author published a separate work on the former in 1968 (*Mobian Xinzhu* 墨辯新注).

3. Zhou Caizhu 周才珠 & Qi Ruiduan 齊瑞端. Their single volume work *Mozi Quanyi* 墨子全譯 which included all chapters, was published using simplified characters in 1993. Subsequently they published an enlarged and revised version in two volumes in 1998 simply titled *Mozi* 墨子 using traditional characters. There is a relatively detailed commentary.

4. *Mozi Baihua Jinyi* 墨子白話今譯. A single volume work using simplified characters, prepared by Wu Longhui 吳龍輝 and others and published in 1992. The Canons and Explanations are omitted.

5. Li Shenglong 李生龍, *Xinyi Mozi Duben* 新譯墨子讀本. This is a single volume work containing all chapters and with a relatively detailed commentary, published in 1996.

In addition, the earlier editions by Bi Yuan, Sun Yirang and Zhang Chunyi were frequently consulted as were other works referred to in Section III above and listed in the Bibliography, albeit less frequently. For the "dialectical" chapters (Part III) and the defence chapters (Part V) several specialised studies proved invaluable. In each case, these are discussed in the brief introductory comments to the respective Parts.

The aim in the translation itself was to attain that elusive balance between accuracy and readability. On this point, the *Mozi* has come under criticism for its allegedly repetitive and boring style.[99] Whatever its

---

99. Hansen (1992), whose positive evaluation of Mo Zi has already been referred to, also defends his style, and prefaces his chapter on Mohism with the following two quotations: "One thing is certain, and that is, philosophically Mohism is shallow and unimportant." (Wing-tsit Chan) and "And yet, as we have seen, he (Mo Zi) defends it in the same pedestrian and uninspired way he defends every other doctrine he preaches …" (Burton Watson) — see his p. 95.

supposed deficiencies, the style is, I think, integral to the presentation of the Mohist arguments so I have attempted to preserve it (as far as this is possible) despite the risk of attracting the very same criticism. The notes were designed to indicate all areas of significant difficulty in the text as well as to provide historical and biographical information where relevant.

In conclusion, then, it must be conceded that very little is known about the historical Mo Zi and the school he founded. On the other hand, there is no doubt that Mohism as a body of doctrine disseminated by its adherents, whoever they were and however they were organised, did flourish during the Warring States period and offered the main doctrinal alternative to Confucianism. However much these two "schools" were seen as opponents at the time, it should be clear from the earlier sections that while there were undoubted points of doctrinal conflict, the two "schools" had a lot in common. Nevertheless, despite its vigour during this early period, Mohism appears to have been eclipsed by the early part of the Western Han period and to have remained in eclipse as an influential philosophy from that time on.

Why, in historical terms, Mohism proved so ephemeral, that is, why it declined and disappeared, is a subject that has occasioned some speculation, but the main reasons are probably not hard to identify. First, it was opposed by a very strong alternative in Confucianism which, by its nature, must have held a greater appeal for the ruling elite. Moreover, Mohism was a doctrine that could not exist *pari passu* with Confucianism in the way that Daoism could (and did). Second, and this particularly applies to what is contained in the "dialectical" chapters, it was a relatively complicated philosophy as well as being personally and intellectually demanding, as Wu Feibai has stressed. Third, since it was never implemented by a state whose ruler espoused its doctrines, it never achieved vindication by practice. Finally, Mohism must have lost its relevance to a significant degree as a doctrine to resolve the destructive struggles between states that characterised the Warring States period when this period itself came to an end with the formation of a unified empire. Also, on this point, skills in defensive warfare at a practical level were no longer at a premium.

Nevertheless, with no small measure of good fortune, the book containing the doctrines of Mohism did survive, albeit in a rather dilapidated state, even if the movement did not. This allowed, and even encouraged, its "rediscovery" by a series of Qing scholars who were themselves successors of the "text-critical" movement of which Gu Yanwu was the most important progenitor, insofar as the textual issues were of particular interest to such men (*vide* Wang Niansun's comment quoted earlier). Others, however, including scholars such as Hu Shi and Liang Qichao in particular, saw in the work (especially the "dialectical" chapters) evidence of interest in logic and science, areas which were otherwise somewhat neglected in early Chinese intellectual history. Whatever the motivation, the work of a substantial number of scholars has brought this seminal text rightfully back into focus more than two millennia after its initial compilation. It is not only a work of great intrinsic interest; it is also of critical importance for an understanding of Chinese philosophy's initial brilliant flowering in the "axial period," as Jaspers has called it. Finally, and by no means least, a number of the ideas it articulates have an enduring relevance and, indeed, in some cases even a particular applicability in the modern world.

Key to Abbreviations

ACG: Graham A. C., *Later Mohist Logic Ethics and Science*, Hong Kong, 1978.

ACG/DT: Graham A. C., *Disputers of the Tao*, La Salle, Illinois, 1989.

AF: Forke A., *Me Ti des Sozialethikers und seiner Schüler philosophische Werke*, Berlin, 1922.

BW: Watson B., **BW/CT**: *Chuang Tzu*, New York, 1968; **BW/MT**: *Mo Tzu*, New York, 1963.

BY: Bi Yuan 畢沅, *Mozi Zhu* 墨子注, MZJC 7 and 8.

CH: Harbsmeier C., *Science and Civilisation in China* VII.1, Cambridge, 1998.

CHANT: Chinese Ancient Texts Database, Hong Kong, 2003.

CSJC: *Congshu Jicheng* 叢書集成.

CYX: Cao Yaoxiang 曹耀湘, *Mozi Jian* 墨子箋, MZJC 17.

CZM: Cen Zhongmian 岑仲勉, *Mozi Chengshou Gepian Jianzhu* 墨子城守各篇簡注, MZJC 45.

DLMAC: Hu Shi, *The Development of the Logical Method in Ancient China*, New York, 1963 reprint.

DMB: *Dictionary of Ming Biography*, eds. Goodrich L. C. and Fang Chaoying, New York, 1976.

DR: *Dictionnaire Ricci de caractères chinois*, Paris, 1999.

DZ: *Dao Zang* 道藏 (*The Daoist Patrology*).

FGY: Fan Gengyan 范耕研, *Mobian Shuzheng* 墨辯疏證, Beijing, 1934.

FSC: Fang Shouchu 方授楚, *Moxue Yuanliu* 墨學源流, Taiwan, 1957.

FYL: Fung Yu-lan, *History of Chinese Philosophy*, vol. 1, trans. Bodde D., Princeton, 1952.

G&S: Graham A. C., Sivin N., in *Chinese Science*, eds. Nakayama S. and Sivin N., MIT, 1973.

GBD: Giles H. A., *A Chinese Biographical Dictionary*, 1898.

GH: Gao Heng 高亨, *Mojing Jiaoquan* 墨經校詮; *Mozi Xinjian* 墨子新箋, MZJC 41.

GSLZ: *Gongsun Longzi* 公孫龍子.

GQF: Guo Qingfan 郭慶藩, *Zhuangzi Jishi* 莊子集釋, 4 vols., Beijing, 1961.

HM: Maspero H., *T'oung Pao* 25 (1928): 1–64.

HS: Hu Shi 胡適, *Mozi Xiaoqupian Xingu* 墨子小取篇新詁, MZJC 21.

HYDCD: *Hanyu Da Cidian* 漢語大辭典, 22 vols., Shanghai, 2001.

HYX: Hong Yixuan 洪頤烜, *Mozi Conglu* 墨子叢錄, MZJC 9.

HZH: Hong Zhenhuan 洪震寰 in *Kexue shi Jikan* 科學史集刊, 4 (1962): 1–40 and 7 (1963): 28–44.

JBC: Jiang Baochang 姜寶昌, *Mojing Xunshi* 墨經訓釋, Jinan, 1993.

JC: Chmielewski J., *Rocznik Orientalistyczny*, 8 articles as follows: 26 (1962): 7–22; 26 (1963): 91–105; 27 (1963): 103–121; 28 (1965): 87–111; 29 (1965): 117–138; 30 (1966): 31–52; 31 (1968): 117–136; 32 (1969): 83–103.

K: Knoblock J., *Xunzi*, 3 vols., Stanford, 1988–1994.

K&R: Knoblock J. and Riegel J., *The Annals of Lü Buwei*, Stanford, 2000.

LC: Liu Chang 劉昶, *Xu Mozi Jiangu* 續墨子閒詁, MZJC 30.

LCC: Legge J., *The Chinese Classics*, 5 vols., Hong Kong, 1960 reprint.

LCR: Liu Cunren 柳存仁, *New Asia Journal* (新亞學報), 7 (1965): 1–134.

LDF: Luan Diaofu 欒調甫, *Mozi Yanjiu Lunwenji* 墨子研究論文集, MZJC 33.

LQC: Liang Qichao 梁啟超, *Mozi Xue'an* 墨子學案 and *Mojing Jiaoshi* 墨經校釋, MZJC 18, 19.

LSCQ: *Lü Shi Chunqiu* 呂氏春秋 — see K&R.

LSL: Li Shenglong 李生龍, *Xinyi Mozi Duben* 新譯墨子讀本, Taipei, 1996.

LYS: Li Yushu 李漁叔, *Mozi Jinzhu Jinyi* 墨子今注今譯, Taipei, 1974.

LZDB: *Xinyi Liezi Duben* 新譯列子讀本, Zhuang Wanshou 莊萬壽, Taipei, 1996.

MBJ: *Mozi Baihua Jinyi* 墨子白話今譯, Wu Longhui et al. 吳龍輝等, Beijing, 1995.

MZH: Ma Zonghuo 馬宗霍, *Mozi Jiangu Canzheng* 墨子閒詁參正, Jinan, 1984.

MZJC: Yan Lingfeng 嚴靈峰, (*Wuqiubeizhai* 無求備齋) *Mozi Jicheng* 墨子集成, 46 vols., Taipei, 1975.

MZQY: *Mozi Quanyi* 墨子全譯 — see Z&R.

MZS: Mou Zongsan 牟宗三, *Mingjia yu Xunzi* 名家與荀子, Taipei, 1994.

PJI: Ivanhoe P. J., *Mozi* in *Readings in Classical Chinese Philosophy*, eds. Van Norden B. W. and Ivanhoe P. J., New York, 2001, pp. 55–110.

QM: Qian Mu 錢穆, *Mozi* 墨子, Shanghai, 1931.

RDSY: Yates R.D.S., **RDSY/T** *The City under Siege: Technology and Organization as Seen in the Reconstructed Text of the Military Chapters of the Mo Tzu*, Ph.D. diss., Harvard, 1980; **RDSY/SC** *Science and Civilisation in China,* vol. V.6, Cambridge, 1994.

SAA: *The Spring and Autumn Annals* 春秋, LCC vol. 5.

SBCK: *Sibu Congkan* 四部叢刊.

SSJZS: *Shisan Jing Zhushu* 十三經注疏.

SSJZ: *Sishu Jizhu* 四書集註, Zhu Xi 朱熹.

SSX: Su Shixue 蘇時學, *Mozi Kanwu* 墨子刊誤, MZJC 10.

SYR: Sun Yirang 孫詒讓, *Mozi Jiangu* 墨子閒詁, MZJC 12–15.

THQ: Tao Hongqing 陶鴻慶, *Du Mozi Zhaji* 讀墨子札記, MZJC 10.

TJF: Tan Jiefu 譚戒甫, *Mobian Fawei* 墨辯發微, Beijing 1964; *Mojing Fenlei Yizhu* 墨經分類譯注, Beijing, 1981.

TJY: Tang Junyi 唐君毅, *New Asia Journal* (新亞學報), 4/2 (1960): 65–99.

WFB: Wu Feibai 伍非百, *Zhongguo Gumingjia Yan* 中國古名家言, Beijing, 1983.

WHB: Wang Huanbiao 王煥鑣, *Mozi Jiaoshi* 墨子校釋, Hangzhou, 1984.

WKY: Wang Kaiyun 王闓運, *Mozi Zhu* 墨子注, MZJC 16.

WNS: Wang Niansun 王念孫, *Mozi Zazhi* 墨子雜志, MZJC 9.

WSN: Wang Shunan 王樹枬, *Mozi Jiaozhu Buzheng* 墨子斠注補正, MZJC 11.

WYJ: Wu Yujiang 吳毓江, *Mozi Jiaozhu* 墨子校注, 2 vols., Beijing, 1993 reprint.

WYZ: Wang Yinzhi 王引之, *Jingzhuan Shici* 經傳釋詞, Taipei, 1968; *Jingyi Shuwen* 經義述聞, Shanghai, 1936.

XYHNZ: *Xinyi Huainanzi* 新譯淮南子, Xiong Lihui 熊禮匯, Taipei, 1997.

XZXZ: *Xunzi Xinzhu* 荀子新注, Beijing, 1979.

YBY: Yang Baoyi 楊葆彝, *Mozi Jingshuo Jiaozhu* 墨子經説校注, cited by JBC.

YPM: Mei Y-P, *The Ethical and Political Works of Motse*, London, 1929.

YTY: Yin Tongyang 尹桐陽, *Mozi Xinshi* 墨子新釋, MZJC 20.

YY: Yu Yue 俞樾, *Mozi Pingyi* 墨子平議, MZJC 10.

YZCQ: *Yanzi Chunqiu* 晏子春秋.

Z&Q: Zhou Caizhu 周才珠 and Qi Ruiduan 齊瑞端, *Mozi* 墨子, Taipei, 1998.

ZCY: Zhang Chunyi 張純一, *Mozi Jijie* 墨子集解, MZJC 23–26.

ZHY: Zhang Huiyan 張惠言, *Mozi Jingshuo Jie* 墨子經説解, MZJC 9.

ZQH: Zhang Qihuang 張其鍠, *Mozi Tongjie* 墨子通解, MZJC 29.

ZWDCD: *Zhongwen Da Cidian* 中文大辭典, China Academy, Taiwan, 1973.

ZYZ: Zhou Yunzhi 周云之, *Mingbian Xuelun* 名辯學論, Shenyang, 1995.

ZZ: *Zuo Zhuan*, SSJZS vol. 6 and LCC vol. 5.

ZZR: Zhang Zhirui 張之銳, *Xin Kaozheng Mojing Zhu* 新考正墨經注, cited by LSL.

Table of Equivalences for Weights and Measures

Weights

1 *liang* 兩 = 16g (16 *liang* 兩 = 1 *jin* 斤)

1 *jin* 斤 = 244g (30 *jin* 斤 = 1 *jun* 鈞)

1 *jun* 鈞 = 7.32kg (4 *jun* 鈞 = 1 *dan* 石)

1 *dan* 石 = 29.32kg

Capacities

1 *sheng* 升 = 199.687ml (10 *sheng* 升 = 1 *dou* 斗)

1 *dou* 斗 = 1.996 litres (10 *dou* 斗 = 1 *dan* 石)

1 *dan* 石 = 19.968 litres

Distances

1 *cun* 寸 = 23.1mm (10 *fen* 分 = 1 *cun* 寸)

1 *chi* 尺 = 23.1cm (10 *cun* 寸 = 1 *chi* 尺)

1 *bu* 步 = 1.38m (6 *chi* 尺 = 1 *bu* 步)

1 *zhang* 丈 = 2.31m (10 *chi* 尺 = 1 *zhang* 丈)

1 *li* 里 = 0.576km (variable) (1 *li* = 300 paces/*bu*)

These figures are taken from Yates (1980)[1] with the addition of *liang* 兩 and *li* 里. The figure for the latter is taken from the *Dictionnaire Ricci* where the distance, although given precisely, is noted as variable.

---

1. Yates' figures are based on M. Loewe, *Records of Han Administration* (Cambridge University Press, 1967), vol. 1, p. 161. See Yates, p. xii.

THE MOZI

PART *I*

The Epitomes

1: 親士[1]

1.1 入國而不存其士,[2] 則亡國矣。見賢而不急,則緩其君矣[3]。非賢無急,非士無與慮國。緩賢忘士,而能以其國存者,未曾有也。

1.2 昔者文公出走而正天下;桓公去國而霸諸侯;越王勾踐遇吳王之醜,而尚攝中國之賢君。三子之能達名成功於天下也,皆於其國抑而大醜也。太上無敗,其次敗而有以成,此之謂用民。

---

1. Both words in the title present some difficulty in translation. On 親, BY quotes the 《眾經音義》 as follows: "親、愛也、近也". I have preferred the latter in the sense that a ruler must be well disposed towards and ready to give his ear to the views of the 士, the second term, which presents the greater difficulty of the two — see, for example, WYJ's detailed note 1, pp. 2–3. Throughout, I have translated 士 as "officer", apart from certain instances in the chapters on defence where "knight-errant" has seemed more appropriate.
2. In this sentence 入 is read as 執掌 (Z&Q), and 存 as 恤問 following the 《說文》 definition (SYR).
3. This is a problematic sentence as evidenced by the varying interpretations — see, for example, LYS, LSL, MBJ, Z&Q.

1: On Being Sympathetic towards Officers

1.1   To take control of a state but not be sympathetic towards its officers leads to loss of the state. To see someone who is worthy but not be anxious [to use him] leads to neglect of its ruler. Unless someone is worthy, do not be anxious [to use him]. Unless someone is an officer, do not deliberate on affairs of the state [with him]. No-one has ever disregarded worthiness and neglected officers, and still been able to preserve his state.

1.2   Formerly, Duke Wen had to flee, yet he came to govern the world; Duke Huan was forced to leave his state, yet he became hegemon over the feudal lords; the king of Yue, Gou Jian met with humiliation at the hands of the king of Wu, yet later was held in awe by the worthy rulers of the Middle Kingdom.[i] These three men were all able to achieve success and fame in the world because they endured repression and great wretchedness in their own states. Best by far is not to fail, but next best is to find in failure the way to success. This is called using the people.

---

i.   Wen Gong 文公, personal name Chong'er 重耳, was the son of Xian Gong 獻公 of Jin 晉. In 654 BC he was forced to flee the country as a result of a plot against him initiated by his father's favourite concubine, Li Ji 驪姬, but later (634 BC) returned to rule it. He was for a time one of the 五霸 or "Five Hegemons". Huan Gong 桓公, personal name Xiaobo 小白, was forced to flee the state of Qi 齊 with his brother by Xiang Gong 襄公. After the murder of the latter, the brothers returned and contended over the succession. With the help of Guan Zhong 管仲, Xiaobo prevailed to enjoy an extended period of rule in Qi. Gou Jian 勾踐 came to the throne of Yue 越 in 496 BC. He subsequently attacked the state of Wu, but was utterly defeated at the eastern gate of the capital by the Wu forces under Fu Chai 夫差. The story is that after the defeat he "daily drank out of a vessel filled with gall and nightly slept on firewood in order to keep himself reminded of the bitterness of defeat." (GBD, p. 373). He later overthrew Wu.

1.3 吾聞之曰:「非無安居也,我無安心也;非無足財也,我無足心也。」[4] 是故君子自難而易彼,眾人自易而難彼。君子進不敗其志,內[5]究其情,雖雜庸民,終無怨心,彼有自信者也。是故為其所難者,必得其所欲焉,未聞為其所欲,而免其所惡者也。是故逼臣傷君,諂下傷上。君必有弗弗[6]之臣,上必有詻詻[7]之下。分議者延延,而支苟者詻詻[8],焉可以長生保國[8]。臣下重其爵位而不言,近臣則喑,遠臣則吟[9],怨結於民心,諂諛在側,善議障塞,則國危矣。桀紂不以其無天下之士邪?殺其身而喪天下。故曰:歸國寶不若獻賢而進士。

---

4. There is no source for this apparent quotation. BY has "青不肯苟安,如好利之不知足" which Z&Q interpret as the eagerness of the ruler to be well disposed towards scholars.
5. I have followed YY's reading of 內 as 退. LSL, however, reads it as 內心.
6. 弗 is read as 咈 (SYR).
7. 詻 is read as 諤 — see WYJ, note 15, p. 5.
8. In translating this clause, I have followed LYS's interpretation — see his note 7, p. 3.
9. Most texts have this character in its variant form (ZWDCD #3957).

1.3   I have heard this said: "It isn't that there is not a peaceful place to dwell, but that I am not at peace in my heart; it isn't that there is not enough wealth, but that my heart is not enough." This is why a gentleman is hard on himself but easy on others, whereas a common man is easy on himself but hard on others. When a gentleman takes office, he does not lose his ideals. When he goes into retirement, he considers the circumstances. Even if he is mistaken for a common man, he never feels resentment because he has confidence in himself. This is why those who undertake what is difficult will certainly achieve what they desire. [On the other hand], one never hears of those who do what they desire avoiding what they dislike. For this reason, powerful officials harm the ruler and fawning subordinates damage their superiors. A ruler must have officials who will stand up to him. A superior must have subordinates who will be plain speaking. If those who engage in open debate adhere to their views and those who privately advise are bold in their censure, then the lives [of the people] can be prolonged and the state protected. If officials and subordinates attach importance to their rank and position and do not speak out, or if close advisers are silent and more distant officials sigh, or if resentment builds up in the hearts of the people, or if toadying and flattery are all around, or if wise counsels are obstructed, then the state is endangered. Did not Jie and Zhou fail to make use of the world's officers?[ii] They lost their own lives and they lost all under Heaven. Thus it is said that making a gift of the state's treasures does not match recommending the worthy and advancing officers.

---

ii.   Jie 桀 and Zhou 紂 are standard and recurring examples of bad rulers whose excesses led to the downfall of their dynasties — Xia and Shang, respectively.

1.4   今有五錐，此其銛，銛者必先挫；有五刀，此其錯，錯者必先
靡。是以甘井近竭，招[10]木近伐，靈龜近灼，神蛇近暴[11]。是故
比干之殪，其抗也；孟賁之殺，其勇也；西施之沈，其美也；吳
起之裂，其事也。故彼人者，寡不死其所長，故曰：「太盛難守
也。」

1.5   故雖有賢君，不愛無功之臣；雖有慈父，不愛無益之子。是故不
勝其任而處其位，非此位之人也；不勝其爵而處其祿，非此祿之
主也。良弓難張，然可以及高入深；良馬難乘，然可以任重致
遠；良才難令，然可以致君見尊。是故江河不惡小谷之滿己也，
故能大。聖人者事無辭也，物無違也[12]，故能為天下器。是故江

---

10. 招 is read as 喬 following BY and SYR.
11. 暴 is taken as 曝 or 晒. As WHB points out, the reference is to a ceremony for bringing
    rain.
12. There is variation in the reading of the clause "物無違也". Thus YPM has, "… do not
    … reject any trifle"; LSL takes it to be about opposing the views of others; MZQY
    interprets it as "… not opposing the laws of objective reality".

1.4 Now if there are five awls, the sharpest one is certainly the first to be broken. If there are five blades, the keenest one is certainly the first to be dulled. In the same way, the sweetest well is the first to be used up and the tallest tree the first to be felled. [Likewise], the efficacious tortoise is the first to be burned and the magical serpent the first to be dried in the sun. Thus, Bi Gan's death was due to his outspokenness; Meng Ben's death was due to his bravery; Xi Shi's drowning was due to her beauty; and Wu Qi's being torn asunder was due to his conduct of affairs.[iii] These examples show that there are few whose deaths are not attributable to what distinguishes them. Thus it is said: "The more egregious, the more difficult to endure."[iv]

1.5 So even a worthy ruler will not look kindly on an official without merit, and even a compassionate father will not look kindly on a son without promise. For this reason, a man who occupies a position for which he is not competent is not the man for the position. Likewise, a man who receives emolument for a rank he does not merit is not the man to have that emolument. A good bow is hard to draw, yet it can reach the heights and penetrate the depths. A good horse is hard to ride, yet it can bear a heavy load and travel far. Men of great talent are difficult to direct, yet they can serve the ruler and be respected. Great rivers do not resent the little streams that fill them because they are what can make them great. In affairs, the sage does not shirk his responsibility and does

---

iii. The details of these four examples are as follows: (i) Bi Gan 比干 (12th century BC) was put to death by the previously mentioned tyrant Zhou 紂 for his outspoken criticism of the latter's excesses. (ii) Meng Ben 孟賁 was noted for his strength and courage. It is not clear whether a native of Wei (LSL, MZQY) or of Qi (WYJ) is being referred to. The latter is mentioned in *Mencius* IIA.2(2). If the man referred to was put to death by Wu Wang of Qi, it is evidence for this chapter being later than Mo Zi himself — see WYJ, note 31, p. 7. (iii) Xi Shi 西施 of Yue, famed for her beauty, was the key figure in a stratagem by Gou Jian 勾踐 against Fu Chai 夫差 — for details and references, particularly to the *Wu Yue Chunqiu* 吳越春秋, see WYJ, note 32, p. 7. (iv) Wu Qi 吳起 (died 381 BC) was a noted statesman and military strategist. A native of Wei, he served in several states. Tradition has it that he was killed by fellow officials jealous of his great ability. As with Meng Ben, there is an issue of dates.

iv. Although there is no source for this apparent quotation, LSL refers to *Laozi* 9 where a similar view is expressed.

河之水，非一源之水也；千鎰之裘，非一狐之白也。夫惡有同方
取不取同而己者乎[13]？蓋非兼王之道也。

1.6　是故天地不昭昭，大水不潦潦，大火不燎燎，王德不堯堯者，乃
千人之長也。其直如矢，其平如砥，不足以覆萬物。是故谿陝者
速涸，逝淺者速竭，墝埆者其地不育，王者淳澤，不出宮中，則
不能流國矣。

_____

13. There are issues about the text of this sentence. YY suggests it should read: "夫惡有同
方不取，而取同己者乎？" which I have followed. ZCY has a slightly different
version, but with the same meaning.

not go against things. Therefore, he can be a utensil of the world. Thus, the waters of a great river do not flow from one source, nor does a fur garment worth a thousand *yi* come from the white fur of a single fox. Can one follow the practice of not selecting those who comply with the Way, but selecting those who agree with oneself? This is not the Way of a universal king.

1.6 Thus, Heaven and earth are not perpetually refulgent; great waters are not always turbulent; great fires are not continuously blazing; great virtue is not entirely lofty. Then the leader of a thousand, be he as straight as an arrow and as smooth as a whetstone, is not sufficient to cover the ten thousand things. This is why narrow streams quickly dry up, why shallow waters are quickly exhausted, and why barren lands do not nourish. If a ruler's genuine beneficence does not go beyond the confines of his palace, then it cannot spread throughout the state.[v]

---

v. The meaning of this final paragraph is obscure and interpretations differ notably. The translation given is tentative and depends particularly on the following: (i) Reading 大 instead of 王 in the fourth clause of the first sentence (e.g. LSL). (ii) Taking 者 as the start of the second sentence, reading it as 若 (SYR), and neither including it in the first sentence as 也 (MZQY), nor retaining it in its nominalising sense. (iii) Reading 逝 as 游 in the sense of 流 (WYZ).

2: 修身

2.1　君子戰雖有陳[1]，而勇為本焉；喪雖有禮，而哀為本焉；士[2]雖有
學，而行為本焉。是故置本不安者，無務豐末[3]；近者不親，無務
來遠；親戚不附，無務外交[4]；事無終始，無務多業；舉物而闇，
無務博聞。是故先王之治天下也，必察邇來遠。君子察邇而邇修
者也。見不修行，見毀，而反之身者也[5]。此以怨省而行修矣。譖
慝之言，無入之耳；批扞之聲，無出之口；殺傷人之孩[6]，無存之
心，雖有詆訐之民，無所依矣。

2.2　故君子力事日彊，願欲日逾，設壯日盛。君子之道也，貧則見
廉，富則見義，生則見愛，死則見哀，四行者不可虛假，反之身
者也。藏於心者無以竭愛，動於身者無以竭恭，出於口者無以竭
馴。暢之四支，接之肌膚，華髮隳顛，而猶弗舍者，其唯聖人
乎！

---

1. 陳 is read as 陣 in the sense of 陣法.
2. There is debate about the character 士. I have followed a number of commentators in taking it as 仕 — see WYJ's detailed note 2, p. 12.
3. The reading of this statement is based on YY's omission of 者 and SYR's interpretation of the other characters.
4. WYJ quotes the commentary on the 曲禮 as follows: "親指族內，戚指族外。"
5. There is uncertainty about the text for this and the last part of the preceding sentence. Most commentators (including SYR) follow the text and suggested punctuation of BY. WYJ, whose version is partially followed here, provides a detailed note (note 8, p. 13).
6. 核 is read for 孩 following WKY and others.

2: On Cultivating the Self

2.1 For a gentleman, in warfare, although there is strategy, it is courage that is fundamental. In mourning, although there is ritual, it is grief that is fundamental. In being in office, although there is learning, it is [right] conduct that is fundamental. Thus, if the root is not made secure, there is no way for the branches and leaves to flourish. If one is not sympathetic to those who are near, one cannot induce those from afar to come. If one does not cherish one's own family, one cannot devote oneself to outsiders. If one does not have an end and a beginning in the conduct of affairs, one cannot complete many undertakings. If one is obscure in raising something, one cannot be widely heard. This is why former kings, in bringing order to the world, certainly examined the near and solicited the distant. A gentleman is one who examines the near and cultivates the self. If he sees conduct that is not cultivated, or if he is vilified, he reflects on his own mistakes. In this way, resentment is minimised and [right] conduct is cultivated. If slanderous and vilifying words do not enter his ears, if critical and offensive sounds do not issue from his mouth, if thoughts of killing and maiming others are not harboured in his heart, then even if there are people who would slander and accuse him, they would have nothing to rely on.

2.2 Thus a gentleman's exertions daily grow stronger, his aspirations daily grow higher, and his accomplishments daily grow more flourishing. The Way of a gentleman is this — when poor to display honesty, when rich to display generosity, to show love towards the living, and to show pity towards the dead. These are four matters in which there is no place for him to be false, and on which he must examine himself. What is stored in his heart is inexhaustible love. What is manifest in his behaviour is inexhaustible reverence. What comes forth from his mouth are words of inexhaustible refinement. If virtue extends to his four limbs, inheres in the flesh of his body, and is not abandoned even to the extreme of age, then he is indeed a sage.

2.3   志不彊者智不達，言不信者行不果。據財不能以分人者，不足與友；守道不篤、遍物不博、辯是非不察者，不足與游[7]。本不固者末必幾[8]，雄而不修者其後必惰[9]，原濁者流不清，行不信者名必耗。名不徒生，而譽不自長，功成名遂，名譽不可虛假，反之身者也。

2.4   務言而緩行，雖辯必不聽；多力而伐功，雖勞必不圖[10]。慧者心辯而不繁說，多力而不伐功，此以名譽揚天下。言無務為多而務為智，無務為文而務為察。故彼智無察，在身而情，反其路者也[11]。善無主於心者不留，行莫辯於身者不立。名不可簡而成也，譽不可巧而立也，君子以身戴行者也。思利尋焉，忘名忽焉，可以為士於天下者，未嘗有也。

7.   In the second part of this sentence the reading basically follows ZCY. See also WYJ, note 23, p. 15, who gives a detailed account of the textual issues including the possible reading of 偏 as 別 in other chapters (19 & 28) and WYZ's notes on this.

8.   Modern commentators generally accept the reading of 幾 as 危.

9.   There are issues with both 雄 and 修. Most equate the former with 勇. YPM (and some Chinese commentators) take the latter to refer to "self-cultivation". MZQY reads it as 長久. I have taken it as indicating 修養 in a general sense — see LSL.

10. 圖 is taken as 取 — see MZQY, LSL.

11. The translation of this sentence incorporates BY's emendation of 彼 to 非 and SYR's emendation of 情 to 惰.

2.3   In one whose will is not strong, wisdom is not far-reaching. In one whose words are not sincere, conduct is not efficacious. One who has wealth but cannot share it with others is not worth befriending. One whose adherence to the Way is not thoroughgoing, whose view of things is partial and not broad, whose discrimination between right and wrong is not perspicacious, is not worth having as a comrade. When the root is not secure, the branches are inevitably endangered. When there is bravery without cultivation, there is inevitably indolence. When the source is turbid, what flows is not clear. When conduct is not sincere, reputation is inevitably damaged. Reputation is not born out of nothing. Praise does not grow of its own accord. If merit is achieved, reputation follows. Reputation and praise cannot be empty and false. This is something that should be looked at in oneself.

2.4   One who devotes his attention to words but is tardy in conduct will certainly not be listened to even though he argues well. One who expends a lot of energy but brags about his achievement will certainly not be chosen even though he works hard. One who is wise discriminates in his mind, but does not complicate his words. He exerts his strength, but does not brag about his achievement. In this way, his reputation and praise spread through the world. In speaking, he should devote attention to wisdom and not to amount. He should devote attention to clear analysis and not to eloquence. Not to be wise and not to analyse clearly, but to be indolent in oneself is to take the opposite road. Goodness that is not paramount within the mind is not enduring. Conduct that is not debated within the self is not established. Reputation cannot be treated lightly and still be achieved. Praise cannot be sought cunningly and still be established. A gentleman must match his words and his deeds.[i] No-one who thinks of seeking profit[ii] and carelessly disregards his reputation can ever be deemed an officer in the world.

---

i.   This follows the MZQY's interpretation of this statement.

ii.   利 is taken here in the Confucian and somewhat pejorative sense rather than in the sense found in the chapters on doctrine, and also in the dialectical chapters (as "benefit").

3: 所染[1]

3.1   子墨子言見染絲者而嘆，曰：「染於蒼則蒼，染於黃則黃，所入者變，其色亦變，五入必，而已則為五色矣[2]！故染不可不慎也。」

3.2   非獨染絲然也，國亦有染。舜染於許由、伯陽；禹染於皋陶、伯益；湯染於伊尹、仲虺；武王染於太公、周公。此四王者所染當，故王天下，立為天子，功名蔽天地。舉天下之仁義顯人，必

1.   A very similar essay, under the title 當染 ("Correct Dyeing"), is found in the LSCQ 2/4. The two texts are essentially identical in the initial paragraphs, but differ in the later parts, particularly the last section in the LSCQ in which Mo Zi himself is spoken of in relation to "dyeing".

2.   In the LSCQ 2/4.1 this statement reads: "五入而以為五色矣。" — see WYJ, note 4, p. 18 for a discussion of the issues concerning 必, 已 and 則 in the *Mozi* text.

3: On Dyeing

3.1   Master Mo Zi told how, when he saw someone dyeing silk, he sighed and said: "When something is dyed by blue [dye], it becomes blue. When it is dyed by yellow [dye], it becomes yellow. What [the dye] enters changes in that its colour changes. Five entries [of dye] create five [different] colours. Therefore, dyeing must be given careful attention."

3.2   This does not only apply to the dyeing of silk. States also have "dyeing". Shun was "dyed" by Xu You and Bo Yang; Yu was "dyed" by Gaoyao and Bo Yi; Tang was "dyed" by Yi Yin and Zhong Hui; King Wu was "dyed" by Tai Gong and Zhou Gong.[i] What "dyed" these four kings was fitting, therefore they ruled all under Heaven, they were established as Sons of Heaven, and their achievements and fame extended throughout Heaven and earth. When the topic of men illustrious in the world for benevolence and righteousness is brought up, these four kings are invariably

---

i.   The four examples of the persons "dyed" are the revered early emperors of the legendary period — the Xia, Shang and Zhou dynasties. Brief details of the "dyers" are as follows: Xu You 許由 was said to have been offered the empire by Yao but declined — see *Shi Ji* 61, vol. 7, p. 2121. Bo Yang 伯陽 was said to have been one of the "Seven Friends" of Shun — see LSCQ 14/2 and WYJ, note 7, p. 19. Gaoyao 皋陶 was traditionally said to have been the officer in charge of punishments at the time of Shun — see the *Documents* 5, SSJZS, vol. 1, pp. 59–65 and LCC, vol. 3, pp. 68–75. Bo Yi 伯益 was appointed by Shun to manage "grass and trees, birds and beasts, mountains and marshes" — see the *Documents* 3 (舜典), LCC, vol. 3, p. 46. Yi Yin 伊尹 was a statesman famed for his counsels under Tang — see, for example, LSCQ 14/2, 15/1. Zhong Hui 仲虺 was also a noted minister under Tang — see, for example, the *Zuo Zhuan* for Xuan 12 (LCC, vol. 5, p. 312) and Xiang 14 (LCC, vol. 5, p. 462) where he is recorded as giving what is basically the same advice. Tai Gong 太公 is taken to be Jiang Tai Gong 姜太公 or Lü Shang 呂尚 who was associated with both Wen Wang and Wu Wang — see *Shi Ji* 32, vol. 5, p. 1477ff. Zhou Gong 周公 (died 1105 BC) was the greatly revered son of Wen Wang and younger brother of Wu Wang. He played an important role in the early Zhou administration.

稱此四王者。夏桀染於干辛、推哆；殷紂染於崇侯、惡來；厲王
染於厲公長父、榮夷終；幽王染於傅公夷、蔡公穀。此四王者，
所染不當，故國殘身死，為天下僇[3]。舉天下不義辱人，必稱此四
王者。

3.3   齊桓染於管仲、鮑叔；晉文染於舅犯、高偃；楚莊染於孫叔、沈
尹；吳闔閭染於伍員、文義；越勾踐染於范蠡、大夫種。此五君

---

3.   辱 is read for 僇 — see, for example, Z&Q.

spoken of. Jie of Xia was "dyed" by Gan Xin and Tui Duo; Zhou of Yin was "dyed" by Chong Hou and Wu Lai; King Li was "dyed" by Duke Chang Fu of Li and Rong Yizhong; King You was "dyed" by Duke Yi of Fu and Duke Gu of Cai.[ii] What "dyed" these four kings was not fitting, therefore their countries were destroyed, they themselves died, and were despised throughout the world. When the topic of men reviled in the world for unrighteousness and shamefulness is brought up, these four kings are invariably spoken of.

3.3 Huan of Qi was "dyed" by Guan Zhong and Bao Shu. Wen of Jin was "dyed" by Jiu Fan and Gao Yan. Zhuang of Chu was "dyed" by Sunshu and Shenyin. Helü of Wu was "dyed" by Wu Yun and Wen Yi. Gou Jian of Yue was "dyed" by Fan Li and Zhong Dafu.[iii]

---

ii. The four examples are rulers noted for misrule, cruelty and excess; Jie 桀 was the last emperor of the Xia dynasty and said to have ruled from 1818 BC to his death in 1763 BC; Zhou 紂 was the last emperor of the Yin (Shang) dynasty. The traditional date for his death is 1122 BC after being overthrown by Wu Wang. An anonymous reader has kindly drawn my attention to recent controversy about this date — see Edward L. Shaughnessy, "Calendar and Chronology," in *The Cambridge History of Ancient China* (Cambridge University Press, 1999), pp. 19–29; Li 厲 and You 幽 ruled during the early part of the Zhou dynasty, the former from 878 to 827 BC and the latter from 781 to 770 BC. Brief details of the "dyers" are as follows: Gan Xin 干辛 is described in commentaries as a "flattering official" at the court of Jie — see LSCQ 15/1 where his adverse influence on Jie is described. Tui Duo (Chi) 推哆 is probably Tui Yi 推移, a noted bravo at the time of Jie — see *Mozi* 31. Chong Hou 崇侯—名虎 was described as a "flattering official" — see *Shi Ji* 3 & 4, vol. 1, pp. 106, 118. Wu Lai 惡來 was the son of Fei Lian — see *Shi Ji* 3, vol. 1, p. 106 and *Xunzi* 8, K, vol. 2, p. 78. Zhang Fu 長父 was probably the Duke of Guo 郭 — see *Xunzi* 25, K, vol. 3, p. 184 and notes 84 & 85, p. 356. Rong Yizhong 榮夷終 was chief minister under Li Wang — see LSL, note 7, p. 11. Of the last two "dyers" nothing certain is known — see WYJ, note 15, p. 21 for various suggestions.

iii. There are some variations in the names of the "dyers" in the LSCQ. Brief details of the five examples, the first, second and fifth of which are also spoken of in *Mozi* 1.2 above, are as follows: (i) Duke Huan of Qi 齊桓公 ruled from 685 to 643 BC and was noted as a virtuous and effective ruler — see, for example, *Lun Yu* XIV.17. Guan Zhong 管仲 (died 645 BC) was his chief minister and adviser as well as the putative author of the *Guanzi*. Bao Shu is Bao Shuya 鮑叔牙, a friend of Guan Zhong, who was said to have recommended him to Huan Gong — for one anecdote linking the three men see LSCQ 23/2.2. (ii) Duke Wen of Jin 晉文公 is often linked with Huan Gong as examples of virtuous rulers (e.g. *Mencius* IVB.21). He ruled from 635 to 628 BC — see FYL pp. 112, 312. Jiu Fan 舅犯 is Jiu Fan 咎犯, a maternal uncle of Duke Wen — see *Shi Ji* 39

者所染當，故霸諸侯，功名傳於後世。范吉射染於長柳朔、王
胜；中行寅染於籍秦、高彊；吳夫差染於王孫雒、太宰嚭；知伯
搖染於智國、張武；中山尚染於魏義、偃長；宋康染於唐鞅、佃

What "dyed" these five rulers was fitting, therefore they ruled over the feudal lords and their achievements and fame were handed down to later generations. Fan Jiyi was "dyed" by Zhang Liushuo and Wang Sheng. Zhonghang Yin was "dyed" by Jiqin and Gao Qiang. Fu Chai of Wu was "dyed" by Wang Sunluo and Chief Minister Pi. Zhi Boyao was "dyed" by Zhi Guo and Zhang Wu. Zhongshan Shang was "dyed" by Wei Yi and Yan Chang. Kang of Song was "dyed" by Tang Yang and Tian Buli.[iv] What

---

and *Xunzi* 13. Gao Yan 高偃 is Guo Yan 郭偃 — see *Han Feizi* 南面 where his role in Jin is discussed. (iii) Duke Zhuang of Chu 楚莊公 (ruled 631 to 591 BC) was one of the five hegemons — see FYL, vol. 1, p. 112. Sunshu is Sunshu Ao 孫叔敖 who served as his prime minister and was renowned for being appointed three times without feeling pleasure and dismissed three times without feeling resentment. There is some uncertainty about Shenyin but he is probably Shenyin Jing 沈尹莖 — see LSCQ 24/ 2.3 for an anecdote linking the two men and WYJ, note 20, pp. 22–23 for views on who Shenyin might be. Note also LSCQ 4/3.1 where a Shenyin Wu is linked with Sunshu Ao as a teacher of Duke Zhuang. (iv) Helü of Wu 吳闔閭 (ruled 514 to 496 BC) was the other name of Duke Guang 光公. He was noted for the simplicity of his life. Wu Yun is Wu Zixu 伍子胥, originally from Chu, who assisted Helü in his successful campaign against that state — see *Shi Ji* 66, vol. 7, pp. 2171–2184 and multiple references in the LSCQ. Wen Yi is Wen Zhiyi 文之儀, a high official in Wu — see LSCQ 2/4.2 & 4/ 3.1 and *Xinxu Zashi* 5. (v) Gou Jian 勾踐 came to the throne of Yue in 496 BC and was involved in a long and ultimately successful struggle with Fu Chai of Wu — see *Shi Ji* 41, vol. 5, pp. 1739–1756. Fan Li 范蠡 was a minister under Gou Jian whom he helped considerably in the struggle against Wu before retiring from office — see *Shi Ji* 129 and *Han Shu* 90. Zhong Dafu 種大夫 (Great Officer Zhong) is taken to be Zhong Wen 種 文. Originally from Zou 鄒, he rose to high office in Yue under Gou Jian — see *Shi Ji* 41, particularly vol. 5, p. 1740 and note 6, pp. 1741–1742.

iv. Brief details of these six ill-fated rulers and their "dyers" are as follows: (i) Fan Jiyi 范 吉射 is Fan Yang 范鞅, a Jin noble of the late Spring and Autumn period who, in alliance with Zhonghang Yin (*vide infra*), fought against the confederacy of Zhao, Wei, Han and Zhi and was defeated — see LSCQ 25/1.4 and K&R p. 713. (ii) Zhonghang Yin 中行寅 was also a noble of the late Spring and Autumn period and the son of Zhonghang Mu 中行穆. He allied with Fan Jiyi in the unsuccessful venture mentioned above. Jiqin (Huang Jiqin 黃籍秦) and Gao Qiang 高彊 were his *jia chen* 家臣 — see WYJ, note 27, p. 24. (iii) Fu Chai 夫差 (died 473 BC) was the son of Helü Wang (*vide supra*). He was involved in a long drawn-out struggle with Gou Jian which he eventually lost through the strategem devised by the latter and his minister Fan Li. Wang Sunluo 王孫雒 and Chief Minister Pi 伯嚭 were his ministers. There is some uncertainty about the name of the former — see WYJ, note 28, pp. 24–25. For the role of the latter in the events leading to Fu Chai's downfall see *Shi Ji* 31, vol. 5, p. 1466ff. (iv) There is uncertainty about the name Zhi Boyao 智伯搖. K&R translate this as Earl

不禮。此六君者所染不當，故國家殘亡，身為刑戮，宗廟破滅，絕無後類，君臣離散，民人流亡，舉天下之貪暴苛擾者，必稱此六君也。

3.4 凡君之所以安者何也？以其行理也，行理性[4]於染當。故善為君者，勞於論人，而佚於治官。不能為君者，傷形費神，愁心勞意，然國逾危，身逾辱。此六君者，非不重其國愛其身也，以不知要故也。不知要者，所染不當也。

---

4. Read as 生 following BY.

"dyed" these six rulers was not fitting, therefore their countries were destroyed and lost, they themselves were punished and disgraced, their ancestral temples were ruined and destroyed, their descendants were completely wiped out, their princes and ministers were set aside and scattered, and the people were dispersed and lost. When the topic of those of the world who were avaricious and cruel, troublesome and vexatious is brought up, these six rulers are invariably spoken of.

3.4   What is it that rulers in general use to bring about peace? They act according to principle. And this acting according to principle stems from proper "dyeing". Therefore, rulers who are skilled [in ruling] take great pains in selecting officials, but use a light touch in controlling them. Rulers who are without ability [in ruling] harm their bodies and tax their spirits, have anxious hearts and troubled minds, their states are increasingly endangered and they themselves are increasingly humiliated. With these six rulers, it was not that they did not consider their states important and did not cherish their own persons, but that they did not know the essential elements [of ruling]. And they did not know these essential elements because what "dyed" them was not fitting.

Yao of Zhi (LSCQ 2/4.2, p. 89) but the *Guang Yun* 廣韻 lists Zhi as a surname and gives Zhi Bo as the example. He may be the person referred to in the *Shi Ji* 101, vol. 8, p. 2746 — see WYJ, note 30, p. 25. I could find no information on the "dyers", Zhi Guo 智國 and Zhang Wu 張武. In the ZWDCD the former is listed simply as an official under Zhi Boyao with reference to the present chapter. (v) Zhongshan 中山 is a place name and is equated with Xian Yu 鮮虞. Shang 尚 may have been the ruler of the region. SYR takes the reference to be to the events recorded in the *Zuo Zhuan* for the 4th year of Duke Ting but see WYJ for other views. I can find nothing about the "dyers", Wei Yi 魏義 and Yan Chang 偃長. (vi) Song Kang 宋康 was King Yan 偃 of Song, posthumously titled Kang. The events leading to his death are recorded in the *Shi Ji* 38, vol. 5, p. 1632. For Tian Buli 田不禮 — written as 田不禋 in the LSCQ 2/4.2 — see the *Shi Ji* 43, particularly vol. 6, pp. 1813–1815. For Tang Yang 唐鞅 and his death see *Xunzi* 21.

3.5 　非獨國有染也，上亦有染。其友皆好仁義，淳謹畏令，則家日益，身日安，名日榮，處官得其理矣，則段干木、禽子、傅説之徒是也。其友皆好矜奮，創作比周，則家日損，身日危，名日辱，處官失其理矣，則子西、易牙、豎刀之徒是也。《詩》曰：「必擇所堪，必謹所堪」者，此之謂也。

3.5   And it is not only countries that have "dyeing" but officers also.
[With the latter], if their friends all love benevolence and
righteousness, and are honest, cautious and law-abiding, then each
day their families will prosper, each day they themselves will be at
peace, and each day their names will be honoured. If they hold an
official position, they abide by its principles. The associates of
Duangan Mu, Qin Zi and Fu Yue were of this sort.[v] If, on the other
hand, their friends all love to brag and are impetuous, if they form
cliques, then each day their households will decline, each day they
themselves will be in danger, each day their reputations will
deteriorate, and, if they hold an official position, they neglect its
principles. The associates of Zi Xi, Yi Ya and Shu Dao were of
this sort.[vi] In the *Odes* it is written: "One must choose what one
is steeped in; one must pay close attention to what one is steeped
in."[vii] This is what has been said.

---

v.   Duangan Mu 段干木, an early Warring States period scholar, was a student of Zi Xia
     and a teacher to Wei Wen Hou — see *Shi Ji* 121, vol. 10, p. 3116 and the LSCQ 4/3.
     2 where he is described as "an important horse trader from Jin". Qin Zi is Qin Guli 禽
     滑釐, one of Mo Zi's leading disciples — see FYL, vol. 1, pp. 103–104 and also *Mozi*
     46 & 50 as well as in several of the chapters on "Defence of the City" — e.g. chapter
     52. In the *Shi Ji* 121 he is listed with Duangan Mu as a student of Zi Xia. Fu Yue 傅説
     was a minister under the Yin (Shang) emperor Wu Ding (1324 to 1265 BC) — see *Mozi*
     9 (尚賢中) for further details.

vi. There is doubt about who Zixi 子西 was. The most common view is that he was the Chu
     high official Dou Yishen 鬥宜申 — see WYJ, note 50, p. 28 and also SAA and ZZ for
     the 10th year of Duke Wen. Yi Ya 易牙 was chief cook to Duke Huan of Qi and noted
     for his great ability to distinguish flavours — see *Mencius* VIA.7(5), LCC, vol. 2, p. 405
     and LSCQ 16/3.2. Shu Dao 豎刀 was also in the service of Duke Huan of Qi. For
     detailed consideration of the name, which in some texts is written Shu Shao 豎刁, see
     WYJ, note 50, p. 28. See also LSCQ 16/3.2 where both he and Yi Ya are linked as
     participants in a coup.

vii. This apparent quotation from the *Odes* cannot be located in presently available texts.

4: 法儀[1]

4.1   子墨子曰:「天下從事者不可以無法儀,無法儀而其事能成者無
有也。雖至士之為將相者,皆有法,雖至百工從事者,亦皆有
法。百工為方以矩,為圓以規,直以繩,〔衡以水,〕正以縣[2]。無
巧工不巧工,皆以此五者為法。巧者能中之,不巧者雖不能中,
放依以從事,猶逾己。故百工從事,皆有法所度。今大者治天
下,其次治大國,而無法所度,此不若百工,辯[3]也。」

4.2   然則奚以為治法而可?當皆法其父母奚若?天下之為父母者眾,
而仁者寡,若皆法其父母,此法不仁也。法不仁,不可以為法。
當皆法其學奚若?天下之為學者眾,而仁者寡,若皆法其學,此
法不仁也。法不仁,不可以為法。當皆法其君奚若?天下之為君

---

1. I have chosen to translate 法儀 as two separate terms, taking the latter in the sense of
    usages or rules rather than instruments. See also LSL's introductory note and reference
    to the *Guanzi* 2 〈形勢〉.
2. I have included the fourth example as added by certain editors such as WYJ. Otherwise
    YY's comment about four rather than five things referred to in the next sentence is
    applicable.
3. Reading 辯 as 明智 following, for example, MZH.

4: On Standards and Rules

4.1 Master Mo Zi said: "Those who work in the world cannot do so without standards and rules. No-one has ever been able to accomplish anything without standards and rules. Even those officers who are generals and ministers all have standards. Even the hundred craftsmen in doing their work all have standards too. The hundred craftsmen make what is square with a square, make what is round with compasses, use a straight edge to establish what is straight, determine the horizontal with a water level, and the vertical with a plumb line. Whether skilled or unskilled, craftsmen all take these five things as standards. Skilled craftsmen are able to comply with these standards whilst unskilled craftsmen, even if they are unable to comply with them, will still surpass themselves if they follow them in their work. Thus the hundred craftsmen all have standards as a basis for their work. Nowadays, the greatest [achievement] is to bring order to the world and the next greatest is to bring order to a large country, but to attempt these things without reliance on standards is to compare unfavourably in wisdom with the hundred craftsmen."

4.2 This being so, then what can be taken as a standard for bringing about order? Would it be fitting if everyone took their parents as the standard? There are many parents in the world, but few who are benevolent. If everyone took their parents as the standard, this would be a standard without benevolence. A standard without benevolence cannot be taken as a standard. Would it be fitting if everyone took their teacher as the standard? There are many teachers in the world, but few who are benevolent. If everyone took their teacher as the standard, this would be a standard without benevolence. A standard without benevolence cannot be taken as a standard. Would it be fitting if everyone took their ruler as a standard? There are many rulers in the world, but few who are benevolent. If everyone took their ruler as the standard, it would be a standard without benevolence. A standard without

者眾，而仁者寡，若皆法其君，此法不仁也。法不仁，不可以為
法。故父母、學、君三者，莫可以為治法。

4.3   然則奚以為治法而可？故曰莫若法天。天之行廣而無私，其施厚
而不德，其明久而不衰，故聖王法之。既以天為法，動作有為必
度於天，天之所欲則為之，天所不欲則止。然而天何欲何惡者
也？天必欲人之相愛相利，而不欲人之相惡相賊也。奚以知天之
欲人之相愛相利，而不欲人之相惡相賊也？以其兼而愛之，兼而
利之也。奚以知天兼而愛之，兼而利之也？以其兼而有之，兼而
食之也。

4.4   今天下無大小國，皆天之邑也。人無幼長貴賤，皆天之臣也。此
以莫不犓〔牛〕[4] 羊，豢犬豬，絜為酒醴粢盛，以敬事天，此不為
兼而有之，兼而食之邪？天苟兼而有食之[5]，夫奚說以不欲人之相
愛相利也！故曰愛人利人者，天必福之；惡人賊人者，天必禍

---

4.   Added by some editors — e.g. LSL.
5.   In the translation I have followed Z&Q in expanding this to read: "兼而有之，兼而食
     之" as previously.

benevolence cannot be taken as a standard. Therefore all three — parents, teachers and rulers — cannot be taken as standards for bringing about order.

4.3   This being so, then what may be taken as a standard for bringing about order? It is said that there is no standard like Heaven. Heaven is broad and unselfish in its actions, and is generous in its bestowing without considering itself virtuous.[i] Its radiance is enduring and does not decay. Therefore, the sage kings took it as the standard. If Heaven is taken as the standard, then all one's actions must be measured against Heaven. What Heaven desires should be done and what it does not desire should not be done. This being so, what does Heaven desire, what does Heaven abhor? Undoubtedly what Heaven desires is that there be mutual love and mutual benefit among people. What it does not desire is that there be mutual hatred and mutual harm among people. How do we know that Heaven desires mutual love and mutual benefit among people and does not desire mutual hatred and mutual harm among people? Because it is universal in loving them and universal in benefiting them. How do we know that Heaven is universal in loving them and universal in benefiting them? Because it is universal in possessing them and universal in feeding them.

4.4   Nowadays, all the countries under Heaven, no matter whether large or small, are Heaven's countries. People, whether young or old, whether noble or base, are all Heaven's subjects. Consequently, there aren't any who do not provide fodder for their oxen and sheep, feed their dogs and pigs, and meticulously prepare the sacrificial wine and millet to honour and serve Heaven. Is this not because [Heaven] is universal in possessing them and universal in feeding them? If Heaven is universal in possessing them and universal in feeding them, how can it be said that it does not want mutual love and mutual benefit among people? This is why it is said that Heaven will certainly bring good fortune to those who love people and benefit people and that Heaven will certainly bring misfortune to those who hate people

---

i.   The translation of this sentence follows Z&Q — see their note 3, p. 31.

之。曰殺不辜者，得不祥焉。夫奚說人為其相殺而天與禍乎？是以知天欲人相愛相利，而不欲人相惡相賊也。

4.5　昔之聖王禹湯文武，兼愛天下之百姓，率以尊天事鬼，其利人多，故天福之，使立為天子，天下諸侯皆賓事之。暴王桀紂幽厲，兼惡天下百姓，率以詬天侮鬼，其賊人多，故天禍之，使遂失其國家，身死為僇於天下，後世子孫毀之，至今不息。故為不善以得禍者，桀紂幽厲是也，愛人利人以得福者，禹湯文武是也。愛人利人以得福者有矣，惡人賊人以得禍者亦有矣。

and harm people. It is also said that those who kill the innocent will meet with disaster. How can it be said that Heaven will bring misfortune to those who kill others? It is by knowing that Heaven desires mutual love and mutual benefit among people and does not desire mutual hatred and mutual harm among people.

4.5   Formerly, the sage kings, Yu, Tang, Wen and Wu were universal in loving the world's ordinary people, leading them to venerate Heaven and serve ghosts, and their benefiting people was very great. Therefore, Heaven brought them good fortune, established them as Sons of Heaven, and the feudal lords of the world all respected and served them. The tyrannical kings, Jie, Zhou, You and Li were universal in hating the world's ordinary people, leading them to revile Heaven and insult ghosts, and their harming people was very great. Therefore, Heaven brought them misfortune, caused them to lose their countries, to be themselves killed, and to be held in contempt in the world so that posterity continues to vilify them unceasingly to the present day. Therefore, those who were without goodness and so suffered misfortune were Jie, Zhou, You and Li. Those who loved people and benefited people and so attained good fortune were Yu, Tang, Wen and Wu. So there are those who, through loving and benefiting people, attain good fortune, and there are also those who, through hating and harming people, suffer misfortune.[ii]

---

ii.   The rulers referred to above are the recurring examples of four good rulers and four bad rulers — see, for example, the previous chapter and, in particular, notes i and ii, pp. 15 and 17.

5: 七患[1]

5.1   子墨子曰:「國有七患。七患者何?城郭溝池不可守,而治宮
室,一患也;邊國至境四鄰莫救[2],二患也;先盡民力無用之功,
賞賜無能之人,民力盡於無用,財寶虛於待客,三患也;仕者持
祿,游者愛佼,君修法討臣,臣懾而不敢拂,四患也[3];君自以為
聖智而不問事,自以為安彊而無守備,四鄰謀之不知戒,五患
也;所信者不忠,所忠者不信,六患也;畜種菽粟不足以食之,
大臣不足以事之,賞賜不能喜,誅罰不能威,七患也。以七患居
國,必無社稷;以七患守城,敵至國傾。七患之所當,國必有
殃。」

5.2   「凡五穀者,民之所仰也,君之所以為養也,故民無仰則君無

---

1.   患 is read as 禍患 in the sense of "misfortune" or "calamity" (Z&Q).

2.   Of the two proposed emendations in this initial clause — 邊 as 敵 (HYX) and 境 as 竟
     (BY) — I have accepted the first only.

3.   The reading of this sentence follows SYR, particularly 咈 for 拂 — see Z&Q.

5: On the Seven Misfortunes

5.1   Master Mo Zi said: "A state has seven misfortunes. What are the seven misfortunes? When the city walls and moat cannot be defended and there is loss of buildings and dwellings — this is the first misfortune. When enemy states approach the frontiers and one's neighbours do not come to one's aid — this is the second misfortune. When first the strength of the people is exhausted in useless undertakings and material rewards are given to those without ability, then the people's strength is dissipated without result, and goods and valuables are wasted in entertaining guests — this is the third misfortune. When officers look to safeguard their salaries, when travelling scholars are fond of fraternising, when rulers frame laws to punish officials, when officials fear punishment and do not dare oppose — this is the fourth misfortune. When the ruler considers himself to have the wisdom of a sage and does not ask about affairs, when he considers himself secure and strong and does not make preparation for defence, when the four neighbours scheme and he does not know to take precautions — this is the fifth misfortune. When those who are sincere are not trusted and those who are trusted are not sincere — this is the sixth misfortune. When the stored and planted pulses and grains are not enough to provide food, when the great officers are not adequate to carry out affairs, when rewards and gifts cannot bring happiness, when penalties and punishments cannot bring fear — this is the seventh misfortune. If the seven misfortunes exist in a state, there will surely be loss of the national altars. If there are the seven misfortunes in guarding a city, when an enemy comes, the state will be overthrown. If the seven misfortunes exist, a state will certainly meet with disaster."

5.2   "In general, the five grains[i] are what the people rely on and what the ruler takes as his support. Therefore, if the people have nothing

---

i.   The five grains are rice, two forms of millet, wheat or barley, and pulses.

養，民無食則不可事，故食不可不務也，地不可不力也，用不可
不節也。五穀盡收，則五味盡御於主，不盡收則不盡御。一穀不
收謂之饉，二穀不收謂之旱，三穀不收謂之凶，四穀不收謂之
饋，五穀不收謂之饑。歲饉，則仕者大夫以下皆損祿五分之一。
旱，則損五分之二。凶，則損五分之三。饋，則損五分之四。
饑，則盡無祿，稟食而已矣。故凶饑存乎國，人君徹鼎食五分之
五，大夫徹縣，士不入學，君朝之衣不革制，諸侯之客，四鄰之
使，雍食而不盛，徹驂騑，塗不芸，馬不食粟，婢妾不衣帛，此
告不足之至也。[4]」

5.3　「今有負其子而汲者，隊[5] 其子於井中，其母必從而道[6] 之。今歲
凶，民飢，道餓，重其子此疚於隊[7]，其可無察邪？故時年歲善，

4.　There are several issues in this sentence as follows: (i) 五分之五 is taken as 五分之三 (SYR). (ii) 縣 is taken as 懸 indicating "musical instruments" (see Z&Q). (iii) 雍 is read as 饗. (iv) 驂 and 騑 represent the two next to outermost and the two outermost horses respectively in a six horse team, the two innermost being termed 服 and 馬. (v) 芸 is taken in the sense of 修理.

5.　There is general acceptance of BY's reading of 隊 as 墜.

6.　道 here is taken as 導 — see, for example, LSL, Z&Q.

7.　Modern editors follow WYZ's rearrangement of this sentence to give: "此疚重於隊其子。"

to rely on, then the ruler has no means of support. If the people have nothing to eat, then they cannot conduct their affairs. Thus food must be taken as fundamental, land must be vigorously worked, and there must be moderation in use. When the five grains are all gathered, then the five tastes are all offered to the ruler [whereas], when they are not all gathered, then the five [tastes] are not all offered. When one of the grains is not harvested, it is spoken of as a dearth. When two of the grains are not harvested, it is spoken of as a scarcity. When three of the grains are not harvested, it is spoken of as a misfortune. When four of the grains are not harvested, it is spoken of as a failure. When five of the grains are not harvested, it is spoken of as a famine.[ii] In a year of dearth, officers from the grand masters down should all suffer a reduction in salary of one part in five. With scarcity, they should suffer a reduction of two parts in five. With misfortune, they should suffer a reduction of three parts in five. With failure, they should suffer a reduction of four parts in five. With famine, there should be no salary whatsoever, only an allowance of food. Therefore, when a misfortune occurs in a state, the ruler should do away with food for the sacrificial tripods (*ding*) by three parts in five. The grand masters should do away with musical instruments. [Ordinary] officers should not enter the schools. The ruler's ceremonial garments should not be renewed. Guests of the feudal lords and messengers from the four neighbours should have prepared food, but it should not be abundant. Four of the horses in a six-horse team should be done away with. Paths are not to be repaired; horses are not to eat grain, and servants and concubines are not to dress in silk, thus indicating the extreme degree of insufficiency."

5.3 "Nowadays, if a mother who is carrying her child on her back while drawing water lets the child fall into the well, she will certainly follow and drag it out. Nowadays, if there is a disastrous year with famine among the people who are starving by the roadside, this is a much greater source of distress than dropping a

---

ii.   The five terms in the text are 饉, 旱, 凶, 饋 (餽) and 饑. The translation follows the generally accepted readings of 旱 as 罕 (YY) and 饋 as 匱 (Z&Q).

則民仁且良；時年歲凶，則民吝且惡。夫民何常此之有？為者
疾，食者眾，則歲無豐[8]。故曰財不足則反之時，食不足則反之
用。故先民以時生財。固本而用財，則財足。故雖上世之聖王，
豈能使五穀常收，而旱水不至哉？然而無凍餓之民者何也？其力
時急，而自養儉也。故《夏書》曰：『禹七年水』，《殷書》曰：『湯五
年旱』，此其離凶餓甚矣，然而民不凍餓者何也？其生財密，其
用之節也。」

5.4   「故倉無備粟，不可以待凶饑。庫無備兵，雖有義不能征無義。
城郭不備全，不可以自守。心無備慮，不可以應卒。是若慶忌無
去[9]之心，不能輕出。夫桀無待湯之備，故放；紂無待武之備，

---

8.   This sentence is quite problematical. YY emends 疾 to 寡 which is followed in the
     translation. SYR proposes a more substantial rearrangement which is clearly what YPM
     has followed.

9.   There is thought to be a lacuna after 去, possibly to be filled by 備 (e.g. LSL), possibly
     by 要離 (e.g. Z&Q).

child. Can this not be recognised? Thus, if the seasons of the year are good, then the people are benevolent as well as good. [Conversely], if the seasons of the year are disastrous, then the people are parsimonious as well as bad. Is the nature of people not constant in this respect? If the people who produce [food] are few, but those who eat it are many, then the year is not one of abundance. Therefore, it is said that, if materials are insufficient, then attention should be directed back at the seasons, and, if food is insufficient, then attention should be directed back at use. Thus, people of ancient times used the season's production of material. With this as the firm foundation for their use of materials, then materials were sufficient. Even if the early generations had sage kings, how could they bring it about that the five grains were always harvested or that droughts and floods did not occur? Nonetheless, there were no people who froze or starved. How was this so? They worked hard in accord with the seasons and in their own lives were frugal. So the *Xia Documents* state: 'Yu had floods for seven years' whilst the *Yin Documents* state: 'Tang had drought for five years'.[iii] This shows that they encountered disaster and famine to an extreme degree. Nevertheless, the people did not freeze or starve. How was this so? It was because the production of materials was substantial, but the use of them was frugal."

5.4 "Therefore, if the granaries are not supplied with grain, it is not possible to deal with disaster and famine. If the armouries are not supplied with weapons, although there is righteousness, it is not possible to prepare troops against the unrighteous. If the inner and outer walls are not completely maintained, it is not possible to defend oneself. If the mind is not prepared beforehand, it is not possible to respond to emergencies. This is like Qing Ji's 'not doing away with it' heart, due to which he was able to escape easily.[iv] Jie made no preparations against Tang and so was banished. Zhou made no preparations against Wu and so was

---

iii. See WYJ, note 43, p. 43 for discussion of these apparent quotations which are found, with some variations, in a number of early works.

iv. Qing Ji 慶忌 was the son of King Liao of Wu and noted for bravery. When King Liao was killed by Helü 闔閭, Qing Ji fled to Wei. He subsequently met his death at the hands of Yao Li 要離.

故殺。桀紂貴為天子，富有天下，然而皆滅亡於百里之君者何
也？有富貴而不為備也。故備者國之重也，食者國之寶也，兵者
國之爪也，城者所以自守也，此三者國之具也。」

5.5　「故曰以其極賞，以賜無功，虛其府庫，以備車馬衣裘奇怪，苦
其役徒，以治宮室觀樂，死又厚為棺槨，多為衣裘，生時治臺
榭，死又修墳墓，故民苦於外，府庫單於內，上不厭其樂，下不
堪其苦。故國離寇敵則傷，民見凶饑則亡，此皆備不具之罪也。
且夫食者，聖人之所寶也。故《周書》曰：『國無三年之食者，國非
其國也；家無三年之食者，子非其子也。』此之謂國備。」

killed.ᵛ Jie and Zhou were both ennobled as Sons of Heaven and were enriched by possession of all under Heaven, yet both were brought to ruin by rulers of a hundred *li*. How was this so?ᵛⁱ They were rich and noble, but they were not prepared. Therefore, being prepared is important for a state. Food is a state's treasure. Weapons are a state's claws. Walls are its means of defending itself. These three are the 'instruments' of the state."

5.5 "Therefore, I say that if, [in a country], its great rewards are conferred on those without merit, if its storehouses and armouries are emptied in the preparation of carriages, horses, exotic garments and furs, if hardship is inflicted on servants and followers by building palaces and houses of fine appearance, if, in death, the inner and outer coffins are thick and the garments and furs are numerous, if, in life, towers and pavilions are built, if, in death, graves and tombs are maintained, the result is that the people suffer without and the storehouses and armouries are exhausted within. Those above are not satisfied with their pleasures and those below do not endure their sufferings. Therefore, the country suffers from bandits and enemies and so is damaged. The people experience calamity and famine and so perish. These are all faults due to not being prepared. Moreover, food is what sages value. Thus the *Zhou Documents* state: 'If a country does not have food for three years, then the country is not a country. If a household does not have food for three years, then the children are not its children.'ᵛⁱⁱ This is what is spoken of as a country being prepared."

---

v.   Both Jie 桀 and Zhou 紂 are paradigms of the cruel and evil ruler and are frequently referred to as such.

vi. The "rulers of a hundred *li*" were Tang and Wu who overthrew Jie and Zhou to establish the Yin and Zhou dynasties respectively — see *Mencius* IIA.3(1).

vii. See WYJ, notes 64, 65, p. 45 for a discussion of this apparent quotation.

6: 辭過[1]

6.1   子墨子曰:「古之民未知為宮室時,就陵阜而居,穴而處,下潤濕傷民,故聖王作為宮室。為宮室之法,曰:『室高足以辟潤濕,邊足以圉風寒,上足以待雪霜雨露,宮牆之高足以別男女之禮[2]。』謹此則止,凡費財勞力,不加利者,不為也。〔以其常〕[3]役,修其城郭,則民勞而不傷;以其常正[4],收其租稅,則民費而不病。民所苦者非此也,苦於厚作斂於百姓。是故聖王作為宮室,便於生,不以為觀樂也;作為衣服帶履,便於身,不以為辟怪也。故節於身,誨於民,是以天下之民可得而治,財用可得而足。」

6.2   「當今之主,其為宮室則與此異矣。必厚作斂於百姓,暴奪民衣食之財以為宮室臺榭曲直之望,青黃刻鏤之飾。為宮室若此,故

1.   There is some question about the precise meaning of the title. LSL, who refers to BY, has "辭過即避免過錯。" (p. 24). There is a school of thought, particularly represented by SYR, which links this chapter to the "節用" chapters of Part II, taking the title as meaning to "avoid excess".
2.   In this sentence, 辟 is read as 避, 圉 as 禦, and 待 as 禦 (WYZ).
3.   Added following BY.
4.   征 is read for 正 (SSX).

6: On Eschewing Faults

6.1   Master Mo Zi said: "In the times when the people of old still did not know how to make dwellings and houses, they dwelt near hills and mounds and lived in caves where the ground beneath was damp and wet, and was harmful to them. Therefore, the sage kings created dwellings and houses. As to their method of building dwellings and houses, they said that a house should be high enough to escape moisture and dampness, the external walls sufficient to withstand wind and cold, the roof sufficient to withstand snow, frost, rain and dew, and the internal walls high enough to maintain the proper separation of men and women. There should be careful attention to these requirements and nothing more, so that, in general, waste of materials and expenditure of strength that did not bring added benefit were avoided. [Then] through their regular employment and in maintaining their city walls, the people may labour, but are not harmed. And through their regular levies and the collection of their rents and taxes, the people may have expenditure, but are not distressed. This is not what causes the people to suffer. What cause suffering among the common people are excessive demands. That is why, when the sage kings made dwellings and houses, they were made suitable for living in but not to be pleasing to the eye. When they made clothes, garments, belts and shoes, they were made suitable for the body but not to be strange and exotic. Thus, they were frugal in themselves and instructive to the people so the people of the world could be provided for and brought to order, and could get enough materials to use."

6.2   "Now, in their making of dwellings and houses, the rulers of the present time are different from this. Certainly they make heavy tax demands on the common people, cruelly seizing their materials for clothing and food in order to make palaces, dwellings, towers and pavilions of intricate appearance, and to adorn them with green and yellow engravings. A consequence of their making their

左右皆法象之。是以其財不足以待凶饑，振孤寡，故國貧而民難治也。君實欲天下之治而惡其亂也，當為宮室不可不節。」

6.3　「古之民未知為衣服時，衣皮帶茭，冬則不輕而溫，夏則不輕而清。聖王以為不中人之情，故作誨婦人治絲麻，梱[5]布絹，以為民衣。為衣服之法：『冬則練帛之中，足以為輕且暖；夏則絺綌之中，足以為輕且清。』謹此則止。故聖人之為衣服，適身體，和肌膚而足矣，非榮耳目而觀愚民也。當是之時，堅車良馬不知貴也，刻鏤文采不知喜也。何則？其所道[6]之然。故民衣食之財，家足以待旱水凶饑者何也？得其所以自養之情，而不感於外也。是以其民儉而易治，其君用財節而易贍也。府庫實滿，足以待不然，兵革不頓，士民不勞，足以征不服，故霸王之業可行於天下矣。」

6.4　「當今之主，其為衣服，則與此異矣。冬則輕暖，夏則輕清，皆已具矣，必厚作斂於百姓，暴奪民衣食之財，以為錦繡文采靡曼

5.　梱 is read for 梱 following SYR.
6.　There is general acceptance of 導 for 道 — see, for example, LSL.

dwellings like this is that their assistants all imitate them. This is why their wealth is insufficient to deal with calamity and famine, and to give relief to orphans and widows, so the state is poor and the people difficult to govern. If rulers truly desire the world to be well ordered and find its disorder abhorrent, it is proper that the houses and dwellings they make cannot be other than moderate."

6.3 "In the times when the people of old still did not know how to make clothes and garments, they wore coverings of skins tied with grasses. In winter, these were not light and warm. In summer, they were not light and cool. The sage kings thought that this did not accord with the people's feelings so they taught women to make silk and hemp, and to weave cotton and light silk to make clothes for the people. The criteria in making clothes and garments were that in winter the inner garments should be of woven silk, enough to be light as well as warm, and in summer the inner garments should be of fine linen, enough to be light as well as cool. They attended to this and went no further. Thus, the sages made clothes and garments that were comfortable for the body and in accord with stature — that was enough — and not to delight the senses and be looked at by fools. At a time like that, strong carts and fine horses were not known as valuable. Carvings and engravings, ornaments and adornments were not known as pleasurable. How so? It was because the leadership was as it was. So how did every family have enough materials for clothing and food to deal with drought and flood, disaster and famine? By having conditions that enabled them to maintain themselves so as not to be affected by what was external. In this way, the people were frugal and easy to govern whilst the ruler was moderate in his use of materials and could easily provide. Storehouses and granaries were full enough to anticipate adverse circumstances. Arms were not in poor repair and officers and people were not worn out and were sufficient to suppress the non-submissive. Therefore, the work of the hegemonical king could be carried out in the world."

6.4 "In their making of clothes and garments, the rulers of the present time are different from this. They all already have what is light and warm in winter and what is light and cool in summer, yet they must impose heavy tax demands on the ordinary people, cruelly

之衣，鑄金以為鈎，珠玉以為珮，女工作文采，男工作刻鏤，以
為身服。此非云益暖之情也，單財勞力，畢歸之於無用也。以此
觀之，其為衣服，非為身體，皆為觀好。是以其民淫僻而難治，
其君奢侈而難諫也。夫以奢侈之君御好淫僻之民，欲國無亂，不
可得也。君實欲天下之治而惡其亂，當為衣服不可不節。」

6.5　「古之民未知為飲食時，素食而分處。故聖人作誨，男耕稼樹
藝，以為民食。其為食也，足以增氣充虛，彊體適腹而已矣。故
其用財節，其自養儉，民富國治。今則不然，厚作斂於百姓，以
為美食芻豢[7]，蒸炙魚鱉，大國累百器，小國累十器，前方丈，目
不能遍視，手不能遍操，口不能遍味，冬則凍冰，夏則飾饐。人

7.　MZQY draws attention to the use of this phrase "芻豢" in *Mencius* VIA.7(8) where
　　Legge translates it as "the flesh of grass and grain-fed animals" (LCC, vol. 2, p. 407).

seizing the people's materials for clothing and food to make elegant, embroidered, ornamented, coloured and beautiful clothes. Gold is used to make hooks, pearl and jade to make girdle ornaments, female artisans make patterns and colours, and male artisans make carvings and engravings, as clothes for the body. These things cannot be said to increase warmth or coolness, but only to use up materials and exhaust strength completely, and to no avail.[i] Looked at from this viewpoint, their making of clothes and garments is not for the sake of their bodies, but entirely to look good. In this way, the people will be dissolute, mean and difficult to rule, and their rulers will be wasteful, extravagant and difficult to restrain. To have wasteful and extravagant rulers achieve good control over dissolute and mean people, and desire the state to be without disorder is out of the question. If rulers truly desire the world to be well ordered and find its disorder abhorrent, it is proper that, in making clothes and garments, they cannot be other than moderate."

6.5   "In the times when the people of old still did not know how to make drink or food, they ate simply and lived separately. Therefore, the sages[ii] gave instruction, teaching men to plough, cultivate and plant so as to provide food for the people sufficient to increase the spirit, to fill what was empty, to strengthen the body, to satisfy the belly, and that is all. And so their use of materials was moderate and they themselves were frugal, the people were made rich, and the country was well ordered. Nowadays, this is not the case insofar as heavy tax imposts are made on the ordinary people to provide fine food and delicacies, steamed and roasted fish and turtles. Great countries prepare hundreds of dishes and small countries prepare tens of dishes spread out over a square *zhang* so the eye cannot see them all, the hand cannot touch them all, and the mouth cannot taste them all. In winter, these dishes will grow cold, and in summer they will

---

i.   Following MZQY and utilising WKY's emendation of 之情 to 清.

ii.   YPM takes this to be a specific reference to Shen Nong 神農, the legendary emperor to whom the founding of agriculture (among other things) is attributed. Chinese commentators do not make this connection.

君為飲食如此，故左右象之，是以富貴者奢侈，孤寡者凍餒，雖欲無亂，不可得也。君實欲天下治而惡其亂，當為食飲不可不節。」

6.6　「古之民未知為舟車時，重任不移，遠道不至，故聖王作為舟車，以便民之事。其為舟車也，全固輕利[8]，可以任重致遠，其為[9]用財少，而為利多，是以民樂而利之。法令不急而行，民不勞而上足用，故民歸之。當今之主，其為舟車與此異矣。全固輕利皆已具，必厚作斂於百姓，以飾舟車，飾車以文采，飾舟以刻鏤。女子廢其紡織而修文采，故民寒，男子離其耕稼而修刻鏤，故民飢。人君為舟車若此，故左右象之，是以其民飢寒並至，故為姦邪。姦邪多則刑罰深，刑罰深則國亂。君實欲天下之治而惡其亂，當為舟車不可不節。」

8.　There are several minor issues with this description. BY takes 全 as 完 in the sense of 完備. MZQY offers the following modern equivalents for the other terms: 固 as 牢固, 輕 as 輕快, and 利 as 便利.

9.　The addition of 為 here follows ZCY.

grow rancid. If the ruler prepares drink and food like this, then his assistants will imitate him. In this way the rich and noble will be wasteful and extravagant whilst orphans and widows will be cold and hungry. And, although there is the desire for no disorder, this will not be achieved. If rulers truly desire the world to be well ordered and find its disorder abhorrent, it is proper that in preparing drink and food they cannot be other than moderate."

6.6 "In the times when the people of old still did not know how to make boats and carts, they could not transport heavy loads or reach distant roads. Therefore, the sage kings[iii] brought about the making of boats and carts to facilitate the affairs of the people. The boats and carts they made were perfectly solid, swift and convenient so they could carry what was heavy and travel far. Moreover, in their making, the use of materials was slight, but their being of benefit was great, so the people were happy and benefited from them. Orders and decrees did not spur them, yet they acted. The people were not worn out, yet the ruler had enough for use, therefore the people returned to him. Now in their making of boats and carts, the rulers of the present are different from this. Having already made them completely solid, swift and convenient, they must impose heavy taxes on the ordinary people in order to decorate the boats and carts, adorning the carts with decorative fabrics and the boats with carvings and engravings. Women put aside their spinning and weaving to prepare the decorative fabrics, therefore the people are cold. Men leave their ploughing and sowing to prepare the carvings and engravings, therefore the people are hungry. If the ruler makes boats and carts like this, then his assistants will imitate him. This will cause the people to be hungry and cold to an extreme degree. Therefore, the people are deceitful and dishonest. And if deceit and dishonesty are great, then penalties and punishments are severe and the country is in disorder. If rulers truly desire the world to be well ordered and find its disorder abhorrent, it is proper that in making boats and carts they cannot be other than moderate."

---

iii. Again YPM takes this as a specific reference, on this occasion to Huang Di 黃帝.

6.7　「凡回[10] 於天地之間，包於四海之內，天壤之情，陰陽之和，莫不有也。雖至聖不能更也，何以知其然？聖人有傳，天地也，則曰上下；四時也，則曰陰陽；人情也，則曰男女；禽獸也，則曰牝牡雄雌也。真天壤之情，雖有先王不能更也。雖上世至聖，必蓄私不以傷行，故民無怨，宮無拘女，故天下無寡夫。內無拘女，外無寡夫，故天下之民眾。當今之君，其蓄私也，大國拘女累千，小國累百，是以天下之男多寡無妻，女多拘無夫。男女失時，故民少。君實欲民之眾而惡其寡，當蓄私不可不節。」

6.8　「凡此五者，聖人之所儉節也，小人之所淫佚也，儉節則昌，淫佚則亡，此五者不可不節。夫婦節而天地和，風雨節而五穀孰[11]，衣服節而肌膚和。」

---

10. 回 is read as "輪回運轉" (Z&Q).
11. 孰 is taken as 熟 — see, for example, Z&Q.

6.7 "Whatever turns and revolves between Heaven and earth, whatever is encompassed within the four seas, must have the nature bestowed by Heaven and the harmonious proportions of *Yin* and *Yang*. Even the greatest sage cannot change this. How do I know this is so? In what the sages transmitted with regard to Heaven and earth, they spoke of upper and lower. With regard to the four seasons, they spoke of *Yin* and *Yang*. With regard to people's feelings, they spoke of male and female. With regard to birds and beasts, they spoke of male and female animals and birds. Truly these were things bestowed by Heaven which the former kings could not change. Even the greatest sages of former generations certainly had wives and concubines, but this did not harm their behaviour, so the people were without resentment. Within the palace there were not 'retained' women, so within the world there were not unmarried men. Since within the palace there were not 'retained' women and without there were not unmarried men, the people of the world were many. Now rulers of the present time, in their taking of wives and concubines, in a large state have several thousand 'retained' women and in a small state several hundred. This means that many men in the world are without wives and many of the women are 'retained' and without husbands, so men and women lose the chance [to marry and have children]. Therefore, the people are few. If rulers truly wish the people to be many and abhor their being few, they cannot be other than moderate in their taking of wives and concubines.

6.8 "In all these five things the sage is restrained and moderate but the petty man is unrestrained and immoderate. If there is restraint and moderation, then there is prosperity. If there is lack of restraint and moderation, then there is decay. So in these five things there must be moderation. When there is moderation with regard to men and women, Heaven and earth are in harmony. When there is moderation in the winds and rains, the five grains ripen. When there is moderation in clothes and garments, skin and flesh are in harmony."

7: 三辯[1]

7.1 程繁問於子墨子曰:「夫子曰『聖王不為樂』。昔諸侯倦於聽治,息
於鐘鼓之樂。士大夫倦於聽治,息於竽瑟之樂。農夫春耕夏耘,
秋斂冬藏,息於聆缶之樂。今夫子曰:『聖王不為樂』。此譬之猶
馬駕而不稅[2],弓張而不弛,無乃非[3]有血氣者之所不能至邪?」

7.2 子墨子曰:「昔者堯舜有茅茨者,且以為禮,且以為樂。湯放桀
於大水,環天下自立以為王,事成功立,無大後患,因先王之
樂,又自作樂,命曰『護』,又修『九招』。武王勝殷殺紂,環天下

---

1. The title here is somewhat perplexing. To what does 辯 refer? Most commentators (as well as the ZWDCD) refer to BY's note which reads: "此辯聖王雖用樂,而治不在此。三者,謂堯舜及湯及武王也。" LSL takes 辯 in the sense of 反復. The brief essay relates to the "Condemning Music" chapters (*Mozi* 32–34). SYR has: "蓋〈非樂〉之餘義。"
2. Z&Q quote Guo Pu's note which reads: "稅猶脫也。"
3. Following YY, 非 is regarded as superfluous.

7: Three Arguments

7.1   Cheng Fan[i] questioned Master Mo Zi saying: "You say, Sir, that the sage kings did not make music. [Yet] in former times, when the feudal lords were weary of the affairs of government, they found rest in the music of bells and drums. When officers and high officials were weary of the affairs of government, they found rest in the music of pipes and strings.[ii] Farmers ploughed in spring, weeded in summer, harvested in autumn and stored in winter. They took rest in the music of jars and bowls. Now you say that the sage kings did not make music. This is like a horse being yoked and never released, or a bow being drawn and never relaxed. Isn't this something that those who have blood and breath (i.e. living beings) cannot achieve?"

7.2   Master Mo Zi said: "In former times, Yao and Shun had thatched roofs. Nevertheless, they created rites and they created music. Tang banished Jie to the great ocean, establishing himself as king of all under Heaven. When his administration was successful and there were no major subsequent misfortunes, he continued the music of the former kings. He also created his own music which was called *Hu* and, in addition, he arranged the *Jiu Zhao*.[iii] King Wu overcame the Yin and killed Zhou, establishing himself as

---

i.   Cheng Fan 程繁 is described as a scholar who combined both Mohism and Confucianism. He is also found in *Mozi* 48.

ii.   YPM, who simply transliterates the terms, describes *yu* 竽 as "a Chinese hand organ of thirty-six reed pipes" and *se* 瑟 as "a Chinese horizontal psaltery of twenty-five strings".

iii.   Yao 堯 and Shun 舜 are the repeatedly referred to exemplary emperors of the legendary period (third millennium BC). Jie 桀 was the last, and notoriously evil, ruler of the Xia 夏 dynasty. He was overthrown by Tang 湯 who established the Shang 商 or Yin 殷 dynasty. *Hu* 護 was music attributed to him whilst *Jiu Zhao* 九招 was music from the Xia dynasty. This list of music associated with the early emperors differs somewhat from that given in the passage on Mohism in *Zhuangzi* 33 — see GQF, vol. 4, pp. 1073–1081.

自立以為王，事成功立，無大後患，因先王之樂，又自作樂，命
曰『象』。周成王因先王之樂，又自作樂，命曰『騶虞』。周成王之
治天下也，不若武王；武王之治天下也，不若成湯；成湯之治天
下也，不若堯舜。故其樂逾繁者，其治逾寡。自此觀之，樂非所
以治天下也。」

7.3　　程繁曰：「子曰：『聖王無樂』，此亦樂已，若之何其謂聖王無樂
也？」子墨子曰：「聖王之命也，多寡之[4]。食之利也，以知飢而食
之者智也，因為無智矣[5]。今聖有樂而少，此亦無也。」

4.　On this terse phrase, WHB has: "疑有脫誤，據文意疑其原文當為`多者寡之`。"
5.　I have followed WHB in taking there to be a missing clause before these five characters
　　which he suggests is "不知飢而食者". He also emends 因 to 固.

king of all under Heaven. When his administration was successful and there were no major subsequent misfortunes, he continued the music of former kings. He also created his own music, which was called *Xiang*.[iv] King Cheng of Zhou continued the music of former kings and also created his own music which was called *Zou Yu*.[v] But King Cheng of Zhou's rule of all under Heaven was not like that of King Wu. King Wu's rule of all under Heaven was not like that of Cheng Tang.[vi] Cheng Tang's rule of all under Heaven was not like that of Yao and Shun. Thus, as their music became increasingly elaborate, so their establishment of order became increasingly less. From this it can be seen that music is not a means of bringing order to the world."

7.3   Cheng Fan said: "You said, Sir, that the sage kings were without music, but this indicates that there was already music, so how can you say that the sage kings were without music?"

Master Mo Zi replied: "The decrees of the sage kings were aimed at reducing excess. Eating is beneficial. Those who eat when they feel hunger are wise, but those who eat when they do not feel hunger are certainly not wise. Now the sages had music, but very little, which is tantamount to not having it."

---

iv.   Wu Wang 武王 was the first ruler of the Zhou 周 dynasty, after overthrowing Zhou 紂.

v.   Cheng Wang 成王 was Wu Wang's successor and is said to have ruled from 1115 to 1078 BC.

vi.   Cheng Tang 成湯 is Tang 湯, referred to in note iii above.

PART *II*

Core Doctrines

8: 尚賢上[1]

8.1   子墨子言曰[2]:「今者[3]王公大人[4]為政於國家者,皆欲國家之富,
人民之眾,刑政之治,然而不得富而得貧,不得眾而得寡,不得
治而得亂,則是本[5]失其所欲,得其所惡,是其故何也?」

8.2   子墨子言曰:「是在王公大人為政於國家者,不能以尚賢事[6]能為
政也。是故國有賢良之士眾,則國家之治厚,賢良之士寡,則國
家之治薄[7]。故大人之務,將在於眾賢而已。[8]」

8.3   曰:「然則眾賢之術將奈何哉?」子墨子言曰:「譬若欲眾其國之善
射御之士者,必將富之,貴之,敬之,譽之,然後國之善射御之
士,將可得而眾也。況又有賢良之士厚乎德行,辯[9]乎言談,博
乎道術者乎,此固國家之珍,而社稷之佐也,亦必且富之,貴
之,敬之,譽之,然後國之良士,亦將可得而眾也。」

1. There is some divergence of view on the meaning of the title depending particularly on
    the reading of 尚, although the interpretation of 賢 is also an issue. Modern
    commentators such as LSL and Z&Q read 尚 as 尊重 ("value", "esteem") or 崇尚
    ("uphold", "advocate") and take the same meaning for its use in the next group of three
    chapters (尚同). I have followed them on the latter point but have used "exalt" in the
    sense of raising the two factors, i.e. "worthiness" and "unity of principles" or "accord"
    between all levels of society to positions of high importance.
2. See WYJ, note 1, p. 68 on this recurring but slightly variable formula.
3. Some texts (e.g. WYJ) have 古者 rather than 今者. The generally accepted emendation
    follows Qiu Shan 秋山 (see WYJ, note 2, p. 68). ACG takes the opposite view, retaining
    古 — see his *Disputers of the Tao*, p. 39.
4. I have rendered 大人 here and in its many subsequent uses as "great officers" although
    it did come to have a more specific meaning — see Hucker #5969.
5. ZCY suggests that 本 is superfluous here.
6. SYR equates 事 with 使義. WYJ has 役使 which I have followed.
7. The paired terms 厚 and 薄 are important in the *Mozi*, having distinct ethical
    connotations — see particularly the "Daqu" 1 (*Mozi* 44.1). I have generally (but not
    invariably) rendered them "thick" and "thin" respectively in relation to ethical values.
8. In this clause, I have followed Z&Q in reading 將 as 當 and taking 眾 as verbal. LYS
    has 增多 or 增強.
9. 辨 is read for 辯 here. The latter term has a quite specific meaning, at least in the Later
    Mohist chapters — see, for example, "Xiaoqu" 1 (*Mozi* 45.1).

8: Exalting Worthiness I

8.1 Master Mo Zi spoke, saying: "At the present time kings, dukes and great officers, in governing a state, all wish it to be rich, its people to be numerous, and its administration to be well ordered. Nevertheless, they do not get wealth but poverty, they do not get a large population but a small one, and they do not get order but disorder. Basically, then, they fail in what they desire but get what they detest. What is the reason for this?"

8.2 Master Mo Zi spoke, saying: "It is because kings, dukes and great officers, in governing a state, are unable to use 'exalting worthiness' and 'utilising ability' in their governing. Thus, if a state has many worthy and good officers, then its order will be 'thick' whereas, if worthy and good officers are few, then its order will be 'thin'. So the responsibility of high officers properly lies in increasing the number of worthy men and nothing more."

8.3 [Someone] said: "If this is so, then what is the method of increasing the number of worthy men?"

Master Mo Zi replied, saying: "It is like wishing to increase the number of officers of the state who are skilled in archery and charioteering. You must enrich them, ennoble them, respect them and praise them. Then officers of the state who are skilled in archery and charioteering will be obtained and become numerous. How much more so is this the case with officers who are worthy and good, who are 'thick' in virtue, discriminating in discussion, and well versed in principles. Such men are certainly treasures of the state and [worthy] assistants at the altars of soil and grain. But it is also necessary to enrich them, ennoble them, respect them and praise them. Then good officers of the state can be obtained and become numerous."

8.4   「是故古者聖王之為政也，言曰：『不義不富，不義不貴，不義不
親，不義不近。』是以國之富貴人聞之，皆退而謀曰：『始我所恃
者，富貴也，今上舉義不辟貧賤，然則我不可不為義。』親者聞
之，亦退而謀曰：『始我所恃者親也，今上舉義不辟親[10]疏，然則
我不可不為義。』近者聞之，亦退而謀曰：『始我所恃者近也，今
上舉義不辟遠，然則我不可不為義。』遠者聞之，亦退而謀曰：
『我始以遠為無恃，今上舉義不辟遠，然則我不可不為義。』[11]逮
至遠鄙郊外之臣，門庭庶子[12]，國中之眾，四鄙之萌[13]人聞之，
皆競為義。是其故何也？曰：上之所以使下者，一物也，下之所
以事上者，一術也。[14]譬之富者有高牆深宮，牆立既，謹上為鑿
一門，有盜人入，闔其自入而求之，盜其無自出。是其故何也？
則上得要也。」

---

10. Following WYZ, 親 is taken as superfluous and omitted.
11. LSL omits this example which does, in fact, somewhat damage the symmetry of the
    argument.
12. See Z&Q's detailed note on this clause, which includes SYR's reading of 庭 as 宮 —
    Z&Q, note 7, p. 69.
13. BY has the following note "萌，氓字之假音。" which is generally accepted. Z&Q
    quote the《說文 · 民部》as follows: "氓，民也，讀若肓。"
14. YTY equates 術 with 途 as 途徑. I have followed modern commentators in
    understanding both the standard (物 as 標準) and the path (術 as 途徑) to be
    righteousness 義.

8.4   "This is why in ancient times, the sage kings, in their conduct of government, said: 'Those who are not righteous, we shall not enrich. Those who are not righteous, we shall not ennoble. Those who are not righteous, we shall not be kin to. Those who are not righteous, we shall not associate with.' When they heard this, it caused the rich and noble men of the state all to retire and ponder, saying: 'At first, what we relied on were riches and nobility. Now the ruler promotes the righteous and does not set aside the poor and lowly. This being so, then we cannot do otherwise than be righteous.' When those who were relatives heard this, they also retired and pondered, saying: 'At first, what we relied on was kinship. Now the ruler promotes the righteous and does not set aside those who are not relatives. This being so, then we cannot do otherwise than be righteous.' When those who were close associates heard this, they also retired and pondered, saying: 'At first, what we relied on was close association. Now the ruler promotes the righteous and does not set aside those who are distant. This being so, then we cannot do otherwise than be righteous.' When those who were distant heard this they also retired and said: 'At first, because we were distant, we had nothing to rely on. Now the ruler promotes the righteous and does not set aside the distant. This being so, we cannot be other than righteous.'[i] When the distant and lowly officials of the outer regions, the young nobles within the palace, the multitudes in the capital, and the common people of the far-flung regions heard this, they all strove to become righteous. What was the reason for this? I say that, for superiors employing subordinates, there is only one standard; for subordinates serving superiors, there is only one path. It is like the rich man who builds a high wall surrounding his house. When the wall is complete, he takes care to make only a single entry gate so, when robbers enter, he can close off the entrance and pursue them and they have no way out. Why is this so? It is because the superior man secures the key point."

---

i.   See note 11 above.

8.5　「故古者聖王之為政，列[15] 德而尚賢，雖在農與工肆之人，有能則舉之，高予之爵，重予之祿，任之以事，斷[16] 予之令，曰：『爵位不高則民弗敬，蓄祿不厚則民不信，政令不斷則民不畏。』舉三者授之賢者，非為賢賜也，欲其事之成。故當是時，以德就列，以官服事，以勞殿[17] 賞，量功而分祿。故官無常貴，而民無終賤，有能則舉之，無能則下之，舉公義，辟私怨。此若言之謂也。」

8.6　「故古者堯舉舜於服澤之陽，授之政，天下平。禹舉益於陰方之中，授之政，九州成。湯舉伊尹於庖廚之中，授之政，其謀得。文王舉閎夭泰顛於置罔[18] 之中，授之政，西土服。故當是時，雖

---

15. SYR equates 列 with 位次, citing the *Guo Yu* 國語. Z&Q have: "列德：任德，即給有德的人安排職位。"
16. SYR refers to the *Li Ji* in equating 斷 with 決 and this is accepted by most commentators — see, for example, WYJ.
17. 定 is read for 殿 following YY.
18. On "置罔", LYS has: "置，獵兔之物，罔即網。"

8.5   "Therefore, the sage kings of ancient times, in the conduct of government, gave precedence to virtue and exalted worthiness so, although someone might be a farmer, or a craftsman, or a merchant, if he had ability then they promoted him, conferring on him high rank, giving him a generous salary, entrusting him with [important] matters, and providing him with executive power. They said: 'If his rank and position are not high, the people will not respect him. If his stipend and emolument are not generous, the people will not trust him. If his administration and decrees are not put into effect, the people will not fear him.' Bringing forward these three things and conferring them on the worthy was not done for the sake of rewarding worthiness, but through a wish to bring the business of government to completion. Therefore, at that particular time, precedence was based on virtue, responsibility for affairs was based on official position, rewards were determined by meritorious accomplishment, and there was estimation of achievement and distribution of emoluments accordingly. Thus officials were not [necessarily] assured of permanent nobility and ordinary people were not [necessarily] lowly for their whole lives. Those with ability were advanced. Those without ability were demoted. Advancing those who are generally accepted as righteous and avoiding private resentment — this is the kind of thing being spoken of."

8.6   "Thus, in ancient times, Yao brought forward Shun from the northern side of Fu marsh, giving him government, and the world was at peace. Yu brought forward Yi from Yin Fang, giving him government, and the Nine Regions were established. Tang brought forward Yi Yin from his work as a cook, giving him government, and his measures were successful. King Wen brought forward Hong Yao and Tai Dian from among their snares and nets, giving them government, and the western lands were subdued.[ii] Therefore, during those times, although officials

---

ii.   Yao 堯 and Shun 舜 were the oft referred to last two emperors of the Legendary Period. It is not known where Fu marsh was. Yu 禹 was the first emperor of the Xia dynasty whilst Yi 益 was Bo Yi 伯益 who was employed by Yu for his skill in animal husbandry and hunting. In both these examples, the second-named succeeded the first. The "Nine Regions" refers to the unification of the kingdom. It is not known where Yin Fang was.

在於厚祿尊位之臣，莫不敬懼而施，雖在農與工肆之人，莫不競勸而尚意[19]。故士者所以為輔相承嗣也。故得士則謀不困，體不勞，名立而功成，美章而惡不生，則由得士也。」

8.7 是故子墨子言曰：「得意賢士不可不舉，不得意賢士不可不舉，尚[20] 欲祖述堯舜禹湯之道，將不可以不[21] 尚賢。夫尚賢者，政之本也。」

---

19. On this sentence Z&Y have the following note: "競勸：爭相勸勉。尚意：崇尚道德。孫云：'意'疑'德'字之誤。"
20. Following WYZ, 尚 is read as 倘.
21. In some texts the positions of 以 and 不 are reversed — see WYJ, note 51, p. 74.

enjoyed a generous stipend and a respected position, they were always reverent and fearful in their actions. [Likewise], although the people were farmers, craftsmen and merchants, they always strove to encourage one another and value virtue. It is [worthy] officers who are the means of assisting [the ruler] in the business of government. If he acquires such officers, then his plans will encounter no difficulties, he himself will not be burdened, his reputation will be established, and his achievement will be complete. His glory will be made known and evil will not arise. This is due to acquiring [such] officers."

8.7   This is the reason Master Mo Zi spoke, saying: "In good times, worthy officers must be promoted. When times are not good, worthy officers [likewise] must be promoted. If the wish is to follow the Way of Yao, Shun, Yu and Tang, it is impossible not to exalt worthiness. Indeed, 'exalting worthiness' is the foundation of government."

Tang 湯 was the first emperor of the Shang dynasty. Yi Yin 伊尹 was a chief minister under Tang, traditionally said to have come to notice due to his culinary skills. Both Hong Yao (Hongyao — 閎夭) and Tai Dian 泰顛 were noted ministers under King Wen, the first emperor of the Zhou Dynasty — see the 《書經》 (*Documents*), LCC, vol. 3, p. 481.

9: 尚賢中

9.1 子墨子言曰:「今王公大人之君人民,主社稷,治國家,欲修保而勿失,故不察尚賢為政之本也?[1] 何以知尚賢之為政本也?曰:自貴且智者為政乎愚且賤者,則治;自愚賤者為政乎貴且智者,則亂。是以知尚賢之為政本也。故古者聖王甚尊尚賢而任使能,不黨父兄,不偏貴富,不嬖顏色。賢者舉而上之,富而貴之,以為官長。不肖者抑而廢之,貧而賤之,以為徒役。是以民皆勸其賞,畏其罰,相率而為賢。者[2] 以賢者眾,而不肖者寡,此謂進[3] 賢。然後聖人聽其言,迹其行,察其所能,而慎予官,此謂事[4] 能。故可使治國者,使治國;可使長官者,使長官;可使治邑者,使治邑。凡所使治國家、官府、邑里,此皆國之賢者也。」

---

1. This is framed as a question following BY's reading of 故 as 胡 and WKY's reading of 也 as 耶. There is some variation as to where Master Mo's words end. A number of modern editors take it to be here — for example, LYS, LSL. I have followed Z&Q's punctuation.
2. Emended to 是 following YY.
3. Following SYR this is taken to be 尚.
4. As with the previous statement in which he takes "進賢" as "尚賢" on the basis of earlier statements, so in this statement SYR takes "事能" as "使能".

9: Exalting Worthiness II

9.1 Master Mo Zi spoke, saying: "Nowadays, kings, dukes and great officers, in ruling the people, in directing the altars of soil and grain, and in bringing order to the country, desire prolonged stability and avoidance of failure, so how can they not see that exalting worthiness is the foundation of government? How do I know that exalting worthiness is the foundation of government? I say it is from the fact that, when those who are noble and wise govern those who are foolish and base, there is order whereas, when those who are foolish and base govern those who are noble and wise, there is disorder. This is how I know that exalting worthiness is the foundation of government. Therefore, the sage kings of old particularly followed exalting worthiness and employed utilising ability and there were no factions with fathers and older brothers, no partiality towards the noble and rich, and no favouritism towards those of fine appearance. They selected those who were worthy and gave them high positions, enriching and ennobling them by making them officers and chiefs. Those who were unworthy they curbed and demoted, impoverishing and debasing them by making them followers and servants. In this way, the people were all encouraged by their rewards and intimidated by their punishments, and followed each other in becoming worthy. In this way, the worthy were numerous and the unworthy few. This was spoken of as 'exalting worthiness'. Subsequently, the sage kings listened to their words, followed their actions, examined their capabilities, and cautiously gave them office. This was called 'utilising ability'. Therefore, those who could be used to bring order to the country were used to bring order to the country, those who could be used as senior officials were used as senior officials, and those who could be used to bring order to a district were used to bring order to a district. In general, then, those who were used to bring order to the country and administer regions, districts and villages were all worthy men of the country."

9.2   「賢者之治國也，蚤朝晏退⁵，聽獄治政，是以國家治而刑法正。
賢者之長官也，夜寢夙興，收斂關市、山林、澤梁之利，以實官
府，是以官府實而財不散。賢者之治邑也，蚤出莫入⁶，耕稼、樹
藝⁷、聚菽粟，是以菽粟多而民足乎食。⁸故國家治則刑法正，
官府實則萬民富。上有以絜為酒醴粢盛，以祭祀天鬼。外有以
為皮幣，與四鄰諸侯交接。內有以食飢息勞，將養其萬民，外
有以懷天下之賢人⁹。是故上者天鬼富之，外者諸侯與之，內者萬
民親之，賢人歸之，以此謀事則得，舉事則成，入守則固，出誅
則彊。故唯昔三代聖王堯舜禹湯文武之所以王天下，正諸侯者，
此¹⁰亦其法已。」

9.3   「既曰若法，¹¹未知所以行之術，則事猶若未成，是以必為置三
本。何謂三本？曰爵位不高則民不敬也。蓄祿不厚則民不信也，
政令不斷則民不畏也。故古聖王高予之爵，重予之祿，任之以

---

5. Here 蚤 is taken as 早 and 晏 as 晚 — see, for example, Z&Q.

6. 蚤 is read as 早, as above, and 莫 as 暮 — see, for example, LYS.

7. LYS has the following paraphrase of "樹藝": "種植果木".

8. BW has a note here commenting on the apparent direct involvement of district overseers
    in agricultural business. He takes this to be misleading and a consequence of devotion
    to the parallel structure.

9. This is a somewhat contentious sentence. In the translation, I have followed LSL who
    accepts WSN's omission of "外有以" before the final clause, so maintaining the 上, 外,
    內 symmetry. Others take the meaning to be an attracting of worthy men from without.

10. "This" 此, as Z&Q point out, is "exalting worthiness" (尚賢).

11. There is some debate about this initial clause. The translation follows WNS's reading of
    曰 as 有 and 若 as 此 — see WYJ's detailed note (note 18, p. 81).

9.2   "Worthy men, in bringing order to the country, rise early and retire late, attend to cases at law and administer the government. In this way, the country is well ordered and laws and punishments are correct. Worthy men, when they are senior officials, go to bed after dark and rise at dawn, collect the tax revenue from strategic passes, market places, mountains and forests, marshes and bridges, and so fill the official treasury. In this way, the official treasury is filled and resources are not dispersed. Worthy men, in administering districts, go out early and come back late, ploughing and harvesting, planting fruit trees and gathering pulses and grains. In this way, the pulses and grains are abundant and the people have enough to eat. Thus, if the country is well ordered, then punishments and laws are correct. If the official treasury is full, then the ten thousand people are rich. Above, the wine and grain will be pure for the sacrifices to Heaven and ghosts. Without, there will be hides and silks to exchange with the feudal lords on all four sides. Within, there will be food for the hungry and rest for the weary, and the wherewithal to nourish the ten thousand people and foster the worthy men of the world. For this reason, from above, Heaven and the ghosts will enrich them. From without, the feudal lords will ally with them. From within, the ten thousand people will feel close to them and worthy men will return to them. In this way, in planning affairs there will be success, in conducting affairs there will be completion. Defence within will be secure and attacks without will be strong. This also was the method used in former times by the sage kings of the Three Dynasties, Yao, Shun, Yu, Tang, Wen and Wu in ruling all under Heaven and holding sway over the feudal lords."

9.3   "When there are these methods, but not the knowledge of how to implement them, then affairs will still not be brought to completion. This is because it is necessary to establish three foundations. What are spoken of as 'three foundations'? They are said to be: If rank and position are not high, then the people will not be respectful; if subsistence and emolument are not generous, then the people will not be trusting; if administration and decrees are not decisive, then the people will not be in awe. Therefore, the ancient sage kings gave them (i.e. the worthy) high ranks and large salaries, made them responsible for affairs, and gave them

事，斷予之令。夫豈為其[12]臣賜哉，欲其事之成也。《詩》曰：『告女憂恤，誨女予爵，孰能執熱，鮮不用濯？』[13] 則此語古者國君諸侯之不可以不執善，承嗣輔佐也。譬之猶執熱之有濯也，將休其手焉。古者聖王唯毋得賢人而使之，般爵以貴之，裂地以封之，然身不厭。賢人唯毋得明君而事之，竭四肢之力以任君之事，終身不倦。若有美善則歸之上，是以美善在上而所怨謗在下，寧樂在君，憂戚在臣。故古者聖王之為政若此。」

9.4 「今王公大人亦欲效人以尚賢使能為政，高予之爵，而祿不從也。夫高爵而無祿，民不信也。曰：『此非中實愛我也，假藉而用我也。』夫假藉之民，將豈能親其上哉！故先王言曰：『貪於政者，不能分人以事；厚於貨者，不能分人以祿。』事則不與，祿則不分，請問天下之賢人將何自至乎王公大人之側哉？若苟賢者不至乎王公大人之側，則此不肖者在左右也。不肖者在左右，則

12. WYJ has 賢 here — see his note 21, p. 81.
13. See《詩經》*Odes*, Mao #257. There is some difference in the text — see LCC, vol. 4, p. 522.

effective executive power. Was this just to reward their officials? No, it was so their affairs were brought to completion. In the *Odes* it is said: 'I tell you to have pity and sympathy, I exhort you to confer rank. Of those who are able to grasp what is hot, there are few who do not use water to rinse their hands.' What this says is that rulers and feudal lords in ancient times could not do otherwise than be close to their successors and assistants. This is to be compared to grasping something hot and having water to rinse with so there will be relief for the hands. The sage kings of old thought only of finding worthy men and employing them, of conferring rank on them to ennoble them, of dividing up land to enfeoff them, and throughout their lives not tiring. Worthy men thought only of finding an enlightened ruler and serving him, exhausting the strength of their four limbs in bearing the burden of the ruler's affairs, and throughout their lives not wearying. If there was beauty and goodness, then this belonged to the ruler. In this way, beauty and goodness lay with the ruler, whilst resentment and ill-repute lay with the subordinates. Peace and happiness lay with the ruler, whilst sorrow and grief lay with the officials. Therefore, the sage kings of ancient times conducted their affairs like this."

9.4   "At the present time, kings, dukes and great officers also wish to imitate the ancients by exalting worthiness and utilising ability in the conduct of government, elevating them by conferring rank, but the emolument doesn't follow. When there is elevation of rank without [commensurate] emolument, the people do not have trust. [A worthy man would] say: 'This is not a sincere regard for me, but a false regard and use of me.' How will people who are falsely regarded be able to feel close to their superiors! Thus, the former kings said: 'Those who covet political power are unable to delegate affairs to others. Those who place great value on wealth are unable to distribute emolument to others.' If affairs, then, are not delegated, if emoluments are not distributed, I would ask how worthy men in the world will bring themselves to the side of a king, duke or great officer? If worthy men do not come to the side of a king, duke or great officer, then it is the unworthy who will be standing to their left and right. When the unworthy are standing to their left and right, then what is praised will not accord with

其所譽不當賢，而所罰[14]不當暴，王公大人尊此以為政乎國家，則賞亦必不當賢，而罰亦必不當暴。若苟賞不當賢而罰不當暴，則是為賢者不勸而為暴者不沮矣。是以入則不慈[15]孝父母，出則不長弟[16]鄉里，居處無節，出入無度[17]，男女無別。使治官府則盜竊，守城則倍畔，君有難則不死，出亡則不從，使斷獄則不中，分財則不均，與謀事不得，舉事不成，入守不固，出誅不彊。故雖昔者三代暴王桀紂幽厲之所以失措其國家，傾覆其社稷者，已此故也。何則？皆以明小物而不明大物也。[18]」

9.5   「今王公大人有一衣裳不能制也，必藉[19]良工。有一牛羊不能殺也，必藉良宰。故當若之二物者，王公大人未知[20]以尚賢使能為政也。逮至其國家之亂，社稷之危，則不知使能以治之，親戚則使之，無故富貴、面目佼好則使之。夫無故富貴、面目佼好則使

---

14. WYJ has 毀 rather than 罰 here, pointing out that it is the opposite of 譽 in the previous clause — see his note 37, p. 83.

15. WYZ quotes the《賈子‧道術篇》on 慈 as follows: "親愛利子謂之慈，子愛利親謂之孝，孝與慈不同，而同取愛利之義，故孝於父母亦可謂之孝慈。"

16. WHB has this note on "長弟": "即‵長悌′，敬重的意思。"

17. Following SYR, 無節 and 無度 are taken to be essentially the same. Z&Q, who equate the two terms, offer these equivalences: "即無法度，無規矩，無節制。"

18. SYR equates 物 with 事 on the basis of Zheng Xuan's note to the《周禮‧大司徒》: "物猶事也".

19. 藉 is read here as 借 in the sense of 借重 — see, for example, LYS.

20. There is some doubt about 未知. SYR suggests emendation of 未 to 本 whereas WNS expands it, having the following note: "當作‵未嘗不知′". LYS and Z&Q both favour the latter. WYJ and LSL suggest 皆知.

worthiness and what is reviled will not accord with wickedness. If kings, dukes and great officers follow this in conducting the government of the state, then rewards will also certainly not be appropriate to worthiness, and punishments will certainly not be appropriate to wickedness. If rewards are not appropriate to worthiness, and punishments are not appropriate to wickedness then those who are worthy will not be encouraged, and those who are wicked will not be stopped. If this is so, at home there will not be kindness and filial behaviour towards parents, and abroad there will not be proper regard for those who are older and younger in districts and villages. At home, there will not be moderation, and abroad there will not be restraint. Nor will there be the proper distinction between men and women. Those who are put in charge of the official treasury will plunder and steal from it, and those who are charged with defending the city will betray and forsake it. If the ruler suffers a calamity, they will not die with him. If he is forced to flee, they will not follow him. Those employed to decide cases at law will not be just. Those who distribute wealth will not do it equitably. Those who plan affairs will not be successful and those who carry out affairs will not bring them to completion. In defence at home, they will not be steadfast. In attack abroad, they will not be vigorous. So, although the tyrannical kings of the Three Dynasties of former times — Jie, Zhou, You and Li — lost their kingdoms and overturned the altars of soil and grain, it was for this reason alone. And why was this? It was because in all cases they had a clear understanding of small matters but did not have a clear understanding of great matters."

9.5 "At the present time, when kings, dukes and great officers have a garment they cannot repair, they must make use of a skilled tailor. When there is an ox or ram they cannot slaughter, they must make use of a skilled butcher. So from these two things, kings, dukes and great officers cannot help but know that they should exalt worthiness and utilise ability in the conduct of government. Still, when it comes to disorder in the state or danger to the altars of soil and grain, they do not know to employ the able to bring about order. If there are relatives, then they employ them. If there are those who are rich and noble without [good] reason, or those who are of fine appearance, then they employ them. But if those who

之，豈必智且有慧哉！若使之治國家，則此使不智慧者治國
家也，國家之亂既可得而知已。且夫王公大人有所愛其色而使
〔之〕[21]，其心[22] 不察其知而與其愛。是故不能治百人者，使處乎
千人之官，不能治千人者，使處乎萬人之官。此其故何也？曰處
若[23] 官者爵高而祿厚，故愛其色而使之焉。夫不能治千人者，使
處乎萬人之官，則此官什倍也。夫治之法將日至者也，日以治
之，日不什修，知以治之，知不什益，而予官什倍，則此治一而
棄其九矣。雖日夜相接以治若官，官猶若不治，此其故何也？則
王公大人不明乎以尚賢使能為政也。故以尚賢使能為政而治者，
夫若言[24] 之謂也，以下賢為政而亂者，若吾言之謂也。」

9.6   「今王公大人中實將欲治其國家，欲修保而勿失，胡不察尚賢為
政之本也？且以尚賢為政之本者，亦豈獨子墨子之言哉！此聖王

----

21. Suggested addition by SYR.
22. THQ suggests emending 心 to 必.
23. See WYJ, note 52, p. 85 on the order of 處若.
24. ZCY has the following note on "夫若言" : "疑當作 '若夫言'。夫，指事之辭；若，
    如也。言如前文所言之謂也。" WYJ's text has "若吾言" as in the final clause.

are rich and noble without [good] reason, or those who are of fine appearance were to be employed in government, surely they would not necessarily prove intelligent and wise? If such men are employed in the administration of the state, then this is to employ those who are neither intelligent nor wise in administering the state so the state's disorder can be known in advance. Moreover, if kings, dukes and great officers have those whom they love for their appearance and they employ them, this is certainly not assessing their intelligence and so loving them. As a consequence, those who are not capable of administering a hundred people are given positions as officials over a thousand people. Those who are not capable of administering a thousand people are given positions as officials over ten thousand people. What is the reason for this? I say that, if they are given positions as officials with high rank and generous salary, the reason is that [the ruler] loves their appearance and so employs them. If a person who is unable to administer a thousand people is given a position as an official in charge of ten thousand people, then this is ten times his capacity as an official. Now the measures of administration arise on a daily basis and a day is available for putting them into effect. But a day does not increase tenfold. Knowledge is required for putting them into effect, but knowledge does not increase tenfold. So, if you give a man an official post requiring ten times his ability, then he will deal with one part but neglect nine parts. Although day and night are joined together for the execution of official business, it will still not be carried out. What is the reason for this? It is because kings, dukes and great officers do not clearly understand the use of exalting worthiness and utilising ability in the conduct of government. But if exalting worthiness and utilising ability are used in government, there is order, as was said before, whereas if there is devaluation of worthiness in the conduct of government, there is disorder, as I have said."

9.6 "If kings, dukes and great officers of the present time have a genuine desire to bring order to the state, and wish to care for and protect it and not lose it, how is it that they do not recognise that exalting worthiness is the basis of government? Moreover, it is not as if exalting worthiness is something that Master Mo Zi alone speaks of. This was the Way of sage kings. It was spoken of in the

之道，先王之書《距年》[25] 之言也。傳曰：『求聖君哲人，以裨輔而身。』[26]《湯誓》曰：『聿求元聖[27]，與之戮力同心，以治天下。』[28] 則此言聖之不失以尚賢使能為政也。[29] 故古者聖王唯能審以尚賢使能為政，無異物雜焉，天下皆得其利[30]。」

9.7　「古者舜耕歷山，陶河瀕，漁雷澤，堯得之服澤之陽，舉以為天子，與接天下之政，治天下之民。伊摯，有莘氏女之私臣，親為庖人，湯得之，舉以為己相，與接天下之政，治天下之民。傅說被褐帶索，庸築乎傅巖，武丁得之，舉以為三公，與接天下之政，治天下之民。此何故始賤卒而貴，始貧卒而富？則王公大人

---

25. There is some debate about《距年》. Most commonly it is taken to be the title of a lost book or chapter — see, for example, WYJ, LSL — although, as the latter notes,《豎年》is spoken of in the following chapter (*Mozi* 10). Another view is to take 距 as indicating "old" (老 — MZQY) or "remote" (遠 — BY). See also YPM, note 1, p. 42 and LYS, note 1, p. 54, the latter taking it to refer to an old man.

26. 傳 is taken to be a general term for an ancient chronicle. In the statement, 而 is read as 爾. WYJ gives the sources of similar statements in the *Yi Xun* 伊訓 and the *Guo Yu*.

27. In this clause, 聿 is taken as 遂 (which WYJ has in his text) and 元聖 as 大聖人 — see, for example, LSL, Z&Q.

28. This statement is not in the《湯誓》as presently preserved — see LSL's note.

29. The translation given for this sentence depends on the reading of 言 as 說明 (advocated by MZQY) and adding 王 after 聖, as proposed, for example, by LSL.

30. There is some variation in this final character. I have used 利 following BY. An alternative is 列 — see WYJ.

writing of former kings, the *Ju Nian*. The chronicle says: 'Seek sage rulers and wise men in order to benefit and aid yourselves.' The *Oath of Tang* states: 'Then seek a great sage and join with him using your strength and being of like mind so as to bring order to the world.' This, then, makes it clear that the sage kings did not lose sight of exalting worthiness and utilising ability in the conduct of government. That is, the sage kings of ancient times were able to give careful attention to exalting worthiness and utilising ability in the conduct of government and did not confuse these with different things, so within the world all obtained their benefit."

9.7   "In ancient times, Shun farmed on Li Shan, made pottery on the banks of the [Yellow] River and fished in Lei Marsh. Yao found him on the northern side of Fu Marsh and raised him to be the Son of Heaven, transferring to him the government of the world and the administration of the world's people.[i] Yi Zhi (Yi Yin) was the personal servant of a woman from You Xin and was himself a cook. Tang found him and raised him to be chief minister, transferring to him the government of the world and the administration of the world's people.[ii] Fu Yue, clad in coarse cloth bound with rope, was working as a common labourer at Fu Yan when Wu Ding found him and raised him to be one of the 'Three Dukes', transferring to him the government of the world and the administration of the world's people.[iii] How was it that someone

---

i.   The first of these three examples, repeated in the following book, speaks of Yao's 堯 choice of Shun 舜 as his successor — see《書經 · 堯典》(LCC, vol. 3, pp. 15–27, particularly pp. 26–27) and also the《史記 · 五帝本紀》(*Shi Ji*, vol. 1, p. 21 et seq). Lei Marsh 雷澤 is probably a reference to Lei Xia 雷夏 — see《書經 · 禹貢》(LCC, vol. 3, p. 99).

ii.   Yi Zhi 伊摯 is Yi Yin 伊尹 who was chosen by Tang 湯. The traditional story is that he attached himself to the bridal party of a woman from Xin who was being married to Tang, and that he himself came to the attention of Tang through his culinary skills. For a discussion of this see the《書經》(LCC, vol. 3, pp. 191–192). For an alternative account see *Mencius* VA.7. Xin, or You Xin 莘/有莘, is the name of an ancient kingdom. 私臣 is taken to indicate a servant included in the dowry.

iii. Fu Yue 傅說 was, according to the traditional story, found by Wu Ding 武丁 (reigned 1324–1265 BC) while repairing roads. See《書經 · 説命上》, LCC, vol. 3, pp. 248–253. Hucker describes the "Three Dukes" 三公 as "… dignitaries who were considered the three paramount aides to the ruler and held the highest possible ranks in the officialdom …" (Hucker #4871).

明乎以賞賢使能為政。是以民無飢而不得食，寒而不得衣，勞而
不得息，亂而不得治者。」

9.8   「故古聖王以審以尚賢使能為政[31]、而取法於天。雖天亦不辯貧
富、貴賤、遠邇、親疏、賢者舉而尚之，不肖者抑而廢之。然則
富貴為賢，以得其賞者誰也？曰若昔者三代聖王堯舜禹湯文武者
是也。所以得其賞何也？曰其為政乎天下也，兼而愛之，從而利
之，又率天下之萬民以尚[32]尊天、事鬼。愛利萬民，是故天鬼賞
之，立為天子，以為民父母，萬民從而譽之曰『聖王』，至今不
已。則此富貴為賢，以得其賞者也。然則富貴為暴，以得其罰者
誰也？曰若昔者三代暴王桀紂幽厲者是也。何以知其然也？曰其
為政乎天下也，兼而憎之，從而賊之，又率天下之民以詬天侮
鬼。賊傲[33]萬民，是故天鬼罰之，使身死而為刑戮，子孫離散，

---

31. There is some uncertainty about the initial part of this sentence, particularly regarding
     the first 以. LSL omits this 以 whereas THQ (followed by Z&Q) suggests emendation
     to 能. WYJ proposes: "故古者聖王唯能審以…" These variations do not affect
     meaning.
32. 尚 is omitted before 尊 following, for example, ZCY.
33. 賊傲 is read as 殘殺 following WNS and others.

who was first a lowly servant was ennobled, who was first a poor servant was enriched? It was because kings, dukes and great officers clearly understood the need to exalt worthiness and make use of ability in government. In this way, there were no instances of people who were hungry not obtaining food, of people who were cold not obtaining clothing, of people who were weary not obtaining rest, or of disorder that was not brought to order."

9.8 "Therefore the ancient sage kings gave careful attention to exalting worthiness and utilising ability in the conduct of government, taking their model from Heaven. Heaven does not discriminate between rich and poor, noble and base, far away and near at hand, close and distant [relations]. Those who are worthy are put forward and advanced whereas those who are unworthy are held back and rejected. If this is so, then who were those both rich and noble who became worthy and so obtained their reward? I say that the former sage kings of the Three Dynasties — Yao, Shun, Yu, Tang, Wen and Wu — were such men. And how did they obtain their rewards? I say that, in their governing of the world, they were universal in their love for it, and followed by benefiting it, and they also led the ten thousand people of the world to revere Heaven and serve ghosts. That they loved and benefited the ten thousand people is why Heaven and ghosts honoured them, establishing them as Sons of Heaven and taking them to be the parents of the people. And it is why the ten thousand people served them and praised them, calling them 'sage kings', as they still do to the present day. This, then, is a case of the rich and noble being worthy and so obtaining their reward. So who were those who were rich and noble but were evil, and for this reason suffered their punishment? I say that the former cruel kings of the Three Dynasties — Jie, Zhou, You and Li — were such men. How do I know this to be so? I say that, in their governing of the world, they were universal in their hatred for it and followed by plundering it, and they also led the people of the world to abuse Heaven and insult ghosts. They massacred the ten thousand people and, for this reason, Heaven and ghosts punished them, causing them to die and be desecrated, their sons and grandsons to be dispersed and scattered, and their homes and houses to be damaged and destroyed. So they were cut off without descendants and the

室家喪滅，絕無後嗣，萬民從而非之曰『暴王』，至今不已。則此
富貴為暴，而以得其罰者也。」

9.9　「然則親而不善，以得其罰者誰也？曰若昔者伯鯀，帝之元子，
廢帝之德庸，既乃刑之於羽之郊，乃熱照無有及也，帝亦不
愛。[34] 則此親而不善以得其罰者也。然則天之所使能者誰也？
曰若昔者禹稷皋陶是也。[35] 何以知其然也？先王之書《呂刑》道之
曰[36]：『皇帝清問下民，有辭有苗。曰群後之肆在下，明明不常，
鰥寡不蓋，德威維威，德明維明。乃名三后，恤功於民。[37] 伯夷
降典，哲[38]民維刑。禹平水土，主名山川。稷隆[39]播種，農殖嘉
穀。三后成功，維假於民。』[40] 則此言三聖人者，謹其言，慎其
行，精其思慮，索天下之隱事遺利，以上事天，則天鄉[41]其德，
下施之萬民，萬民被其利，終身無已。」

---

34. There is some uncertainty about the people and places in this example. Bo Gun 伯鯀 is possibly the son of the Emperor Zhuan Xu 顓頊 and the father of Yu 禹, at least according to the《史記‧夏本紀》— see *Shi Ji* 2, vol. 1, pp. 49–50. ZCY, however, takes the emperor in question to be Shun 舜. The matter turns on the reading of 元子 — see, for example, LSL. 羽 is possibly 羽山 — see LYS for details. There is also some variation in the reading of 照 and 有 in the penultimate clause, with the suggestion that they should be read as 昭 and 存 respectively. SYR understands this clause to indicate that he was imprisoned in a place which the sun and moon did not illuminate.
35. Yu 禹 was the first emperor of the Xia dynasty 夏; Ji 稷 was Hou Ji 后稷, director of husbandry under the Emperor Yao 堯; Gao Yao 皋陶 was an officer of justice, also under Yao.
36. The following quotation from the《書經‧呂刑》differs in a number of places from the text of that work — see LCC, vol. 3, pp. 593–597.
37. The translation of this sentence follows particularly MZQY's interpretation which is, in turn, based on SYR's reading. The "three lords" are Bo Yi 伯夷, Yu 禹, and Ji 稷, as is apparent from what follows.
38. Following WYZ, 哲 is taken as 折 which accords with the《書經》text.
39. Reading 隆 as 降 in the sense of 傳授 (WNS, Z&Q).
40. For a detailed consideration of a number of issues in this quotation see WYJ, notes 83–97, pp. 92–94.
41. There is general acceptance of the reading of 鄉 as 享.

people went on to condemn them, calling them 'cruel kings', as they still do to the present day. This, then, is a case of those who were rich and noble being cruel and so getting their punishment."

9.9 "This being so, then who was it that was closely related but bad, and so suffered his punishment? I say that such a man was Bo Gun of former times who was a direct descendant of the emperor, but had abandoned the emperor's beneficent virtue and so was banished to the region of Yu where no warmth or light reached him and the emperor did not love him. This, then, was a case of someone being closely related but bad, and so suffering his punishment. Who, then, were examples of Heaven employing the able? I say that men of former times like Yu, Ji and Gaoyao were such men. How do I know this to be so? A writing of the former kings, the *Lü Xing* has this to say: 'The great emperor carefully questioned his subjects and there were complaints against the Miao people.[iv] He said: The feudal lords and those below them must be men of obvious virtue not selected by convention, and widows and widowers who are worthy are not to be concealed. Virtue is imposing only when it is truly imposing. Virtue is clear only when it is clearly manifest. Thus he ordered the three lords to be sympathetic but effective in relation to the people. Bo Yi established the statutes and restrained the people with punishments. Yu brought order to the waters and the lands and gave names to the mountains and rivers. Ji came down [from his high position] to sow seed and to cultivate and propagate fine grain. The three lords completed their achievements and their contribution to the people was great.' This, then, is to say that the three sages were cautious in their speech, careful in their actions, and meticulous in their planning, searching out the world's hidden affairs and neglecting personal benefit in order to serve Heaven above, so Heaven took delight in their virtue. Below, they bestowed [benefits] on the ten thousand people, so the ten thousand people received their benefits throughout their lives unceasingly."

---

iv. This is the first mention in these chapters of the *Miao* (有) 苗, a minority people and the ancestors of today's Hmong people. They are referred to again in 12.8 and 19.5 — see LCC, vol. 3, p. 64.

9.10   「故先王之言曰：『此道也，大用之天下則不窕；小用之則不困；
修用之則萬民被其利，終身無已。』[42]《周頌》道之曰：『聖王之
德，若天之高，若地之普，其有昭於天下也。若地之固，若山之
承，不坼不崩。若日之光，若月之明，與天地同常。』[43] 則此言聖
人之德，章明博大，埴固，以修久也。故聖人之德，蓋總乎天地
者也。」

9.11   「今王公大人欲王天下，正諸侯，夫無德義將何以哉？其說將必
挾震威彊。今王公大人將焉取挾震威彊哉？傾者民之死也。[44] 民
生為甚欲，死為其憎，所欲不得而所憎屢至，自古及今未有[45] 嘗
能有以此王天下，正諸侯者也。今〔王〕[46] 大人欲王天下，正諸
侯，將欲使意得乎天下，名成乎後世，故[47] 不察尚賢為政之本
也？此聖人之厚行也。」

- - - - - - - - - - -

42. There is no identifiable source for this quotation. There is some variation in the reading
of 窕. I have followed Z&Q in taking it in the sense of 缺損 — see also WYJ, note 99,
p. 94.

43. This apparent quotation cannot be located in the 《詩經·周頌》. To quote WHB, "此為
逸詩名。" Within it there are several contentious characters — see WYJ, notes 101–
104. YY proposes the following alternative version: "聖人之德昭於天下，若天之
高，若地之普，若山之承，不坼不崩，若日之光，若月之明，與天地同常。" This
is the version YPM seems to have followed.

44. There is some variation in the reading of this sentence, particularly the first two
characters. Most commentators accept SYR's emendation of 者 to 諸. WYJ, who does
not, paraphrases the sentence as follows: "陷斯民於死地也。"

45. 有 here is regarded as superfluous by WYJ and so omitted.

46. Added following WYJ — see his note 110, p. 95.

47. There is general acceptance of the reading of 故 as 胡, making this a question.

9.10   "Therefore, the words of the former kings said: 'With respect to this Way, when it is used on a large scale, then the world will not be defective. When it is used on a small scale, then [the world] will not be in difficulty. When it is used over a long period, then the ten thousand people will be benefited by it throughout their lives unceasingly.' The *Zhou Song* says of the Way: 'The virtue of the sage is as high as Heaven; it is as broad as the earth, and it illuminates the world. It is like the earth's foundation; it is like the mountains' support, and it does not crack or collapse. It is as bright as the sun, as clear as the moon, and as constant as Heaven and earth.' This, then, is spoken of as the sage's virtue — clear, bright, all-encompassing and vast. It is firm, tenacious and long-enduring. Thus the virtue of the sage covers all Heaven and earth."

9.11   "At the present time, kings, dukes and great officers wish to rule all under Heaven and govern the feudal lords but, without virtue and righteousness, how will they do this? They say it would need to be through intimidation and force. But why would the kings, dukes and great officers of the present time choose intimidation and force? This would only incline the people towards death. But life is what the people most desire and death is what they most detest. If what they desire is not attained but what they detest frequently occurs, from ancient times to the present, no-one has ever been able to use these methods to rule all under Heaven and govern the feudal lords. Now if kings and great officers wish to rule the world and govern the feudal lords, if they wish to realise their ambitions for the world and extend their reputation to later generations, why do they not look to exalting worthiness as the basis of government? This was the meritorious conduct of the sage kings."

10: 尚賢下

10.1   子墨子言曰：「天下之王公大人皆欲其國家之富也，人民之眾
也，刑法之治也，然而不識以尚賢為政其國家百姓，王公大人本
失[1] 尚賢為政之本也。若苟王公大人本失尚賢為政之本也，則不
能毋舉物示之乎？今若有一諸侯於此，為政其國家也，曰：『凡
我國能射御之士，我將賞貴之，不能射御之士，我將罪賤之。』
問於若國之士，孰喜孰懼？我以為必能射御之士喜，不能射御之
士懼。我賞因而誘之矣[2]，曰：『凡我國之忠信之士，我將賞貴
之；不忠信之士，我將罪賤之。』問於若國之士，孰喜孰懼？我
以為必忠信之士喜，不忠不信之士懼，今唯毋以尚賢為政其國家
百姓，使國〔之〕[3] 為善者勸，為暴者沮，大以為政於天下，使天
下之為善者勸，為暴者沮。然昔吾所以貴堯舜禹湯文武之道者，

---

1.   WKY suggests that 本失 should read 未知.
2.   In this clause, 賞 is taken as 嘗 (SYR) and 誘 as 進 in the sense of 進一步 (CYX).
3.   之 added following ZCY.

10: Exalting Worthiness III

10.1   Master Mo Zi spoke, saying: "Kings, dukes and great officers of
the world all desire their states to be wealthy, their people to be
many, and their administration to be well ordered. Nevertheless,
if they do not know to make use of exalting worthiness in
governing the state and the people, then kings, dukes and great
officers fundamentally fail to make exalting worthiness the
foundation of government. If kings, dukes and great officers
fundamentally fail to make use of exalting worthiness as the
foundation of government, then can we do otherwise than put
forward examples to demonstrate this? Now suppose there was a
feudal lord involved in the administration of his state who said:
'All those officers in my state who can shoot arrows and drive
chariots, I shall reward and honour, but those who are not able to
shoot arrows and drive chariots, I shall censure and degrade.' You
might ask, which officers in a state like this would be happy and
which would be fearful. I think that without doubt those officers
able in archery and charioteering would be happy and those
officers without ability in archery and charioteering would be
fearful. I might take this discussion a step further and have him
say: 'All the loyal and trustworthy officers of my state, I shall
reward and honour. Officers that are not loyal and trustworthy, I
shall censure and degrade.' You might ask, which officers in a
state like this would be happy and which would be fearful. I think
that undoubtedly those officers who were loyal and trustworthy
would be happy and those officers who were not loyal and
trustworthy would be fearful. Now, if he makes use of exalting
worthiness in conducting the government of his state and its
people, he will cause those of the state who do good to be
encouraged and those who do evil to be stopped. If this is put to
use in conducting the government of the world, it causes those of
the world who do good to be encouraged and those who do evil to
be stopped. This being so, for what reason did I previously regard
as honourable the Way of Yao, Shun, Yu, Tang, Wen and Wu? It

何以故哉？以其唯毋臨眾發政而治民，使天下之為善者可而[4] 勸
也，為暴者可而沮也。然則此尚賢者也，與堯舜禹湯文武之道同
矣。」

10.2　「而今天下之士君子，居處言語皆尚賢，逮至其臨眾發政而治
民，莫知尚賢而使能，我以此知天下之士君子，明於小而不明於
大也。何以知其然乎？今王公大人，有一牛羊之財[5] 不能殺，必
索良宰；有一衣裳之財不能制，必索良工。當王公大人之於此
也，雖有骨肉之親、無故富貴、面目美好者，實知其不能也，不
使之也，是何故？恐其敗財也。當王公大人之於此也，則不失尚
賢而使能。王公大人有一罷[6] 馬不能治，必索良醫；有一危弓[7] 不
能張，必索良工。當王公大人之於此也，雖有骨肉之親、無故富
貴、面目美好者，實知其不能也，必不使。是何故？恐其敗財
也。當王公大人之於此也，則不失尚賢而使能。逮至其國家則不
然，王公大人骨肉之親，無故富貴，面目美好者，則舉之，則王
公大人之親其國家也，不若親其一危弓、罷馬、衣裳、牛羊之財

4.　There is general acceptance that 可而 here and in its immediately subsequent use should
　　be read as 可以 following WNS.
5.　There is general acceptance of BY's reading of 財 as 材.
6.　Here 罷 is taken as 疲 following SYR.
7.　LSL has the following note on 危弓: "《周禮‧考工記‧弓人》：'豐肉而短，寬緩以
　　荼，若是者為之危弓。'鄭玄注：'危猶疲也。'危弓是一種難開的弓。"

was because they were in touch with the multitude in issuing their decrees and bringing order to the populace, which meant that those in the world who were good could be encouraged and those who were evil could to be stopped. It is in such a manner that exalting worthiness is identical with the Way of Yao, Shun, Yu, Tang, Wen and Wu."

10.2 "Yet at the present time, [although] officers and gentlemen of the world all exalt worthiness in their private speech, when it comes to being in touch with the multitude in issuing decrees and bringing order to the people, they do not know to exalt worthiness and utilise ability. This is how I know that officers and gentlemen of the world are clear about small matters but not about great matters. How do I know this is so? Now if kings, dukes and great officers have an ox or sheep they cannot slaughter, they must send for a skilled butcher. If they have the material for a garment but they cannot make it, they must send for a skilled tailor. When a king, duke or great officer is in such a situation, although there is a blood relative, or someone rich and noble without proper cause, or someone of fine appearance, he would truly know they were not able and he would not use them. Why is this? He would be afraid they might damage the material. When a king, duke or great officer is in such a situation, he does not fail to exalt worthiness and utilise ability. If a king, duke or great officer has a sick horse that he cannot cure, he would certainly call for a skilled veterinarian. If he has an overly stiff bow that he cannot draw, he would certainly call for a skilled craftsman. When a king, duke or great officer is in such a situation, although there is a blood relative, or someone rich and noble without proper cause, or someone of fine appearance, he would truly know they were not able and certainly would not use them. What is the reason for this? He would be afraid they might damage the material. When a king, duke or great officer is in this situation, he does not fail to exalt worthiness and utilise ability. But when it comes to his state, he is not like this, in that if the king, duke or great officer has a blood relative, or someone rich and noble without cause, or someone of fine appearance, then he advances him. So the king's, duke's or great officer's concern for his state is not like his concern the overly stiff bow, or the sick horse, or the garment, or the ox and

與！我以此知天下之士君子皆明於小，而不明於大也。此譬猶喑
者而使為行人，聾者而使為樂師。」

10.3　「是故古之聖王之治天下也，其所富，其所貴，未必王公大人骨
肉之親、無故富貴、面目美好者也。是故昔者舜耕於歷山，陶於
河瀕，漁於雷澤，灰[8]於常陽[9]。堯得之服澤之陽，立為天子，使
接天下之政，而治天下之民。[10]昔伊尹為〔有〕莘氏女師僕[11]，使
為庖人，湯得而舉之，立為三公，使接天下之政，治天下之民。
昔者傅說居北海之洲[12]，圜土之上[13]，衣褐帶索，庸築於傅巖之
城，武丁[14]得而舉之，立為三公，使之接天下之政，而治天下之
民。是故昔者堯之舉舜也，湯之舉伊尹也，武丁之舉傅說也，豈
以為骨肉之親、無故富貴、面目美好者哉？惟法其言，用其謀，
行其道，上可而利天，中可而利鬼，下可而利人，是故推而上
之。」

10.4　「古者聖王既審尚賢欲以為政，故書之竹帛，琢之槃盂，傳以遺

8.　Following YY, most commentators read 灰 as 販.
9.　BY takes 常陽 to be the southern side of Heng Shan 恒山. Others (for example Z&Q)
　　take it to be a specific place.
10.　For other details of this story see note i to 9.7 above.
11.　In the previous book there is "私臣" rather than "師僕" — see 9.7 note ii above and also
　　WYJ's detailed note to the previous chapter (his note 69, pp. 88–89) for further details.
　　I have followed LSL in including 有 here.
12.　洲 is generally read as 州. Bei Hai 北海 is probably a general reference to northern
　　regions, although it may here be a specific name.
13.　There is no reference to prison in the earlier account.
14.　Reigned 1324–1265 BC. For details of Fu Yue's 傅說 elevation, see 9.7, note iii above.

sheep. This is how I know that officers and gentlemen of the world all are clear about small matters but are not clear about great matters. It is like taking those who are dumb and making them envoys, or those who are deaf and making them music masters."

10.3   "For this reason, in the ancient sage kings' governing of the world, those whom they enriched and ennobled were not necessarily the blood relatives of kings, dukes and great officers, or those who were rich and noble without proper reason, or those of fine appearance. For example, in ancient times, Shun cultivated land on Li Shan, made pottery on the banks of the [Yellow] River, fished in Lei Marsh and sold his wares at Chang Yang. Yao found him on the northern side of Fu Marsh and established him as the Son of Heaven, transferring to him the government of the world and the administration of the world's people. Formerly, Yi Yin was the personal servant of a daughter of the [You] Xin clan and was employed as a cook. Tang found him and raised him to be one of the 'Three Dukes', transferring to him the government of the world and the administration of the world's people. Fu Yue of former times lived in the district of Bei Hai within the prison walls. His garments were of coarse cloth bound with rope and he was working as a common labourer in the city of Fu Yan. Wu Ding found him and raised him to be one of the 'Three Dukes', transferring to him the government of the world and the administration of the world's people. Was the reason for Yao's promotion of Shun, or Tang's promotion of Yi Yin, or Wu Ding's promotion of Fu Yue because they were blood relatives, or rich and noble without proper cause, or of fine appearance? No, it was only because they modelled themselves on their words, used their plans and carried into practice their Way, so it was possible for them to benefit Heaven above, to benefit ghosts in the middle realm, and to benefit the people in the lower realm. This was why they put them forward and elevated them."

10.4   "The ancient sage kings gave careful attention to [the principle of] exalting worthiness and wished to use it in government. Therefore, they wrote it on bamboo and silk, and carved it on [ceremonial] basins and bowls, in this way passing it on to their

後世子孫。於先王之書《呂刑》之書然：『王曰：於！來！有國有
土，告女訟刑，在今而安百姓，女何擇？言人？何敬？不刑？何
度？不及？』[15] 能擇人而敬為刑，堯舜禹湯文武之道可及也。是何
也？則以尚賢及之。於先王之書《豎年》之言然：『曰：晞夫聖、
武、知人，以屏輔而身。』[16] 此言先王之治天下也，必選擇賢者以
為其群屬輔佐。曰今也天下之士君子，皆欲富貴而惡貧賤。曰
然。女何為而得富貴而辟貧賤？〔曰〕[17] 莫若為賢。為賢之道將奈
何？曰有力者疾以助人，有財者勉以分人，有道者勸以教人。若
此則飢者得食，寒者得衣，亂者得治。若飢則得食，寒則得衣，
亂則得治，此安生生。」

10.5   「今王公大人其所富，其所貴，皆王公大人骨肉之親，無故富
貴，面目美好者也。今王公大人骨肉之親，無故富貴，面目美好
者，焉故[18] 必知哉！若不知，使治其國家，則其國家之亂可得而
知也。今天下之士君子皆欲富貴而惡貧賤。然女何為而得富貴，
而辟貧賤哉？[19] 曰莫若為王公大人骨肉之親，無故富貴，面目美
好者。王公大人骨肉之親、無故富貴，面目美好者，此非可學能

---

15. See the 《書經・呂刑》, LCC, vol. 3, pp. 601–602. This is a difficult passage. YPM
    simply uses Legge's translation. The version given above follows particularly LSL and
    takes into account proposed emendations and interpretations by BY and WYZ
    especially. See WYJ, notes 42–47, pp. 103–104.
16. As noted in relation to the previous chapter, where the work is referred to as the *Ju Nian*
    距年, the source of this apparent quotation is unknown. There is general acceptance of
    BY's reading of 晞 as 睎 in the sense of 望 and the addition of 人 after 聖.
17. Several editors transfer 曰 from the start of the previous sentence to here which I have
    followed.
18. There is general acceptance of 焉故 as 何故.
19. In this sentence 女 is taken as 汝 and 辟 as 避 (see, for example, LYS).

descendants of later generations. In the record of the former kings, the *Lü Xing*, it is written thus: 'The king said: Ah come! You who have states and lands, I tell you of just punishments. If at present you are to bring peace to the ordinary people, whom should you select? Is it not worthy men? What should you respect? Is it not punishments? What should you reflect on? Is it not making them fitting?' With ability in the selecting of men and reverent attention to the carrying out of punishments, the Way of Yao, Shun, Yu, Tang, Wen and Wu can be reached. How is this? It is through exalting worthiness that it is reached. In the words of the writings of the former kings, the *Shu Nian*, it is so. '[They] say: Look for sages, valiant and wise men, to guard and assist your person.' This is to say that former kings, in governing the world, certainly selected worthy men to be their officers and assistants. I say that at the present time officers and gentlemen of the world all wish for wealth and nobility and abhor poverty and baseness. This being so, how can they attain wealth and nobility and avoid poverty and baseness? I say there is nothing to compare with being worthy. What is the way of worthiness? I say that one who has strength must hasten to use it to help people. One who has material wealth must distribute it to people to the best of his ability. One who possesses the Way must encourage people through teaching. In this way, then, the hungry will obtain food, the cold will obtain clothing, and the disordered will find order. If the hungry acquire food, if the cold acquire clothing, and if the disordered acquire order, this will bring about the maintenance of life."

10.5   "Now those whom kings, dukes and great officers enrich, those whom they ennoble, are all blood relatives of kings, dukes and great officers, those rich and noble without reason, and those of fine appearance. But how are they necessarily wise! If they are not wise, but are made to govern the state, then one knows that disorder of the state will ensue. At the present time, officers and gentlemen of the world all desire wealth and nobility and abhor poverty and baseness. This being so, how do they act to achieve wealth and nobility and avoid poverty and baseness? [I] say there is no other way than by being a blood relative of a king, duke or great officer, being rich and noble without reason, or being of fine appearance. But [such people] cannot learn to be able. If the

者也。使不知辯，德行之厚若禹湯文武不加得也。王公大人骨肉
之親，躄喑聾暴為桀紂[20]，不加失也。是故以賞不當賢，罰不當
暴，其所賞者已無故矣，其所罰者亦無罪。是以使百姓皆攸心[21]
解體，沮以為善，垂其股肱之力而不相勞來也；[22] 腐臭餘財，而
不相分資也；隱慝良道，而不相教誨也。若此，則飢者不得食，
寒者不得衣，亂者不得治。推而上之以。[23]」

10.6 「是故昔者，堯有舜，舜有禹，禹有皋陶，湯有小臣，武王有閎
夭、泰顛、南宮括、散宜生[24]，而天下和[25]，庶民阜，是以近者安
之，遠者歸之。日月之所照，舟車之所及，雨露之所漸，粒食之
所養，得此莫不勸譽。且今天下之王公大人士君子，中實將欲為
仁義，求為上士，上欲中聖王之道，下欲中國家百姓之利，故尚
賢之為說，而不可不察此者也。尚賢者，天鬼百姓之利，而政事
之本也。」

- - - - - - - - - - - - -

20. Following SYR, LYS proposes the emendation of this sentence as follows: "躄瘖聾
    瞽，暴如桀紂。"
21. There is wide acceptance of the reading of 攸 as 悠 in the sense of 悠忽 ("lazy", "idle")
    — see, for example, LYS. WHQ, however, takes 攸 as an error for 散 whilst WYJ has
    放.
22. Z&Q have the following note on this sentence: "垂其股肱之力：指不願動手足勞
    動，怠惰也。不相來勞：王煥鑣說：'來同救。''勞來'，既'勞敕'，勉勵幫助。
    不相勞來：既不勉勵幫助人。"
23. The five characters "推而上之以" are regarded as superfluous or misplaced here
    following WYZ and ZCY. WYJ transposes them to section 10.6 below.
24. Of these examples, several have been given before. For Gao Yao 皋陶 see note 35,
    p. 76. For Hong Yao 閎夭 and Tai Dian 泰顛 see note ii, pp. 59–61. Nangong Gua 南
    宮括 and San Yisheng 散宜生, who have not previously been mentioned, were both
    ministers under Kings Wen and Wu. All the last four ministers are spoken of together
    in the《書經‧君奭》(LCC, vol. 3, p. 481 — and see Legge's note regarding Sanyi as
    being possibly the surname). Several of these men are also mentioned in *Mencius* VIIB.
    38.
25. WYJ's text here reads: "得此推而上之，以而天下和" — see his notes 77–79, p. 107.

distinction is not recognised then even someone whose moral worth is like that of Yu, Tang, Wen or Wu will not find advancement.[i] And even if a blood relative of a king, duke or great officer is lame, sick, deaf or blind, or is evil like Jie and Zhou, he will not fail to go further. The reason for this is that reward does not equate with worthiness, nor does punishment equate with cruelty. That is, those who are rewarded are without merit and those who are punished are without transgression. The effect of this is that the ordinary people are all lazy and unfocused in their minds, are undisciplined in their bodies, are prevented from doing good, make no use of the strength of their limbs, and do not help and encourage each other. Surplus materials are left to rot and decay without being distributed. The excellent Way is hidden and concealed without being taught and explained. In such a situation, those who are hungry do not get food, those who are cold do not obtain clothes, and those who are in disorder do not become ordered."

10.6 "So it was that in former times Yao had Shun, Shun had Yu, Yu had Gaoyao, Tang had Xiao Chen (Yi Yin), and Wu Wang had Hong Yao, Tai Dian, Nangong Gua and San Yisheng, and the world was made harmonious, and the masses were made prosperous. By these means, those near at hand were made peaceful and those who were distant returned. Wherever the sun and moon shone, boats and carts reached, rain and dew made wet and grains were what nourished, this obtained and was invariably encouraged and praised. So, at the present time, if kings, dukes, great officers, officers and gentlemen of the world have a genuine wish to be benevolent and righteous, and to seek high office, if above, they desire to be in accord with the Way of the sage kings and below, they desire to achieve benefit for the state and the common people, then exalting worthiness should be the method. This is something that must be examined. Exalting worthiness is of benefit to Heaven, to the ghosts, and to the common people as well as being the foundation of government and affairs."

---

i.   The reading of this somewhat problematic statement largely follows LYS.

11: 尚同上[1]

11.1 子墨子言曰:「古者民始生,未有刑政[2]之時,蓋其語『人異義[3]』。是以一人則一義,二人則二義,十人則十義,其人茲[4]眾,其所謂義者亦茲眾。是以人是其義,以非人之義,故交相非也。是以內者父子兄弟作怨惡,離散不能相和合。天下之百姓,皆以水火毒藥相虧害,至有餘力不能以相勞,腐朽[5]餘財不以相分,隱匿良道不以相教,天下之亂,若禽獸然。」

11.2 「夫明虖[6]天下之所以亂者,生於無政長。是故選天下之賢可者,立以為天子。天子立,以其力為未足,又選擇天下之賢可者,置

---

1. There is again debate about the reading of the title 尚同. Both BY and SYR take 尚 in the sense of 上 and many commentators/editors follow this — see, for example, YPM, note 1, p. 55 and WYJ. I have, however, followed LSL in reading 尚 as in the previous group of essays (尚賢 I–III) and 同 as 壹同. It would seem to be the unity or uniformity of beliefs and principles which is the central issue.
2. A number of commentators take "刑政" to be a general term for the administrative apparatus. For example, Z&Q have the following note: "刑政:指行政治理。" I have chosen to preserve the basic meaning of 刑 although some early texts have 形 — see WYJ, note 2, p. 111.
3. In this section 義 is read as 道理 via 議 — see YPM's note 2, p. 55.
4. 茲 here is taken as 滋 giving the meaning of "越多".
5. In a number of texts the unusual alternative form of this character (with radical 78 — ZWDCD #16725) is used — see, for example, LSL, Z&Q.
6. Taken as a variant of 乎 in the sense of 於 — see, for example, Z&Q.

11: Exalting Unity I

11.1   Master Mo Zi spoke, saying: "Ancient times, when people first came into being, were times when there were as yet no laws or government, so it was said that people had differing principles. This meant that, if there was one person, there was one principle; if there were two people, there were two principles; and if there were ten people, there were ten principles. The more people there were, the more things there were that were spoken of as principles. This was a case of people affirming their own principles and condemning those of other people. The consequence of this was mutual condemnation. In this way, within a household, fathers and sons, and older and younger brothers were resentful and hostile, separated and dispersed, and unable to reach agreement and accord with each other. Throughout the world, people all used water and fire, and poisons and potions to injure and harm one another. As a result, those with strength to spare did not use it to help each other in their work, surplus goods rotted and decayed and were not used for mutual distribution, and good doctrines were hidden and obscured and not used for mutual teaching. So the world was in a state of disorder comparable to that amongst birds and beasts."

11.2   "It is quite clear that what is taken as disorder in the world arises from lack of effective rule. Therefore, the one who was the most worthy and able in the world was selected and established as being the Son of Heaven.[i] When the Son of Heaven was established, because his strength alone was not sufficient, there was also selection and choice of the worthy and able of the world who were

---

i.   BW raises the issue of who does the selecting — something which is not clear from the text (see his note, p. 35).

立之以為三公。天子三公既以立，以天下為博大，遠國異土之
民，是非利害之辯，不可一二而明知，故畫分萬國，立諸侯國
君。諸侯國君既已立，以其力為未足，又選擇其國之賢可者，置
立之以為正長[7]。正長既已具，天子發政於天下之百姓，言曰：
『聞善而不善，皆以告其上。上之所是，必皆是之；〔上之〕[8]所
非，必皆非之。上有過則規諫之，下有善則傍薦之。上同而不下
比者，此上之所賞，而下之所譽也。意若聞善而不善，不以告其
上。上之所是，弗能是，上之所非，弗能非，上有過弗規諫，下
有善弗傍薦。下比不能上同者，此上之所罰而百姓所毀也。』上
以此為賞罰，甚明察以審信。」

---

7. I have rendered 正長, both here and subsequently, "government leaders", i.e. 政長 —
    see Z&Q, note 7, p. 115. An alternative would be "upright leaders".
8. Added by WYJ in conformity with the previous sentence.

set up and established as the 'Three Dukes'.[ii] When the Son of Heaven and the 'Three Dukes' were already established, because the world was vast and wide and there were people of distant countries and different lands, the distinctions between right and wrong, and between benefit and harm could not be clearly understood by one or two people. There was, therefore, division into ten thousand states with the establishment of feudal lords and rulers of states. When feudal lords and rulers of states were already established, because their strength alone was not sufficient, there was also the choice and selection of the worthy and able of the states and their establishment as government leaders.[iii] When the government leaders were already all in place, the Son of Heaven issued his decree to the people of the world, saying: 'On hearing of good or evil, all must inform their superior. What the superior takes to be right, all must take to be right. What the superior takes to be wrong, all must take to be wrong. If those above have faults, then admonish and remonstrate with them. If those below do good, then enquire about[iv] and recommend them. Agreement with superiors and non-agreement with inferiors — this is what superiors reward and what inferiors praise. If one hears of good or evil and does not inform one's superiors; if what one's superiors take to be right cannot be taken to be right and what one's superiors take to be wrong cannot be taken to be wrong; if superiors have faults and one does not admonish and remonstrate with them; if those below are good and one does not enquire about and recommend them; if those below align [with each other] and are unable to align with their superiors — these are what those above censure and what the ordinary people speak ill of.' It was on this basis that those above carried out rewards and punishments. This has to be clearly understood and carefully examined so it can be relied upon."

---

ii. Hucker begins his extensive entry on the *san gong* 三公 as follows: "Three Dukes: from antiquity a collective reference to dignitaries who were officially considered the three paramount aides to the ruler and held the highest possible ranks in the officialdom ..." (#4871, p. 399).

iii. This term, 正長, is not listed as a specific term by Hucker.

iv. This follows LSL's reading of 傍 as 訪. Z&Q follow the reading by WHB of 傍 as 旁 in the sense of 廣, giving the interpretation, "廣泛地推薦".

11.3　「是故里長者，里之仁人也。里長發政里之百姓，言曰：『聞善而不善，必以告其鄉長。鄉長之所是，必皆是之；鄉長之所非，必皆非之。去若不善言，學鄉長之善言；去若不善行，學鄉長之善行，則鄉何說以亂哉？』察鄉之所治者何也？鄉長唯能壹同鄉之義，是以鄉治也。鄉長者，鄉之仁人也。鄉長發政鄉之百姓，言曰：『聞善而不善者，必以告國君。國君之所是，必皆是之；國君之所非，必皆非之。去若不善言，學國君之善言，去若不善行，學國君之善行，則國何說以亂哉？』」

11.4　「察國之所以治者何也？國君唯能壹同國之義，是以國治也。國君者，國之仁人也。國君發政國之百姓，言曰：『聞善而不善，必以告天子。天子之所是，皆是之；天子之所非，皆非之。去若不善言，學天子之善言，去若不善行，學天子之善行，則天下何說以亂哉？』察天下之所以治者何也？天子唯能壹同天下之義，是以天下治也。天下之百姓皆上同於天子，而不上同於天，則菑

11.3   "This is why the village head was the most benevolent man of the
village. It was the village head who brought administrative order
to the people of the village, saying: 'When you hear of good or
evil, you must inform your district head. What the district head
takes to be right, all must take to be right. What the district head
takes to be wrong, all must take to be wrong. Do away with bad
words and study the good words of the district head. Do away with
bad actions and study the good actions of the district head. Then
how can there be said to be disorder in the district?' How do we
examine what it is that brings order to a district? It is only that the
district head is able to make uniform the principles in the district.
This is how there is order in a district. The district head was the
most benevolent man of the district. It was the district head who
brought administrative order to the people of the district, saying:
'When you hear of good or evil, you must inform the ruler of the
state. What the ruler of the state takes to be right, all must take to
be right. What the ruler of the state takes to be wrong, all must take
to be wrong. Do away with bad words and study the good words
of the ruler of the state. Do away with bad actions and study the
good actions of the ruler of the state. Then how can there be said
to be disorder in the state?'"

11.4   "How do we examine what it is that brings order to a state? It is
only that the ruler of the state is able to make uniform the
principles of the state. This is how there is order in a state. The
ruler of a state was the most benevolent man of the state. It was the
ruler of the state who brought administrative order to the people of
the state, saying: 'When I hear of good or evil, I must inform the
Son of Heaven. What the Son of Heaven takes to be right, all must
take to be right. What the Son of Heaven takes to be wrong, all
must take to be wrong. Do away with bad words and study the
good words of the Son of Heaven. Do away with bad actions and
study the good actions of the Son of Heaven. Then how can there
be said to be disorder in the world?' How do we examine what it
is that brings order to the world? It is only that the Son of Heaven
is able to make uniform the principles of the world. This is how
there is order in the world. When the people of the world all have
respect for, and uniformity with, the Son of Heaven, but do not
have respect for, and uniformity with, Heaven, calamity is still not

猶未去也。今若天飄風苦雨，溱溱而至者，此天之所以罰百姓之
不上同於天者也。」

11.5   是故子墨子言曰：「古者聖王為五刑[9]，請[10]以治其民。譬若絲縷
之有紀，罔罟之有網，所連收[11]天下之百姓不尚同其上者也。」

---

9. The "five punishments" varied in different eras, but at this time were 墨 (branding), 劓 (cutting off the nose), 刖 (cutting off the feet), 宮 (castration) and 大辟 (death).

10. Following SYR 請 is read as 確實.

11. 以 is supplied after 所 (YY). On the phrase "連收" ZCY has the following note: "連，合也；收，聚也。"

done away with. Nowadays, if Heaven's violent storms and heavy rains are continuous and extreme, this is Heaven's way of bringing punishment to the people for not respecting and being in accord with Heaven."

11.5   This is the reason Master Mo Zi said: "The ancient sage kings put into effect the five punishments, which was truly how they brought order to the people. The five punishments were like the main thread in a skein of silk, or the controlling rope of a fishing net, and were the means used to bring into line the ordinary people of the world who did not respect, and make themselves like, those above."

12: 尚同中

12.1 子墨子曰：「方今之時，復[1]古之民始生，未有正長之時，蓋其語曰：『天下之人異義』。是以一人一義，十人十義，百人百義，其人數茲眾，其所謂義者亦茲眾。是以人是其義，而非人之義，故相交[2]非也。內之父子兄弟作怨仇，皆有離散之心，不能相和合。至乎舍餘力不以相勞，隱匿良道不以相教，腐朽[3]餘財不以相分，天下之亂也，至如禽獸然，無君臣上下長幼之節，父子兄弟之禮，是以天下亂焉。」

12.2 「明乎民之無正長以一同天下之義，而天下亂也。是故選擇天下賢良聖知辯慧之人，立以為天子，使從事乎一同天下之義。天子既已[4]立矣，以為唯其耳目之請[5]，不能獨一同天下之義，是故選擇天下贊閱[6]賢良聖知辯慧之人，置以為三公，與從事乎一同天

---

1. LYS reads 復 as 反. Z&Q give the following paraphrase of this sentence: "回過頭去考查古之民始生之時。"
2. Following the previous chapter, 相交 should be reversed in order — i.e. 交相.
3. This character is generally found in the unusual form — ZWDCD #16725.
4. Emended from 以 on the basis of the following text (WYJ).
5. There is general acceptance of 請 as 情 in the sense of 情況.
6. Those who retain these two characters take 贊 in 贊閱 as 進 in the sense of 進用 and 閱 as 簡 (e.g. LYS). It is probably better to follow WHB in regarding them as superfluous.

12: Exalting Unity II

12.1 Master Mo Zi said: "If, from the vantage point of the present, one
looks back to the past when people first came into being, a time
when there was not yet any government, in general what was said
was, 'The people of the world differed in their principles.' This
meant that for one person there was one principle, for ten people
ten principles, for a hundred people a hundred principles, and so
the more people there were, the more so-called principles there
were. This also meant that each person took his own principle to
be right and the principles of others to be wrong, so there was
mutual disagreement. Within, amongst fathers and sons, and older
and younger brothers, there was resentment and enmity since all
were quite disparate in their minds and were unable to reach
mutual accord. As a result, any surplus strength was set aside and not
used in mutual toil, excellent doctrines were kept secret and not used
in mutual teaching, and surplus materials rotted and decayed and
were not used for mutual distribution. The disorder of the world was
comparable to that amongst birds and beasts. There were no
regulations regarding rulers and ministers, superiors and inferiors,
old and young, and there was no propriety between fathers and sons,
and older and younger brothers, so the world was in disorder."

12.2 "There was a realisation that the people did not have a leader who
could unify the principles of the world, and that the world was in
disorder. This was the reason for selecting the man in the world
who was [the most] worthy and good, sagacious and wise, skilled
in discussion and clever, and establishing him as the Son of
Heaven, giving him the task of bringing unity to the principles of
the world. Once the Son of Heaven was established, his ears and
eyes were such that, on his own, he was not able to bring unity to
the principles of the world. For this reason, he selected men in the
world who were worthy and good, sagacious and wise, skilled in
discussion and clever, setting them up as the 'Three Dukes', to
join with him in the task of bringing unity to the principles of the

下之義。天子三公既已立矣，以為天下博大，山林遠土之民，不可得而一也，是故靡[7]分天下，設以為萬諸侯國君，使從事乎一同其國之義。國君既已立矣，又以為唯其耳目之請，不能一同其國之義，是故擇其國之賢者，置以為左右將軍大夫，以遠至乎鄉里之長，與從事乎一同其國之義。[8]」

12.3 「天子諸侯之君，民之正長，既已定矣，天子為發政施教曰：『凡聞見善者，必以告其上；聞見不善者，亦必以告其上。上之所是，必亦是之；上之所非，必亦非之。己有善傍薦之[9]，上有過規諫之。尚同義[10]其上，而毋有下比之心。上得則賞之，萬民聞則譽之。意若聞見善，不以告其上，聞見不善，亦不以告其上，上之所是不能是，上之所非不能非，己有善不能傍薦之，上有過不能規諫之，下比而非其上者，上得則誅罰之，萬民聞則非毀之。』故古者聖王之為刑政賞譽也，甚明察以審信。是以舉[11]天下之人，皆欲得上之賞譽，而畏上之毀罰。」

---

7. LYS has the following note on 靡: "靡：磨的誤字，與歷同，分割的意思。見非攻下篇。"
8. There are two minor emendations in this sentence, both due to SYR, as follows: (i) 將軍 to 卿. (ii) 遠 to 逮.
9. There is some uncertainty about this statement. I have followed WNS in reading 己 as 民 and SYR in reading 傍 as 訪 — see also LYS's note where he draws attention to a similar sentence in *Mozi* 48.
10. According to SYR, 義 here should read 乎 based on similar statements in the following sections.
11. 舉 here is read as 全 — see, for example, Z&Q.

world. When the Son of Heaven and the 'Three Dukes' were already in place, realising that the world was vast and they could not bring the people of the mountains, forests and distant lands to a state of unity, they divided it up and set up the numerous feudal lords and rulers of states, giving them the task of unifying the principles of their own states. When the rulers of states were already established, it was also the case that their ears and eyes were such that they were unable to bring unity to the principles of their states. So they selected those who were worthy in their states and established them as assistants, generals and great officers, right down to heads of districts and villages, to join them in the task of bringing unity to the principles of their states."

12.3   "When the Son of Heaven, feudal lords, rulers and the leaders of the populace had already been established, the Son of Heaven put forth a decree, saying: 'Whenever you hear or see something good, you must inform your superior. Whenever you hear or see something bad, you must also inform your superior. What the superior approves of, you must also approve of. What the superior condemns, you must also condemn. When the people are good, enquire about it and reward them. When superiors are at fault, admonish them. Value uniformity with those above and do not act in collusion with those below. If those above get to know [about this], they will reward you. If the ten thousand people hear [about this], they will praise you. If, on the other hand, you hear or see something good and do not inform your superior, or if you hear or see something bad and also do not inform your superior, if you are unable to approve of what your superior approves of, if you are unable to condemn what your superior condemns, if the people are good but you are unable to enquire about and reward them, if your superiors are at fault but you are unable to admonish them, if you collude with those below and act against those above, then if those above get to know [about this], they will reprove and punish you and if the ten thousand people hear [about this], they will condemn and vilify you.' Therefore, the sage kings of ancient times, in establishing punishments, government, rewards and praise, were very perspicacious and thoroughly reliable. In this way, people throughout the world all wished to gain rewards and praise from their superiors and feared their superiors' condemnation and punishment."

12.4   「是故里長順天子政，而一同其里之義。里長既同其里之義，率
其里之萬民，以尚同乎鄉長，曰：『凡里之萬民，皆尚同乎鄉
長，而不敢下比。鄉長之所是，必亦是之；鄉長之所非，必亦非
之。去而不善言，學鄉長之善言；去而不善行，學鄉長之善行。
鄉長固鄉之賢者也，舉鄉人以法鄉長，夫鄉何說而不治哉？』察
鄉長之所以治鄉〔而鄉治〕[12] 者，何故之以也？曰：唯以其能一同
其鄉之義，是以鄉治。」

12.5   「鄉長治其鄉，而鄉既已治矣，有率其鄉萬民，以尚同乎國君，
曰：『凡鄉之萬民，皆上同乎國君，而不敢下比，國君之所是，
必亦是之，國君之所非，必亦非之。去而不善言，學國君之善
言；去而不善行，學國君之善行。國君固國之賢者也，舉國人以
法國君，夫國何說而不治哉？』察國君之所以治國，而國治者，
何故之以也？曰唯以其能一同其國之義，是以國治。」

12.6   「國君治其國，而國既已治矣，有率其國之萬民，以尚同乎天

12. WYJ proposes the addition of these three characters here and the four characters
    included in the equivalent sentence of 12.6 to give the penultimate sentence of the three
    parallel sections the same form.

12.4   "In this way, the village heads complied with the Son of Heaven's administration and unified the principles of the villages. And when the village heads had unified the principles of their villages, they led the many people of their villages to exalt unity with the district chiefs, saying: 'In general, all the many people of the villages should exalt unity with the district chief and not dare to collude with those below. What the district chief approves of, they must also approve of. What the district chief condemns, they must also condemn. They are to cast aside their own bad words and learn from the good words of the district chief. They are to cast aside their own bad actions and learn from the good actions of the district chief. The district chief is definitely the most worthy man in the district. If all the people of the district model themselves on him, how can the district be said to be not well ordered?' And what do you think was the cause of the district chief bringing order to the district? I say, it was nothing other than that he was able to unify its principles. This is how a district becomes well ordered."

12.5   "When the district chief had brought order to his district and the district was already well ordered, he led the many people of his district to exalt unity with the ruler of the state, saying: 'In general, all the many people of the district should exalt unity with the ruler of the state and not dare to collude with those below. What the ruler of the state approves of, they must also approve of. What the ruler of the state condemns, they must also condemn. They should cast aside their own bad words and learn from the good words of the ruler of the state. They should cast aside their own bad actions and learn from the good actions of the ruler of the state. The ruler of the state is certainly its most worthy man. If all the people of the state take its ruler as a model, how can it be said that the state is not well ordered?' And what do you think was the cause of the ruler of the state bringing order to the state so it was well ordered? I say, it was only his being able to unify the principles of his state. This is how a state becomes well ordered."

12.6   "When the ruler of a state had brought order to it, and the state was already well ordered, he led the many people of his state to exalt

子，曰：『凡國之萬民，〔皆〕[13] 上同乎天子，而不敢下比。天子之
所是，必亦是之，天子之所非，必亦非之。去而不善言，學天子
之善言；去而不善行，學天子之善行。天子者，固天下之仁人
也，舉天下之萬民以法天子，夫天下何說而不治哉？』察天子之
所以治天下〔而天下治〕[14] 者，何故之以也？曰唯以其能一同天下
之義，是以天下治。」

12.7　「天下既尚同乎天子，而未尚同乎天者，則天菑將猶未止也[15]。故
當若天降寒熱不節，雪霜雨露不時，五穀不孰[16]，六畜不遂，疾
災戾疫，飄風苦雨，薦臻而至者，此天之降罰也，將以罰下人之
不尚同乎天者也。故古者聖王，明天鬼之所欲，而避天鬼之所
憎，以求興〔天下之利，除〕[17] 天下之害。是以率天下之萬民，齊
戒沐浴，潔為酒醴粢盛，以祭祀天鬼。其事鬼神也，酒醴粢盛不
敢不蠲潔，犧牲不敢不腯肥，珪璧幣帛不敢不中度量，春秋祭祀
不敢失時幾，聽獄不敢不中，分財不敢不均，居處不敢怠慢。曰

---

13. Added by WYJ — see his note 32, p. 126.
14. Added following WYJ — see his note 34, p. 126.
15. This is WYJ's version of this sentence which is characterised by the emendation of 夫
    to 天下 at the start and 上 to 尚 as the tenth character — see his notes 36–38, p. 126.
16. 熟 is read for 孰.
17. There is wide acceptance of the addition of these five characters here — see, for
    example, WYJ and Z&Q.

unity with the Son of Heaven, saying: 'In general, all the many people of the state should exalt unity with the Son of Heaven and not dare to collude with those below. What the Son of Heaven approves of, they must also approve of. What the Son of Heaven condemns, they must also condemn. They should cast aside their own bad words and learn from the good words of the Son of Heaven. They should cast aside their own bad actions and learn from the good actions of the Son of Heaven. The Son of Heaven is certainly the world's most benevolent man. If you bring the many people of the world to take the Son of Heaven as a model, how can it be said that the world is not well ordered?' And what do you think was the cause of the Son of Heaven bringing order to the world? I say, it was only his being able to unify the principles of the world. This is how the world becomes well ordered."

12.7   "If the world exalts unity with the Son of Heaven, but does not yet exalt unity with Heaven, then Heaven's calamities still will not stop. Therefore, it is right to expect Heaven to send down cold and heat without moderation, to [send down] snow, frost, rain and dew out of season, [so] the five grains will not ripen, the six animals will not flourish, and pestilence and plague will occur, as will whirlwinds and flooding rains. And these will be unceasing and extreme. These are the punishments brought down by Heaven with the intention of punishing the people below who do not exalt unity with Heaven. Thus it was that in ancient times the sage kings had a clear understanding of what Heaven and ghosts wished for and avoided what Heaven and ghosts detested. So they sought to promote the world's benefits and eliminate the world's harms. This is why they led the ten thousand people of the world by fasting and bathing, and purifying the sweet wine and millet to offer sacrifice to Heaven and the ghosts. And in their serving of ghosts and spirits, they dared not have sweet wine and millet that were not clean and pure. They dared not have sacrificial animals that were not sleek and fat; they dared not have jade tablets and silk offerings that did not conform to standard measurements; and in the spring and autumn sacrifices, they dared not miss the proper time. In hearing lawsuits, they did not dare to be unfair; in distributing wealth, they did not dare to be inequitable; and, in

其為正長若此，是故上者天鬼有厚乎其為政長也，下者萬民有便
利乎其為政長也。天鬼之所深厚而能彊從事焉，則天鬼之福可得
也。萬民之所便利而能彊從事焉，則萬民之親可得也。其為政若
此，是以謀事得，舉事成，入守固，出誅勝者，何故之以也？曰
唯〔而〕[18] 以尚同為政者也，故古者聖王之為政若此。」

12.8   今天下之人曰：『方今之時，天下之正長猶未廢乎天下也，而天
下之所以亂者，何故之以也？』子墨子曰：「方今之時之以[19] 正
長，則本與古者異矣，譬之若有苗之五刑然。昔者聖王制為五
刑，以治天下，逮至有苗之制五刑，以亂天下。則此豈刑不善
哉？用刑則不善也。是以先王之書《呂刑》之道曰：『苗民否用練折

18. Added by WYJ and read as 能 — see his note 62, p. 128.
19. It is generally agreed that 以 here should be read as 為.

their ordinary dwellings, they did not dare to be disrespectful. I say that their being administrative leaders like this was the reason Heaven and the ghosts above were beneficent towards them in their conduct of government, and the ten thousand people below were of benefit to them in their conduct of government. Since Heaven and ghosts were profoundly beneficent and they could be resolute in carrying out their business, then the blessings of Heaven and ghosts could be obtained. Since the ten thousand people were of benefit to them and they could be resolute in carrying out their business, then the love of the ten thousand people could be obtained. Their conducting government like this was why their plans were realised and the business they undertook was successful. In defence, they were secure. In attack, they were victorious. What was the reason for this? I say it was just that they were able to use exalting unity in the conduct of government. Therefore, in ancient times, the sage kings conducted government like this."

12.8   Nowadays, the people of the world say: "At the present time, the government leaders of the world have still not abandoned the world but the world is in disorder. What is the reason for this?' Master Mo Zi says: "At the present time, those who are government leaders are fundamentally different from those of ancient times. It is like the case of the You Miao and their use of the 'five punishments'.[i] In former times, the sage kings formulated the 'five punishments' for the purpose of bringing order to the world. When it came to the You Miao's formulation of the 'five punishments', this brought disorder to the world. Does this mean, then, that the punishments [themselves] were not good? No, it means that the use of punishments was not good. This is why, in the words of the book of the former kings, the *Lü Xing* (*Punishments of Lü*), it is said: 'The Miao people were not selective in their use of punishments. They just established the

---

i.   For the You Miao 有苗 see 9.9 note iv, p. 77. For the "five punishments" see 11.5, note 9, p. 96.

則刑，唯作五殺之刑，曰法。』則此言善用刑者以治民，不善用
刑者以為五殺，則此豈刑不善哉？用刑則不善。故遂以為五殺。
是以先王之書《術令》之道曰：『唯口出好興戎。』則此言善用口者
出好，不善用口者以為讒賊寇戎。則此豈口不善哉？用口則不善
也，故遂以為讒賊寇戎。」

12.9 「故古者之置正長也，將以治民也，譬之若絲縷之有紀，而罔罟
之有網也，將以運役[20] 天下淫暴，而－－同其義也。是以先王之書
《相年》之道曰：『夫建國設都，乃作后王君公，否用泰也，輕大夫
師長，否用佚也，維辯使治天均。』[21] 則此語古者上帝鬼神之建設

---

20. 運役 is taken as 連收 in accordance with the preceding chapter.
21. There are several issues with this apparent quotation as follows: (i) The title of the work is given as《相年》. BY suggests it should be《拒年》and many commentators agree. Z&Q have《書》as the title but there is no such chapter in the *Documents*. LYS has the following: "…或以為古代逸書之名，或以為係大年之意，是說前輩老年人，也可通。" (ii) BY reads 輕 as 卿. (iii) WHB takes "師長" as "眾官之長". (iv) In the final clause, I have followed Z&Q in reading 辯 as 辨 in the sense of 分 and "天均" as "天的公平之道".

five violent punishments and called them laws."[ii] This is to say, then, that those who were skilled in the use of punishments used them to bring order to the people [whereas] those who were not skilled in the use of punishments conceived of the five violent [punishments]. Does this mean, then, that punishment itself was not good? No, it was the use of punishments that was not good. Therefore, they subsequently became the five violent punishments. This is why, in the words of the writings of the former kings, the *Shu Ling*, it is said: 'The mouth may emit what is good or it may promote warfare.'[iii] This is to say, then, that those who are skilled in the use of the mouth emit what is good [whereas] those who are not skilled in the use of the mouth use it to slander and incite enmity. Does this mean that the mouth itself is not good? No, it is the use of the mouth that is not good. Therefore, it is subsequently used to slander and incite enmity."

12.9 "Thus, in ancient times, the establishment of government leaders was intended to bring order to the people. It may be compared to silk threads being gathered into a skein, or a fishing net having a main rope, in that they were used to draw together the depraved and cruel [people] of the world and cause them to have unity of principles. This is why the book of the former kings, the *Xiang Nian*, has this to say: 'In the establishment of states and the setting up of cities, the creation of rulers, kings, princes and dukes was not so they could be proud. The appointment of ministers and officials was not so they could live in idleness. It was for the apportionment of responsibility for the peace of the world.' This, then, states that in ancient times the Supreme Lord and the ghosts and spirits, in the setting up of states and cities, established political leaders not for the sake of giving them high rank or large

---

ii. The text of the 《書經》, which differs from that in the *Mozi*, is: "苗民弗用靈，制以刑，惟作五虐之刑，曰法。". Legge gives the following translation: "Among the people of Miao, they did not use the power of good, but the restraint of punishments. They made the five punishments engines of oppression, calling them the laws." — see LCC, vol. 3, p. 591.

iii. The *Shu Ling* 術令 is either a lost work, possibly a chapter of the 《書經》, or, as SYR points out, a reference to the *Yue Ming* 説命 chapter of that work which has a somewhat similar passage — see LCC, vol. 3, p. 256.

國都，立正長也，非高其爵，厚其祿，富貴佚而錯之也[22]，將以
為萬民興利除害，富貧眾寡[23]，安危治亂也。故古者聖王之為
〔政〕[24]若此。」

12.10　「今王公大人之為刑政則反此。政以為便譬，宗於父兄故舊，以
為左右，置以為正長[25]。民知上置正長之非正以治民也，是以皆
比周隱匿，而莫肯尚同其上[26]。是故上下不同義。若苟上下不同
義，賞譽不足以勸善，而刑罰不足以沮暴。何以知其然也？曰上
唯毋立而為政乎國家，為民正長，曰人可賞吾將賞之。若苟上下
不同義，上之所賞，則眾之所非，曰人眾與處，於眾得非。則是
雖使得上之賞，未足以勸乎！上唯毋立而為政乎國家，為民正
長，曰人可罰吾將罰之。若苟上下不同義，上之所罰，則眾之所
譽，曰人眾與處，於眾得譽。則是雖使得上之罰，未足以沮乎！
若立而為政乎國家，為民正長，賞譽不足以勸善，而刑罰不沮

---

22. In this clause, WNS proposes the addition of 游 before 佚 and 錯 is read as 措 (e.g. Z&Q).
23. I have followed WYJ's text for this clause which in other texts reads "富貴貧寡" — see his note 82, p. 132.
24. Added by WYJ.
25. In this sentence, the reading of 便譬 (as 駢辟) follows LYS who glosses this as: "就是 左右得寵的小人。" Also, 宗於 is taken as 宗族. WYJ has a somewhat different text which reads: "政以為便嬖宗族，父兄故舊，立以為左右" — see p. 120 and notes 85–87, p. 133.
26. In this sentence, it is generally agreed that 正 following 非 is superfluous. Z&Q's version of "比周隱匿" is "結黨營私，相互隱瞞" which I have followed.

salaries, or to live in a state of wealth, opulence, licentiousness and ease, but so they could act for the ten thousand people, promoting benefit and eliminating harm. It was so they could enrich the poor and make numerous the few, bring peace where there was danger, and order where there was disorder. Thus, the way the ancient sage kings conducted government was like this."

12.10 "Nowadays, kings, dukes and great officers who conduct government are the opposite of this. They surround themselves with flatterers and use kindred, fathers and elder brothers, old friends and acquaintances, making them their assistants and establishing them as government leaders. The people know that those above, in establishing government leaders, are not doing so for the purpose of bringing order to the people, which is why they all form cliques and deceive one another and are not willing to value unity with their superiors. This is why both above and below there is not unity of principles. If those above and below do not have unity of principles, then rewards and praise are not enough to encourage goodness, and punishments and penalties are not enough to put a stop to evil. How do I know this is so? I say that the ruler, in establishing and conducting the government in a country and in making leaders of government, claims that, if there are people who can be rewarded, he will reward them. If those above and below do not have unity of principles, then those the ruler rewards will be those the people condemn. But I say it is the people who live with them every day and it is by the people that they are condemned. Then, even if they are rewarded by the ruler, it will not be enough to encourage them. The ruler, in establishing and conducting the government in a country and creating leaders of government, claims that, if there are people who may be punished, he will punish them. But if above and below there is not unity of principles, then those the ruler punishes will be those the people praise. But I say it is the people who live with them every day and it is by the people that they are praised. Then, although they should receive punishment from the ruler, this will not be enough to stop them. If, in establishing and conducting government and creating leaders of the people, rewards and praise are not enough to encourage goodness and punishments and penalties do not stop evil, then is this not the same as I originally

暴²⁷，則是不與鄉吾本言民『始生未有正長之時』同乎！若有正長
與無正長之時同，則此非所以治民一眾之道。」

12.11 「故古者聖王唯而審以尚同，以為正長，是故上下情請為通²⁸。上
有隱事遺利，下得而利之；²⁹ 下有蓄怨積害，上得而除之。是以
數千萬里之外，有為善者，其室人未遍知，鄉里未遍聞，天子得
而賞之。數千萬里之外，有為不善者，其室人未遍知，鄉里未遍
聞，天子得而罰之。是以舉天下之人皆恐懼振動惕慄，不敢為淫
暴，曰天子之視聽也神。先王之言曰：『非神也，夫唯能使人之
耳目助己視聽，使人之吻助己言談，使人之心助己思慮，使人之
股肱助己動作。』助之視聽者眾，則其所聞見者遠矣。助之言談
者眾，則其德音之所撫循者博矣。助之思慮者眾，則其談謀度速
得矣。助之動作者眾，即其舉事速成矣。」

12.12 「故古者聖人之所以濟事成功，垂名於後世者，無他故異物焉，

---

27. There is some variation in this clause. For example, WYJ has "而刑罰不足以沮暴"
(note 96, p. 133) which I have followed in the translation.

28. The translation of this sentence is based on LYS's reading which includes taking 唯而
as 唯能 and omitting 請為 in the final clause as superfluous. WYJ omits 審 and
provides detailed textual notes on this sentence — see his notes 97–99, p. 134.

29. In this statement, I have followed SYR in equating "隱事" with "隱謀" as in the similar
phrase in *Mozi* 23. I have accepted Z&Q's overall interpretation.

described a little earlier as the time when people 'first came into existence and did not have government leaders'! If having government leaders is just the same as the time when there were no government leaders, this is not the way to bring order to the people and unity to the multitude."

12.11 "Therefore, the sage kings of ancient times, because they were able to carefully select people who exalted unity and make them leaders of government, [ensured that] the feelings of those above and below were in harmony. If those above had any matters that had not been planned or benefits that had not been initiated, those below learned of these and benefited them. If those below had any stored up resentments or accumulated harms, those above learned of these and eliminated them. So it was that, if there was someone who had done good several thousand or even ten thousand *li* away, although family members were completely unaware of it and district and village had not heard of it at all, the Son of Heaven learned of it and rewarded him. And, if there was someone who had done evil several thousand or even ten thousand *li* away, although family members were completely unaware of it and district and village had not heard of it at all, the Son of Heaven learned of it and punished him. Thus the people of the world were all fearful, agitated and awe-struck, and did not dare act in a depraved or evil manner, saying that the Son of Heaven's sight and hearing were those of a god. [But] the former kings' words said: 'He is not a god. It is only that he is able to use the ears and eyes of the people to help his own sight and hearing, to use the lips of the people to help his own speech, to use the minds of the people to help his own plans, and to use the limbs of the people to help his own actions.' If those who help his sight and hearing are many, then what he hears and sees is far distant. If those who help his speech are many, then the comfort given by his wise words is far-reaching. If those who help his plans are many, then his schemes and devices are swiftly accomplished. If those who help him in his activities are many, then the matters he embarks upon will be swiftly brought to completion."

12.12 "The reason why the sages of ancient times brought their achievements to completion and passed their reputations down to

曰唯能以尚同為政者也。是以先王之書《周頌》之道之[30]曰：『載來
見彼王，聿求厥章。』[31]則此語古者國君諸侯之以春秋來朝聘天子
之廷，受天子之嚴教，退而治國，政之所加，莫敢不賓。當此之
時，本無有敢紛天子之教者。《詩》曰：『我馬維駱，六轡沃若，載
馳載驅，周爰咨度。』又曰：『我馬維駰，六轡若絲，載馳載驅，
周爰咨謀。』[32]即此語也。古者國君諸侯之聞見善與不善也，皆馳
驅以告天子，是以賞當賢，罰當暴，不殺不辜，不失有罪，則此
尚同之功也。」

12.13   是故子墨子曰：「今天下之王公大人士君子，請[33]將欲富其國家，
眾其人民，治其刑政，定其社稷，當若尚同之不可不察，此之本
也。」

---

30. This 之 is regarded as superfluous.
31. The lines are the opening lines of Mao #283 from the *Odes* — see Legge, vol. 5, p. 591
    for the rest of the poem and informative notes. The king in question is taken to be Cheng
    Wang 成王. Some texts have 雖 as the first character of the final line (e.g. WYJ).
32. These are the third and fourth stanzas of Mao #163 — see Legge, (LCC, vol. 4, p. 250)
    whose translation is followed. The reference is thought to be to King Wen.
33. 請 is taken as 誠 following WNS (as elsewhere).

later generations was no other than that they were able to conduct their administration by means of exalting unity. This is why, in the writing of the former kings, the *Zhou Song*, there is the statement: '[The feudal lords] first came to see the Zhou king. It is said they sought from him the regulations.' This, then, tells of how, in ancient times, the rulers of states and the feudal lords came to the Son of Heaven's court in spring and autumn to pay their respects and to receive his strict instructions. They then returned to rule their states and implement these instructions and there was no-one who dared not comply. At that time there was originally no-one who dared disturb the Son of Heaven's instructions. The *Odes* says: 'My horses are white and black-maned; the six reins look glossy. I gallop them and urge them on, everywhere seeking information and advice.' It also says: 'My horses are piebald; the six reins are like silk. I gallop them, and urge them on, everywhere seeking information and counsel' so telling of these conditions. In ancient times, the rulers of states and the feudal lords, when they heard or saw something good or bad, all rode swiftly to inform the Son of Heaven. This is why rewards were appropriately given to the worthy and punishments appropriately inflicted on the bad. There was no killing the innocent nor was there letting off the guilty. This, then, was the good outcome of exalting unity."

12.13   This is why Master Mo Zi said: "Nowadays, if kings, dukes, great officers, officers and gentlemen of the world sincerely wish to enrich their states, make their people numerous, bring order to their government, and establish their altars of soil and grain, then it is proper that they cannot do otherwise than examine exalting unity. This is the foundation."

13: 尚同下

13.1　子墨子言曰：「知者之事，必計國家百姓〔之〕所以治者而為之，必計國家百姓之所以亂者而辟之。¹ 然計國家百姓之所以治者何也？上之為政，得下之情則治，不得下之情則亂。何以知其然也？上之為政，得下之情，則是明於民之善非也。若苟明於民之善非也，則得善人而賞之，得暴人而罰之也。善人賞而暴人罰，則國必治。上之為政也，不得下之情，則是不明於民之善非也。若苟不明於民之善非，則是不得善人而賞之，不得暴人而罰之。善人不賞而暴人不罰，為政若此，國眾必亂。故賞〔罰〕² 不得下之情，而不可³ 不察者也。」

1.　There are three textual issues in this sentence, as follows: (i) 知 should be understood as 智. (ii) 之 should be supplied after 百姓 (ZCY). (iii) 辟 should be read as 避.

2.　罰 is supplied following SSX.

3.　YY has the following note on "而不可": "而不可，當作不可而，猶言不可以也。"

13: Exalting Unity III

13.1   Master Mo Zi spoke, saying: "The business of one who is wise must be to work out what it is that brings order to the ordinary people of the state and do it, and to work out what it is that brings disorder to the ordinary people of the state and avoid it. So how does he work out what it is that brings order to the ordinary people of the state? If the ruler, in carrying out government, understands the feelings (conditions)[i] of those below him, then there is order, whereas, if he does not understand the feelings (conditions) of those below him, then there is disorder. How do I know this to be so? If the ruler, in carrying out government, understands the feelings (conditions) of those below him, this means he will have a clear understanding of what is good and bad among the people. If he has a clear understanding of what is good and bad among the people, then in this case he will recognise those who are good and reward them, and he will recognise those who are bad and punish them. If he rewards those who are good and punishes those who are bad, then the state will certainly be brought to order. [Conversely], if the ruler, in carrying out government, does not understand the feelings (conditions) of those below him, this means he will not have a clear understanding of what is good and bad among the people. If he does not have a clear understanding of what is good and bad among the people, then in this case he will not recognise those who are good and reward them, and he will not recognise those who are bad and punish them. If those who are good are not rewarded and those who are bad are not punished, and government is conducted like this, the state and its populace will certainly be in disorder. Therefore, a failure of rewards and punishments to accord with the feelings (conditions) of those below is a matter which must be examined."

---

i.   LSL takes 情 here in the sense of "情況" ("conditions").

13.2　然計得下之情將奈何可？故子墨子曰：「唯能以尚同一義為政，
然後可矣。何以知尚同一義之可而為政於天下也？然胡不審稽
古之治為政之說乎[4]。古者，天之始生民，未有正長也，百姓為
人[5]。若苟百姓為人，是一人一義，十人十義，百人百義，千人千
義，逮至人之眾不可勝計也，則其所謂義者，亦不可勝計。此皆
是其義，而非人之義，是以厚者有鬥，而薄者有爭。」

13.3　「是故天下之欲同一天下之義也，是故選擇賢者，立為天子。天
子以其知力為未足獨治天下，是以選擇其次，立為三公。三公又
以其知力為未足獨左右天子也，是以分國建諸侯。諸侯又以其知
力為未足獨治其四境之內也，是以選擇其次，立為卿之[6]宰。卿
之宰又以其知力為未足獨左右其君也，是以選擇其次，立而為鄉
長家君[7]。是故古者天子之立三公、諸侯、卿之宰、鄉長家君，非
特富貴游佚而擇之也，將使助治〔亂〕[8]刑政也。故古者建國設

4.　WYJ proposes the following version of this sentence based in part on the comments of
WYZ and YY: "胡不審稽古之始為政之說乎" — see his note 14, p. 143.

5.　Following WHB, 人 here is read as 上.

6.　SYR suggests emendation of 之 to 與 here and immediately following.

7.　WHB has this note on "家君": "春秋時各國卿大夫的宗族，他的封邑及其政權組織
稱'家'，其封地之總管稱為'家君'。"

8.　亂 is taken to be superfluous following SYR.

13.2 In this case, how will the feelings (conditions) of those below be determined and recognised? On this point, Master Mo Zi said: "It is only possible through carrying out government by exalting unity under a single principle. After this, it is possible. How do I know that exalting unity under a single principle is possible and can be used to govern the world? How else than by examining the way government was conducted when it first came into existence. In ancient times, when Heaven first gave rise to people, there were not yet leaders of government and each person was his own master. If each person was his own master, then for one person there was one principle, for ten people ten principles, for a hundred people a hundred principles, for a thousand people a thousand principles, and so on up to the point where the great number of people could not be counted. At this time, then, what were termed principles also could not be counted. This meant that everyone affirmed their own principles and denied the principles of others, with the result that what was weighty was contentious and what was trivial was [also] contentious."

13.3 "This resulted in the world's desire to unify the principles of the world, so there was the selection of one who was worthy, and he was established as the Son of Heaven. Because the Son of Heaven knew that his strength alone was not sufficient to bring order to the world, he selected his deputies and established them as the 'Three Dukes'. The 'Three Dukes' also knew that their strength alone was not sufficient to assist the Son of Heaven, so they divided the state and established the feudal lords. The feudal lords also knew that their strength alone was not sufficient to bring order to the territory within their four boundaries, so they selected assistants and established them as ministers and stewards. The ministers and stewards also knew that their strength alone was not sufficient to assist their ruler, so they selected assistants and established them as district heads and regional chiefs (clan princes). The reason why, in ancient times, the Son of Heaven established the 'Three Dukes', the feudal lords, ministers and stewards, district heads and regional chiefs was not especially to select them for riches and honour, leisure and ease, but to help in bringing order to government. Thus, in ancient times, states were created and cities built, and rulers, kings, princes and dukes were established, and

都，乃立后王君公，奉以卿士師長，此非欲用說也，唯辯而使助
治天明也。」

13.4 「今此何為人上而不能治其下，為人下而不能事其上？則是上下
相賊也。何故以然？則義不同也。若苟義不同者有黨，上以若人
為善，將賞之，〔百姓不刑，將毀之。〕[9] 若人唯使得上之賞，而
辟百姓之毀，是以為善者，必未可使勸，見有賞也。上以若人為
暴，將罰之，〔百姓姓付，將舉之。〕[10] 若人唯使得上之罰，而懷
百姓之譽，是以為暴者，必未可使沮，見有罰也。故計上之賞
譽，不足以勸善，計其毀罰，不足以沮暴。此何故以然？則義不
同也。」

13.5 然則欲同一天下之義，將奈何可？故子墨子言曰：「然胡不賞使
家君試用家君[11]，發憲布令其家，曰：『若見愛利家者，必以告，
若見惡賊家者，亦必以告。若見愛利家以告，亦猶愛利家者也，
上得且賞之，眾聞則譽之；若見惡賊家不以告，亦猶惡賊家者
也，上得且罰之，眾聞則非之。』是以遍若家之人，皆欲得其長
上之賞譽，辟其毀罰。是以善言之，不善言之，家君得善人而賞

---

9. These seven characters are added by WYJ (note 30, p. 145) but not included in the
    translation.
10. As for note 9 above — see WYJ, note 35, p. 145.
11. Later commentators generally accept WNS's emendation of the initial part of this
    statement which depends on taking 賞 as 嘗 and omitting the three characters 使家君
    to read as follows: "胡不嘗試用家君發憲布令其家，…"

appointed ministers and masters. This was not to make them happy, but to divide [the responsibility] and use their help in bringing an enlightened order to the world."

13.4   "At the present time, why is it that there are superiors but they are not able to bring order to those below, and there are inferiors but they are not able to serve those above? Because there is mutual harm between superiors and inferiors. Why is this so? Because principles are not uniform. If principles are not uniform, there are factions. For example, if those above consider someone to be good they will reward him. If, although this person gets a reward from above, he nevertheless cannot escape vilification by the common people, his doing of good is certainly not encouraged by there being rewards. [Conversely], if those above consider someone to be bad they will punish him. If, although this person is punished by those above, he nonetheless is comforted by the praise of the common people, his being bad certainly cannot be prevented by there being punishment. So it is determined that rewards and praise from those above are not enough to encourage goodness, and censure and punishment are not enough to prevent evil. What is the reason for this being so? It is because principles are not unified."

13.5   So, then, if we wish to unify the principles of the world, how can it be done? Thus Master Mo Zi spoke, saying: "Why not try getting the leaders of houses to issue a proclamation to their families saying, 'if you see someone who loves and benefits the family, you must make it known. If you see someone who hates and harms the family, you also must make it known. If you inform about someone who loves and benefits the family, this too is like loving and benefiting the family. If those above learn of this, they will reward the person. If the multitude hear of this, they will praise the person. If you do not inform about someone who hates and harms the family, this too is like hating and harming the family. If those above learn of this, they will punish the person. If the multitude hear of this, they will condemn the person.' And it is the case that all the members of the family will wish to obtain the rewards and praise of their superiors and avoid their censure and punishment. Thus, if what is good is spoken about and what is

之，得暴人而罰之。善人之賞，而暴人之罰，則家必治矣。然計若家之所以治者何也？唯以尚同一義為政故也。」

13.6　「家既已治，國之道盡此已邪？則未也。國之為家數也甚多，此皆是其家，而非人之家，是以厚者有亂，而薄者有爭。故又使家君總其家之義，以尚同於國君。國君亦為發憲布令於國之眾，曰：『若見愛利國者，必以告。若見惡賊國者，亦必以告。若見愛利國以告者，亦猶愛利國者也，上得且賞之，眾聞則譽之；若見惡賊國不以告者，亦猶惡賊國者也，上得且罰之，眾聞則非之。』是以遍若國之人，皆欲得其長上之賞譽，避其毀罰。是以民見善者言之，見不善者言之，國君得善人而賞之，得暴人而罰之。善人賞而暴人罰，則國必治矣。然計若國之所以治者何也？唯能以尚同一義為政故也。」

not good is spoken about, the family chief will learn of the good people and reward them, and will learn of the bad people and punish them. If the good people are rewarded and the bad people are punished, then the family will certainly be well ordered. So what is it that determines that a family is well ordered? It is nothing more than being able to exalt unity of principles as a basis for administration."

13.6 "Now if families are already well ordered, does this mean that the way of ordering the state is already complete? It does not. A state comprises a very great number of families, and, if all consider their own family to be right and the families of others to be wrong, this means that among the grand there is disorder and among the petty there is contention. Therefore, it should also be the case that the family chiefs unify the principles of their own families and bring them into accord with the ruler of the state. The ruler of the state should also issue a proclamation to all its people saying, 'if you see someone who loves and benefits the state, you must make it known. If you see someone who hates and harms the state, you also must make it known. If you inform about someone who loves and benefits the state, this too is like loving and benefiting the state. If those above learn of it, they will reward the person. If the masses hear about it, they will praise the person. If you see someone who hates and harms the state and do not inform about it, this too is like hating and harming the state. If those above learn of it, they will punish the person. If the masses hear about it, they will condemn the person.' And it is the case that everywhere the people of the state all wish to get the rewards and praise of their leaders and avoid their censure and punishment. This is why, if the people see someone who is good, they will speak of it, and, if they see someone who is not good, they will speak of it, so the ruler of the state will learn of the good people and reward them, and will learn of the bad people and punish them. If the good people are rewarded and the bad people are punished, then the state will certainly be well ordered. So what is it that determines that a state is well ordered? It is nothing more than being able to exalt unity of principles as a basis for administration."

13.7   「國既已治矣，天下之道盡此已邪？則未也。天下之為國數也甚
多，此皆是其國，而非人之國，是以厚者有戰，而薄者有爭。故
又使國君選[12] 其國之義，以尚同於天子。天子亦為發憲布令於天
下之眾，曰：『若見愛利天下者，必以告，若見惡賊天下者，亦
〔必〕[13] 以告。若見愛利天下以告者，亦猶愛利天下者也，上得則
賞之，眾聞則譽之。若見惡賊天下不以告者，亦猶惡賊天下者
也，上得且罰之，眾聞則非之。』是以遍天下之人，皆欲得其長
上之賞譽，避其毀罰。是以見善不善者告之[14]。〔則〕[15] 天子得善
人而賞之，得暴人而罰之，善人賞而暴人罰，天下必治矣。然計
天下之所以治者何也？唯而[16] 以尚同一義為政故也。」

13.8   「天下既已治，天子又總天下之義，以尚同於天。故當尚同之為
說也，尚用之天子[17]，可以治天下矣。中用之諸侯，可而[18] 治其
國矣。小用之家君，可而治其家矣。是故大用之，治天下〔而〕[19]
不窕，小用之，治一國一家而不橫者，若道之謂也。」[20]

---

12. Commentators are agreed on reading 選 here as 總 in conformity with the previous
    paragraph.
13. Added following WYJ.
14. WYJ proposes the expansion of this sentence to read: "是以見善者善之，見不善者告
    之。" with the second 善 being read as 告 — see his note 67, p. 148.
15. Added following WYJ.
16. Following BY, 而 is taken as 能.
17. I have followed LYS and Z&Q in reading this clause as: "上用之於天子". For textual
    variations see WYJ, note 73, p. 149.
18. Here and in the following sentence, 而 is taken as 以.
19. Added by WYJ.
20. Two points in this sentence, both following WNS and generally agreed upon, are the
    reading of 窕 as 不滿 and 橫 as 充塞.

13.7 "Now, if the states are already well ordered, does this mean that the way of ordering the world is already complete? It does not. The world comprises a great number of states, and all consider their own state to be right and the states of others to be wrong. This means that among the grand there is warfare and among the petty there is contention. Therefore, it should also be the case that the rulers of states unify the principles of their own states and exalt unity with the Son of Heaven. The Son of Heaven should also issue a proclamation to all the people of the world saying, 'if you see someone who loves and benefits the world, you must make it known. If you see someone who hates and harms the world, you must also make it known. If you inform about someone who loves and benefits the world, this too is like loving and benefiting the world. If those above learn of it, they will reward the person. If the masses hear about it, they will praise the person. If you see someone who hates and harms the world and do not inform about it, this too is like hating and harming the world. If those above learn of it, they will punish the person. If the masses hear about it, they will condemn the person.' And it is the case that everywhere the people of the world all wish to get the rewards and praise of their leaders and avoid their censure and punishment. This means that, if they see someone who is good or someone who is bad, they make it known. If the Son of Heaven learns of the good people and rewards them, and learns of the bad people and punishes them so the good people are rewarded and the bad people are punished, then the world will certainly be well ordered. So what is it that determines that the world is well ordered? It is nothing more than being able to exalt unity of principles as the basis of administration."

13.8 "If the world is already well ordered, it means that the Son of Heaven has also unified the principles of the world through exalting unity with Heaven. Thus it is right that exalting unity is taken to be a principle. When used on the highest scale by the Son of Heaven, it can bring order to the world. When used on a moderate scale by feudal lords, it can bring order to their states. When used on a small scale by family chiefs, it can bring order to their families. This means that, if it is used on a large scale, it brings order to the world and is not deficient, whilst if it is used on

13.9 故曰治天下之國若治一家，使天下之民若使一夫。意獨子墨子有
此，而先王無此其有邪？[21] 則亦然也。聖王皆以尚同為政，故天
下治。何以知其然也？於先王之書也，《大誓》之言然，曰：『小人
見姦巧乃聞，不言也，發罪鈞。』[22] 此言見淫辟不以告者，其罪亦
猶淫辟者也。

13.10 故古之聖王治天下也，其所差論[23]，以自左右羽翼者皆良，外為
之人，助之視聽者眾。[24] 故與人謀事，先人得之；與人舉事，先
人成之，光譽令聞，先人發之，唯信身[25] 而從事，故利若此。古
者有語焉，曰：『一目之視也，不若二目之視也；一耳之聽也，
不若二耳之聽也；[26] 一手之操也，不若二手之彊也。』夫唯能信身
而從事，故利若此。是故古之聖王之治天下也，千里之外有賢人
焉，其鄉里之人皆未之均聞見也，聖王得而賞之。千里之內[27] 有

21. LYS suggests that "無此其有邪" should read "無有此邪".

22. There is no chapter entitled "大誓" in the currently available text of the 《書經》. In the
"泰誓" chapter there is the phrase: "厥罪惟鈞" and in another part of the same chapter
there is consideration of 姦, 淫 and 巧 (see LCC, vol. 3, p. 287 and p. 295 respectively).

23. On "差論" WNS has: "差論，皆擇也。"

24. There is variation in the interpretation of this sentence. I have followed WHB's
rearrangement which is: "其所差論，以自為左右羽翼者，皆良桀之人。" Other
versions, influenced particularly by ZCY, take there to be a reference to both assistants
at court and those in far places — see, for example, LSL.

25. WHB suggests 身 should be emended to 民.

26. SYR proposes that 視 and 聽 should, in the second instance of each, be read as 睹 and
聰 respectively.

27. 內 is taken as 外 here following WYJ's text and note 91, p. 152.

a small scale, it brings order to one state or one family and is not filled up. This is why it is spoken of as the Way."

13.9 Therefore, it is said that bringing order to the states of the world is like bringing order to a single family. Making use of the people of the world is like making use of one person. Could it be thought that Master Mo Zi alone had this [principle] and that the former kings did not have this which he had? No, they were also like this. The sage kings all used exalting unity in governing, therefore the world was brought to order. How do we know this was so? It is in the writings of the former kings. The words of the *Great Oath* are like this, saying: "If a petty man sees or hears of something villainous or wicked and does not speak, he displays an equivalent fault." This is like saying that, if someone sees something depraved and perverse and does not inform about it, his fault is also like that of the one who is depraved and perverse.

13.10 Therefore, in the case of the sage kings of ancient times who governed the world, those whom they selected to be their aides and assistants were all men of outstanding ability. And those without who helped them to see and hear were numerous. Therefore, when they made plans for people, they realised them before others would have, and, when they managed affairs for people, they brought them to completion before others would have. Praise for their fine reputation was heard before that for others. Only because they put their trust in the people in conducting affairs did they enjoy benefits like this. In ancient times, there was this saying: 'Seeing with one eye is not like seeing with two eyes. Hearing with one ear is not like hearing with two ears. Grasping something with one hand is not like the strength of two hands.' And it was only because they were able to put their trust in the people in conducting affairs that they enjoyed benefits like this. This is why, when the ancient sage kings governed the world, if there was a worthy man more than a thousand *li* away, while the people of his district and village had not yet all heard of him or seen him, the sage kings learned of him and rewarded him. And, if there was an evil man more than a thousand *li* away, while the people of his district and village had

暴人焉，其鄉里未之均聞見也，聖王得而罰之。故唯毋[28] 以聖王
為聰耳明目與？豈能一視而通見千里之外哉！一聽而通聞千里之
外哉！聖王不往而視也，不就而聽也，然而使天下之為寇亂盜賊
者，周流天下無所重足者，何也？其以尚同為政善也。

13.11 是故子墨子曰：「凡使民尚同者，愛民不疾[29]，民無可使，曰必疾
愛而使之，致信而持之，富貴以道[30] 其前，明罰以率其後。為政
若此，唯[31] 欲毋與我同，將不可得也。」

13.12 是以子墨子曰：「今天下王公大人士君子，中情[32] 將欲為仁義，求
為上士，上欲中聖王之道，下欲中國家百姓之利，故當尚同之
說，而不可不察尚同為政之本，而治〔國之〕[33] 要也。」

---

28. On 唯毋 LSL has this note: "唯毋：語助詞。無意義。"
29. Modern commentators equate 疾 with 力. Z&Q have the following note: 疾：《呂氏春
秋・尊師篇》，高上云："疾，力也。"
30. Taken as 引導 (e.g. LYS).
31. There is general agreement that 唯 should be read as 雖.
32. I have followed LSL in reading 中 as 內心 and 情 as 誠.
33. Added following WYJ — see his note 107, p. 153.

not yet all heard of him or seen him, the sage kings learned of him and punished him. Was this because the sage kings were particularly sharp of hearing and keen of sight? How can one person look and see what is more than a thousand *li* away, or listen and hear what is more than a thousand *li* away! The sage kings did not go themselves to look; they did not go themselves to listen. Nevertheless, they made it so that the robbers and bandits of the world, although they might travel all over the world, could find no place of refuge. How was this so? It was because they took exalting unity to be the perfection of government.

13.11 This is why Master Mo Zi said: "If anyone directs the people to exalt unity but does not love the people deeply, he will find that the people cannot be directed. It is said that one must deeply love the people to direct them, that one must have trust in them to control them. One must lead them with riches and honour from the front, and pursue them with clearly understood punishments from behind. If I were to conduct government like this, even if I wished there not to be unity with me, I would not be able to achieve this."

13.12 This is why Master Mo Zi said: "If, now, the kings, dukes, great officers, officers and gentlemen of the world sincerely wish to become benevolent and righteous, and seek to be superior officers, and, if above, they wish to be in accord with the Way of the sage kings and, below, they wish to benefit the ordinary people of the state, then they must recognise the validity of the concept of exalting unity and must look upon this as the foundation of government and the essential element of bringing order to a state."

14: 兼愛上[1]

14.1 聖人以治天下為事者也，必知亂之所自起，焉[2]能治之。不知亂
之所自起，則不能治。譬之如醫之攻[3]人之疾者然，必知疾之所
自起，焉能攻之。不知疾之所自起，則弗能攻。治亂者何獨不
然？必知亂之所自起，焉能治之。不知亂之所自起，則弗能治。

14.2 聖人以治天下為事者也，不可不察亂之所自起。當[4]察亂何自
起？起不相愛。臣子之不孝君父，所謂亂也。子自愛不愛父，
故[5]虧父而自利。弟自愛不愛兄，故虧兄而自利。臣自愛不愛
君，故虧君而自利。此所謂亂也。雖父之不慈[6]子，兄之不慈
弟，君之不慈臣，此亦天下之所謂亂也[7]。父自愛也不愛子，故虧
子而自利。兄自愛也不愛弟，故虧弟自利。君自愛也不愛臣，故

---

1. I have adopted the usual translation of 兼愛 in the *Mozi* as "universal love", although neither component of the term is entirely satisfactory. An alternative is "impartial caring" as used, for example, by PJI but that is also unsatisfactory. The matter is discussed in the Introduction. The essential point is that all people should be loved equally without gradations according, for example, to family relationship as advocated by the Confucians. MBJ has: "所謂兼愛，其本質是要求人們愛人如己，彼此之間不要存在血緣與等級差別的觀念。" (p. 69)
2. Here, and in its two subsequent uses, 焉 is read as 則 or 乃 (e.g. WYZ).
3. 攻, also used here three times, is taken as equivalent to 治.
4. There is general acceptance of SYR's reading of 當 as 嘗 or 試.
5. The *Yi Lin* 意林 has 欲 in place of 故. Although the former probably gives a better reading, the latter is retained.
6. I have presumed a distinction is being made between 愛 and 慈. The latter can be specifically used in relation to parental love.
7. The interpretation of this sentence depends on the reading of 雖. I have taken it as 即使 following MZQY.

14: Universal Love I

14.1   A sage who takes the ordering of the world as his business must know what disorder arises from, and then he can bring order to it. If he does not know what disorder arises from, then he is not able to bring about order. It is, for example, like a doctor treating a person's illness. He must know what the illness arises from, and then he is able to treat it. If he does not know what the illness arises from, then he is not able to treat it. How can bringing order to disorder be the only thing not like this? One must know the source of the disorder, and then one is able to bring about order. If one does not know the source of the disorder, then one is not able to bring about order.

14.2   A sage, in taking the ordering of the world to be his business, must examine what disorder arises from. In his attempts, what does he discover disorder to arise from? It arises from lack of mutual love. Ministers and sons not being filial towards rulers and fathers is what is spoken of as disorder. If a son loves himself and does not love his father, then he disadvantages the father and benefits himself.[i] If a younger brother loves himself and does not love his older brother, then he disadvantages the older brother and benefits himself. If a minister loves himself and does not love his prince, then he disadvantages the prince and benefits himself. This is what is spoken of as disorder. Even if a father does not feel affection for his son, or an older brother does not feel affection for his younger brother, or a prince does not feel affection for his minister, this is also what is spoken of as disorder in the world. When a father loves himself but does not love his son, then he disadvantages the son and benefits himself. When an older brother loves himself but

---

i.   In this and the following two instances, the distinction is between 虧 and 利 rather than the more usual Mohist distinction between 害 and 利. I have rendered 虧 as "disadvantage", reserving "harm" for 害.

虧臣而自利。是何也？皆起不相愛。雖至天下之為盜賊者亦然。
盜愛其室不愛其[8]異室，故竊異室以利其室。賊愛其身不愛人，
故賊人身[9]以利其身。此何也？皆起不相愛。雖至大夫之相亂
家，諸侯之相攻國者亦然。大夫各愛其家，不愛異家，故亂異家
以利其家。諸侯各愛其國，不愛異國，故攻異國以利其國。天下
之亂物[10]具此而已矣。察此何自起？皆起不相愛。

14.3　　若使天下兼相愛[11]，愛人若愛其身，猶有不孝者乎？視父兄與君
若其身[12]，惡施不孝？猶有不慈者乎？視弟子與臣若其身，惡施
不慈？故不孝不慈亡有。[13]猶有盜賊乎？故[14]視人之室若其室，
誰竊？視人身若其身，誰賊？故盜賊亡有[15]。猶有大夫之相亂
家，諸侯之相攻國者乎？視人家若其家，誰亂？視人國若其國，
誰攻？故大夫之相亂家，諸侯之相攻國者亡有。若使天下兼相

8.　Modern editors follow WNS in regarding 其 as superfluous here.

9.　身 is added here following YY.

10.　SYR suggests that 物 should be understood as 事.

11.　Z&Q glosses the phrase "兼相愛" in its first use here as: "全部相親相愛".

12.　See WYJ (note 16, p. 157) on the restoration of the preceding 14 characters.

13.　See WYJ for a slightly different version of this sentence and his detailed note on it
(note 17, p. 157). The version given follows LSL and Z&Q and takes 亡 as 無 or 沒.

14.　故 should be omitted here according to SYR.

15.　WYJ reverses the order of 亡 and 有 and reads the latter as 又. This has been followed
in the translation.

does not love his younger brother, then he disadvantages the younger brother and benefits himself. When a ruler loves himself but does not love his minister, then he disadvantages the minister and benefits himself. How is this? In all cases it arises through lack of mutual love. Even if we come to those who are thieves and robbers in the world the same applies insofar as they love their own household but do not love the households of others. Therefore, they plunder other households in order to benefit their own households. A robber loves himself but not others. Therefore he robs others in order to benefit himself. How is this? In all cases it arises through want of mutual love. Even if we come to the disorder that great officers bring to each other's houses and the attacks made by the feudal lords on each other's states, it is also the case. Great officers each love their own house but do not love other houses, therefore they bring disorder to other houses in order to benefit their own house. Feudal lords each love their own state but do not love other states. Therefore, they attack other states in order to benefit their own state. Disorder in the world is entirely this and nothing else. If we examine this, from what source does it arise? In all cases it is due to lack of mutual love.

14.3   If there were universal mutual love in the world, with the love of others being like the love of oneself, would there still be anyone who was not filial? If one were to regard father, older brother and ruler like oneself, how could one not be filial [towards them]? Would there still be anyone who did not feel affection? If one were to regard younger brother, son or minister like oneself, how could one not love [them]? Therefore, there would be no-one who was not filial or not loving. Would there still be thieves and robbers? If there were regard for the houses of others like one's own house, who would steal? If there were regard for the persons of others like one's own person, who would rob? Therefore, thieves and robbers would also disappear. Would there still be great officers who brought disorder to each other's houses or feudal lords who attacked each other's states? If there were regard for the houses of others like one's own house, who would bring disorder? If there were regard for the states of others like one's own state, who would attack? Therefore, there would be no instances of great officers bringing disorder to each other's houses or of feudal lords

愛，國與國不相攻，家與家不相亂，盜賊無有，君臣父子皆能孝
慈。若此則天下治。故聖人以治天下為事者，惡得不禁惡而勸
愛？故天下兼相愛則治，交相惡則亂。故子墨子曰「不可以不勸
愛人」者，此也。

attacking each other's states. If the world had universal mutual love, then states would not attack each other, houses would not bring disorder to each other, there would be no thieves and robbers, and rulers, ministers, fathers and sons could all be filial and loving. In this way, then, there would be order in the world. Therefore, how can sages who make it their business to bring order to the world do otherwise than prohibit hatred and encourage love? So if there is universal mutual love in the world, then there is order [whereas], if there is exchange of mutual hatred, then there is disorder. The reason why Master Mo Zi said: "One cannot but encourage the love of others" is this.

15: 兼愛中

15.1 子墨子言曰:「仁人之所以為事者,必興天下之利,除去天下之害,以此為事者也。」然則天下之利何也?天下之害何也?子墨子言曰:「今若國之與國之相攻,家之與家之相篡,人之與人之相賊,君臣不惠忠,父子不慈孝,兄弟不和調,此則天下之害也。」

15.2 然則崇此害亦何用生哉?[1] 以不相愛生邪?[2] 子墨子言:「以不相愛生。今諸侯獨知愛其國,不愛人之國,是以不憚[3] 舉其國以攻人之國。今家主[4] 獨知愛其家,而不愛人之家,是以不憚舉其家以篡人之家。今人獨知愛其身,不愛人之身,是以不憚舉其身以賊人之身。是故諸侯不相愛則必野戰。家主不相愛則必相篡,人與人不相愛則必相賊,君臣不相愛則不惠忠,父子不相愛則不慈孝,兄弟不相愛則不和調。天下之人皆不相愛,強必執弱,〔眾

---

1. In the reading of this sentence, YY's proposals, which are 察 for 崇 and 何以生 for 何用生, are followed.
2. According to YY, this question should read "以相愛生邪?", the interlocutor taking the opposite position to Mo Zi.
3. Modern editors (e.g. LYS, LSL, Z&Q) include a note equating "不憚" with "不怕".
4. LYS has the following note on 家主:"家主:有采邑的官員,采邑是古代的封地。"

15: Universal Love II

15.1 Master Mo Zi spoke, saying: "The way in which the benevolent man conducts affairs must be to promote the world's benefit and eliminate the world's harm. It is in this way he conducts affairs." If this is so, then what is the world's benefit? What is the world's harm?

Master Mo Zi said: "Now if states attack each other, if houses usurp each other, if people harm each other, if there is not kindness and loyalty between rulers and ministers, if there is not love and filiality between fathers and sons, if there is not concord and harmony between older and younger brothers, then this is harmful to the world."

15.2 If this is so, then how can we not examine from what this harm arises? Does it not arise through mutual love? Master Mo Zi spoke, saying: "It arises through *lack* of mutual love. Nowadays, feudal lords know only to love their own states and not to love the states of others, so they have no qualms about mobilising their own state to attack another's state. Nowadays, heads of houses know only to love their own house and not to love the houses of others, so they have no qualms about promoting their own house and usurping another's house. Nowadays, individual people know only to love their own person and not to love the persons of others, so they have no qualms about promoting their own person and injuring the persons of others. For this reason, since the feudal lords do not love each other, there must inevitably be savage battles; since heads of houses do not love each other, there must inevitably be mutual usurpation; and, since individuals do not love each other, there must inevitably be mutual injury. Since rulers and ministers do not love each other, there is not kindness and loyalty; since fathers and sons do not love each other, there is not compassion and filial conduct; and, since older and younger brothers do not love each other, there is not harmony and accord.

人劫寡〕[5]，富必侮貧，貴必敖[6]賤、詐必欺愚。凡天下禍篡怨恨，其所以起者，以不相愛生也，是以仁者非之。」

15.3 既以[7]非之；何以易之？[8] 子墨子言曰：「以兼相愛交相利之法易之。」然則兼相愛交相利[9]之法將奈何哉？子墨子言：「視人之國若視其國，視人之家若視其家，視人之身若視其身。是故諸侯相愛則不野戰，家主相愛則不相篡，人與人相愛則不相賊，君臣相愛則惠忠，父子相愛則慈孝，兄弟相愛則和調。天下之人皆相愛，強不執弱，眾不劫寡，富不侮貧，貴不敖賤，詐不欺愚。凡天下禍篡怨恨可使毋起者，以相愛生也，是以仁者譽之。」

15.4 然而今天下之士君子曰：「然，乃若兼則善矣，雖然，天下之難物於故[10]也。」子墨子言曰：「天下之士君子，特不識其利，辯其故也。今若夫攻城野戰，殺身為名，此天下百姓之所皆難也，苟

---

5. Added by SYR on the basis of the subsequent text — see WYJ, note 7, p. 161.
6. There is general acceptance of BY's proposed reading of 傲 here.
7. 以 is read here as 已 following LSL and Z&Q.
8. LYS places the last six characters of the previous paragraph at the start of this sentence. Most commonly, however, the arrangement follows that given above (e.g. WYJ, LSL, Z&Q).
9. I include here LYS's note which draws attention to these two important terms/concepts. He has: "兼相愛：兼是併的意思。墨家的兼相愛係一種特有的主張，認為天下人都應該相愛，沒有什麼等差 (等級)。交相利：隨着兼相愛同時發生的。交就是互的意思。墨子言愛必提到利，這種利是大家的利益，和儒家所斥的私利不同。"
10. Modern commentators generally accept YY's suggestion that "於故" is superfluous.

When the people of the world do not all love each other, then the strong inevitably dominate the weak, the many inevitably plunder the few, the rich inevitably despise the poor, the noble inevitably scorn the lowly, and the cunning inevitably deceive the foolish. Within the world, in all cases, the reason why calamity, usurpation, resentment and hatred arise is because mutual love does not exist, which is why those who are benevolent condemn this state of affairs."

15.3   Since they already condemn it, how can it be changed? Master Mo Zi spoke, saying: "It can be changed by the methods of universal mutual love and exchange of mutual benefit." In this case, then, what are the methods of universal mutual love and exchange of mutual benefit? Master Mo Zi said: "People would view others' states as they view their own states. People would view others' houses as they view their own houses. People would view other people as they view themselves. So the feudal lords would love each other and then there would not be savage battles. Heads of houses would love each other and then there would not be mutual usurpation. Individual people would love each other and then they would not injure each other. Rulers and ministers would love each other and then there would be kindness and loyalty. Fathers and sons would love each other and then there would be compassion and filial conduct. Older and younger brothers would love each other and then there would be harmony and accord. If the people of the world all loved each other, the strong would not dominate the weak, the many would not plunder the few, the rich would not despise the poor, the noble would not scorn the lowly, and the cunning would not deceive the foolish. Within the world, in all cases, there would be nothing to cause calamity, usurpation, resentment and hatred to arise because of the existence of mutual love. This is why those who are benevolent praise it."

15.4   Nevertheless, nowadays officers and gentlemen of the world say: "That may be so. Universal [love] would, of course, be very good. However, in the world, it is a difficult matter." Master Mo Zi spoke, saying: "This is only because the officers and gentlemen of the world do not recognise its benefits and do not understand its reasons. At the present time, attacking cities, fighting on the

君説之，則士眾能為之。況於兼相愛，交相利，則與此異。夫愛
人者，人必從而愛之；利人者，人必從而利之；惡人者，人必從
而惡之；害人者，人必從而害之。此何難之有！特上弗以為政，
上不以為行故也。」

15.5　「昔者晉文公好士之惡衣，故文公之臣皆牂羊之裘，韋以帶劍，
練帛之冠，入以見於君，出以踐於朝。是其故何也？君説之，故
臣為之也。」[11]

15.6　「昔者楚靈王好士細要[12]，故靈王之臣皆以一飯為節，脅息然後
帶，扶牆然後起。比期年，朝[13]有黧黑之色，是其故何也？君説
之，故臣能之也。昔越王勾踐好士之勇，教馴其臣，和合之焚舟
失火[14]，試其士曰：『越國之寶盡在此！』越王親自鼓其士而進
之。士聞鼓音，破碎亂行[15]，蹈火而死者，左右百人有餘。越王
擊金而退之。」

15.7　是故子墨子言曰：「乃若夫少食惡衣，殺身而為名，此天下百姓
之所皆難也，若苟君説之，則眾能為之。況兼相愛，交相利，與

---

11. Jin Wen Gong 晉文公 ruled from 636 to 628 BC. There is some uncertainty about 練
　　帛. SYR suggests it should be 大帛. It must indicate some relatively unprepared form
　　of silk.
12. Chu Ling Wang 楚靈王 ruled from 540 to 529 BC — see, for example, the LSCQ 22/
　　1.3. 要 is accepted as 腰.
13. 朝 here is taken as referring to the court officials — see, for example, Z&Q.
14. I have followed SYR's proposed emendations of this clause which suggest "和合之"
　　should read "私令人", and 舟 should be emended to 內 in the sense of "寢室".
15. Following SYR, I have taken 碎 as 萃.

battlefield and sacrificing oneself for fame are all things that the ordinary people of the world find difficult. Still, if the ruler favours these things, then the officers and people are able to do them. By comparison, universal mutual love and exchange of mutual benefit are quite different from these things. If a person loves others then others must, as a result, love that person. If a person benefits others then others must, as a result, benefit that person. If a person hates others then others must, as a result, hate that person. If a person harms others then others must, as a result, harm that person. Where is the difficulty? It is only that those above do not make it part of their government, so their officers see no reason to do it."

15.5   "In former times, Duke Wen of Jin liked his officers to wear clothing of poor quality so Duke Wen's officials all wore garments of ewe's wool, carried their swords in ox-hide belts and had caps of rough silk. On entering, they attended the ruler. On leaving, they walked from the court. Why did they do this? The ruler liked it so the officials did it."

15.6   "Formerly, King Ling of Chu liked officers with slender waists so King Ling's officials limited themselves to one meal a day, fastened their belts after breathing in, and required the support of a wall to rise. Within a year, the faces of the court officials had become dark and sallow. What was the reason for this? The ruler liked it so the officials were able to do it. In former times, the Yue king, Gou Jian, loved officers who were brave and advised his officials of this. Then, privately, he ordered a man to set fire to his palace to put his officers to the test, saying: 'All the treasures of the Yue kingdom are in there.' The Yue king himself struck the drum for his officers to advance. When they heard the sound of the drum, they rushed forward in a disorderly rabble. Somewhere around a hundred men lost their lives in the fire. The King of Yue then beat the gong to sound the retreat."

15.7   For this reason, Master Mo Zi spoke, saying: "Now things like eating little, poor quality clothes, and sacrificing one's life for the sake of fame are all things that the ordinary people of the world find difficult. But, if the ruler takes pleasure in them, then the

此異矣。夫愛人者，人亦從而愛之；利人者，人亦從而利之；惡
人者，人亦從而惡之；害人者，人亦從而害之。此何難之有焉，
特君[16]不以為政而士不以為行故也。」

15.8 然而今天下之士君子曰：「然，乃若兼則善矣。雖然，不可行之
物也，譬若挈太山越河濟也。」子墨子言：「是非其譬也。夫挈太
山而越河濟，可謂畢劫[17]有力矣，自古及今未有能行之者也。況
乎兼相愛，交相利，則與此異，古者聖王行之。何以知其然？古
者禹治天下，西為西河漁竇[18]，以泄渠孫皇之水[19]；北為防原泒，
注后之邸，呼池之竇，灑為底柱，鑿為龍門，以利燕代胡貉與西
河之民；[20]東方漏之陸，防孟諸之澤，灑為九澮，以楗東土之
水，以利冀州之民；[21]南為江漢淮汝東流之，注五湖之處，以利
荊楚干越與南夷之民。此言禹之事，吾今行兼矣。」

15.9 「昔者文王之治西土，若日若月，乍光於四方於西土，不為大國

---

16. Emended from 上 following LYS. Z&Q suggest 上 on the basis of the earlier statement.
17. Following SYR, 劫 is read as 勮 in the sense given in the《廣韻》as "用力也".
18. In this clause, 為 is taken as 治理 following Z&Q. WHB has this note on 西河："古稱
    西部地區南北流向的黃河為西河。" On 漁竇, LSL has the following note (referring
    to ZCY): "張純一據《水經注》，認為即鯉魚澗，其地在黃河南岸山西境內。"
19. On these waters, WHB has this note: "渠、孫皇，古水名，都在西河黑水流域。"
20. The issues in this example are as follows: (i) Should 防 be taken as the name of a water
    (Z&Q) or in its more usual sense — for example, LSL takes it as 堤。原 and 泒 are both
    accepted as waters of unknown location. (ii) What does "后之邸" refer to? SYR has this
    note: "后之邸，疑即職方氏并州澤藪之昭餘祁。" The marsh he speaks of is
    considered in the *Zhou Li* (SSJZS, vol. 3, p. 500). (iii) Is BY correct in taking 呼池 to
    be 滹沱河? On this, see Z&Q's note which identifies the waterway as being in what is
    now 繁峙縣 in 山西. (iv) 灑 is read here and subsequently as 分流.
21. The several issues in this example are, firstly, that in the initial clause 方 should be read
    as 為 in conformity with the other examples. Secondly, that 之 in the initial clause
    should be read as 大，大陸 being a place name. Thirdly, in the second clause, Meng Zhu
    Marsh was, as noted by Z&Q, "古代河南商丘東北的湖澤名。" Fourthly, on 楗 in the
    fourth clause, BY quotes the *Shuo Wen* definition: "楗，門限。" Finally, on 冀州,
    SYR has this note: "古通以中土為冀州。"

multitude are able to do them. By comparison, universal mutual love and exchange of mutual benefit are quite different from these things. If a person loves others, then others, as a result, also love that person. If a person benefits others, then others, as a result, also benefit that person. If a person hates others, then others, as a result, also hate that person. If a person harms others, then others, as a result, also harm that person. What is the difficulty in this? It is only that the ruler does not make it part of his government, so his officers see no reason to do it."

15.8   Nevertheless, nowadays officers and gentlemen of the world say: "This may be so. If it were universal, it would be good. However, this is something that cannot be done. It is comparable to lifting up Tai Shan and jumping over the Yellow River and the Qi Waters." Master Mo Zi said: "That is not a valid comparison. Lifting up Tai Shan and jumping over the Yellow River could be said to be a feat of extraordinary strength. From ancient times to the present, no-one has been able to do this. By comparison, universal mutual love and exchange of mutual benefit are quite different from this. The sage kings of ancient times practised these things. How do I know this was so? In ancient times, when Yu brought order to the world, in the west, he controlled the West River and Yudou by diverting the waters of the Qu and the Sunxing. In the north, he controlled the Fang, Quan and Gu waters, making them drain into Zhao Yu Qi and into the Hu Tuo River, and to be divided by Dizhu Mountain. He tunnelled through Longmen in order to bring benefit to the Yan, Dai, Hu and He (Mo) and the people of the Western River. In the east, he controlled the waters of Da Lu both by blocking off the marsh at Meng Zhu and also by dividing them into nine channels in order to restrict the waters of the eastern lands and so benefit the people of Ji Zhou. In the south, he made the Jiang, Han, Huai and Ru Rivers flow eastward and drain into the region of the five lakes to benefit the people of Jing, Chu, Gan and Yue, and the Nan Yi. This tells of the affairs of Yu [and shows] that now we could practise universal [love]."

15.9   "In former times, when King Wen brought order to the western lands, he was like the sun, he was like the moon. For the first time,

侮小國，不為眾庶侮鰥寡，不為暴勢奪穡人黍稷狗彘。天屑[22] 臨
文王慈，是以老而無子者，有所得終其壽；連獨[23] 無兄弟者，有
所雜於生人之間；少失其父母者，有所放依而長。此〔言〕[24] 文王
之事，則吾今行兼矣。[25] 昔者武王將事泰山隧，傳曰：『泰山，有
道曾孫周王有事，大事既獲，仁人尚作，以祇商夏，蠻夷醜貉。
雖有周親，不若仁人[26]，萬方有罪，維予一人。』此言武王之事，
吾今行兼矣。」

15.10   是故子墨子言曰：「今天下之〔士〕[27] 君子，忠[28] 實欲天下之富，而
惡其貧；欲天下之治，而惡其亂，當兼相愛，交相利，此聖王之
法，天下之治道也，不可不務為也。」

22. There is general agreement that 屑 here should be read as 顧 — see, for example, Z&Q.
23. There is wide acceptance of SYR's reading of 連 as 矜. Z&Q, who accept SYR's
    suggestion and also refer to a passage in the *Shi Ji*, have the following: "連獨，猶言窮
    苦煢獨耳。"
24. Added by SYR to accord with the form of earlier statements.
25. The following sentence has caused not a little confusion. A particular problem is 隧, but
    there is also the matter of the punctuation of the initial part of the statement and whether,
    as some commentators think (e.g. LYS), "有道" refers to Wu himself in contrast to the
    deposed 紂 who is "無道". The translation is based on WHB's reading of 隧 as 遂 in
    the sense of 於是 and placing commas after 山 and 道. In detail, then, this sentence
    is read as follows: "昔者武王將事泰山，隧傳曰：『泰山有道，曾孫周王有事』，
    …" — see Z&Q, note 27, p. 174 for details.
26. The preceding eight characters are found in the《書經‧泰誓》— LCC, vol. 3, p. 292.
27. Added following CYX and WYJ.
28. There is general agreement that 忠 here should be read as 中 to conform with the
    previous text.

there was brightness in the four regions and in the western lands. He made it so that great states did not bully small states, that the many and numerous did not insult the solitary and few, that the cruel and the powerful did not snatch away the different kinds of millet, or the dogs and swine, of farmers. And Heaven looked down on King Wen's compassion so that those who were old and without sons had what they needed to live out their lives; those who were poor and friendless and without older or younger brothers had the various things they needed to mix with other people; and those who had lost their parents when young had what they could rely on to grow up. This speaks of the affairs of King Wen [and shows] that we could now practise universal [love]. In former times, when King Wu was about to offer a sacrifice at Tai Shan, he said: 'Spirits of Tai Shan, I, the King of Zhou, have come to offer sacrifice. The great matter has now been accomplished and men of benevolence arise to come to the aid of the whole central kingdom and the barbarians of all regions. And although there are kinsmen of the Zhou house, it is not as if they are benevolent men. Yet the people in every direction have faults and I am only one man.' This speaks of the affairs of King Wu [and shows] that, now, we could practise universal [love]."

15.10 For this reason Master Mo Zi spoke, saying: 'Nowadays, officers and gentlemen of the world, if they truly wish for its wealth and abhor its poverty, if they wish the world to be well ordered and abhor its disorder, should take as right universal mutual love and exchange of mutual benefit. These were the methods of the sage kings and the Way of order for the world, so it is impossible that they not be assiduously pursued."

16: 兼愛下

16.1   子墨子言曰:「仁人之事者,必務求興天下之利,除天下之害。」
然當今之時,天下之害孰為大?曰:「若大國之攻小國也,大家
之亂小家也,強之劫弱,眾之暴寡,詐之謀愚,貴之傲賤,此天
下之害也。又與為人君者之不惠也,臣者之不忠也,父者之不慈
也,子者之不孝也,此又天下之害也。又與今人[1]之賤人,執其
兵刃毒藥水火以交相虧賊,此又天下之害也。姑嘗本原若眾害之
所自生,此胡自生?此自愛人利人生與?即必曰非然也,必曰從
惡人賊人生。分名乎天下惡人而賊人者,兼與?別與?即必曰別
也。然即之交別者,果生天下之大害者與?是故別非也。」

16.2   子墨子曰:「非人者[2]必有以易之,若非人而無以易之,譬之猶以
水救火也[3],其說將必無可焉。」是故子墨子曰:「兼以易別。」然
即兼之可以易別之故何也?曰:「藉為人之國,若為其國,夫誰
獨[4]舉其國以攻人之國者哉?為彼者由[5]為己也。為人之都,若為

---

1.   Following WNS, 人 here is regarded as superfluous and is omitted.
2.   I have followed THQ's reading of "非人者" as "非之者". The "something" is of course
     "discrimination" (別).
3.   There is general acceptance of YY's expansion of "以水救火" to "猶以水救水,以火
     救火也" — see WYJ's detailed note 9, pp. 181–182.
4.   獨 is read as 還, both here and subsequently — see Z&Q.
5.   由 is read as 猶 in conformity with the following sentences — see WYJ, note 10, p. 182.

16: Universal Love III

16.1 Master Mo Zi spoke, saying: "The business of the benevolent man must be to seek assiduously to promote the world's benefits and to eliminate the world's harms." This being so, of the world's harms what, at the present time, are the greatest? [Master Mo Zi] said: "They are great states attacking small states, great houses bringing disorder to small houses, the strong plundering the weak, the many ill-treating the few, the cunning scheming against the foolish, and the noble being arrogant towards the lowly. These are the world's harms. Also, it is rulers not being kind, ministers not being loyal, fathers not being compassionate and sons not being filial. These too are the world's harms. Furthermore, at the present time, base men make use of weapons, poisons, water and fire to injure and harm each other. This too is harmful to the world. Let us for the moment consider the origin of these many harms, what it is they arise from. Do they arise from loving people and benefiting people? We must certainly say they do not. We must say they arise from hating people and harming people. And if we were to distinguish and name those in the world who hate people and harm people, would it be as 'universal' or would it be as 'discriminating'? We must undoubtedly say it would be as 'discriminating'. This being so, is not this mutual discrimination really the source of the world's great harms? This is why 'discrimination' is to be condemned."

16.2 Master Mo Zi said: "Those who condemn something must have the means of changing it. To condemn something without having the means to change it is like fighting water with water or fire with fire. Their theories will certainly not be admissible." This is why Master Mo Zi said: "'Universal' is the means of changing 'discriminating'." If this is the case, how can 'universal' change 'discriminating'? [He] said: "If people were to regard others' states as they regard their own state, then who would still mobilise their own state to attack the states of others? They would regard

其都，夫誰獨舉其都以伐人之都者哉？為彼猶為己也。為人之
家，若為其家，夫誰獨舉其家以亂人之家者哉？為彼猶為己也。
然即國都不相攻伐，人家不相亂賊，此天下之害與？天下之利
與？即必曰天下之利也。姑嘗本原若眾利之所自生，此胡自生？
此自惡人賊人生與？即必曰非然也，必曰從愛人利人生。分名乎
天下愛人而利人者，別與？兼與？即必曰兼也。然即之交兼者，
果生天下之大利者與。」

16.3   是故子墨子曰：「兼是也。且鄉[6]吾本言曰：『仁人之事者，必務
求興天下之利，除天下之害。』今吾本原兼之所生，天下之大利
者也；吾本原別之所生，天下之大害者也。」是故子墨子曰：「別
非而兼是者，出乎若方也。」

16.4   今吾將正求興天下之利而取之，以兼為正[7]。是以聰耳明目相與視
聽乎，是以股肱畢強相為動宰乎，而有道肆相教誨[8]。是以老而無
妻子者，有所侍養以終其壽；幼弱孤童之無父母者，有所放依以

6.   BY suggests that 鄉 should be read as 曏 in the sense of 不久. I have omitted it in the
     translation.
7.   The translation of this sentence follows WHB's emended text which is: "今吾將求興天
     下之利，除天下之害，而取以兼為正。"
8.   This follows Z&Q's version which in turn incorporates BY's reading of the initial 與 as
     為, MZH's reading of 動宰 as 動制 or 動作 and the reading of 肆 as 勉力.

others' [states] as they regard their own. If people were to regard the capital cities of others as they regard their own capital city, then who would still raise their own capital city to strike at the capital cities of others? They would regard others' [capital cities] as they regard their own. If people were to regard the houses of others as they regard their own house, who would still stir their own house to bring disorder to the houses of others? They would regard others' [houses] as they regard their own. Now if states and cities did not attack and strike at each other, and if people's houses did not bring disorder to and damage each other, would this be harmful to the world? Or would it be beneficial to the world? This must be said to be beneficial to the world. For the moment let us think about the origin of these many benefits, what it is they arise from. And what is this from which they arise? Is it from hating people and harming people that they arise? We must certainly say it is not. We must say that it is from loving people and benefiting people that they arise. And, if we were to distinguish and name those in the world who love people and benefit people, would it be as 'discriminating' or as 'universal'? We must certainly say it would be as 'universal'. In this case, then, it is 'mutual and universal' which gives rise to the world's great benefits."

16.3   It was for this reason that Master Mo Zi said: "'Universal' is right. Moreover, as I originally said, the business of the benevolent man must be to seek diligently to promote the world's benefits and eliminate the world's harms. Now I [have established] what 'universal' gives rise to — it is the world's great benefits. And I [have established] what 'discriminating' gives rise to — it is the world's great harms." This is why Master Mo Zi said: "'Discriminating' being wrong and 'universal' being right comes from this principle."

16.4   Now if I am to seek to promote the world's benefit and eliminate the world's harm, I shall choose "universal" as being right. As a result, [people] will use their acute hearing and keen sight to help each other see and hear; they will use their strong and powerful limbs to help each other in action; and they will use principles to encourage mutual instruction. As a result, those who are old, without wives and children, will have the means of support and

長其身。今唯毋以兼為正，即若其利也，不識天下之士，所以皆聞兼而非〔之〕[9]者，其故何也？

16.5 然而天下之士非兼者之言，猶未止也。曰：「〔兼〕[10]即善矣。雖然豈可用哉？」子墨子曰：「用而不可，雖我亦將非之。且焉有善而不可用者？姑嘗兩而進之。設[11]以為二士，使其一士者執別，使其一士者執兼。是故別士之言曰：『吾豈能為吾友之身，若為吾身，為吾友之親，若為吾親。』是故退睹其友，飢即不食，寒即不衣，疾病不侍養，死喪不葬埋。別士之言若此，行若此。兼士之言不然，行亦不然，曰：『吾聞為高士於天下者，必為其友之身，若為其身，為其友之親，若為其親，然後可以為高士於天下。』是故退睹其友，飢則食之，寒則衣之，疾病侍養之，死喪葬埋之。兼士之言若此，行若此。」

16.6 「若[12]之二士者，言相非而行相反與？當使若二士者，言必信，行

---

9. Added following SYR and WYJ.
10. Added by WYJ following CYX.
11. Emended from 誰 following WYZ — see Z&Q, note 3, p. 184.
12. I have followed Z&Q in reading 若 as "像這".

nourishment through their old age, and those who are young and weak, or who are alone without a father or mother, will have the means of help and support while they grow into adulthood. Now, if "universal" is taken as being right, these are the benefits. I do not know what possible reason officers of the world could have for opposing 'universal' when they all hear about it.

16.5 Nevertheless, the arguments of the officers of the world who condemn "universal" still never stop. They say: "['Universal'] may be good, but how can it be put to use?" Master Mo Zi said: "If it could not be put to use, even someone such as myself would also condemn it. Moreover, how can there be something that is good but can't be used? Let us for the moment approach [the matter] from two sides.[i] Suppose we consider two officers. Let one of them hold to 'discriminating' and the other one hold to 'universal'. In the first case, the officer holding to 'discriminating' would say: 'How am I able to regard the person of my friend as I regard my own person, or regard my friend's parents as I regard my own parents?' Therefore, if he were to turn his attention to his friend, should he find him hungry, he would not feed him; should he find him cold, he would not clothe him; should he find him sick and ailing, he would not tend to him; and if he died, he would not bury him. The 'discriminating' officer's words are like this and his actions are too. [On the other hand], the 'universal' officer's words are not like this and neither are his actions. He would say: 'I have heard that one who aspires to high office in the world must regard the person of his friend as he regards his own person and regard his friend's parents as he regards his own parents. Only then can he be considered a high officer in the world.' For this reason, if he were to turn his attention to his friend, should he find him hungry, he would feed him; should he find him cold, he would clothe him; should he find him sick and ailing, he would tend to him; and if he died, he would bury him. The 'universal' officer's words are like this and his actions too."

16.6 Are two such officers mutually contradictory in their words and mutually opposing in their actions? Let us suppose that there were

---

i. WHB offers a slightly different interpretation of this sentence based on reading 進 as 盡.

必果，使言行之合猶合符節也，無言而不行也。然即敢問，今有平原廣野於此，被甲嬰胄將往戰，死生之權未可識也；又有君大夫之遠使於巴越齊荊往來及否未可識也。然即敢問，不識將惡也家室，奉承親戚，提挈妻子，而寄託之[13]？不識於兼之有是乎？於別之有是乎？我以為當其於此也，天下無愚夫愚婦，雖非兼之人，必寄託之於兼之有是也。此言而非兼，擇即取兼，即此言行費[14]也。不識天下之士，所以皆聞兼而非之者，其故何也？」

16.7   然而天下之士非兼者之言，猶未止也。曰：「意[15]可以擇士，而不可以擇君乎？」「姑嘗兩而進之。設[16]以為二君，使其一君者執兼，使其一君者執別，是故別君之言曰：『吾惡能為吾萬民之身，若為吾身，此泰非天下之情也。人之生乎地上之無幾何也，

---

13. The reading of this sentence follows Z&Q who, in turn, accept YY's addition of 從 after 惡 and WHB's addition of "將固庇" before "家室". See also WYJ's notes 38 and 39, pp. 184–185.

14. 費 should be read as 拂 here in accord with the equivalent sentence in 16.8. WNS has: "古者拂與費通".

15. 意 is read as 抑, in the sense of 或許, both here and subsequently (WHB).

16. Emended from 誰 as in section 16.5.

two such officers and their words were certainly trustworthy and their actions certainly came to fruition, and that their words and actions corresponded like the two halves of a tally. They would not say something that they would not do. In such a case, let us pose this question. Suppose now there was an open plain, broad and uncultivated, where someone was donning his armour and fastening his helmet about to go into battle, and whether he would live or die could not be known. Or suppose also that a ruler or great officer was sending him to a distant place such as Ba, Yue, Qi or Jing, and whether he would go and return or not could not be known. The question then is, to whom would he entrust the protection of his house and family, the support of his parents, and the care of his wife and children? Do we not know whether it would be to someone who held 'universal' to be right or someone who held 'discriminating' to be right? I think that, under such circumstances, the men and women of the world would not be foolish. Although they might condemn [the views of] the 'universal' person, they would certainly entrust these matters to someone who took 'universal' to be right. In their words they might reject 'universal', but in their choice they would select 'universal', which is a case of words and actions being opposed. We do not know why it is that the officers of the world all hear about 'universal' and yet condemn it — what reason can there be?"

16.7   Nonetheless, the arguments of the officers of the world who condemn "universal" still never stop. They say: "Is it permissible as a way of selecting officers, but not permissible as a way of selecting rulers?"[ii] "Let us for a moment approach [the matter] from two sides. Suppose there were two rulers and suppose one of them held to 'universal' and the other to 'discriminating'. In this case, the words of the 'discriminating' ruler would be: 'How am I able to regard the persons of my ten thousand people as I regard my own person? This is absolutely contrary to the feelings of [everyone in] the world. A person's life on earth is very brief. It is like a galloping horse passing a crack.' Therefore, if he were to

---

ii.   I have taken what follows to be attributable to Mo Zi.

譬之猶駟馳而過隙也[17]。』是故退睹其萬民，飢即不食，寒即不衣，疾病不侍養，死喪不葬埋。別君之言若此，行若此。兼君之言不然，行亦不然。曰：『吾聞為明君於天下者，必先萬民之身，後為其身，然後可以為明君於天下。』是故退睹其萬民，飢即食之，寒即衣之，疾病侍養之，死喪葬埋之。兼君之言若此，行若此。」

16.8　「然即交若之二君者[18]，言相非而行相反與？常[19]使若二君者，言必信，行必果，使言行之合猶合符節也，無言而不行也。然即敢問，今歲有癘疫，萬民多有勤苦凍餒，轉[20]死溝壑中者，既已眾矣。不識將擇之二君者，將何從也？我以為當其於此也，天下無愚夫愚婦，雖非兼者，必從兼君是也。言而非兼，擇即取兼，此言行拂也。不識天下〔之君〕，所以皆聞兼而非之者，其故何也？」

16.9　然而天下之士非兼者之言也，猶未止也。曰：「兼即仁矣義矣。

17. A similar statement is found in *Zhuangzi* 22 which has: "人生天地之間，若白駒之過郤，忽然而已" — see GQF, vol. 3, p. 746.
18. This opening phrase differs from the corresponding phrase in 16.6 above in that it begins with the three characters "然即交". Several commentators (e.g. ZCY) take these to be superfluous and so omit them.
19. Following SYR, 常 is emended to 嘗 in line with the similar previous statement.
20. 轉 is read as 棄 following SYR.

turn his attention to his ten thousand people, should he find them hungry, he would not feed them; should he find them cold, he would not clothe them; should he find them sick and ailing, he would not tend to them; and if they died, he would not bury them. The 'discriminating' ruler's words would be like this and his actions also. [On the other hand], the 'universal' ruler's words would not be like this and neither would his actions. He would say: 'I have heard that one who aspires to be an enlightened ruler in the world must give priority to the persons of the ten thousand people and put his own person second. Then he can be considered to be an enlightened ruler in the world.' Therefore, if he were to turn his attention to his ten thousand people, should he find them hungry, he would feed them; should he find them cold, he would clothe them; should he find them sick and ailing, he would tend to them; and if they died, he would bury them. The 'universal' ruler's words would be like this and his actions also."

16.8   "Are two such rulers mutually contradictory in their words and mutually opposing in their actions? Let us suppose there were two such rulers, and their words were certainly trustworthy and their actions certainly came to fruition, and that their words and actions corresponded like the two halves of a tally. They would not say something that they would not do. In such a case, let us pose this question. Suppose now the year was one of plague and pestilence and among the ten thousand people there were many who suffered cold and hunger so the number left for dead in channels and ditches was already very considerable. Do we not know, if there were to be a choice between these two rulers, which one would be followed? I think, under these circumstances, the men and women of the world would not be foolish. Although [people] might condemn 'universal', they would certainly follow the 'universal' ruler as right. In their words they might reject 'universal', but in their choice they would select 'universal', which is a case of words and actions being opposed. We do not know why it is that the rulers of the world all hear about 'universal' and yet condemn it — what reason can there be?"

16.9   Nonetheless, the arguments of officers of the world who condemn "universal" still never stop. They say: "'Universal' might be

雖然豈可為哉？吾譬兼之不可為也，猶挈泰山以超江河也。故兼
者直願之也，夫豈可為之物哉？」子墨子曰：「夫挈泰山以超江
河，自古之及今，生民而來未嘗有也。今若夫兼相愛，交相利，
此自先聖六王[21]者親行之。」何知先聖六王之親行之也？子墨子
曰：「吾非與之並世同時，親聞其聲，見其色也。以其所書於竹
帛，鏤於金石，琢於槃盂，傳遺後世子孫者知之。《泰誓》曰：『文
王若日若月，乍照，光於四方於西土。[22]』即此言文王之兼愛天下
之博大也，譬之日月兼照天下之無有私也。」即此文王兼也，雖[23]
子墨子之所謂兼者，於文王取法焉。

16.10   「且不唯《泰誓》為然，雖《禹誓》即亦猶是也。禹曰：『濟濟有眾，
咸聽朕言，非惟小子，敢行稱亂，蠢茲有苗，用天之罰，若予既
率爾群對諸群，以征有苗。』[24] 禹之征有苗也，非以求以[25]重富

21. I have accepted SYR's emendation of 六 to 四 on the basis of usage elsewhere. The four
    kings in question are taken to be Yu 禹, Tang 湯, Wen 文 and Wu 武.
22. Following LYS (for example), I have taken 乍 as 作. The quotation from the 《書經·
    太誓》 is: "嗚呼，惟我文考，若日月之照臨，光于四方，顯于西土." — see LCC,
    vol. 3, pp. 296–297.
23. 雖 is read as 唯 following SYR.
24. See the 《書經·大謨禹誓》 (LCC, vol. 3, pp. 64–65). The text is, however, somewhat
    different and there are issues with the *Mozi* text — see, for example, LYS and WYJ.
25. 以 here is taken as superfluous and is omitted.

benevolent and it might be righteous, but how can it be put into practice? We compare the impossibility of practising 'universal' to that of picking up Mount Tai and leaping with it across the Yangtze and Yellow Rivers. Therefore, 'universal' is no more than a wish. How is it something that can be put into practice?" Master Mo Zi said: "Picking up Mount Tai and leaping with it across the Yangtze and Yellow Rivers is something no-one has ever done, from ancient times to the present, from when people first came to exist. Now in the case of universal mutual love and exchange of mutual benefit, this comes from the first four sage kings personally practising it." How do we know that the first four sage kings personally practised it? Master Mo Zi said: "I myself did not live at the same time as they did so I did not personally hear their voices or see their faces. It is through what they wrote on bamboo and silk, what they carved in metal and stone, what they engraved on [ceremonial] plates and bowls to hand down to their descendants of later generations that I know this. The *Great Oath* (*Tai Shi*) says: 'King Wen was like the sun and the moon, creating light and bringing its brightness to the four regions and to the western lands.' This speaks of the wide extent and greatness of King Wen's universal love of the world being like the sun and moon which universally illuminate all parts of the world without discrimination." This was King Wen's "universal" and is what Master Mo Zi means when he speaks of "universal", taking King Wen as his model.

16.10   "Moreover, it is not only the *Great Oath* (*Tai Shi*) that is so. The *Oath of Yu* (*Yu Shi*) is also like this. Yu said: "People everywhere, I ask you to listen to my words. It is not that I, one small person, dare to stir up this warlike activity. It is due to the foolishness of the You Miao which I am acting on Heaven's behalf to punish. So I am leading the hosts of the feudal lords and princes to bring the You Miao to submission."[iii] Yu's bringing the You Miao to submission was not because he sought to increase his wealth and nobility, nor because he sought happiness and prosperity, nor to bring pleasure to his ears and eyes. It was because he sought to

---

iii.   On the You Miao 有苗 see particularly 9.9 note iv and also 12.8 above.

貴，下[26]福祿，樂耳目也，以求興天下之利，除天下之害。」即此
禹兼也。雖子墨子之所謂兼者，於禹求焉[27]。

16.11　「且不唯《禹誓》為然，雖《湯說》[28]即亦猶是也。湯曰：『惟予小子
履，敢用玄牡，告於上天后〔上〕[29]曰：今天大旱，即當朕身履，
未知得罪於上下，有善不敢蔽，有罪不敢赦，簡在帝心。萬方有
罪，即當朕身，朕身有罪，無及萬方。』即此言湯貴為天子，富
有天下，然且不憚以身為犧牲，以祠說於上帝鬼神。」即此湯兼
也。雖子墨子之所謂兼者，於湯取法焉。

16.12　「且不唯《誓命》與《湯說》為然，《周詩》即亦猶是也。《周詩》曰：
『王道蕩蕩，不偏不黨，王道平平，不黨不偏。其直若矢，其易
若底，君子之所履，小人之所視』，若吾言非語道之謂也[30]，古者
文武為正[31]，均分賞賢罰暴，勿有親戚弟兄之所阿[32]。」即此文武

---

26. 下 is read as 求 — see Z&Q.
27. Following SYR, I have emended the final clause from "於禹求焉" to "於禹取法焉"
    to conform with the preceding and succeeding sections.
28. Several commentators (e.g. Z&Q) suggest that 《湯說》 should be taken as 《湯誓》. The
    passage is not, in fact, found in continuous form in the 《書經》 although some of the
    sentences can be found in the 《湯誥》, whilst drought is mentioned in the 《説命》 chapter.
    SYR has the note: "據此後文，則是湯禱旱之辭。"
29. I have followed SYR's proposed addition of 上 here.
30. This is a difficult sentence — see, for example, Legge's note on it (LCC, vol. 2, p. 114).
    I have followed WHB's proposed reorganisation to "故若言，語兼道之謂也。"
31. 正 here is understood as 政.
32. 阿 is taken as 私. Both this and the previous emendation were proposed by SYR based
    on the *Lü Shi Chunqiu*.

promote the world's benefits and eliminate the world's harms."
This was Yu's "universal" and is what Master Mo Zi means when
he speaks of "universal", taking Yu as his model.

16.11   "Moreover, it is not only the *Oath of Yu* (*Yu Shi*) that is so. The
Speech of Tang (*Tang Shuo*) is also like this. Tang said: 'I, the
unworthy Lü, dared to use a dark-coloured male animal to inform
the Supreme Lord and the spirits of the earth, saying: 'Now
Heaven [has sent] a great drought and it is right that I, Lü, bear the
responsibility. I do not know if I have committed a wrong against
[the powers] above and below. Where there is good, I dare not
conceal it. Where there is wrongdoing, I dare not pardon it. This is
something that is clearly understood by the mind of the Supreme
Being. If anywhere in the ten thousand regions there is
wrongdoing, it is right that I take the responsibility. If I myself do
wrong, it need not involve the ten thousand regions.' This, then,
tells of Tang's ennoblement as Son of Heaven and his enrichment
in possessing all under Heaven. Nevertheless, he did not shrink
from offering himself as a sacrificial victim to be used as a
sacrifice to persuade the Supreme Being and the ghosts and
spirits." This was Tang's "universal" and is what Master Mo Zi
means when he speaks of "universal", taking Tang as his model.

16.12   "Moreover, it is not only the *Oath of Fate* (*Shi Ming*) and the
Speech of Tang (*Tang Shuo*) that are so. The *Odes of Zhou* (*Zhou
Shi*) is also like this. The *Odes of Zhou* (*Zhou Shi*) states: 'The
King's path is broad and expansive. It is not inclined; it is not
partial. The King's path is level and fair. It is not partial; it is not
inclined. Its straightness is like an arrow, its smoothness is like a
whetstone. It is what the princely man walks upon. It is what the
petty man looks at.'[iv] It is words such as these that speak of the
principle [of universality]. In ancient times, when Wen and Wu
conducted government, with just division they rewarded
worthiness and punished evil, showing no partiality to parents or
younger and older brothers." This was Wen and Wu's "universal"

---

iv.   The quotation is a combination of lines from the 《書經 · 洪範》 (LCC, vol. 3, p. 331)
and the 《詩經 · 大東》 Mao #203 (LCC, vol. 4, p. 353).

兼也。雖子墨子之所謂兼者，於文武取法焉。不識天下之人，所
以皆聞兼而非之者，其故何也？

16.13 然而天下之〔士〕非兼者之言，猶未止，曰：「意不忠親之利，而害
為孝乎？[33]」子墨子曰：「姑嘗本原之孝子之為親度者。吾不識孝
子之為親度者，亦欲人愛利其親與？意欲人之惡賊其親與？以說
觀之，即欲人之愛利其親也。然即吾惡先從事即得此？若我先從
事乎愛利人之親，然後人報我〔以〕[34]愛利吾親乎？意我先從事乎
惡〔賊〕[35]人之親，然後人報我以愛利吾親乎？即必吾先從事乎愛
利人之親，然後人報我以愛利吾親也。然即之交孝子者，果不得
已乎，毋先從事愛利人之親者與？意以天下之孝子為遇而不足以
為正乎[36]？姑嘗本原之先王之所書，《大雅》之所道曰：『無言而不
讎，無德而不報，投我以桃，報之以李。』即此言愛人者必見愛
也，而惡人者必見惡也。不識天下之士，所以皆聞兼而非之者，

---

33. In this sentence, 意 is read as 抑 in the sense of 抑或, as in several other instances in this section, and 忠 is taken as 中 in the sense of 符合 following SSX. 士 is added in conformity with previous sections.
34. Added following WYJ.
35. Added following WYJ.
36. In this sentence, I have followed SYR's reading of 遇 as 愚 and YTY's reading of 正 as 善.

and is what Master Mo Zi means when he speaks of "universal", taking Wen and Wu as his models. We do not know why it is that the people of the world all hear about "universal" and yet condemn it — what reason can there be?

16.13   Nonetheless, the arguments of officers of the world who condemn "universal" still never stop. They say: "Could it be that not being in accord with one's parents' benefit is harmful to being filial?" Master Mo Zi said: "For the moment, let us examine the question of consideration for one's parents being the basis for a filial son. Do we not know that, in the case of consideration for parents being [the basis for] a filial son, he would also wish others to love and benefit his parents? Or would he wish others to hate and harm his parents? Looking at it from basic principles, he would wish others to love and benefit his parents. In this case, then, to what would I give priority in day-to-day business in order to attain this? If I were to give priority in day-to-day business to loving and benefiting the parents of others, would others subsequently requite me by loving and benefiting my parents? Or if I were to give priority in day-to-day business to hating and harming the parents of others, would others subsequently requite me by loving and benefiting my parents? Most certainly, if I were to give priority in day-to-day business to loving and benefiting the parents of others, others would subsequently requite me by loving and benefiting my parents. This being the case, then, in the interchange between filial sons, is there, in fact, any alternative to giving priority in day-to-day business to loving and benefiting the parents of others? Or are we to regard the filial sons of the world as foolish and not up to accepting this as good? If, for a moment, we take as a basis what the former kings wrote, in the words of the *Da Ya* it is said: 'No words are without response, no virtue is without reward. If you present me with a peach, I repay you with a plum.'[v] This, then, is to say that those who love others must themselves be loved, and those who hate others must themselves be hated. We do not know why it is that the world's officers' all hear about 'universal' and

---

v.   See the 《詩經》 Mao #256 (LCC, vol. 4, p. 514) for these lines, the first two being in stanza 6 and the second two in stanza 8.

其故何也？意以為難而不可為邪？嘗有難此而可為者。」

16.14 「昔荊靈王好小要。當靈王之身[37]，荊國之士飯不逾乎一，固據而
後興，扶垣而後行。故約食為其難為也，然後為而靈王說之，未
逾於世而民可移也，即求以鄉其上也。昔者越王勾踐好勇。教其
士臣三年，以其知為未足以知之也，焚舟失火，鼓而進之，其士
偃前列，伏水火而死者，不可勝數也[38]。當此之時，不鼓而退
也，越國之士可謂顫矣[39]。故焚身為其難為也，然後為之越王說
之，未逾於世而民可移也，即求以鄉〔其〕[40]上也。昔者晉文公好
苴服。當文公之時，晉國之士，大布之衣，牂羊之裘，練帛之
冠，且苴之屨，入見文公，出以踐之朝。故苴服為其難為也，然
後為而文公說之，未逾於世而民可移也，即求以鄉其上也。是故
約食，焚舟，苴服，此天下之至難為也，然後為而上說之，未逾
於世而民可移也。何故也？即求以鄉其上也。今若夫兼相愛，交

---

37. There is general acceptance of 時 for 身.
38. In this and the preceding clause, I have followed the text of WYJ which has the
    emendation of 有 to 者.
39. In the translation, I have followed LYS's rearrangement of this sentence which is: "當
    此之時，不鼓而退也，越國之士，可謂顫 (彈 — BY, 憚 — SYR) 矣。" — see his
    note 8, p. 129.
40. Added following WYJ.

yet condemn it — what reason can there be? Do they think it is difficult or impossible to put into practice? But there have already been things as difficult as this that have been possible to put into practice."

16.14   "Formerly, King Ling of Jing loved slender waists. During the time of King Ling, the officers of Jing did not eat more than one meal a day. As a result, they had to rely on a stick to get up, and to use the support of walls when walking. Now restricting one's food is a difficult thing to do, but they did it because it pleased King Ling. So it doesn't need more than a single generation for people to be able to change if they seek to fall in with the wishes of their superior. Formerly, the Yue king, Gou Jian, loved courage. He instructed his officers and ministers [in it] for three years, but his knowledge was not yet sufficient to know [the outcome of the instruction]. So he set fire to a boat and beat the drum to signal the advance. As those in front fell so those behind took their positions and the number who succumbed to water and fire could not be counted. At that time, if he had not sounded the drum for retreat, the officers of Yue could have been said to be completely lost. Sacrificing oneself is a difficult thing to do, but after they did it the Yue king was delighted. So it doesn't need more than a single generation for people to be able to change if they seek to fall in with the wishes of their superior. Formerly, Duke Wen of Jin liked coarse clothing. In Duke Wen's time, the officers of Jin wore clothes of coarse cloth, furs of sheepskin, hats of rough silk and shoes of coarse canvas. [Thus attired], they went in to see Duke Wen and went out to walk in the court. Wearing coarse clothing is a difficult thing to do, but after they did it Duke Wen was delighted. So it doesn't need more than a single generation for people to be able to change if they seek to fall in with the wishes of their superior. Now eating very little, the burning boat incident, and wearing coarse clothing are among the most difficult things in the world to do, but after they were done the rulers were delighted, indicating that it doesn't need more than a single generation for people to be able to change. What is the reason for this? It is that they seek to conform to the pattern of the superior. Now things like universal mutual love and the exchange of mutual benefit are both beneficial and easy to practise in

相利，此其有利且易為也，不可勝計也，我以為則無有上說之者
而已矣。苟有上說之者，勸之以賞譽，威之以刑罰，我以為人之
於就兼相愛交相利也，譬之猶火之就上，水之就下也，不可防止
於天下。」

16.15 故兼者聖王之道也，王公大人之所以安也，萬民衣食之所以足
也。故君子莫若審兼而務行之，為人君必惠，為人臣必忠，為人
父必慈，為人子必孝，為人兄必友，為人弟必悌。故君子莫若欲
為惠君，忠臣，慈父，孝子，友兄，悌弟，當若兼之不可不行
也，此聖王之道而萬民之大利也。

innumerable ways. I think it is only a matter of not having a ruler who delights in them, and that is all. If there was a ruler who delighted in these things, and encouraged people with rewards and praise, and intimidated them with penalties and punishments, I think the people would take to universal mutual love and interchange of mutual benefit just like fire goes up and water goes down and cannot be stopped in the world."

16.15 Therefore, "universal" was the Way of the sage kings. It was the means whereby kings, dukes and great officers brought peace, and the means whereby the ten thousand people had enough clothing and food. So, for the gentleman, there is nothing equal to carefully examining "universal" and assiduously practising it. It makes rulers necessarily kind, it makes ministers necessarily loyal, it makes fathers necessarily compassionate, it makes sons necessarily filial, it makes older brothers necessarily well disposed, and it makes younger brothers necessarily respectful. And, for a gentleman, there is nothing equal to wishing to be a kind ruler, or a loyal minister, or a compassionate father, or a filial son, or a well-disposed older brother, or a respectful younger brother, so it is right that "universal" cannot but be put into practice. This was the Way of the sage kings and is of great benefit to the ten thousand people.

17: 非攻上[1]

17.1   子墨子言曰:「古者王公大人,情欲得而惡失,欲安而惡危,故
當攻戰而不可不非[2]。今有一人,入人園圃,竊其桃李,眾聞則非
之,上為政者得則罰之。此何也?以虧人自利也。至攘人犬豕雞
豚者,其不義又甚入人園圃竊桃李。是何故也?以虧人愈多,其
不仁茲甚,罪益厚。[3]至入人欄廐,取人馬牛者,其不仁義又甚
攘人犬豕雞豚。此何故也?以其虧人愈多。苟虧人愈多,其不仁
茲甚,罪益厚。至殺不辜人也,拖其衣裘,取戈劍者,其不義又
甚入人欄廐取人馬牛。此何故也?以其虧人愈多。苟虧人愈多,
其不仁茲甚矣,罪益厚。當此,天下之君子皆知而非之,謂之不
義。今至大為攻國[4],則弗知〔而〕[5]非,從而譽之,謂之義。此可
謂知義與不義之別乎?」

---

1.   The text for this and the next two chapters follows WYJ. The points of notable difference
     from other modern editions (e.g. LYS, LSL, MBJ, Z&Q) will be indicated in the notes
     as they occur.
2.   The preceding 31 characters, prefaced by "是故", are more commonly found in what
     below is 18.5. WYJ particularly follows CYX in making this rearrangement — see the
     former's note 1, p. 199.
3.   The translation of this sentence depends on reading 茲 as 滋 or 更 (following SYR), 厚
     as 重 (MZQY), and accepting the addition of 義 after 仁 (MZQY).
4.   There is general acceptance of BY's addition of 不義 following 大為.
5.   Added here and in corresponding clauses in what follows by WYJ — see his note 14,
     p. 200.

17: Condemning Offensive Warfare I

17.1 Master Mo Zi spoke, saying: "In ancient times, kings, dukes and great men, if they genuinely desired success and abhorred failure, if they wished for peace and disliked danger, could not do otherwise than condemn offensive warfare. Now, if there is one man who enters another's orchard or garden and steals his peaches and plums, all who hear about it condemn him. If those above who conduct government get hold of him, then they punish him. Why is this? Because it is by harming the other that he benefits himself. When it comes to stealing another's dogs, hogs, chickens and suckling pigs, his unrighteousness is greater than entering the other's orchard or garden and stealing his peaches and plums. What is the reason for this? Because his harming the other is much greater, his lack of benevolence and righteousness is even greater, and the crime more serious. When it comes to entering another's animal enclosure and taking his horses and oxen, his lack of benevolence and righteousness is even greater than stealing the other's dogs, hogs, chickens and suckling pigs. What is the reason for this? It is because the harm to the other is even greater. If the harm to the other is even greater, then the lack of benevolence and righteousness is even greater, and the crime more serious. When it comes to killing an innocent man, seizing his clothes and fur garments, and taking his spear and sword, the lack of righteousness is greater again than entering another's animal enclosure and taking his horses and oxen. What is the reason for this? It is because the loss to the other is even greater. If the loss to the other is even greater, then the lack of benevolence [and righteousness] is even greater and the crime more serious. If this is valid, the gentlemen of the world should all know and condemn it, and call it unrighteous. Now when it comes to what is a great lack of righteousness, that is, attacking states, they do not know and condemn [it] but instead they commend it and say it is righteous. Can this be called knowing the difference between what is righteous and what is not righteous?"

17.2   「殺一人謂之不義，必有一死罪矣。若以此說往，殺十人十重不
義，必有十死罪矣；殺百人百重不義，必有百死罪矣。當此，天
下之君子皆知而非之，謂之不義。今至大為不義攻國，則弗知
〔而〕非[6]，從而譽之，謂之義，情[7]不知其不義也，故書其言以遺
後世。若知其不義也，夫奚說書其不義以遺後世哉？」

17.3   「今有人於此，少見黑曰黑，多見黑曰白，則以此人不知白黑之
辯矣；少嘗苦曰苦，多嘗苦曰甘，則必以此人為不知甘苦之辯
矣。今小為非，則知而非之；大為非攻國，則不知〔而〕非，從而
譽之，謂之義。此可謂知義與不義之辯乎？是以知天下之君子
也，辯義與不義之亂也。」

---

6. In this clause, 知 is the accepted emendation of 之 (WYZ) and 而 is added following
    WYJ.
7. Following WNS 情 is read as 誠 in the sense of 確實.

17.2 "The killing of one person is spoken of as unrighteous and certainly constitutes one capital offence. Reasoning on this basis, killing ten people is ten times as unrighteous, so certainly constitutes ten capital offences. Killing a hundred people is a hundred times as unrighteous, so certainly constitutes a hundred capital offences. If this is valid, the gentlemen of the world should all know and condemn it, and call it unrighteous. But when it comes to what is a great lack of righteousness, that is, attacking states, then they do not know and condemn it. On the contrary, they praise it and call it righteous. Truly, they did not know this was unrighteous and therefore recorded their words to hand on to later generations. If they knew it was not righteous, then how does one explain their recording what was unrighteous in order to hand it on to later generations?"

17.3 "Now suppose there was someone who, when he saw a little bit of black, called it black, but when he saw a lot of black, called it white. We would certainly take this person to be someone who did not know the difference between white and black. [Likewise], suppose there was someone who, when he tasted a little bitterness, called it bitter, but when he tasted a lot, called it sweet. We would certainly take this person to be someone who did not know the difference between sweet and bitter. Now when something small is a crime, people know and condemn it. When something great is a crime, like attacking states, then they don't know and condemn [it], but go along with it and praise it, calling it righteous. Can this be spoken of as knowing the difference between what is righteous and what is not righteous? This is how we know that the gentlemen of the world are confused about the distinction between what is righteous and what is not righteous."

18: 非攻中

18.1   子墨子言曰:「古者王公大人,為政於國家者,情欲〔毀〕[1] 譽之審,賞罰之當,刑政之不過失,故當攻戰而不可為也[2]。[3] 今師徒唯毋興起,冬行恐寒,夏行恐暑,此不可以冬夏為者也。春則廢民耕稼樹藝,秋則廢民穫斂。[4] 今唯毋廢一時,則百姓飢寒凍餒而死者,不可勝數。今嘗計軍上[5],竹箭羽旄幄幕,甲盾撥劫[6],往而靡斃腑冷不反者,不可勝數。又與矛戟戈劍乘車,其列往[7]碎折靡斃而不反者,不可勝數。與其牛馬肥而往,瘠而反,往死亡而不反者,不可勝數。與其塗道之修遠,糧食輟絕而不繼,百姓死者,不可勝數也;與其居處之不安,食飲之不時,飢飽之不節,百姓之道疾病而死者,不可勝數。喪師多不可勝數,喪師盡不可勝計,則是鬼神之喪其主後,亦不可勝數。[8]」

---

1. Added following Qiu Shan 秋山 — see WYJ, note 1, p. 205.
2. There are several issues in this opening sentence apart from the addition of 毀. These are as follows: (i) A number of commentators follow WNS in emending 由 to 今. WYJ does not and I have followed him. (ii) 情 is accepted as being in the sense of 誠. (iii) 當 is read as 得當 (Z&Q). (iv) The final nine characters are transferred from what is 18.3 below following WYJ — see note 3 below.
3. As with the previous essay, there is notable variation in the opening part of this essay. Again the text follows WYJ. An alternative arrangement is to include the following 57 characters: "今者王公大人、情欲得而惡失、欲安而惡危,故當攻戰而不可不非。" 是故子墨子曰:"古者有語:'謀而不得,則以往知來、以見知隱。'謀若此,可得而知矣。" The first 26 are WNS's proposed addition to fill a perceived lacuna after "不過失" and the second 31 are those found in modern editions of LSL and Z&Q.
4. According to SYR, there should be a sentence here of the form "此不可以春秋為者也" corresponding to that following the previous statement about winter and summer.
5. Two emendations are made in this clause: 嘗 to 試 (e.g. LYS) and 上 to 出 (SYR).
6. "Other things" is the translation given for 撥劫. There are other suggestions — for example, a large shield (大盾 — SYR) and 劫 as an iron hook (鈺 — YTY).
7. There is variation here with some texts having 列住 (e.g. LYS, Z&Q). 列住 (or 列住) is read as 往則 (SYR, LSL) — see WYJ, note 11, p. 206.
8. There is some uncertainty about this sentence — see WYJ, note 18, p. 207.

18: Condemning Offensive Warfare II

18.1 Master Mo Zi spoke, saying: "In ancient times, kings, dukes and great officers, in conducting government in their states, genuinely wished to be careful with regard to censure and praise, to be just in rewards and punishments, and not to fail in judicial and administrative matters. Therefore, rightly, offensive warfare was something they could not pursue. Nowadays, if troops are to be raised, there is fear of cold if they go forth in winter and of heat in summer, so this cannot be done in either winter or summer. If they go in spring, then it disrupts the people's planting and sowing and the cultivation of trees. If they go in autumn, then it disrupts the people's reaping and storing. Now, as there is not one season without disruption, the ordinary people who die from hunger and cold cannot be numbered. And if you try to calculate how much of the equipment — bamboo arrows, flags and banners, tents, and other things — which an army sets out with, is lost or destroyed and does not return, this also is beyond computation. Moreover, the spears, lances, halberds, swords and war chariots that the army goes forth with which are destroyed, broken and lost and do not return also cannot be numbered. Further, of the oxen and horses that are fat when they go forth, those that are lean when they return, or die and are lost and do not return, cannot be numbered. And, in addition, because the road is long and food supplies are cut off without means of relief, the ordinary people who die cannot be numbered. And because the places where they dwell cannot be made peaceful, they do not eat and drink at proper times, satiety and starvation cannot be controlled, and the ordinary people who become sick and die on the roads cannot be numbered. Either the soldiers who are lost will be very many, or the whole army will be lost. In both cases, the losses cannot be numbered. Then the ghosts and spirits will lose those descendants who can carry out the sacrifices, which is another incalculable loss."

18.2 國家發政，奪民之用，廢民之利，若此甚眾，然而何為為之？曰：「我貪伐勝之名，及得之利，故為之。」子墨子言曰：「計其所自勝，無所可用也。計其所得，反不如所喪者之多。今攻三里之城，七里之郭，攻此不用銳，且無殺而徒得此然也。殺人多必數於萬，寡必數於千，然後三里之城，七里之郭，且可得也[9]。今萬乘之國，虛數於千，不勝而入。廣衍數於萬，不勝而辟[10]。然則土地者，所有餘也，王民者，所不足也。今盡王民[11]之死，嚴下上之患，以爭虛城，則是棄所不足，而重所有餘也。為政若此，非國之務者也。」

18.3 飾攻戰者也言曰[12]：「南則荊、吳之王，北則齊、晉之君，始封於天下之時，其土地之方，未至有數百里也；人徒之眾，未至有數十萬人也。以攻戰之故，土地之博至有數千里也；人徒之眾至有數百萬人。故當攻戰而不可為也。[13]」子墨子言曰：「雖四五國則得利焉，猶謂之非行[14]道也。譬若醫之藥人之有病者然。今有醫

9. There are certain difficulties with the two preceding sentences which modern commentators attempt to resolve by adding 非 after 攻此. There are also problems with 然. The translation above is based on the detailed analysis given by WYJ (notes 19 & 20, pp. 207–208). As he mentions, a similar city is spoken of in *Mencius* IIB.1(2).

10. The somewhat free translation of this sentence depends on the acceptance of BY's four proposals: (i) Reading 虛 as 墟. (ii) Taking 人 as 入. (iii) Reading 廣衍 as 廣大. (iv) Reading 辟 as 闢. Other versions have been suggested, for example by SYR — see WYJ, notes 23–26, p. 208.

11. There is general acceptance of WNS's emendation of 王民 to 士民.

12. On "也言曰" see WYJ, note 27, pp. 208–209. Some editors omit 也 (e.g. Z&Q). WYJ reads it as 之.

13. WYJ's text for this sentence is: "是故攻戰之速也。" I have followed the textual emendations of SYR which make the sentence as above — see WYJ, particularly note 31, p. 209.

14. 行 is read as 正 here when qualifying 道 and as 好 subsequently when qualifying 藥.

18.2   [The rulers of] states start wars, depriving the people of their livelihood and stripping the people of benefit, all to a very great degree. Why do they do this? They say: "We covet the fame of conquest and wish to reap the benefits. That is why we do it." Master Mo Zi spoke, saying: "If you determine what they themselves gain from this, it is not something that can be of use. If you calculate what they acquire, it is not nearly as much as they lose. For example, if you could attack a city with an inner wall of three *li* and an outer wall of seven *li* without using sharp weapons and without anyone being killed, there would be no difficulty. But this is not the case. The number of people killed will range from ten thousand at the most to one thousand at the least before a city with an inner wall of three *li* and an outer wall of seven *li* can be taken. Now in a state of ten thousand chariots, there is a great amount of waste land that can be entered without conquest and there are vast open spaces that can be opened up without conquest. It is a case, then, of land being what there is an excess of, but officers and people being what there is not enough of. Now to send officers and men to their deaths and to add to the misfortunes of those above and below in order to attack an empty city is to cast away what there is not enough of to gain what there is already an excess of. To govern like this is contrary to what is fundamental to a state."

18.3   Those who argue in favour of offensive warfare say: "To the south, there are the kings of Jing and Wu.[i] To the north, there are the rulers of Qi and Jin. At the time of the world when they were first enfeoffed, the size of their lands did not reach several hundred *li*, and the number of their people did not come to several hundred thousand. By means of offensive warfare their lands have been extended to several thousand *li* and their people number several millions. That this validates offensive warfare cannot be denied." Master Mo Zi spoke, saying: "Although four or five states may have benefited by this means, I still say that this is not the correct way. For example, a doctor treats those who are sick with

---

i.   Jing 荊 was Chu 楚. SYR states that 吳 should read 越 in that the former was already lost by Mo Zi's time — see WYJ for details.

於此，和合其祝藥之于天下之有病者而藥之，萬人食此，若醫四五人得利焉，猶謂之非行藥也[15]。故孝子不以食其親，忠臣不以食其君。」

18.4   「古者封國於天下，尚[16]者以耳之所聞，近者以目之所見，以攻戰亡者，不可勝數。何以知其然也？東方有莒之國者，其為國甚小，間於大國之間，不敬事於大，大國亦弗之從而愛利。是以東者越人夾削其壤地，西者齊人兼而有之。計莒之所以亡於齊越之間者，以是攻戰也。雖南者陳蔡，其所以亡於吳越之間者，亦以攻戰。雖北者且不一著何，其所以亡於燕代胡貊之間者，亦以攻戰也。」是故子墨子曰：「古者有語：『謀而不得，則以往知來，以見知隱。』謀若此，可得而知矣。」[17]

18.5   飾攻戰者之言曰：「彼不能收用彼眾，是故亡。我能收用我眾，

15. There are certain difficulties with this sentence involving particularly "和合" and "祝藥". On the former, see ZCY's detailed note. On the latter, BY proposes reading 祝 as 祝由科. LYS, who disagrees, has: "大概是一種兼用符咒的藥類。"

16. There is general acceptance of the reading of 尚 as 上 in the sense of 久 or 遠.

17. On the placement of this statement here see WYJ, note 44, p. 211.

medicines. Now suppose there was this doctor who so unified his treatment that he gave the same medicine to all the sick people of the world and ten thousand people took it, but only four or five got any benefit. I would still say that it was not a good medicine. Therefore, a filial son would not give it to his parents and a loyal minister would not give it to his ruler."

18.4   "In ancient times, there was the establishment of states in the world. Those in the distant past we hear about. Those more recent we see for ourselves. The number of these that were lost through offensive warfare cannot be counted. How do I know this is so? In the east, there was the state of Ju[ii] which was a very small state squeezed in between large states. It did not show due deference to the large states and they, in turn, did not foster it or wish to benefit it. So, from the east, the people of Yue encroached upon it and seized territory while, from the west, the people of Qi annexed and incorporated it. If we think about why Ju was destroyed between Qi and Yue, it was due to offensive warfare. Even the destruction of Chen and Cai in the south, situated as they were between Wu and Yue, was also due to offensive warfare,[iii] as also in the north was the destruction of Zu and Butuhe between Yan, Dai, Hu and Mo."[iv] Therefore Master Mo Zi said: "The ancients had this saying: 'If you plan and are unsuccessful, then use the past to predict the future, use the manifest to know the hidden.' If you plan like this, you can succeed and know."

18.5   The advocates of offensive warfare say: "Others may not be able to gather and utilise the great mass of their people for the purpose

---

ii.   Ju 莒 was a small Warring States period kingdom occupying part of what is now Shandong province.

iii. Chen 陳 and Cai 蔡 were also small Warring States period kingdoms situated in what is now Henan province, the former corresponding to Huaiyang and the latter to Xincai. Both were destroyed by Chu 楚 in 479 BC and 447 BC respectively (Z&Q).

iv.   This is WHB's note on "且不一著何": "當依舊本作'且一不著何'。且：即相，國名，所在無考。'一'疑'以'之音訛。以：與。不著和：國名，亦稱'不屠何'，故城在今遼寧境內。" The kingdom of Zu is referred to in the SAA for the 10th year of Duke Xiang — see LCC, vol. 5, p. 442 and Legge's note on the question of the name (Zu/Cha) on p. 445. There are other views on this matter — see WYJ, note 42, pp. 210–211.

以此攻戰於天下，誰敢不賓服哉？」子墨子言曰：「子雖能收用子
之眾，子豈若古者吳闔閭哉？古者吳闔閭教七年，奉甲執兵，奔
三百里而舍焉，次注林，出於冥隘之徑，戰於柏舉，中楚國而朝
宋與魯[18]。及[19] 至夫差之身，北而攻齊，舍於汶上，戰於艾陵，
大敗齊人而葆之大山；東而攻越，濟三江五湖，而葆之會稽。九
夷之國莫不賓服。於是退不能賞孤，施舍辟萌，自恃其力，伐其
功，譽其智，怠於教，遂築姑蘇之臺，七年不成。及若此，則吳

---

18. The translation of this sentence follows the textual changes as detailed by SSX and Z&Q.
19. 及 is transferred here from its more usual position before 魯 in the preceding sentence.
    This follows SSX — see WYJ, note 51, p. 212.

of destruction. We, however, are able to gather and utilise the great mass of our people and employ them in offensive warfare in the world, so who would dare not to submit to us?"

Master Mo Zi spoke, saying: "Although you may be able to gather and utilise the great mass of your people, how can you compare with Helü of Wu in ancient times?[v] In ancient times, Helü of Wu trained his troops for seven years so that, wearing armour and carrying weapons, they could travel fast for 300 *li* before resting. When stationed at Zhulin, they came forth on the track at Mingai and engaged [the Chu forces] at Boju.[vi] [Helü] took control of Chu and forced Song and Lu to come to his court and offer tribute. When it came to Fu Chai himself, he attacked Qi to the north. Positioning his troops above Wen, he joined battle at Ailing and inflicted a crushing defeat on the people of Qi, forcing them to retreat to Tai Shan.[vii] To the east, he attacked Yue, crossing the 'three rivers' and the 'five lakes', and compelling [the Yue forces] to take refuge at Guiji.[viii] Of the 'nine tribes', there was none that did not submit. When he returned, he was not able to reward those bereaved or bestow charity on the people. He took advantage of his own strength, boasted about his achievements, and flaunted his own brilliance but neglected to train [his troops]. Subsequently, he built a tower at Gusu which was not complete after seven years.[ix]

---

v. Helü 闔閭 (also 闔廬) was an ancient king of Wu. He was succeeded by his son Fu Chai (vide infra) in 495 BC. See also《吳越春秋 · 闔閭內傳》and for an account of the battle with Chu see the *Zuo Zhuan* for the 4th year of Duke Ding (LCC, vol. 5, p. 751).

vi. Of the three places referred to here, Zhulin 注林 is unknown, Mingai or Ming Pass (冥 隘 or 冥阨) is mentioned in the *Zuo Zhuan* reference and was situated in what is now Henan whilst Boju 柏舉, anciently in Chu, was in what is now Hubei. For further details see WYJ, note 48, p. 212.

vii. As noted above, Fu Chai was the son of Helü. After he came to power in 495 BC, he waged successful campaigns against both Qi and Yue, but was later badly defeated by Gou Jian of the latter kingdom and eventually took his own life. Wen 汶 refers to Wen Waters in what is now Shandong and Ailing 艾陵 was also in present-day Shandong. It is generally accepted that 葆 should be read as 保.

viii. For the "three rivers" see WYJ, note 54, p. 213 and for the "five lakes", as the term applied in ancient times, see ZWDCD, vol. 1, 668–669. Guiji 會稽 was in what is now Zhejiang province.

ix. On the matter of the tower and its construction see WYJ, note 60, p. 214.

有離罷[20]之心。越王勾踐視吳上下不相得，收其眾以復其仇，入
北郭，徙大內[21]，圍王宮，而吳國以亡。」

18.6 「昔者晉有六將軍，而智伯莫為強焉。計其土地之博，人徒之
眾，欲以抗諸侯，以為英名。〔攻戰之速〕[22]，故差論其爪牙之
士，皆列其舟車之眾，以攻中行氏而有之[23]。以其謀為既已足
矣，又攻茲[24]氏而大敗之，并三家以為一家，而不止，又圍趙襄
子於晉陽。及若此，則韓魏亦相從而謀曰：『古者有語，唇亡則
齒寒。』趙氏朝亡，吾夕從之；趙氏夕亡，我朝從之。《詩》曰：
『魚水不務，陸將何及乎！』是以三主之君，一心戮力辟門除道，
奉甲興士，韓魏自外，趙氏自內，擊智伯大敗之。」

18.7 是古子墨子言曰：「古者有語曰：『君子不鏡於水而鏡於人。鏡於

---

20. There is general acceptance of the reading of 疲 for 罷 — see, for example, LSL, Z&Q.
21. "徙大內" presents a problem. There is wide acceptance of the emendation of 內 to 舟
    and the reading of 徙 as 獲得 — see WYJ, note 62, p. 215.
22. In the translation, I have followed WYJ in omitting the problematical "攻戰之速" — see
    his note 66, p. 215. Another option is that offered by ZCY whose note reads: "疑當作
    '以攻戰之速為英名'。"
23. Apart from the omission referred to in the previous note, in the translation of this
    sentence, the following three points should be noted: (i) 差論 is taken as 選擇 (Z&Q).
    (ii) "爪牙之士" is rendered simply "brave soldiers". (iii) 皆列 is read as 比列 in the
    sense of 排列 (WNS).
24. Following SYR, 茲 is regarded as superfluous.

When it came to this then, there was disaffection and weariness in the hearts of the people of Wu. The king of Yue, Gou Jian, saw the dissension and discord between superiors and inferiors in Wu so he assembled his forces to take revenge on his enemy. Entering through the outer wall to the north, he seized the great boat and surrounded the royal palace, and so the state of Wu was lost."

18.6 "In former times, Jin had six generals, none of whom was as strong as Zhi Bo.[x] Considering the great extent of his lands and the large number of his people, he thought to oppose the feudal lords in order to glorify his name. So he selected his bravest soldiers and deployed the great number of his boats and chariots to attack Zhonghang and possess his [lands]. He thought his plans were already excellent so he also attacked the Fan house and completely defeated it. Thus he combined the three houses into one. Still he did not stop, but surrounded Zhao Xiang Zi at Jinyang.[xi] When this happened, Han and Wei got together to plan, saying: "There is an old adage which says, 'When the lips are lost the teeth become cold'. If the house of Zhao is destroyed in the morning, in the evening we will follow it. If the Zhao family is killed in the evening, in the morning we will follow it. The *Odes* says: 'If a fish cannot move swiftly in water, how will it manage on dry land?'"[xii] Therefore, the three rulers worked together with singleness of purpose, opening gates and clearing roads, donning armour and raising officers. So, with Han and Wei acting from without and the Zhao house acting from within, they struck at Zhi Bo and completely defeated him."

18.7 This is why Master Mo Zi spoke, saying: "In ancient times, there was the saying: 'The gentleman does not seek his reflection in water but in the people. From a reflection in water he sees only his

---

x. On the use of 將軍 here see WYJ's note 65, p. 215 which also includes SYR's note. The six generals referred to were: Han Kang Zi 韓康子, Zhao Xiang Zi 趙襄子, Wei Huan Zi 魏桓子, Fan Jishe 范吉射, Zhonghang Wen Zi 中行文子 and Zhi Bo 智伯 himself.

xi. The military exploits of Zhi Bo are also referred to, albeit more briefly, in *Mozi* 49. For references to these texts, including *Zhuangzi, Shi Ji, Huainanzi* and *Zhanguoce*, see WYJ's notes 70–76, pp. 216–217.

xii. This is not in the surviving 《詩經》. Most commentators follow SYR in reading 務 as 鶩.

水，見面之容；鏡於人，則知吉與凶。』今以攻戰為利，則蓋嘗鑑之於智伯之事乎？此其為不吉而凶，既可得而知矣。」

face; from a reflection in the people he can know good fortune and bad fortune.'[xiii] Nowadays, if there are those who take offensive war to be beneficial, should they not examine this in the mirror of Zhi Bo's affairs. It can easily be recognised that this is not auspicious but inauspicious."

---

xiii. There are several similar but not identical statements in other texts — for details see WYJ, note 80, p. 217.

19: 非攻下

19.1 子墨子言曰：「今天下之所譽善者，其說將何哉¹？為其上中天之利，而中中鬼之利，而下中人之利，故譽之與？意亡²非為其上中天之利，而中中鬼之利，而下中人之利，故譽之與？雖使下之愚人，必曰：『將為其上中天之利，而中中鬼之利，而下中人之利，故譽之。』今天下之所同義者，聖王之法也。今天下之諸侯將猶多皆免攻伐并兼³，則是有譽義之名，而不察其實也。此譬猶盲者之與人，同命白黑之名，而不能分其物也，則豈謂有別哉？」

19.2 「是故古之知者之為天下度也，必順慮其義，而後為之行，是以動則不疑，速通成⁴得其所欲，而順天鬼百姓之利，則知者之道也。是故古之仁人有天下者，必反大國之說，一天下之和，總四海之內，焉率天下之百姓，以農臣事上帝山川鬼神⁵。利人多，功故又大，是以天賞之，鬼富之，人譽之，使貴為天子，富有天

1. In this sentence, 善 is read as 義 to conform with the text that follows (ZCY). Even if 善 is retained, the argument is essentially unchanged. Also 將 is read as 應當.
2. There is general agreement that 意亡 should be taken as 抑無 in the sense of 還是.
3. I have followed MZH's version of this sentence, reading 免 as 勉 in the sense of 強.
4. While there is wide agreement that 順 should be read as 慎 (following WSN), there is an issue with "速通成". Most modern commentators follow SYR's revamping of this sentence, but I have followed WYJ's different version for the reasons he sets out in his note 11, p. 223.
5. There is some uncertainty about this sentence. LYS refers to the *Zuo Zhuan* for the 13th year of Duke Xiang where there is "小人農力以事其上." and reads 農 as 勉 on the basis of the 《廣雅·釋詁》. He also quotes ZCY's proposal for the first part of the statement as follows: "焉(乃)率天下之百姓以農".

19: Condemning Offensive Warfare III

19.1   Master Mo Zi spoke, saying: "What is it that nowadays should be praised as righteous in the world? Should it be that, if someone acts in accord with what benefits Heaven above, ghosts in the middle realm, and the people below, he should be praised? Or should it be that, if someone does not act in accord with what benefits Heaven above, ghosts in the middle realm, and the people below, he should be praised? Even foolish people would have to say: 'It ought to be that, if someone acts in accord with what benefits Heaven above, ghosts in the middle realm, and the people below, he should be praised!' Nowadays, everyone in the world agrees that righteousness was the method of the sage kings. But, in fact, nowadays the many feudal lords of the world all violently attack each other to an equal degree, which is to praise righteousness as a word without considering what it actually is. This is the same as a blind person using the terms 'white' and 'black' like other people, but not being able to distinguish what they are. How can this be called distinguishing?"

19.2   "This is why, in ancient times, those who were wise, in planning for the world, necessarily gave careful consideration to righteousness and afterwards put it into practice, so that their actions were then without doubt and quickly came to completion. They attained their desires yet still complied with what benefited Heaven, ghosts and ordinary people. This, then, was the Way of those who were wise. Therefore, those benevolent men who ruled the world in ancient times certainly opposed the great states' policy (of aggressive war), unified the world as an harmonious whole, and brought together all within the four seas. Thus they led the ordinary people of the world to pursue their affairs and, in doing so, to serve the Supreme Lord and the ghosts and spirits of mountains and rivers. The people they benefited were many and their achievements were, as a consequence, great. This was why Heaven rewarded them, the ghosts enriched them, and the people

卜，名參乎天地，至今不廢。此則知者之道也，先王之所以有天
下者也。」

19.3 「今王公大人天下之諸侯則不然，將必皆差論其爪牙之士，皆列
其舟車之卒伍，於此為堅甲利兵，以往攻伐無罪之國。入其國家
邊境，芟刈其禾稼，斬其樹木，墮其城郭，以湮其溝池，攘殺其
牲牷，燔潰其祖廟，勁殺其萬民，覆其老弱，遷其重器[6]，卒進而
柱乎鬥[7]，曰：『死命為上，多殺次之，身傷者為下，又況失列北
橈乎哉[8]，罪死無赦』以憚[9]其眾。夫無兼國覆軍，賊虐萬民，以亂
聖人之緒[10]。意將以為利天乎？夫取天之人，以攻天之邑，此刺
殺天民，剝振神之位，傾覆社稷，攘殺其犧牲，則此上不中天之
利矣[11]。意將以為利鬼乎？夫殺〔天〕[12]之人，滅鬼神之主，廢滅
先王，賊虐萬民，百姓離散，則此中不中鬼之利矣。意將以為利
人乎？夫殺〔天〕之人，為利人也博矣。又計其費，此為害[13]生之
本，竭天下百姓之財用，不可勝數也，則此下不中人之利矣。」

6. The readings of the various characters in this sentence follow LYS, notes 1–8, p. 145. Several commentators refer to the use of 墮 in the sense of 毀 in the *Zuo Zhuan* — see, for example, WYJ, note 23, pp. 224–225. 牲 are the six animals/birds — oxen, horses, sheep, pigs, dogs and fowl — whilst 牷 specifically refers to a bullock of a single colour suitable for sacrifice. 勁殺 is read as 刺殺 based on the *Shi Ji* — see Z&Q.
7. This clause is read as "卒進而極乎鬥" — see Z&Q.
8. The issues in this clause, concerning particularly 橈 and 北, are given detailed analysis by WYJ in his note 31, pp. 225–226.
9. Following BY, this is the generally accepted emendation for the unknown character, 單 with the 言 radical.
10. In this sentence, it is generally accepted that "夫無" acts as an introductory particle without specific meaning and that 緒 is to be taken as 業 in the sense of 緒業.
11. There are several issues with this statement, as follows: (i) 取 is taken as 用 (Z&Q). (ii) On "天之人" CYX has: "人者天之所生，故曰天之人。有生皆繫於天，故他國亦天之邑。" (iii) 剝振 is read as 剝裂 (WNS). (iv) 之 and 其 are regarded as superfluous in the fourth and sixth clauses respectively (WYJ).
12. 天 is added here and in the similar subsequent clause — see Z&Q, note 20, p. 227. WYJ has "夫殺之神" — see his note 37, p. 226.
13. I have followed WYJ's emendation of 周 to 害 — see his note 39, p. 227.

praised them. So they were honoured as Sons of Heaven, they were enriched with all under Heaven, and their fame was established in Heaven and on earth and has continued undimmed to the present day. This, then, was the Way of wise men and the means by which the former kings came to rule the world."

19.3   "Nowadays, kings, dukes, great officers and feudal lords of the world are not like this. All of them certainly select their bravest and fiercest soldiers, arrange and deploy their boats and chariots, and prepare their strongest armour and sharpest weapons to attack and reduce states that are without fault. When they enter the border regions of a state, they cut down its grain crops, fell its trees and forests, break down its inner and outer city walls, fill in its ditches and pools, seize and kill its sacrificial animals, burn down its ancestral temples, slaughter its people, destroy the old and weak, and move away its valuable utensils. [The soldiers] advance rapidly and fight to the limit, saying: 'The highest [honour] is to die in battle; the next highest is to kill many of the enemy; the least is to suffer injury oneself. Further, to break ranks and scatter in defeat is a crime punishable by death without possible pardon.' These words are used to instil fear into the masses. To annex a state and overthrow its army, and to plunder and oppress its people is a way of bringing disorder to the work of the sages. How can this be construed as benefiting Heaven? In fact, to take the people of Heaven and use them to attack the cities of Heaven is to kill the people of Heaven, to destroy the standing of the spirits, to overturn the altars of soil and grain, and to seize and slaughter the sacrificial animals. This, then, does not accord with Heaven's benefit in the upper realm. How can this be construed as benefiting ghosts? To kill the people of Heaven, to exterminate those who honour the ghosts and spirits, to cast aside the former kings, to plunder and oppress the ten thousand people, to scatter and disperse the general populace does not, then, accord with the ghosts' benefit in the middle realm. How can this be construed as benefiting people? If you kill the people of Heaven to benefit people, the benefit is meagre indeed. Moreover, if you consider the resources wasted in military activity, this harms the foundations of life of the people, and the depletion of the resources of the world and the ordinary people is incalculable. So this does not achieve benefit for the people below."

19.4　「今夫師者之相為不利者也，曰：將不勇，士不分[14]，兵不利，教
不習，師不眾，率不利和[15]，威不圉，害之不久，爭之不疾，
孫[16]之不強。植心不堅，與國諸侯疑。與國諸侯疑，則敵生慮，
而意羸矣[17]。偏具此物，而致從事焉，則是國家失卒，而百姓易
務也。今不嘗觀其說好攻伐之國？若使中興師，君子庶人也，必
且數千，徒倍十萬，然後足以師而動矣[18]。久者數歲，速者數
月，是士不暇聽治，士不暇治其官府，農夫不暇稼穡，婦人不暇
紡績織紝，則是國家失卒，而百姓易務也。然而又與其車馬之罷
弊也，幔幕帷蓋，三軍之用，甲兵之備，五分而得其一，則猶為
序疏[19]矣。然而又與其散亡道路，道路遼遠，糧食不繼傺，食飲
之時，廁役以此飢寒凍餒疾病，而轉死溝壑中者，不可勝計
也[20]。此其為不利於人也，天下之害厚矣。而王公大人，樂而行
之。則此樂賊滅天下之萬民也，豈不悖哉！今天下好戰之國，齊
晉楚越，若使此四國者得意於天下，此皆十倍其國之眾，而未能

14. "Knights" rather than the more usual "officers" is used for 士 here. Also, 分 is read as
    奮 following SYR.
15. In this clause, the translation follows the proposals of YY and LYS — 卒 for 率 and the
    omission of 利 as an erroneous duplication of 和.
16. Here 係 is read as 繫 or 縛 (SYR).
17. The somewhat free translation given for this sentence follows the reading of "與國" as
    "友邦" (e.g. LYS), WHB's rearrangement of "敵生慮" to "生敵慮" and the reading of
    羸 as 弱 (e.g. Z&Q).
18. In this statement, 君子 is read as 賢良 (e.g. Z&Q), 數百 is supplied after 君子 (SYR),
    庶人 is taken as 庶子 on the basis of the earlier 尚賢 chapters, and 徒 is read as 步兵
    (YTY).
19. Here 序疏 is emended 厚餘 (多餘 — SYR).
20. There are several issues in this sentence as follows: (i) 者 is added after the first
    "道路". (ii) On 傺, YY has this note:"疑墨子原文本作'糧食不傺'，不傺，即不接
    也。" LSL takes 傺 as superfluous and simply reads "不繼". (iii) In the clause "食飲
    之時"，之 is emended to 不 (e.g. LSL, Z&Q). (iv) 廁役 is taken as 廝役 (WYZ).

19.4 "Nowadays, when armies consider what is not of benefit, they list the following: A general who is not brave, knights who are not determined, weapons that are not sharp, training that is inadequate, a force that is not substantial, soldiers that are not harmonious, ill-treatment that is not resisted, a siege that is not sustained, a conflict that is not swift, and a force without strong cohesion. [Further], if resolve is not firm, the feudal lords of allied states start to waver, and, if this is the case, then it will give rise to enemy plans and weaken the determination of [the defending forces]. If all these adverse factors exist yet the state still goes ahead [with military activity], it will lose its soldiers and the ordinary people will lose their livelihood. Now why not look at this from the viewpoint of a state that favours attacking and reducing? Even if it is to launch a campaign on a moderate scale, the worthy men must number several hundred, the sons of officials must number several thousand and the ordinary foot-soldiers must number several tens of thousands. Then there is enough for an army to go forth. A protracted campaign lasts several years, a swift campaign lasts several months. In either case, superiors do not have the time to attend to government, officers do not have the time for their official duties, farmers do not have the time to sow and harvest, women do not have the time to spin and weave, and so the state loses soldiers and the ordinary people lose their livelihood. Furthermore, if you think about the wearing out and destruction of horses and carts, and the materials for the army's tents, and what the 'three armies' use in terms of arms and weapons, if one part in five remains, it is a lot. And not only this, but consider also those who are scattered or lost on the road because the road is long and supplies are not maintained. They do not eat and drink at the proper time, so due to this the serving men who become ill through hunger and cold and are rolled into ditches and gullies to die cannot be counted. This is not of benefit to the people and the harm to the world is substantial. Yet kings, dukes and great men still favour it and do it. This is to favour injuring and destroying the ten thousand people of the world. How is this not perverse? At the present time, the states in the world that love warfare are Qi, Jin, Chu and Yue. If these four states were to realise their ambitions within the world, they would all increase the people of their states tenfold and still [the people] would not be

食其地也。是人不足而地有餘也。今又以爭地之故,而反相賊也,然則是虧不足,而重有餘也。」

19.5　今遝[21] 夫好攻伐之君,又飾其說以非子墨子曰:「以攻伐之為不義,非利物[22] 與?昔者禹征有苗,湯伐桀,武王伐紂,此皆立為聖王,是何故也?」子墨子曰:「子未察吾言之類,未明其故者也。彼非所謂攻,謂誅也。昔者三苗大亂,天命殛之,日妖宵出,雨血三朝,龍生於廟,犬哭乎市,夏冰,地坼及泉,五穀變化,民乃大振。高陽乃命玄宮,禹親把天之瑞令,以征有苗。四電誘祇,有神人面鳥身,若瑾以侍,扼矢有苗之祥,苗師大亂,後乃遂幾[23]。禹既已克有三苗,焉磨為山川,別物上下,卿制大極[24],而神民不違,天下乃靜。則此禹之所以征有苗也。」

---

21. There is general agreement that in this statement 遝 should be read as 逮.
22. 物 here is understood as 事 — see, for example, Z&Q.
23. This is also a contentious sentence. In the translation, the first clause follows SYR's emendation of "四電誘祇" to "雷電誖 (勃) 震" — see also Z&Q. The second clause follows WHB and Z&Q.
24. "卿制大極" is taken as "鄉 (饗) 制四極" with 饗 in the sense of 享有 — see SYR, Z&Q.

able to eat what the land produced. This is a case of there being not enough people and too much land. Now they still contend for the sake of land, opposing and harming each other. This, then, is to neglect what there is not enough of and give importance to what there is excess of."

19.5   Nowadays those rulers who favour offensive warfare also embellish their arguments in order to refute Master Mo Zi by saying: "Do you take offensive warfare to be unrighteous and not to be beneficial in affairs? In former times, Yu reduced the You Miao,[i] Tang overthrew Jie, and King Wu overthrew Zhou, yet they are all established as being sage kings. How do you account for this?"

Master Mo Zi replied: "You have not considered the category of my words nor have you understood their basis. What they did is not called 'attack', it is called 'punishment'. In former times, the San Miao were in great disorder and Heaven decreed their destruction. The sun was strange and came forth at night. For three days it rained blood. Dragons appeared in the temples. Dogs cried in the market places. There was ice during summer and the earth cracked so that springs welled up. The five grains underwent change and the people were greatly alarmed. Heaven issued its decree to Yu at the Xuan Palace[ii] and Yu himself took hold of Heaven's imperial tablet in order to attack the You Miao. Thunder and lightning suddenly appeared and there was a spirit with the face of a man and the body of a bird which, with great deliberation, took hold of an arrow and shot the Miao general. The Miao army was thrown into great confusion. Not long after that the Miao people were in decline. After Yu had subdued the You San Miao, he separated the mountains and rivers, made division into high and low, offered sacrifices to regulate the four regions, and created harmony between spirits and people. The world was then at peace. This was why Yu reduced the You Miao."

---

i.   有苗 was an ancient term for the Miao 苗 minority, as was 三苗 — see 9.9 note iv, p. 77 and 《書經 · 大禹謨》, LCC, vol. 3, p. 64.

ii. There are several proposed modifications to overcome the historical difficulties of this statement as reflected in YPM's note 1, p. 111. The translation is based on SYR's version. See WYJ, note 73, p. 230 for other versions.

19.6　「遝至乎夏王桀，天有酷命，日月不時，寒暑雜至，五穀焦死，鬼呼國，鶴鳴十夕餘[25]。天乃命湯於鑣宮：『用受夏之大命，夏德大亂，予既卒其命於天矣，往而誅之，必使汝堪之[26]。』湯焉敢奉率其眾，是以鄉有夏之境，帝乃使陰暴毀有夏之城。少少有神來告曰：『夏德大亂，往攻之，予必使汝大堪之。予既受命於天，天命融隆火，於夏之城間西北之隅。』湯奉桀眾以克有〔夏〕，屬諸侯於薄，薦章天命，通於四方，而天下諸侯莫敢不賓服[27]。則此湯之所以誅桀也。」

19.7　「遝至乎商王紂，天不序[28]其德，祀用失時。兼夜中，十日雨土於薄[29]，九鼎遷止[30]，婦妖宵出，有鬼宵吟，有女為男，天雨肉，棘生乎國道，王兄自縱也[31]。赤鳥銜珪，降周之岐社，曰：『天命周文王伐殷有國。』泰顛來賓，河出綠圖，地出乘黃。武王踐功，

---

25. There are several minor points in this sentence as follows: (i) 酷 is substituted for the unknown character 告 with the 車 radical (SYR) — but see also WYJ who has 誥 (note 83, p. 232). (ii) 雜 is read as 亂. (iii) 於 is inserted after 呼 in the clause "鬼呼國" (WNS).
26. There is some doubt about this supposed statement by Heaven. SYR takes it to be an erroneous displacement from the statement by the spirit — see WYJ, note 90, p. 233. Following Qiu Shan, 堪 is read as 戡.
27. In this sentence, 夏 is supplied after 克有 (SSX) and 薄 is taken as 亳, a place name — see WYJ's detailed note 97, p. 234.
28. There is dissatisfaction with 序. YY proposes 宇 and WNS 順 — see LYS (note 27, p. 151) for detailed discussion.
29. In the translation I have followed WYJ's version of this problematic sentence. His proposed version reads: "兼夜十日，雨土於亳" — see note 103, pp. 235–236.
30. 止 here is taken as 址.
31. Translation of the final clause follows WNS whose note reads: "'兄'與'況'同。況，益也。"

19.6 "When it came to the Xia king, Jie, Heaven issued a stern decree. The sun and moon did not rise and set at the right time, cold and heat were disordered to an extreme degree, the five grains were scorched and died, ghosts called out in the country, and cranes cried unceasingly for more than ten nights. Heaven then gave its command to Tang at the Biao Palace: 'You must receive the great decree of Xia. The virtue of Xia is in severe disorder and I have already withdrawn its mandate from Heaven, so to go and punish them I must send you to subdue them.' Tang then dared to lead forth his forces and attack the regions of Xia. The Supreme Lord sent a spirit under cover of darkness to destroy the cities of Xia and after a short time the spirit came to inform [Tang], saying: 'The virtue of Xia is in severe disorder so go and attack them. I must send you to subdue them. I have already received the decree from Heaven and Heaven has ordered that [Zhu] Rong[iii] bring down fire on the north-west corner of the Xia capital.' Tang then led Jie's masses to subdue Xia and gathered the feudal lords at Bo to make clear Heaven's decree and promulgate it to the four regions. And among the feudal lords of the world there was none who dared not to submit to him. This, then, was how Tang punished Jie."

19.7 "When it came to the Shang king, Zhou, Heaven did not approve of his morality. Sacrifices did not accord with the time. For ten nights in succession the sun shone and it rained earth at Bo. The nine tripods (*ding*) moved from their bases, strange women came forth at night, there were ghosts lamenting at night, there were women who became men, the heavens rained flesh, thorny brambles grew on the nation's roads (national highway), and the king himself became increasingly self-indulgent. A red bird, holding in its beak the imperial jade, alighted on the Zhou altar at Qi [Shan] and proclaimed Heaven had decreed that King Wen of Zhou should overthrow Yin and take possession of the state.[iv] Tai Dian came back, the (Yellow) River brought forth the chart, and

---

iii. Zhu Rong 祝融 was an ancient god of fire.

iv. For further details see WYJ's notes 110 and 111, pp. 237–238.

夢見三神曰：『予既沈漬殷紂於酒德[32]矣，往攻之，予必使汝大堪之。』武王乃攻狂夫，反商之周，天賜武王黃[33]鳥之旗。王既已克殷，成帝之來[34]，分主諸神，祀紂先王，通維四夷，而天下莫不賓，焉襲湯之緒，此既武王之所以誅紂也。若以此三聖王者觀之，則非所謂攻也，所謂誅也。」

19.8   則夫好攻伐之君，又飾其說以非子墨子曰：「子以攻伐為不義，非利物與？昔者楚熊麗始討[35]此睢山之間，越王繄虧，出自有遽，始邦於越。唐叔與呂尚邦齊晉。此皆地方數百里，今以并國之故，四分天下而有之。是故何也？」子墨子曰：「子未察吾言之

32. There is general acceptance of the reading of 食 for 德 — see, for example, Z&Q.
33. Some commentators emend 黃 to 皇 (e.g. LSL, Z&Q).
34. 來 is read as 賚.
35. Following BY, 討 here is taken as 封.

the land brought forth *cheng-huang*.[v] King Wu continued his achievement. In a dream, he saw three spirits who said: 'We have already 'drowned' Zhou of Yin in wine and food. Go and attack him. We will certainly see to it that you overcome him.' Wu then attacked the dissolute man, replaced Shang with Zhou, and Heaven gave King Wu the phoenix banner. After he had already completely subdued the Yin, he received the full mandate as Son of Heaven. He divided the responsibilities for sacrifices to the gods among the feudal lords and (himself) made sacrifice to Zhou's first king (Cheng Tang 成湯). He gave notice of this to the four barbarous tribes so that within the world none did not submit. Thus he became the successor to the line of Tang. This was, in fact, King Wu's way of punishing Zhou so, if it is considered from the point of view of the three sage kings, it is not what is called attack. It is what is called punishment."

19.8   Then those rulers who favour attacking and reducing (other states) also embellish their arguments to refute Master Mo Zi, asking: "Do you take attacking and reducing to be unrighteous and not beneficial in affairs? Formerly, Xiong Li of Chu was first enfeoffed with the region between the Sui Mountains. The Yue king, Yi Kui, came out from Youju and first founded a country at Yue. Tang Shu and Lü Shang founded Qi and Jin (respectively). These were all (initially) regions of several hundred *li*. Now, by reason of their annexation of states, the four have divided all under Heaven and possess it. Why is this?"[vi]

---

v.   Tai Dian 泰顛 was a notable minister under King Wen — see, for example, the《書經 · 君奭》LCC, vol. 3, pp. 474–486, particularly p. 481. Regarding the "chart", 綠 is read as 籙. The *cheng-huang* 乘黃 was a form of supernatural animal — see WYJ, note 115, p. 238.

vi.   With respect to the four kingdoms, as SSX has pointed out, in Mo Zi's time the four kingdoms of Chu (Jing) 楚 (荊), Yue 越, Qi 齊 and Jin 晉 were pre-eminent. Traditionally, it was said that in the early days (e.g. the time of Yu) there were ten thousand kingdoms, and at the time of Tang more than three thousand. BY draws attention to the LSCQ (19/4.4, K&R pp. 489–490). The individuals mentioned are as follows: Xiong Li 熊麗 of Chu served King Wen — see *Shi Ji* 40 (vol. 5, p. 1691). Yi Kui 緊觭 was, as stated, a Yue king. Nothing much else seems to be known about him — see WYJ note 132, p. 241. Tang Shu 唐叔 is Tang Shuyu 唐叔虞, a son of Wu Wang — see *Shi Ji* 39 (vol. 5, pp. 1635–1636. Lü Shang 呂尚 is also known as Grand Duke

類，未明其故者也。古者天子之始封諸侯也，萬有餘，今以并國之故，萬國有餘皆滅，而四國獨立。此譬猶醫之藥萬有餘人，而四人愈也，則不可謂良醫矣。」

19.9 則夫好攻伐之君又飾其說曰：「我非以金玉，子女，壤地為不足也，我欲以義名立於天下，以德求[36]諸侯也。」子墨子曰：「今若有能以義名立於天下，以德求諸侯者，天下之服可立而待也。夫天下處攻伐久矣，譬若傅子之為馬然[37]。今若有能信效先利天下諸侯者，大國之不義也，則同憂之；大國之攻小國也，則同救之；小國城郭之不全也，必使修之；布粟之絕，則委之[38]；幣帛不足，則共之[39]。以此效大國，則小國之君說[40]，人勞我逸，則我甲兵強。寬以惠，緩易急，民必移。易攻伐以治我國，攻必

---

36. 求 is BY's proposal, both here and in the following sentence, and followed by most modern editors. WYJ, however, retains 來 — see his notes 141 and 142, p. 243.

37. The translation of this sentence depends on CYX's reading of 處 as 苦 and SYR's reading of 傅 as 孺 (or WNS's reading as 童子 — see *Mozi* 46). See also WYJ's detailed note 143, p. 243 on 傅 / 傳.

38. Here 之絕 is read as 乏絕 (WNS) and 委 as 輸 in the sense of 供應 (Z&Q).

39. 共 is taken as 供 — see, for example, LYS.

40. The translation of this sentence depends on the following: (i) Reading 效 as 交 (SYR). (ii) Adding the 11 characters "則大國之君說，以此效小國" after 大國 as proposed by ZCY, although not all modern editors accept this addition — see, for example, LSL. (iii) Reading 說 as 悅.

Master Mo Zi replied: "You have not considered the category of my words nor have you understood the reasons for them. In ancient times, when the Son of Heaven first enfeoffed the feudal lords, there were more than ten thousand of them. Now, because of the annexation of states, more than ten thousand states have all been destroyed and four states alone are established. This is like a doctor treating more than ten thousand people and curing only four. He could not, then, be called a good doctor."

19.9 But those rulers who favour attacking and reducing [other states] further elaborate their arguments, saying: "It is not that we consider our gold and jade, our sons and daughters, and our fertile land to be insufficient. We wish to be established in the world through righteousness and fame and we wish to attract the feudal lords through virtue."

Master Mo Zi said: "Now, if there was one who was able to establish himself in the world through righteousness and reputation and attract the feudal lords through virtue, the world's submission would be immediate and expected. The world is wearied by prolonged attack and reduction like a young boy playing at being a horse. Nowadays, if there were feudal lords in the world who were able to establish good faith in their dealings and gave primacy to benefit, then, when a great state was not righteous, they would join in grieving for it. When a great state attacked a small state, they would join in rescuing it. When the inner and outer city walls of a small state were incomplete, they would join in repairing them. If cloth and grain were deficient, they would supply them. If money was insufficient, they would provide it. If there was this kind of association with a great state, then the ruler of the great state would be pleased. If there was this kind of association with a small state, then the ruler of the small state would be pleased. If the other's [forces] were weary and our [forces] were rested, then our army would be stronger. If they

---

Wang of Lü — see K&R, p. 776 for numerous references in the LSCQ and also *Shi Ji* 32, vol. 5, pp. 1477–1479. For several issues relating to these people as well as their identification see particularly WYJ, notes 131–135, pp. 240–242.

倍[41]。量我師舉之費，以爭諸侯之斃，則必可得而序利焉[42]。督以正[43]，義其名，必務寬吾眾，信吾師，以此授[44]諸侯之師，則天下無敵矣，其為〔利天〕[45]下不可勝數也。此天下之利，而王公大人不知而用，則此可謂不知利天下之巨務矣。」

19.10 是故子墨子曰：「今且天下之王公大人士君子，中情將欲求興天下之利，除天下之害，當若繁為攻伐，此實天下之巨害也。今欲為仁義，求為上士，尚欲中聖王之道，下欲中國家百姓之利，故當若非攻之為說，而將不可不察者此也。」

---

41. There is general agreement that 攻 in the second clause should be read as 功 in the sense of 功效.
42. Uncertainty remains regarding this sentence, involving particularly 爭, 斃 and 序 — see, for example, WYJ, notes 152 and 153, pp. 244–245. The version given follows Z&Q who include WNS's note that "序利" should be taken as "厚利".
43. In this clause, 督 is taken as 率 and 正 as 正道 (e.g. LSL).
44. 授 is taken as 援 in the sense of 援助 (SYR).
45. Added following SSX.

were treated liberally and with kindness, and if what was relaxed replaced what was pressing, the people would certainly be compliant. If attack and reduction were replaced by good order in our state, the efficacy would certainly be multiplied. If we calculated the cost involved in raising an army to protect against the evils of the feudal lords, then [we could see that we] would certainly be able to obtain substantial benefit (from avoidance of warfare). If we led the people along the right path, established a reputation for righteousness, and invariably acted liberally towards our populace as well as training our forces with sincerity, and in this way supported the feudal lords, then it would be possible to have no enemies in the world. This would be of incalculable benefit to the world. And, since it would be [of such] benefit to the world, if kings, dukes and great officers do not know and employ it, then they may be spoken of as not knowing a major factor in benefiting the world."

19.10 For this reason, Master Mo Zi said: "At the present time, kings, dukes, great officers, officers and gentlemen of the world genuinely seek to further the world's benefits and eliminate its harms, but they still frequently engage in offensive warfare. This is truly of enormous harm to the world. Now, if they wish to be benevolent and righteous, and seek to be superior officers who accord with the Way of the sage kings above and with the benefit of the ordinary people below, then the theory of condemnation of offensive warfare is something they will not be able to avoid considering."

20: 節用上

20.1　聖人為政一國，一國可倍也。[1] 大之為政天下，天下可倍也。其倍之，非外取地也，因其國家去其無用之費[2]，足以倍之。聖王為政，其發令興事，使民用財也，無不加用而為者，是故用財不費，民德[3] 不勞，其興利多矣。其為衣裘何？以為冬以圉[4] 寒，夏以圉暑。凡為衣裳之道，冬加溫，夏加清者，鮮且[5] 不加者去之。其為宮室何？以為冬以圉風寒，夏以圉暑雨，有盜賊[6] 加固者，鮮且不加者去之。其為甲盾五兵[7] 何？以為以圉寇亂盜賊，若有寇亂盜賊，有甲盾五兵者勝，無者不勝。是故聖人作為甲盾五兵。凡為甲盾五兵加輕以利，堅而難折者，鮮且不加者去之。其為舟車何？以為車以行陵陸，舟以行川谷，以通四方之利。凡

1. BY's note on this terse statement is generally accepted: "言利可倍".
2. "之費" is omitted by WYJ — see his detailed note 2, p. 247 on the whole clause.
3. Following modern commentators, 德 is read as 得 both here and subsequently. For example, Z&Q have "百姓不勞苦".
4. 圉 is read as 禦 (Z&Q).
5. The two characters, 芊 plus the rare character (ZWDCD #47057), which appear four times in this passage, have caused commentators some confusion. Suggestions include: (i) 則止 (HYX). (ii) 則取 (LSL). (iii) 鮮且 in the sense of 華美處處 (YY), this last being the version I have used. A very detailed discussion is provided by WYJ (note 11, pp. 249–250).
6. WYJ replaces "有盜賊" with "凡為宮室" — see his note 12, p. 251.
7. The five weapons 五兵 are bows and arrows (弓矢), spears (殳), lances (矛), spears (戈) and halberds (戟).

20: Moderation in Use I

20.1   When a sage governs a single state, that one state's [benefits] can be doubled. On a larger scale, when [a sage] governs the world, the world's [benefits] can be doubled.[i] His doubling [of benefits] does not come through acquiring land beyond the borders, but by doing away with useless expenditure in his own state. This is enough to double [benefits]. When a sage governs, in issuing edicts and promoting affairs, in employing the people and using materials, he does nothing that is not useful. For this reason, the use of resources is without waste, the people are not over-burdened, and the increase in benefit is considerable. Why does he make clothes and fur garments? To keep out the cold of winter and withstand the heat of summer. In general, the principle of making clothes is to provide warmth in winter and coolness in summer. What is merely decorative and doesn't add to these objectives, he eschews. Why does he make dwellings and houses? In order to keep out the wind and cold of winter and withstand the heat and rain of summer, and to provide protection against thieves and robbers. What is merely ornamental and doesn't add to these objectives, he eschews. Why does he make armour and shields and the five weapons? To withstand plunder and disorder due to thieves and robbers. If there is plunder and disorder due to thieves and robbers, those who have armour and shields and the five weapons can overcome them and those who don't cannot. This is the reason sages make armour and shields and the five weapons. In general, in making armour and shields and the five weapons, to increase lightness is beneficial, and they should be strong and hard to break. What is merely ornamental and doesn't add to these objectives, he eschews. Why does he make boats and carts? Carts are made to travel over hills and level ground whilst boats are made to travel on rivers and waterways, as ways of benefiting

---

i.   Reading 大 as 擴大 and understanding 利 as before.

為舟車之道，加輕以利者，鮮且不加者去之。凡其為此物也，無
不加用而為者，是故用財不費，民德不勞，其興利多矣。

20.2   有去大人之好聚珠玉，鳥獸，犬馬，以益衣裳，宮室，甲盾，五
兵，舟車之數，於數倍乎！[8] 若則不難〔倍〕[9]，故孰為難倍？唯人
為難倍。然人有可倍也。昔者聖王為法曰：『丈夫年二十，毋敢
不處家，女子年十五，毋敢不事人。』[10] 此聖王之法也。聖王既
沒，於民次[11]也，其欲蚤處家者，有所二十年處家。其欲晚處家
者，有所四十年處家。以其蚤與其晚相踐，後聖王之法十年。若
純三年而字，子生可以二三年矣。[12] 此不惟使民蚤處家，而可以
倍與？且不然已。

20.3   今天下為政者，其所以寡人[13]之道多。其使民勞，其籍斂[14]厚，
民財不足，凍餓死者不可勝數也。且大人唯毋興師以攻伐鄰國，
久者終年，速者數月，男女久不相見，此所以寡人之道也。與居

---

8. In this sentence 有 is read as 又 and 益 taken in the sense of 增加 — see, for example,
    Z&Q.
9. Added following WYJ.
10. See WYJ, notes 20–24, p. 252, for detailed discussion of this supposed edict with
    reference to the *Zhou Li, Han Feizi* and *Guo Yu*.
11. 次 is read as 恣 following SYR.
12. There are several issues with this sentence as follows: (i) 純 is read as 皆. (ii) 字 is taken
    as 生孩子. (iii) 子 and 生 are transposed. (iv) 年 is emended to 人 — see, for example,
    WYJ.
13. 寡 here is verbal, Z&Q giving the following paraphrase: "使人口減少".
14. Following WYZ, 籍斂 is read as 稅斂.

communication in the four directions. In general, in making boats and carts, lightness in weight is beneficial. What is merely ornamental, and doesn't add to this, he eschews. Overall, in making these things, if something does not add to use it is not done. This is why there is no wastage in the use of materials, the people are not overburdened, and the increase in benefit is considerable.

20.2 Again, if the great officers' love of accumulating pearls and jade, birds and animals, and dogs and horses is done away with in order to increase the numbers of clothes and garments, dwellings and houses, armour and shields, the five weapons and boats and carts, the numbers can be doubled. If, then, these are not difficult to double, what is it that is difficult to double? It is only the population that is difficult to double. Nevertheless, the population can be doubled. The sage kings of former times made a law stating: "When men are twenty years old, they must marry and have a family. When women are fifteen years old, they must take a husband." This was the law of the sage kings. But now the sage kings are no more and the people cast off restraint, so that those who wish to get married and have a family early do so at twenty, whilst those who wish to get married and have a family late do so at forty. In this way, the number of those marrying early is reduced by the number of those marrying late and vice versa with the result that the average age is ten years later than that of the sage kings' law. If a child is born every three years, in this period there would be [the addition of] two or three people. So is it possible to double [the population] without making people marry and have a family early? It is not.

20.3 Nowadays, those who conduct government in the world have many ways of reducing the population. They cause the people to be burdened with labour, their tax imposts are heavy, and materials for the people are insufficient, so that those dying of cold and hunger cannot be counted. Moreover, great officers raise armies to attack neighbouring states. Long [campaigns] last a whole year and short [campaigns] several months, so for long periods, men and women do not see each other. In this way the population is reduced. Those who are made sick by unsettled

處不安，飲食不時，作疾病死者，有與侵就援橐[15]，攻城野戰死
者，不可勝數。此不今[16]為政者，所以寡人之道數術而起與？聖
人為政，特無此，此不聖人為政[17]，其所以眾人之道亦數術而起
與？故子墨子曰：「去無用之費，聖王之道[18]，天下之大利也。」

---

15. There are several issues with this clause as follows: (i) 有 is read as 又 (SYR). (ii) Taking
    援 (in some texts written with the 人 radical) as 伏 (SYR). (iii) Understanding 橐 as a
    method of attack by fire. Thus, LSL has: "用以舉火攻城的武器" — see his note 4,
    p. 138. WYJ, however, says of the whole clause: "猶言進即援橐也" — see his note 33,
    pp. 253–254.
16. The emendation of 令 to 今 follows BY.
17. The text for the preceding nine characters is that given by WYJ and depends on the
    addition of a second 此 following SYR and CYX.
18. WYJ has the following text for this and the preceding clause: "去無用之務，行聖王之
    道。"

living conditions and irregular intake of food and drink, as well as those who are ambushed or injured in attacks by fire, or killed in assaults on cities, or battles on open ground, cannot be counted. Are these not several ways of reducing the population that have arisen through those who presently conduct government? Only when the sages governed was it not like this. When the sages governed, did not several ways of increasing the number of people also arise? Therefore, Master Mo Zi said: "Doing away with useless expenditure was the Way of the sage kings and was of great benefit to the world."

21: 節用中

21.1 子墨子言曰:「古者明王聖人,所以王天下,正諸侯者,彼其愛
民謹忠,利民謹厚,忠信相連,又示之以利,是以終身不饜,歿
世而不卷。[1] 古者明王聖人,其所以王天下,正諸侯者,此也。」

21.2 「是故古者聖王,制為節用之法曰:『凡天下群百工,輪車,鞼
鮑[2],陶,冶,梓匠,使各從事其所能。』曰:『凡足以奉給民用,
則止。』諸加費不加於民利者,聖王弗為。[3]」

21.3 「古者聖王制為飲食之法曰:『足以充虛繼氣,強股肱,〔使〕[4] 耳
目聰明,則止。不極五味之調,芬香之和,不致遠國珍怪異
物。』何以知其然?古者堯治天下,南撫交阯,北降[5] 幽都,東西

---

1. In this opening statement I have read 王 as 統 · and 正 as 匡正 following LYS and LSL,
    and have taken 彼 as referring to the enlightened rulers and sages. I have also read 饜
    as 滿足 (LYS, Z&Q), and 卷 as 倦 (SSX).
2. This is WNS's proposed emendation of the two characters that usually appear here —
    ZWDCD #43991 and 匏.
3. See WYJ, p. 255 and note 6, p. 257 for an alternative version of this sentence and the
    textual issues involved.
4. Added following WYJ — see his note 7, p. 257.
5. Following WNS 降 is read as 際.

21: Moderation in Use II

21.1   Master Mo Zi spoke, saying: "In ancient times, the way enlightened kings and sages unified the world and corrected the feudal lords was through their loving the people with great devotion and benefiting the people very substantially. Devotion and trust are closely connected and are, moreover, made manifest by benefit. In their doing this, throughout their lives they were never satisfied and did not weary until they died. This, in ancient times, was how enlightened kings and sages unified the world and corrected the feudal lords."

21.2   "For this reason, the sage kings of ancient times, in establishing their rules for moderation in use, said: 'Throughout the world all the many artisans — wheelwrights and cart makers, tanners and salters, potters and metal workers, and carpenters — should each do the work they are capable of.' They [also] said: 'Everywhere they should provide enough for the people's use and then stop.' Anything over and above this is wasteful and does not add to the benefit of the people so the sage kings did not do it."

21.3   "In ancient times, the sage kings, in establishing their rules for drink and food, said: '[Provide] enough to fill what is empty and to aid the spirit, to give strength to the legs and arms, to make the ears and eyes sharp and keen, and then stop. Do not go to great lengths to blend the five flavours or to harmonise the various aromas and do not look to distant lands for things that are rare, strange and different.' How do I know this was so? In ancient times, when Yao brought order to the world, in the south he brought peace to Jiaozhi.[i] In the north he established the boundaries of Youdu.[ii] In the east and west he reached to where

---

i.   Jiaozhi 交阯 is taken as a general reference to the region south of Wuling 五嶺.

ii.   Youdu 幽都 or You Zhou 幽州 was one of the twelve 州 in ancient times, situated in what is now the northern part of Hebei.

至日所出入，莫不賓服。逮至其厚愛[6]，黍稷不二，羹胾不重，飯於土塯，啜於土形[7]，斗以酌。俛仰周旋威儀之禮，聖王弗為。」

21.4 「古者聖王制為衣服之法曰：『冬服紺緅之衣，輕且暖，夏服絺綌之衣，輕且清，則止。』諸加費不加於民利者，聖王弗為。」

21.5 「古者聖王為猛禽狡獸，暴人害民，於是教民以兵行，日[8]帶劍，為刺則入，擊則斷，旁擊而不折，此劍之利也。甲為衣則輕且利，動則兵且從，此甲之利也。[9]車為服重致遠，乘之則安，引之則利；安以不傷人，利則速至，此車之利也。古者聖王為大川廣谷之不可濟，於是利[10]為舟楫，足以將之則止。雖上者三公諸侯至，舟楫不易，津人不飾，此舟之利也。」

21.6 「古者聖王制為節葬之法曰：『衣三領，足以朽肉；棺三寸，足以

---

6. Most modern commentators read 厚愛 as 享受 following ZCY.

7. According to SYR 形 here should be taken as 鉶, a form of sacrificial vessel.

8. I have followed SYR in taking 日 as 廿, although some modern editors retain the former in the sense of 每天 (e.g. LSL).

9. In this sentence, 利 in the first instance is read as 方便, and 兵 is read as 便 via 弁 and 變 (SYR).

10. As WNS observed, 利 here seems out of place and probably should be read as 制.

the sun rises and sets, and there was nowhere that did not submit
[to his rule]. When it came to what he accepted and received, it
was not two kinds of grain or large pieces of meat. He ate from a
simple bowl, drank from a simple cup, and took wine from a ladle.
As for the ceremonial forms of bowing, walking and deportment,
the sage kings did not practise them."

21.4 "In ancient times, the sage kings, in establishing their rules for
clothes and garments, said: 'In winter, make clothes that are
purple or brown in colour, and light as well as warm. In summer,
make clothes that are of fine and coarse linen, and light as well as
cool, and then stop.' Anything over and above this is wasteful and
does not add to the benefit of the people so the sage kings did not
do it."

21.5 "In ancient times, because the people were being injured and
harmed by fierce and cunning animals, the sage kings taught them
to carry weapons when they went out and about, saying [they
should] wear a sword which pierced when used for stabbing and
cut when used for striking, and did not itself break when struck.
These are the benefits of a sword. When armour is worn it should
be light and convenient and allow ease of movement. These are
the benefits of armour. Carts are for the purpose of carrying heavy
things over a distance. When mounted they should be safe and
when drawn they should be convenient. Safe insofar as they do not
injure people and convenient insofar as they reach [their
destination] quickly. These are the benefits of carts. In ancient
times, the sage kings, because there were great rivers and wide
ravines that could not be crossed, devised boats and oars which
served their purpose but nothing more. Even if those above such as
[one of] the 'Three Dukes', or a feudal lord came, the boats and
oars did not change and the boatman did not decorate them. These
are the benefits of boats."

21.6 "In ancient times, the sage kings established their rules for
moderation in funerals, saying: 'The [burial] garments should be
of three kinds, sufficient for decaying flesh. The coffin should be
three *cun* [thick], sufficient for decaying bones. The hole for the
grave should not be so deep as to reach water, but deep enough for

朽骸；堀穴深不通於泉，流不發洩則止。[11] 死者既葬，生者毋久
喪用哀。』」

21.7 「古者人之始生，未有宮室之時，因陵丘堀穴而處焉。[12] 聖王慮
之，以為堀穴曰：『冬可以辟風寒。』[13] 逮夏，下潤濕，上熏烝，
恐傷民之氣。於是作為宮室而利。」然則為宮室之法將奈何哉？
子墨子言曰：「其旁可以圉風寒，上可以圉雪霜雨露，其中蠲
潔，可以祭祀，宮牆足以為男女之別則止。諸加費不加民利者，
聖王弗為。」

22: 節用下：闕

23: 節葬上：闕

24: 節葬中：闕

---

11. In this sentence, 領 is read as 件, 堀 as 窟, and 流 as 臭 (BY).
12. In this sentence, 宮 is read as 房, 因 is read as 愚, and 堀穴 is read as 挖洞, all following
    Z&Q.
13. The ending of the statement attributed to the sage kings here also follows Z&Q. Other
    modern editors (e.g. LYS, LSL) take it to end after 氣.

the stench not to escape, and that is all. Once the dead are buried, the living should not mourn for a long period'."

21.7 "Ancient times, when people first came into being, were times when there were not yet buildings and houses, so they relied on digging out holes in mounds and hills and living in them. The sage kings, in their contemplations, thought about this digging out and said: 'During winter it would be possible to avoid the wind and rain in this way.' But when summer comes, there would be dampness and moisture below, and steam and vapour above, which they feared would harm the people's spirits. Therefore, they created buildings and houses that were beneficial." So, then, what were their rules for making buildings and houses? Master Mo Zi spoke, saying: "What is at the sides should be able to keep out wind and cold. What is above should be able to keep out snow, frost, rain and dew. What is within should be clean and pure so it can be used for prayers and offerings. The inner walls of the buildings should be adequate to maintain the proper separation between men and women. That is all. Anything over and above this is wasteful and does not add to the benefit of the people, so the sage kings did not do it."

22: Moderation in Use III: Lost

23: Moderation in Funerals I: Lost

24: Moderation in Funerals II: Lost

25: 節葬下

25.1   子墨子言曰：「仁者之為天下度也，辟[1]之無以異乎孝子之為親度也。今孝子之為親度也，將奈何哉？曰，親貧則從事乎富之，人民寡則從事乎眾之，眾亂則從事乎治之。當其於此也，亦有力不足，財不贍，智不智，然後已矣[2]。無敢舍[3]餘力，隱謀遺利[4]，而不為親為之者矣。若三務者，孝子之為親度也，既若此矣。雖仁者之為天下度，亦猶此也。曰，天下貧則從事乎富之，人民寡則從事乎眾之，眾而亂則從事乎治之。當其於此，亦有力不足，財不贍，智不智，然後已矣。無敢舍餘力，隱謀遺利，而不為天下為之者矣。若三務者，此仁者之為天下度也，既若此矣。」

25.2   「今逮至昔者三代聖王既沒，天下失義，後世之君子，或以厚葬久喪以為仁也，義也，孝子之事也。或以厚葬久喪以為非仁義，非孝子之事也。曰二子者，言則相非，行即相反，皆曰：『吾上

---

1. Generally accepted as 譬 following BY.
2. I have rendered the phrase "然後已矣" rather freely as "he has done what he can". Other translators such as YPM and BW in effect ignore it. Z&Q equate 已 with 止.
3. Taken as 捨 by modern commentators.
4. There is some uncertainty about this rather terse phrase. Modern commentators generally follow SYR in its interpretation. LSL, for example, has: "隱藏謀慮，遺棄財利。"

25: Moderation in Funerals III

25.1   Master Mo Zi spoke, saying: "A benevolent man's planning for the world is in no way different from a filial son's planning for his parents. Now what will a filial son's planning for his parents consist of? I say that, if his parents are poor, he works to make them rich. If the people [of his family] are few, he works to make them numerous. If they are numerous but in disorder, he works to bring them to order. When he has done this, even if his strength is insufficient, if the materials are not enough, if his wisdom is inadequate, he has done what he can. But while ever he has untapped strength, hidden resources or remaining materials, he cannot do otherwise than use them for his parents. It is by discharging these three responsibilities that the filial son makes provision for his parents. The case of the benevolent man making provision for the world is just like this. I say that, if the world is poor, he works to make it rich. If the people [of the world] are few, he works to make them numerous. If they are numerous but in disorder, he works to bring them to order. When he has done this, even if his strength is insufficient, if the materials are not enough, if his wisdom is inadequate, he has done what he can. But while ever he has untapped strength, hidden resources or remaining materials, he cannot do otherwise than use them for the world. It is by discharging these three responsibilities that the benevolent man makes provision for the world."

25.2   "Now, when we come to the present time, the sage kings of the Three Dynasties of former times are already dead and the world is bereft of righteousness. Among gentlemen of later generations, some take lavish funerals and prolonged mourning to be benevolent and righteous and to be the duty of the filial son, whereas others take lavish funerals and prolonged mourning to be contrary to benevolence and righteousness and not to be the duty of the filial son. So for these two groups, their words are mutually contradictory and their actions mutually opposed. [Yet] both say:

祖述堯舜禹湯文武之道者也。』[5]而言即相非，行即相反，於此乎
後世之君子，皆疑惑乎二子者言也。」

25.3   「若苟疑惑乎之二子者言，然則姑嘗傳[6]而為政乎國家萬民而觀
之。計厚葬久喪，奚當此三利者〔哉〕[7]？我意[8]若使法其言，用其
謀，厚葬久喪實可以富貧眾寡，定危治亂乎，此仁也，義也，孝
子之事也，為人謀者不可不勸也。仁者將〔求〕[9]興之天下，誰賈[10]
而使民譽之，終勿廢也。意亦使法其言，用其謀，厚葬久喪實不
可以富貧眾寡，定危理亂乎，此非仁非義，非孝子之事也，為人
謀者不可不沮也。仁者將求除之天下，相廢而使人非之，終身勿
為。[11]」

25.4   「且故[12]興天下之利，除天下之害，令國家百姓之不治也，自古及
今，未嘗之有也。何以知其然也？今天下之士君子，將猶多皆疑
惑厚葬久喪之為中是非利害也。」故子墨子言曰：「然則姑嘗稽
之，今雖毋法執厚葬久喪者言，以為事乎國家。此存乎王公大人

---

5. In interpreting this sentence, I have followed Z&Q in reading 上 as 尚 in the sense of
    崇尚 and 祖述 as 效法 or 遵循.
6. On the issue of 傳 (taken as 轉 — e.g. LSL, Z&Q) or 傳 see WYJ, note 12, pp. 269–
    270.
7. CYX, followed by WYJ, has 哉 here as an emendation of 我 in the following sentence.
8. Read here and in the following instance as 抑.
9. Added, for example, by WYJ and LSL on the basis of the recurring similar statement.
10. According to SYR, 誰賈 should read 設置. I have followed modern commentators in
    accepting this.
11. In the form of this final sentence I have followed the modern editions of LSL and Z&Q.
    For a slightly different version see WYJ, p. 263.
12. Taken as 是故 by some (e.g. WYJ, LSL). I have retained 且 in the sense of 況且 (LYS,
    Z&Q).

'We are upholding and abiding by the Way of Yao, Shun, Yu, Tang, Wen and Wu.' Nevertheless, their words are mutually contradictory and their actions are mutually opposed. And because of this, the gentlemen of later generations are all in doubt and confusion regarding the two positions."

25.3   "If there is doubt and uncertainty regarding the statements of the two parties, then let us for the moment test them in terms of the conduct of government of states and their people, and consider them in this light. In evaluating elaborate funerals and prolonged mourning, how do they accord with these three benefits? Perhaps it is the case that, if we take their words as a model and make use of their plans, elaborate funerals and prolonged mourning really can make the poor rich and make the few many, resolve danger and bring order to disorder. If so, they are benevolent and righteous, and the duty of a filial son, and their use in planning for people must be encouraged. Those who are benevolent will seek to promote them in the world, establish them and cause the people to praise them, so forever they will not be done away with. Perhaps, on the other hand, if we take their words as a model and make use of their plans, elaborate funerals and prolonged mourning really cannot make the poor rich and the few many, or resolve danger and bring order to disorder. If so, they are not benevolent and not righteous, and not the duty of a filial son, and their use in planning for people must be resisted. Those who are benevolent will seek to do away with them in the world, set them aside and cause the people to oppose them, so forever they will not be used."

25.4   "Moreover, by promoting the world's benefits and eliminating its harms, there has never been, from ancient times to the present, a failure to bring order to the states and their people. How do we know this to be so? Nowadays, among the world's officers and gentlemen, there are still many who are doubtful and uncertain as to whether elaborate funerals and prolonged mourning are in accord with what is right or not, and whether they are beneficial or harmful." Therefore Master Mo Zi spoke, saying: "In this case then, let us for a moment try to examine the matter in the light of those who now uphold the idea of elaborate funerals and

有喪者，曰棺槨必重，葬埋必厚，衣衾必多，文繡必繁，丘隴必
巨；存乎匹夫賤人死者，殆竭家室；〔存〕[13] 乎諸侯死者，虛車[14]
府，然後金玉珠璣比乎身，綸組節約，車馬藏乎壙，又必多為屋
幕，鼎鼓几梴壺濫[15]，戈劍羽旄齒革，寢[16] 而埋之，滿意。若送
從，曰天子殺殉，眾者數百，寡者數十。將軍大夫殺殉，眾者數
十，寡者數人。」

25.5   「處喪之法將奈何哉？曰哭泣不秩聲翁[17]，縗絰[18] 垂涕，處倚盧，
寢苫枕塊[19]，又相率強不食而為飢，薄衣而為寒，使面目陷陬[20]，
顏色黧黑，耳目不聰明，手足不勁強，不可用也。又曰上士之操
喪也，必扶而能起，杖而能行，以此共三年。若法若言[21]，行若
道，使王公大人行此，則必不能蚤朝[22] *〔晏退，聽獄治政。使士

---

13. Added by several editors (e.g. WYJ, Z&Q) whilst LYS suggests 在.
14. This is taken to be 庫 — see, for example, Z&Q.
15. In this list, 梴 is read as 筵 and 濫 is taken to be a kind of vessel for liquid — see, for example, LYS.
16. WYZ proposes emendation to 挾.
17. In this statement, "不秩" is read as "沒有一定得時候" whilst 翁 is taken as 嗡 — see LYS.
18. Although I have rendered this "sackcloth and hemp" it may indicate a specific garment — see LYS for a description.
19. Generally given in its ancient form — ZWDCD #1836.
20. This is the generally accepted emendation of the rare character pronounced *ge* on which the ZWDCD has "義未詳" — see #42782 and WYJ, note 45, p. 274.
21. In this clause the first 若 is read as 假如 and the second 若 as 其, the "they" being those who advocate the practice of elaborate funerals and prolonged mourning — see, for example, Z&Q.
22. It is generally agreed, following SYR, that there is a lacuna in the text here. The added 16 characters in parentheses and marked by asterisks are those given by LYS.

prolonged mourning, taking them to be a service to the state. If
these views are maintained, in the case of those remaining when a
king, duke or great officer dies, they say that the inner and outer
coffins must be heavy, the funeral itself must be elaborate, the
funeral garments must be numerous, the markings and embroidery
must be complicated, and the burial structure must be large. In the
case of those remaining when an ordinary, lowly person dies, the
family's resources are almost exhausted. In the case of those
remaining when a feudal lord dies, his armoury and storehouse
will be emptied after gold, jade, and regular and irregular pearls
[are used] to surround the body, silk of various sorts is bundled up,
and carriages and horses are interred in the tomb. There must also
be many domestic screens, tripods, drums, tables, mats, vessels
and basins as well as spears and swords, feathered banners, ivory
and hides placed around and buried to a satisfactory amount. With
regard to those who are sent to follow [the dead], in the case of the
Son of Heaven, the number killed and buried with him ranges
from several hundred at the most to several tens at the least. In the
case of a general or high-ranking officer, the number of people
killed and buried with him ranges from several tens at the most to
several at the least."

25.5 "What will be the procedure for those in mourning? It is said they
should wail and cry, make a sobbing sound at irregular intervals,
and wear sackcloth and hemp stained with tears. They should live
in a mourning hut with a straw mat for a bed and a clod of earth for
a pillow. They should also restrain each other from eating so as to
appear starving, and wear thin clothes so as to be cold. They
should make their appearance gaunt and wasted and their
countenance sallow and dark. Their ears and eyes should not hear
or see, and their hands and feet should be without strength as if
they cannot be used. It is also said, in respect of the conduct of
mourning by high officers, that they must have support to be able
to rise and a stick to be able to walk, and in this way carry out their
duties for three years. If their statements are taken as the standard,
and conduct follows their way so that kings, dukes and great
officers act like this, then certainly they will not be able to come
to court early and retire late, carry out trials, and bring order to
government. If officers and high officers act like this, then they

大夫行此，則不能治〕＊五官六府²³，辟草木，實倉廩。使農夫行
此，則必不能夙出夜入，耕稼樹藝。使百工行此，則必不能修舟
車為器皿矣。使婦人行此，則必不能夙興夜寐，紡績織絍。細²⁴
計厚葬，為多埋賦之財者也。計久喪，為久禁從事者也。財以成
者，扶而埋之。後得生者，而久禁之，以此求富，此譬猶禁耕而
求穫也，富之說無可得焉。是故求以富〔國〕²⁵家，而既已不可
矣。」

25.6   「欲以眾人民，意者²⁶可邪？其說又不可矣。今唯無以厚葬久喪者
為政²⁷，君死，喪之三年；父母死，喪之三年；妻與後子²⁸死
者，五²⁹皆喪之三年；然後伯父，叔父，兄弟，孽子其³⁰；族人³¹
五月；姑姊甥舅皆有月數。則毀瘠必有制矣，使面目陷陬，顏色
黧黑，耳目不聰明，手足不勁強，不可用也。又曰上士操喪也，
必扶而能起，杖而能行，以此共三年。若法若言，行若道，苟其
飢約，又若此矣，是故百姓冬不仞寒，夏不仞暑，作疾病死者，

---

23. For the "Five Offices" and the "Six Departments" see the *Li Ji*, "Qu Li"《禮記·曲禮》，
     SSJZS, vol. 5, p. 81.
24. 細 is taken as superfluous following YY.
25. Supplied in some texts — e.g. LYS, WYJ.
26. Throughout this argument "意者" is read as "抑或" in the sense of "或" — see, for
     example, LYS and Z&Q.
27. On this sentence, and in particular 唯惟無, see WYJ, notes 65 and 66, p. 276.
28. 後子 is taken to be the eldest son by the legal wife. BY has: "嗣子嫡也".
29. There is general acceptance that 五 should be emended to 又.
30. 其 here is taken as 期, indicating a period of one year.
31. LYS suggests that this phrase should read "戚族人" based on *Mozi* 39 and has the
     following note: "戚族人就是近支的同族人。"

will certainly not be able to bring order to the 'Five Offices' and the 'Six Departments', develop grasslands and woods, and fill the public granaries. If farmers act like this, then they will certainly not be able to go out early and come back late, plough and plant, and cultivate trees. If the hundred artisans act like this, then they will certainly not be able to repair boats and carriages, and make utensils and vessels. If women act like this, then they will certainly not be able to get up early and go to bed late, and carry out their spinning and weaving. In considering elaborate funerals, there is the burial of much wealth. In considering prolonged mourning, there is protracted prevention of the conduct of affairs. Materials already produced are buried and there is a prolonged prevention of further production. To seek wealth in this way is like preventing ploughing but seeking to reap. As a method of bringing about wealth it cannot work. Therefore, to seek to enrich the state like this is altogether impossible."

25.6 "If the wish is to increase the number of people, is this perhaps possible? No, their theories again make it impossible. For suppose now that those who believe in elaborate funerals and prolonged mourning are those in charge of government. If the ruler dies, the mourning is three years. If a father or mother dies, the mourning is three years. If a wife or her eldest son dies, they also both require three years of mourning. After that, the period is one year for a father's older and younger brothers, for one's own older and younger brothers, and for sons other than the first. For close relatives within the clan the period is five months. For a father's sisters, one's older sisters, a sister's child, or a mother's brothers the period for all is several months. Then there are the regulations requiring [the mourners] to appear ravaged and emaciated, for their faces to appear gaunt and wasted, and their complexions sallow and dark. Their ears and eyes should not hear or see, and their hands and feet should be without strength as if they cannot be used. It is also said, in respect of the conduct of mourning by high officers, that they must have support to be able to rise and a stick to be able to walk, and in this way carry out their duties for three years. If their statements are taken as the standard, and if they act in this way, if they are starving and shrink from food like this, the ordinary people will not endure the winter's cold or the summer's

不可勝計也。此其為敗男女之交多矣。以此求眾，譬猶使人負劍
而求其壽也。眾之說無可得焉。是故求以眾人民，而既以不可
矣。」

25.7　「欲以治刑政，意者可乎？其說又不可矣。今唯無以厚葬久喪者
為政，國家必貧，人民必寡，刑政必亂。若法若言，行若道，使
為上者行此，則不能聽治；使為下者行此，則不能從事。上不聽
治，刑政必亂；下不從事，衣食之財必不足。若苟不足，為人弟
者，求其兄而不得，不弟弟[32]必將怨其兄矣；為人子者，求其親
而不得，不孝子必是怨其親矣；為人臣者，求之君而不得，不忠
臣必且亂其上矣。是以僻淫邪行之民，出則無衣也，入則無食
也，〔內積謀詬〕[33]，並為淫暴，而不可勝禁也。是故盜賊眾而治
者寡。夫眾盜賊而寡治者，以此求治，譬猶使人三還[34]而毋負己
也，治之說無可得焉。是故求以治刑政，而既已不可矣。」

---

32. According to Z&Q the first 弟 should be read as 悌.
33. This is given in all texts as "內續奚吾". From early commentators such as BY and WYZ on, this has been accepted as an error, the presumption being that the correct form is as above.
34. 還 is given here instead of the old form (ZWDCD #24019).

heat, and those who become ill and die will be uncountable. This will also greatly damage the relations between men and women. To seek to increase the number of people in this way is just like causing a man to fall on his sword while wishing him a long life. As a method of increasing the number of people it cannot work. Therefore, to seek to increase the population like this is altogether impossible."

25.7 "If the wish is to bring order to government, is this perhaps possible? No, again their methods make it impossible. Now suppose those who advocate elaborate funerals and prolonged mourning are in charge of government. The state will certainly be poor, its people will certainly be few, and its administration will certainly be disordered. If their statements are taken as the standard and they act in this way, causing those who are superiors to do this, they will not be able to attend to bringing about order. If it causes inferiors to do this, they will not be able to carry out their business. If those above do not attend to bringing about order, the administration will certainly be disordered. If those below do not carry out their business, the materials for clothing and food will certainly be insufficient. If they are insufficient, when a younger brother seeks help from an older brother he will not get it, so the younger brother will not behave like a younger brother should but will certainly be resentful towards his older brother. When a son seeks help from his parents he will not get it, so the son will be unfilial and will certainly be resentful towards his parents. When an official seeks help from his ruler he will not get it, so the official will be disloyal and will certainly bring disorder to his superior. This will bring about all manner of evil conduct in the people because, when they go out they will have no [adequate] clothing and when they come home they will have no food, so shame will build up within them giving rise to depravity and cruelty which cannot be overcome or prevented. For this reason, thieves and robbers will be numerous while those who are well ordered will be few. If thieves and robbers are numerous and those who are well ordered are few, to seek order under these circumstances is like asking a person to turn around three times without turning his back to you. As a method of bringing about order it cannot work. For this reason, to seek to bring order to the administration like this is altogether out of the question."

25.8　「欲以禁止大國之攻小國也，意者可邪？其説又不可矣。是故昔者聖王既沒，天下失義，諸侯力征。南有楚，越之王，而北有齊，晉之君，此皆砥礪其卒伍，以攻伐并兼為政於天下。是故凡大國之所以不攻小國者，積委多，城郭修，上下調和，是故大國不耆攻之；無積委，城郭不修，上下不調和，是故大國耆攻之。今唯無以厚葬久喪者為政，國家必貧，人民必寡，刑政必亂。若苟貧，是無以為積委也；若苟寡，是城郭溝渠者寡也[35]；若苟亂，是出戰不克，入守不固。此求禁止大國之攻小國也，而既已不可矣。」

25.9　「欲以干上帝鬼神之福，意者可邪？其説又不可矣。今唯無以厚葬久喪者為政，國家必貧，人民必寡，刑政必亂。若苟貧，是粢盛酒醴不淨潔也；若苟寡，是事上帝鬼神者寡也；若苟亂，是祭祀不時度也。今又禁止事上帝鬼神，為政若此，上帝鬼神，始得

---

35. I have not added 修 as the fourth character in this clause as some commentators suggest — see WYJ, note 91, p. 280. Four of the most recent editors (MBJ, LYS, LSL, Z&Q) do not include it.

25.8   "If the wish is to prevent large states attacking small states, is this perhaps possible? Again their methods do not work. The reason is that the sage kings of former times have already passed away, the world has lost righteousness and the feudal lords use force to make incursions. In the south, there are the kings of Chu and Yue, and in the north, there are the rulers of Qi and Jin. They all train up their troops to attack and annex [other states] and take control of the world. Now, in general, the reason why large states do not attack small states is because the latter have a large store of resources, have inner and outer city walls in good repair, and have superiors and subordinates who are in accord. Under these circumstances, large states do not like to attack them. If there is no store of reserves, if inner and outer city walls are not in good repair, and if superiors and subordinates are not in accord, large states do like to attack them. Now, if those who advocate elaborate funerals and prolonged mourning are conducting government, the state will certainly be poor, its people will certainly be few, and its administration will certainly be in disorder. If it is poor, there will be no means of accumulating resources. If [the people] are few, the inner and outer city walls and the ditches and watercourses will also be few. If it is in disorder, any military offence will be unsuccessful and any defence will not be strong. To seek to prevent large states attacking small states in this way is altogether out of the question."

25.9   "If the wish is to gain the blessings of the Supreme Lord and the ghosts and spirits, is it perhaps possible? No, their methods again will not do. Suppose now that those who believe in elaborate funerals and prolonged mourning are conducting government. The state will certainly be poor, its people will certainly be few, and the administration will certainly be in disorder. If it is poor, this means that the sacrificial grain and wine will not be pure. If its people are few, this means that those who can serve the Supreme Lord and the ghosts and spirits will be few. If the administration is in disorder, this means that sacrifices will not be carried out at the proper times. Now, if the service of the Supreme Lord and the ghosts and spirits is prevented because the government is like this, the Supreme Lord and the ghosts and spirits will, for a start, look down from above and ask themselves the question: 'Is it better for

從上撫³⁶之曰：『我有是人也，與無是人也，孰愈？』曰：『我有是
人也，與無是人也，無擇也。』則惟上帝鬼神降之罪厲之禍罰而
棄之，則豈不亦乃其所哉！」

25.10 「故古聖王制為葬埋之法，曰：『棺三寸，足以朽體，衣衾三領，
足以覆惡。以及其葬也，下毋及泉，上毋通臭，壟若參耕之
畝³⁷，則止矣。死者既以葬矣，生者必無久喪³⁸，而疾而從事，人
為其所能，以交相利也。』此聖王之法也。」

25.11 今執厚葬久喪者之言曰：「厚葬久喪，雖使不可以富貧眾寡，定
危治亂，然此聖王之道也。」子墨子曰：「不然，昔者堯北教乎八
狄，道死，葬蛩山之陰，衣衾三領，穀木之棺，葛以緘之，既犯
而後哭，滿埳無封。³⁹已葬，而牛馬乘之。舜西教乎七戎，道
死，葬南己之市，衣衾三領，穀木之棺，葛以緘之，已葬，而市

---

36. There is noted variation on the reading of 撫. Some, on the basis of the 《方言》, equate
it with 疾 (e.g. Z&Q, LSL) whilst others who provide a modern equivalent have "發
問" (e.g. LYS, MBJ). LSL offers "迫不及待".
37. LYS has the following note on "參耕之畝": "參即三字，耕地寬五寸叫做一伐，兩
伐叫做一耦。`三耦耕之畝`，是說墓地的寬廣，大約三尺的樣子。"
38. This is WYJ's text for this and the preceding clause. The variations concern 則 for 者，
已 for 以，and 哭 for 喪 and are exemplified by Z&Q's text.
39. In this sentence, 犯 is BY's emendation for the same character plus the 水 radical and
埳 is taken as 坎 (also BY). 犯 is taken as 窆.

us that these people exist or do not exist?' And they will say: 'Whether they exist or not makes no difference.' Then the Supreme Lord and the ghosts and spirits will bring down misfortune on them, and punish and abandon them. And why shouldn't this be so!"

25.10 "Therefore, the ancient sage kings formulated rules for carrying out funerals and burials, which stated: 'The coffin should be three *cun* [thick], sufficient for a decaying body. The burial garments should be three *ling* (layers), sufficient to encase the corpse. In carrying out the burial, [the coffin] should not reach water below and the stench should not leak through above. The burial mound should approximate to three *chi* and no more. Once the one who has died is already buried, those who are living must not mourn for long, but quickly return to their daily affairs, each doing what they are capable of in the pursuit of mutual benefit.' These were the rules of the sage kings."

25.11 Now the arguments of those who advocate lavish funerals and prolonged mourning say: "With regard to lavish funerals and prolonged mourning, although they cannot enrich the poor or make numerous the few, settle danger or bring order to disorder, they are, nevertheless, the Way of the sage kings."

Master Mo Zi said: "Not so. Formerly, when Yao went north to teach the eight *Di*, he died on the road and was buried on the north side of Mount Qiong.[i] His burial garments were of three layers and he had a plain wooden coffin tied up with vines. Only after the coffin was lowered into the ground was there weeping and the hole was just filled in without a burial mound. After the burial, oxen and horses crossed the grave. Shun went west to teach the seven *Rong* and died on the road. He was buried in the market place at Nanji.[ii] His burial garments were of three layers and he

---

i.　Also termed 邛山, this mountain is situated in what is now 濮縣 in 山東.

ii.　It is not known where Nanji was. Traditionally, it is said that Shun was buried at Jiuyi Mountain 九嶷山 in the Ningyuan district of Hunan. For a detailed discussion see WYJ, note 112, pp. 283–284.

人乘之。禹東教乎九夷，道死，葬會稽之山，衣衾三領，桐棺三寸，葛以縅之，絞之不合[40]，通之不埳[41]，土[42]地之深，下毋及泉，上毋通臭。既葬，收餘壤其上，壟若參耕之畝，則止矣。若以此若三聖王者觀之，則厚葬久喪果非聖王之道。故三王者，皆貴為天子，富有天下，豈憂財用之不足哉？以為如此葬埋之法。」

25.12　「今王公大人之為葬埋，則異於此。必大棺中棺，革闠三操，璧玉即具，戈劍鼎鼓壺濫，文繡素練，大鞅萬領，輿馬女樂皆具，曰必捶塗差通[43]，壟雖凡山陵[44]。此為輟民之事，靡民之財，不可勝計也，其為毋用若此矣。」是故子墨子曰：「鄉者，吾本言曰，意亦使法其言，用其謀，計厚葬久喪，請[45]可以富貧眾寡，定危治亂乎，則仁也，義也，孝子之事也，為人謀者，不可不勸也；

---

40. On this clause, LYS has: "是說絞束之而不密合。"
41. On this clause, LYS has: "是說雖通道而不為深埳。"
42. Here 土 is taken as 掘 — see, for example, LSL.
43. In this clause, 塗 is BY's emendation of the rare character (ZWDCD #5249 — where the only reference is to this passage) whilst 羡道 is SYR's proposal for 差通.
44. All commentators regard this clause as unsatisfactory. LSL has: "墳墓要高如山陵" as his gloss.
45. Here as elsewhere, 請 is read as 誠.

had a plain wooden coffin tied up with vines. After the burial, the people in the market place crossed the grave. Yu went east to teach the nine *Yi* and died on the road. He was buried at Guiji Mountain.[iii] His burial garments were of three layers and his coffin was of *tong* wood three *cun* thick and tied up with vines. The binding was not, however, close and, although there was a path [to the grave], it was not deeply dug. The depth of the excavated ground was such that it did not reach water below and did not leak any stench above. After the burial, the earth left over was collected above to create a mound of three *chi* in size and no more. So, if we look at this matter the way the three sage kings looked at it, then lavish funerals and prolonged mourning were certainly not the Way of the sage kings. But the three kings were all ennobled as Sons of Heaven and enriched by the possession of all under Heaven so how could they be anxious that the wealth available was not sufficient? It was just that they considered these to be the rules for funerals and graves."

25.12   "Nowadays, kings, dukes and great officers, in their conduct of funerals and burials, are different from this. There must be an outer and an inner coffin, embroidered hide in three layers, jade emblems and jade already prepared, spears, swords, tripods, drums, pots, vessels, embroideries and silks, and funeral garments in countless layers as well as carriages, horses, women and musicians all prepared. They say the ground must be beaten down to make a road [to the grave] and the burial mound should resemble a hill. The interference with the business of the people and the wastage of their wealth cannot be calculated. This constitutes the uselessness of these [funeral practices]." This is why Master Mo Zi said: "A little earlier what I originally said was that, if you take as rules their words and implement their plans and, in considering elaborate funerals and prolonged mourning, genuinely see that they can make the poor rich and the few many, can settle danger and bring order to disorder, then they are the business of those who are benevolent and righteous, and of filial

---

iii.   Guiji was situated in what is now Zhejiang Province. Again, for details see WYJ, note 116, p. 285.

意亦使法其言，用其謀，若人厚葬久喪，實不可以富貧眾寡，定危治亂乎，則非仁也，非義也，非孝子之事也，為人謀者，不可不沮也。」

25.13　「是故求以富國家，甚得貧焉；欲以眾人民，甚得寡焉；欲以治刑政，甚得亂焉；求以禁止大國之攻小國也，而既已不可矣；欲以干上帝鬼神之福，有得禍焉。上稽之堯舜禹湯文武之道而政[46]逆之，下稽之桀紂幽厲之事，猶合節[47]也。若以此觀，則厚葬久喪，其非聖王之道也。」

25.14　今執厚葬久喪者言曰：「厚葬久喪果非聖王之道，夫胡說中國之君子，為而不已，操而不擇[48]哉？」子墨子曰：「此所謂便其習而義其俗者也。昔者越之東有輆沐之國者，其長子生，則解而食之。謂之『宜弟』。其大父死，負其大母而棄之，曰鬼妻不可與居

---

46. In this instance, 政 is read as 正.
47. 合節 is taken as 符合 — see, for example, Z&Q.
48. The majority of Chinese commentators read 擇 in the sense of 釋 or 放棄 — see, for example, Z&Q.

sons, so, in formulating plans for the people, they must be encouraged. If, however, you take as rules their words and implement their plans and, in considering elaborate funerals and prolonged mourning, see that in reality they cannot make the poor rich and the few many, or settle danger and bring order to disorder, then they are not the business of those who are benevolent and righteous, nor of filial sons, so, in formulating plans for the people, they must be stopped."

25.13   "Because of this, although they seek to enrich the state, they greatly impoverish it. Although they seek to make the people many, they greatly reduce them in number. And, although they seek to bring order to administration, they bring extreme disorder to it. They seek to prevent the attacks of large states on small states, but they find, in the end, this is impossible. They seek to obtain good fortune from the Supreme Lord and the ghosts and spirits, but they get only misfortune. On a higher plane, if we examine the Way of Yao, Shun, Yu, Tang, Wen and Wu, [we see that] it was directly opposed to this. On a lower plane, if we examine the affairs of Jie, Zhou, You and Li, [we see that] they were in accord with this. Looked at in this way, elaborate funerals and prolonged mourning run contrary to the Way of the sage kings."

25.14   Now the arguments of those who adhere to elaborate funerals and prolonged mourning say: "If elaborate funerals and prolonged mourning are really not the Way of the sage kings, how do you account for the fact that the gentlemen of the central kingdom practise them and do not stop them, implement them and do not abandon them?" Master Mo Zi said: "This is what is called '[considering] one's habits convenient and one's customs righteous'. Formerly, to the east of Yue, there was the country of the Kaimu.[iv] When a first son was born, they cut him up and ate him. They called this 'fitting for the younger brother'. When the paternal grandfather died, they carried the maternal grandmother away and abandoned her, saying: 'We cannot live with a ghost's

---

iv.   Little is known of this place other than that it was an ancient state east of Yue. For discussion of the name in particular, see WYJ, note 146, p. 289.

處。此上以為政，下以為俗，為而不已，操而不擇，則此豈實仁義之道哉？此所謂便其習而義其俗者也。」

25.15 「楚之南有炎人國者，其親戚死，朽其肉而棄之，然後埋其骨，乃成為孝子。秦之西有儀渠之國者，其親戚死，聚柴薪而焚之，燻上，謂之登遐，然後成為孝子。此上以為政，下以為俗，為而不已，操而不擇，則此豈實仁義之道哉？此所謂便其習而義其俗者也。若以此若三國者觀之，則亦猶薄矣。若以中國之君子觀之，則亦猶厚矣。如彼則大厚，如此則大薄，然則葬埋之有節矣。」

25.16 故衣食者，人之生利也，然且猶尚有節；葬埋者，人之死利也，夫何獨無節於此乎？子墨子制為葬埋之法曰：「棺三寸，足以朽骨；衣三領，足以朽肉；掘地之深，下無菹[49]漏，氣無發洩於

---

49. It is generally accepted that 菹 should be read as 沮 in the sense of 濕 — see, for example, LSL.

wife'. If, above, these things are taken to be government practice and, below, they are taken to be customs, and are carried out and not stopped, implemented and not discarded, then are they the Way of true benevolence and righteousness? This is what is called '[considering] one's habits convenient and one's customs righteous'."

25.15   "To the south of Chu there is the country of the Yan people. When their parents die, they allow the flesh to rot and discard it. Afterwards they bury the bones, taking this to be [the mark of a] filial son. To the west of Qin there is the country of the Yiqu [people].[v] When their parents die, they gather up kindling and firewood and burn them, and, as the smoke rises, say they are rising far off. After that they have fulfilled their roles as filial sons. If, above, these things are taken to be government practice and, below, they are taken to be customs, and are carried out and not stopped, implemented and not discarded, then are they the Way of true benevolence and righteousness? This is what is called '[considering] one's practices convenient and one's customs righteous'. If we look at the matter from the viewpoint of these three countries, then we could say that [their practices] are unduly simple. If we look at the matter from viewpoint of the gentlemen of the central kingdom, then we could say that [their practices] are unduly elaborate. So, on the one side, there is very elaborate and, on the other side, there is very simple. But there is also moderation in funerals and burials."

25.16   Thus, clothing and food are benefits for people who are living, but moderation is still valued with regard to such things. Funerals and burials are benefits for people who are dead, so why is there no moderation only in regard to such things? The rules which Master Mo Zi formulates for the conduct of funerals and burials state: "A coffin should be three *cun* [thick], sufficient for rotting bones. Burial garments should be of three layers, sufficient for rotting flesh. The depth of the ground dug out should be such that it does not reach water below, and it does not let vapours escape above.

---

v.   On 儀渠, Z&Q have: "古西戎國名。"

上，龜足以期[50] 其所，則止矣。哭往哭來，反從事乎衣食之財，俱乎祭祀，以致孝於親。」故曰子墨子之法，不失死生之利者，此也。

25.17 故子墨子言曰：「今天下之士君子，中請將欲為仁義，求為上士，上欲中聖王之道，下欲中國家百姓之利，故當若節喪之為政，而不可不察者此[51] 也。」

---

50. There is some divergence of view on 期. LYS understands it as 認識 whilst LSL suggests 示.

51. The reversal of order of 此者 follows WYZ and WYJ.

The burial mound should be sufficient to make the place [of burial] recognisable and that is all. There should be weeping going to and from [the funeral], but then there should be a return to the matters of clothing and food. There should be such attention to sacrifices as accords with being filial to parents." Thus it is said that this is what constitutes Master Mo Zi's rules not losing the benefits to either the living or to the dead.

25.17   Therefore, Master Mo Zi spoke, saying: "Nowadays, the officers and gentlemen of the world, if they sincerely wish in their hearts to be benevolent and righteous, and seek to be superior officers who desire to be in accord with the Way of the sage kings above, and to be in accord with the benefit of the ordinary people of the state below, then it is right that they practise moderation in funerals in their conduct of government. This is something they cannot but examine."

26: 天志上

26.1 子墨子言曰:「今天下之士君子,知小而不知大。何以知之?以
其處家者知之。若處家得罪於家長,猶於鄰家所¹避逃之。然且
親戚兄弟所知識,共相儆戒,皆曰:『不可不戒矣!不可不慎
矣!惡有處家而得罪於家長,而可為也!』非獨處家者為然,雖
處國亦然。處國得罪於國君,猶有鄰國所避逃之,然且親戚兄弟
所知識,共相儆戒,皆曰:『不可不戒矣!不可不慎矣!誰亦有
處國得罪於國君,而可為也!』此有所避逃之者也,相儆戒猶若
此其厚,況無所避逃之者,相儆戒豈不愈厚,然後可哉?且語言
有之曰:『焉而晏日焉而得罪²,將惡避逃之?』曰無所避逃之。夫
天不可為林谷幽門³無人,明必見之。然而天下之士君子之於天
也,忽然不知以相儆戒,此我所以知天下士君子知小而不知大
也。」

26.2 「然則天亦何欲何惡?天欲義而惡不義。然則率天下之百姓以從

---

1. 可 is read for 所 following WNS.
2. With regard to the curious repetition of 焉 in this sentence, SYR reads the first 焉 as 於
    and takes the second 焉 to be a modal particle (語氣詞).
3. There is general acceptance of 間 for 門 following SYR.

26: Heaven's Intention I

26.1 Master Mo Zi spoke, saying: "Nowadays, the world's officers and gentlemen understand small matters but not great matters. How do I know this? I know it through their conduct within families. If, within a family, someone commits an offence against the head of that family, they still have a neighbouring family to which they can escape. Nevertheless, parents, older and younger brothers, and people who know them, all join together in admonishing and warning them, saying, 'You must be more cautious, you must be more careful! How is it possible for you to be in a family and commit an offence against the head of the family!' And it is not only conduct in families that is like this. Even conduct in states is also like this. If, in a state, someone commits an offence against the ruler of that state, they still have a neighbouring state to which they can escape. Nevertheless, parents, older and younger brothers, and people who know them, all join together in admonishing and warning them, saying, 'You must be more cautious, you must be more careful! Who is it that can possibly live in a state and commit an offence against the ruler of that state!' If the admonitions and warnings are this serious in the case of someone who has a place to escape to, how is it possible that the admonitions and warnings will not be much more serious in the case of someone who has no place to escape to? Moreover, there is the saying: 'If someone commits a crime in the bright light of day, how will he flee from it?' — which is to say there is no place to escape to. Now, with Heaven, there cannot be a forest, valley or dark and secluded place that it does not certainly see clearly. Nevertheless, with respect to Heaven, the world's officers and gentlemen are unconcerned and do not know to admonish and warn each other. This is how I know that the world's officers and gentlemen understand small matters but not great matters."

26.2 "This being so, then what does Heaven desire and what does it abhor? Heaven desires righteousness and abhors unrighteousness.

事於義，則我乃為天之所欲也。我為天之所欲，天亦為我所欲。
然則我何欲何惡？我欲福祿而惡禍祟。*若我不為天之所欲，而
為天之所不欲，然則*[4]我率天下之百姓，以從事於禍祟中也。然
則何以知天之欲義而惡不義？曰天下有義則生，無義則死；有義
則富，無義則貧；有義則治，無義則亂。然則天欲其生而惡其
死，欲其富而惡其貧，欲其治而惡其亂，此我所以知天欲義而惡
不義也。」

26.3　「曰且夫義者政[5]也，無從下之政上，必從上之政下。是故庶人竭
力從事，未得次[6]己而為政，有士政之。士竭力從事，未得次己
而為政，有將軍大夫政之。將軍大夫竭力從事，未得次己而為
政，有三公諸侯政之。三公諸侯竭力聽治，未得次己而為政，有
天子政之。天子未得次己而為政，有天政之。天子為政於三公，

4.　For the 17 characters between the asterisks WYJ has the following text: "然則率天下
　　之百姓以從事於不義，則我乃為天之所不欲也。我為天之所不欲，天亦為我所不
　　欲，則是…" which gives greater clarity to the argument — see his pp. 293–294 and
　　note 17, p. 299.
5.　There is general acceptance of WNS's reading of 政 as 正 in the verbal sense of 匡正.
6.　BY reads 次 as 恣, making 恣己 equivalent to 任意 or 擅自.

In this case, then, if I lead the ordinary people of the world to conduct their affairs with righteousness, I will, in fact, be doing what Heaven desires. If I do what Heaven desires, Heaven will also do what I desire. What, then, do I desire and what do I abhor? I desire good fortune and prosperity and I abhor bad fortune and calamity.[i] If I do not do what Heaven desires, but do what Heaven does not desire, then I will lead the ordinary people of the world to land themselves in misfortune and calamity in the conduct of affairs. This being so, how do I know that Heaven desires righteousness and abhors unrighteousness? I say that when the world is righteous, it 'lives', and when it is not righteous, it 'dies'. When it is righteous, it is rich. When it is not righteous, it is poor. When it is righteous, it is well ordered. When it is not righteous, it is disordered. So then, Heaven desires its (the world's) 'life' and abhors its 'death'. It desires its wealth and abhors its poverty. It desires its order and abhors its disorder. This is how I know that Heaven desires righteous and abhors unrighteousness."

26.3 "I say, moreover, that righteousness is what rectifies. And it is not for inferiors to rectify superiors but, of necessity, for superiors to rectify inferiors. For this reason, it is for the common people to use all their strength in carrying out their business and not to follow their own wishes in bringing about correctness. There are officers to rectify them. It is for officers to use all their strength in the conduct of affairs and not to follow their own wishes in bringing about correctness. There are generals and great officers to rectify them. It is for generals and great officers to use all their strength in carrying out their business and not to follow their own wishes in bringing about correctness. There are the 'Three Dukes'[ii] and the feudal lords to rectify them. It is for the 'Three Dukes' and the feudal lords to use all their strength in effecting good order and not to follow their own wishes in bringing about correctness. There is the Son of Heaven to rectify them. And the Son of Heaven does

---

i. Modern commentators make a point of indicating that 祟 means misfortune or calamity brought about by the spirits — see, for example, LYS.

ii. The 'Three Dukes' 三公 are described by Hucker (#4871) as "... the three paramount aides to the ruler ...".

諸侯，〔將軍，大夫，〕[7] 士，庶人，天下之士君子固明知〔之〕[8]，天之為政於天子，天下百姓未得之明知也。故昔三代聖王禹湯文武，欲以天之為政於天子，明說天下之百姓，故莫不犓牛羊，豢犬彘，潔為粢盛酒醴，以祭祀上帝鬼神，而求祈福於天。我未嘗聞天下之所[9] 求祈福於天子者也，我所以知天之為政於天子者也。」

26.4 「故天子者，天下之窮[10] 貴也，天下之窮富也。故於富且貴者，當天意而不可不順。順天意者，兼相愛，交相利，必得賞。反天意者，別相惡，交相賊，必得罰。」然則是誰順天意而得賞者？誰反天意而得罰者？子墨子言曰：「昔三代聖王禹湯文武，此順天意而得賞〔者〕[11] 也。昔三代之暴王桀紂幽厲，此反天意而得罰者也。」

26.5 然則禹湯文武其得賞何以也？子墨子言曰：「其事上尊天，中事

---

7. "將軍大夫" is added in accord with all recent editors.

8. The addition of 之 is widely accepted — see WYJ, note 24, p. 300.

9. Following Gu Qianli, 下 is omitted after 天 in line with the statements in 天志中 and 下 (see Z&Q, note 9, p. 294). LYS would also omit 所.

10. 窮, both here and in its immediately subsequent use, is read as 極 or 最.

11. Added following BY.

not follow his own wishes in bringing about correctness. There is Heaven to rectify him. That it is the Son of Heaven who brings about correctness among the 'Three Dukes', the feudal lords, generals and great officers, officers and the common people was something that the world's officers and gentlemen certainly knew quite clearly. That it is Heaven that brings about correctness in the Son of Heaven was something that the ordinary people of the world did not clearly know. This is why the sage kings of the Three Dynasties, Yu, Tang, Wen and Wu, in their wish for Heaven to bring correctness to the Son of Heaven, made it perfectly clear to the ordinary people of the world that none should fail to prepare fodder for oxen and sheep, feed grain to dogs and pigs, and make pure the offerings of grain and wine in order to sacrifice to the Supreme Lord, ghosts and spirits, and seek and pray for good fortune from Heaven. I have never heard of Heaven seeking and praying for good fortune from the Son of Heaven. This is how I know that it is Heaven that brings about correctness in the Son of Heaven."

26.4   "Therefore, the Son of Heaven is the world's most honoured and wealthy person. And one who is wealthy and honoured rightly cannot do otherwise than comply with Heaven's intention. Further, one who complies with Heaven's intention, and who practises universal mutual love and exchange of mutual benefit is certainly rewarded [whereas] one who opposes Heaven's intention, who practises discriminatory mutual dislike and exchange of mutual harm is certainly punished." In this case then, who were those that complied with Heaven's intention and were rewarded? Who were those that opposed Heaven's intention and were punished? Master Mo Zi said: "Formerly, there were the sage kings of the Three Dynasties, Yu, Tang, Wen and Wu. These were men who complied with Heaven's intention and were rewarded. Formerly, there were the tyrannical kings of the Three Dynasties, Jie, Zhou, You and Li. These were men who opposed Heaven's intention and were punished."

26.5   If this was so, then how did Yu, Tang, Wen and Wu get their reward?

Master Mo Zi spoke, saying: "In their conduct, they honoured

鬼神，下愛人。故天意曰：『此之我所愛，兼而愛之；我所利，
兼而利之。愛人者此為博焉，利人者此為厚焉。』故使貴為天
子，富有天下，業萬世子孫，傳稱其善，方施天下[12]，至今稱
之，謂之聖王。」然則桀紂幽厲得其罰何以也？子墨子言曰：「其
事上詬天，中詬鬼，下賊人，故天意曰：『此之我所愛，別而惡
之，我所利，交而賊之。惡人者此為之博也，賊[13]人者此為之厚
也。』故使不得終其壽，不歿其世，至今毀之，謂之暴王。」

26.6　「然則何以知天之愛天下之百姓？以其兼而明之。何以知其兼而
明之？以其兼而有之。何以知其兼而有之？以其兼而食焉[14]。何
以知其兼而食焉？四海之內，粒食之民，莫不犓牛羊，豢犬彘，

---

12. This phrase, "方施天下", has caused some difficulty. BY takes 方 as 旁 whilst SYR has
    "言施溥遍於天下也", which is what I have followed.
13. SYR's emendation of 賤 to 賊 is generally accepted.
14. 焉 is taken in the sense of 於之, the 之 being the people.

Heaven in the upper realm, they served the ghosts and spirits in the middle realm, and they loved the people in the lower realm. Therefore, Heaven's intention said: 'Those I love, these men love without distinction. Those I benefit, these men benefit without distinction. In their love of the people, they are all-embracing and their benefiting the people is substantial.' And so they were honoured by being made Sons of Heaven, and were enriched with all under Heaven. Their descendants continued for ten thousand generations, and they were praised for their goodness. And wherever in the world they are spoken of, they are praised right up to the present time and called sage kings."

If this was so, then how did Jie, Zhou, You and Li get their punishment?

Master Mo Zi spoke, saying: "In their conduct, they abused Heaven in the upper realm, they abused the ghosts in the middle realm, and they harmed the people in the lower realm. Therefore, Heaven's intention said: 'Those I love, these men discriminate against and hate. Those I benefit, these men harm in their dealings with them. In their hatred of people, they are all-embracing and their harming of people is substantial.' And so they did not live out their full lives and they did not go beyond their time. Right up to the present time, they are reviled and called tyrannical kings."

26.6 "So then, how do I know that Heaven loves the ordinary people of the world? Because it completely understands them.[iii] And how do I know that it completely understands them? Because it completely possesses them. And how do I know that it completely possesses them? Because it provides food for them all. How do I know that it provides food for them all? Within the four seas, all people who eat grains, without exception, prepare fodder for oxen and sheep, feed grain to dogs and pigs, and make pure the

---

iii. I follow modern Chinese editors (e.g. LYS, LSL, Z&Q) in this reading. The last, for example, has "對人全部了解". Both YPM and BW in their translations take it to mean that heaven enlightens the people. An alternative is to take both 兼 and 明 as separate descriptive terms characterising Heaven — i.e. "universal" and "all-seeing".

潔為粢盛酒醴，以祭祀於上帝鬼神。天有邑人[15]，何用弗愛也？
且吾言殺一不辜者必有一不祥。殺不辜者誰也？則人也。予之不
祥者誰也？則天也。若以天為不愛天下之百姓，則何故以人與人
相殺，而天予之不祥？此我所以知天之愛天下之百姓也。」

26.7　順天意者，義政也。反天意者，力政也。然義政將奈何哉？子墨
子言曰：「處大國不攻小國，處大家不篡小家，強者不劫弱，貴
者不傲賤，多詐者[16]不欺愚。此必上利於天，中利於鬼，下利於
人。三利無所不利，故舉天下美名加之，謂之聖王。力政者則與
此異，言非此，行反此，猶倖馳也[17]。處大國攻小國，處大家篡
小家，強者劫弱，貴者傲賤，多詐〔者〕欺愚。此上不利於天，中
不利於鬼，下不利於人。三不利無所利，故舉天下惡名加之，謂
之暴王。」

26.8　子墨子言曰：「我有天志，譬若輪人之有規，匠人之有矩，輪匠

---

15. In this clause, 邑 is something of a problem. BY has a note that early texts had 色. I have followed LYS in taking it as 下民. He has: "邑人：猶言下民。"

16. The initial three characters in this phrase here are 多詐者, whereas in the corresponding phrase subsequently there are just the two characters 多詐. The consensus, following SYR, is that 多 is superfluous in both instances and that 者 should be added in the second case.

17. There is general acceptance of BY's reading of 倖 as 偝 (背), making the phrase the equivalent of the modern "背道而馳" — see, for example, Z&Q.

offerings of grain and wine in order to sacrifice to the Supreme Lord, ghosts and spirits. So if Heaven does possess the people, how could it be that it does not love them? Furthermore, I say that, if there is the killing of one innocent person, there must be one misfortune. And who is it that kills the innocent person? It is a another person. And who is it that brings the misfortune? It is Heaven. If Heaven did not love the ordinary people of the world, then why, if people kill each other, does Heaven bring them misfortune? This is how I know that Heaven loves the ordinary people of the world."

26.7   When there is compliance with Heaven's intention, there is rule by righteousness. When there is opposition to Heaven's intention, there is rule by force. So what is rule by righteousness?

Master Mo Zi spoke, saying: "Those who live in large states do not attack small states. Those who live in large families do not take over small families. The strong do not plunder the weak. Those in high positions do not disdain the lowly. Those who are clever do not cheat the foolish. In the upper realm, this must be of benefit to Heaven. In the middle realm, this is of benefit to the ghosts. In the lower realm, this is of benefit to the people. With these three benefits, there is nothing that is not benefited. Therefore, [in the case of a ruler], the highest reputation of the world is given to him and he is called a sage king. Rule by force is different from this. It is the negation of this in word and the converse of this in deed. In fact, it is entirely the opposite. Those who live in large states do attack small states. Those who live in large families do take over small families. The strong do plunder the weak. Those in high positions do disdain the lowly. Those who are clever do cheat the foolish. In the upper realm, this is not of benefit to Heaven. In the middle realm, this is not of benefit to ghosts. In the lower realm, this is not of benefit to the people. When these three benefits are absent, there is nothing that is benefited. Therefore, [in the case of a ruler], the most abhorred name in the world is given to him and he is called a tyrannical king."

26.8   Master Mo Zi spoke, saying: "I have Heaven's intention just like wheelwrights have compasses and carpenters have squares.

執其規矩，以度天下之方圜，曰：『中者是也，不中者非也。』今天下之士君子之書，不可勝載，言語不可盡計。上說諸侯，下說列士，其於仁義，則大相遠也。何以知之？曰；我得天下之明法以度之。」

Wheelwrights and carpenters take up their compasses and squares to evaluate square and round in the world, saying: 'What conforms is right. What does not conform is wrong.' Now the books of the world's officers and gentlemen cannot be completely recorded and their doctrines cannot be completely enumerated. Above, they persuade the feudal lords. Below, they persuade ranked officers. But they are a long way from benevolence and righteousness. How do I know this? I say it is because I have the clearest standard in the world to evaluate them with."

27: 天志中

27.1　子墨子言曰:「今天下之君子之欲為仁義者,則不可不察義之所從出。」既曰不可以不察義之所從出,然則義何從出?子墨子曰:「義不從愚且賤者出,必自貴且知者出。何以知義之不從愚且賤者出,而必自貴且知者出也?曰:義者,善政也。何以知義之為善政也?曰:天下有義則治,無義則亂,是以知義之為善政也。夫愚且賤者,不得為政乎貴且知者。〔貴且知者〕[1],然後得為政乎愚且賤者。此吾所以知義之不從愚且賤者出,而必自貴且知者出也。然則孰為貴?孰為知?曰:天為貴,天為知而已矣。然則義果自天出矣。」

27.2　今天下之人曰:「當若天子之貴諸侯,諸侯之貴大夫,礚[2]明知之[3]。然吾未知天之貴且知於天子也。」子墨子曰:「吾所以知天之貴且知於天子者有矣[4]。曰:天子為善,天能賞之。天子為暴,天

1. The text of this sentence is difficult to comprehend without BY's proposed addition of "貴且知者" which I have adopted.
2. This is BY's emendation of the rare character (ZWDCD #950) which appears here.
3. In the translation of this sentence, I have taken 當若 as 當即 (Z&Q) and 礚 (see previous note) as 確 in the sense of 確然 (BY).
4. I have followed Z&Q in reading 有矣 as 有道理的.

27: Heaven's Intention II

27.1   Master Mo Zi spoke, saying: "At the present time, if the gentlemen of the world wish to be benevolent and righteous, they must examine what it is that righteousness comes from."

Since you say they must examine what it is that righteousness comes from, [tell us] then, what does it come from?

Master Mo Zi said: "Righteousness does not come from the foolish and the base. It must come from the noble and the wise. How do I know that righteousness does not come from the foolish and the base, but must come from the noble and the wise? I say that righteousness equates with good government. How do I know that righteousness equates with good government? I say that, if the world has righteousness, then it is well ordered. If it does not have righteousness, then it is disordered. This is how I know that righteousness equates with good government. Now the foolish and base cannot govern the noble and wise. There are the noble and wise and subsequently they govern the foolish and base. This is how I know that righteousness does not come from the foolish and base, but must come from the noble and wise. If this is so, then who is noble? Who is wise? I say Heaven is noble, Heaven is wise, and that is all. In that case, then, righteousness undoubtedly comes from Heaven."

27.2   Nowadays, the people of the world say: "We know with absolute certainty that the Son of Heaven is more noble than the feudal lords and the feudal lords more noble than the great officers. However, we do not know that Heaven is more noble and wise than the Son of Heaven."

Master Mo Zi said: "The way I know that Heaven is more noble and wise than the Son of Heaven is as a matter of principle. I say that, if the Son of Heaven does what is good, Heaven is able to

能罰之。天子有疾病禍祟，必齋戒沐浴，潔為酒醴粢盛，以祭祀
天鬼，則天能除去之，然吾未知天之祈福於天子也。此吾所以知
天之貴且知於天子者。[5] 不止此而已矣。又以先王之書馴天明不
解[6] 之道也知之。曰：『明哲維天，臨君下土。』則此語天之貴且
知於天子。不知亦有貴知夫天者乎？曰：天為貴，天為知而已
矣。然則義果自天出矣。」

27.3 是故子墨子曰：「今天下之君子，中實將欲遵道利民，本察仁義
之本，天之意不可不慎[7] 也。」既以天之意以為不可不慎已[8]，然則
天之將何欲何憎？子墨子曰：「天之意不欲大國之攻小國也，大
家之亂小家也，強之〔劫弱、眾之〕[9] 暴寡，詐之謀愚，貴之傲
賤，此天之所不欲也。不止此而已，欲人之有力相營，有道相

---

5. WYJ has the following initial clause in this sentence: "且吾所以知天之貴且知於天子者" (p. 303). This is not included in the translation.
6. Z&Q take the preceding five characters as the title of a book or chapter. Others, such as WYJ and LYS do not. Within the five characters, Qiu Shan reads 訓 for 馴 and 懈 for 解 both of which are generally accepted. BY has: "馴與訓同，言訓釋天之明道。"
7. Here, and in the duplication of this statement in immediately succeeding sections, 慎 is read as 順.
8. In this clause, 既以 is taken as 既然 — see, for example, Z&Q.
9. Added following WYJ in conformity with the similar passage in 27.8 — see his note 15, p. 309.

reward him. If the Son of Heaven does what is tyrannical, Heaven is able to punish him. If the Son of Heaven suffers sickness or misfortune, he must fast and bathe, and prepare pure offerings of wine and grain to make sacrifices to Heaven and to ghosts. Then Heaven can rid him of these troubles. On the other hand, I have never heard of Heaven praying to the Son of Heaven for blessings. This is how I know that Heaven is more noble and wise than the Son of Heaven. But it doesn't stop at this. It is also known from the writings of the former kings explaining the enlightened and inexhaustible way of Heaven. These say: 'Glorious and wise is Heaven. It illuminates the world below.'[i] This, in effect, says that Heaven is more noble and wise than the Son of Heaven. Do I not also know of something more noble and wise than Heaven? I say, 'Heaven is noble, Heaven is wise' and that is all. In that case, then, righteousness certainly comes from Heaven."

27.3 For this reason Master Mo Zi said: "Nowadays, if the gentlemen of the world genuinely wish in their hearts to abide by the Way and bring benefit to the people, they must start by examining the basis of benevolence and righteousness, and, in doing this, Heaven's intention cannot but be complied with."

If Heaven's intention is taken as something that must be complied with, what, in fact, is it that Heaven desires and what is it that it detests?

Master Mo Zi said: "Heaven's intention is not to want great states to attack small states, or great houses to bring disorder to small houses, or the strong to oppress the weak, or the many to tyrannise the few, or the cunning to deceive the gullible, or the noble to be arrogant towards the lowly. These are the things that Heaven's intention does not want. But it does not stop at this. It wants those with strength to help others, those who know the Way to teach others, and those with wealth to distribute it. It also wants those

---

i. This is taken to be a reference to the *Odes* (Mao #207) although the text is somewhat different. *Mozi* has: "明哲維天，臨君下土." whereas the *Shi Jing* has: "明明上天，照臨下土." — see WYJ, note 9, pp. 308–309.

教，有財相分也。又欲上之強聽治也，下之強從事也。上強聽
治，則國家治矣。下強從事，則財用足矣。若國家治財用足，則
內有以潔為酒醴粢盛，以祭祀天鬼；外有以為環璧珠玉，以聘撓
四鄰。諸侯之冤不興矣，邊境兵甲不作矣。內有以食飢息勞，持
養其萬民，則君臣上下惠忠，父子弟兄慈孝。故唯毋明乎順天之
意，奉而光施之天下，則刑政治，萬民和，國家富，財用足，百
姓皆得暖衣飽食，便寧無憂。」

27.4   是故子墨子曰：「今天下之君子，中實將欲遵道利民，本察仁義
之本，天之意不可不慎也。且夫天子之有天下也，辟之無以異乎
國君諸侯之有四境之內也。今國君諸侯之有四境之內也，夫豈欲
其臣國萬民之相為不利哉？今若處大國則攻小國，處大家則亂小

above to be resolute in the conduct of government and those below to be diligent in going about their business. If those above are resolute in the conduct of government, then the state will be well ordered. If those below are diligent in going about their business, then the materials for use will be sufficient. If the state is well ordered and materials for use are sufficient then, within, there is the means to make pure the sweet wine and millet for sacrifices to Heaven and ghosts and, without, there are the several jade emblems for relationships with neighbouring states.[ii] When grievances among the feudal lords do not arise, then warfare on the borders does not occur. When, within, there is food for the hungry and rest for the weary, and there is support and care for their ten thousand people, then rulers and ministers, and superiors and inferiors are kind and loyal, and fathers and sons, and older and younger brothers are compassionate and filial. Therefore, only when there is clear compliance with Heaven's intention, and obedience to Heaven's intention is widely practised in the world, will the administration be well ordered, the ten thousand people harmonious, the country wealthy, materials for use sufficient, and the ordinary people all obtain warm clothes and enough food so they will be at peace and free from anxiety."

27.4   For this reason Master Mo Zi said: "Nowadays, if the gentlemen of the world truly wish in their hearts to abide by the Way and bring benefit to the people, they must start by examining the basis of benevolence and righteousness, and in doing this, Heaven's intention cannot but be complied with. Moreover, if you compare the Son of Heaven's possessing all under Heaven with the ruler of a state or a feudal lord possessing what is within his four boundaries, it really is no different. Nowadays, when the ruler of a state or a feudal lord possesses what is within his four boundaries, does he wish his ministers and the state's ten thousand people not to bring benefit to each other? If he lives in a large state and attacks a small state, or lives in a large house and brings

---

ii.   In this sentence, 聘撓 is taken as 聘交 (BY) or 結交 (LSY). I have used the general term "relationships" just as I have included the four specific jade emblems (環, 璧, 珠 and 玉) named under a general term.

家，欲以此求賞譽，終不可得，誅罰必至矣。夫天之有天下也，
將無已異此。今若處大國則攻小國，處大都則伐小都，欲以此求
福祿於天，福祿終不得，而禍祟必至矣。然有所不為天之所欲，
而為天之所不欲，則夫天亦且不為人之所欲，而為人之所不欲
矣。人之所不欲者何也？曰病疾禍祟也。若已不為天之所欲，而
為天之所不欲，是率天下之萬民以從事乎禍祟之中也。故古者聖
王明知天鬼之所福，而辟天鬼之所憎，以求興天下之利，而除天
下之害。是以天之為寒熱也節，四時調，陰陽雨露也時，五穀
孰，六畜遂，疾菑戾疫凶饑則不至。」

27.5   是故子墨子曰：「今天下之君子，中實將欲遵道利民，本察仁義
之本，天意不可不慎也。且夫天下蓋有不仁不祥者[10]。曰當若子
之不事父，弟之不事兄，臣之不事君也。故天下之君子，與謂之
不祥者。今夫天兼天下而愛之，撽遂[11]萬物以利之，若豪之末，
〔莫〕[12]非天之所為也，而民得而利之，則可謂否[13]矣。然獨無報

---

10. In this sentence and subsequently, I have taken 蓋 as 大概 and 祥 as 善 following, for example, Z&Q.
11. On "撽遂" LSL, for example, offers "即持養育成".
12. This is SSX's addition of 莫 before 非.
13. There is general acceptance of YY's reading of 否 as 厚 via 后.

disorder to a small house, wishing in doing this to seek reward and praise, in the end he cannot get them, and punishments and penalties will certainly come to him. Now Heaven's possession of the world is no different from this. For if those who dwell in a large state attack a small state, or those who dwell in a large city attack a small city, wishing by this to seek good fortune and prosperity from Heaven, they will not, in the end, attain them; misfortune and calamity must, instead, follow. In this case, if people do not do what Heaven desires, or if they do what Heaven does not desire, then Heaven in turn will not do what people desire, but will do what people do not desire. And what is it that people do not desire? I say it is sickness and disease, misfortune and calamity. If one does not do what Heaven desires or does what Heaven does not desire, this is to lead the ten thousand people of the world, in carrying out their ordinary business, into the midst of misfortune and calamity. Therefore, in ancient times, the sage kings were clear in their knowledge of what Heaven and ghosts gave their blessings to, and avoided what Heaven and ghosts detested. In this way, they sought to promote Heaven's benefits and eliminate Heaven's harms. And so Heaven made cold and heat moderate, the four seasons blend, the *yin* and *yang* interchange, rain and dew timely, the five grains ripen, the six animals thrive, and sickness, disaster, pestilence and famine not occur."

27.5 Therefore Master Mo Zi said: "Nowadays, if the gentlemen of the world truly wish in their hearts to comply with the Way and benefit the people, they must start by examining the basis of benevolence and righteousness, and, in doing this, they cannot but comply with Heaven's intention. However, the world for the most part has those who are not benevolent and not good. I am speaking now, for example, of sons who do not serve their fathers, younger brothers who do not serve their older brothers, and ministers who do not serve their rulers. Therefore, the world's rulers join in speaking of such people as not good. Now, in fact, Heaven is universal in its love for [the people of] the world. It brings to fruition the ten thousand things to benefit them. Even something as small as the tip of a hair is created by Heaven. So what the people gain and benefit can, then, be called substantial. Nevertheless, they still do not repay Heaven and do not know they

夫天，而不知其為不仁不祥也。此吾所謂君子明細而不明大
也。」

27.6　「且吾所以知天之愛民之厚者有矣，曰：以磨[14]為日月星辰，以昭
道之；制為四時春秋冬夏，以紀綱之；雷[15]降雪霜雨露，以長遂
五穀麻絲，使民得而財利之；列為山川溪谷，播賦百事，以臨司
民之善否[16]；為王公侯伯[17]，使之賞賢而罰暴；賊[18]金木鳥獸，從
事乎五穀麻絲，以為民衣食之財。自古及今，未嘗不有此也。今
有人於此，讙若愛其子，竭力單務以利之，其子長而無報子求
父[19]，故天下之君子，與謂之不仁不祥。今夫天兼天下而愛之，
撽遂萬物以利之，若豪之末，非天之所為，而民得而利之，則可
謂否厚矣，然獨無報夫天，而不知其為不仁不祥也。此吾所謂君
子明細而不明大也。」

27.7　「且吾所以知天愛民之厚者，不止此而已[20]矣。曰殺不辜者，天予
不祥。不辜者誰也？曰人也。予之不祥者誰也？曰天也。若天不
愛民之厚，夫胡說人殺不辜，而天予之不祥哉？此吾之所以知天
之愛民之厚也。且吾所以知天之愛民之厚者，不止此而已矣。曰

---

14. 磨 presents a problem. WNS works it round to 離 via 歷. WYJ has 曆 — see his note
    50, p. 312. I have omitted it.
15. There is general acceptance of WNS's reading of 雷 as 隕.
16. Some emendations and interpretations are required to make this statement intelligible.
    In short, these are: 播 as 布; 賦 as 敷; 百事 as 百官; 臨 as 察視; 司 as 治; and 否 as 不
    好 — see, for example, Z&Q.
17. WYJ places these five characters before the preceding clause following a semi-colon
    after "百事" — see his note 55, p. 313.
18. There is general acceptance of the emendation of 賊 to 賦 (SYR).
19. SSX takes this clause to read: "其子長而無報乎父。"
20. Emended from 足 — see WYJ, note 68, p. 314.

are not being benevolent and good. This is what I mean when I say that gentlemen are clear about small matters, but not clear about great matters."

27.6   "Further, how I know that Heaven's love of the people is profound is this. I say it is through its creating the sun, moon, stars and planets in order to light the way for them. It fixed the four seasons – spring, autumn, winter and summer — to regulate them. It sent down snow, frost, rain and dew so the five grains, hemp and silk would grow, and it let the people gain the benefits of these materials. It divided off the mountains, rivers, streams and valleys and widely established the many officials to oversee the people and keep watch on what was good and bad. It created kings, dukes, marquises and earls and caused them to reward the worthy and punish the wicked. It provided metal and wood, birds and beasts, as well as the production of the five grains, hemp and silk so the people had the materials for clothing and food. From ancient times until now, it has always been like this. Now suppose there was a man who had a great love for his son and exerted all his strength and capacity to bring benefit to him. If, when the son grows up, he does not repay his father, then the gentlemen of the world will join in saying he is neither benevolent nor good. Now Heaven is universal in its love for [the people of] the world. It brings to fruition the ten thousand things to benefit them. Even something as small as the tip of a hair is created by Heaven. So what the people gain and benefit can, then, be called substantial. Nevertheless, they still do not repay Heaven, and do not know they are not being benevolent and good. This is what I mean when I say that gentlemen are clear about small matters, but not clear about great matters."

27.7   Moreover, how I know that Heaven's love for the people is profound doesn't stop at this. I say that if an innocent person is killed, Heaven brings down misfortune. Who is it that is innocent? I say it is a person. Who is it that brings down misfortune? I say it is Heaven. If Heaven's love for the people was not profound, how do you explain the fact that it brings down misfortune if an innocent person is killed? This is why I say that Heaven's love for the people is profound. Further, how I know that Heaven's love

愛人利人，順天之意，得天之賞者有之[21]。憎人賊人，反天之
意，得天之罰者亦有矣。」

27.8　「夫愛人利人，順天之意，得天之賞者誰也？曰若昔三代聖王，
堯舜禹湯文武者是也。堯舜禹湯文武焉所從事？曰從事兼，不從
事別。兼者，處大國不攻小國，處大家不亂小家，強不劫弱，眾
不暴寡，詐不謀愚，貴不傲賤。觀其事，上利乎天，中利乎鬼，
下利乎人。三利無所不利，是謂天德。聚斂天下之美名而加之
焉，曰：此仁也，義也，愛人利人，順天之意，得天之賞者也。
不止此而已，書於竹帛，鏤之金石，琢之槃盂，傳遺後世子孫。
曰將何以為？將以識夫愛人利人，順天之意，得天之賞者也。

---

21. WYJ emends 之 to 矣 in conformity with the following sentence.

for the people is profound doesn't stop at this. I say that those who love people and benefit people, and who comply with Heaven's intention, are those who get Heaven's rewards, whereas those who hate people and harm people, and who oppose Heaven's intention, are those who get Heaven's punishments."

27.8 "Who were those who loved people and benefited people, who complied with Heaven's intention, and who got Heaven's rewards? I say they were men such as the sage kings of the Three Dynasties in former times — Yao, Shun, Yu, Tang, Wen and Wu. What was it that Yao, Shun, Yu, Tang, Wen and Wu did? I say that in their conduct of affairs they were universal and not discriminatory. Where there is universality, those living in large states do not attack small states, those living in large houses do not bring disorder to small houses, the strong do not oppress the weak, the many do not tyrannise the few, the cunning do not deceive the foolish, and the noble are not arrogant towards the lowly. If you look at their deeds, then above there was benefit to Heaven, in the middle realm there was benefit to ghosts, and below there was benefit to people. If there are these three benefits then there is nothing that is not benefited. This is called 'Heaven's virtue'. They acquired a fine reputation throughout the world and added to it. I say they were both benevolent and righteous. They are examples of those who loved and benefited people, who complied with Heaven's intention, and who got Heaven's rewards. But it doesn't stop at this. They also wrote about their deeds on bamboo and silk, they made carvings on metal and stone, and they made engravings on [ceremonial] bowls and dishes for transmission to their descendants of later generations. You might ask what this achieves. It allows us to know of those who loved people and benefited people, who complied with Heaven's intention, and who got Heaven's rewards. In the words of the *Huang Yi* it is said:[iii]

---

iii. From the *Odes*《詩經・大雅》Mao #241, LCC, vol. 4, p. 454.

《皇矣》道之曰：『帝謂文王，予懷明德，不大聲以色，不長夏以革，不識不知，順帝之則。』帝善其順法則也，故舉殷以賞之，使貴為天子，富有天下，名譽至今不息。故夫愛人利人，順天之意，得天之賞者，既可得留而已[22]。」

27.9　「夫憎人賊人，反天之意，得天之罰者誰也？曰若昔者三代暴王桀紂幽厲者是也。桀紂幽厲焉所從事？曰從事別，不從事兼。別者，處大國則攻小國，處大家則亂小家，強劫弱，眾暴寡，詐謀愚，貴傲賤。觀其事，上不利乎天，中不利乎鬼，下不利乎人。三不利無所利，是謂天賊。聚斂天下之醜名而加之焉，曰此非仁也，非義也。憎人賊人，反天之意，得天之罰者也。不止此而已，又書其事於竹帛，鏤之金石，琢之槃盂，傳遺後世子孫。曰將何以為？將以識夫憎人賊人，反天之意，得天之罰者也。《大

---

22. This final clause is modified to read "既可得而知也。" in conformity with the following section (Z&Q).

The Lord spoke to King Wen,
I cherish your bright virtue,
making no great noise with ostentation,
not extending Xia through change.
Neither recognising nor knowing,
but following the pattern of the Lord.

The [Supreme] Lord was pleased with his compliance with the standards and so gave him Yin (i.e. the succession) to reward him, causing him to be ennobled as the Son of Heaven and enriched with all under Heaven, and his fame and praise to extend to the present time without ceasing. Thus, those who love people and benefit people, who comply with Heaven's intention, and who get Heaven's rewards can be recognised and known."

27.9 "Who were those who hated and harmed people, who opposed Heaven's intention, and who got Heaven's punishments. I say that men like the evil kings of the Three Dynasties in former times — Jie, Zhou, You and Li — were such people. How was it that Jie, Zhou, You and Li conducted their affairs? I say they conducted affairs with discrimination and not with universality. Where there is discrimination, those dwelling in large states attack small states, those dwelling in large houses bring disorder to small houses, the strong oppress the weak, the many are tyrannical towards the few, the cunning deceive the foolish, and the noble are arrogant towards the lowly. If you look at their deeds, there was no benefit to Heaven in the upper realm, no benefit to ghosts in the middle realm, and no benefit to people in the lower realm. If there are not these three benefits then there is nothing that is benefited. This is called 'Heaven's harm'. They acquired a reputation throughout the world for moral turpitude and added to it. I say they were neither benevolent nor righteous. They are examples of those who hated and harmed people, who opposed Heaven's intention, and who got Heaven's punishments. But it doesn't stop at this. They (i.e. the sage kings) wrote on bamboo and silk of the deeds of such men too, and made carvings on metal and stone, and made engravings on [ceremonial] bowls and dishes for transmission to their descendants of later generations. You might ask what this achieves. It allows us to know of those who hated people and

誓》²³之道之曰：『紂越厥夷居，不肯事上帝，棄厥先神祇不祀，
乃曰吾有命，無廖其務²⁴。』天下，天亦縱棄紂而不葆²⁵。察天以
縱棄紂而不葆者，反天之意也。故夫憎人賊人，反天之意，得天
之罰者，既可得而知也。」

27.10 是故子墨子之有天之²⁶，辟人無以異乎輪人之有規，匠人之有矩
也。今夫輪人操其規，將以量度天下之圜與不圜也。曰：『中吾
規者謂之圜，不中吾規者謂之不圜。』是以圜與不圜，皆可得而
知也。此其故何？則圜法明也。匠人亦操其矩，將以量度天下之
方與不方也。曰：『中吾矩者謂之方，不中吾矩者謂之不方。』是
以方與不方，皆可得而知之。此其故何？則方法明也。

27.11 故子墨子之有天之意也，上將以度天下之王公大人為刑政也，下
將以量天下之萬民為文學，出言談也。觀其行，順天之意，謂之

---

23. On this title, which WYJ has as 《大明》, see his note 84, pp. 315–316.
24. This is the generally accepted emendation of this clause, emending 廖 to 僇 and the rare variant of 其 to 其.
25. By general agreement, 天下 at the start of this sentence is taken to be superfluous and is omitted, and 葆 is read as 保. Some editors (e.g. LSL, Z&Q) include this in the apparent quotation whereas others (e.g. WYJ, LYS) do not. As nothing similar appears in the relevant passage in the *Documents* (see note iv), I have followed the latter.
26. 之 is read as 志. Alternatively, 意也 is added in conformity with the opening statement in most sections.

harmed people, who opposed Heaven's intention, and who got Heaven's punishments. In the words of the *Great Oath* this is said:[iv] 'Zhou was particularly arrogant and disrespectful. He was not willing to serve the Supreme Lord. He abandoned his ancestors and the spirits of the earth and did not sacrifice [to them]. Then he said, I have the mandate. I do not stand in awe of ghosts and spirits.' Heaven in turn cast off and abandoned Zhou and did not protect him. If we examine why Heaven cast Zhou off, abandoned and did not protect him, [it was because] he opposed Heaven's intention. Thus, those who hate people and harm people, who oppose Heaven's intention, and who get Heaven's punishments can be recognised and known."

27.10 So Master Mo Zi's having Heaven's intention is no different to a wheelwright having compasses or a carpenter having a square. Now a wheelwright takes hold of his compasses in order to determine whether things in the world are round or not, saying: "What accords with my compasses is called round and what does not accord with my compasses is called not round." In this way the roundness or non-roundness of all things can be ascertained and known. Why is this so? It is because the standard for roundness is clear. Also a carpenter takes hold of his square in order to determine whether things in the world are square or not, saying: "What accords with my square is called square and what does not accord with my square is called not square." In this way the squareness or non-squareness of all things can be ascertained and known. Why is this so? It is because the standard for squareness is clear.

27.11 Thus Master Mo Zi's having Heaven's intention is [for this]: Above to estimate the conduct of government by the kings, dukes and great officers of the world, and below to measure the world's ten thousand people, taking their writings as expressing what they are saying.[v] He looks at their conduct. If it complies with Heaven's

---

iv. Something similar, but not identical, appears in the *Documents* 《書經 · 大誓》 — see LCC, vol. 3, pp. 285–286. There are some textual issues in the *Mozi* passage. I have followed LYS — see his notes 1 and 2, p. 204.

v. In translating this sentence I have followed LYS's punctuation.

善意行；反天之意，謂之不善意行。觀其言談，順天之意，謂之
善言談；反天之意，謂之不善言談，觀其刑政，順天之意，謂之
善刑政；反天之意，謂之不善刑政。故置此以為法，立此以為
儀，將以量度天下之王公大人卿大夫之仁與不仁，譬之猶分黑白
也。是故子墨子曰：「今天下之王公大人士君子，中實將欲遵道
利民，本察仁義之本，天之意不可不順也。順天之意者，義之法
也。」

intention, he calls it well-intentioned conduct, whereas, if it is contrary to Heaven's intention, he calls it badly intentioned conduct. He considers what they are saying. If it complies with Heaven's intention, he calls it good speech, whereas, if it is contrary to Heaven's intention, he calls it bad speech. He looks at their conduct of government. If it complies with Heaven's intention, he calls it good government, whereas, if it is contrary to Heaven's intention, he calls it bad government. Thus he establishes this as his standard and sets it up as his principle, using it to measure and evaluate the benevolence and non-benevolence of the world's kings, dukes, great officers and ministers. It is comparable to distinguishing between black and white. This is why Master Mo Zi says: "Now kings, dukes, great officers, officers and gentlemen of the world, if they truly wish in their hearts to honour the Way and benefit the people, must from the start examine the basis of benevolence and righteousness, and accept that Heaven's intention must be complied with. Compliance with Heaven's intention is the standard of righteousness."

28: 天志下

28.1   子墨子言曰：「天下之所以亂者，其說將何哉？則是天下士君
子，皆明於小而不明於大〔也〕[1]。何以知其明於小不明於大也？以
其不明於天之意也。何以知其不明於天之意也？以處人之家者知
之。今人處若家得罪，將猶有異家所以避逃之者，然且父以戒
子，兄以戒弟，曰：『戒之慎之！處人之家，不戒不慎之，而有
處人之國者乎？』今人處若國得罪，將猶有異國所以避逃之者
矣，然且父以戒子，兄以戒弟，曰：『戒之慎之！處人之國者，
不可不戒慎也！』今人皆處天下而事天，得罪於天，將無所以避
逃之者矣。然而莫知以相極戒[2]也，吾以此知大物則不知者也。」

28.2   是故子墨子言曰：「戒之慎之，必為天之所欲，而去天之所惡。
曰天之所欲者何也？所惡者何也？天欲義而惡其不義者也。何以
知其然也？曰義者正也。何以知義之為正也？天下有義則治，無
義則亂，我以此知義之為正也。」

28.3   「然而正者，無自下正上者，必自上正下。是故庶人不得次己而

---

1.   Added following CYX and WYJ.
2.   According to YY, in the phrase "極戒", 極 should be read as 敂 in the sense of 敬 (儆/
     警).

28: Heaven's Intention III

28.1   Master Mo Zi spoke, saying: "How shall we explain what brings about the world's disorder? It is that the officers and gentlemen of the world all understand small matters but do not understand great matters. How do I know that they understand small matters but not great matters? Because they do not understand Heaven's intention. And how do I know that they do not understand Heaven's intention? I know it from the way they conduct themselves in their houses. Nowadays, if people commit a crime in their own house, they still have other houses to which they can flee. Nevertheless, fathers caution sons and older brothers caution younger brothers, saying: 'Be cautious, be careful! If those who live in a house are not cautious and careful, what will happen in the case of those who live in a state?' Nowadays, if people who live in a state commit a crime, they still have different states to which they can flee. Nevertheless, fathers caution sons and older brothers caution younger brothers, saying: 'Be cautious, be careful! For those who live in a state must be cautious and careful.' Nowadays, all the people who live in the world serve Heaven and, if they commit a crime against Heaven, they will have nowhere to flee to. Nevertheless, they do not know to warn and admonish each other. This is how I know that they do not understand great matters."

28.2   Therefore Master Mo Zi spoke, saying: "Being cautious and being careful must refer to doing what Heaven desires and setting aside what Heaven abhors. What do I say it is that Heaven desires? And what is it that Heaven abhors? Heaven desires righteousness and abhors unrighteousness. How do I know this to be so? I say that righteousness is being correct. How do I know that righteousness is being correct? If the world has righteousness, then it is well ordered. If there is not righteousness, then it is in disorder. This is how I know that righteousness is being correct."

28.3   "However, with regard to correctness, rectification does not come

為正，有上正之。上不得次已而為正，有大夫正之。大夫不得次
己而為正，有諸侯正之。諸侯不得次已而為正，有三公正之。三
公不得次已而為正，有天子正之。天子不得次已而為正，有天正
之。」

28.4 「今天下之上君子，皆明於天子之正天下也，而不明於天之正天
子也。是故古者聖人，明以此說人曰：『天子有善，天能賞之；
天子有過，天能罰之。』天子賞罰不當，聽獄不中，天下疾病禍
福[3]，霜露不時，天子必且犓豢其牛羊犬彘，絜為粢盛酒醴，以禱
祠祈福於天。我未嘗聞天之禱〔祠〕[4]祈福於天子也。吾以此知天
之重且貴[5]於天子也。是故義者不自愚且賤者出，必自貴且知者
出。曰：〔誰為貴？〕誰為知？〔曰：天為貴〕；天為知[6]。然則義果
自天出也。今天下之上君子欲為義者，則不可不順天之意矣。」

28.5 「曰順天之意何若？曰兼愛天下之人。何以知兼愛天下之人也？

---

3. 下 is read as 降. Also 福 is clearly wrong here so, as proposed by WNS, 禍福 is taken
     as 禍祟.
4. It is not included in the translation. Added following BY — see WYJ, note 12, p. 324.
5. There is general acceptance of SYR's emendation of "重且貴" to "貴且知".
6. On the addition of the seven characters indicated see WYJ, note 14, pp. 324–325.

from those below to those above. Unquestionably it comes from those above to those below. This is why the ordinary people cannot act of their own accord to become correct. It is officers who rectify them. But officers cannot act of their own accord to become correct. It is great officers who rectify them. But great officers cannot act of their own accord to become correct. It is feudal lords who rectify them. But feudal lords cannot act of their own accord to become correct. It is the 'Three Dukes' who rectify them. But the 'Three Dukes' cannot act of their own accord to become correct. It is the Son of Heaven who rectifies them. But the Son of Heaven cannot act of his own accord to become correct. It is Heaven that rectifies him."

28.4   "Now the world's officers and gentlemen all clearly understand that it is the Son of Heaven who rectifies the world. What they do not clearly understand is that it is Heaven that rectifies the Son of Heaven. This is why, in ancient times, the sages, in giving a clear explanation to the people, said: 'If the Son of Heaven is good, Heaven is able to reward him. If he is at fault, Heaven is able to punish him.' If the Son of Heaven's rewards and punishments are not appropriate, if his judgements in lawsuits are not fair, then Heaven sends down sickness and disease, misfortune and calamity. Frost and dew are untimely, and the Son of Heaven must, perforce, feed his cattle, sheep, dogs and pigs, and cleanse and purify the millet and sweet wine in order to offer prayers to Heaven in the ancestral temple beseeching good fortune. I have never heard of Heaven offering prayers beseeching good fortune to the Son of Heaven. This is how I know that Heaven is more noble and wise than the Son of Heaven. Thus, righteousness does not come from the foolish and lowly. It must come from the noble and wise. And who do I say is noble, who is wise? I say Heaven is noble, Heaven is wise. In this case, then, righteousness undoubtedly comes from Heaven. Now if the world's officers and gentlemen wish to be righteous, they cannot do otherwise than comply with Heaven's intention."

28.5   "What do I say constitutes compliance with Heaven's intention? I say it is universal love for the people of the world. How do I know [that Heaven] is universal in its love for the people of the world?

以兼而食之也。何以知其兼而食之也？自古及今，無有遠靈孤夷
之國[7]，皆犓豢其牛羊犬彘，絜為粢盛酒醴，以敬祭祀上帝山川鬼
神，以此知兼而食之也。茍兼而食焉，必兼而愛之。譬之若楚，
越之君，今是楚王食於楚之四境之內，故愛楚之人；越王食於越
〔之四境之內〕[8]，故愛越之人。今天兼天下而食焉，我以此知其兼
愛天下之人也。」

28.6   「且天之愛百姓也，不盡物而止矣[9]。今天下之國，粒食之民，殺
一不辜者，必有一不祥。曰誰殺不辜？曰人也。孰予之不祥[10]？
曰天也。若天之中實不愛此民也，何故而人有殺不辜，而天予之
不祥哉？且天之愛百姓厚矣，天之愛百姓別[11]矣，既可得而知
也。」

28.7   「何以知天之愛百姓也？吾以賢者之必賞善罰暴也。何以知賢者

---

7. In this clause, "無有" is read as "所有" or ("無論") and "遠靈孤夷" as "遙遠偏僻" (see,
    for example, LYS, Z&Q), although WSN suggests "遠夷孤靈" with 靈 read as 零.
8. Added following WYJ — see note 20, p. 325.
9. I have followed WNS in reading 盡 as 僅 and 物 as 此.
10. There is general acceptance of SYR's emendation of 辜 to 祥 here.
11. There is general agreement following WYZ that 別 should be understood as 遍 (普遍)
    — see WYJ, note 24, p. 326 for discussion.

Because it is universal in providing food for them. How do I know that it is universal in providing food for them? From ancient times to the present, no matter how distant or remote states are, they all provide nourishment for their cattle and sheep, dogs and pigs, and clean and purify the millet and sweet wine in order to honour and offer sacrifices to the Supreme Lord and the ghosts and spirits of the mountains and rivers. It is from this we know that [Heaven] is universal in its providing food for them (i.e. the people of the world).[i] If it is universal in providing food for them, then it must be universal in loving them. For example, consider the rulers of Chu and Yue. Now the Chu king provides food for those within the four boundaries of Chu, therefore he loves the people of Chu. The Yue king provides food for those within the four boundaries of Yue, therefore he loves the people of Yue. Now Heaven is universal in providing food in the world. This is how I know that it is universal in its love for the people of the world."

28.6 "Moreover, Heaven's love for the ordinary people doesn't simply end with this. Now in the states of the world, wherever there are people who eat grain, if one innocent person is killed, there will certainly be one calamity. Who is it, you ask, who kills the innocent person? I say it is a person. Who is it, you ask, who brings the calamity? I say it is Heaven. If Heaven truly in its heart did not love these people, what reason would it have for bringing about a calamity if there was an innocent person killed? Further, that Heaven's love for the ordinary people is profound, and that Heaven's love for the ordinary people is generalised, are things that can be ascertained and known."

28.7 "How do we know of Heaven's love for the ordinary people? We know because worthy people invariably rewarded goodness and punished wickedness. How do we know that worthy people invariably rewarded goodness and punished wickedness? It is

---

i. This argument is not entirely clear. The crux of the difficulty is the fourth sentence — "以兼而食之也". Z&Q, for example, gloss this as follows: "食之：吃他們的東西，受他們供養" which is the line YPM takes in translation. I have followed what I take to be LYS's interpretation. Either way, there are difficulties with what follows.

之必賞善罰暴也？吾以昔者三代之聖王知之。故昔也三代之聖王
堯舜禹湯文武之兼愛之天下也，從而利之，移其百姓之意焉，率
以敬上帝山川鬼神。天以為從其所愛而愛之，從其所利而利之，
於是加其賞焉，使之處上位，立為天子以法也，名之曰『聖人』，
以此知其賞善之證。是故昔也三代之暴王桀紂幽厲之兼惡天下
也，從而賊之，移其百姓之意焉，率以詬侮上帝山川鬼神。天以
為不從其所愛而惡之，不從其所利而賊之，於是加其罰焉，使之
父子離散，國家滅亡，抎失社稷，憂以及其身。是以天下之庶民
屬而毀之，業萬世子孫繼嗣，毀之賁[12]不之廢也，名之曰『失[13]
王』。以此知其罰暴之證。今天下之士君子，欲為義者，則不可
不順天之意矣。」

28.8   「曰順天之意者，兼也。反天之意者，別也。兼之為道也，義
正[14]。別之為道也，力正。曰義正者何若？曰大不攻小也，強不
侮弱也，眾不賊寡也，詐不欺愚也，貴不傲賤也，富不驕貧也，
壯不奪老也。是以天下之庶國，莫以水火毒藥兵刃以相害也。若

---

12. Following WNS, 賁 is taken as 者.
13. There is general acceptance of SSX's emendation of 失 to 暴.
14. Here and in the following sentence, 正 is taken as 政 — see, for example, LSL and Z&Q.

because of the sage kings of the Three Dynasties of former times that we know it. Thus, in former times, the sage kings of the Three Dynasties — Yao, Shun, Yu, Tang, Wen and Wu – were universal in their love of the world and, as a result, brought benefit to it. They changed the way of thinking of the ordinary people, leading them to revere the Supreme Lord and the ghosts and spirits of the mountains and rivers. Heaven considered that they followed what it loved and loved it, and they followed what it benefited and benefited it. And so it added to their rewards and caused them to occupy a high position, establishing them as Sons of Heaven in order to be models. It gave them the name of 'Sage', from which we have proof that it rewarded goodness. So too, in former times, the evil kings of the Three Dynasties — Jie, Zhou, You and Li — universally hated the world and, as a result, harmed it. They changed the way of thinking of the ordinary people, leading them to revile and ridicule the Supreme Lord and the ghosts and spirits of the mountains and rivers. Heaven considered that they did not follow what it loved but hated it, and did not follow what it benefited but harmed it. And so it added to their punishments, caused fathers and sons to be dispersed and scattered, and the kingdom to be destroyed and lost, there to be destruction of the altars of soil and grain, and grief to come to them personally. And so the ordinary people were as one in reviling them and, for ten thousand generations, their descendants too continued to revile them unceasingly. It gave them the name of 'Evil King', from which we have proof that it punished wickedness. Nowadays, if the world's officers and gentlemen wish to be righteous, then they must comply with Heaven's intention."

28.8   "I say that to comply with Heaven's intention is to be universal. To oppose Heaven's intention is to be discriminating. To follow the way of universality is to govern by righteousness. To follow the way of discrimination is to govern by force. If you ask what government by righteousness is, I say it is the great not attacking the small, the strong not plundering the weak, the many not harming the few, the clever not cheating the foolish, the noble not being arrogant towards the lowly, the rich not being boastful towards the poor, and the able-bodied not snatching away from the old. In this way, the many states of the world will not use water

事上利天，中利鬼，下利人。三利而無所不利，是謂天德。故凡
從事此者，聖知也，仁義也，忠惠也，慈孝也，是故聚斂天下之
善名而加之。是其故何也？則順天之意也。曰力正者何若？曰大
則攻小也，強則侮弱也，眾則賊寡也，詐則欺愚也，貴則傲賤
也，富則驕貧也，壯則奪老也。是以天下之庶國，方以水火毒藥
兵刃以相賊害也。若事上不利天，中不利鬼，下不利人。三不利
而無所利，是謂之賊[15]。故凡從事此者，寇亂也，盜賊也，不仁
不義，不忠不惠，不慈不孝，是故聚斂天下之惡名而加之。是其
故何也？則反天之意也。」

28.9 故子墨子置立天之[16]，以為儀法，若輪人之有規，匠人之有矩
也。今輪人以規，匠人以矩，以此知方圜之別矣。是故子墨子置
立天之，以為儀法。吾以此知天下之士君子之去義〔之〕[17]遠也。
何以知天下之士君子之去義遠也？今知氏大國之君寬者然曰[18]：

---

15. I have followed YY's proposal to emend "之賊" to "天賊", making it uniform with the earlier "天德".
16. As in the previous chapter, "天之" is taken either as "天志" or "天之意".
17. Added by WYJ.
18. There are several issues with this clause. Following the proposals of SYR and YY particularly, what has been translated is "今夫大國之君寬然曰".

and fire, poisons and potions, or arms and weapons to harm one another. If these conditions obtain, then, above, Heaven is benefited, in the middle realm ghosts are benefited, and, below, mankind is benefited. If there are these three benefits, there is nothing that is not benefited. This is called 'heavenly virtue'. Therefore, in all cases, those who conduct themselves like this will be sage-like in wisdom, benevolent and righteous, loyal and kind, and compassionate and filial, which is why the world's good names will be gathered together and applied to them. What is the reason for this? It is because there is compliance with Heaven's intention. If you ask what government by force is, I say it is the great attacking the small, the strong plundering the weak, the many harming the few, the clever cheating the foolish, the noble being arrogant towards the lowly, the rich being boastful towards the poor, and the able-bodied snatching away from the old. In this way, the many states of the world will, in fact, use water and fire, poisons and potions, or arms and weapons to plunder and harm one another. If these conditions obtain, then above it does not benefit Heaven, in the middle realm it does not benefit ghosts, and below it does not benefit mankind. If there are not these three benefits, there is nothing that is benefited. This is spoken of as 'heavenly plunder'. Therefore, in all cases those who conduct themselves like this will be tyrannical and reckless, robbers and thieves, non-benevolent and non-righteous, disloyal and unkind, and non-compassionate and unfilial, which is why the world's bad names will be gathered together and applied to them. What is the reason for this? It is because there is opposition to Heaven's intention."

28.9 Therefore, Master Mo Zi established and set up Heaven's intention to act as a principle and standard just as the wheelwright has his compasses and the carpenter his square. Now the wheelwright uses compasses and the carpenter uses a square because, with these things, they can distinguish what is square or round. This is why Master Mo Zi established and set up Heaven's intention to act as a principle and standard. With this we can know whether the world's officers and gentlemen are distancing themselves from righteouness. How can we know whether the world's officers and gentlemen are distancing themselves from

「吾處大國而不攻小國，吾何以為大哉？」是以差論蚤牙[19]之士，比列其舟車之卒，以攻伐[20]無罪之國，入其溝境[21]，刈其禾稼，斬其樹木，殘其城郭，以御其溝池，焚燒其祖廟，攘殺其犧牷。民之格[22]者，則剄拔[23]之，不格者，則係操而歸，丈夫以為僕圉胥靡，婦人以為舂酉[24]。

28.10　則夫好攻伐之君，不知此為不仁義，以告四鄰諸侯曰：「吾攻國覆軍，殺將若干人矣。」其鄰國之君亦不知此為不仁義也，有具其皮幣，發其總[25]處，使人饗賀焉。則夫好攻伐之君，有重不知此為不仁不義也，有書之竹帛，藏之府庫。為人後子者，必且欲順其先君之行，曰：「何以當發吾府庫，視吾先君之法美[26]？」必不曰文，武之為正者若此矣[27]，曰：「吾攻國覆軍，殺將若干人矣。」則夫好攻伐之君，不知此為不仁不義也，其鄰國之君，不知此為不仁不義也。是以攻伐世世而不已者，此吾所謂大物則不知也。

---

19. I have followed Z&Q in reading 差論 as 擇 and 蚤牙 as "得力助手" — see their note 4, p. 335.
20. I have followed WYJ in having 伐 rather than 罰 here — see his note 49, p. 329.
21. 溝境 is taken as 國境 — see, for example, Z&Q.
22. 格 is taken as 鬥 in the sense of 反抗, both here and subsequently — see, for example, Z&Q.
23. Following SYR, 剄拔 is read as 剄殺.
24. See Z&Q for a discussion of "僕圉胥靡" and "舂酉" (notes 15 and 16, pp. 335–336). It is their interpretation I have followed.
25. This is SYR's emendation of the variably written, unknown character which texts generally have here — see WYJ, note 61, p. 331, for discussion.
26. Here 美 is read as 儀 following SYR.
27. WYJ duplicates 為正, placing a full-stop after the first 正 — see his notes 65, 66, pp. 331–332.

righteouness? Now we know that rulers of large states expansively say: "If I dwell in a large state and do not attack small states, how am I to be taken as great?" And so they select capable officers to assist them, and arrange the troops on their boats and chariots in order to attack and reduce a state that has committed no crime. They enter its national boundaries, cut down its grains and crops, fell its forests and trees, destroy its inner and outer city walls, fill in its moats and pools, burn down its ancestral temples, and seize and kill its sacrificial animals. Those people who oppose them, they kill. Those who do not oppose them, they bind together and take back with them. The men they use to mind horses or in forced labour, and the women they use to pound grain and carry water.

28.10   Then those rulers who loved assault and attack did not take this to be neither benevolent nor righteous and, accordingly, told the neighbouring feudal lords on the four sides: "We have attacked such and such a state and defeated its army, killing the general like capable men." And the rulers of the neighbouring states also did not know that this was neither benevolent nor righteous so they prepared gifts of fur and silk, brought out what they had stored away, and sent men for feasting and congratulation. Then those rulers who loved assault and attack were doubly unaware that this was neither benevolent nor righteous. They wrote this on bamboo and silk and stored it in their storehouses for the people of later generations who would certainly wish to emulate the actions of their former rulers and so say: "Why is it not appropriate to open our storehouses and look at the models and principles of our former rulers?" They would certainly not say, "Kings Wen and Wu conducted their governments like this." They would say, "We attacked states and defeated their armies, killing their generals like capable men." Then the rulers who loved assault and attack would not know that this was neither benevolent nor righteous, and the rulers of their neighbouring states would [likewise] not know that this was neither benevolent nor righteous. In this way, assault and attack were perpetuated for generation after generation without stopping. This is why I say that, if it was a great matter, then they did not know it.

28.11 所謂小物則知之者何若？今有人於此，入人之場園，取人之桃李瓜薑者，上得且罰之，眾聞則非之，是何也？曰不與其勞，獲其實，已非其有所取之故。而況有踰於人之牆垣，[28] 格人之子女者乎？與角人之府庫，竊人之金玉蚤絫[29] 者乎？與踰人之欄牢，竊人之牛馬者乎？而況有殺一不辜人乎？今王公大人之為政也，自殺一不辜人者，踰人之牆垣，格人之子女者；與角人之府庫，竊人之金玉蚤絫者；與踰人之欄牢，竊人之牛馬者；與入人之場園，竊人之桃李瓜薑者，今王公大人之加罰此也，雖古之堯舜禹湯文武之為政，亦無以異此矣。

28.12 今天下之諸侯，將猶皆侵凌攻伐兼并，此為殺一不辜人者，數千萬矣。此為踰人之牆垣，格人之子女者，與角人府庫，竊人金玉蚤絫者，數千萬矣。踰人之欄牢，竊人之牛馬者，與入人之場園，竊人之桃李瓜薑者，數千萬矣，而自曰義也。

28.13 故子墨子言曰：「是蕡義[30] 者，則豈有以異是蕡黑白甘苦之辯者哉！今有人於此，少而示之黑，謂之黑，多示之黑謂白，必曰吾

28. I have followed WYJ and LSL of modern commentators in omitting the rare character (ZWDCD #12223) which other texts (e.g. LYS, Z&Q) have here and again in line six of this section. The latter equate it with 又 on the basis of the 《廣雅》.

29. 蚤絫 is taken as 布縷 following WYZ.

30. I have accepted the emendation of 我 to 義 — see WYJ, note 83, p. 334.

28.11   How do we know what it is that is called a small matter? Now suppose there was a person who entered another's garden or orchard and took his peaches and plums, melons and ginger. If those above learn of it, they will punish him. If the multitude hear of it, they will condemn him. Why is this? I say it is because he did not participate in the work yet he seized the produce so what he took was not his. How much more does this apply if someone jumps over another's wall or fence and seizes his sons and daughters? Or if someone breaks into another's storehouse and steals his gold, jade and cloth? Or jumps over the railing of another's animal enclosure and steals his oxen and horses? How much more so again if they kill one innocent person? Nowadays, kings, dukes and great men conduct the government. And in the case of someone who kills an innocent person, or one who jumps over another's wall or fence and seizes his sons and daughters, or breaks into another's storehouse and steals his gold, jade and cloth, or leaps over the railing of another's animal enclosure and steals his oxen and horses, or enters another's garden or orchard and steals his peaches, plums, melons and ginger, these same kings, dukes and great men will punish him. And even in ancient times, when Yao, Shun, Yu, Tang, Wen and Wu were in charge of government, it was no different from this.

28.12   Nowadays, the world's feudal lords all still encroach, attack and annex. This is like killing one innocent person many thousands of times over. It is like jumping over another person's wall or fence and seizing his sons and daughters, or breaking into another's storehouse and stealing his gold, jade and cloth many thousands of times over. [It is like] leaping over the railing of another's animal enclosure and stealing his oxen and horses, or entering another's garden or orchard and stealing his peaches, plums, melons and ginger many thousands of times over. And yet they themselves say it is righteous.

28.13   Therefore Master Mo Zi spoke, saying: "If this is to be confused about righteousness, then how is it different from being confused about the distinction between black and white, or sweet and bitter? Now suppose there is a person who, when you show him a little bit of black, calls it black, but when you show him a lot of black, calls

目亂，不知黑白之別。今有人於此，能少嘗之甘謂甘，多嘗謂苦，必曰吾口亂，不知其甘苦之味。今王公大人之政也，或殺人，其國家禁之，此蚤越有能多殺其鄰國之人，因以為文義[31]。此豈有異賤白黑，甘苦之別者哉？」

28.14 故子墨子置天之以為儀法。非獨子墨子以天之志為法也，於先王之書《大夏》[32]之道之然：「帝謂文王，予懷明德，毋大聲以色，毋長夏以革，不識不知，順帝之則。」此誥文王之以天志為法也，而順帝之則也。且今天下之士君子，中實將欲為仁義，求為上士，上欲中聖王之道，下欲中國家百姓之利者，當天之志，而不可不察也。天之志者，義之經也。

29: 明鬼上：闕

30: 明鬼中：闕

---

31. There is some doubt about this and the preceding sentence. The version translated follows particularly LSL's version which, in turn, follows in part ZCY — see LSL, note 3, p. 188. See also WYJ, notes 87–89, p. 334.

32. As YY originally pointed out, it is the "大雅" that is being quoted here — see *Odes*《詩經 · 大雅》Mao #241, verse 7, LCC, vol. 4, p. 454.

it white. He will certainly have to admit that his eyes are confused and that he does not know the difference between black and white. And suppose now there is a person who, when you allow him to taste a little sweetness, calls it sweet, but when he tastes a lot of sweetness, calls it bitter. He will certainly have to admit that his mouth is confused and that he doesn't know the tastes of sweet and bitter. Nowadays, when kings, dukes and great officers carry out government, with regard to someone killing another person, his own state will try to prevent this because everyone knows that to do this is not righteous. But they are able to kill large numbers of people in a neighbouring state and take this to be great righteousness. How is this different from confusing the distinction between black and white, or between sweet and bitter?"

28.14 Therefore Master Mo Zi established Heaven's [intention] as being a principle and standard. But it was not only Master Mo Zi who took Heaven's intention to be the standard. In the writings of the former kings, such as the *Da Ya*, it is the same:

The Lord spoke to King Wen,
I cherish your bright virtue,
making no great noise with ostentation,
not extending Xia through change.
Neither recognising nor knowing,
but following the pattern of the Lord.

This tells of King Wen's use of Heaven's intention as a standard and his compliance with the [Supreme] Lord's pattern. Moreover, nowadays, the world's officers and gentlemen, if they truly wish in their hearts to be benevolent and righteous, and seek to be superior officers, and wish to accord with the Way of the sage kings above, and with the benefits of the ordinary people of the state below, cannot do otherwise than examine Heaven's intention. Heaven's intention is the standard of righteousness.

29: Percipient Ghosts I: Lost

30: Percipient Ghosts II: Lost

31: 明鬼下[1]

31.1 子墨子言曰:「逮至昔三代聖王既沒,天下失義,諸侯力正[2],是以存夫為人君臣上下者之不惠忠也,父子弟兄之不慈孝弟長貞良也,正長之不強於聽治,賤人之不強於從事也,民之為淫暴寇亂盜賊,以兵刃毒藥水火,退[3]無罪人乎道路率徑。奪人車馬衣裘以自利者並作,由此始,是以天下亂。此其故何以然也?則皆以疑惑鬼神之有與無之別,不明乎鬼神之能賞賢而罰暴也。今若使天下之人,偕若信鬼神之能賞賢而罰暴也,則夫天下豈亂哉!」

31.2 今執無鬼者曰:「鬼神者,固無有。」旦暮以為教誨乎天下〔之人〕[4],疑天下之眾,使天下之眾皆疑惑乎鬼神有無之別,是以天下亂。是故子墨子曰:「今天下之王公大人士君子,實將欲求興天下之利,除天下之害,故當鬼神之有與無之別,以為將不可不明察此者也。[5]」

---

1. There is some question about the best translation of the title, as discussed in the Introduction. The usual rendering is "Understanding Ghosts" (in the sense of making clear their existence) which certainly fits with the use of 明 in the early sections. However, in the later sections (32.16 on), it is the ghosts and spirits that are 明, which I have rendered as "percipient" in the title, although "all-seeing" might also be satisfactory.
2. Modern commentators (e.g. LYS, LSL, Z&Q) take 正 as 征 here.
3. I have followed SYR in taking 退 as 迒.
4. "之人" is added here following BY and WYJ — see the latter's note 8, p. 345. The alternative is to omit 之 (WYZ).
5. There is some variation in this clause. The version given follows WNS and WYJ — see the latter's note 10, p. 345.

31: Percipient Ghosts III

31.1   Master Mo Zi spoke, saying: "Since the passing of the three sage
kings of the Three Dynasties of former times, the world has lost
righteousness and the feudal lords use [military] force in
governing, so that those living now who are rulers and ministers,
and superiors and inferiors, are without kindness or loyalty whilst
fathers and sons, and younger and older brothers, are without
compassion, filial conduct, respect, upright behaviour and
goodness. Those who are leaders are not diligent in the conduct of
government whilst those who are lowly are not diligent in the
conduct of affairs. The people give themselves to debauchery,
cruelty, robbery, disorder, theft and plunder, using weapons,
poisons, water and fire to stop innocent travellers on the roads and
footpaths, seizing their carts, horses, clothes and furs to further
their own benefit. And these things have increased since they
began, causing disorder in the world. Why have things come to
this? It is because everyone is doubtful and suspicious on the
question of whether ghosts and spirits exist or not, and do not
clearly understand that ghosts and spirits are able to reward the
worthy and punish the wicked. Now if all the people of the world
could be brought to believe that ghosts and spirits are able to
reward the worthy and punish the wicked, then how could the
world be in disorder?"

31.2   Nowadays, those who hold that there are no ghosts say: "Ghosts
and spirits certainly do not exist." [From] morning to evening they
teach and instruct the world's people, sowing doubt amongst its
multitudes, and causing them all to be suspicious and doubtful
on the question of whether ghosts and spirits exist or not. This
causes disorder in the world. For this reason Master Mo Zi said:
"Nowadays, if kings, dukes, great officers, officers and gentlemen of
the world genuinely wish to promote what benefits the world and
eliminate what harms it, it is right that the issue of whether ghosts and
spirits exist or not is something that must be clearly examined."

31.3   既以鬼神有無之別，以為不可不察已，然則吾為明察此，其說將
奈何而可？子墨子曰：「是與[6]天下之所以察知有與無之道者，必
以眾之耳目之實知有與亡為儀者也[7]，請惑聞之見之[8]，則必以為
有。莫聞莫見，則必以為無。若是，何不嘗[9]入一鄉一里而問
之，自古以及今，生民以來者，亦有嘗見鬼神之物，聞鬼神之
聲，則鬼神何謂無乎？若莫聞莫見，則鬼神可謂有乎？」

31.4   今執無鬼者言曰：「夫天下之為聞見鬼神之物者，不可勝計也，
亦孰為聞見鬼神有無之物哉？」子墨子言曰：「若以眾之所同見，
與眾之所同聞，則若昔者杜伯是也。周宣王殺其臣杜伯而不辜。
杜伯曰：『吾君殺我而不辜，若以死者為無知則止矣。若死而有
知，不出三年，必使吾君知之。』其三年，周宣王合諸侯而田於
圃，田車數百乘，從數千，人滿野[10]。日中，杜伯乘白馬素車，

---

6.   Here ZCY takes 是 to be superfluous and reads 與 as 舉, proposals accepted by modern
commentators.

7.   In this clause, 亡 is read as 無 and 儀 as 標準 — see Z&Q.

8.   In translating this clause, I have followed SYR in reading 請 as 誠 and 惑 as 或.

9.   Here and subsequently, 嘗 is taken as 試著 (Z&Q).

10. In this sentence, there is some uncertainty about 圃 and the following 田. Some (e.g.
WYJ) take "圃田" to be a place name. Some take 圃 to be a place name and 田 to be
an adjective describing the chariots (e.g. LYS), and some take 圃 as a general term
equivalent to 獵苑 (Z&Q). I have followed LYS, although the matter must remain in
doubt.

31.3   So the question of whether ghosts and spirits exist or not is taken
to be one that must be examined. In that case, if we are to examine
this clearly, how can it be done? Master Mo Zi said: "In bringing
up the method of how [the people of] the world examine and know
whether something exists or not, we must certainly take the ears
and eyes of the multitude to be a standard on the matter of
existence and non-existence. If someone has genuinely heard
something or seen something, then we must take it as existing. But
if no-one has heard it and no-one has seen it, then we must take it
as not existing. If this is the case, why not put the matter to the test
by going into a district or a village and asking about it? If, from
ancient times to the present, since people came into existence,
there have been those who have seen ghost-like or spirit-like
things, or have heard ghost-like or spirit-like sounds, then how can
ghosts and spirits be said to be non-existent? If no-one has heard
or seen [such things], then how can ghosts and spirits be said to
exist?"

31.4   Nowadays, those who hold that there are no ghosts say: "The
[people of] the world who have seen or heard things that are ghosts
and spirits are too many to count, but how many [of these] can
truly say that they have seen such things?" Master Mo Zi spoke,
saying: "If we are to take what many people together have seen, or
what many people together have heard, then someone like the Earl
of Du[i] of former times is a case in point. King Xuan of Zhou had
his minister, the Earl of Du, put to death although he had
committed no crime. The Earl of Du said: 'My ruler is putting me
to death although I have committed no crime. If those who are
dead are without awareness, then that will be the end of the matter,
but, if those who are dead have awareness, then in three years I
shall certainly cause my ruler to know it.' Some three years later,
when King Xuan of Zhou had gathered the feudal lords to go
hunting at Pu, the hunting chariots numbered several hundred and
the followers several thousand. People filled the field. On the

---

i.   Little is known of the Earl of Du 杜伯. The place of his enfeoffment is thought to have
been near Changan in Shanxi Province. See the *Guo Yu, Zhou Yu Shang*. King Xuan ruled
from 827 to 782 BC.

朱衣冠，執朱弓，挾朱矢，追周宣王，射之車上，中心折脊，殪車中，伏弢而死。當是之時，周人從者莫不見，遠者莫不聞，著在周之《春秋》。為君者以教其臣，為父者以警其子，曰：『戒之慎之！凡殺不辜者，其得不祥，鬼神之誅，若此憯遫[11]也！』以若書之說觀之，則鬼神之有，豈可疑哉？」

31.5 「非惟若[12]書之說為然也，昔者鄭穆公[13]，當[14]晝日中處乎廟，有神入門而左[15]，鳥身，素服三絕[16]，面狀正方。鄭穆公見之，乃恐懼奔。神曰：『無懼[17]！帝享女明德，使予錫女壽十年有九，使若國家蕃昌，子孫茂，毋失。』鄭穆公再拜稽首曰：『敢問神名？』曰：『予為句芒。』若以鄭穆公之所身見為儀，則鬼神之有，豈可疑哉？」

31.6 「非惟若書之說為然也，昔者燕簡公殺其臣莊子儀而不辜。莊子

---

11. For "憯遫" the ZWDCD has "急疾迅速也" with reference to this passage — vol. 4, p. 260.
12. 若 here is taken as 此.
13. Most commentators following BY and SYR accept that 鄭 should read 秦. LSL, however, retains 鄭 — see WYJ, note 31, p. 349.
14. Some commentators take 當 as 嘗 — see, for example, WYJ, LSL.
15. 左 is taken as verbal. Z&Q have "向左走".
16. There is general acceptance of SYR's emendation of "素服三絕" to "素服玄純".
17. On the issue of whether this should be 懼 or 奔 see WYJ, note 37, pp. 350–351.

stroke of noon, the Earl of Du appeared in a plain chariot drawn by white horses. He was wearing vermillion clothes and a vermillion cap, and he grasped a vermillion bow and held vermillion arrows under his arm. He pursued King Xuan of Zhou and fired at him as he rode on his chariot, striking him at the very centre and breaking his spine, killing him in his chariot. [The King] slumped over his quiver and died. At that time, among the Zhou followers, there was none who did not see, and, of those far away, none who did not hear. It was recorded in the *Spring and Autumn Annals* of Zhou. It became something rulers used to instruct their ministers, and fathers used to caution their sons, saying: 'Be warned! Be careful! All those who kill the innocent will suffer misfortune and the punishment of ghosts and spirits will be very swift like this.' If we look at what is said in writings of this sort, how can we doubt the existence of ghosts and spirits?"

31.5 "But it is not only what is said in this book that makes it so. In former times, once, when Duke Mu of Zheng was sitting in his ancestral temple in the middle of the day, there was a spirit which came through the door and turned to the left. It had the body of a bird and wore plain garments of one dark colour. Its face had a square appearance. When Duke Mu of Zheng saw it he was frightened and [about to] flee. The spirit said: 'Do not be afraid. The [Supreme] Lord is pleased with your shining virtue and has sent me to grant you a longer life by nineteen years, to make your state prosperous and your progeny vigorous, and not to lose [your state].' Duke Mu of Zheng bowed repeatedly, striking his head on the ground, and saying: 'Dare I ask the spirit's name?' [The spirit] replied: 'I am Gou Mang.'[ii] If we take what Duke Mu of Zheng saw in person as genuine, how can we doubt the existence of ghosts and spirits?"

31.6 "But it is not only what is said in this book that makes it so. In former times, Duke Jian of Yan had his minister Zhuang Ziyi put

---

ii. Gou Mang 句芒 is taken as the name of a spirit of spring and is traditionally described as having the body of a bird and the face of a person — see WYJ, note 41, p. 351.

儀曰：『吾君王殺我而不辜，死人毋知亦已，死人有知，不出三
年，必使吾君知之。』期年燕將馳祖，燕之有祖，當齊之社稷，
宋之有桑林，楚之有雲夢也，此男女之所屬而觀也。日中，燕簡
公方將馳於祖塗，莊子儀荷朱杖而擊之，殪之車上。當是時，燕
人從者莫不見，遠者莫不聞，著在燕之《春秋》。諸侯傳而語之
曰：『凡殺不辜者，其得不祥，鬼神之誅，若此其憯遬也！』以若
書之說觀之，則鬼神之有，豈可疑哉？」

31.7　「非惟若書之說為然也，昔者宋文君鮑之時，有臣曰祝觀辜，固
嘗從事於厲，袜子杖揖出與言曰[18]：『觀辜！是何珪璧之不滿度
量？酒醴粢盛之不淨潔也？犧牲之不全[19]肥？春秋冬夏選失
時[20]？豈女為之與？意鮑為之與？』觀辜曰：『鮑幼弱在荷繈之
中，鮑何與識焉。官臣觀辜特為之。』袜子舉揖而槁之，殪之壇

---

18. There are several issues in this opening statement as follows: (i) 鮑 is the 名 of Prince
    Wen who ruled from 610 to 589 BC. (ii) Most commentators follow SYR in taking 觀
    辜 as the name (as seems appropriate from what follows) and taking the unknown graph
    which appears before it as 祝, describing his position. LSL, however, takes all three
    characters as the name. (iii) In the clause "固嘗從事於厲", 固 is read as 故 and 厲 is
    taken as a temple (神祠 — LYS). Z&Q refer to the《禮記・祭法》as follows: "諸侯為
    國立五祀…曰公厲。" (iv) I have accepted SYR's reading of 袜子 as 巫史. Others take
    袜 as 祝 (e.g. LSL). (v) Some commentators take 揖 as 挾持 (Z&Q), others as 短槳
    (LSL). LYS has: "杖揖：揖當為木旁，杖就是持。"
19. 仝 is taken as 純.
20. Modern commentators such as Z&Q and LSL accept WHB's reading of 選 as 獻 and
    SYR's suggestion that there is a missing character (效) after 選.

to death although he had committed no crime.[iii] Zhuang Ziyi said: 'My ruler is putting me to death although I have committed no crime. If those who are dead are without awareness, then that will be the end of the matter, but, if those who are dead have awareness, then, within three years, I shall cause my prince to know it.' One year later, [the people of] Yan were about to set out for Zu — Yan had Zu just as Qi had Sheji, Song had Sanglin, and Chu had Yunmeng, these being places where men and women gathered to watch.[iv] On the stroke of noon, as Duke Jian of Yan was about to set out on the road to Zu, Zhuang Ziyi [appeared] carrying a vermillion staff and struck him, killing him in his chariot. At that time, there was not one of the Yan people in attendance who did not see it and not one of those far away who did not hear of it. It was recorded in the *Spring and Autumn Annals* of Yan. The feudal lords transmitted it and spoke of it, saying: 'All those who kill the innocent will suffer misfortune, and the punishment of the ghosts and spirits will be very swift like this.' If we look at what is said in writings like this, then how can we doubt the existence of ghosts and spirits?"

31.7 "But it is not only what is said in this book that makes it so. Formerly, at the time of Prince Wen of Song [named] Bao, there was a minister in charge of sacrifices called Guan Gu. Once, when he was performing his duties in the temple, [a spirit in the form of] a wizard carrying a staff appeared and spoke, saying: 'Guan Gu! Why are the jade emblems not of the proper dimensions? Why are the sweet wine and millet not clean and pure? Why are the sacrificial animals not pristine and fattened? Why are the spring, autumn, winter and summer offerings not those appropriate for the time? Is this your doing or is it Bao's?' Guan Gu replied: 'Bao is still young and frail and wears swaddling clothes. How can he be responsible? I, the official Guan Gu, am alone responsible for this.' The wizard raised his staff and struck him, killing him on the

---

iii. Little is known of Zhuang Ziyi 莊子儀 — see WYJ, note 43, p. 351 for possible variations in the name. Duke Jian ruled Yan from 504 to 493 BC.

iv. PJI (for one) takes the final part of this sentence (after Zu) to be a later interpolation — see his note 62, p. 93. There is also a question about what precisely is covered by "觀" here.

上。當是時，宋人從者莫不見，遠者莫不聞，著在宋之《春秋》。
諸侯傳而語之曰：『諸不敬慎祭祀者，鬼神之誅，至若此其僭遬
也！』以若書之說觀之，鬼神之有，豈可疑哉？」

31.8   「非惟若書之說為然也，昔者齊莊君之臣，有所謂王里國，中里
徼者，此二子者，訟三年而獄不斷。齊君由謙殺之恐不辜；猶謙
釋之，恐失有罪[21]。乃使之[22]人共一羊，盟齊之神社，二子許
諾。于是泄泇到羊而灑其血[23]，讀王里國之辭既已終矣，讀中里
徼之辭未半也，羊起而觸之，折其腳，祧神之而槁之，殪之盟
所。當是時，齊人從者莫不見，遠者莫不聞，著在齊之《春秋》。
諸侯傳而語之曰：『請品先不以其請者[24]，鬼神之誅，至若此其僭
遬也。』以若書之說觀之，鬼神之有，豈可疑哉？」是故子墨子言

---

21. In these two sentences, 由 in the first and 猶 in the second are taken as 欲 in the sense of 想到 — see, for example, LSL, Z&Q.
22. There is general agreement for the emendation of 之 to 二.
23. There are two rare and one unknown characters in this clause as follows: (i) 泄 is read as 掘 or 穴 (e.g. YTY, Z&Q) so "泄泇" means "挖洞於地". (ii) The unknown character is taken as 到 (WYZ). (iii) *Li* (ZWDCD #18489) is emended to 灑.
24. I have followed WYZ's emendation of "請品先" to "諸共盟" and BY's emendation of the second 請 to 情.

sacrificial altar. At that time, there was not one of the Song people in attendance who did not see it, and not one of those far away who did not hear of it. It was recorded in the *Spring and Autumn Annals* of Song. The feudal lords transmitted it and spoke of it, saying: 'All those who are not reverential and careful in the sacrifices will suffer the punishment of the ghosts and spirits which will be very swift like this.' If we look at what is said in writings like this, how can we doubt the existence of ghosts and spirits?"

31.8   "But it is not only what is said in this book that makes it so. Formerly, among the officials of Prince Zhuang of Qi, there was one called Wang Liguo and another called Zhongli Jiao.[v] These two men had been engaged in a lawsuit for three years without any judgement being reached. The Qi prince considered putting both men to death but feared that one was innocent. He considered releasing both men but feared that one was guilty. Then he made the two men together bring a ram and take an oath on the Qi altars of soil and grain. The two men agreed. Thereupon, [before the altar] a hole was dug, the ram's throat was cut and its blood was scattered. Wang Liguo then read his statement right through to the end. But when Zhongli Jiao was not yet halfway through reading his statement, the [dead] ram rose up and butted him, breaking his leg. As he stumbled and fell, he struck the altar and was killed at the place of the oath.[vi] At that time, there was not one of the Qi people in attendance who did not see it, and not one of those far away who did not hear of it. It was recorded in the *Spring and Autumn Annals* of Qi. The feudal lords transmitted it and spoke of it, saying: 'All those who swear oaths together but are untruthful will suffer the punishment of the ghosts and spirits which will be very swift like this.' If we look at what is said in writings like this, how can we doubt the existence of ghosts and spirits?" That is why Master Mo Zi spoke, saying: "Even in deep valleys and thick

---

v.   Prince Zhuang is thought to be Duke Zhuang 莊公. There is some doubt about the names of the two litigants — see BY and WYJ, notes 73 and 74, p. 356.

vi.   There are differing versions of what exactly happened related to different readings of "桃神". English translators (YPM, BW, PJI) take it that the ram continues its post-mortem attack. Chinese commentators either assume the appearance of a 巫史 — see, for example, Z&Q — or read 桃 as 踙 (LSL). I have followed the latter.

曰：「雖有深溪博林，幽澗毋人之所，施行不可以不董，見有鬼
神視之。」

31.9 今執無鬼者曰：「夫眾人耳目之請，豈足以斷疑哉？奈何其欲為
高[25]君子於天下，而有復信眾之耳目之請哉？」子墨子曰：「若以
眾之耳目之請，以為不足信也，不以斷疑。不識若昔者三代聖王
堯舜禹湯文武者，足以為法乎？故於此乎，自中人以上皆曰：若
昔者三代聖王，足以為法矣。若苟昔者三代聖王足以為法，然則
姑嘗上觀聖王之事。昔者武王之攻殷誅紂也，使諸侯分其祭曰：
『使親者受內祀，疏者受外祀。』故武王必以鬼神為有，是故攻殷
誅[26]紂，使諸侯分其祭。若鬼神無有，則武王何祭分哉？」

31.10 「非惟武王之事為然也，故聖王其賞也必於祖，其僇也必於社[27]。
賞於祖者何也？告分之均也。僇於社者何也？告聽之中也。非惟

25. I have understood 士 after 高 — see WYJ, note 93, p. 358.
26. I have followed WYJ in having 誅 rather than 伐 here.
27. In this sentence, there is general agreement that 祂 should be understood as 祖廟 and 僇 read as 戮 in the sense of 刑戮.

forests, in dark places where no one dwells, you must be careful in your conduct because there are ghosts and spirits watching you."

31.9   Nowadays, those who hold that there are no ghosts say: "How is the evidence of the ears and eyes of the masses sufficient to resolve doubt? How can we expect those who want to be high officers and gentlemen in the world to turn around and trust the evidence of the ears and eyes of the masses?" Master Mo Zi said: "Suppose we accept that the evidence of the ears and eyes of the masses is not enough to trust and cannot be used to resolve doubt. Would we not accept that the sage kings of the Three Dynasties of former times — Yao, Shun, Yu, Tang, Wen and Wu — are enough to be taken as standards? Thus, in this, all those from the middle [level] and above say they accept that the sage kings of the Three Dynasties of former times are enough to be taken as standards. If, in fact, the sage kings of the Three Dynasties of former times are enough to be taken as standards, then let us look for a moment at the affairs of these sage kings. Formerly, after King Wu had attacked Yin and punished Zhou, he made the feudal lords divide up the sacrifices, saying: 'I shall let close relatives participate in the internal sacrifices and distant relatives participate in the external sacrifices.'[vii] Thus King Wu undoubtedly took ghosts and spirits to exist. This is why, after attacking Yin and punishing Zhou, he made the feudal lords divide the sacrifices. If ghosts and spirits did not exist, then why would King Wu have made this division of sacrifices?"

31.10   "But it is not only the matter of King Wu that makes it so. Thus, when the sage kings bestowed their rewards, they invariably did so in the ancestral temple, and when they meted out [capital] punishment, they invariably did so at the altar of soil. Why did they bestow rewards in the ancestral temple? To announce [to the ghosts and spirits] that the apportionment was equitable. Why did they mete out [capital] punishment at the altar of soil? To

---

vii. LSL has this on the distinction between internal and external sacrifices: "內祭：立祖廟進行祭祀。外祭：祭祀本國的山川等。"

若書之說為然也，且惟昔者虞夏商周三代之聖王，其始建國營都²⁸日，必擇國之正壇。置以為宗廟；必擇木之修茂者，立以為菆位²⁹；必擇國之父兄慈孝貞良者，以為祝宗；必擇六畜之勝腯肥倅，毛以為犧牲，珪璧琮璜，稱財為度³⁰；必擇五穀之芳黃，以為酒醴粢盛，故酒醴粢盛，與歲上下也。故古聖王治天下也，故必先鬼神而後人者此也。故曰官府選效³¹，必先祭器祭服，畢藏於府，祝宗有司，畢立於朝，犧牲不與昔聚群。故古者聖王之為政若此。」

31.11 「古者聖王必以鬼神為〔有〕³²，其務鬼神厚矣。又恐後世子孫不能知也，故書之竹帛，傳遺後世子孫。咸恐其腐蠹絕滅，後世子孫

---

28. WYJ takes the clause to end with 都 and emends 日 to 曰 making it the first character of the next clause.
29. See Z&Q notes 13 and 14, p. 361 on this statement. In particular, 菆 is read as 叢. I have substituted the more usual 木 for their 本.
30. There is some variation in the text of this statement — see, for example, Z&Q and WYJ, notes 109 and 110, p. 360.
31. I have followed SYR's reading of 選效 — see also Z&Q.
32. 有 is added following WNS.

announce [to the ghosts and spirits] that the judgement was fair.
But it is not only what is said in writings like this that makes it so.
There is also the case of the sage kings of the Three Dynasties of
former times — Yu Xia, Shang and Zhou — who, in the days
when they first established the kingdom and built the capital,
certainly selected [the place for] the kingdom's sacrificial altar
and established it as being the ancestral temple. They certainly
selected a place where the woodland was dense and luxuriant,
establishing it as the altar of soil. They certainly selected the most
compassionate, filial, upright and good of the fathers and older
brothers and took them to be the leaders of the sacrifices. They
certainly selected the most plump and pure-coloured of the six
domestic animals and took them as sacrificial victims. The several
jade emblems were of an appropriate nature and size.[viii] They
certainly selected the most fragrant and ripe of the five grains to
use for the wine and millet so the wine and millet were a reflection
of whether the year was good or bad. Thus, the ancient sage kings,
in bringing order to the world, certainly put the ghosts and spirits
first and the people second, as this shows. So it is said, with
respect to the preparations and provisions by government
departments, that it is necessary first to ensure that the utensils and
garments for the sacrifices are all stored in the storehouses, that
the leaders of the sacrifice and the other officials are all
established at court, and that the sacrificial animals are not mixed
with the rest of the herd. Thus, in ancient times, the sage kings'
conduct of government was like this."

31.11 "In ancient times, the sage kings certainly took ghosts and spirits
to exist and their service to the ghosts and spirits was profound.
But they also feared that their descendants of later generations
would not be able to know this, so they wrote it on bamboo and
silk to transmit it and hand it down to them. But they all feared that
[these writings] would decay and be worm-eaten, and be lost and
destroyed, so their descendants of later generations would have no
record. Therefore, they carved it on [ceremonial] basins and

---

viii. The four items mentioned — 珪璧琮璜 — differed in size, shape, composition and
significance.

不得而記，故琢之盤盂，鏤之金石，以重之。有恐後世子孫不能
敬莙以取羊[33]，故先王之書，聖人一尺之帛，一篇之書，語數鬼
神之有也，重有重之。此其故何？則聖王務之。今執無鬼者曰：
『鬼神者，固無有。』則此反聖王之務。反聖王之務，則非所以為
君子之道也！」

31.12 今執無鬼者之言曰：「先王之書，慎無一尺之帛，一篇之書，語
數鬼神之有，重有重之，亦何書之有[34]哉？」子墨子曰：「《周書·
大雅》有之。《大雅》曰：『文王在上，於昭於天，周雖舊邦，其命
維新。有周不顯，帝命不時。文王陟降，在帝左右。穆穆文王，

33. Z&Q have the following note on 取羊: "取得吉祥。羊通祥。"
34. WYJ reverses the order of "之有".

plates, and engraved it on metal and stone to be especially sure. But they also feared that their descendants of later generations would not be able to be reverential and respectful enough to derive the blessings [from these writings]. Therefore, in the writings of the former kings, the sages, in every *chi* of silk and every *pian* of bamboo strips, speak many times of the existence of ghosts and spirits, reiterating this again and again. What is the reason for this? It is because the sage kings took it to be important. Now those who hold that there are no ghosts say: 'Ghosts and spirits certainly do not exist.' This, then, is the opposite of what the sage kings took as fundamental. To oppose what the sage kings took to be fundamental cannot be regarded as the Way of the gentleman."

31.12   Nowadays, the arguments of those who hold that there are no ghosts say: "If, in the writings of the former kings, the sages, in every *chi* of silk and every *pian* of bamboo strips, speak many times of the existence of ghosts and spirits, reiterating this again and again, what are these writings?"

Master Mo Zi said: "Of the Zhou writings, the *Da Ya* is one. The *Da Ya* says:[ix]

King Wen is above,
brightly shining in Heaven.
But Zhou is an old country,
its decree is now new.
Is Zhou not illustrious?
Was the Lord's decree not timely?
King Wen ascends and descends
on the right and left of the Lord.
Profound indeed was King Wen,
and his fame is heard unceasingly.

---

ix.   See the *Odes* 《詩經。大雅》 Mao #235, LCC, vol. 4, pp. 427–428.

令問不已。』若鬼神無有，則文王既死，彼豈能在帝之左右哉？
此吾所以知周書之鬼也。」

31.13　「且周書獨鬼，而商書不鬼，則未足以為法也。然則姑嘗上觀乎
商書，曰：『嗚呼！古者有夏，方未有禍之時，百獸貞蟲，允及
飛鳥，莫不比方。矧佳人面，胡敢異心？山川鬼神，亦莫敢不
寧。若能共允，佳天下之合，下土之葆。』[35] 察山川鬼神之所以
莫敢不寧者，以佐謀禹也。此吾所以知商書之鬼也。」

31.14　「且商書獨鬼，而夏書不鬼，則未足以為法也。然則姑嘗上觀乎
夏書《禹誓》[36] 曰：『大戰於甘，王乃命左右六人，下聽誓於中軍，
曰：『有扈氏威侮五行，怠棄三正，天用[37] 剿絕其命。』有曰：『日

---

35. This passage does not appear as such in extant writings, although there is something
similar in the *Documents*《書經・伊訓》, LCC, vol. 3, pp. 193–194. There are several
textual issues which, taken sentence by sentence (excluding the exclamation), are as
follows: Sentence 1: 貞 in 貞蟲 is taken as 征 (or 徵) by SYR. I have followed LSL in
reading it as "爬蟲". 允 is taken as 以 (WYZ). On 比方, SYR has "猶言順道也". The
same phrase is found in *Zhuangzi* 21 (GQF, vol. 3, p. 707). Sentence 2: Following BY,
佳 is taken as 惟. Sentence 4: 共允 is taken as 恭誠 — see, for example, LYS. 佳 is again
read as 惟 (some texts — e.g. LYS — have 佳 instead of 佳 in both instances), and 合
is taken as 統 ・(Z&Q).

36. In fact, what follows is from the *Documents*《書經・甘誓》, LCC, vol. 3, pp. 152–155,
although there are substantial textual variations.

37. 用 here is read as 因 — see, for example, Z&Q.

If ghosts and spirits did not exist, then, when King Wen was already dead, how could he be at the left and right of the [Supreme] Lord? This is how I know of the ghosts of Zhou writings."

31.13 "Further, if only the Zhou writings [spoke of] ghosts but the Shang writings did not, then this would not be enough to take as a criterion. In that case, then, let us look for a moment at the Shang writings. [There] it is said: 'Ah alas! In ancient times there was Xia. Just before the time of misfortune, of the hundred animals and crawling insects right up to the flying birds, there was none that did not follow the Way. Still more, of those with human faces, who would dare harbour a different heart? Of the ghosts and spirits of the mountains and rivers, there was also none that dared not be at peace. If they were able to be respectful and sincere, the world would be harmonious and the land would be protected.' If we examine the reason why ghosts and spirits of the mountains and rivers did not dare not to be at peace, it was because they were assisting Yu in the execution of his plans. This is how I know of the ghosts of the Shang writings."

31.14 "Further, if only the Shang writings [spoke of] ghosts but the Xia writings did not, then this would not be enough to take as a criterion. In that case, then, let us look for a moment at the Xia writings, [specifically] the *Oath of Yu*, which says: 'There was a great battle at Gan.ˣ The king then ordered the six high officers to the left and right to go below the altar and listen to his declaration in the middle of the armyˣⁱ where he said: 'There is this man Hu and he has destroyed and insulted the Five Constant Virtues, and he has rejected and abandoned the Three Paths.ˣⁱⁱ Heaven, as a

---

x.   Gan 甘 was a place in what is now Shanxi 陝西 in the western part of the Hu 戶 district.

xi. This follows Z&Q — see their note 4, p. 367.

xii. Hu 扈 was the name of a kingdom in Xia times and occupied part of what is now Shanxi. 威 is read as 滅. The "Five Phases" 五行 does not here refer to the usual "phases" (金, 木, 水, 火 and 土), but to 仁, 義, 禮, 智 and 信, more commonly known as the "五 常". The "Three Paths" 三正 are 天道, 地道 and 人道.

中，今予與有扈氏爭一日之命。且爾卿大夫庶人，予非爾田野葆士³⁸之欲也，予共³⁹行天之罰也。左不共于左，右不共于右，若不共命，御非爾馬之政，若不共命。』」

31.15 「是以賞于祖而僇于社。賞于祖者何也？言分命之均也。僇于社者何也？言聽獄之事⁴⁰也。故古聖王必以鬼神為賞賢而罰暴，是故賞必于祖而僇必于社。此吾所以知夏書之鬼也。故尚⁴¹者夏書，其次商周之書，語數鬼神之有也，重有重之，此其故何也？則聖王務之。以若書之說觀之，則鬼神之有，豈可疑哉？於古曰⁴²：『吉日丁卯，周代祝社方，歲於社者考，以延年壽。』⁴³若無鬼神，彼豈有所延年壽哉！」

31.16 是故子墨子曰：「嘗若鬼神之能賞賢如罰暴也⁴⁴。蓋本施之國家，施之萬民，實所以治國家利萬民之道也。若以為不然⁴⁵，是以吏

---

38. 葆士 is taken as 寶土 following YY.

39. In this sentence 共 does double duty. In this and the fourth instance it is read as 恭 and in the second and third instances as 攻 following SYR — see WYJ, notes 153–154, p. 367.

40. 中 is read for 事 following WNS.

41. 尚 here is read as 上 in the sense of 上古 (Z&Q).

42. There is doubt about "於古曰". SYR has: "疑有脫字".

43. No source for this apparent quotation could be found and the text is quite uncertain. The version given follows particularly LSL.

44. There is general acceptance of SYR's proposal that the initial 嘗若 be read as 當若. Modern editors (e.g. LSL, Z&Q) suggest 應當. Also 如 is taken as 而.

45. All modern editors accept WNS's recommendation that the five characters occurring here (若以為不然) be regarded as superfluous and omitted.

result, attacked him and cut off his mandate.' It also says: 'At midday, I and the man of Hu will contend for the fate of this day. As for all you ministers and high officers, and you common people — it is not that I wish for your lands or your precious jade. I am reverentially carrying out Heaven's punishment. And if you on the left do not attack on the left, and if you on the right do not attack on the right, you will not be respecting the mandate. If you charioteers do not control your horses, you will not be respecting the mandate'."

31.15 "This is why rewards were bestowed in the ancestral temple and punishments meted out at the altar of soil. Why were rewards bestowed in the ancestral temple? To tell [the ancestors] that the apportionment of the decree was equitable. Why were punishments meted out at the altar of soil? To tell [the ghosts] that the resolution of lawsuits was fair. Therefore, the ancient sage kings undoubtedly thought that the ghosts and spirits rewarded the worthy and punished the wicked. This is the reason why rewards necessarily occurred in the ancestral temple and punishments at the altar of soil. This is how I know of the ghosts of Xia writings. Thus, most anciently in the Xia writings, and next in those of Shang and Zhou, there are numerous references to the existence of ghosts and spirits, and these are reiterated again and again. What is the reason for this? It is because the sage kings took it to be fundamental. If we look at what is said in writings such as these, then how is it possible to doubt the existence of ghosts and spirits? In an ancient [writing] it is said: 'On the propitious day *ding-mao*, the official conducting the sacrifice and representing [the ruler] offered prayers all around — to the spirits of the earth, to the spirits of the four directions, to the spirits of the year and to the spirits of ancestors — praying for long life [for the ruler].' If there were no ghosts and spirits, what could there have been to prolong life?"

31.16 For this reason, Master Mo Zi said: "It is right to think that ghosts and spirits are able to reward the worthy and punish the wicked. If this could be established at the outset in the state and among the ten thousand people, it would truly be the way to bring order to the state and benefit to the ten thousand people. If the officials in

治官府之不絜廉，男女之為無別者，鬼神見之。民之為淫暴寇亂
盜賊，以兵刃毒藥水火，退無罪人乎道路，奪人車馬衣裘以自利
者，有鬼神見之。是以吏治官府，不敢不絜廉，見善不敢不賞，
見暴不敢不罪。民之為淫暴寇亂盜賊，以兵刃毒藥水火，退無罪
人乎道路，奪車馬衣裘以自利者，由此止。是以莫放幽閒，擬乎
鬼神之明，顯明有一人畏長誅罰[46]；是以天下治。」

31.17　「故鬼神之明，不可為幽閒廣澤；山林深谷，鬼神之明必知之。
鬼神之罰，不可為富貴眾強；勇力強武，堅甲利兵，鬼神之罰必
勝之。若以為不然，昔者夏王桀，貴為天子，富有天下，上詬天
侮鬼，卜殃傲[47]天下之萬民，祥上帝伐元山帝行[48]，故於此乎，
天乃使湯至明罰焉。湯以車九兩[49]，鳥陳雁行[50]，湯乘大贊，[51]犯

---

46. Most editors consider the 21 characters of this sentence to be misplaced here. WYJ, however, does not — see his notes 174–176, p. 370. The punctuation above is his.
47. There is general acceptance of WNS's emendation of 殃傲 to 殃殺.
48. Since BY, many commentators have regarded this clause as incomprehensible. The translation above is based on ZCY's re-worked version — from "祥上帝伐元山帝行" to "佯代上帝，危上帝行。"
49. It is unlikely that Tang had only 9 chariots. It may be that 兩 here indicates a band of 25 foot-soldiers, but again the number is very small — see WYJ, note 182, p. 371 for references to other sources, in particular the LSCQ 8/3.2 which gives Tang 70 chariots and 6000 soldiers (K&R, p. 197).
50. It is widely accepted that "鳥陳" and "雁行" represent troop formations (YTY).
51. The following eight characters are SYR's version of the otherwise incomprehensible statement in the original text.

charge of government departments are not pure and incorruptible, and if the proper separation between men and women is not maintained, ghosts and spirits see it. If people are depraved and cruel, giving themselves to plunder, disorder, robbery and theft, and use weapons, poisons, water and fire to waylay innocent travellers on the roads, seizing carriages and horses, and clothes and furs for their own benefit, there are ghosts and spirits who see them. So the officials in charge of government departments do not dare not to be pure and incorruptible. When they see what is good, they dare not fail to reward it. When they see what is evil, they dare not fail to punish it. And the people being depraved and cruel, giving themselves to plunder, disorder, robbery and theft, and using weapons, poisons, water and fire to waylay innocent travellers on the roads, seizing carriages and horses, clothes and furs for their own benefit will stop because of this. [So there is no licentiousness, even in the darkest places, that is not clearly apparent to the ghosts and spirits, and every single person is aware and fearful of punishment from above]. In this way the world is well ordered."

31.17 "Therefore, the awareness of ghosts and spirits is such that it is not possible to do something in the darkest places, whether in wide marshes, in mountains and forests, or in deep ravines without the awareness of ghosts and spirits certainly knowing of it. The punishments of the ghosts and spirits are such that it is not possible [to avoid them], whether rich and noble and [having a populace that is] numerous and strong, or with brave and powerful forces, or with strong shields and sharp weapons, for the punishments of ghosts and spirits will undoubtedly overcome these things. If you think this is not the case, [then consider] the Xia king, Jie of former times. He was ennobled as the Son of Heaven and enriched with all under Heaven. But he abused Heaven and insulted the ghosts above, and he brought calamity and death to the ten thousand people of the world below. [He feigned before the Supreme Lord and endangered the Supreme Lord's practices.] It was because of this that Heaven sent Tang to effect its clearly recognisable punishment. Tang, with his nine chariots arranged in the Bird Formation and the Wild Goose March, ascended Da Zan, clashed with Jie's forces, entered the outskirts of the city and

遂夏桀，入之郊遂，王乎禽[52] 推哆大戲。故昔夏王桀，貴為天
子，富有天下，有勇力之人推哆大戲，生列兕虎，指畫殺人，人
民之眾兆億，侯盈厥澤陵，然不能以此圉鬼神之誅。此吾所謂鬼
神之罰，不可為富貴眾強，勇力強武，堅甲利兵者，此也。」

31.18　「且不惟此為然。昔者殷王紂，貴為天子，富有天下，上詬天侮
鬼，下殃傲天下之萬民，播棄黎老，賊誅孫子，楚毒無罪，刳剔
孕婦，庶舊鰥寡，號咷無告也。故於此乎，天乃使武王至明罰
焉。武王以擇車百兩，虎賁之卒四百人，先庶國節窺戎，於殷人
戰乎牧之野，王乎禽費中，惡來，眾畔百走[53]。武王遂奔入宮，
萬年梓株[54]，折紂而繫之赤環，載之白旗，以為天下諸侯僇。故

---

52. BY emends 乎禽 to 手擒.
53. There are several issues with this statement as follows: (i) 乎禽 is read as 手擒 as
    elsewhere. (ii) 費中 is thought to be 費仲. He and Wu Lai 惡來 were assistants to King
    Zhou. The latter is mentioned in this regard in several places in the LSQC. (iii) On "眾
    畔百走", I have followed modern editors such as LSL and Z&Q. For a detailed
    discussion of the issues see WYJ, note 204, p. 375.
54. I have followed LSL's modern paraphrase version of the very problematic "萬年梓
    株". Previous translators (YPM, BW) simply omit it.

seized Tui Duo and Da Xi with his own hands.[xiii] Thus, in former times, the Xia king, Jie, was ennobled as the Son of Heaven and enriched with all under Heaven. And he had strong and courageous men such as Tui Duo and Da Xi who could tear apart a live rhinoceros or tiger and could kill a man with one finger. His people were numbered in the millions and they filled the marshes and hills. Nevertheless, he was not able to ward off the punishment of the ghosts and spirits. This is why I say that the punishments of ghosts and spirits are such that it is impossible [to avoid them], whether rich and noble and [having a populace that is] numerous and strong, or with brave and powerful forces, or with strong shields and sharp weapons."

31.18   "Moreover, it was not only this that was the case. In former times, there was the Yin king, Zhou. He was ennobled as the Son of Heaven and enriched with all under Heaven. But he abused Heaven and insulted the ghosts above, and he brought calamity and death to the ten thousand people of the world below. Everywhere he abandoned old people, killed young children, administered the torture of the burning pillar to the innocent, and he ripped open a pregant woman.[xiv] The masses, widowers and widows, and those orphaned and alone, cried out but were not heard. It was because of this that Heaven sent King Wu to effect its clearly recognisable punishment. So King Wu chose a hundred chariots and four hundred of the bravest soldiers and, after sending out appointed officers to assess their strength, engaged with the Yin forces in the fields of Mu. The King with his own hands seized Fei Zhong and Wu Lai, and the multitude turned and fled. King Wu then pursued [Zhou] and entered the palace. There, on an ancient tree stump, he cut off his head and hung it on a red chariot wheel against the backdrop of a white banner to make clear to the feudal lords of the world that he had carried out the punishment. Therefore, in former times, the Yin king, Zhou, although he was

---

xiii. Tui Duo 推哆 and Da Xi 大戲 were ministers to Jie. They are also mentioned in the LSCQ account.

xiv. For further details, textual and historical, regarding these four transgressions, see WYJ notes 194–197, pp. 373–374.

昔者殷王紂，貴為天子，富有天下，有勇力之人費中，惡來，崇
侯虎[55]，指寡殺人，人民之眾兆億，侯盈厥澤陵，然不能以此圉
鬼神之誅。此吾所謂鬼神之罰，不可為富貴眾強，勇力強武，堅
甲利兵者，此也。且《禽艾》之道之曰：『得璣無小，滅宗無大。』
則此言鬼神之所賞，無小必賞之；鬼神之所罰，無大必罰之。」

31.19 今執無鬼者曰：「意不忠[56]親之利，而害為孝子乎？」子墨子曰：
「古之今之為鬼，非他也，有天鬼，亦有山水鬼神者，亦有人死
而為鬼者。今有子先其父死，弟先其兄死者矣，意雖使然，然而
天下之陳物曰：『先生者先死。』若是，則先死者非父則母，非兄
而姒也。今絜為酒醴粢盛，以敬慎祭祀，若使鬼神請[57]有，是得
其父母姒兄而飲食之也，豈非厚利哉？若使鬼神請亡，是乃費其
所為酒醴粢盛之財耳。自夫費之，非特注之污壑而棄之也，內者
宗族，外者鄉里，皆得如具飲食之。雖使鬼神請亡，此猶可以合
歡聚眾，取親於鄉里。」

---

55. In the translation, I have followed WYJ's text — "生捕兕虎" — see his note 207, pp. 376–377.
56. As elsewhere, 忠 is read as 中 in the sense of 符合.
57. In this and the following section 請 in the several instances of its use is read as 誠.

ennobled as the Son of Heaven and enriched with all under Heaven, and had men of courage and strength such as Fei Zhong and Wu Lai who could seize a live rhinoceros or tiger, or kill a man with one finger, and had a people numbered in the many millions so they filled the lowlands and the hills, was nevertheless not able to ward of the punishment of the ghosts and spirits. This is why I say that the punishments of the ghosts and spirits are such that it is impossible [to avoid them], whether rich and noble and [having a populace that is] numerous and strong, or with brave and powerful forces, or with strong shields and sharp weapons. Moreover, the words of the *Qin Ai* say: 'One can attain [Heaven's] blessing no matter how lowly. One's lineage can be wiped out no matter how great.'[xv] This, then, says that whoever the ghosts and spirits are going to reward, no matter how lowly, they will certainly reward him [and conversely], whoever the ghosts and spirits are going to punish, no matter how great, they will certainly punish him."

31.19   Nowadays, those who hold that there are no ghosts say: "Is it not so [that such things] do not accord with benefiting parents and are harmful to being filial?" Master Mo Zi said: "The ghosts of ancient and modern times are the same. There are the ghosts of Heaven, there are the ghosts and spirits of the mountains and rivers, and there are also the ghosts of people who have died. Now there are instances of sons dying before their fathers, and of younger brothers dying before older brothers. Although this may be so, nevertheless there is a common saying in the world — 'Those who are born first die first'. Thus the first to die, if it is not the father, then it is the mother; if it is not the older brother, then it is the older sister. Now if we make pure the wine and millet in order to carry out the sacrifices with reverence and circumspection assuming ghosts and spirits genuinely exist, this provides father and mother, older sisters and brothers and younger brothers with drink and food, so how is it not a substantial benefit? If, however,

---

xv. Most modern Chinese commentators take 禽艾 to be a writing (book or chapter) — see, for example, WYJ, LYS, Z&Q. Some (e.g. LSL) take it to be a person, as do the two English translators (YPM, BW).

31.20   今執無鬼者言曰:「鬼神者固請無有,是以不共[58]其酒醴粢盛犧牲
之財。吾非乃今愛其酒醴粢盛犧牲之財乎?其所得者臣將何
哉?」此上逆聖王之書,內逆民人孝子之行,而為上士於天下,
此非所以為上士之道也。是故子墨子曰:「今吾為祭祀也,非直
注之污壑而棄之也,上以交鬼之福,下以合歡聚眾,取親乎鄉
里。若神有,則是得吾父母弟兄而食之也。則此豈非天下利事也
哉!」

31.21   是故子墨子曰:「今天下之王公大人士君子,中實將欲求興天下
之利,除天下之害,當若鬼神之有也,將不可不尊明也,聖王之
道也。」

---

58. By general consent, 共 is read as 供.

ghosts and spirits do not really exist, this might seem like a waste of the materials used for the wine and millet. But, on the matter of wastage, it is not that we just pour these materials into ditches and drains and throw them away. Within, the family members and without, [the people] of the district and village, all get what is provided and drink and eat it, so, although ghosts and spirits may not truly exist, this still means that large numbers can meet together for enjoyment and this fosters a closeness [among the people] of district and village."

31.20 Nowadays, those who hold that there are no ghosts say: "As for ghosts and spirits, they basically do not exist. This is why we do not provide the materials for the wine and millet and the sacrificial victims. Now it is not that we are parsimonious with respect to the materials for the wine and millet, and the sacrificial victims. It is rather a matter of asking what we will achieve."[xvi] But, above, this runs counter to the writings of the sage kings, and, within, it runs counter to conduct of filial sons among the people. And, as far as being a superior officer of the world is concerned, this is not the way to be such a superior officer. This is why Master Mo Zi said: "Now when I carry out a sacrifice it is not that I am pouring [the material] directly into ditch or drain and throwing it away. I am effecting an exchange for the blessings of the ghosts above, and I am bringing about a joyous meeting and fostering a closeness [among the people of] district and village below. And, if spirits do exist, then I am providing food for my parents and siblings. How, then, is this not a beneficial matter for the world?"

31.21 This is the reason why Master Mo Zi said: "Nowadays, if kings, dukes, great officers, officers and gentlemen of the world truly wish in their hearts to seek to promote the benefits of the world and eliminate its harms, they ought to accept the existence of ghosts and spirits and cannot help but honour them as all-seeing. It is the Way of the sage kings."

---

xvi. I have recast the preceding two sentences so they are not in the form of direct questions despite the final particles in each case. Also 乃今 is read simply as 今, 愛 is taken as 吝 嗇 (Z&Q), and 臣 is emended to 且 (SYR).

32: 非樂上

32.1   子墨子言曰：「仁之事者[1]，必務求興天下之利，除天下之害，將
以為法乎天下。利人乎，即為；不利人乎，即止。且夫仁者之為
天下度也，非為其目之所美，耳之所樂，口之所甘，身體之所
安，以此虧奪民衣食之財，仁者弗為也。」

32.2   是故子墨子之所以非樂者，非以大鐘、鳴鼓、琴瑟、竽笙之聲，
以為不樂也；非以刻鏤華文章之色，以為不美也；非以犓豢煎炙
之味，以為不甘也，非以高臺厚榭邃野[2]之居，以為不安也。雖
身知其安也，口知其甘也，目知其美也，耳知其樂也，然上考之
不中聖王之事，下度之不中萬民之利。是故子墨子曰：「為樂非
也。」

32.3   「今王公大人，雖無[3]造為樂器，以為事乎國家，非直掊潦水折壤

---

1.   Following SYR, "仁之事者" is emended to "仁者之事". WYJ, following CYX, adds 人
     after 仁.
2.   On the basis of the《楚辭 · 招魂》, "高堂邃宇", WYZ equates 邃 with 深 and 野 with
     宇.
3.   It is generally agreed that 雖無 should be read as 唯毋 and, in fact, has no meaning —
     see, for example, LYS.

32: Condemning Music I

32.1   Master Mo Zi spoke, saying: "The business of the benevolent [man] must be to seek diligently to promote what benefits the world and eliminate what harms it so he will be a model for the world. If he is benefiting people, then he acts. If he is not benefiting people, then he stops. Furthermore, those who are benevolent, in making their plans for the world, do not make what is beautiful to their eyes, or pleasing to their ears, or sweet to their mouths, or of comfort to their bodies. They take these things as depriving the people of materials for food and clothing and so the benevolent do not make them."

32.2   For this reason, Master Mo Zi's condemnation of music is not because he thinks the sounds of the struck bell and the beaten drum, of lutes and pipes, are not pleasing. It is not because he thinks the colours of inlays and patterns are not beautiful. It is not because he thinks the flavours of the broiled meats of grass- and grain-fed animals are not sweet.[i] It is not because he thinks dwellings with high towers, large pavilions and secluded courtyards are not comfortable. Although the body knows their comforts, the mouth their sweetness, the eyes their beauty and the ears their music, nevertheless, when we examine these things in terms of the high, they do not accord with the business of the sage kings, and when we evaluate them in terms of the low, they do not accord with the benefit of the ten thousand people. This is why Master Mo Zi said: "Making music is to be condemned."

32.3   "Nowadays, kings, dukes and great officers make musical instruments, taking it to be the business of the state. But this is not a simple matter like collecting water or digging earth. They will

---

i.   The "grass- and grain-fed animals" are cattle and sheep in the first case; pigs and dogs in the second.

坦而為之也[4]，將必厚措斂[5]乎萬民，以為大鐘、鳴鼓、琴瑟、竽
笙之聲。[6]古者聖王亦嘗厚措斂乎萬民，以為舟車，既以成矣，
曰：『吾將惡許用之？曰：舟用之水，車用之陸，君子息其足
焉，小人休其肩背焉。』故萬民出財齎而予之，不敢以為慼恨
者，何也？以其反中民之利也。然則樂器反中民之利亦若此，即
我弗敢非也。然則當用樂器譬之若聖王之為舟車也，即我弗敢非
也。」

32.4 「民有三患：飢者不得食，寒者不得衣，勞者不得息，三者民之
巨患也。然即[7]當為之撞巨鐘、擊鳴鼓、彈琴瑟、吹竽笙而揚干
戚，民衣食之財將安可得乎？即我以為未必然也。」

32.5 「意舍此。今有大國即攻小國，有大家即伐小家，強劫弱，眾暴
寡，詐欺愚，貴傲賤，寇亂盜賊並興，不可禁止也。然即當為之
撞巨鐘、擊鳴鼓、彈琴瑟、吹竽笙而揚干戚，天下之亂也，將安

---

4. There are several issues with the characters in this clause. The version given follows
   LYS. For a detailed discussion of the issues see WYJ, note 9, pp. 384–385.
5. I have followed WNS, whose note reads: "措斂與籍斂同。"
6. WYJ transfers the 22 characters of what is the final sentence of the section in the above
   text to this position.
7. Following WYZ, 然即 is read as 然則.

certainly have to levy heavy taxes from the ten thousand people to make the sounds of the struck bell and the beaten drum, of lutes and pipes. In ancient times, the sage kings also levied heavy taxes from the ten thousand people to make boats and carts. And when they were completed, they asked [themselves]: 'Where will we use these things?'[ii] 'The boats we will use on water and the carts on land,' they said, 'so gentlemen can rest their feet and ordinary men can rest their shoulders and backs.' Therefore, the ten thousand people brought forth their goods and presented them, and dared not resent this. Why? Because in return these things were in accord with the benefits of the people. In this case, then, if musical instruments gave in return something to accord with the benefits of the people like this, then I would not dare condemn them. That is to say, if there was some proper use for musical instruments like that of the sage kings' use of boats and carts, then I would not dare condemn them."

32.4 "The people have three hardships: to be hungry and not find food; to be cold and not find clothing; to be weary and not find rest. These three things are great hardships for the people. If this is so, then suppose we strike the great bells, beat the sounding drums, strum lutes, blow pipes, and brandish shields and battle-axes. Will this enable the people to find the materials for food and clothing? I certainly don't think this will ever be so."

32.5 "But let us put this aside for the moment.[iii] Nowadays, there are large states attacking small states. There are large families striking at small families. The strong plunder the weak. The many tyrannise the few. The cunning deceive the foolish. The noble are arrogant towards the lowly. And robbery, disorder, theft and plunder all arise and cannot be stopped. If this is so, then suppose we strike the great bells, beat the sounding drums, strum lutes, blow pipes, and brandish shields and battle-axes. Will this enable

---

ii. Previous English translators (YPM, BW) put this question in the mouths of "the people", but this is not how it is understood by Chinese commentators. In the question, 許 is taken as 所 (see WYZ and also WYJ's detailed note).

iii. The translation of this initial brief sentence depends on YY's reading of 意 as 抑 (as in similar structures elsewhere).

可得而治與？即我〔以為〕[8] 未必然也。」是故子墨子曰：「姑嘗厚
措斂乎萬民，以為大鐘、鳴鼓、琴瑟、竽笙之聲，以求興天下之
利，除天下之害而無補也。」是故子墨子曰：「為樂非也。」

32.6　今王公大人，唯毋處高臺厚榭之上而視之，鐘猶是延鼎[9] 也，弗
撞擊將何樂得焉哉？其說將必撞擊之。惟勿撞擊，將必不使老與
遲[10] 者。老與遲者耳目不聰明，股肱不畢強，聲不和調，明不轉
朴[11]。將必使當[12] 年，因其耳目之聰明，股肱之畢強，聲之和
調，眉之轉朴。使丈夫為之，廢丈夫耕稼樹藝之時；使婦人為
之，廢婦人紡績織紝之事。今王公大人唯毋為樂，虧奪民衣食之
財，以拊樂如此多也。是故子墨子曰：「為樂非也。」

32.7　今大鐘、鳴鼓、琴瑟、竽笙之聲既已具矣，大人鏽然[13] 奏而獨聽
之，將何樂得焉哉？其說將必與賤人不與君子[14]。與君子聽之，
廢君子聽治；與賤人聽之，廢賤人之從事。今王公大人惟毋為
樂，虧奪民之衣食之財，以拊樂如此多也。是故子墨子曰：「為
樂非也。」

8.　Added following WYJ.
9.　On "延鼎" SYR has: "蓋謂偃覆之鼎。"
10.　Following WNS, 遲 is read as 稚.
11.　"明不轉朴" and later "眉之轉朴" are taken to indicate tonal changes related to how the
　　bell is struck based on YY's generally accepted proposal that both 明 and 眉 be read as
　　音, and 朴 as 扑 in the sense of 變.
12.　壯 is read for 當 (WNS).
13.　鏽然 is taken as 肅然 — see, for example, LYS.
14.　In the translation, I have followed SYR's reworking of this sentence from "其說將必與
　　賤人不與君子" to "其說將不與賤人必與君子". See also WYJ's detailed note 46,
　　p. 389.

good order to be imposed on the disorder of the world? I certainly don't think so." This is why Master Mo Zi said: "As before, imposing heavy taxes on the ten thousand people in order to make the sounds of the great bell, the sounding drum, lutes and pipes won't help in seeking to promote the world's benefits and eliminate the world's harms." This is why Master Mo Zi said: "Making music is to be condemned."

32.6 Nowadays, kings, dukes and great officers, when they sit up in their high towers and large pavilions and look at them, the bells just seem like upturned tripods (*ding*). If no-one strikes them, how will they get any music from them? Clearly their pleasure requires someone to strike them. But for striking [the bells] they will certainly not use those who are old or young. In the case of the old and young, their ears and eyes are not sharp and keen, and their arms and legs are not quick and strong, so the sounds are not harmonious and the tones do not change appropriately. They will undoubtedly use those in their prime because their ears and eyes are sharp and keen and their arms and legs are quick and strong, so the sounds will be harmonious and the tones will change appropriately. If they use men to do this, it will interfere with their time for sowing grain and planting trees. If they use women to do this, it will interfere with their work of spinning and weaving. So now if kings, dukes and great officers make music, their depleting and depriving the people of materials for clothing and food in order to make music will, in this way, be very great. This is why Master Mo Zi said: "Making music is to be condemned."

32.7 Now if the great bell, the sounding drum, lutes and pipes are already prepared and a great officer reverentially plays music and listens to it alone, what pleasure will he get from this? If his enjoyment is not with lowly men then it must be with gentlemen. But if he listens to [music] with gentlemen, that prevents them from attending to administration. And if he listens to [music] with lowly men, that prevents them from carrying out their work. So now, if kings, dukes and great officers make music, their depleting and depriving the people of materials for clothing and food in order to make music will, in this way, be very great. This is why Master Mo Zi said: "Making music is to be condemned."

32.8   昔者齊康公興樂萬，萬人不可衣短褐，不可食糠糟，曰食飲不
美，面目顏色，不足視也；衣服不美，身體從容醜嬴[15]，不足觀
也。是以食必粱肉，衣必文繡，此掌[16] 不從事乎衣食之財，而掌
食乎人者也。是故子墨子曰：「今王公大人唯毋為樂，虧奪民衣
食之財，以拊樂如此多也」。是故子墨子曰：「為樂非也。」

32.9   今人固與禽獸麋鹿、蜚[17] 鳥、貞[18] 蟲異者也，今之禽獸麋鹿，蜚
鳥、貞蟲，因其羽毛以為衣裘，因其蹄蚤以為絝屨，因其水草以
為飲食。故唯使雄不耕稼樹藝，雌亦不紡績織絍，衣食之財固已
具矣。今人與此異者也，賴其力者生，不賴其力者不生。君子不
強聽治，即刑政亂；賤人不強從事，即財用不足。今天下之士君
子，以吾言不然，然即姑嘗數天下分事，而觀樂之害。王公大人
蚤朝晏退，聽獄治政，此其分事也。士君子竭股肱之力，亶其思

---

15. WYJ omits these two characters so making the statement parallel to the preceding statement — see his note 53, p. 391.
16. In both instances in this sentence, 掌 is taken as 常 — see, for example, LYS.
17. Following SYR, 蜚 is read as 飛.
18. Following SYR, 貞 is read as 微.

32.8 In former times, Duke Kang of Qi took pleasure in the *Wan* dance, but the musicians and dancers were not permitted to wear coarse clothing, nor to eat poor quality food.[iv] He said that, if their food and drink were not excellent, their appearance and countenance would not be good enough to look at. And, if their clothes and garments were not excellent, their bodies and bearing would not be good enough to look at. So their food had to be millet and meat and their clothes had to be patterned and embroidered. Such people never themselves worked [to produce] the materials for clothing and food, but always relied on others for their food. It was for this reason that Master Mo Zi said: "So now, if kings, dukes and great officers make music, their depleting and depriving the people of materials for clothing and food in order to make music will, in this way, be very great." This is why Master Mo Zi said: "Making music is to be condemned."

32.9 Now mankind is fundamentally different from birds and beasts such as the tailed deer, flying birds and small insects, insofar as birds and beasts like the tailed deer, flying birds and small insects rely on their feathers and fur as clothes and coverings, on their hooves and claws as trousers and shoes, and on water and grass as their drink and food. This is why, even if the males do not sow grains or plant trees, and the females do not spin or weave, the materials for clothing and food are assuredly already provided. Now the difference between people and these [creatures] is that people rely on their strength to live. And if they don't rely on their strength, they don't live. If gentlemen are not diligent in the conduct of government, then the administration falls into disorder. If lowly people are not diligent in doing their work, then the materials for use will be insufficient. Nowadays, officers and gentlemen of the world take my words to be wrong, so let us then enumerate for a moment the various duties in the world and look at how music harms them. Kings, dukes and great officers go to court early and retire late. They decide lawsuits and bring order to

---

iv. There is some uncertainty about the initial part of this section. There is, however, wide acceptance of the proposals of YY and SSX which are considered in detail by WYJ. The translation closely follows LYS's version which incorporates these proposals.

慮之智，內治官府，外收斂關市、山林、澤梁之利，以實倉廩府
庫，此其分事也。農夫蚤出暮入，耕稼樹藝，多聚叔粟，此其分
事也。婦人夙興夜寐，紡績織絍，多治麻絲葛緒綑布縿[19]，此其
分事也。

32.10 今惟毋在乎王公大人説樂而聽之，即必不能蚤朝晏退，聽獄治
政，是故國家亂而社稷危矣。今惟毋在乎士君子説樂而聽之，即
必不能竭股肱之力，亶其思慮之智，內治官府，外收斂關市、山
林、澤梁之利，以實倉廩府庫，是故倉廩府庫不實。今惟毋在乎
農夫説樂而聽之，即必不能蚤出暮入，耕稼樹藝，多聚叔粟，是
故叔粟不足。今惟毋在乎婦人説樂而聽之，即必不能夙興夜寐，
紡績織絍，多治麻絲葛緒綑布縿，是故布縿不興。曰：孰為大人
之聽治而廢國家之從事？[20] 曰樂也。是故子墨子曰：「為樂非
也。」

32.11 何以知其然也？曰先王之書，湯之官刑有之曰：「其恆舞于宮，

---

19. See 37.8 (note 81, p. 346) below for the textual and interpretative issues in this statement.
20. There is general acceptance of YY's reworking of this sentence from "孰為大人之聽
    治而廢國家之從事？" to "孰為而廢大人之聽治，賤人之從事？"

government. This is their allotted task. Officers and gentlemen exhaust the strength of their limbs, and use to the full the capacities of their minds in bringing order to government offices within, and receive the benefits of the taxes on passes and market places, mountains and forests, and marshes and bridges without, so as to fill the public granaries and treasuries. This is their allotted task. Farmers go out early and come back late, sowing grains and planting trees, and collecting large amounts of pulses and grains. This is their allotted task. Women rise early and go to bed late, spinning and weaving to produce large amounts of hemp, silk and other cloth, and weaving cotton and silk. This is their allotted task.

32.10 If, as things are now, kings, dukes and great officers delight in music and listen to it, then they certainly will not be able to come to court early and retire late, resolve lawsuits and bring order to government. As a result, the state will be in disorder and the altars of soil and grain will be in danger. If, as things are now, officers and gentlemen delight in music and listen to it, then they certainly will not be able to exhaust the strength of their limbs and use the capacities of their minds to the full in bringing order to government offices within, and receiving the benefits of the taxes on passes and market places, mountains and forests, and marshes and bridges without, so as to fill the public granaries and the treasuries. As a result, the public granaries and the treasuries will not be full. If, as things are now, farmers delight in music and listen to it, then they certainly will not be able to go out early and come back late, sowing grains and planting trees, and collecting large amounts of pulses and grains. As a result, pulses and grains will not be enough. If, as things are now, women delight in music and listen to it, then they certainly will not be able to rise early and go to bed late, spinning and weaving to produce large amounts of hemp, silk and other cloth, and weaving cotton and silk. As a result, the production of cotton and silk will not flourish. What is it that destroys the great officer's attention to government and the lowly person's attention to work? I say it is music. This is why Master Mo Zi said: "Making music is to be condemned."

32.11 How do we know this to be so? I say it is through the writings of

是謂巫風。其刑君子出絲二衛，小人否，似二伯黃徑。」[21] 乃言
曰：「嗚乎！舞佯佯，黃言孔章，上帝弗常，九有以亡，上帝不
順，降之百殃，其家必壞喪。」[22] 察九有之所以亡者，徒從飾樂
也。於《武觀》曰：「啟乃淫溢康樂，野於飲食，將將銘莧磬以力，
湛濁于酒，湢食于野，萬舞翼翼，章聞于大，天用弗式。」[23] 故上
者天鬼弗戒，下者萬民弗利。

32.12   是故子墨子曰：「今天下士君子，請將欲求興天下之利，除天下
之害，當在樂之為物，將不可不禁而止也。」

33: 非樂中：闕

34: 非樂下：闕

---

21. There are several issues with this apparent quotation: (i) What is its source? Of the first
     nine characters, seven appear in the *Documents*《書經‧伊訓》. There is, however, no
     chapter with the title《官刑》. Chinese commentators refer to the *Zuo Zhuan* for the 6th
     year of Duke Zhao 昭公 and a letter from Shu Xiang 叔向 to Zi Chan 子產 (WYJ, note
     77, p. 394). (ii) According to BY, 衛 should be read as 緯. He quotes the《說文》as
     follows: "緯，織橫絲也." (iii) SYR takes 否 as 齐. (iv) No one can make any sense of
     "似二伯黃徑". Following Z&Q, I have omitted it.
22. The issues with this quotation are as follows: (i) SYR's proposed emendation of "乃言
     曰" to "泰誓曰". (ii) In the first sentence of the quotation, although there is some
     resemblance to the *Documents*《書經‧伊訓》(see LCC, vol. 3, p. 198), there is a close
     correspondence to the *Odes*《詩經‧魯頌》, Mao #300 (LCC, vol. 4, pp. 625). Mao
     equates 洋洋 with 眾多. (iii) In the second sentence, following SYR and Z&Q, 黃 is read
     as 其, 孔 is taken as 甚 or 很, and 章 is understood as 顯明. (iv) The remaining five lines
     appear in closely similar form to what Legge has as an appendix to the *Great Oath* (see
     LCC, vol. 3, p. 299). In these lines, 常 is read as 右 (WYZ), 九有 is taken as 九州
     following Mao's note to a similar line in the *Odes* #303 (LCC, vol. 4, p. 636), and the
     unknown character in the penultimate line is taken as 殃.
23. The issues with this apparent quotation are: (i) *Wu Guan* 武觀 is taken as the title of a
     no longer extant writing. The predominant view is that 武觀 is 五觀 a son of 啟, the
     second emperor of the Xia dynasty — see WYJ, note 92, pp. 396–397. (ii) In the first
     sentence, 啟乃 is taken as 啟子, i.e. 五觀 (Z&Q). (iii) SYR's reworking of the third
     sentence is followed — i.e. to "將將鍠鍠，笙 (笙) 磬以方" — see also the *Odes*《詩
     經‧周頌》Mao #274, LCC, vol. 4, p. 579. (iv) In the fifth sentence, Z&Q's version is
     followed, this including SYR's taking of 渝 as 偷. (v) In the seventh sentence, 章 is taken
     as 顯 by general consent and 大 as 天 (see Z&Q). (vi) In the final sentence, 式 is taken
     法式.

the former kings. Tang's *Official Punishments* has this to say: "Frequent dancing in a dwelling is spoken of as witchcraft. In the case of a gentleman, the penalty is two rolls of silk. In the case of a petty man, this is doubled." The *Great Oath* says: "Ah, alas! How much dancing there is. How many sounds, clear and sharp. The Supreme Lord does not honour him. The Nine Regions will be lost. The Supreme Lord is displeased and will send down on him a hundred calamities. His household will certainly be damaged and destroyed." If we examine the reason for the loss of the Nine Regions, it is nothing other than elaborate music. In the *Wu Guan* it says: "Qi's son (Wu Guan) gave himself to excess and dissipation. He ate and drank in the open fields. *Jiang-jiang huang-huang* the pipes and chimes sounded in harmony. He gave himself up to wine. The whole day he feasted and wandered. There were the ordered movements of the *Wan* dance and the sounds rose to Heaven. But Heaven took this as being a transgression of the rule." Thus, above, it transgressed the rule of Heaven and the ghosts, and, below, it brought no benefit to the ten thousand people.

32.12   This is why Master Mo Zi said: "Nowadays, if the world's officers and gentlemen genuinely wish to seek to promote what benefits the world and eliminate what harms it, then, in regard to such a thing as music, they cannot but prohibit and prevent it."

33: Condemning Music II: Lost

34: Condemning Music III: Lost

35: 非命上

35.1 子墨子言曰：「古¹者王公大人，為政國家者，皆欲國家之富，人
民之眾，刑政之治。然而不得富而得貧，不得眾而得寡，不得治
而得亂，則是本失其所欲，得其所惡，是故何也？」

35.2 子墨子言曰：「執有命者以雜於民間者眾。執有命者之言曰，『命
富則富，命貧則貧，命眾則眾，命寡則寡，命治則治，命亂則
亂，命壽則壽，命夭則夭，命²，雖強勁何益哉？』以上說王公大
人，下以駔百姓之從事，故執有命者不仁。³故當執有命者之
言，不可不明辨。」

35.3 然則明辨此之說將奈何哉？子墨子言曰：「必立儀⁴，言而毋儀，
譬猶運鈞之上而立朝夕者也，是非利害之辨，不可得而明知也。
故言必有三表。」何為三表？子墨子言曰：「有本之者，有原之

---

1. English translators (YPM, BW, PJI) read 古 as 今, as does AF who has a note to this
    effect. Recent Chinese editions that provide a modern language paraphrase all retain 古
    (LYS, LSL, MBJ, MZQY/Z&Q).
2. WYZ has suggested that there is some missing text after 命 whereas LYS considers 命
    to be superfluous here. WYJ, who leaves the text as it is, writes: "言凡事有命" and this
    is the reading I have followed.
3. The first two parts of this statement are difficult to understand as they are. Commentators
    who accept them read 說 as 遊說 and 駔 as 阻 in the sense of 阻礙 following BY. WYJ
    proposes the following emended and expanded text which is what I have followed in the
    translation: "上以說王公大人，廢大人之聽治。下以說天下百姓，駔百姓之從事"
    — see his detailed note 3, p. 404.
4. As elsewhere, 儀 is taken as 標準 or 準則 — see, for example, Z&Q.

35: Against Fate I

35.1   Master Mo Zi spoke, saying: "In ancient times, kings, dukes and great officers, in governing a state, all wished that state to be rich, its people numerous, and its administration well ordered. However, when they did not get prosperity but poverty instead, when they did not get many people but few instead, when they did not get order but disorder instead, this was fundamentally to lose what it was they desired and get what it was they abhorred. What was the cause of this?"

35.2   Master Mo Zi spoke, saying: "Those who believe in Fate are mixed in with the population in large numbers. And they say: 'If Fate decrees wealth, then there is wealth. If Fate decrees poverty, then there is poverty. If Fate decrees many people, then there are many people. If Fate decrees few people, then there are few people. If Fate decrees order, then there is order. If Fate decrees disorder, then there is disorder. If Fate decrees longevity, then there is longevity. If Fate decrees an early death, then there is an early death. Fate is everywhere, and although one might be strong and unyielding, of what benefit is that?' Above, these theories affect kings, dukes and great officers, causing them to neglect their administration. Below, these theories affect the common people and hinder the conduct of their affairs. Thus, those who believe in Fate are not benevolent. Therefore, it is appropriate that the words of those who believe in Fate cannot be otherwise than clearly distinguished."

35.3   If this is the case, then how does one clearly distinguish these theories? Master Mo Zi spoke, saying: "You must establish standards. To speak without standards is like using the upper part of a potter's revolving wheel to determine the direction of the sunrise and sunset. The distinction between right and wrong, between benefit and harm cannot be achieved and clearly known. Therefore, theories must have three criteria." What are the three criteria?

者，有用之者。於何本之？上本之於古者聖王之事。於何原之？下原察百姓耳目之實。於何用之？廢⁵以為刑政，觀其中國家百姓人民之利。此所為言有三表也。」

35.4 「然而今天下之士君子，或以命為有。蓋嘗尚觀於聖王之事？⁶古者桀之所亂，湯受而治之。紂之所亂，武王受而治之。此世未易，民未渝，在於桀紂，則天下亂；在於湯武，則天下治。豈可謂有命哉！」

35.5 「然而今天下之士君子，或以命為有。蓋嘗尚觀於先王之書？先王之書，所以出國家，布施百姓者，憲⁷也。先王之憲，亦嘗有曰：『福不可請，而禍不可諱⁸，敬無益，暴無傷』者乎？所以聽獄制罪者，刑也。先王之刑亦嘗有曰：『福不可請，禍不可諱，敬無益，暴無傷』者乎？所以整設師旅，進退師徒者，誓也。先王之誓亦嘗有曰：『福不可請，禍不可諱，敬無益，暴無傷』者乎？」是故子墨子言曰：「吾當未鹽數⁹，天下之良書不可盡計數，

---

5. There is general acceptance of WYZ's reading of 廢 as 發.
6. In translating this sentence I have followed LSL's readings which are as follows: 蓋 as 盍; 嘗 as 試; 尚 as 上; 事 as 事例.
7. Most commentators refer to the 《爾雅‧釋詁》 which has: "憲，法也。"
8. 諱 is taken as 違 in the sense of 避免.
9. In this sentence, 當 is taken as 尚 (SYR) and 鹽 as 盡 (BY).

Master Mo Zi spoke, saying: "There is the foundation; there is the source; there is the application. In what is the foundation? The foundation is in the actions of the ancient sage kings above. In what is the source? The source is in the truth of the evidence of the eyes and ears of the common people below. In what is the application? It emanates from government policy and is seen in the benefit to the ordinary people of the state. These are what are termed the 'three criteria'."

35.4 "Nevertheless, among officers and gentlemen of the world at the present time, there are some who take there to be Fate. How can they not look to the past and consider the examples of the sage kings? In ancient times, the disorder of Jie was inherited by Tang who brought order to it. The disorder of Zhou was inherited by King Wu who brought order to it. The world never changed and the people never changed, but under Jie and Zhou the world was in disorder, whereas under Tang and Wu the world was well ordered. How can they say there is Fate?"

35.5 "Nevertheless, among the world's officers and gentlemen at the present time, there are some who take there to be Fate. How can they not look to the past and consider the writings of former kings? The writings of former kings which came from the state and were promulgated to the common people were the 'Laws'. Among the 'Laws' of the former kings were there ever those that said: 'Good fortune cannot be requested, bad fortune cannot be prevented. Being respectful is not beneficial, being evil is not harmful?' The means whereby lawsuits were heard and crimes were restrained were the 'Punishments'. Among the 'Punishments' of the former kings were there ever those that said: 'Good fortune cannot be requested, bad fortune cannot be prevented. Being respectful is not beneficial, being evil is not harmful'? The means whereby armies were kept in order and deployed, and troops ordered to advance or retreat were the 'Declarations'. Among the 'Declarations' of the former kings were there ever those that said: 'Good fortune cannot be requested, bad fortune cannot be prevented. Being respectful is not beneficial, being evil is not harmful'?" This is why Master Mo Zi spoke, saying: "This still does not bring me to the end of the matter. The excellent writings

大方[10]論數，而五[11]者是也。今雖毋[12]求執有命者之言，不必
得，不亦可錯[13]乎？今用執有命者之言，是覆天下之義。覆天下
之義者，是立命者也，百姓之諄[14]也。說百姓之諄者，是滅天下
之人也。」

35.6   然則所為欲義〔人〕在上者，何也？[15]曰：「義人在上，天下必治，
上帝山川鬼神，必有幹主[16]，萬民被其大利。」何以知之？子墨子
曰：「古者湯封於亳[17]，絕長繼短，方地百里，與其百姓兼相愛，
交相利，移[18]則分。率其百姓，以上尊天事鬼，是以天鬼富之，
諸侯與之，百姓親之，賢士歸之，未歿其世，而王天下，政諸
侯。昔者文王封於岐周，絕長繼短，方地百里，與其百姓兼相
愛，交相利，則[19]，是以近者安其政，遠者歸其德。聞文王者，
皆起而趨之。罷[20]不肖股肱不利者，處而願之曰：『奈何乎使文王
之地及我，吾則吾利[21]，〔則吾〕豈不亦猶文王之民也哉。』是以天
鬼富之，諸侯與之，百姓親之，賢士歸之，未歿其世，而王天

---

10. 大方 is generally accepted as 大略.
11. There is general acceptance of BY's emendation of 五 to 三, the three being the "Laws"
      憲, the "Punishments" 刑 and the "Declarations" 誓.
12. 雖毋 is taken as 唯毋 — see, for example, LYS.
13. Read as 措 in the sense of 措置.
14. Read as 悴 in the sense of 憂 following YY.
15. In this sentence, 為 is read as 謂 (Z&Q) and 人 is added after 義 (SYR).
16. Read as 宗主 following SYR. LYS has: "古代承祖先祭祀的叫做幹主，亦稱宗主" —
      see his note 3, p. 256.
17. 亳 was a place in what is now Henan. When Tang established the Shang dynasty
      following the fall of the Xia, this was the site of the capital.
18. BY has the following note: "言財多則分也。移，或多字。"
19. 則 should either be omitted (WYZ) or the characters 移 and 分 added to parallel the
      previous statement (LSL).
20. Several commentators draw attention to Yang Liang's 楊倞 note on a similar use of 罷
      in the 《荀子。稱相》("罷，弱不任事者") in equating it with 罷 here — see, for
      example, WYJ's note 37, pp. 408–409.
21. In the translation I have followed YY's rearrangement — i.e. omit the first 吾 and 利
      from the four characters given and then add the remaining "則吾" to the following
      clause.

of the world are too numerous to be entirely considered, but, in general, they are the same as these three. Now, although we might look for arguments to support the idea of Fate, we certainly do not find them, so can we not also abandon [it]? Now the arguments of those who hold that there is Fate are used to overthrow righteousness in the world. To overthrow righteousness in the world is to establish Fate and this is to create distress for the ordinary people. Those who take delight in creating distress for the ordinary people are those who would destroy the world's people."

35.6 In this case, then, why is there said to be the wish for righteous men above? I say: "If there are righteous men above, the world will certainly be well ordered. The Supreme Lord and the ghosts and spirits of the mountains and rivers will certainly have someone to preside over [the sacrifices], so the ten thousand people will receive their great benefits." How do we know this?

Master Mo Zi said: "In ancient times, Tang was enfeoffed with Bo which, making allowance for its irregular boundaries, was one hundred *li* square. He united his people in universal mutual love and in reciprocal mutual benefit, and when there was plenty it was distributed. He led his people to honour Heaven and serve the ghosts above. For this reason, Heaven and the ghosts made him rich, the feudal lords joined with him, the common people loved him, worthy officers returned to him, and, within his own generation, he became ruler of all under Heaven and leader of the feudal lords. In former times, King Wen was enfeoffed with Qi Zhou which, making allowance for its irregular boundaries, was one hundred *li* square. He united his people in universal mutual love and in reciprocal mutual benefit. For this reason, those who were near were content with his government and those who were distant returned to his virtue. Those who heard of King Wen all rose up to hasten to him. Apart, that is, from those who were weak and exhausted and whose arms and legs were not up to it. They stayed where they were and asked in expectation: 'Could not the domain of King Wen extend to us, for then how would we not also be King Wen's people?' This is why Heaven and the ghosts

下，政諸侯。鄉者言曰：『義人在上，天下必治，上帝山川鬼
神，必有幹主，萬民被其大利。』吾用此知之。」

35.7　「是故古之聖王發憲出令，設以為賞罰以勸賢，是以入則孝慈於
親戚，出則弟長於鄉里，坐處有度，出入有節，男女有辨。是
故使治官府，則不盜竊，守城則不崩叛，君有難則死，出亡則
送，此上之所賞，而百姓之所譽也。執有命者之言曰：『上之所
賞，命固且賞，非賢故賞也。上之所罰，命固且罰，不²² 暴故罰
也』²³ 。」

35.8　「是故入則不慈孝於親戚，出則不弟長於鄉里，坐處不度，出入
無節，男女無辨。是故治官府則盜竊，守城則崩叛，君有難則不
死，出亡則不送。此上之所罰，百姓之所非毀也。執有命者言

---

22. Several modern editors quote WYZ's note on 不 as follows: "不與 "非" 同義，故互
    用。"

23. YY has questioned whether the 13 characters of this sentence, repeated in the following
    section, are superfluous here and whether, also, the 13 characters of the preceding
    sentence are superfluous when repeated in the following section (35.8) — see WYJ notes
    47 and 49, p. 410.

enriched him, why the feudal lords joined him, why the ordinary people loved him, and why worthy officers returned to him. Before the end of his own generation, he became ruler of all under Heaven and leader of the feudal lords. As I said previously, when a righteous man is ruler, the world is certainly well ordered, the Supreme Lord and the ghosts and spirits of the mountains and rivers certainly have those to preside over [the sacrifices], and the ten thousand people are greatly benefited by them. This is how I know it."

35.7 "This is why the ancient sage kings promulgated laws and issued decrees, establishing through them rewards and punishments to encourage worthiness. In this way, within, there was filiality and compassion towards parents; without, there was deference to elders in the districts and villages; in entering and leaving, there was courtesy; and between men and women, there was [the proper] distinction. For this reason, when people were put in charge of administrative offices, they did not pilfer and steal; when they were called on to defend the city, they did not betray it; when the ruler encountered difficulties, they were loyal to the death; when he was forced to flee, they followed him. This is what those above rewarded and what the ordinary people praised. [Yet] the arguments of those who hold that there is Fate say: 'Whomever superiors reward is undoubtedly fated to be rewarded. It is not that he is worthy and therefore is rewarded. Whomever superiors punish is undoubtedly fated to be punished. It is not that he is cruel and therefore is punished'."

35.8 "If this were the case, then, within, there would not be filiality and compassion towards parents; without, there would not be deference to elders in the districts and villages; in bearing, there would not be established practice; in entering and leaving, there would not be courtesy; and between men and women, there would not be [the proper] distinction. For this reason, when people were put in charge of administrative offices, they would pilfer and steal; when they were called on to defend the city, they would betray it; when the ruler encountered difficulties, they would not be loyal to the death; when he was forced to flee, they would not follow him. This is what those above punished and what the ordinary people

曰：『上之所罰，命固且罰，不暴故罰也。上之所賞，命固且
賞，非賢故賞也。』以此為君則不義，為臣則不忠，為父則不
慈，為子則不孝，為兄則不良[24]，為弟則不弟。而強執此者，此
特凶言之所自生，而暴人之道也。」

35.9 「然則何以知命之為暴人之道？昔上世之窮民，貪於飲食，惰於
從事，是以衣食之財不足，而飢寒凍餒之憂至，不知曰：『我罷
不肖，從事不疾』，必曰：『我命固且貧』。昔上世暴王不忍其耳目
之淫，心涂之辟[25]，不順其親戚，遂以亡失國家，傾覆社稷，不
知曰：『我罷不肖，為政不善』，必曰：『吾命固失之』。」

35.10 「於《仲虺之告》曰：『我聞於夏人，矯天命，布命于下，帝伐之
惡，龔喪厥師。』[26]此言湯之所以非桀之執有命也。於《太誓》曰：
『紂夷處，不肯事上帝鬼神，禍厥先神禔不祀，乃曰吾民有命，
無廖排漏，天亦縱棄之而弗葆。』[27]此言武王所以非紂執有命
也。」

---

24. SYR has the following note on this clause: "良為兄義不甚切，疑'良'當為'長'。"
25. In this final phrase, 心涂 is taken as 心志 (WYZ). In similar statements in the following
    two chapters there is "心意". 辟 is read as 僻.
26. There are several issues in this apparent quotation as follows: (i) The《仲虺之告》is a
    chapter of the《書經》— 告 is taken as 誥 — see LCC, vol. 3, pp. 177–183. The statement
    in the *Documents* is somewhat different — see LCC, vol. 3, p. 179. (ii) Zhong Hui 仲
    虺 was a minister serving Tang 湯. (iii) The Xia man 夏人 is Jie 桀. (iv) According to
    BY, the clause "帝伐之惡" should read "帝式是惡" as in the following chapter — see
    36.6 below. (v) 厥 is taken as 其.
27. There are also issues with this quotation from the《書經》— see LCC, vol. 3, p. 286 —
    as follows: (i) On "夷處" which appears in the *Documents* as "夷居", LYS has: "即倨
    傲是居". (ii) 肯 in the text is in its old form — ZWDCD #29895. The *Documents* has
    "弗事". (iii) In the third clause, 禍 is read as 棄 (SYR), 先 as 祖先 and 神禔 as 神祇
    in the sense of 神靈. (iv) In the fourth clause, 民 is omitted on the basis of a similar
    statement in "天志中" (SYR). (v) On the fifth clause (無廖排漏) reference is also made
    to "天志中". I have followed LYS who has: "是說不戮力祭祀鬼神之事，所以天亦棄
    之而不保佑他們。"

reviled. [Yet] the arguments of those who hold that there is Fate say: 'Whomever superiors punish is undoubtedly fated to be punished. It is not that he is cruel and therefore is punished. Whomever superiors reward is undoubtedly fated to be rewarded. It is not that he is worthy and therefore is rewarded.' In this way, rulers are not righteous; ministers are not loyal; fathers are not compassionate; sons are not filial; older brothers are not caring; younger brothers are not deferential. And strong adherence to these ideas is particularly the origin of inhuman theories and the way of cruel men."

35.9 "In this case, then, how do we know that Fatalism is the way of evil men? Formerly, the poor people of earlier generations were covetous of drink and food and were indolent in the conduct of their affairs so the material for clothing and food was insufficient and the hardships of hunger and cold were extreme. But they did not know [enough] to say: 'We are weak and unworthy and are not diligent in the conduct of our affairs'. Instead, they had to say: 'It is our Fate that has determined that we are poor'. Formerly, the evil kings of earlier generations could not restrain the excesses of their senses (ears and eyes) nor the depravity in their hearts. They did not act in accordance with their parents so subsequently the kingdom was lost and the altars of soil and grain overturned. But they did not know [enough] to say: 'I am weak and unworthy and my conduct of government is not good'. Instead, they had to say: 'It is my Fate that determined I should lose it (the kingdom)'."

35.10 "In the *Announcement of Zhong Hui* it says: 'I have heard the man of Xia feigned the decree of Heaven and put forth a decree to his subjects. The Supreme Lord thereupon resented him and destroyed his forces.' This tells how Tang rejected Jie's belief in Fate. In *The Great Oath* it says: 'Zhou was haughty and imperious and was not willing to serve the Supreme Lord and the ghosts and spirits. He neglected the spirits of his ancestors and did not sacrifice to them, going so far as to say that he himself was Fate. He was not diligent in his service to the ghosts and spirits, so Heaven also abandoned him and did not protect him.' This tells how King Wu rejected Zhou's belief in Fate."

35.11　「今用執有命者之言,則上不聽治,下不從事。上不聽治,則刑政亂;下不從事,則財用不足。上無以供粢盛酒醴,祭祀上帝鬼神,下無以降綏天下賢可之士,外無以應待諸侯之賓客,內無以食飢衣寒,將養老弱[28]。故命上不利於天,中不利於鬼,下不利於人,而強執此者,此特兇言之所自生,而暴人之道也。」

35.12　是故子墨子言曰:「今天下之士君子,忠[29]實欲天下之富而惡其貧,欲天下之治而惡其亂,執有命者之言,不可不非,此天下之大害也。」

---

28. There is some variation in the text of this sentence. That given above follows modern editions such as LYS and Z&Q which preserve the 上 / 下 and 外 / 內 contrasts. For an alternative version see WYJ, p. 403 and his note 68, pp. 412–413.

29. As elsewhere, 忠 is taken as 中 in the sense of 內心.

35.11 "Now if the arguments of those who hold that there is Fate are put into practice, then those above will not attend to government and those below will not carry out their business. If those above do not attend to government, the administration will be in disorder. If those below do not carry out their business, materials for use will be insufficient. Those above will not have the means to provide millet and sweet wine to offer sacrifices to the Supreme Lord and the ghosts and spirits, and those below will not have the means to provide stability for the world's worthy and capable officers. Without, there will not be the means to receive the visits of feudal lords, and within, there will not be the means to feed the hungry and clothe the cold, nor to care for the old and feeble. Therefore, with regard to Fate, it is of no benefit to Heaven above; it is of no benefit to the spirits in the middle realm; it is of no benefit to the people below. Strong adherence to these ideas is particularly the origin of inhuman theories and the way of cruel men."

35.12 This is why Master Mo Zi spoke, saying: "Nowadays, officers and gentlemen of the world who, in their hearts, genuinely desire wealth for the world and abhor its poverty, who desire good order for the world and abhor its disorder, cannot but oppose the arguments of those who hold that there is Fate, [since] this is a great harm to the world."

36: 非命中

36.1 子墨子言曰：「凡出言談，由文學之為道也，則不可而不先立義法。[1] 若言而無義，譬猶立朝夕於員[2] 鈞之上也，則雖有巧工，必不能得正[3] 焉。然今天下之情偽，未可得而識也，故使言有三法。三法者何也？有本之者，有原之者，有用之者。於其本之也，考之天鬼之志，聖王之事。於其原之也，徵以先王之書。用之奈何？發而為刑[4]。此言之三法也。」

36.2 「今天下之士君子〔或以命為有〕或以命為亡[5]，我所以知命之有與亡者，以眾人耳目之情，知有與亡。有聞之，有見之，謂之有；莫之聞，莫之見，謂之亡。然胡不嘗考之百姓之情？自古以及今，生民以來者，亦嘗見命之物，聞命之聲者乎？則未嘗有也。若以百姓為愚不肖，耳目之情不足因而為法，然則胡不嘗考之諸侯之傳言流語乎？自古以及今，生民以來者，亦嘗有聞命之聲，見命之體者乎？則未嘗有也。然胡不嘗考之聖王之事？古之聖

---

1. There are three points in relation to this first sentence: (i) 出 is emended to 為 (SYR). (ii) 道 should be omitted as superfluous. (iii) 義 is taken as 儀 in the sense of 標準 or 準則.
2. Some commentators take 員 as 運 in keeping with the previous chapter (e.g. LSL); others take it as 圓 (e.g. LYS who writes: "員鈞和運鈞都是圓盤").
3. For 正, Z&Q have: "正確得方向".
4. Generally accepted as "政刑" or "刑政". WYJ, for example, has 刑政.
5. In this statement, modern editors add the five characters in brackets on the basis of context and the other essays in the group (see, for example, LYS, LSL, Z&Q). 亡 is read as 無.

36: Against Fate II

36.1   Master Mo Zi spoke, saying: "In general, in stating a doctrine or writing it down, one must first establish standards and criteria. To make a statement without standards is like trying to establish the direction of the sunrise and the sunset with the upper part of a potter's revolving wheel. Even a skilled craftsman would certainly not be able to achieve correctness. And so it would not be possible to reach a reliable conclusion about what is true and false in the world at the present time. Therefore, in making a statement, there are three criteria. What are the three criteria? That there be a basis; that there be an origin; and that there be a use. With regard to its basis, examine the intentions of Heaven and ghosts, and the affairs of the sage kings. With regard to its origin, verify it through the writings of the former kings. What of its use? This comes out in the conduct of government. These are the three criteria for a statement."

36.2   "At the present time, among the world's officers and gentlemen, there are some who take there to be Fate and some who take there not to be [Fate]. The means by which I know whether there is Fate or not is through the evidence of the ears and eyes of the multitude. This is how I know whether it exists or not. If there are those who hear it or those who see it, I say it exists. If there are not those who hear it or not those who see it, I say it does not exist. This being so, how can we not test and examine the evidence from the ordinary people? From ancient times to the present, since people first came to exist, has anyone seen such a thing as Fate, or heard the sounds of Fate? There has never been anyone. And if the ordinary people are considered to be foolish and unworthy and the evidence of their ears and eyes not adequate as a criterion, then why not test and examine the transmitted words and statements of the feudal lords? From ancient times to the present, since people first came to exist, have any of them heard the sound of Fate or seen the substance of Fate? There has never been anyone. This being so,

王，舉孝子而勸之事親，尊賢良而勸之為善，發憲布令以教誨，
明賞罰以勸阻[6]。若此，則亂者可使治，而危者可使安矣。若以為
不然，昔者桀之所亂，湯治之；紂之所亂，武王治之。此世不渝
而民不改，上變政而民易教。其在湯武則治，其在桀紂則亂，安
危治亂，在上之發政也，則豈可謂有命哉！夫曰有命云者亦不然
矣。」

36.3　「今夫有命者言曰：『我非作之後世也，自昔三代有若言以傳流
矣。今故先生對之？』[7] 曰：夫有命者，不志[8] 昔也三代之聖善人
與？意亡[9] 昔三代之暴不肖人也？何以知之？初之列士桀大夫，
慎言知行，此上有以規諫其君長，下有以教順其百姓，故上得其
君長之賞，下得其百姓之譽。列士桀大夫聲聞不廢，流傳至今，
而天下皆曰其力也，必不能曰我見命焉[10]。」

36.4　「是故昔者三代之暴王，不繆[11] 其耳目之淫，不慎其心志之辟，外

6.　There are two relatively minor issues with this statement: (i) Not all texts have 明. WYJ
refers to the following passage in the《長短經・運命》: "發憲令以教誨，明賞罰以沮
勸", in arguing for its inclusion. (ii) Some texts have 沮 instead of 阻 — for example,
Z&Q who expand the clause as: "勸善止惡".

7.　There is general acceptance of SYR's emendation of this question to read: "今胡先生
非之？"

8.　BY takes 志 as 識 (i.e. 知) here.

9.　As elsewhere, 意 is taken as 抑 in the sense of 或. 亡 is read as 無.

10.　There is some uncertainty about this clause. The eight characters given above are found,
for example, in LYS and Z&Q. WYJ has " 見命焉" — see his detailed notes 24 and
25, pp. 418–419.

11.　繆 is read as 糾 (SYR) in the sense of 糾正.

why not test and examine the affairs of the sage kings? In ancient times, the sage kings promoted filial sons and encouraged them to serve their parents. They respected the worthy and virtuous and encouraged them to be good. They issued regulations and promulgated edicts to teach and instruct. They clarified rewards and punishments to encourage goodness and prevent evil. In this way, then, what was in confusion could be brought to order and what was dangerous could be made safe. If you think this wasn't so, [consider] the disorder wrought by Jie in former times and how Tang brought order; or the disorder wrought by Zhou and how King Wu brought order. In these cases, the age did not change and the people did not change. The ruler changed the government and the instruction of the people changed. When they were under [the rule of] Tang and Wu, there was order. When they were under [the rule of] Jie and Zhou, there was disorder. Peace and danger, order and disorder lie with the government of the ruler. How, then, can you say there is Fate? I say that those who claim there is Fate are altogether wrong."

36.3   "Now the arguments of those who hold that there is Fate say: 'We did not create this at a later time. From the former Three Dynasties on, there has been this view which has been handed down. Why, Sir, do you now oppose it?' I say, with respect to there being Fate, do we not know whether it came from the sages and good men of the former Three Dynasties or from the evil and unworthy men of the former Three Dynasties? How do we know this? In the beginning, the various officers and brave grandees were careful in their speech and wise in their actions. This meant they could advise and admonish their rulers and leaders above, and they could teach and instruct the ordinary people below. Therefore, above, they received rewards from their rulers and leaders, and below, they received praise from the ordinary people. The reputation of these various officers and brave grandees is [still] heard of and has not died away, having been handed down to the present time. And the whole world says it was their own ability. They are certainly not able to say 'I see Fate there'."

36.4   "This is why, in former times, the cruel kings of the Three Dynasties did not curb the excesses of their senses nor control the

之毆騁田獵畢弋，內沈於酒樂，而不顧其國家百姓之政。繁為無
用，暴逆百姓，使下不親其上。是故國為虛厲[12]，身在刑僇之
中。不肯曰[13]：『我罷不肖，我為刑政不善』，必曰：『我命故且
亡』。」

36.5 「雖昔也三代之窮民，亦由[14]此也。內之不能善事其親戚，外
〔之〕[15]不能善事其君長，惡恭儉而好簡易，貪飲食而惰從事，衣
食之財不足，使身至有飢寒凍餒之憂，必不能曰：『我罷不肖，
我從事不疾』，必曰：『我命固且窮』。」

36.6 「雖昔也三代之偽[16]民，亦猶此也。繁飾有命，以教眾愚樸人久[17]
矣。聖王之患此也，故書之竹帛，琢之金石[18]，於先王之書《仲虺
之告》曰：『我聞有夏，人矯天命，布命于下，帝式是惡，用闕
師。』[19] 此語夏王桀之執有命也，湯與仲虺共非之。先王之書《太
誓》之言然曰：『紂夷之居，而不肯事上帝，棄闕其先神而不祀

---

12. Most modern commentators refer to BY's note on this clause which quotes Lu Deming's 陸德明《莊子音義》as follows: "李云`居它無人曰虛，死而無後曰厲'。"
13. WYJ has "必不能曰".
14. Read as 猶.
15. Added by WYJ.
16. I have followed Z&Q's reading of 偽 as "弄虛作假".
17. WYJ has "之人" rather than "人久" — see his note 42, pp. 420–421.
18. WYJ expands this to the more usual formulation to give: "琢之盤盂，鏤之金石。"
19. There are some variations in the quotation from that given in the previous chapter — see notes to 35.10 above.

depravity in their hearts. Without, they galloped their horses and hunted. Within, they drowned themselves in wine and music. They did not look to the government of the ordinary people of their kingdoms. They did much that was useless, and cruelly oppressed the ordinary people, causing those below not to love their superiors. As a result, their kingdoms were emptied of people and without posterity whilst they themselves met with punishment and death. Yet they were not willing to say: 'I am careless and unworthy and my conduct of government has not been good'. Instead they had to say: 'It is my Fate that I should lose it (the kingdom)'."

36.5 "Formerly, even the poor people of the Three Dynasties were also like this. Within, they were not able to serve their parents and relatives well, and, without, they were not able to serve their rulers and leaders well. They abhorred respect and moderation and loved rudeness and ease. They coveted drink and food and were lazy in attending to their business so that materials for clothing and food were insufficient, bringing them to the hardships of hunger and cold. Yet they were certainly not able to say: 'We are indolent and unworthy. We have not been diligent in our business'. Instead they had to say: 'It is our Fate that we are poor'."

36.6 "Formerly, even the people of the Three Dynasties who resorted to deception were also like this. [They had] numerous deceptive [arguments] about the existence of Fate which they used to teach the many ignorant and simple people over a long period, and this was troubling to the sage kings. Therefore, they wrote about it on bamboo and silk and carved it on metal and stone. In the book of the former kings, *The Announcement of Zhong Hui*, it says: 'I have heard the man of Xia feigned the decree of Heaven and put forth a decree to his subjects. The Supreme Lord thereupon resented him and destroyed his forces.' This tells of the Xia king, Jie's belief in Fate and that Tang and Zhong Hui together rejected this. In the book of the former kings, the *Great Oath*, there are words like this, saying: 'Zhou was haughty and imperious and was not willing to serve the Supreme Lord. He neglected his ancestral spirits and did not sacrifice to them, saying that his people had Fate so there was no need for him to be diligent in his service [to

也，曰我民有命，毋僇其務。天不亦棄縱而不葆。』[20] 此言紂之執有命也。武王以《太誓》非之。」

36.7　「有於《三代不國》有之曰：『女毋崇天之有命也。』命《三〔代〕不國》亦言命之無也。[21] 於召公之《執令》於然，且：『敬哉！無天命，惟予二人，而無造言，不自降天之哉得之。』[22] 在於商，夏之詩書曰：『命者暴王作之。』且今天下之上君子，將欲辨是非利害之故，當天[23]有命者，不可不疾非也。」執有命者，此天下之厚害也，是故子墨子非也。

---

20. As with the previous quotation, comparison should be made with 35.10 above.
21. There are several issues in this initial statement as follows: (i) According to SYR, the first 有 should be read as 又. (ii) Most commentators follow SYR in emending 不 to 百 making "三代百國" the title of a lost book or chapter. WYJ suggests it may be two separate titles. Several commentators refer to Li Delin's comment on the *Sui Shu* 隨書 which quotes Mo Zi as saying: "吾見《百國春秋》。" (iii) SYR, in part following WSN, suggests "命三不國" after the apparent quotation should read "今三代百國。"
22. There is uncertainty about this quotation and its attribution. The version above follows WYJ whilst the translation uses CYX's reading of 於 as 亦 and BY's reading of 且 as 曰. An alternative view is offered by SYR who suggests the initial statement should read: "於召公之非執命亦然。" The two people referred to are thought to be Duke Shao himself and Zhou Gong Dan 周公旦 who acted as regents for the young King Cheng — although see also WYJ who takes 二人 as 仁人. Modern editors (e.g. LYS, LSL, Z&Q) accept SYR's reworking of the final clause to give: "不自天降，自我得之。"
23. 天 is taken as 大 following BY.

ghosts and spirits]. [As a result] Heaven abandoned him and did not protect him.' This tells of Zhou's belief in Fate and how King Wu with the *Great Oath* rejected this."

36.7   "Also in the *Three Dynasties, One Hundred Kingdoms*, there is the statement: 'You should not venerate Heaven as having Fate.' So the *Three Dynasties, One Hundred Kingdoms* also speaks of the non-existence of Fate. In Duke Shao's *Zhi Ling*, it is the same. [This] says: '[There should be] respect [for ghosts and spirits]. But there is no heavenly Fate. There are the two of us and we do not speak falsely. Fate is not sent down from Heaven. It comes from ourselves.' In the *Odes* and the *Documents* of the Shang and Xia [dynasties], it is said: 'Fate is the creation of evil kings'. Moreover, for the world's officers and gentlemen of the present time who wish to distinguish the causes of right and wrong and of benefit and harm, it is proper that a belief in Fate cannot but be resolutely rejected." To hold that there is Fate is of great harm to the world, which is why Master Mo Zi rejected it.

37: 非命下

37.1   子墨子言曰：「凡出言談，則不¹可而不先立儀而言。若不先立儀
而言，譬之猶運鈞之上而立朝夕焉也。我以為雖有朝夕之辯，必
將終未可得而從定也。是故言有三法。何為三法？曰：有考之
者，有原之者，有用之者。惡乎考之？考先聖大王之事。惡乎原
之？察眾之耳目之情²。惡乎用之？發而為政乎國，察萬民而觀
之³。此謂三法也。」

37.2   「故昔者三代聖王禹湯文武方為政乎天下之時，曰：『必務舉孝子
而勸之事親，尊賢良之人而教之為善。』是故出政施教，賞善罰
暴。且以為若此，則天下之亂也，將屬⁴可得而治也，社稷之危
也，將屬可得而定也。若以為不然，昔桀之所亂，湯治之；紂之
所亂，武王治之。當此之時，世不渝而民不易，上變政而民改
俗。存乎桀紂而天下亂，存乎湯武而天下治。天下之治也，湯武

---

1.   Emended from 必 on the basis of the previous essay. This is generally accepted.
2.   Although some texts have 請 (e.g. Z&Q), there is agreement that this should be read as
     情.
3.   In this sentence, WYJ emends 察 to 家 and omits the comma — see his note 6, p. 427.
4.   With regard to the use of 屬 here and in what follows, Z&Q refer to a note to the 《國
     語‧魯語》 which equates 屬 with 適.

37: Against Fate III

37.1 Master Mo Zi spoke, saying: "In general, it is not permissible, when making a statement, to fail to establish a standard first and [then] speak. If you do not establish a standard first and [then] speak, it is like using the upper part of a potter's revolving wheel and trying to establish the direction of the sunrise and sunset with it. I think that, although there is a distinction between the sunrise and the sunset, you will, in the end, certainly never be able to find it and establish it. This is why, for a statement, there are three criteria. What are the three criteria? I say there is examining it, there is determining its origin, and there is putting it to use. How do you examine it? You examine the affairs of the first sages and great kings. How do you determine its origin? You look at the evidence from the ears and eyes of the multitude. How do you put it to use? You set it out and use it in governing the state, considering its effect on the ten thousand people. These are called the 'three criteria'."

37.2 "Thus, in the past, at the time when the sage kings of the Three Dynasties — Yu, Tang, Wen and Wu — were governing the world, they said: 'We must devote our attention to promoting filial sons and encouraging them to serve their parents. We must honour men who are worthy and virtuous and teach them to be good.' For this reason, they brought forth government and gave instruction. They rewarded the good and punished the bad. Moreover, if you view it like this, then if there is disorder in the world, it can be overcome and order brought about; if there is danger to the altars of soil and grain, it can be overcome and peace brought about. If you do not think this is so, then consider the disorder formerly wrought by Jie and how Tang brought order to it; consider the disorder wrought by Zhou and how King Wu brought order to it. At these times, the age did not change and the people did not change. The ruler changed the government and the people changed their customs. As it existed under Jie and Zhou, the world was in disorder. As it existed under Tang and Wu, the world was

之力也；天下之亂也，桀紂之罪也。若以此觀之，夫安危治亂存
乎上之為政也，則夫豈可謂有命哉！」

37.3　「故昔者禹湯文武方為政乎天下之時，曰：『必使飢者得食，寒者
得衣，勞者得息，亂者得治。』遂得光譽令問[5]於天下。夫豈可以
為命哉？故[6]以為其力也！今賢良之人，尊賢而好功道術[7]，故上
得其王公大人之賞，下得其萬民之譽，遂得光譽令問於天下，亦
豈以為其命哉？又以為〔其〕[8]力也！然今夫[9]有命者，不識昔也三
代之聖善人與？意亡[10]昔三代之暴不肖人與？若以[11]說觀之，則
必非昔三代聖善人也，必暴不肖人也。」

37.4　「然今以命為有者，昔三代暴王桀紂幽厲，貴為天子，富有天
下。[12]於此乎不而矯[13]其耳目之欲，而從其心意之辟。外之歐騁
田獵畢弋，內湛於酒樂，而不顧其國家百姓之政。繁為無用，暴
逆百姓，遂失其宗廟。其言不曰：『吾罷不肖，吾聽治不強』，必
曰：『吾命固將失之。』雖昔也三代罷不肖之民，亦猶此也。不能

---

5. 問 here is read as 聞. Z&Q offer the following paraphrase: "榮譽和美好的名聲。"
6. 故 here is read as 固 following Z&Q.
7. There is some question about this statement. BY takes 功 to be superfluous and a number
   of later commentators accept this (e.g. LYS). Emendation to 蓄 is suggested by SYR.
   There must also be a question as to whether both 道 and 術 should be retained.
8. 其 is added by general consent following SYR.
9. WYJ has 執 here — see his note 17, p. 428.
10. LYS reads "意亡" as "抑毋" and equates this with "或者是".
11. SYR suggests the reversal of order of "若以".
12. The punctuation here follows WYJ.
13. "不而矯" is emended to "不能正" — see WYJ, note 20, p. 428.

well ordered. The good order of the world was due to the efforts of Tang and Wu. The disorder of the world was due to the faults of Jie and Zhou. If you look at it like this, peace and danger, order and disorder lie in the ruler's conduct of government. How, then, is it permissible to say there is Fate!"

37.3 "Therefore, in the past, at the time when Yu, Tang, Wen and Wu were governing the world, they said: 'We must ensure that those who are hungry get food, that those who are cold get clothes, that those who are weary find rest, and those in disorder find order.' Subsequently, they acquired a glorious reputation throughout the world. How can this be thought of as Fate? It must undoubtedly be thought of as due to their efforts. Nowadays, men who are worthy and virtuous respect worthiness and love the Way. Therefore, they obtain the rewards of kings, dukes and great officers above, and they get the praise of their people below, so that subsequently they acquire a glorious reputation throughout the world. Can this also be put down to their Fate? It should also be taken to be through their efforts! In the case of those who nowadays believe in Fate, do we not know whether this comes from the sages and good men of the Three Dynasties in the past, or from the cruel and unworthy men of the former Three Dynasties? If we look at this in the light of what has been said, then it certainly cannot be from the sages and good men of the former Three Dynasties, so it must be from the cruel and unworthy men."

37.4 "In this case now, with regard to those who took there to be Fate, there were the former evil kings of the Three Dynasties — Jie, Zhou, You and Li — who were ennobled as Sons of Heaven and enriched with all under Heaven. But in this they were not able to curb the excesses of their senses and followed the depravity in their hearts. Outside, they galloped their horses and hunted. Inside, they drowned themselves in wine and music. They did not look to the government of the ordinary people of their kingdoms. They did much that was useless, and cruelly oppressed the ordinary people. Subsequently, they lost their ancestral temples. But their words did not say: 'I have been careless and unworthy. I have not been resolute in my conduct of government.' Instead they had to say: 'It is my Fate that has determined that I shall lose

善事親戚君長，其惡恭儉而好簡易，貪飲食而惰從事，衣食之財不足，是以身有陷乎飢寒凍餒之憂。其言不曰『吾罷不肖，吾從事不強』，又曰『吾命固將窮』。昔三代偽民亦猶此也。」

37.5 「昔者暴王作之，窮人術[14]之，此皆疑眾遲樸[15]，先聖王之患之也，固在前矣。是以書之竹帛，鏤之金石，琢之盤盂，傳遺後世子孫。曰何書焉存？禹之《總德》[16]有之曰：『允不著[17]，惟天民不而葆，既防凶心，天加之咎，不慎厥德，天命焉葆？』[18]《仲虺之告》曰：『我聞有夏，人矯天命，于下，帝式是增，用爽厥師。』[19]彼用無為有，故謂矯，若有而謂有，夫豈謂[20]矯哉！」

37.6 「昔者，桀執有命而行，湯為《仲虺之告》以非之。《太誓》之言也，於《去發》[21]曰：『惡乎君子！天有顯德，其行甚章，為鑑不遠，在彼殷王。謂人有命，謂敬不可行，謂祭無益，謂暴無傷，上帝不

---

14. 術 is taken in the sense of 述 — see, for example, LYS, LSL.
15. This is a somewhat difficult statement. Particularly this applies to "遲" on which WYZ writes: "'遲'字義不可通，'遲'當為'遇'字之誤。'遇'與'愚'同。"
16. This is taken to be a chapter of a lost work.
17. SYR has the following note on 著: "疑當為若，允不若，信不順也。"
18. There are several issues in this statement. Apart from that referred to in the previous note, these include the readings of 而 as 能, 葆 as 保 in both instances, 防 as 放 in the sense of 放縱 (WYJ) and 厥 as 其 (as elsewhere). The translation closely follows the version given by Z&Q.
19. There are some textual differences from the same quotation given in 35.10 — see notes to that section above.
20. I have followed WYJ in having 謂 here rather than 為.
21. There is general acceptance, following YY and SYR, that 《去發》 should be 《太子發》, this indicating King Wu — see, for example, WYJ, note 42, p. 430.

it (the kingdom).' Formerly even the indolent and unworthy people of the Three Dynasties were also like this. They were not able to serve their parents and relatives or their rulers and leaders well. They greatly abhorred respect and moderation, and loved rudeness and ease. They coveted drink and food, and were lazy in attending to their business so that materials for clothing and food were insufficient. This is why they themselves were caught up in the hardships of hunger and cold. Yet their words did not say: 'We are indolent and unworthy. We have not been resolute in our business.' They also said: 'It is our Fate that has determined that we are poor.' The deceptive people of the former Three Dynasties were also like this."

37.5 "The cruel kings of former time created this (i.e. Fate) and the poor people handed it on. And this raised doubt in the multitude and deceived the gullible, which was something that troubled the first sage kings. This is why they wrote about it on bamboo and silk, carved it on metal and stone, and engraved it on [ceremonial] vessels and cups to hand down to their descendants of later generations. You ask, what writings were preserved? Yu's *Zong De* has this to say: 'If you do not have faith, Heaven and the people will not be able to protect you. If you give free rein to a cruel heart, Heaven will send down disasters. If you do not carefully cultivate your virtue, how can Heaven's decree protect you?' The *Announcement of Zhong Hui* says: 'I have heard that the man of Xia feigned the decree of Heaven and put forth a decree to his subjects. The Supreme Lord thereupon resented him and destroyed his forces.' He (Jie) took something that did not exist as existing, therefore he is said to have 'feigned'. If something did exist and he said it existed, how could he be spoken of as 'feigning'?"

37.6 "In former times, Jie held to a belief in Fate and acted on it. Tang created the *Announcement of Zhong Hui* in order to condemn him. The *Great Oath's* words, in the *Tai Zi Fa*, say: 'Ah princes! Heaven has manifest virtue. Its actions are luminously displayed. It made a 'mirror' near at hand and that was the Yin king. He said people had a Fate. He said that reverence could not be put into practice. He said that sacrifices brought no benefit. He said that

常，九有以亡，上帝不順，祝降其喪，惟我有周，受之大帝。』[22]
昔紂執有命而行，武王為《太誓》，《去發》以非之。曰，子胡不
尚考之乎商周虞夏之記。從十簡之篇以尚，皆無之，將何若者
也？[23]」

37.7　是故子墨子曰：「今天下之君子之為文學出言談也，非將勤勞其
惟舌[24]，而利其唇吻[25]也，中實將欲[26]其國家邑里萬民刑政者
也。今也王公大人之所以蚤朝晏退，聽獄治政，終朝均分，而不
敢怠倦者何也？曰：彼以為強必治，不強必亂，強必寧，不強必
危，故不敢怠倦[27]。今也卿大夫之所以竭股肱之力，殫其思慮之
知，內治官府，外斂關市，山林，澤梁之利，以實官府，而不敢
怠倦者，何也？曰：彼以為強必貴，不強必賤，強必榮，不強必
辱，故不敢怠倦。」

37.8　「今也農夫之所以蚤出暮入，強乎耕稼樹藝，多聚叔[28]粟，而不敢
怠倦者，何也？曰：彼以為強必富，不強必貧，強必飽，不強必

---

22. There are some issues with this quotation insofar as it does not appear as a continuous passage in the *Documents*《書經・太誓》. Also, there are textual variations in the parts that do appear there — see LCC, vol. 3, p. 291ff. In particular, 行 in the penultimate clause is taken as 朝 whilst the final 帝 is read as 商.
23. For this final sentence, WYJ has: "從《卜簡》之篇以尚皆無之也。" — see his note 53, p. 432.
24. According to WNS, 惟舌 should read 喉舌.
25. For symmetry with the preceding phrase, I have taken "唇吻 (吻)" as "mouth and lips".
26. According to SYR, 為 should be added here.
27. Here and in subsequent sentences, I have followed LSL and Z&Q in reading "怠倦" as "懈怠".
28. Read as 菽 here.

cruelty did no harm. The Supreme Lord was not pleased and the Nine Regions met with destruction. The Supreme Lord was not content and he sent down calamities. I represent the Zhou house and have received the great Shang.' Formerly, Zhou held to a belief in Fate and acted on it. King Wu created the *Great Oath, Tai Zi Fa* in order to condemn him. I say, why not examine what has happened before in the records of the Shang, Zhou, Yu and Xia. In the ten chapters referred to above, there is no mention of it (Fate). How do you account for that?"

37.7   For this reason, Master Mo Zi said: "Nowadays, gentlemen of the world create writings to expound their doctrines and ideas. And they don't do this just to exercise their throats and tongues or to benefit their mouths and lips. They do it because in their hearts they are people who wish to carry out the administration of their states, cities and villages, and the ten thousand people. Nowadays, why is it that kings, dukes and great officers go to court early and retire late, hearing lawsuits and bringing order to government, and for the whole day give proper attention to their duties, and dare not be remiss? I say it is because they think that [such] diligence ensures good order and lack of diligence must result in disorder; that diligence ensures peace and lack of diligence must result in danger. So they do not dare to be remiss. Nowadays, why is it that ministers and high officials exhaust the strength of their limbs, and use all the capacity of their wisdom to bring order to government offices within, and without, to gain the benefits of the taxes on passes and market places, mountains and forests, marshes and bridges in order to fill the government coffers, and dare not be remiss? I say it is because they think that diligence ensures nobility and lack of diligence ensures baseness, that diligence ensures glory and lack of diligence must result in disgrace. Therefore, they do not dare to be remiss."

37.8   "Nowadays, why is it that farmers go out early and come back late, and are diligent in their sowing of grain and planting of trees, gathering large amounts of pulses and grains, and dare not be remiss? I say it is because they think that diligence ensures wealth and lack of diligence must result in poverty, that diligence ensures satiety and lack of diligence must result in hunger. So they dare

飢，故不敢怠倦。今也婦人之所以夙興夜寐，強乎紡績織絍，多治麻絲葛緒，捆布縿[29]，而不敢怠倦者，何也？曰：彼以為強必富，不強必貧，強必煖，不強必寒，故不敢怠倦。今雖毋在乎王公大人，蕢若[30]信有命而致行之，則必怠乎聽獄治政矣，卿大夫必怠乎治官府矣，農夫必怠乎耕稼樹藝矣，婦人必怠乎紡績織絍矣。」

37.9   「王公大人怠乎聽獄治政，卿大夫怠乎治官府，則我以為天下必亂矣。農夫怠乎耕稼樹藝，婦人怠乎紡績織絍，則我以為天下衣食之財將必不足矣。若以為政乎天下，上以事天鬼，天鬼不使；下以持養百姓，百姓不利。必離散不可得用也。是以入守則不固，出誅則不勝。故雖昔者三代暴王桀紂幽厲之所以共抎其國家，傾覆其社稷者，此也。」

37.10   是故子墨子言曰：「今天下之士君子，中實將欲求興天下之利，除天下之害，當若有命者之言，不可不強非也。曰：命者，暴王

---

29. There is some uncertainty about precisely what materials and activities are being referred to here. 絲 is WNS's emendation of the rare character *liu* (ZWDCD #28024). In the phrase, "捆布縿", 捆 is taken as 緄 in the sense of 織 whilst 縿 is read as 縼 (WNS). Z&Q quote WNS as follows: "緄布縿，猶言緄布帛。"
30. There is general acceptance of YY's reading of 蕢若 as 藉若 in the sense of 假如.

not be remiss. Nowadays, why is it that women get up early and go to bed late and are diligent in their spinning and weaving, producing large amounts of hemp, silk and other cloth and weaving cotton and silk, and dare not be remiss? I say it is because they think that diligence ensures wealth and lack of diligence must result in poverty, that diligence ensures warmth and lack of diligence must result in cold. So they dare not be remiss. In the present circumstances, if kings, dukes and great men trust in the existence of Fate and act accordingly, then they will certainly be remiss in resolving lawsuits and bringing order to government; ministers and great officers will certainly be remiss in managing government offices; farmers will certainly be remiss in the sowing of grain and the planting of trees; and women will certainly be remiss in their spinning and weaving."

37.9 "If kings, dukes and great men are remiss in hearing lawsuits and bringing order to government, and if ministers and high officials are remiss in bringing order to government departments, then I think the world will certainly be in disorder. If farmers are remiss in sowing grain and planting trees, and if women are remiss in spinning and weaving, then I think the material for the world's clothing and food will certainly not be sufficient. If the government of the world is conducted like this, then above, in the case of serving Heaven and ghosts, they are not complied with; and below, in the case of nurturing the ordinary people, they are not benefited and certainly will be dispersed and scattered and not able to be put to use. Defence against invasion will not be secure and punitive expeditions will not be successful. So the reason why, in former times, the evil kings of the Three Dynasties — Jie, Zhou, You and Li — all lost their kingdoms and overturned the altars of grain and soil was precisely this."

37.10 This is why Master Mo Zi spoke, saying: "Nowadays, the world's officers and gentlemen, if they genuinely wish in their hearts to seek to promote the world's benefits and eliminate its harms, then quite properly words like those which claim the existence of Fate cannot but be resolutely rejected. They should say that [the concept of] Fate was a creation of the evil kings and was perpetuated by the poor people; it was not something which the

所作，窮人所術，非仁者之言。今之為仁義者，將不可不察而強
非者，此也。」

38: 非儒上：闕

benevolent spoke of. Nowadays, for those who are benevolent and righteous, this is something that will need to be examined and strongly rejected."

38: Against the Confucians I: Lost

39: 非儒下

39.1   儒者曰:「親親有術,尊賢有等。」¹ 言親疏尊卑之異也。其《禮》
曰:「喪父母三年,妻後子 三年,伯父叔父弟兄庶子其,戚族人
五月。」² 若以親疏為歲月之數,則親者多而疏者少矣,是妻後子
與父〔母〕³同也。若以尊卑為歲月數,則是尊其妻子與父母同,
而親伯父宗兄而卑子也,逆孰大焉!⁴ 其親死,列尸弗斂,登屋
窺井,挑鼠穴,探滌器,而求其人矣。以為實在則贛愚甚矣。
如⁵ 其亡也必求焉,偽亦大矣!

39.2   取妻,身迎,祗嵩⁶為僕,秉轡授綏⁷,如仰嚴親,昏禮威儀,如
承祭祀。顛覆上下,悖逆父母,下則妻子,妻子上侵。⁸ 事親,
若此可謂孝乎?儒者曰⁹:「迎妻,妻子奉祭祀¹⁰,子將守宗廟,

---

1.   This is identical to the *Doctrine of the Mean* XX.5 (LCC, vol. 1, p. 406) apart from having
     術 instead of 殺. Most commentators follow WYZ in reading the latter in the sense of
     等差.
2.   There are three issues with this apparent quotation: (i) It does not appear to be an exact
     quotation. SYR takes the reference to be to the *Yi Li* (儀禮, 喪服 — see SSJZS, vol. 5,
     p. 347ff). (ii) There is some doubt about the text in the second phrase — see WYJ,
     note 3, p. 442. (iii) 其 is read as 期 in the sense of ·整年.
3.   Added by WSN.
4.   In this sentence, there is general acceptance of 視 for 親, 如 for 而 and 庶子 for 卑子
     following particularly WNS and WYZ.
5.   Read as 知 (WYZ).
6.   The character here is written with the 衣 radical — see ZWDCD #35276. The *Shuo Wen*
     definition is "衣正幅" which may be taken to mean that clothing is correct. LSL takes
     the phrase to mean "black clothing".
7.   This phrase is found in the 士昏 chapter of the *Yi Li* — see SSJZS, vol. 4, p. 50. In fact,
     the details here referred to by Mo Zi are given in that chapter.
8.   The full-stop here is due to WYJ.
9.   Most commentators agree on the addition of 曰 here. WYJ has a slightly different text
     — see his p. 436.
10. SYR suggests emending the second 妻 to 與. This is followed in the translation.

39: Against the Confucians II

39.1 The Confucians say: "In treating relatives as relatives, there are gradations. In respecting the worthy, there are gradations." They speak of the differences of near and distant, honoured and lowly. Their *Rites* states: "Mourning for a father or mother is three years; for a wife or eldest son it is three years; for older and younger brothers of the father, younger and older brothers, and other sons it is one full year; for other family members it is five months." If the calculation of the period of years and months is based on nearness and distance, then it should be long for near relatives and short for distant relatives. This is to take the wife or eldest son to be the same as the father [or mother]. If the calculation of the years and months is based on being honoured or lowly, then this is to honour the wife or son the same as the father or mother and to consider the father's older brothers, and older brothers to be like other sons. What greater perversity is there than this! When a parent dies, they lay out the corpse without preparation while they climb onto the roof, peer into the well, poke into rat holes and look into wash-basins seeking the person. Taking the parent to actually be alive is foolish in the extreme. To know they are dead but feel compelled to seek them is also a great hypocrisy!

39.2 [When a Confucian] takes a wife, he goes to meet her in person, correctly attired as a servant. He takes the reins of the cart himself and hands her the cord to draw herself up as if honouring a revered parent. The wedding ceremony is conducted with solemnity just like conducting a sacrifice. This is to turn high and low upside down, and is perverse conduct towards parents who are brought down to the level of the wife whilst the wife infringes on those above. In serving parents, how can something like this be called filial?

The Confucians say: "After taking a wife, she can join with you in

故重之。」應者曰:「此誣言也,其宗兄守其先宗廟數十年,死喪之其,兄弟之妻,奉其先之祭祀弗散[11],則喪妻子三年,必非以守奉祭祀也。夫憂[12]妻子以大負紊。有[13]曰:『所以重親也』。為欲厚所至私[14],輕所至重,豈非大姦也哉!」

39.3   有強執有命以說議曰:「壽夭貧富,安危治亂,固有天命,不可損益。窮達賞罰,幸否有極,人之知力,不能為焉。」群吏信之,則怠於分職。庶人信之,則怠於從事。吏[15]不治則亂,農事緩則貧,貧且亂政之本[16],而儒者以為道教[17],是賊天下之人者也。

39.4   且夫繁飾禮樂以淫人,久喪偽哀以謾親,立命緩貧而高浩居[18],

---

11. Read as 服 following Lu Wenchao.
12. Read as 優 following SYR.
13. Generally accepted as 又.
14. Some early texts have 和 here which was changed to 私 by BY on the grounds of meaning.
15. Added following WYZ — see WYJ, note 34, p. 446.
16. There is general acceptance of SYR's addition of 倍 as 背 in the sense of 違背 before 政 in this statement.
17. I have followed Z&Q in reading of 道教 as 教導.
18. In this statement 緩貧 is read as 安貧 (Z&Q based on the 《廣韻》) whilst 浩居 is read as 傲倨 (BY).

carrying out the sacrifices whilst a son will protect the ancestral temple, therefore they are highly regarded."

In reply I say:[i] "These are false words insofar as a man's uncles and older brothers maintain the ancestral temple for several decades, yet, when they die, he mourns them for one year[ii] whilst the wives of older and younger brothers, who assist at the sacrifices to his ancestors, are not mourned at all. Thus, mourning wives and sons for three years is certainly not because they maintain [the ancestral temple] or assist at sacrifices. Such favourable treatment of wives and sons is already excessive.[iii] They also say, 'It is the way of honouring parents.' In wishing to treat 'thickly' those towards whom they are most discriminatory, they treat 'thinly' those who are most important. Is this not a great deception?"

39.3 They also hold firmly to the doctrine that there is Fate, arguing thus: "Living to old age and dying young, poverty and wealth, peace and peril, order and disorder are determined by Heaven's decrees and cannot be decreased or increased. Success and failure, reward and punishment, good luck and bad are established [by Fate] and cannot be affected by a person's knowledge or strength." If the many officials believed this, they would be careless in their allotted duties. If the ordinary people believed this, they would be careless in following their tasks. If officials do not bring about order, there is disorder. If agricultural matters are attended to tardily, there is poverty. Poverty and disorder strike at the root of government, yet the Confucians take it [i.e. Fate] as a teaching. This is damaging to the people of the world.

39.4 Moreover, they use various elaborate rites and music to delude people. They use prolonged mourning and false grief to deceive relatives. They believe in Fate and accept poverty, yet they are

---

i.   It is not actually specified who is making the response. I have taken it to be Mo Zi himself. It could also be an unidentified Mohist or Mohists as a whole.
ii. Taking 其 in the sense of 期.
iii. There is some variation in the interpretation of this sentence depending on the readings of the second and final characters.

倍本棄事而安怠傲[19]，貪於飲食，惰於作務，陷於飢寒，危於凍
餒，無以違之。是若人氣，歎鼠藏，而羝羊視，賁彘起。[20] 君子
笑之。怒曰：「散人！焉知良儒。」夫〔春〕[21]夏乞麥禾，五穀既
收，大喪是隨，子姓皆從，得厭飲食，畢治數喪，足以至矣。[22]
因人之家翠以為[23]，恃人之野以為尊，富人有喪，乃大說，喜
曰：「此衣食之端也。」

39.5   儒者曰：「君子必服古言然後仁。」[24] 應之曰：「所謂古之言服者，
皆嘗新矣。而古人言之，服之[25]，則非君子也。然則必服[26]非君
子之服，言非君子之言，而後仁乎？」

39.6   又曰：「君子循而不作。」[27] 應之曰：「古者羿作弓，杼[28]作甲，奚
仲作車，巧垂作舟，然則今之鮑函車匠皆君子也，而羿杼奚仲

---

19. Emended from 徹 by BY and most editors following him. WYJ retains 徹.
20. There are several issues in this sentence: (i) 人氣 is emended to 乞人 (乞丐 — SYR).
    (ii) 歎鼠 is read as 田鼠 (see Qiu Shan, WYJ). (iii) 羝羊 is read as 公羊. (iv) 賁彘 is
    understood as 閹割過的猪 (MZQY).
21. 春 is added, or at least understood, here following SYR. The point is that, during spring
    and summer when produce is readily available, this is what beggars seek, whereas during
    autumn and winter they follow funerals.
22. In this phrase 至 is read as 生 (WYJ).
23. It is generally accepted, following SYR, that this statement should read: "因人之家以
    為翠。"
24. The text of this sentence is generally altered to conform with the argument in what
    follows, and that in the *Mozi* 48 (公孟) — i.e. 服古言 becomes 古言服.
25. Emended from 言之 following WYZ.
26. WYJ has 法 here instead of 服.
27. In the *Lun Yu* VII.1 there is: "子曰：'述而不作，信而好古，竊比於我老彭'。"
    (LCC, vol. 1, p. 195).
28. Usually written with the 人 radical.

arrogant and self-important. They turn their backs on what is fundamental and abandon their duties, finding contentment in idleness and pride. They are greedy for drink and food. They are indolent in carrying out their responsibilities and fall into hunger and cold, but, when endangered by starvation and freezing, they have no way of avoiding these things. They are like beggars. They hoard food like field mice. They stare like billy goats. They rise up like castrated pigs. When a gentleman laughs at them, they angrily reply: "Useless fellow! What do you know of good Confucians." In spring, they beg for wheat. In summer, they beg for rice. When the five grains have already been harvested, they attach themselves to large funerals with their sons and grandsons all following along, and so they get their fill of drink and food. If they are put in charge of several funerals, they have enough to live on. They depend on other people's households for food and rely on other people's fields for wine. When a rich man has a funeral, they are very happy and say delightedly: "This is a source of clothing and food."

39.5 Confucians say: "A gentleman must use ancient modes of speech and dress and afterwards he is benevolent."

I say in reply: "What is called ancient in speech and dress was all once upon a time new so, if the men of old spoke this way and dressed this way, they were not gentlemen. This being so, must we clothe ourselves in the garb of those who were not gentlemen and speak the speech of those who were not gentlemen before being benevolent?"

39.6 [Confucians] also say: "The gentleman follows but does not create."

I say in reply: "Among the ancients, Yi created the bow, Yu created armour, Xi Zhong created the cart and Craftsman Chui created the boat.[iv] In this case, then, are the tanners, armourers, cart-makers and carpenters of the present time all gentlemen, and

---

iv. For notes on the four people referred to here see WYJ, notes 62–65, pp. 449–450.

巧垂皆小人邪？且其所循人必或作之，然則其所循皆小人道
也？」

39.7 又曰：「君子勝不遂奔，揜凾弗射，施²⁹則助之胥車。」應之曰：
「若皆仁人也，則無說而相與。仁人以其取捨是非之理相告，
無故從有故也，弗知從有知也，無辭必服，見善必遷，何故相
〔與〕³⁰？若兩暴交爭，其勝者欲不遂奔，揜³¹凾弗射，施則助之
胥車，雖盡能猶且不得為君子也。意暴殘之國也，聖將為世除
害，興師誅罰，勝將因用儒術令士卒曰：『毋遂奔，揜凾勿射，
施則助之胥車。』暴亂之人也得活，天下害不除，是為群殘父
母，而深賤³²世也，不義莫大焉！」

---

29. Some texts have 強 rather than 施 here — see WYJ, note 73, pp. 451–452.
30. Added following WYZ.
31. WYJ has 揜 here in keeping with its use elsewhere in this passage.
32. WYJ emends 賤 to 賊.

Yi, Yu, Xi Zhong and Craftsman Chui all petty men? Moreover, someone must have created what the follower follows. This being so, then, is to follow in all cases the way of the petty man?"

39.7   [Confucians] also say: "When the gentleman triumphs in battle, he does not pursue those who are fleeing, he does not fire at those caught in traps, and he helps those in retreat to drag their heavy carts."[v]

I say in reply: "If they are all benevolent men, there is no reason for them to contend.[vi] Benevolent men inform each other of the principles of selecting and rejecting, of right and wrong. If they are without a cause, they follow those who have a cause. If they are without knowledge, they follow those who have knowledge. When they have no argument, they invariably yield. When they see good, they invariably change. What reason do they have to contend? If the two parties fighting with each other are evil, then, although those who triumph might not pursue the fleeing enemy, nor shoot at those who are trapped, and might help those in retreat to drag their heavy carts, even if they are able to do all this, they still do not come to be considered gentlemen. Consider a state which is cruel and destructive, and suppose a sage, intending to rid the world of evil, raises an army to eradicate and punish it and he triumphs. And then, because he is using Confucian methods, he issues orders to his soldiers, saying: 'Do not pursue those who are fleeing; do not shoot at those who are trapped; help those in retreat to drag their heavy carts.' Then those who are cruel and destructive will hold on to life and the harm to the world will not be done away with. This is to act in a way that is damaging and destructive to parents and deeply detrimental to ordinary people. There is no unrighteousness so great!"

---

v.   There are some issues with this sentence although the general meaning is clear. The issues relate to 掩函, 施 and 胥車. The translation is based on SYR's readings and on the MZQY.

vi   Taking 相與 as 相敵.

39.8   又曰：「君子若鐘，擊之則鳴，弗擊不鳴。」應之曰：「夫仁人事上
竭忠，事親務孝，務善則美，有過則諫，此為人臣之道也。[33] 今
擊之則鳴，弗擊不鳴，隱知豫[34] 力，恬漠待問而後對，雖有君親
之大利，弗問不言，若將有大寇亂，盜賊將作，若機辟將發也，
他人不知，己獨知之，雖其君親皆在，不問不言，是夫大亂之賊
也！以是為人臣不忠，為子不孝，事兄不弟，交遇人不貞良。夫
執後不言之朝物，見利使己雖恐後言。[35] 君若言而未有利焉，
則高拱不視，會噎為深，曰：『唯其未之學也。』用誰急，遺行
遠矣。夫一道術學業仁義者[36]，皆大以治人，小以任官，遠施周

---

33. The text of this sentence is emended by changing 得 to 務 in the second clause and 務
    to 有 (or 得) in the third clause — see YY and WYJ, note 85, p. 453.
34. Read as 舍 following SYR.
35. WYJ has a slightly different reading of this sentence with different punctuation — see
    his notes 92, 93, p. 454.
36. Some texts have 也 rather than 者 — e.g. WYJ.

39.8   [Confucians] also say: "The gentleman is like a bell. If you strike
[a bell], then it sounds. If you do not strike it, then it does not
sound."

I say in reply: "The benevolent man in serving his superior
displays the utmost loyalty and in serving his parents devotes
himself to being filial. If there is goodness, he gives praise. If there
are faults, he gives censure. This is the way of the man who is a
minister. Now, if he sounds when struck, but when not struck does
not sound, this is to conceal his knowledge and set aside his
ability, and to wait quiet and unconcerned until he is questioned
before replying. Although something may be of great benefit to
prince or parents, if he is not asked he does not speak. For
example, if there is about to be a great incursion or disorder, or
thieves and robbers are about to strike, or some trap is about to be
sprung, and he alone knows this whilst others do not, yet even if
his ruler and parents are all present, he doesn't speak unless asked,
he is a criminal bringing about great disorder. Such a man is not
loyal as an official, he is not filial as a son, he is not respectful in
serving an older brother, he is not honest and virtuous in his
dealings with others. He restrains himself and does not speak on
court matters. Indeed, even if he sees something of benefit to
himself, he is afraid to speak out.[vii] If his ruler speaks of something
which will not be beneficial, then he just folds his hands and looks
to the floor, saying in a strangled voice as if deep [in thought]:
'This is something I never learned of'. Even if the matter is
pressing, he distances himself and avoids it. When principle,
method, learning, duty, benevolence and righteousness are
brought together as one, on a large scale, all are the means of
bringing order to the people, and, on a small scale, all are the
means of serving as an official. Distantly, they should be
implemented everywhere. Near at hand, they should be used to

---

vii.   There are several problems of text and interpretation in these two sentences which make
the translation uncertain. Specifically these are: (i) 執後 which Z&Q gloss as "遇事持
後退不言的態度。" (ii) 朝物 about which SYR writes, "疑有脫誤。" (iii) 雖 which
YY suggests emending to 唯. For a discussion of these issues see WYJ, notes 92, 93,
p. 454. I have followed LSL's interpretation — see his notes 6–8, p. 246. It is taken to
be a further description of the "bell-like" person.

偏[37]，近以修身，不義不處，非理不行，務興天下之利，曲直周旋[38]，〔不〕[39] 利則止，此君子之道也。以所聞孔某[40] 之行，則本與此相反謬也。」

39.9   齊景公問晏子曰：「孔子為人何如？」晏子不對，公又復問，不對。景公曰：「以孔某語寡人者眾矣，俱以〔為〕[41] 賢人也。今寡人問之，而子不對，何也？」晏子對曰：「嬰不肖，不足以知賢人。雖然，嬰聞所謂賢人者，入人之國必務合其君臣之親，而弭其上下之怨。孔某之荊，知白公之謀，而奉之以石乞，君身幾滅，而

---

37. This is read as "遠用遍施" following CYX.
38. I have followed Z&Q's reading of this clause — see their note 17, p. 447.
39. The addition of 不 here following YY is generally accepted.
40. Here and in several subsequent instances in this chapter 孔某 is written for Confucius. In each case WYJ emends 某 to 丘 although other modern editors (e.g. MZQY, LSL) do not — see WYJ, note 103, p. 455.
41. Proposed addition by SYR.

cultivate the self. One should not abide what is not righteous. One should not do what contravenes principle. One should devote one's efforts to furthering the benefit of the world. One should take every measure to achieve this objective. If something is not of benefit, one should stop. This is the way of the gentleman. From what I have heard of Confucius' conduct, it was the opposite of this at a fundamental level."

39.9   Duke Jing of Qi[viii] questioned Yan Zi[ix] saying: "What sort of man is Confucius?"

Yan Zi did not reply so the Duke asked him again, but again he did not reply.

Duke Jing said: "Many people have spoken to me about Confucius and they all take him to be a worthy man. Now I ask you about him and you do not reply. Why is this?"

Yan Zi replied, saying: "Ying is a worthless person and is not adequate to know who is a worthy man. Nevertheless, I have heard it said about a worthy man that, when he enters another's state, he certainly devotes himself to fostering close relationships between the ruler and his ministers and eliminating antagonism between superiors and inferiors. But, when Confucius went to Jing, he knew of Bo Gong's plans and yet he introduced him to Shi Qi. [As a result] the ruler almost lost his life and Bo Gong himself was killed.[x] Ying has heard that, when a worthy man gains his

---

viii. Duke Jing of Qi 齊景公 is held to have ruled Qi from 546 to 489 BC. There are several references to exchanges with Confucius recorded in the *Lun Yu* — for example, XII.11, XVI.12 and XVIII.3.

ix. Yan Zi is Yan Ying 晏嬰 (died 493 BC) who was chief minister of Qi under Duke Jing and the putative author of the *Yanzi Chunqiu* which several later commentators (e.g. Liu Zongyuan, Wang Yinglin) have interpreted as a Mohist work. In keeping with this, he was noted for his frugality.

x. The matter here recorded is documented in the *Zuo Zhuan* for the 16th year of Duke Ai (LCC, vol. 5, pp. 843–848). Jing is the state of Chu 楚. Bo Gong is Bo Sheng 白勝. The year in question is 479 BC, the year of Confucius' death. It is, moreover, some years after the deaths of both Duke Jing and Yan Ying — see, for example, WYJ, notes 107–109, p. 456.

白公僇[42]。嬰聞賢人得上不虛，得下不危，言聽於君必利人，教
行下必於[43]上，是以言明而易知也，行明[44]而易從也，行義可明
乎民，謀慮可通乎君臣。今孔某深慮同[45]謀以奉賊，勞思盡知以
行邪，勸下亂上，教臣殺君，非賢人之行也。入人之國而與人之
賊，非義之類也。知人不忠，趣之為亂，非仁義之也[46]。逃人而
後謀，避人而後言，行義不可明於民，謀慮不可通於君臣，嬰不
知孔某之有異於白公也，是以不對。」景公曰：「嗚乎！貺寡人者
眾矣，非夫子，則吾終身不知孔某之與白公同也。」

39.10[47] 孔某之齊見景公，景公說，欲封之以尼谿，以告晏子。晏子曰：
「不可。大儒浩居[48]而自順者也，不可以教下。好樂而淫人，不可

---

42. Read as 戮.
43. Emended to 利 in conformity with the preceding statement following YY.
44. Some early texts have no character here. CYX restores 易 which WYJ follows. 明 is due
    to WYZ — see WYJ, note 111, p. 456, for details.
45. Read as 周 in the sense of 周密 following YY.
46. Since BY a number of commentators have proposed emendation of this clause. I have
    taken it as "非仁之類也" to achieve parallelism with the previous statement. Other
    suggestions include the addition of 類 (LSL) and emendation to "非仁之義也" (WYJ).
47. This passage, with some variations, also appears in the *Yanzi Chunqiu* (SPTK, vol. 14,
    YZCQ, pp. 85–86)
48. 居 is read as 倨 in the sense of 傲慢 — see LSL.

superior's trust, he should not waste his position. When he gains
the trust of his subordinates, he should not endanger them. If his
words are heeded by the ruler, they must benefit the people. If his
teachings are carried out by his subordinates, they must benefit the
ruler. This is why his words must be clear and easy to understand
and why his conduct must be unequivocal and easy to follow. If
his conduct is righteous, it can bring enlightenment to the people.
If his plans are well considered, they can be communicated to ruler
and ministers. Now Confucius gave deep consideration and
careful planning to bringing about rebellion. He thought hard and
exhausted his knowledge to carry out evil. He encouraged
subordinates to rebel against the ruler and he taught ministers to
kill the ruler. These are not the actions of a worthy man. To enter
another's state and join with the people in rebellion is not the mark
of righteousness. To know the people are not loyal and incite them
to be rebellious is not the mark of benevolence. To evade the
people and afterwards plan, to avoid the people and afterwards
speak, means that conduct which is righteous cannot enlighten
the people and plans which are well considered cannot be
communicated to ruler and ministers. Ying does not see how
Confucius is any different from Bo Gong. This is why I didn't
reply."

Duke Jing said: "Alas! I have taught my people a great deal,[xi] but,
if it were not for you, I would have lived my whole life without
knowing that Confucius was the same as Bo Gong."

39.10   Confucius went to Qi to see Duke Jing. Duke Jing was delighted
and wished to enfeoff him with Nixi[xii] and told Yan Zi of this.

Yan Zi said: "Don't do it. Confucians are arrogant and opiniated
and cannot be used to instruct subordinates. They love music and

---

xi.   There is variation in how this initial statement is interpreted, depending particularly on
      how 既 is read — e.g. as 況 (BY) or as 賜 in the sense of 賜教 (SYR, based on a sentence
      in the *Yi Li*).
xii. It is not clear where Nixi 尼溪 was — see WYJ, note 121, p. 457, for discussion and other
      possible references including the *Yanzi Chunqiu* version of this passage which has Erji
      爾稽.

不可使親治。立命而怠事，不可使守職。宗喪循哀[49]，不可使慈
民。機服勉容，不可使導眾。孔某盛容脩飾以蠱世，弦歌鼓舞以
聚徒，繁登降之禮以示儀，務趨翔[50]之節以觀眾，博學不可使議
世，勞思不可以補民，絫壽不能盡其學，當年不能行其禮，積財
不能贍其樂，繁飾邪術以營世君，盛為聲樂以淫遇民，其道不可
以期[51]世，其學不可以導眾。今君封之，以利齊俗，非所以導國
先[52]眾。」公曰：「善！」於是厚其禮，留其封，敬見而不問其道。
孔某乃恚[53]，怒於景公與晏子，乃樹鴟夷子皮於田常之門，告南
郭惠子以所欲為，歸於魯。有頃間[54]齊將伐魯，告子貢曰：「賜
乎，舉大事於今之時矣！」乃遣子貢之齊，因南郭惠子以見田
常，勸之伐吳，以教高，國，鮑，晏，使毋得害田常之亂，勸越
伐吳。三年之內，齊吳破國之難，伏尸以言術數，孔某之誅也。

---

49. This statement is generally modified to read: "崇喪遂哀" following SYR and WNS.
    Z&Q gloss "遂哀" as "哀而不止也".

50. 趨翔 is taken to be a particular ritual activity. It is referred to not only in the above
    passage and the corresponding passage in the *Yanzi Chunqiu* but also in other texts —
    for example, the LSCQ 4/3.4 where K&R render it "leaping forward and jumping back".
    YPM has "rushing and soaring" — see his note 1, p. 208.

51. Following YY, many commentators read 期 as 示.

52. 先 has here the same meaning as 導 according to MZQY. LSL uses 引導 for the latter
    and 率領 for the former.

53. 恚 here is due to BY. WYJ, who retains 志, has the following comment: "志，讀如論
    語 '默而識之' 之 '識'。" The reference is to *Lun Yu* VII.2, LCC, vol. 1, p. 195 — see
    WYJ, note 142, p. 459.

54. Read as 聞 following SSX.

deprave people, so cannot be close to government. They set up Fate and are indolent in affairs, so cannot be used to bear responsibility. They honour mourning and prolong grief, so they cannot show compassion to the people. They wear strange clothes and maintain a strained bearing, so they cannot bring leadership to the multitude. Confucius decks himself out in splendid attire in order to beguile the world. He uses strings and drums, songs and dances to gather followers. He complicates the ceremonies of ascending and descending to display ritual. He devotes attention to the rules of walking quickly and circling around to draw the gaze of the people. He is broad in learning, but he cannot establish principles for the age. He is diligent in thought, but he cannot use this to be a help to the people. In several lifetimes one could not exhaust his learning, but in the prime of life one is not able to carry out his ritual practices. A great accumulation of wealth does not enable one to provide for his music. He uses complicated adornments and heterodox methods in order to delude the rulers of the age. He makes much of the sounds of music to influence and hoodwink the people. His Way cannot be used to represent the times. His learning cannot be used to lead the multitude. Now you would enfeoff him in order to benefit the customs of Qi. This is not the way to guide the state or to lead the ordinary people." "Well said," replied the Duke.

After this, he was lavish with his ceremonies, but he put aside the enfeoffment. He accorded Confucius respect, but did not enquire about his Way. Confucius was outraged. He became furious with Duke Jing and Yan Zi, so then, having appointed Chiyi Zipi to the entourage of Tian Chang, he informed Nanguo Huizi of what he wanted done and returned to Lu. After a time, when he heard that Qi was going to attack Lu, he informed Zi Gong, saying: "Ci, now is the time to raise the great matter." He then sent Zi Gong to Qi where, through an introduction by Nanguo Huizi, he met with Tian Chang. He urged him to attack Wu and, by instructing Gao, Guo, Bao and Yan to do nothing to hinder Tian Chang's rebellion, urged Yue to attack Wu. That within the space of three years, Qi and Wu were states facing destruction and the corpses of the dead were numbered in hundreds of thousands was the result of Confucius' schemes.[xiii]

39.11   孔某為魯司寇，舍公家而奉[55] 季孫。季孫[56] 相魯君而走，季孫與邑人爭門關，決植。[57]

39.12   孔某窮於蔡陳之間[58]，藜羹不糂[59]。十日，子路為亨[60] 豚，孔某不問肉之所由來而食。號[61] 人衣以酤酒，孔某不問酒之所由來而飲。哀公迎孔子，席不端弗坐，割不正弗食。子路進，請曰：「何其與陳蔡反也？」孔某曰：「來！吾語女。曩與女為苟[62] 生，今

---

55. Not all editors accept BY's emendation of 於 to 竽 here — see, for example, WYJ, note 150, p. 461.
56. LSL suggests that the repeated 季孫 is superfluous.
57. There are several issues with this short paragraph: (i) Confucius is recorded as having been minister of justice in Lu in the 9th year of Duke Ting. (ii) Some take Ji Sun (or Jisun) to be the same as the person referred to in the *Lun Yu* — see III.1, for example. As SYR points out, however, the events recorded in the *Mozi* do not appear in any other classical texts. (iii) For the interpretation of the very terse final expression see WYJ, note 153, pp. 461–462. (iv) For further information see both the *Zuo Zhuan*, Duke Ding, 9th year (LCC, vol. 5, pp. 771–773) and *Shi Ji* 47, vol. 6, p. 1914ff.
58. In the *Lun Yu* there is: "在陳絕糧，從者病，莫能興" — XV.1(2).
59. This character, usually written with the 米 radical (#27635 in the ZWDCD), is defined in the *Shuo Wen* as follows: "以米和羹也".
60. 亨 is taken as 烹 following BY.
61. WYJ emends 號 to 裋. Others accept BY's reading of the former as the latter. SYR quotes the 〈說文·衣部〉 as follows: "裋，豎衣也。"
62. Here, and in its subsequent use, 苟 is read as 假 or 急 (WNS).

39.11   When Confucius was acting as minister of justice in Lu, he
forsook the ducal house and served the interests of Ji Sun. Ji Sun
was chief minister to the Lu prince yet he fled. As he was
struggling with the guards of the city gate, [Confucius] lifted the
bar [for him].

39.12   Confucius fell on hard times while between Cai and Chen and was
living on broth made from brambles without any rice mixed in.
After ten days, Zi Lu boiled up a pig which Confucius ate without
asking where the meat had come from. Zi Lu also divested a man
of his robe to exchange for sweet wine which Confucius drank
without asking where the liquor had come from. Yet, when
Confucius was received by Duke Ai, he did not sit if the mat was
not straight and did not eat what was not cut properly.[xiv]

Zi Lu came forward and asked: "Why do you do the opposite of
what you did between Cai and Chen?"

Confucius replied: "Come! I shall tell you. At that time, I, with
you, was anxious about surviving. Now, with you, I am anxious
about being righteous."

When starving and in straitened circumstances, he did not shrink
from any means of preserving his life. When satiated and in
abundance, he acted falsely to glorify himself. In terms of being

---

xiii. Brief details of the people referred to in this paragraph are as follows: (i) Chiyi Zipi 鴟
夷子皮 is Fan Li 范蠡 who helped Gou Jian 句踐 in the overthrow of Wu. (ii) Tian
Chang 田常 was a Qi noble who drove Jian Gong 簡公 from the throne in 481 BC —
see *Shi Ji* 33, vol. 5, p. 1545. (iii) It is unclear who Nanguo Huizi was — see WYJ , note
144, p. 460. YPM has him as "Huitse of the South City" and describes him in a note as
"... a follower of T'ien Ch'ang" (p. 208). (iv) Zi Gong 子貢 is the well-known disciple
of Confucius, also called Ci 賜 — see *Shi Ji* passage referred to above. (v) Gao 高, Guo
國, Bao 鮑 and Yan 晏 are taken to be four separate people by modern Chinese editors
(both YPM and BW refer to a single person — Kao-kuo Pao-yen). For Gao and Guo see
Zuo Zhuan, 16th year of Duke Cheng and the *Shiji* 40, vol. 5, p. 1710 and note 18,
p. 1712. Bao is taken to be Bao Shuya 鮑叔牙 and Yan is probably Yan Ying himself.
It must be remembered that there is no historical evidence to support the *Mozi* account
of these supposed events.

xiv. For these two requirements of proper behaviour see *Lun Yu* X.9 and X.8(3) respectively.

與女為苟義。」夫飢約則不辭妄取以活身，贏飽則偽行以自飾，
汙邪詐偽，孰大於此！

39.13　孔某與其門弟子閒坐曰：「夫舜見瞽叟就[63]然，此時天下圾[64]乎！
周公旦非其人也邪？何為舍其家室而託寓也？」孔某所行，心術
所至也。其徒屬弟子皆效孔某。子貢，季路輔孔悝亂乎衛，陽貨
亂乎齊，佛肸以中牟叛，黍雕刑殘，〔暴〕[65]莫大焉！夫為弟子後
生，其〔於〕[66]師必修其言，法其行，力不足，知弗及而後已。今
孔某之行如此，儒士則可以疑矣。

---

63. 就 is read as 蹴 in the sense of 蹙. Some texts (e.g. Z&Q) have 孰.
64. Read as 危 (危險).
65. Suggested addition by WYJ, Z&Q.
66. Suggested addition by LSL.

impure, dishonest, deceitful and hypocritical, what could be greater than this!

39.13 Once, when Confucius was sitting together with his disciples, he said: "When Shun saw Gu Sou, he was ill at ease. At that time the world was in danger.[xv] Was Dan, the Duke of Zhou a non-benevolent man? Why did he forsake his ducal house and retire to his private dwelling?"[xvi]

This is what Confucius' conduct and the workings of his mind came to. And his students and disciples all imitated him. Zi Gong and Ji Lu aided Kung Kui in bringing disorder to Wei.[xvii] Yang Huo brought disorder to Qi.[xviii] Fu Xi involved Zhongmou in rebellion.[xix] Qidiao inflicted punishment and death.[xx] In terms of cruelty, what is greater [than these instances]? Those who are disciples and follow their teacher must cultivate his words and imitate his behaviour, yet their strength is not sufficient and their knowledge is not adequate so they subsequently give up. Now if Confucius' conduct was like this, Confucian scholars should be regarded with suspicion!

---

xv. Tradition has it that Shun's father Gu Sou 瞽叟 took a second wife after which both treated Shun badly. Despite this, Shun continued to display what Giles has described as "exemplary conduct" towards them.

xvi. An expanded version of this story is to be found in *Mozi* 46.13.

xvii.There is some uncertainty about the names here. Zi Gong 子貢 is generally thought to be Zi Gao 子皋. Both YPM and BW speak of Kong Li but he should probably be called Kong Kui 孔悝 which is how Legge speaks of him in his translation of the *Zuo Zhuan* where the incident referred to is described (Duke Ai, 15th year, LCC, vol. 5, pp. 840–843).

xviii.Yang Huo 陽貨 is Yang Hu 陽虎, charioteer to Ji Huan 季桓, who was the chief of one of the three great families of Lu. Yang Hu rebelled against his master — *Zuo Zhuan*, Duke Ding, 9th year, LCC, vol. 5, pp. 771–773.

xix. Fu Xi 佛肸 was a high official in the Jin city of Zhongmou (situated in what is now Henan province). Whilst resisting attack by Jian Zi of Zhao, he is said to have called for Confucius — *Shi Ji* 47, vol. 6, p. 1924.

xx. 桼 is read 漆 and the person referred to is taken to be either Qidiao Kai 漆雕開 or Qidiao Duo 漆雕哆, both from Lu and said to have been disciples of Confucius. Both are mentioned in the *Shi Ji* 67, vol. 7, pp. 2213 and 2220 respectively, but there is very little about either — see note on p. 2213. There is also some variation in interpretation of the *Mozi* text as to whether they inflicted punishment and destruction or suffered these things (e.g. BW).

PART *III*

Language, Logic & Science

Introduction

All editors and commentators agree that chapters 40–45 of the *Mozi* (the so-called dialectical chapters) present very considerable textual and interpretative problems. Mei Yipao, who omitted these chapters from what was the first substantial English translation of the work, wrote in the introduction to his translation (p. xii), apropos these chapters, "… besides the unsettled question as to their respective authorship, the few pages probably make the hardest reading in the whole body of Chinese literature." Nonetheless, considerable progress has been made in sorting out the various problems and bringing the text of these chapters to an intelligible state. Very briefly stated, the problems fall into two categories: those related to individual characters and those related to the arrangement of the text.

The first category includes the use of unknown graphs (what Graham refers to as "the extraordinary variation in writing of single words"), the effects of Song taboos (bearing in mind that the lost Song *Daoist Patrology* [DZ] is probably the source of the present text via the Ming *Daoist Patrology* [DZ]), and basic errors of copying such as the mistaken use of characters of similar sound or form, and simple omissions and duplications. The second category includes the curious arrangement of the Canons indicated by the very brief five word comment immediately before the final Canon of the A series to read the text horizontally, the importance of the head character in identifying the start of each Explanation, dislocation of whole groups of characters, the effects of transfer of the text from wooden writing strips to a continuous text, and the interpolation of glosses.

Important milestones in the continuing search for clarity, again very briefly listed, have been Bi Yuan's initial rediscovery of the text overall and his recognition of the particular arrangement of the Canons, Sun Yirang's invaluable edition, first pulished in 1894, in which many of the important and still accepted textual emendations were made, Liang Qichao's recognition of the role of the head character in the structure of the Explanations, Wu Yujiang's edition which included notes giving reference to all the available ancient texts, Luan Diaofu's studies of textual structure, and, most recently, the work of Tan Jiefu and A. C. Graham. Some commentators who have made detailed studies of these chapters have tended to rely on a piecemeal as opposed to a systematic approach in their attempts to bring sense to this material. Although they have been the target of what is probably justified criticism by Graham, their contributions remain noteworthy. Such men include Gao Heng and Wu Feibai. Furthermore, among those who have made such detailed studies, there is a significant lack of uniformity as to what textual changes and rearrangements should be made. So, despite the valiant efforts of these and many other scholars, and the definite advances that have been made in establishing a reliable text, there is still considerable room for interpretative variation in these six chapters.

For this reason, the translation that follows is based essentially on the *Daoist Patrology* (DZ) text which is the approach taken in modern Chinese editions of the *Mozi* such as those of Wu Yujiang, the MBJ, Li Shenglong, Zhou Caizhu and Qi Ruiduan, and the CHANT. In the case of the last two, the Canons and Explanations (C&Es) are kept separate (i.e. chapters 40 to 43 appear consecutively rather than having 40 joined with 42, and 41 joined with 43), and the Canons appear consecutively rather than being re-arranged to follow the order of the Explanations. A broad subdivision of the A group of Canons may be made into the basic definitions, all ending in 也, comprising A1–A76; the Canons on words with multiple meanings or uses (A77–A88); a somewhat miscellaneous group with particular textual uncertainty (A89–A99); and the propositions or theses all ending with 説在 X, comprising B1–B81. Both Tan Jiefu in his 1981 work 《墨經分類譯注》 and Graham in his major work on the subject (LMLES), and also in the later *Disputers of the Tao*, make more substantial subdivisions, primarily on the basis of subject matter. In the case of chapters 44 and 45 (Daqu and Xiaoqu), these same two scholars also make major rearrangements of the material whilst Zhang Qihuang rearranges the Daqu only. These several rearrangements are clearly of interest and have much to commend them in each case, but, because they differ quite considerably, and particularly because they are not incorporated into standard editions of the *Mozi*, I have not followed any one of them in the present work. Those interested in a detailed account of the textual problems pertaining to these chapters should consult the section entitled "Textual Problems" in Graham's *Later Mohist Logic Ethics and Science* (pp. 72–110).

40 & 42: 經與經說上

A1   C: 故，所得而後成也。

E: 故：小故有之不必然，無之必不然。體也。若有端。大故有之
必〔然〕，無〔之必不〕然¹。若見之成見也。

Comment: The text of the C is uncontroversial. Not so with the E which ACG describes as "badly mutilated". SYR's widely accepted additions to the DZ text are used in the translation. The simplest emendation is that of TJF who omits 無 from the DZ text for the penultimate sentence, giving: "大故，有之必然。" More extensive changes are made by both ACG and WFB. Nonetheless, the basic point remains the same. Most commentators equate the meaning of 故 given here with that in the *Shuo Wen* (使為之也). Related definitions are to be found in the Daqu 20, Xiaoqu 2 and the LSCQ 9/4.1. The E elaborates the definition, identifying minor and major causes, equivalent to "necessary" and "necessary and sufficient" conditions respectively. The examples are obscure and variably interpreted.

A2   C: 體，分於兼也。

E: 體：若二之 ‥，尺之端也。

Comment: Most editors retain the DZ text as above. WFB is an exception, incorporating part of this C&E into A1 above and making the remainder his A49. WYJ gives a clear amplification of the E (his note 8, p. 487) whilst ACG draws attention to the important paired term 兼 for which the definition is lost — see his pp. 265–266. In WFB's rearrangement 體 and 兼 are contrasted in his modified E for A1.

---

1.   The addition of the four characters indicated to the DZ text is due to SYR and is widely accepted (WYJ, ACG, Z&Q, LSL, JBC). TJF, however, does not make the addition but simply omits 無. WFB makes more substantial changes — see Comment.

40 & 42: Canons & Explanations A

A1   **C:** A cause is that which obtains before something comes about.

   E: Cause: When there is a minor cause, something is not necessarily so; when there is not, something is necessarily not so. It is a part — like a point. When there is a major cause, something is necessarily so; when there is not, something is necessarily not so. Like seeing something completes seeing.

A2   **C:** A part is a division in the whole.

   E: Part: For example, one is a part of two; a point is a part of a *chi* (measured length).

A3   **C:** 知，材也。

E: 知：材[2] 知也者，所以知也，而必知[3]。若明[4]。

Comment: This is the first of four definitions of epistemological terms (A3–A6). One issue is whether a distinction is being made between two senses of 知, the first as 智 (suggested by SYR) and the second as 知. ACG, who transliterates all four terms, equates the two 知 with intelligence/conciousness and knowing respectively. JBC has for 知 in A3: "指人們認識客觀事物之綜合官能和材質" (p. 5) and for 知 in A5: "指知道、了解，認識，相當于心理學之感覺" (p. 8). If one accepts SYR's reading of 知 here as 智, the definition of the latter as "capacity" (材質) is similar to that offered in the *Xunzi* 22 (XZXZ p. 367, K vol. 3, p. 127) as "ability" (能). I have taken 知 as "knowing" in both instances, regarding the two C&Es as dealing with two aspects of the one process.

A4   **C:** 慮，求也。

E: 慮：慮也者，以其知有求也，而不必得之。若睨[5]。

Comment: 慮 is equated with 思考 or 思慮, in the sense of "reflect" or "deliberate" by both WFB and JBC, with an element of planning implied as in the *Shuo Wen* definition (謀思). I have followed the DR definition for philosophical use.

A5   **C:** 知，接也。

E: 知：知也者，以其知過[6] 物，而能貌之。若見。

Comment: The issue of whether there is a distinction between 知 here and in A3 has been discussed above. As ACG observes, SYR's proposed emendation of 過 seems unnecessary. In translating 貌 as above I have followed JBC. ACG has "describe" (see his note 63, p. 267). Z&Q give a similar reading — 描畫.

---

2.   材 is something of a problem here. Some editors take it as the second of a double head character — see, for example, LSL, note 3, p. 254. This gives the next three characters the same form as in the following similar C&Es. WFB omits it.

3.   HS adds 不 before 必 in this clause.

4.   There is general acceptance of 明 as indicating "eyesight" as in *Mencius* IA.7(10). LQC, in fact, emends 明 to 眼.

5.   For 睨 see also *Doctrine of the Mean*, XIII.2 and *Zhuangzi* 23 (GQF, vol. 4, p. 810 and particularly his note on p. 812). The term is variously translated: e.g. "look askance" (Legge), "childlike stare" (Watson), "sideways glance" (Mair). The point here seems to be that it is an indirect process. ACG has "peering".

6.   SYR's emends 過 to 遇 but this is not widely accepted — see, for example, ACG, note 62, p. 267.

A3   **C:** Knowing is a capacity.

        E: Knowing: With regard to the capacity of knowing, it is how one knows and knows with certainty. It is like seeing.

A4   **C:** Cogitating is seeking.

        E: Cogitating: With regard to cogitating, it is through one's knowing that there is a seeking [of something], but one does not necessarily find it. It is like seeing indirectly.

A5   **C:** Knowing is contacting.

        E: Knowing: With regard to knowing, it is through one's knowing [capacity] "passing" a thing that one is able to form an impression of it (describe it). It is like seeing.

A6   **C:** 恕[7]，明也。

　　　　E: 恕：恕也者，以其知論物，而其知之也著[8]。若明。

Comment: This is the most problematical of the four epistemological definitions. With respect to all four definitions, the position taken here is that the first and third refer to "primary" acts of cognition, taking place directly through the senses, whilst the second and fourth indicate mental activity either of a conceptual or analytic nature. The fourth and final process, that of reasoning, is the most elaborate and requires a new graph. The correspondence to the various aspects of vision is then with the eyesight in general as a function, with an indirect or uncertain aspect of the process, with the direct aspect of seeing, and with the bringing of clarity to knowing by reasoning finally compared to clarity in vision. Relevant, albeit brief, correspondences in ancient texts are, particularly, with *Zhuangzi* 23, LSCQ 16 and *Xunzi* 22.

A7   **C:** 仁，體愛也。

　　　　E: 仁：愛己[9]者，非為用己也。不若愛馬著若明。[10]

Comment: Here begins a series of 14 C&Es on conduct and ethics, the majority dealing with common and important terms. The interpretation of the definition of 仁 depends particularly on the reading of 體 and, to a lesser extent, on whether 己 is retained or emended to 民 (SYR). It seems likely that the point here is the distinction between "體愛" and "兼愛", the latter, of course, a central Mohist concept. WYJ has: "大取篇曰'仁而無利愛'，體愛與利愛相反。" — see his note 20, p. 489. ACG renders 體 as "individually" and I have followed this. It is also possible that 體 is misplaced here on the basis of the following definition and the statement on the two terms (仁 and 義) in B75. The issue of the love of the self within the framework of universal love is addressed in the Daqu (*Mozi* 44.7).

7.　This is the commonly accepted emendation, on the basis of the E, of the otherwise unknown Mohist character (知 above the 心 radical). Not all editors make the emendation — see, for example, TJF and ACG (note 64, p. 267).

8.　Interpreted by modern commentators (e.g. MZQY, JBC) in the sense of 顯著 (see *Zhuangzi* 25, GQF, vol. 4, p. 896).

9.　Not all commentators accept 己 here. Thus, some emend it to 民 following SYR (e.g. WYJ — see his note 21, p. 489), whilst WFB emends the first 己 to 也 and omits the second.

10.　The last three characters (著若明) are almost certainly a misplaced fragment from the preceding E (see ACG, note 67, p. 270). Most, following SYR, emend 著 to 者, although even the 者 may be superfluous.

A6   **C:** Reasoning is seeing clearly.

 E: Reasoning: With regard to reasoning, it is through one's knowing and explaining a thing that one's knowing it is made manifest. It is like seeing clearly.

A7   **C:** Benevolence is loving individually.

 E: Benevolence: Loving the self is not for the sake of the self being of use. It is not like loving a horse.

A8 C: 義，利也。

E: 義：志以天下為芬[11]，而能能[12] 利之；不必用。

Comment: There is general agreement on the reading of this C&E, modern commentators accepting CYX's interpretation of the last three characters of the E: "用者，見用於世也。不必用者不必在上位、隨分而能利人也。" Notable in this and the previous C&E is the definition of two central Confucian concepts (仁 and 義) in terms of two central Mohist concepts (愛 and 利). See also C&E B75, *Mozi* 44.1, and *Lun Yu* IV.16.

A9 C: 禮，敬也。

E: 禮，貴者公，賤者名[13]，而俱有敬慢[14] 焉。等異論[15] 也。

Comment: The relationship between 禮 and 敬 is stated at the outset of the *Li Ji* (SSJZS, vol. 5, p. 12). The Mohist point is that it should apply regardless of rank or position and run through all strata of society, in contrast to the Confucian position as also exemplified in the *Li Ji* (SSJZS, vol. 5, p. 55).

A10 C: 行，為也。

E: 行：所為不善名，行也。所為善名，巧也。若為盜。

Comment: This C&E may not be as clear as the version above suggests. A number of commentators (see, for example, LSL, JBC) refer to *Xunzi* 22 (《荀子‧正名》): "正義而為謂之行。" WFB, in fact, emends the E to read: "行；所為義，名行也。所為不義，名巧也，若為盜。" making the distinction between 行 (as 德行) and 巧. TJF writes: "'行為' 二字，常見連用。此即以 '為' 訓 '行'，似難分曉。竊意此 '為' 即 '能為'、當與《說》之 '所為' 對看。'所為' 者 '事' 也，未必即謂之 '行'；'能為' 則可謂之 '行' 矣。故曰 '行，為也。'"

---

11. It is generally accepted that this should be read as 分.
12. There has been some debate about the duplication of 能. I have followed ACG, for example, in taking the first 能 as nominal. SYR equates the second 能 with 善 — see WYJ, note 26, p. 490. See also A13 below.
13. ZHY reads 名 as 民.
14. 慢 is read as 慢 following BY and is taken as the opposite of 敬.
15. Accepted as 倫 following ZHY.

A8   **C:** Righteousness is being of benefit.

      E: Righteousness: The resolve to take the world as one's sphere of action and, having ability, being able to benefit it. It is not necessary to be used (i.e. have a position).

A9   **C:** Propriety is respect.

      E: Propriety: The noble have the title "duke" whilst the lowly just have a name, yet for both there is respect and rudeness. It is only in rank that they differ.

A10   **C:** Conduct is doing.

      E: Conduct: That which is done without thought of bettering one's name is conduct. That which is done to better one's name is speciousness. It is like being a robber.

A11   C: 實，榮也。

E: 實：其志，氣之見[16]也，使人如己。不若金聲玉服。

Comment: There are several issues with this C&E. First, there is the question of 實 which is found here in a somewhat different context from its usual association with 名 in Mingjia texts. However, the conjunction with 榮 is not unknown. For example, WYJ refers to the *Guo Yu* as follows: "《國語‧晉語》 曰：'華則榮矣，實之不知，請務實乎'" — see his note 32, p. 491 — and it is generally retained by Chinese commentators in the sense given. Thus, LSL has: "榮與實相對而言。實指內在的充實，榮指外在的文采。" — see his note 1, p. 258. On the other hand, ACG argues that 實 has been used to replace 誠 due to a Song taboo (his note 73, p. 273) and is more appropriately paired with the following definition of 忠, i.e. "sincerity" and "loyalty". Second, there is the question of 志 and 氣, whether these are to be taken together (see, for example, JBC, note 2, p. 19) or separately as above following WFB. Third, there is the final sentence of the E. Several commentators refer to *Mencius* VB.1(6), LCC, vol. 2, p. 372 but the context there is different. In his modern language version, LSL has: "不像金玉之類的佩飾，只是外表好看。" — see also TJF, p. 90 and ACG, note 75, p. 274.

A12   C: 忠，以為利而強低[17]也。

E: 忠：不利弱子亥、足將入止容。

Comment: The issue in the C concerns 低 — whether to retain it or emend it in one of several ways (see note 17 below). I have retained it at the suggestion of an anonymous reader. The E presents a major problem. ACG omits it altogether considering the whole E to be a "misplaced fragment" (his note 77, p. 274). Both WFB and WYJ describe it as "unclear". Apart from several contentious characters, the punctuation varies from none (WFB, WYJ) to a break after 子 (TJF) or 亥 (e.g. Z&Q). The translation in parentheses above follows Z&Q who, in turn, follow SYR's emendations (低 to 村 in the C, 亥 to 孩, and 止 to 正 in the E) and interpretations — see Z&Q, notes 1 and 2, p. 539.

---

16. Generally read as 現.
17. A number of commentators express dissatisfaction with this character but emendations vary: to 村 following SYR which JBC supports by reference to the *Xunzi* 13 (XZXZ, p. 213), to 任 (ACG), and to 民 (WYJ), whilst WFB retains it.

A11   **C:** (Inner) substance equates with the (outer) display.

       E: (Inner) substance: His will is manifest in his spirit and causes others to be like himself. It is not like the tinkle of metal or jade adornments.

A12   **C:** Loyalty is to strengthen the lowly, taking this to be beneficial.

       E: Loyalty: (It is not beneficial to a young lord to be disloyal. On walking in to the prince's presence one must correct one's bearing.)

A13   C: 孝，利親也。

E: 孝：〔志〕[18] 以親為芬，而能能利親；不必得。

Comment: This C&E is closely similar in form to A8. The two common characters 芬 and 能 are treated similarly. One issue is what it is not necessary to gain. Among the possibilities are personal reputation and the love or recognition of parents — see *Zhuangzi* 26 (GQF, vol. 4, p. 920), *Xunzi* 27.82 (K, vol. III, p. 227) and 27.112 (K, vol. III, pp. 235–236). There is also the point raised particularly in JBC's commentary on the range of filial feeling and its not being limited to one's own parent or parents — see his note 4, p. 23 and the *Mozi* 16.

A14   C: 信，言合於意[19] 也。

E: 信：不以[20] 其言之當也。使人視城得金[21]。

Comment: Although there might be some debate about the best reading of 意 (and to a lesser extent of 信), the meaning of the C is generally agreed upon. The E is a different matter. In fact, ACG makes major changes, transferring the 13 characters from what, in the present text, is A29 to be interposed between 視 and 城 in A14 and leaving A29 without an E. The most common position is that expressed by SYR (see note 21 below) which is that followed by modern editors LSL, Z&Q and JBC. The point is that, if you tell someone there is gold in the city, they should expect to find it. WFB's view is that it is an explanation or metaphor (喻) for the value of trustworthy words.

---

18. ACG restores 志 here to complete the parallel structure to A8. I have not included it in the translation.
19. There are several interpretations of 意 other than its primary meaning: 義 (WFB), 意志 (JBC), 預料 (Z&Q), 億 (TJF), 內心 (LSL).
20. WFB emends 不以 to 必 — see Comment.
21. On this sentence, SYR has: "言告人以城上有金，視而果得之，明言必信也。"

A13 **C:** Being filial is to benefit parents.

E: Being filial: To take parents as one's sphere of action and, having ability, to be able to benefit them. It is not necessary to attain [recognition].

A14 **C:** Trustworthiness is words being in accord with thoughts (intentions).

E: Trustworthiness: It is not just a matter of one's words being appropriate. [For example], sending a person to look in the city and his getting gold.

A15   C: 佴，自作也。

E: 佴：與人遇，人眾循²²。

Comment: This is an extremely problematical C&E and the reading offered is very tentative. Several commentators emend the head character — TJF to 狂, WFB to 身 with the 人 radical (ZWDCD #722), and ACG to 司 with the 耳 radical (not listed in the ZWDCD — see his note 82, p. 277). In the E, there are issues with the punctuation (an alternative is "與人、遇人、眾循。" found, for example, in WYJ and Z&Q), with 遇 and whether it should be read as 偶, with the second 人 and whether it should be read as 入, and with the final unknown character (see note 22). The version given above follows CYX and LSL.

A16   C: 狷²³，作嗛²⁴ 也。

E: 狷：為是²⁵。為是之台²⁶ 彼也，弗為也。

Comment: With uncertainty surrounding much of this C&E, any interpretation must be tentative. In the translation, I have substantially followed WYJ's version — see his note 45, pp. 492–493. It is of interest to speculate on the relationship between 狂 and 狷 in Confucian texts, brought out by TJF's emendation of the head character in A15. On this, see Leys (1997), pp. 184–185, the issue being whether they are similar or different.

---

22. An unknown Mohist graph is here emended to 循 as above by most commentators following ZCY, although WFB emends to 楯 in the sense of "defend" and TJF to 遁 in the sense of "escape", "conceal oneself". The Mohist graph has the "heart" radical.
23. The modification of the unknown Mohist character to 狷 as above, following BY and SYR, is generally accepted. The meaning is taken to be that exemplified by the *Lun Yu* XIII.21, where there is a contrast with 狂, made the head character of the preceding C&E by TJF, and the *Mencius* VIIB.37, linked to the description in the *Lun Yu*. See also ACG, note 84, p. 277.
24. There is debate about this character which is found in the *Zhuangzi* 29 (GQF, vol. 4, p. 1012) and the *Xunzi* 7 (XZXZ, p. 83). I have followed the reading as 慊 in the sense of 滿足 (see JBC, note 1, p. 27), which is accepted by a number of commentators. ACG retains it in the sense of "deficient in initiative".
25. Some editors (e.g. JBC) follow SYR in omitting 為是 in one instance. I have followed this in the translation.
26. There are several readings of this character. SYR has it as 詒. I have accepted WYJ's reading as 殆. The sense is similar in each case in that something that is disadvantageous to another is not done.

A15   **C:** To help is the self acting.

E: To help: With one person, being in close association; with many people, complying with the crowd.

A16   **C:** To be scrupulous is acting to bring satisfaction.

E: To be scrupulous: If doing "this" is dangerous to another, it is not done

A17   C: 廉²⁷，作非也²⁸。

        E: 廉：己惟²⁹為之，知其也思耳³⁰也所³¹。

Comment: This C&E is also very problematic as notes 27–31 indicate. The translation is extremely tentative and is largely based on SYR and LSL. WFB rearranges the order to place what is here A18 before what is A16 in the present text, and brackets what are here A16 and A17 together under the brief comment "未詳".

A18   C: 令³²，不為所作也。

        E: 令：非身弗行。

Comment: In the translation, 令 is accepted and BY's initial interpretation of the C followed ("言使人為之，不自作。") The E follows TJF's text and is based on his reading of it as a cryptic statement of what is more clearly expressed in the *Lun Yu* XIII.6 and the final exchange between Gao Zi and Mo Zi in the *Mozi* 48.24, i.e. if one's own conduct is not correct, one cannot expect one's orders to be properly carried out. This is an appropriate point to draw attention to ACG's remarks apropos the preceding four C&Es in which he says: "This is a curiously isolated sequence, and nothing in the rest of the dialectical chapters throws much light on it. All editors heavily emend the text, and some follow an entirely different track ..." (p. 278)

---

27. Some commentators (e.g. SYR) equate this with 慊 in the sense used in the *Mencius* IIA. 2(15), but not the almost contrary meaning in IIB.2(6). On this, see Legge's note (LCC, vol. 2, p. 213) and Zhu Xi, SSJZ (*Mencius*), p. 53. For the conjunction with 狂 see the *Lun Yu* XVII.16(2).

28. The meaning of this construction presents problems. On the C as a whole, ZCY has: "One who is *lian* frequently examines his words and actions and, where these are not in accord with propriety (*li*), he corrects them."

29. Generally read as 雖 following SYR.

30. In the DZ text 思耳 is written as one character (not listed in the ZWDCD). SYR takes this as equivalent to *zhi* (ZWDCD #36574) in the sense of 懼. On writing the two components separately see WYJ, note 47, p. 493 and WFB's text.

31. 所 here presents a problem. At least three positions have been taken: (i) To regard it as superfluous (BY). (ii) To transpose it to come before the preceding one or two characters depending on how 思耳 is written (ACG). (iii) To place it before 令 at the start of the next E — see WYJ, note 49, p. 493 and WFB, p. 29.

32. Whilst most accept 令 (to give a command) as the head character, ZCY (and following him the MZQY) find this term incongruous in the midst of four other terms dealing with personal behaviour and replace it with 節 in the sense of "moderation".

A17   **C:** To be ashamed is to do wrong.

        E: To be ashamed: If one recalls doing something regrettable one knows it and is distressed.

A18   **C:** To give an order is not to do what is done.

        E: To give an order: If it is not something one would do oneself it should not be done.

A19   C: 任，士損己而益所為也。

E: 任：為身之所惡，以成人之所急。

Comment: There are no significant textual problems in this C&E, although there are minor variations in interpretation. Thus many commentators follow BY in reading 任 as 任俠 in the sense of "chivalry", although others (e.g. ACG) take it in the more usual sense of assuming official responsibility. Linked with this is the interpretation of 士 which may be read as "knight-errant" or simply as "officer". I have followed the second of the two options in both instances. The translation above follows BY and TJF on the basis that this reflects a closer connection with the following C&E and possibly even A21.

A20   C: 勇，志之所以敢也。

E: 勇：以其敢於是也，命[33]之。不以其不敢於彼也，害之。

Comment: Although courage/bravery is equated with being fearless (e.g. *Lun Yu* IX.28), it is more complex in that, whilst the courage of a daring act is readily recognised, the courage not to act in certain situations must also be recognised. This distinction is well brought out in WYJ's note 53, p. 494 and by JBC, pp. 34–35. It is interesting to compare this C&E with the first part of *Laozi* 73: "勇於敢則殺，勇於不敢則活。此兩者，或利或害。"

A21   C: 力，刑[34] 之所以奮也。

E: 力：重之謂[也][35]。下與[36] 重舊[37] 也。

Comment: This C&E has proven to be a problem. From its position it should be considered among the terms of 德行 (moral conduct — WFB) and linked with the adjacent definitions of 任 and 勇. On this basis, ACG's translation as "strength" is attractive. It certainly appears to be the final term in the sequence of general terms relating to conduct and is separate from the terms of physics. In this respect, it is noteworthy that 力 is linked with 勇 in the *Zhuangzi* 29 as follows: "俠人之勇力而以為威強" where some read the initial character as 任. Nonetheless, most modern commentators accept the emendations above and

33. There is general acceptance of SYR's reading as 名. The implication is that the naming is favourable, i.e. give him a reputation, hence the rendering as "praise".
34. There is general acceptance of BY's emendation to 形 as in other, related texts such as GSLZ 2.
35. Added by ACG — see his note 92, p. 279.
36. Read as 舉 by SYR and others.
37. There is general acceptance of the emendation of 舊 to 奮 in line with the C.

A19   **C:** To act responsibly is an officer bringing harm to himself but being of benefit in what he does.

       E: To act responsibly: To do what is abhorrent to oneself in order to accomplish what is pressing for others.

A20   **C:** Courage is the means whereby the will dares [to act].

       E: Courage: For his daring to act in this matter, praise him. Do not, for his not daring to act in that matter, disparage him.

A21   **C:** Force is what moves a body.

       E: Force: Said with reference to a weight. Lowering and raising a weight is moving [it].

interpret both C and E in terms of physics, in fact almost a statement of Newton's First Law. Particularly is this so with the E where 下 is equated with the downward gravitational force (although not of course recognised as such) and 舉 as a force raising a body. 力, however, is certainly used in Confucian texts in relation to conduct — see, for example, *Lun Yu* I.7 and the *Doctrine of the Mean* XX.10 where it relates to 仁.

A22   **C:** 生，刑[38] 與知處也。

E: 生：楹[39] 之生，商[40] 不可必也。

Comment: The distinction being made is taken to be that between the corporeal and the mental, between body and mind/spirit, both being the essential prerequisites for life. The E is obscure and quite different interpretations are offered depending on which emendations are accepted. The above translation relates 盈 to its use in A66, B15 and *GSLZ* 3 with respect to the hard white stone, i.e. properties mutually filling. One favoured alternative, following ZCY, is to retain the meaning of 商 and equate the uncertainty of life with the uncertainty of commerce. ACG suggests that the whole E is misplaced here and transposes it to the end of the E for his A39 which itself is a variably placed C&E. He describes the E as "... another fragment unintelligible in the light of the *Canon*" which certainly appears to be the case. However, no matter where it is placed, it is very difficult to make any sense of it.

A23   **C:** 臥，知無知也。

E: 臥：None

Comment: SYR attributes the absence of an E to the clarity of the C, an idea rejected by TJF. The DZ simply has the character 臥 immediately followed by 夢 and then the E for 平.

---

38. From BY on there is a general acceptance of 形 here in the sense of the perceptible form of the body, in fact the body itself, as in the previous C.
39. BY emends this to 形, others (e.g. JBC) to 盈 in the sense of "full"/"to fill". ACG retains the character as meaning "pillar" in his transposition.
40. Whilst some commentators retain this character in its usual sense of "trade" or "commerce", other readings proposed include 常 (WYJ) and 章 (TJF).

A22   **C:** Life is when body and mind exist (are located) [together].

   E: Life: "Filling" it is life, a constant association that cannot be separated.

A23   **C:** To sleep is to have the capacity for knowing but not its function.

   E: To sleep: None

A24 C: 夢，臥而以為然也。

E: 夢：None

Comment: SYR, and the majority of those following him, equate 夢 with the character of similar pronunciation defined in the *Shuo Wen* as "sleeping soundly yet being aware" (*Shuo Wen Jiezi* 7, SBCK, vol. 4, p. 65). Several commentators refer to Zhuang Zhou's well-known dream (see GQF, vol. 1, p. 112, BW, p. 49). Again there is no E, which SYR here also attributes to the clarity of the C.

A25 C: 平，知無欲惡也。

E: 平：淡[41] 然。

Comment: WFB sees these four definitions (A22–A25) as relating to Daoist thinking but, in fact, similar statements and definitions are found in a number of early texts of varying philosophical hue. For a discussion of the majority of the terms in these four C&Es see the *Xunzi* 21.5d (XZXZ, pp. 351–352, K, vol. 3, pp. 104–105).

A26 C: 利，所得而喜也。

E: 利：得是而喜，則是利也。其害也[42]，非是也。

Comment: This and the following C&E are identical in form, supplying converse definitions of two important Mohist terms. The main issue centres on CYX's proposed emendation, the choice being between "its harming another means it is not this" (see e.g. WYJ, note 65, p. 495) and the version above (see also comment to A27).

---

41. Although written in several ways with different radicals, there is agreement following ZHY that the meaning of this character equates with 憺 in the sense of the modern 恬 憺 or 安靜. The DZ has the rare character ZWDCD #11013.
42. Many editors accept CYX's emendation to 他. I have followed JBC in retaining 也 and not implicating "the other".

A24   **C:** To dream is to be asleep yet to take something to be so.

E: To dream: None

A25   **C:** To be at peace is to know no desire or aversion.

E: To be at peace: To be tranquil.

A26   **C:** Benefit is what one is pleased to get.

E: Benefit: If one gets this and is pleased then this is benefit. If it is harmful it is not this.

A27   C: 害，所得而惡也。

E: 害：得是而惡，則是害也。其利也，非是也。

Comment: This C&E is identical in form with that preceding it and differs in content only by the exchange of 害 for 利 and 惡 for 喜. With reference to the final phrase of the E in each case, TJF exemplifies the first with the initial sentences of the *Mozi* 47.1 and the second with the *Mozi* 44.3 (see TJF, p. 105).

A28   C: 治，求得也。

E: 治：吾事治矣，人有[43] 治南北。

Comment: In the C there is variation depending on whether 求 and 得 are read as the same parts of speech, as above, or otherwise (e.g. "to achieve what is sought" — ACG). There is doubt about the E. ACG regards it as incomplete (see his note 96, p. 283) whilst WFB dismisses it as "unclear" without further comment. If it is accepted as it stands, is it descriptive or prescriptive? ZCY, whose interpretation is followed by the MZQY (pp. 367, 420), equates 治 with 平. JBC (note 2, p. 45), in a somewhat free interpretation, identifies the specific Mohist objectives of "兼相愛" and "交相利" as what are to be sought and obtained.

A29   C: 譽，明美也。

E: 譽：之[44] 必[45] 其行也。其言之忻，使人督之。[46]

Comment: This and the following C&E form a pair as do A26 and A27. Here, however, whilst there is identity of form in the C, there is considerable doubt regarding the E both for this and the following C&E. There are at least four different proposals as below:

i.   Omit the E for both A29 and A30, regarding what is there as misplaced in both instances (ACG).

ii. Retain both Es as they are, apart from the omission of 之 from A29 and the emendation of 必 to 止 and 忻 to 作 in A30 (TJF, followed by Z&Q, and in the translation above).

---

43. There is general acceptance of the reading of 有 as 又 (SYR, CYX).

44. 之 in some texts is placed with the head character, and in some it is omitted altogether (see, for example, JBC, note 2, p. 46).

45. Read here and in A30 in the sense of 堅持.

46. There is an argument for omitting the final four characters. GH transfers them to fill the possible lacuna at the end of the previous E (A28). If they are retained, 督 may also be read as 篤 in the sense of 篤厚 (SYR, Z&Q), or as 察, following the *Shuo Wen* definition, as several commentators have suggested (e.g. TJF, JBC).

A27   **C:** Harm is what one is displeased to get.

E: Harm: If one gets this and is displeased then this is harm. If it is beneficial it is not this.

A28   **C:** To put in order is seeking and obtaining.

E: To put in order: My affairs are put in order; others also put in order south and north.

A29   **C:** To praise is to make clear the good.

E: To praise: This strengthens his actions. Its words are pleasing, causing people to be urged on.

iii. WYJ's rearrangement which gives parallel Es for A29 and A30 as follows: "譽之，必其行也，其言也使人忻" and "誹之，必其行也，其言也使人督".

iv. WFB's rearrangement which also gives parallel Es for A29 and A30 as follows: "譽之必其行也，其言之忻，使人督之" and "誹之必其行也，其言之忻，使人督之".

In the translation of this and the following C&E, I have followed the DZ text, reading 必 as 堅持 (although this is somewhat problematical in A30) and accepting LQC's reading of 忻 in the E of A30.

A30   **C:** 誹，明惡也。

   E: 誹：必[47] 其行也。其言之忻[48]。

Comment: See Comment to A29.

A31   **C:** 舉，擬[49] 實也。

   E: 舉[50]：告以文名，舉彼實也。

Comment: 舉 is an important Later Mohist term; e.g. *Mozi* 45.1 ("以名舉實"). Unfortunately textual and interpretative problems are significant in this C&E. The version above is the DZ text apart from the widely accepted emendation of the head character of the E from 譽 to 舉 as indicated in note 50. This is the text that is found, for example, in WYJ and CHANT. ACG proposes a major rearrangement here with respect to this and the following E — see his notes 101 and 102, p. 285. The translation given above is with the Xiao Qu in mind. 實 is translated as "entity" in accord with what I take to be its use in the GSLZ 1 ("名實論").

47. If this is retained, it could be read in the sense indicated for the previous E (see note 45 above). I have, however, followed TJF's emendation to 止 in the translation — see Comment to A29.

48. Several modern editors accept LQC's proposed emendation of 忻 to 怍 (see, for example, TJF).

49. There is some variation in how 擬 is interpreted. ACG has discussed the difficulties of giving a suitable English equivalent (his note 100, p. 285). Most commentators refer to the *Shuo Wen* definition in terms of 度 — see, for example, TJF — but differ in precisely how 度 is to be understood. Some (e.g. LSL) lean towards the meaning of "compare". I have followed WFB's straightforward explanation (p. 33).

50. The emendation of 譽 (found in the DZ) to 舉 is widely, but not universally, accepted — see WYJ, note 72, p. 496 and Comment above.

A30   **C:** To censure is to make clear the bad.

E: Censure: [This] stops his actions. Its words are shaming.

A31   **C:** To raise (pick out) is to identify an entity.

E: To raise (pick out): To inform by means of its name is to pick out that entity.

A32 C: 言，出舉也。

E: 故[51]：言也者，諸[52] 口能之出民[53] 者也。民若畫虎[54] 也。言也，謂[55]。言，猶[56] 石[57] 致也。

Comment: Clearly there are problems with the text, at least of the E, which make any translation and interpretation necessarily tentative. One relatively straightforward and not unreasonable interpretation of the C is that of JBC (note 1, p. 50) which makes a close connection with the previous C. Thus 舉 offers a likeness of an entity whilst 言 puts this process into words. The translation depends on the several emendations and rearrangements considered in notes 51–57. Different editors adopt more or less of these proposals whilst ACG provides a notably different version — see Comment to A31 above.

A33 C: 且，且言然也。[58]

E: 且：自前曰且，自後曰已[59]，方然亦且。（若石者也。）[60]

Comment: The most common and obvious interpretation is that two uses of 且 are being identified, as in YY's oft-quoted analysis, differentiated as referring

---

51. There is doubt about the head character. Some texts retain 故 (e.g. BY, CHANT). In some 故 is omitted leaving "言也者" (e.g. MZQY). WYJ would emend 故 to 言 but retain the following "言也者" which is LQC's proposal and is followed in the translation. See, however, ACG, note 102, p. 285 on this point.
52. 謂 is WFB's emendation of 諸, which some (e.g. JBC) simply omit.
53. There is wide acceptance of 名 here as an emendation of 民.
54. There is general acceptance of 虎 as "tiger" replacing the original character with the "man" radical.
55. I have followed the re-ordering of these three characters suggested by LQC to give "言，謂也".
56. Both WYJ and WFB read 猶 as 由 here, which is followed in the translation.
57. Most accept SYR's emendation of 名 for 石 here.
58. There are several versions of this C. The DZ as above has 且 duplicated and is followed in WYJ's text (although he does accept BY's emendation — *vide infra*). A second version, following BY and SYR, omits the second 且 and is the most common. A third version, following HS and accepted by TJF and WFB, places the second 且 as the third character. Finally, ACG restores 自前 from the E — see his note 109, p. 288.
59. ZCY emends 己 to 且 — see Comment.
60. These four characters are duplicated in the DZ text, occurring also as the E for the following C&E (A34) preceded by 以. The general view is that they are misplaced here. They are not included in the translation. ACG replaces them with what below are the final two characters from the E of A37 — see his note 110, p. 288.

A32   **C:** To speak is to bring forth raisings.

          E: To speak: Speaking is said of the mouth's ability to bring forth names. A name is like a picture of a tiger. Speaking is to say. Speech is what is achieved through names.

A33   **C:** About to is saying (something) is going to be so.

          E: About to: From beforehand, one says about to; from afterwards, one says already; at the moment of occurrence, there is also about to.

to something that is going to happen in the future at some unspecified time and something that is actually on the point of, or in the process of, happening, these uses being contrasted with something that has already happened (已). For other interpretations see particularly ZCY and JBC.

A34 C: 君，臣萌[61] 通約也 。

E: 君：以若[62] 名[63] 者也 。

Comment: Whilst the C seems clear, the E is quite contentious. Thus, WYJ provides two versions, one original and one emended, whilst ACG omits it altogether (see his note 111, p. 289). The version above (the DZ text) is found in SYR, TJF, JBC and Z&Q. The translation is based largely on JBC's analysis. WYJ interprets the E as indicating accord between ruler and subjects, referring to the *Great Learning* X.3.

A35 C: 功，利民也 。

E: 功：不[64] 待時，若衣裘 。[65]

Comment: In this, the first of four closely related C&Es, the C is without textual or interpretative difficulties although there is some doubt about the E. Originally the seven characters were duplicated, but following BY these have been omitted. There are essentially two interpretations. The first, exemplified by WFB, ACG (who adds "惟利無功" to give parallelism with A37) and JBC, is that if the meritorious service is not carried out at the appropriate time it is useless or even harmful. This is made most clear by SYR's suggested emendation. The second interpretation, reflected in the translation, is that meritorious service does not, like summer and winter garments do, depend on a certain time, but is always appropriate.

---

61. This is generally emended to 氓 meaning "the people".
62. Read as 順 by TJF and JBC, as 約 by LQC, as 群 by ZCY, and as 后 by WFB.
63. Also read as 民 — see JBC, note 2, p. 56 and WYJ, note 82, p. 497.
64. SYR suggests emending 不 to 必.
65. The seven characters of this E are duplicated in the DZ text (presumably erroneously) but not in the Wu 吳 text. The duplicated characters are generally omitted following BY — see WYJ, note 83, pp. 497–498.

A34   **C:** A ruler is one who brings officials and people together in agreement.

E: A ruler: He is the means of compliance with edicts.

A35   **C:** Meritorious service is benefiting the people.

E: Meritorious service: It does not await a time like summer and winter garments do.

A36   C: 賞，上報下之功也。

E: 賞：〔上報下之功也。〕⁶⁶

Comment: There is no E immediately following 賞 in the DZ text. The six characters included above come after 殆姑 in the E for A37 following, and this is what the great majority of editors do. ACG, however, does not, writing: "The *Canons* of A36, 38 have been accidentally repeated in the *Explanations*, no doubt by the scribe who was restoring the sequence of the head characters in the dislocated *Explanations* by comparing them with the *Canons*" — see his notes 115 and 116, p. 290.

A37   C: 罪，犯禁也。

E: 罪：不在禁，惟⁶⁷ 害無罪。〔殆姑上報下之功也。〕⁶⁸

Comment: Again the C is quite clear. The problem with the E is the final sentence as above. As considered in the Comment to the previous C&E, the majority view is to transpose the last six characters of this sentence to provide an E for A36. What, then, of 殆姑? Broadly, commentators follow one of three approaches. First, following LQC, they are emended to 若殆; second, following SYR they are emended to 及辜; and third, they are transposed to the E of A33 preceded by an added 若 (ACG — see his note 114, p. 290). Generally, there is an agreed interpretation along the lines indicated in the translation, however one reads the final two characters if they remain here. If SYR's emendation is accepted, the most obvious interpretation would be that causing harm where there is no prohibition, although not a crime, comes close to being a crime. With LQC's emendation, endorsed by WFB, the reading is a little more obscure — see Z&Q, note 3, p. 550 with reference to *Xunzi* 4.

---

66. The bracketed characters are transposed from the last part of the E for A37.
67. Generally read as 雖.
68. The eight bracketed characters appear here in the DZ text. If the last six of these are transposed to form the E of A36, the problem of the first two still remains — see Comment. Commentators generally follow one of three approaches. First, following LQC, they are emended to 若殆; second, following SYR, they are emended to 及辜; and third, they are omitted altogether, for example by ACG who regards them as misplaced from A33.

A36   **C:** To reward is superiors requiting the meritorious service of inferiors.

E: To reward: [Superiors requiting the meritorious service of inferiors.]

A37   **C:** Committing a crime is transgressing a prohibition.

E: Committing a crime: If no prohibition exists, even if there is harm, there is no crime; like coming near.

A38   C: 罰，上報下之罪也。

E: 罰：上報下之罪也。

Comment: A38 is a replica of A36 apart from the substitution of 罰 and 罪 for 賞 and 功. As several commentators have discussed, these four definitions (A35–A38) should be considered in the light of other texts including the *Xunzi* 18.3, the *Han Feizi* 36 (SBCK, vol. 18, HFZ, pp. 74–77), the *Zuo Zhuan* for Xiang 26 (LCC, vol. 5, p. 521), and, of particular note, the *Mozi* 13.

A39[69]   C: 同，異而俱於之一也。

E: 侗[70]：二人而俱見是楹也，若事君。

Comment: There are several issues with this C&E apart from its placement (see note 69). First, the C and E have different head characters. Should one be emended to the other, and, if so, which one? The most common approach is to read 侗 as 同 (see, for example, LSL, JBC) and this is done here. Second, what is the referent of 異 — is it an implied "thing" (like a pillar) or is it the 二人? Third, should ACG's proposed addition of a verbal 同 after 俱 in the C be accepted? On this, see his note 117, p. 291 and the following discussion on pp. 291–292. In the translation above, the C and E are taken as making somewhat different points. That is, according to the C, things may be called the same if there is identity in one aspect whereas, in the E, the sameness is reflected in two observers coming to the same judgement about the one thing.

A40   C: 久[71]，彌異時也。

E: 今久：古今且[72] 莫[73]。

---

69. There is an issue about placement of this C&E. It occurs here in the DZ text and is retained here in many texts (e.g. SYR, WYJ, ACG, LSL, Z&Q). However, several editors of editions devoted to the "dialectical chapters" (e.g. TJF, WFB, JBC) transfer it on the grounds of subject matter to what in the present text would be A88.

70. In the DZ text there is 侗 as above. Following ZHY, this has been read as 同, although ACG retains 侗 and makes a point of the difference — see also SYR's detailed comment on p. 486.

71. There is general agreement that 久 is to be taken in the sense of 宙 as, for example, in the *Zhuangzi* 23 (GQF, vol. 4, p. 800, BW, p. 256). See also WFB's discussion, p. 35 and the *Huainanzi* 11 where 宙 and 宇 are also defined (XYHNZ, vol. 1, p. 543).

72. The emendation of 且 to 旦 proposed by WYZ is generally accepted.

73. Read as 暮 by modern commentators.

A38 **C:** To punish is superiors requiting inferiors for a crime.

E: To punish: Superiors requiting inferiors for a crime.

A39 **C:** Being the same is (includes) being different but both in this (aspect) being one.

E: Being the same: Two people, yet both see that this is a pillar. It is like serving a ruler.

A40 **C:** Time spreads over different periods.

E: Time: (Includes) past and present, morning and evening.

Comment: The E presents some problems. Whilst ACG is prepared to accept this placement of 今 before 久 (see his note 121, p. 293), most do not. For example, SYR takes it as superfluous and omits it. Both TJF and WFB transpose it to make it the second character and then emend it to 介 which is what is followed in the translation along with the two generally accepted readings of 比 and 莫 (see notes 72 and 73).

A41 **C:** 守[74]，彌異所也。

E: 宇：東西家[75] 南北。

Comment: The two points with regard to the C are, first, the generally accepted emendation of 守 to 宇, and, second, the fact that it immediately follows the preceding C rather than showing the usual paired arrangement. Z&Q, in fact, join it to A40 as a single C. The issue in the E is 家 which is similar to the issue of the second 今 in A40. JBC omits both characters in the Es (i.e. 介 in A39, 家 in A40). Certainly they are both to a degree controversial and in both cases the meaning remains clear without them.

A42 **C:** 窮，或[76] 有[77] 前不容尺[78] 也。

E: 窮：或[79] 不容尺，有窮。莫不容尺，無窮也。

Comment: Despite the several contentious characters, the meaning of the C seems clear and the E extends and clarifies this meaning. There has been some discussion about the precise meaning of 窮. WFB argues for equating it with 空, referring to the *Zhuangzi* 22 (GQF, vol. 3, p. 758 and his note 3), whilst JBC equates it with 極, referring to the *Liezi* 5 (LZDB, p. 182).

---

74. It is generally accepted that 守 (in the DZ text) should read 宇 — see ACG, note 123, p. 293.
75. There are at least four approaches to 家 here: (i) To omit it as superfluous (e.g. LSL). (ii) To read it as 蒙 (e.g. ACG). (iii) to read it as 蒙 and transpose it to the start of the E (e.g. WFB, TJF). (iv) To read it as 中 (e.g. SYR, WFB).
76. There is almost universal acceptance of 或 as 域. ACG, however, renders it "somewhere" — see his note 125, p. 294.
77. Read as 又.
78. Many commentators interpret this as 線. WYJ argues for retaining the meaning as a unit of length, as does ACG, and I have accepted this.
79. As in the C, 或 is read as 域.

A41   **C:** Space spreads over different places.

E: Space: Covers east and west, south and north.

A42   **C:** A limit is a boundary which does not allow any further advance by a measured length (*chi*).

E: A limit: When a boundary does not allow a [further] measured length (*chi*), there is a limit. When a [further] measured length (*chi*) is allowed, there is not a limit.

A43   C: 盡，莫不然也。

E: 盡：但止動。

Comment: The issue with the C&E is the reading of 盡 itself. Is it in conjunction with 窮 (i.e. limited/completely applicable) or not? I have followed LSL's reading as "全部情況". WFB transfers this C&E to his A48 where 盡 is read as 兼 and paired with 體 in his A49, which is usually A2 as above. There are issues about the head character (盡 or 靜), about whether 但 should be emended to 俱 (SYR), and whether 動 should be included here or in the following E (ACG). On these matters see WYJ, note 98, p. 500. The version above follows particularly the interpretations of LSL and JBC — see their notes 1 and 2, p. 273 and p. 68 respectively.

A44   C: 始，當時也。

E: 始：時或有久，或無久。始當無久。

Comment: Although the meaning seems relatively clear, there are problems with the precise reading of 當, the fact that both 或 and 久 are read differently from the immediately preceding C&Es, and what exactly is intended by the E. In the translation, I have taken 當 as "specific" or "particular", and "beginning" to be a specific, durationless time, i.e. there are times with duration and times without duration, "beginning" being a particular example of the latter. Along this line, LSL has: "當時—正值時間最初的那一片刻、剎那。" — note 2, p. 274.

A45   C: 化，徵易也。

E: 化：若蛙為鶉。

Comment: There are no apparent textual issues in this C&E. Variations in interpretation relate to 徵, essentially between the meaning as "proof" or "evidence" (驗 — e.g. MZQY) and the meaning as "characteristic" or "trait" (特 徵) which ACG emphasises in his rendering as "distinguishing marks". I have taken the latter position but, in either case, the meaning is essentially the same.

A46   C: 損[80]，偏去也。

E: 損：偏也者，兼之禮[81] 也。其體或去〔或〕[82] 存。謂其存者損。

---

80. SYR equates 損 with 減 so the sense is of "decrease" or "reduction" rather than "injury" or "damage".

81. There is general agreement that 禮, found in the DZ text, should be emended to 體.

82. A second 或 is added here in most modern texts (but not by TJF) — see WYJ, note 104, p. 501 and ACG, note 130, p. 296.

A43   **C:** Completely applicable is where there is nothing that is not like this.

E: Completely applicable: There is only either being at rest or being in motion.

A44   **C:** A beginning is a specific instant of time.

E: A beginning: Time in some cases has duration and in some cases does not. A beginning is a specific instant of time without duration.

A45   **C:** A transformation is a change of characteristics.

E: A transformation: Like a water frog becoming a quail.

A46   **C:** Decrease is a part leaving.

E: Decrease: A part is part of a whole. Of its parts, some leave and some remain. Decrease is said of what remains.

Comment: The issue of the part/whole relationship is an important one to the Later Mohists and is discussed in some detail by several commentators (e.g. TJF, CYX, GH). GH, in particular, sees this statement as a point of difference between the Mohists and the Mingjia on the question of what the "decrease" refers to — the part remaining (Mohists) or the whole original object (Mingjia).

A47   **C:** 大益⋯

E: None

Comment: There are considerable doubts about this C&E. There is, however, widespread agreement with SYR that there should be a second C to give the pair 損/益 (see SYR, p. 457 and WYJ, note 105, p. 501). Several editors follow GH in making this simply: 益大也 (e.g. WFB). TJF has for the C: "益，言利大。" and transfers the E from A48 here, leaving that C without an E. ACG writes: "At Stage 2 this fragment may have either preceded A47 or followed A94. It is probably, as most editors suspect, from a lost definition of *yi* 益 'increase' following the definition of *sun* 損 'reduce' (A46), but there is no means of reconstructing the missing Canon, which must have lacked an Explanation." (p. 296)

A48   **C:** 儇，積柢[83] 。〔SYR: C: 環，俱柢。〕

E: 儇：昫民[84] 也。

Comment: This is a very problematical C&E. In the C there are doubts about all three characters and, as ACG points out, it is the only C in the series A1–A75 without a final 也. WFB transfers this to his A92 to form a pair of C&Es with the head characters of 環 and 儿 respectively, with an entirely different E for the former than that given above. ACG's detailed note on the rare characters should be consulted for an alternative view to SYR (ACG note 133, pp. 296–297). The E is also uncertain. TJF transfers it to the previous C&E (A47) whilst ACG retains it here with emendations given in note 84 below. His translation is: "It is the figure of a curve." The version given is that of SYR which is followed by WYJ, LSL, Z&Q and JBC. The point in SYR's version is that, while other objects have a particular base, a circle or round object does not, each part being equally a base. JBC makes this explicit diagrammatically — see his pp. 76–77.

---

83. These two rare characters (ZWDCD #25575 and #25633) are emended by most editors, the majority following SYR (see his p. 457). SYR's version is given in parentheses above and is used for the translation.

84. The two characters 昫民, which TJF has in the E for A47, are read by SYR as 俱氏 duplicating the C. ACG has 句貌 (variant) whilst GH emends 昫 to 恂.

A47   **C:** Large increase ...?
       E: None

A48   **C:** In a circle all points are potentially a base.
       E: Circle: All points make contact.

A49   C: 庫[85]，易也。

E: 庫：區[86] 穴[87] 若斯貌常。

Comment: Again there is considerable variation in text and interpretation making translation quite tentative. In that given above, 庫 is retained and the interpretation largely follows JBC, i.e. what is stored in a storehouse changes, but not the storehouse itself. In the E, "區穴" remains problematical.

A50   C: 動，或從也。[88]

E: 動：偏祭從者戶樞免瑟。[89]

Comment: The majority of characters in this C&E are controversial (see notes 88, 89) so any translation or interpretation must remain very tentative. All that can be said with assurance is that it is about movement. The emendations in the C included above (i.e. 或 to 域, 從 to 徙) are, however, widely agreed upon so the definition of movement as a change of position is probably acceptable. The E is an altogether different matter. If there is acceptance that two kinds of movement are being indicated, the second exemplified by the rotation of a door around its hinge, "non-linear" may be acceptable as a characterisation of the second kind. It is possible, if three examples are being given (door-hinge, hare, zithern), that the three kinds of movement discussed by JBC (linear, rotational, oscillatory) are being identified. WYJ interprets the E as differentiating between the movement of inanimate and animate objects. ACG takes a different view again of the text and hence of interpretation, in part related to making the second example the movement of a louse on a hare. The best discussions of the issues are provided by TJF (pp. 128–130), WFB (pp. 41–42) and JBC (pp. 79–81).

---

85. Whilst some commentators retain 庫 in the sense of "storehouse" (see MZQY, note 1, p. 377), others emend it to either 連 (WYJ, ACG) or 障 (variant) (SYR, WFB).

86. LQC equates 區 with the plane surface of geometry (面). SYR equates it with 虛 based on the *Guanzi* 11 (see SYR, p. 488 and the SBCK, vol. 18, *GZ*, p. 25).

87. LQC reads this as "cave" or "hole". See the *Shi Jing*, Mao #237, LCC, vol. 4, p. 437 and particularly Legge's note on the same page. These two characters (區穴) occur in conjunction again in A64 (see note 108). ACG understands them as a geometrical term for circumference — see his note 138, p. 297.

88. Whilst 動 is generally accepted both 或 and 從 are generally emended; the former to 域 (e.g. SYR, CYX) and the latter to 徙 (e.g. SYR and CYX) or to 縱 (e.g. TJF). Of modern editors, WYJ and Z&Q follow the CYX/SYR version (see, for example, WYJ, note 111, p. 502) whilst LSL follows TJF. ACG retains 或 but emends 從 to 徙 (see his note 140, p. 298).

89. Emendations have been proposed for six of the eight characters in the E apart from 動. These are, in summary, 偏 to 遍, 祭 to 際, 從 to 徙 or 縱, 者 to 若, 免 to 兔, and 瑟 to 閟 or 蝨.

A49   **C:** A storehouse relates to change.

       E: A storehouse: With a region or cavity like this the appearance is constant.

A50   **C:** Movement is change of position.

       E: Movement: Non-linear movement is like a door hinge avoiding shutting.

** This is where the break in the DZ text chapter 40 (經上) occurs. That is, the Canons that follow interdigitate with those already given. In modern editions this arrangement is preserved by Z&Q.

A51   **C:** 止，以久也。

E: 止：無久之不止，當牛非馬，若夫[90] 過楹。有久之不止，當馬非馬，若人過梁。

Comment: This is a particularly interesting C&E in that, although free of textual problems, it still elicits quite disparate interpretations. These hinge on the readings of 止 and 久 which are recurring characters in Mingjia and Later Mohist writings. The crucial question is whether the C&E applies to language or to motion. It is hard not to agree with ACG that it is the former — see his discussion on pp. 298–299. Apart from the references which he gives to other related uses, there is the similar use of 止 at least in Gongsun Long's 名實論. As an example of the alternative view, TJF, starting from WKY's equating of 久 with 撐柱, interprets it rather as "opposing force", which the MZQY follows, making this a relatively clear statement about kinetics related to Newton's Laws. Thus, if there is no opposing force, a body "continues in its state of (rest or) uniform motion" which is easy to understand, hence the examples. When there is an opposing force yet the body does not stop, this is less easy to understand. JBC makes the distinction between high and low velocity movement. For other interpretations see particularly WYJ's detailed analysis (notes 114 &115, p. 503) and WFB (pp. 42–46).

A52   **C:** 必，不巳[91] 也。

E: 必：謂臺執[92] 者也。若弟兄，一然者，一不然者，必不必也，是非必也。

---

90. Taken as 夫 following WYZ — see WYJ, note 114, p. 503.
91. Although 巳 is almost universally accepted, WFB has 已, referring to the *Shuo Wen* definition as 分極, whilst the MZQY emends 巳 to 已.
92. I have followed JBC's reading of "臺執" as "堅執不移" — his pp. 83–84. The DZ text has 執 rather than 執. ACG remarks: "Pi Yüan's (BY) emendation to *chih* 執 'hold' is accepted so universally that most editors forget to mention that it is an emendation." (note 149, p. 299)

A51   **C:** Stopping is by means of duration.

        E: Stopping: Not stopping when there is no duration corresponds to "ox is not horse" and is like "an arrow passing a pillar". Not stopping when there is duration corresponds to "horse is not horse" and is like "a man passing a bridge".

A52   **C:** Necessity is unending (?that to which there is no alternative).

        E: Necessity: [This is] to speak of what can be firmly adhered to. For example, in the case of younger and older brother; one is and one isn't: that is, necessity applies in one case and not in the other, affirming or denying the necessity.

Comment: This is another C&E without real textual difficulties which presents significant problems in interpretation. Several commentators quote BY's simple paraphrase: "言事必成". What is offered above is a rather loose and very tentative translation. Informative discussions can be found in ACG (pp. 299–301), JBC (pp. 83–85), WFB who links this C&E to those following rather than what has gone before and emends 凵 in the C to 二 (pp. 47–48), WYJ (note 118, p. 504) and TJF (pp. 131–133). Both TJF and WYJ relate this C&E to the Hegelian dialectic i.e. an identification of thesis, antithesis and synthesis. Also of interest is the statement in *Zhuangzi* 32 to which WYJ draws attention: "聖人以必不必，…；眾人以不必必之，…" — see GQF, vol. 4, p. 1046.

A53 **C:** 平，同高也。

E: None

Comment: The DZ has no E for 平 and most texts follow this. The absence of an E is again attributed by some to the clarity of the C. However, TJF provides an E. Reading 臺 as 抬, he takes the two components of his E (comprising the first eight characters of what is above the E for A52) to illustrate two different uses of 平, the latter case being exemplified by the *Lun Yu* XIII.7 — see his explanatory diagram (p. 133).

A54 **C:** 同長[93]，以[94] 正[95] 相盡也。

E: 同：捷[96] 與狂[97] 之同長也。

Comment: Most commentators take the subject to be "the same length" although the MZQY suggests the alternative of 同 alone as the head character in keeping with the E. It is a character which features at the start of several other Cs (A87, A89). The MZQY extends the reading of "length and straightness are identical" to make this a definition of the square. Both the MZQY and WFB read 盡 as 莫不然. Also possible is WFB's reading as a description of parallel lines, although to meet the length requirement it would need to be a parallelogram. In the E, there is general acceptance of the example as indicating that the door-frame and supporting upright are of the same length.

---

93. Whilst almost all commentators combine these two characters as the head of the C, the MZQY has 同 alone, as in the E.
94. A number of commentators (WFB, MZQY, JBC) read 以 as 與.
95. Accepted by all as the emendation from the recurring Mohist character variably written as 缶 or closely related forms — see ZWDCD #1835, #28734, #28735.
96. 捷 is read as 楗 following BY and SYR — see also ACG, note 152, p. 304.
97. The original 狂 is read as either 柱 or 框 — see ACG, note 153, p. 304.

A53   **C:** Level is being the same height.

E: None

A54   **C:** The same length is when they use each other up with their
straightness (i.e. when the straightness is identical).

E: The same: The door-post and frame are of the same length.

A55   C: 中，同長也。

E: 心[98] 中：自是往相若也。

Comment: The only textual issues with this C&E are whether ACG is correct
in restoring "所自" before "同長也" in the C (see his note 155, p. 305), and
whether 心 should be transposed to follow 中 in the E. ACG's addition certainly
makes the C more explicit. The presence or otherwise of 心 does not affect the
basic meaning. One point of variance among commentators is whether the
C&E refers specifically to the radii of a circle (TJF, JBC) or more generally to
various geometrical figures, most simply, a straight line. — see WYJ, note 122,
p. 505.

A56   C: 厚，有所大也。

E: 厚：惟〔無厚〕[99] 無所大。

Comment: 厚 is a particularly important term in Later Mohist and also Mingjia
writings. On the latter, see Hui Shi's Paradox 2 (GQF, vol. 4, p. 1102). In
relation to this, a translation of the C might read: "Thickness is being what has
accumulated." — this being in contrast to 無厚 which is what cannot be
accumulated ("無厚，不可積也"). As it stands, the E seems incomprehensible, or at least incompatible with the C, although WYJ makes an attempt
to understand the text as it is, referring to the *Zhuangzi* 3 (GQF, vol. 1, p. 119),
the argument being that even things without apparent thickness to the senses
must be considered as having thickness, as exemplified by the cook's knife
blade (WYJ, note 123, pp. 505–506). I have followed GH's addition in the
translation, accepting the reading of 厚 as "thickness" relating to a solid body
and as defined in the *Shuo Wen* (厚、山陵之厚也). ACG adds 端 after 惟
taking the former as "starting-point" — see his note 157, p. 305.

---

98. Basically, there have been two approaches to 心 here. One is to transpose it to follow 中
(see, for example, GH, TJF) and the other is to make it the final character in the preceding
E and emend it to 正 (see, for example, WYJ, WFB, ACG). Meaning is not significantly
affected in either case.

99. The added characters are those of GH, accepted by JBC. ACG adds instead 端 ("a
point"), whilst WFB adds another 無 with a comma after 惟無.

A55   **C:** The centre is [established by] equal lengths.

         E: The centre: From this outwards distances are the same.

A56   **C:** Thickness is being to some extent large.

         E: Thickness: Only what is without thickness is not to some extent large.

A57   C: 日中止¹⁰⁰ 南也。

      E: None

      Comment: "Noon" is particularly TJF's reading of 日中 which is, in fact, the modern term for this. JBC's expanded version reads: "The shadow of the sun at the centre (noon) points directly south and north."

A58   C: 直，參也。

      E: None

      Comment: There are several interpretations of 參 with reference to its use in a number of other texts. Essentially there are three possibilities: To read it as "aligned" for which ACG has argued quite cogently (p. 307); to understand it as "upright" or "vertical" following JBC who provides a diagram on p. 93, but which borders on the tautological unless related perhaps to the gnomon and possibly linked to the previous C (WFB); or to regard it as something to do with "three" as in the MZQY where it is interpreted as "A circle's diameter is one third of its circumference."

A59   C: 圜，一中同長也。

      E: 圜：規寫交¹⁰¹ 也 。

      Comment: Clearly this C&E is about the features of a circle, i.e. a single centre and a circumference, each point of which is at an equal distance from the central point, or with equal radii, and its construction. The emendation of radical 66 to 交, due to SYR, is generally accepted and does seem appropriate, the meaning being (as made explicit, for example, by WFB and JBC) that, when the compass line meets the starting point, the circle is complete. ACG, however, makes a strong case against this emendation, referring to LC, and for reading it as 朴 in the sense of "rough". His version of the E is: "The compasses draw it *in the rough* (?)." (p. 309)

---

100. Emended from the Mohist character — see note 95 above.
101. All modern commentators apart from ACG accept SYR's emendation of radical 66 (which BY leaves as is) to 交.

A57   **C:** The sun at noon is directly south.

 E: None

A58   **C:** Straight is to be aligned (upright).

 E: None

A59   **C:** A circle consists of the same lengths from one centre.

 E: A circle: A pair of compasses describes until the line joins.

A60　C: 方，柱隅四讙也。

　　　E: 方：矩見交[102] 也。

Comment: This C&E seems as though it should be the equivalent for a square to A59 for a circle but the majority of characters are more or less contentious. There is a tendency among modern editors to rather skate over the difficulties and simply provide a close equivalent to A59, substituting the carpenter's square for a pair of compasses. This is particularly facilitated by Z&Q's interpretation of the C, following LDF, the key emendation of which is 讙 to 權 reading the latter as 等. ACG, who persists in his adherence to LC's retention of radical 66 in the sense of 樸 as "rough", takes the view that what is intended is to convey that the formation of a circle or square by the implements indicated is only rough and relates this to Paradox 13 of the second list (see particularly FYL, vol. 1, p. 218).

A61　C: 倍，為二也。

　　　E: 倍：二尺與尺，但去一。

Comment: There is widespread acceptance of this C&E as it stands; certainly the meaning seems clear. To double is to multiply by 2, the E providing a concrete example in the case of 尺, further clarification being added by the final phrase. ACG, however, makes an interesting suggestion, proposing that what is generally taken as the E for the following C&E (A62) rightly belongs at the end of the E for A61. His version of the E reads: "倍：二，尺與尺俱去一端，是無同也。" which he translates as follows: "When they are 'two', measured foot and measured foot both depart from one starting-point, which is being nowhere the same." — see ACG, pp. 309–310. The two problems with this proposal are that, first, it leaves the next C without an E although the head character 端 is there in the appropriate place in the text, and, second, ACG's version is clearly less applicable to doubling than the standard version. I have, therefore, followed the latter.

A62　C: 端，體之無序[103] 而最前者也。

　　　E: 端：是無同也。

---

102. See note 101 above. On this point, ACG's notes 159, 162 arguing for the retention of the original should be consulted.

103. Some commentators (e.g. WFB, ACG) emend 序 to 厚. Those who retain 序 generally accept BY's comment "序言次序", amplified by ZHY as follows: "無序，謂無與為次序。" See also TJF, p. 142.

A60   **C:** A square is where the sides and angles are four and regular.

E: A square: A carpenter's square establishes the meeting points.

A61   **C:** To double is to make two.

E: To double: 2 *chi* and 1 *chi* [differ] only in doing away with 1.

A62   **C:** A starting point is a part which is without thickness (? sequence) and is the very foremost.

E: A starting point: This has nothing the same as it. (This is unique).

Comment: The primary issue in this C&E is the precise meaning of 端. Is it a "point" in general, equivalent to 點; is it an "extreme point", i.e. "beginning" and "end", as would accord with usage in the *Doctrine of the Mean* VI and *Lun Yu* IX.7, or is it the "starting point" only, as ACG argues and as would accord with its description as "最前"? The emendation or otherwise of 序 has a bearing on this in that the retention of 序 would favour one of the second two possibilities, whereas 厚 is in keeping with the more general meaning. In the translation I have followed ACG's version of the C (i.e. 端 as "starting-point" and the emendation of 序 to 厚). ACG does, however, transfer the E to A61 — see Comment to A61. On "是無同" ZHY has: "若有同之，即非最前。"

A63   **C:** 有間，〔不及〕[104] 中也。

　　　E: 有聞[105]：謂夾之者也。

Comment: There are two issues here. The first is whether ACG's proposed addition to the C should be accepted as has been done in the translation. Most commentators accept the original — BY has: "間際是 者之中". WYJ avoids the difficulty identified by ACG with his reading of 中 as 盅 in the sense of "empty" — see his note 132, p. 507. The second point is the emendation of 聞 to 間 which appears to be universally accepted. In relation to this C&E, several commentators (e.g. WYJ, TJF) refer to *Zhuangzi* 3 which has: "彼節者有間，而刀刃者无厚；以无厚入有間，⋯⋯" (GQF, vol. 1, p. 119). WYJ's explanation reads (in part): "間為物之空隙，就其夾之之物而言，是謂有「間」。" (note 133, p. 508).

A64   **C:** 間，不及旁也。

　　　E: 間[106]：謂〔所〕[107] 夾者也。尺前於區穴[108] 而後於端，不夾於端與區內[109]。及及，非齊之及也。[110]

---

104. ACG restores 不及 which he says makes sense out of what is otherwise nonsensical and makes the C parallel to A64 following — see his note 166, p. 311.
105. Both here and in the following E, 聞 (found in the DZ) has been taken as 間 from BY on — see WYJ, note 133, p. 508.
106. Accepted as 間 — see previous note.
107. Restored following ACG — see his note 168, p. 311.
108. There are clearly problems with 區穴, and 穴 in particular, as considered in relation to A49 where this combination is also found (see notes 86, 87 above). Most commonly the two characters are taken together to indicate here a plane surface. LQC considers the second character superfluous, leaving 區 with the same meaning.
109. Commentators either equate 內 with 穴 (e.g. WYJ, ACG) or read it differently (e.g. as 間 — LQC).
110. This final sentence presents a particular problem and may, as LQC proposes, be best omitted.

A63   **C:** Having a space/interval is not reaching to the centre.

      E: Having a space/interval: Said of what is at the sides (flanking).

A64   **C:** The space/interval does not reach the sides.

      E: The space/interval: Said of what is flanked. A *chi* (line) is before in relation to a plane surface and after in relation to a point, but is not flanked by a point and a plane surface. (The 及 is not the 及 of 齊, i.e. not meaning "alike", "comparable to".)

Comment: The reading of this C&E given above depends on the following: (i) The emendation of 聞 to 間 as the head character of the E. (ii) The addition of 所 after 謂 (ACG). (iii) The readings of 尺 as 線 meaning "line" and 區穴 as 面 meaning "plane surface". (iv) The emendation of 內 to 穴. (v) The acceptance of the final seven characters as a later gloss (LQC). These points are well considered in Z&Q's notes 2 and 3, p. 561 quoting Fang Xiaobo 方孝博.

A65   **C:** 纑[111]，間虛也。

E: 纑：虛也者，兩木之間，謂其無木者也。

Comment: Commentators broadly take one of two positions on this C&E. The first depends on the emendation of 纑 to 櫨 and is exemplified by WYZ, WNS, LSL and JBC, whilst the second depends on the retention of 纑 and the emendation of 木 (e.g. WYJ, TJF, Z&Q). On this point, ACG writes: "纑…, primarily 'thread', has no known sense which fits the definition." — see his note 170, p. 311. In the first case, the meaning is taken as "king-post", a short wooden post, square in section, used in roof construction. This give a clear meaning to the C&E in that the space between king-posts is without wood and is empty. In the second case, differing arguments are advanced — see, for example, TJF, pp. 146–147, WYJ, note 138, pp. 508–509. In either case, the C&E is again about "space between". ACG simply leaves the question of 纑 open.

A66   **C:** 盈，莫不有也。

E: 盈：無盈無厚。於尺無所往而不得得二[112]。

Comment: In relation to the C, there is some variation in the reading of 盈. Thus LQC writes: "盈 is 涵. For example, a body 'contains' (涵) surfaces; surfaces 'contain' lines; lines 'contain' points. Whatever contains, necessarily completely contains what it contains. Therefore it is said 'not not to have'." I have taken 盈 in the sense of "fill" as a number of commentators do (e.g. ACG). The E is much more problematical, both in structure and interpretation, and is closely linked with the following C&E. Broadly, there are four versions of this and the following E as below:

---

111. In some texts this is emended to 櫨 in the sense of "king-post" (see JBC, p. 105 and comment above). Others retain 纑 as it is used in the *Zuo Zhuan*, Zhao 19 *Shiwen*, i.e. "hemp".

112. There is variation in how these last two characters are treated. Some (e.g. ACG) have them here as in the DZ text but take the second 得 to be an erroneous duplication. This is the position I have followed. Others transfer them to the next E (see Comment to A67). Some omit 得二 altogether (LSL).

A65   **C:** With king-posts there is an empty space between.

E: King-posts: The empty space is between the two pieces of wood and refers to what is without wood.

A66   **C:** To fill is for there not not to be (to be nowhere absent — ACG).

E: To fill: Not to fill is being without thickness (dimensionless). In a *chi* (line) there is nowhere to go to where you don't get two.

(i)   The version given for A66 and A67 above which is the DZ text and is followed by WYJ and ACG, for example.

(ii) A66 E "盈：無盈無厚。" A67 E "堅：於石、無所往而不得，得二。異處不相盈，相非，是相外也。" This, with slight variation, is given by TJF and JBC.

(iii) A66 E "盈：無盈無厚。於尺無所往而不得。" A67 E "得二，堅異處不相盈，相非，是相外也。" This version, advocated by SYR, is followed (apart from the omission of the two head characters) in modern texts by Z&Q and involves also SYR's proposed emendation of 尺 to 石.

(iv) A66 E "盈：無盈，無厚於尺。盈、無所往而不得。" A67 E "堅：得二，異處不相盈。相非，是相外也。" which is WFB's version.

Clearly, versions (ii) to (iv) are framed with Gongsun Long's argument particularly in mind — see Comment to A67 and WFB, pp. 54–58.

A67   C: 堅白，不相外也。

E: 堅〔白〕[113]：異處不相盈，相非，是相外也。

Comment: The textual issues relating to this and the previous C&E have been considered in the Comment to A66. However these issues are resolved, important Later Mohist terms are involved, in particular 厚 and 盈. Here the former is taken in the sense of "thickness" or "substance" and the latter as "contain" or "fill". What is most generally agreed is that these two C&Es are part of the Later Mohist response to the arguments of GSL as expressed in his *Jianbai Lun* 堅白論. ACG, who considers this essay to be a late forgery, rejects this, although he acknowledges that the "hard and white" issue was alive at the time of the Later Mohists — see his comments on p. 313.

A68   C: 攖，相得也。

E: 攖：尺與尺俱不盡。端無[114] 端但[115] 盡。尺與〔端〕[116] 或盡或不盡。堅白之攖相盡。體攖不相盡。

Comment: There is widespread agreement on text and meaning for this C&E, specifically the interpretation of 攖 (which, it should be noted, also appears in the next two C&Es) and the emendations proposed primarily by ZHY. The meaning, then, is that two lines do not, with one theoretical exception, occupy the same space whereas two points do. The case of a line and a point is also

---

113. SYR suggests the addition of 白 following 堅 in line with the C.
114. Emended to 與 following ZHY and SYR.
115. Emended to 俱 by ZHY and SYR, although 但 is retained by TJF.
116. Added following ZHY and SYR by transposition from the end of the E.

A67   **C:** Hard and white do not exclude each other.

E: Hard [and white]: Different positions do not fill each other. Not being each other — this is excluding each other.

A68   **C:** To coincide is both obtaining (occupying the same space).

E: To coincide: With a line and a line, the coinciding of both is not complete. With a point and a point, the coinciding of both is complete. With a line and a point, the coinciding is complete in respect to one and incomplete in respect to the other. The coinciding of hard and white is mutually complete. The coinciding of parts is not mutually complete.

given. These situations are represented diagrammatically by JBC. The qualities of hard and white in a body are spatially co-extensive whereas two individual bodies cannot occupy the same space. This C&E links the geometric definitions with the hard and white argument.

A69   C: 似[117]，有以相攖，有不相攖也。

E: (端) [118] 仳：兩有端而後可。

Comment: In this C&E variation in interpretation centres around what figures are being compared, if indeed it is one particular figure, about what "two" refers to, and about how 端 is to be understood. As a consequence, several different detailed analyses are given involving lines (JBC), rectangles (MZQY), or triangles (WYJ). In the translation, I have taken lines to be the subject, 兩 to refer to the two lines being compared, and 端 to be the common starting point, which is essentially ACG's interpretation.

A70   C: 次，無間而不攖[119] 攖也。

E: 次：無厚而厚[120] 可。

Comment: In the C there appears to be universal acceptance of the emendation of the first 攖 to 相. In the E the proposed emendation of the second 厚 to 后 is more contentious and there are variations in interpretation. There are broadly three proposals for the E: (i) Emend the second 厚. (ii) Retain the second 厚 (WYJ — see his detailed note 148, p. 511). (iii) Precede the first 厚 with 端 as proposed by ACG to give his reading of: "It is possible only because the starting point is dimensionless." This, however, seems to be a different issue from that raised in the C. Of these three suggestions, the first is by far the most widely accepted, and it would seem reasonably so, leading to the clear exposition by JBC — if two or more lines are joined end to end precisely, there is no space between them and no coincidence/overlap. There is, moreover, no "piling up" or "thickness", i.e. no 厚.

117. There is variation in the head character of both C and E. The DZ text has 似 for the C and 仳 for the E. Modern commentators either emend the 似 of the C to 仳 (TJF, WFB, JBC) or, less commonly, the 仳 of the E to 似 (WYJ). On this point see ACG, note 177, p. 315. There is broad agreement that where 仳 is present, it should be read as 比 (WYZ).
118. See ACG's note 178, p. 315 on this apparently displaced character.
119. There is general acceptance of the emendation of 攖 to 相 here.
120. There is some debate as to whether the original 厚 (DZ) should be emended to 后 (後) as accepted by the majority, or retained — see WYJ, note 148, p. 511 for a defence of this position.

A69   C: In comparing, there is some respect in which [two things?] coincide and there is [some respect in which] they do not coincide.

E: In comparing: Only if the two have a (common) starting-point is it possible.

A70   C: A series is where there is no interval (space) but no coinciding.

E: A series: Only possible if there is no piling up.

A71   **C:** 法，所若而然也。

E: 法：意規員三也，俱可以為法。

Comment: Although there are no textual difficulties, there are some minor variations in interpretation. In the C, these depend on the reading of 若 (as 順 by BY, as 叵 by WYZ, and as 中效 by WFB), and to some degree on how broadly 法 is understood, i.e. physical standards only, or relating to conduct as laws. The issue in the E is whether all three (i.e. 意, 規, 員) are necessary standards jointly for the construction of a circle (LQC, WFB), or whether each individually may be taken as a standard (ACG). In the punctuation of the E, I have followed ACG.

A72   **C:** 佴，所然也。

E: 佴：然也者，民若法也。

Comment: The main issue with the C is how to understand 佴, which is also the subject of a previous C&E (A15). Here early commentators relate it to Guo Pu's commentary on the *Er Ya* as 貳 or 副貳, which both WYJ and JBC equate with 副本 in the sense of "duplicate"; this is what I have followed. Thus 法 is the standard or model and 佴 is the replica or duplicate. For other interpretations of 佴 see GH and ACG. The latter emends 佴 to 因 — see his note 184, p. 316 — which he renders "criterion". In the version above, the example provided by the E of following the model/standard is the people complying (reading 若 here again as 順 following BY for A71) with the laws. If ACG's emendation of 佴 to 因 is accepted then his further emendation of 民 to 貌 (variant) becomes necessary and his E reads: "Being 'so' is the characteristics being like the standard."

A73   **C:** 説，所以明也。

E: None

Comment: There are no textual difficulties and all are agreed that there is no E. On 説, ACG writes: "To 'explain' (*shuo*) in the dialectical chapters ... is nearly always to offer proofs; indeed there is no other word for demonstration in the vocabulary."

A71   **C:** A standard is what something complies with and is so.

E: A standard: Concepts, compasses and circle are three things — all may be taken as standards.

A72   **C:** A replica (duplicate) is that which is "in accord".

E: A replica (duplicate): With regard to that which is "in accord", it is people complying with standards (laws).

A73   **C:** Explanation is the means by which clarification is effected.

E: None

A74   C: 彼[121]，不可兩不可也。

E: 彼：凡牛樞非牛。兩也，無以非也。

Comment: There are several issues in this definition of 彼, assuming the emendation discussed in note 121 is accepted. It is an important definition, both in relation to other C&Es (including that immediately following), and to other writings such as the *GSLZ*. I have understood the head character in its most commonly accepted sense as "that" or "the other", although its particular relationship to 是, as in the *Zhuangzi* 2, and LQC's observations about the distinction between subject and object, with 彼 representing the latter, must be borne in mind. The first issue concerns the structure of the C. I think that the standard text, as above, is clear as it stands and should be retained. JC makes two points that I think are both valid and interesting: First, that the C is the Mohist response to Deng Xi's "peculiar theory and practice" of "both are admissible" (兩可之說) and second, that it is "... the most general and the most explicit statement (in metalogical terms) of the conjunction of the laws of non-contradiction and of excluded middle which the Chinese ever made until modern times." The second issue is the meaning of 兩. This is also given detailed consideration by JC, but I think can most simply and clearly be understood as the two "possibilities" — i.e. "ox" and "not-ox". Thirdly, there is the issue of the structure, and therefore the meaning, of the E which is in part dependent on the emendation or otherwise of 樞 and its placement. The version above follows WFB's rearrangement to give: "凡牛非牛，若樞。兩也，無以非也。" and relates this passage particularly to the *Zhuangzi* 2 (GQF, vol. 1, p. 66 and note 10, p. 68).

A75   C: 辯，爭彼[122]也。辯勝，當也。

E: 辯：或謂之牛，或謂之非牛；是爭彼也。是不俱當。不俱當，必或不當。不若當犬。[123]

Comment: Having defined 彼, 辯 is now defined in terms of contending about 彼. The text is generally agreed, the only modification being that proposed by HS in relation to the last four characters of the E (note 123), the usage of 或 uncomplicated, and 當 is rendered as "valid" following JC (#6, p. 47).

---

121. There is debate about this character written 彼 in the DZ. Most commentators emend it to 彼 following ZHY and SYR and in keeping with the head character of the E. Others emend it to *fan* (反 written with the "man" radical — ZWDCD #433), for example, HS followed by Z&Q and also ACG (see his note 187, p. 318).
122. As in the previous C, 彼 is read as 彼 — see, for example, WYJ, note 158, p. 513.
123. The rearrangement of the last four characters due to HS, i.e. transposition of the original 若 and 當, is generally accepted.

A74   **C:** The other is not admissible; two are not admissible.

   E: The other: Everything is either "ox" or "not-ox". It is like a hinge. There are two — there is no way to deny (this).[i]

A75   **C:** Disputation is contending about "that" (the other). Winning in disputation depends on validity.

   E: Disputation: One says it is "ox", one says it is "not-ox"; this is contending about "that" (the other). In this case, both are not valid. Where both are not valid, of necessity, one is not valid. Not valid (in this case) is like "dog".

---

i.   The translation is of WFB's version of the E — see Comment above.

A76   C: 為，窮知而縣[124] 於欲也。

E: 為：欲養[125] 其指，智不知其害，是智之罪也。若智之慎之[126] 也，無遺於其害也。而猶欲養之，則離[127] 之。是猶食脯也。騷〔脯〕[128] 之利害，未〔可〕知也。欲〔食脯〕而騷，〔則食之也，〕是不以所疑止所欲也。廥外之利害，未可知也。趨之而得刀[129]，則弗趨也。是以所疑止所欲也。觀「為窮知而縣於欲」之理。食[130] 脯而非智[131] 也，養指而非愚也。所為與不所與為相疑也[132]，非謀也。

Comment: If one accepts the readings of the Mohist character given in note 125, this C is clear in meaning. Some modern commentators see the reference as being to "bad conduct" specifically (MZQY, JBC). It is certainly a statement about the contributions of reason and desire to conduct, although whether it should be framed in conditional or assertive form is not so clear. Textual variations notwithstanding, the three examples in the E also seem clear and appear to favour a conditional formulation of the C — i.e. if, in a certain situation, knowledge is limited, then conduct is determined by desire.

** This marks the end of the definitions (A1–A76) and the start of a series of 12 C&Es (A77–A88 inclusive) of a particular form, i.e. a series of terms without any sentence formation and without a concluding 也. They are aimed at clarification of the first term, taken as the head character and used as such in

---

124. This is one of several suggested emendations of the specific Mohist character here (i.e. 縣 with the 人 radical) — see JBC, note 1, p. 125 for details.
125. This second specific Mohist character (not included in the ZWDCD) is emended in three quite different ways: most commonly as indicating some form of injury (see, for example, WYJ); as 養 in the sense of "care for" by TJF, depending on the *Mencius* VIA, 14(4); and as 析 in the sense of "analyse" by WFB, which necessitates a different reading of 指.
126. Emended from 义 by SYR and subsequently generally accepted.
127. There is apparently universal agreement following SYR to emend this to 罹 in the sense of "meet with" or "suffer from".
128. This character and the subsequent characters in brackets are added following ACG — see his note 199, p. 320.
129. SYR's emendation from 力 to 刀 in the sense of 泉刀 is generally accepted.
130. This is TJF's emendation of the specific Mohist character which most texts have here.
131. The generally accepted emendation of the Mohist character with the 心 radical.
132. The rearrangement of the preceding 10 characters to give: "所為與所不為相疑也", originally proposed by ZHY, is widely accepted and is followed in the translation.

A76 **C:** In doing [something] there are limits to knowledge and dependence on desire.

E: In doing [something]: If you desire to preserve your finger and reason does not know this to be harmful, this is reason's fault. If you carefully consider this, you do not overlook the harm involved. Should you still desire to preserve it, then you must suffer the harm. It is the same with eating dried meat. The benefit or harm of rank-smelling dried meat cannot be known, so if you desire to eat the dried meat although it is rank-smelling, this is not to let what you doubt put a stop to what you desire. The benefit or harm of what is beyond the wall cannot be known, so if, by running to it, you obtain money but you do not run, this is to let what you doubt put a stop to what you desire. Consider the principle: "In doing [something] there is a limit to knowledge and a dependence on desire". One may eat dried meat and not be wise; one may preserve one's finger and not be foolish. That which one does and that which one does not do, both involve doubt — there is no plan.

the E. Although the form of the C may be the same in each case, the nature of the explication varies. ACG writes: Although the series is most conveniently treated as an appendix to the definitions ... it also serves as a bridge to the theses ..." (p. 323). In the present text these begin with A89 (A90 in WYJ's text).

A77   **C:** 已，成，亡。

E: 已：為衣，成也。治病，亡也。

Comment: In the case above, it is not clear whether the purpose is to indicate the range of verbal uses of 巳, or to identify verbs to which the adverbial use is applicable. Regarding the two examples in the E, the first has been related to the *Lun Yu* XI.25(7) which has: "春服既成" (JBC) and the second to the LSCQ 11/2.3 which has: "王之病必可巳也。" (ACG), although, in both instances, the relationship is somewhat problematical.

A78   **C:** 使，謂，故。

E: 使：〔使〕[133] 令謂[134]，謂也，不必成。濕[135]，故也，必待所為之成也。

Comment: In a modern dictionary (HYDCD) nominal, verbal and conjunctional uses are listed for 使 with the verbal subdivided into three. The issue is which meanings are intended here. The problem is complicated by the textual uncertainty of the E, particularly relating to sentence division, but also to the duplication or otherwise of 使 and 謂. Both ACG and JBC take the E to be two essentially parallel statements amplifying the perceived meanings of 使 and retaining 濕 in the sense of "making damp", one of the causes of illness which, as ACG points out, is used by the Mohists to exemplify phenomena with multiple causes (see his analysis in *Disputers of the Tao* p. 162).

---

133. Added by WFB.
134. Some commentators delete this 謂 (GH, LQC, ACG). WYJ retains it, reading both it and the following 謂 as 為 (his note 177, p. 516), whilst WFB punctuates differently, placing a full-stop after the first 謂 and making the second 謂 part of the next sentence which ends with 濕.
135. There is debate about the meaning of this character here, and where the full-stop should be placed, i.e. before it (JBC, ACG) or after it (TJF, WYJ, MZQY, WFB).

A77   **C:** *Yi* (已) [may mean] "to complete" (*cheng* 成) or "to go away" (*wang* 亡).

  E: *Yi* (已): In the case of making a garment, it is completed. In the case of curing an illness, it goes away.

A78   **C:** *Shi* (使) may mean "to tell" (*wei* 謂) or "to cause" (*gu* 故).

  E: *Shi* (使): Giving an order is "telling" but does not necessarily come about. Making damp is "causing" and necessarily depends on what it does coming about.

A79   C: 名，達，類，私。

E: 名：物，達也。有實必待文多也[136]。命之馬，類也。若實也者必以是名也。命之臧，私也。是名也，止於是實也。聲出口，俱有名，若姓字灑[137]。

Comment: The textual variations in the E do not affect meaning, the E providing clear exemplification of the three forms of name.

A80   C: 謂，移，舉，加。

E: 謂：狗犬，命也。[138] 狗，犬，舉也。叱狗，加也。

Comment: The interpretation of this C&E depends on several emendations and interpretations. Meaning and parallelism would seem best served by retaining 移 in the C, emending 命 to 移 in the E, placing 灑 / 儷 at the end of the preceding E, and retaining 犬 in the second sentence of the E. Thus "transferring" refers to the transfer of the same name from one entity to another, i.e. a pup may be called a dog, "referring" or "raising" is picking out separate entities, i.e. a pup or a dog, whilst "applying" or "adding" is the application of an additional word-meaning — here "scold". This interpretation closely follows WFB and JBC. TJF identifies the three instances as a "verb used as a noun", an "intransitive verb" and a "transitive verb". See also ACG's discussion on pp. 326–327.

---

136. There is doubt about this sentence, specifically characters four to six. In the translation I have used WFB's version (得之名). The simplest modification is that proposed by SYR (多 to 名). ACG has "待之名". The meaning is essentially the same in all cases.

137. There is debate about this character with regard to both form and placement. Most have it as the final character of this E, although others have it as the initial character of the next E (ACG, Z&Q), whether in its original form as 灑 or emended to 儷 as by TJF and others.

138. There is variation in the initial five to six characters of the E as follows: (i) Some versions have 灑 preceding 謂 (see ACG note 207, p. 326). (ii) Most common is the version given above which is that of the DZ (although, of course, in that text there is no indication of which E 灑 belongs to). (iii) WFB has the following rearrangement: "謂，命狗犬，移也。" reading 命 as 名. (iv) GH duplicates 謂.

A79   **C:** *Ming* (名 — a name) [may be] "generalising" (*da* 達), "classifying" (*lei* 類) or "particularising" (*si* 私).

E: *Ming* (名 — a name): "Thing" is generalising. If there is an entity, it necessarily gets this name. Naming it 'horse' is classifying. If it is an entity like this, it is necessarily named by this. Naming someone *Zang* is particularising. This name stops at (is limited to) this entity. The words issuing from the mouth all are names — like the pairing of surname and style.

A80   **C:** *Wei* (謂) [may be] "to transfer" (*yi* 移), "to refer/raise/pick out" (*ju* 舉), or "to apply/add" (*jia* 加).

E: *Wei* (謂): To call a pup a dog is to transfer. (To call something) "pup" or "dog" is to refer/raise/pick out. Scolding a pup is to apply/add.

A81   **C:** 知，聞[139]，説，親，名，實，合，為。

      E: 知：傳受之，聞也。方不障[140]，説也。身觀焉，親也。所以謂，名也。所謂，實也。名實耦，合也。志行，為也。

Comment: Apart from BY's accepted emendation (note 139), there are no textual problems in the C, although WYJ does divide this C into two, separating the three means and the four aspects of knowing. 知 has been previously analysed in A3–A6 and all the other terms in the C except 親 are subjects of definition. ACG (p. 328) sees the fourfold classification of "objects of knowledge" as being "... of fundamental importance if, as we believe, it is the clue to the organisation of the Canons" — an idea he develops in *Disputers of the Tao* (pp. 137–170). In the E also, there are no textual or interpretative difficulties apart from the elaboration of 説. Here there have been multiple readings of 方 including: 方域 (TJF, MZQY, JBC), 比類推論 (WYJ), "square" (ACG) and 時空 (WFB). There is, however, quite general agreement about reading 障 as "obstruction". I have taken 方 simply as "method", i.e. the method of explanation, which is then the method of explaining something unknown by something known, akin to WYJ's interpretation. ACG's reading of this example is: "Knowing that something square will not rotate is by 'explanation'."

A82   **C:** 聞，傳[141]，親。

      E: 聞：或告之，傳也。身觀焉，親也。

Comment: It seems clear that the distinction being made is between hearing about something through an intermediary and hearing something directly by being present. The second sentence of the E, which is identical to part of the preceding E, does, however, present something of a difficulty to the extent that LQC proposes reading 觀 as 親 since it is about hearing not seeing. Both CYX and WYJ make the point that the distinction is between hearing about something from which one is remote in time and/or place, and hearing something when one is present, which explanation is reflected in the translation.

---

139. There is general acceptance of BY's emendation of 問 to 聞.
140. This is the most commonly accepted emendation of the character usually written here which is 章 with radical 53. 障 is taken in the sense of "obstruct". ACG, however, emends to 運 — see Comment.
141. The emendation from 博 by BY on the basis of the E is generally accepted.

A81   **C:** *Zhi* (知 — knowing) [is by] hearing (*wen* 聞), explaining (*shuo* 説) and personally experiencing (*qin* 親); (it is about) names (*ming* 名), entities (*shi* 實), correlations (*he* 合) and actions (*wei* 為).

E: *Zhi* (知 — knowing): Receiving something transmitted is hearing. The method not being obstructed is explaining. Observing (something) oneself is personally experiencing. What something is called by is its name. What is called [by the name] is the entity. The pairing of name and entity is correlation. Intentions that are carried out are actions.

A82   **C:** *Wen* (聞 — to hear) is by transmission (i.e. from someone else), or in person.

E: *Wen* (聞 — to hear): Someone informing about it is "by transmission". Seeing for oneself is "in person".

A83   C: 見，體，盡。

E: 見：時[142] 者，體也。二者，盡也。

Comment: The problem here revolves around the reading of 時 in the E. Whilst there is widespread acceptance of SYR's emendation to 特, ACG raises doubt as indicated in note 142. Modern editors such as WFB, TJF, WYJ, LSL, and Z&Q all have this emendation and the last four all quote SYR's note which reads: "'時' 疑當為 '特'。特者奇也。二者耦也。特者止見其一體，二者盡見其眾體。特、二文正相對。" (SYR, pp. 499–500). There is then the issue of whether a pair of unspecified objects is being considered (ACG's position) or the formulation is more general — i.e. "two" is taken as "all". LQC's remarks, favouring the latter position, bring the familiar example of the parts of the elephant to mind.

A84   C: 合，正[143]，宜，必。

E: 古[144]：兵[145] 立反[146] 中志工[147]，正也。臧[148] 之為，宜也。非彼必不有，必也。(聖者用而勿必必也者可勿疑仗者兩而勿偏。)[149]

Comment: Whilst the C seems clear enough (although there might be some debate on how 合 should best be rendered — see ACG, p. 331), the E is a problem from first to last and might reasonably be deemed incomprehensible. What is probable is that the three aspects of 合 identified in the C are being exemplified. In the first case, the variety of proposed emendations, readings and punctuation attest to the obscurity of the example — as WFB remarks: "文詭難解". I have followed JBC in treating the first six characters as three

---

142. SYR's emendation of 時 to 特 is widely accepted, although ACG observes that "there is no other example of *t'e* in the dialectical chapters" — see his note 212, p. 329.
143. Emended from the recurring Mohist character — see note 95 above.
144. There is general acceptance of SYR's emendation of 古 to 合.
145. This character is accepted by some editors but variously emended by others: for example to 並 by TJF, to 平 by ZJF, to 評 MZQY, and to 與 by ACG.
146. I have accepted JBC's reading of this character as 返 based on the *Lun Yu* XI.15 and Zhu Xi's comments thereon (SSJZ, *Lun Yu*, p. 72).
147. There is general acceptance of SYR's emendation of 工 to 功 related to its use in conjunction with 志 in the Daqu 9, although it should be noted that this itself is a contentious passage.
148. See WYJ, note 197, p. 520 on the emendation to 臧 which is variously read as an individual (most commonly and as elsewhere), as 義 (SYR), and as 善 (WFB).
149. These 18 characters are what follow in sequence in the DZ text. They are very problematical — see Comment.

A83   **C:** *Jian* (見 — to see) is partial or complete.

E: *Jian* (見 — to see): [Seeing] one aspect is "partial". [Seeing] two (all) aspects is "complete".

A84   **C:** *He* (合 — relation/to tally with/to correspond) includes being correct (exact), being fitting (appropriate) and being necessary.

E: *He* (合 — relation/to tally with/to correspond): The deployment of troops, the return to the centre, intention and outcome; these involve being correct. *Zang's* conduct; this involves being fitting. Negating "that" means it is necessarily not so; this involves being necessary. (The judgements of sages, employ but do not treat as necessary. The "necessary", accept and do not doubt. The ones which are the converse of each other, apply on both sides, not on one without the other.)[ii]

---

ii.   This is ACG's translation of the problematical 18 characters (p. 331). For his emendations and additions see his notes 218–221, p. 330.

pairs, accepting 反 as 返 and 工 as 功, the latter following SYR. The second and third examples are also very difficult and the translations offered are very tentative indeed. On the second, ACG has: "The relation to what Jack is deemed to be is 'to the one which is appropriate'." Then there are the 18 characters in parentheses. There are at least four distinct approaches to these characters:

i.   To include the first 12 of the 18 in the E for A84 and make the last 6 the E for A85, either with an added head character (正) or without. This is the most common approach and is exemplified by GH, WYJ, LSL, JBC and Z&Q.

ii. To include all 18 as the E for A85 following, providing a head character (正), emending 睪 to 正, and emending 伕 to 權 as advocated by SYR. This arrangement is given by TJF who also takes the middle 6 of the 18 characters to be a later gloss.

iii. To include all 18 in the E for A84 (as CYX does) and provide a separate E for A85. WFB's version of the 18 characters reads: "正者，用而勿必。宜者，兩而無偏。必者，可而無疑。" — see WFB, pp. 82–84. My translation of his version reads: "With respect to the correct, it is used but there is not certainty. With respect to the fitting, there are two yet there is not partiality. With respect to the necessary, it is admissible and there is not doubt."

iv. To include all 18 in the E for A84 and regard A85 as being without an E.

Of these four options, whilst the first is favoured by weight of numbers, ACG's arguments are strong and should be consulted — see his pp. 329–332. I have included his translation of the 18 characters in parentheses above.

A85   C: 欲，正權利；且惡正權害。

E: None

Comment: There is considerable doubt about this C&E. First, it appears to be out of context here, and, second, there is uncertainty as to whether there is an E — see Comment to A84. The version given above follows ACG and reproduces the DZ text apart from the substitution of the standard form of 正 for the rare early form in the two instances. Also, 且 is contentious — SYR suggests omitting it whilst ACG favours retaining it and translates it as "about to", being an alternative meaning of 欲. On this point, he writes: "Sun Yi-jang (SYR) deleted the *ch'ieh* (*qie* 且) 'about to'. But it would be worth the Mohist's while to distinguish *yü* 'about to' from *yü* 'desire' which, with *wu* 'dislike', is the basis of the ethical definitions. It is true that this usage is attested rather late, but the Canons are only a century or two earlier than the *Shih-chi*, in which it is frequent." (ACG, p. 332) This use of 且 does not, however, seem to fit with its place in the statement so I have followed SYR's proposal in the translation.

A85   **C:** To desire; directly (correctly) weighing the benefit. To abhor;
directly (correctly) weighing the harm.

E: None

WFB gives a quite different version of this C&E, making 宜 the head character, making the structure conform to the pattern of this group of C&Es (A76–88), and providing an E which is, in fact, the usual C for A85 with 且 omitted — see his p. 84. WYJ, who accepts SYR's deletion of 且, refers (as do others) to the Daqu (*Mozi* 44.17) — see his note 199. If the most common version of the E is accepted — i.e. "仗者，兩而勿偏。" — WYJ's interpretation is probably appropriate. He accepts SYR's reading of 仗 as 權 and writes: "言兩權利害，無所偏也。" — note 200, p. 521.

A86   **C:** 為，存，亡，易，蕩，治，化。

E: 為：早臺，存也。[150] 病，亡也。買鬻，易也。霄盡，蕩也。[151] 順長，治也。[152] 蛙買[153]，化也。

Comment: I have followed commentators such as WFB in taking 為 (previously defined in A76) in the senses of both "being" and "becoming". The E, which should of course clarify this, is however bedevilled by textual and interpretative problems. As a consequence, different positions are taken on the meaning of 為. Thus, ACG includes six meanings (constitute/become/deem/make/cure/govern) omitting two (see his p. 333).

---

150. There are textual issues in this opening statement, particularly concerning 早 which is not generally accepted, although it is retained without comment by BY. Most commentators, dating back to SYR and ZHY, emend it to 甲. TJF has in his text 亭, but argues for 造 via 草 as does WYJ. ACG takes a quite different position, making the first two characters 甲 商, which leaves a problem with translation.

151. From BY on, most editors emend 霄 to 消, although proposing retention of the meaning of the former. If the latter is taken as "dissolve", this makes the example of a different sort — see ACG, note 224, p. 332. ACG also reads 盡 as 燼 ("ashes") in pursuit of uniformity of examples.

152. There are several quite different interpretations of this example. ACG reads both 順 and 長 as verbal, preserving the double form of the example ("instruct" and "leading"). Most commonly, this is taken to indicate compliance with old ways or with elders bringing order. WFB, however, understands it in the sense of growth, although this makes the reading of 治 difficult.

153. 買 is usually emended to one of three characters: 鵙 (ZHY and others), 鼠 (SYR, WFB), or 鼮 (TJF).

A86 **C:** *Wei* (為 — being/becoming) includes to be (exist), to cease to be (exist), to exchange, to disperse, to put in order, to transform.

E: *Wei* (為 — being/becoming): Armour and towers exist. A sickness ceases to exist. Buying and selling are exchanges. Mist and ashes disperse. Complying and directing bring order. The tree frog and field mouse are transformed (i.e. become a quail).

A87   **C:** 同，重，體，合，類。

E: 同：二名一實，重同也。不外於兼，體同也。俱處於室，合同也。有以同，類同也。

Comment: Both C and E are free of textual difficulties. Here the E does clarify the C effectively, the only point of interpretative variation being the third example. Most commentators provide illustrative examples. The first is almost invariably pup/dog, whilst the second refers to the part/whole issue considered in A2. The variation in the third example largely depends on how literally 室 is interpreted. Thus, both TJF and ACG read it as "house" or "room", the former using as an example the Daqu (*Mozi* 44.13) relating to a robber in a house. On the other hand, some read 室 more generally as 所 in the sense of "location".

A88   **C:** 異，二，〔不〕[154] 體，不合，不類。

E: 異：二必異，二也。不連屬，不體也。不同所，不合也。不有同，不類也。

Comment: With the acceptance of the addition of 不 preceding 體 comes the acceptance also, as ZHY early indicated, that four aspects of 異 are being listed corresponding to four aspects of 同 in the preceding C. There must, however, be some uncertainty as to the interpretation of ⼆ and the corresponding first statement in the E. 體, 合 and 類 are all repeated in this C&E leaving ⼆ to correspond to 重 in A87, which the E makes clear is about two names for the same entity. On this basis, most editors assume that the issue is again "name and entity", i.e. in contrast to one entity with two names "difference" is exemplified by two entities and two names, although neither "name" nor "entity" is specifically mentioned. In the translation, I have not made this assumption, taking it rather as a general statement about difference (following WFB).

** This marks the end of the group of 12 C&Es of a particular form which list the several meanings of each of a series of important terms. What follows from now to the end of the A series of C&Es is very uncertain. As stated in the introduction to the section, my intention is to follow the DZ text, indicating (in summarised form), where major variations occur in different editions.

---

154. In the DZ and BY there is no 不 here. Its addition in SYR's text is attributed to BY, but I found no mention of this in BY's notes. Nonetheless, it is generally accepted — see, for example, WYJ, note 213, p. 522.

A87   **C:** *Tong* (同 — the same) [may involve] being duplicated, being a
part, being together, or being of a class.

   E: *Tong* (同 — the same): Two names for one entity is the
sameness of duplication. Not being outside the whole is the
sameness of being a part. Both being situated in the room is the
sameness of being together. Being the same in some respect is
the sameness of being of a class.

A88   **C:** *Yi* (異 — different) [may involve] two, not being a part, not
being together, and not being of a class.

   E: *Yi* (異 — different): Two certainly being different is two. Not
being joined is not being a part. Not being in the same place is
not being together. Not having what is the same is not being of
a class.

A89   **C:** 同異交得，放有無。

      E: 同異交得：於福[155] 家，良恕，有無也。比度，多少也。蛇蚓[156] 還圜，去就也。鳥折用桐[157]，堅柔也。劍尤早[158]，死生也。處室子子母，長少也[159]。兩絕勝，白黑也。中央，旁也。論行行行[160] 學實，是非也。難宿，成未也[161]。兄弟，俱適〔敵〕也。身處志往，存亡也。霍為，姓故也[162]。賈宜，貴賤也。諾超城，員止也[163]。

Comment: This is a very problematical C&E. In the C I have followed the line of those who read 放 as 比, the point being that the paired terms 同 and 異 are comparable to the paired terms 有 and 無, or that sameness and difference are determined by comparing what things have and do not have, i.e. sameness and difference depend on some quality or aspect being present or not, which is a clear and unexceptionable proposition. The E is unusual in its length and bedevilled by textual and interpretative difficulties. I have offered a translation for each of the examples with a varying degree of uncertainty. The discrepancies between the various commentators in their interpretations of these examples attest to their obscurity. There is also an issue about where this E should end. The version above follows WYJ. Some editors (e.g. TJF) include more of the characters which follow 諾 in the DZ text. ACG's version should also be considered. He makes significant changes in the C by duplicating the final two characters from 11 of the 15 examples in the E to be included also in the C — see his pp. 338–341 and also p. 93.

155. On the reading of 福 as 富 see ACG, note 234, p. 338.
156. These two characters are Z&Q's emendation of 兔 followed by the unknown graph 刀 with the 單 radical — see also SYR, p. 502, WYJ, note 222, pp. 522–523, and ACG, note 236, p. 338.
157. In this puzzling example I have followed the reading of TJF and Z&Q which depends on taking 折 as 逝 in the sense of 飛逝, 用 as 甲 in the sense of 甲蟲 and 同 as 動 — see Z&Q, note 5, p. 577. ACG takes 鳥折 as a military term for a "tactical retreat" — see his note 238, pp. 338–339.
158. I have followed TJF — see his p. 183.
159. See ACG, note 240, p. 339 on this example, in particular the duplication of 子.
160. Two of the three instances of 行 are taken to be superfluous (SYR).
161. There is wide variation in how this example is understood. The version given in the translation follows JBC — see his note 12, p. 167.
162. In this rather obscure example the reading follows TJF and Z&Q and depends on taking 霍 as 鶴, 為 as 猴 (based on the *Shuo Wen*), and 姓 as 性.
163. It is questionable whether this example should occur in this E since in the DZ text it follows 諾 which is the head character of the next E. Its form does, however, suggest placement here so I have followed WYJ in transferring it — see his note 237, p. 524.

A89   **C:** Sameness and difference are interrelated [and are determined
by] comparing what things have and do not have.

   E: Sameness and difference are interrelated: In the case of a rich
family and intuitive knowledge, there is having and not having.
In the case of comparing and measuring, there is much and
little. In the case of snakes and earthworms, there is turning
and circling, going away and approaching. In the case of a bird
flying or a beetle moving, there is hard and soft. In the case of
sword and armour, there is death and life. In the case of two
sons and a mother under one roof, there is older and younger.
In the case of two, one decisively prevails as in black and
white, centre and sides. In discussion, conduct, learning and
entities, there is right and wrong. In the case of the *Nan* bird
roosting, there is becoming and not (becoming). In the case of
older and younger brother, there is together and opposing. In
the case of the body being in one place but the mind being
elsewhere, there is present and absent. In the case of a crane or
monkey, there is what is innate and what is acquired (caused).
In the case of the price being right, there is dear and cheap. In
jumping over a wall, there is moving and stopping.

** The next four Cs have no corresponding E in the DZ text. This is accepted by
early editors such as BY and SYR. In later editions in which the Canons and
Explanations are placed together, several editors take what are the second and
fourth of the four Cs above and make them the Es for the first and third Cs
(e.g. WFB, TJF, LSL, JBC). ACG regards all four sentences as misplaced in
the C&Es and includes them in his separate, composite treatise "Names and
Objects" — see his pp. 109–110, 342, 478.

A90   **C:** 聞，耳之聰也。

E: None

Comment: The issues of arrangement have been indicated in the note **
above. As will be seen, the two pairs (A90 & 91 and A92 & 93) are related in
content. There are no significant textual issues. The primary senses,
exemplified here by hearing, receive impressions from the external world
which require the mind for interpretation. Similar views are expressed in
several other early texts.

A91   **C:** 循所聞而得其意，心之[164] 察也。

E: None

Comment: There is general acceptance of BY's emendation of 也 to 之 (note
164). The only issue is the appropriate reading of 察. WYJ has the following
note: "察、知也，明也。循聞得意，須有心神以君之。此公孫龍'臧三耳'之說所
由立也。" — see his note 239, p. 525.

A92   **C:** 言，口之利也。

E: None

Comment: The issues of arrangement and placement are considered in the
"Comment" to A90. As with that C&E, there are no significant textual issues.
These may be seen as a pair of C&Es dealing with what TJF characterises as
"出意" and "入意". Note that both 言 and 聞 are previously defined, the former
in A32 and the latter in A82.

164. The emendation from 也 by BY on the basis of parallelism with A93 is generally
accepted.

A90   **C:** Hearing is the ear's listening.

E: None

A91   **C:** To follow what is heard and get to its meaning is the mind's discernment.

E: None

A92   **C:** To speak is the benefit of the mouth.

E: None

A93   **C:** 執所言而意得見，心之辯[165] 也。

      E: None

Comment: On the use of 辯 here, ACG notes that it is, "... the only example in the corpus of *bian* as a quality of mind, 'subtle in making distinctions, logical in ordering ideas ...'" (his note 615, p. 478).

A94   **C:** 諾，不一[166] 利用。

      E: 〔諾〕：相從，相去，先知，是，可，五色[167]。長短，前後，輕
      重，援。

Comment: This is another uncertain C&E. There are problems of what to include, of what to emend, and to what, and of how to interpret what is not emended. Any translation must remain quite tentative. There are essentially three versions of the C with a relatively minor variation in the third. ACG reads 不 as 否 and makes this about "assent and denial", whilst TJF makes it a statement of the five benefits of answering. The variation in the third interpretation, which is the one used in the translation, depends on whether 利 is taken as nominal or adjectival. What to include in the E is quite problematical. The version given, allowing for some variation in the emendations, is that found in DZ and, among modern editors, WYJ, apart from the inclusion of 援 as the last character here rather than the first in the next E. Several editors omit the three pairs of the second sentence and also transfer what are the last 25 characters of the chapter in the DZ text to this E as they are about 諾 — see, for example, WFB, TJF and Z&Q. JBC also has this version, apart from the five additional characters, "超城員止也", given above as part of the E for A89, but which he includes as the first sentence of this E. The E, if one accepts the transposition of what some have as the first five characters to the E for A89, begins with a list of the five forms of assenting, of which only the third is to any extent contentious. The issue there is whether 先知 indicates "being first informed" as TJF suggests, based on *Mencius* VA.7 (5), "knowing already" (e.g. JBC), or *a priori* knowledge (ACG).

---

165. Read as 辨 — see JBC, note 2, pp. 172–173.
166. TJF emends 不一 to 五, relating this to the five instances listed in the first sentence of the E. ACG reads 不 as 否.
167. The emendation of 色 to 也 by SYR is generally accepted.

A93   **C:** To grasp what is said and its meaning being seen is the mind's discrimination.

   E: None

A94   **C:** Assenting does not have [just] one benefit or use.

   E: Assenting: Both agreeing, both rejecting, knowing beforehand, asserting, allowing the possibility are the five (forms of assent). Long and short, before and after, light and heavy are adducing.

A95 C: 服，執說[168] (音利) [169] 巧轉則求其故。

E: 執服難成，言務成之九，則求執之法。[170]

Comment: This is an almost impossible C&E with virtually no two texts or interpretations being the same. I shall simply list in sequence the points of difficulty and contention. For the C: (i) The reading of 服 — I have followed Z&Q in taking it in the sense of 信服 as above. TJF relates it the use in *Mencius* IIA.3(2), i.e. "to subdue", whilst ACG takes 服執 as a two-word phrase and renders it "devote oneself to the claim one upholds" — see his note 252, p. 343. (ii) The reading of 說 — is this, as ACG suggests, a corruption of an unknown graph *mao* (i.e. 貌 with the 言 radical) meaning "describe"? I have accepted his argument in note 253, p. 343. Modern texts have it as 說. (iii) Is 音利 an added note or part of the text. I have taken the former position. For alternative views see JBC, SYR, WFB. (iv) Do the final six characters belong here (e.g. WYJ), or do they constitute a separate C (e.g. Z&Q), or are they part of the following C (e.g. LSL)? (v) If they remain, how is the C to be punctuated? For differing versions, see WYJ, ACG. For the E: (i) Should 援 be the first character of the E as in WYJ or does it belong in the previous E? (ii) Should the first two characters read 執服 as in the DZ or should the order be reversed to conform to the C? (iii) How should the E be punctuated? For example, see ACG, note 254, pp. 343–344. (iv) Should 九 be omitted (e.g. LSL) or emended as generally assumed and, if so, to what? I have followed ACG's suggestion (i.e. to 執 — his note 255, p. 344). (v) Should 法 be the final character here or is it part of the next E? If retained here, should it be read as 故? It should be clear from these issues that any reading of this C&E must remain extremely tentative.

---

168. ACG makes a point of distinguishing an unknown character (貌 with the 言 radical in the sense of "describe") from 說, which most modern editors give. I have followed JBC in taking 說 as 說司 which he equates with the modern 刺探 ("to make roundabout enquiries", "to spy", "to detect"), and WFB who equates it with 伺.

169. I have accepted BY's suggestion that these two characters are an added note — see SYR, p. 456.

170. This group of six characters (or five if 法 or 故 is not included) is quite problematical regarding both placement and interpretation. JBC includes the five only, whilst ACG has six (i.e. including 法) in his A94, as does WYJ in his A96. Modern commentators all emend 九 but differently: to 丸 (WFB), to 執 (ACG), to 紏 (WYJ), to 究 (MZQY). One attractive solution to the problem is that of WFB who places the also problematical C&E A47, with an alternative E, here in conjunction with a C&E having the head character 丸 giving a pair of C&E's (his A92 and A93) with the head characters 環 and 丸 respectively. In his text these are as follows: A92. C: 環俱柢。E: 環：俱柢，則求其 故。: A93. C: 丸，巧轉。E: 丸：巧轉，則求之勢。He then identifies 連環 and 轉 丸 as two forms of disputation employed by the Mingjia 名家.

A95 C: To be convinced about something one must grasp the subtle turns of the description and then seek their reason.

E: To be convinced in grasping something is difficult to achieve. In speaking, the important task is to complete the grasping, then to seek the reasons behind the grasping.

A96 C: 法同則觀其同。

E: 法[171]：取同觀巧傳。

Comment: This, the first of a pair of C&Es on the use of a standard, model, or criterion, is largely free of textual issues. The only points of note are in the E where there is the question of whether 法 is duplicated at the start of the E, but this does not affect meaning. There is also WFB's proposed substitution of 同 for 巧傳 but again, meaning is not affected.

A97 C: 法異則觀其宜。[172]

E: 法：取此擇彼，問[173] 故觀宜。以人之有黑[174] 者有不墨者也。止黑人與以有愛於人，有不愛於人，心[175] 愛人，是孰宜？

Comment: There are basically three issues with this C&E, all pertaining to the E. First, should the E end after the first 宜 making it symmetrical with the initial member of the pair (A96), leaving the remaining 31 characters to become the initial part of the next E — compare, for example, the texts of WYJ, TJF and ACG with those of WFB and LSL. Second, does 黑 stand for 墨 (i.e. Mohists) as initially suggested by ZCY. If this is taken to be the case, a somewhat different reading from that given above is possible — see, for example, Z&Q. Third, is the emendation of 心 to 止 acceptable? I have taken it to be so.

A98 C: 止，因以別道。[176]

E: 心[177]：彼舉然者，以為此其然也，則舉不然者而問之。

---

171. There is uncertainty about the start of this E relating to the issue of the final character of the section in parentheses in the previous E. Apart from the arrangement above, that of WFB and WYJ, there is omission of 法 (ACG), duplication (TJF, JBC) and the suggestion that 法同 is the head (MZQY).

172. There is widespread agreement on the structure of this C, only TJF proposing a significant variation. He sees 宜止 as connected and, in fact, incorporates all of what is here the next C (A96) in the C above with a comma after 止.

173. The original 問 is preserved by most editors although it is emended to 明 by WFB.

174. Many commentators (e.g. ZCY, WFB) either emend the more usual 黑 to 墨 or at least take it as referring to Mo Zi or the Mohists. Some, however, retain 黑 as meaning "black" (ACG, WYJ) and this has been done above.

175. By general agreement 心 is emended to 止 — see, for example, SYR.

176. In the translation, 止 is read as 停止, 以 is read as 已 (WYZ), 別 is read as 辨別, and 道 is read as 道理 — see, for example, JBC, note 1, p. 186.

177. There is widespread acceptance of ZHY's emendation of 心 to 止 in conformity with the C — see, for example, WYJ, note 256, p. 527.

A96   **C:** Where the model (standard) is the same, look at its sameness (what is the same in it).

       E: Model (standard): Select what is the same and look at subtle variations.

A97   **C:** Where the model (standard) is different, examine its appropriateness.

       E: A model (standard): Select this, pick out that; ask about cause, look at appropriateness. Use a person's being black and a person's not being black to establish the limit of "black person" and a person having love towards others and a person not having love towards others to establish the limit of "loving person". In the case of these, what is appropriate?

A98   **C:** Stopping occurs because there already is a resolution of the argument (differentiation of principles).

       E: Stopping: If "that" is raised as being so and taken as the ground for "this" being so, then raise what is not so and question (clarify) it.

Comment: There are three main variations with regard to this C. The most common version is that given above. TJF, however, attaches all five characters to the previous C and proceeds directly to what is here A99. WFB emends the head character to 正, although from his discussion I judge his interpretation to be not greatly different from that usually given for 止 when this is taken as a means of resolving disputation. As for the E, and its relation to the C, WYJ offers this summary: "說言停止辯論之術。辯論之所以停止者，因其所辯論之道理已明也，故曰`止，因以別道'。" — see WYJ, note 257, p. 527. Several commentators refer to the following statement from《荀子‧正名篇》: "辭足以見極則舍之矣。" — XZXZ, p. 379.

A99　　**C:** 正[178]，無非。

　　　　E: 〔正〕[179]：若聖人有非而不非。[180] 正五諾，皆人於知有說。過五諾，若員無直，無說。用五諾，若自然矣。

Comment: There are major difficulties with this final C&E of the A series. Two examples of attempts to make some sense of it are those of ACG and WFB. In the first, ACG includes the first eight characters of the E in the previous E ("For example, the sage has respects in which he is not, yet he is."), makes the following 正 the head character, emends 五 to 伍 in the sense of "matching", and 人 to 入, and places a full-stop after 知. The subject is then "matching and assent" — see his pp. 347–348. On WFB's emendations and arrangement (正 to 聖 in the C, the addition of 聖 as the head character in the E, and the ending of the E after "不非") and interpretation, the meaning is simply that the sage is an infallible arbiter of 是 and 非, a point which the E amplifies by stating that even when he seems wrong he is not.

** Immediately prior to the final C there are these five characters: "讀此書旁行" ("Read this text horizontally"). These are almost certainly a late addition and were, indeed, an important clue in deciphering the Canons and Explanations — see WYJ, note 262, p. 528 and TJF, p. 197.

---

178. Written as the Mohist variant used for 正. WFB emends it to 聖 and supplies 聖 as the head character of the E.
179. The DZ has no head character. Some modern editors supply 正 (e.g. ACG, LSL), others do not (e.g. WYJ, Z&Q).
180. Some editors end the E here, transferring the 25 characters that follow to the E for A94 in which 諾 is the head character — see, for example, TJF, WFB, LSL and JBC.

A99 **C:** The correct is not negatable.

E: The correct: For example, "sage" is negatable and is not negatable. Being correct in the five assents is when all people have in their minds an explanation. Being wrong in the five assents (like a circle not being straight) is when there is no explanation. Use the five assents as if they were naturally so.

41 & 43: 經與經說下

B1   **C:** 止類以行人¹。說在同。

       E: 止：彼以此其然也，說是其然也。我以此其不然也，疑是其然也。

       Comment: The uncertainty regarding this C&E relates to the precise interpretation of 止, whether 人 should be emended to 之 in the C, to the meaning of 疑 in the E, and whether the last sentence of the next E minus "為麋" should be placed at the end of this E — see, for example, TJF, WFB, JBC, LSL, Z&Q. The variations in the reading of 止 include "putting a stop to disputation" (JBC and the meaning taken here), "fixing the class" (ACG), "the permanence of classes" (TJF), or even reading it as 正 (LQC). Whatever variation is accepted, the subject is clearly classes, the topic of several C&Es here. Overall, I have followed the analysis of JBC which is detailed and persuasive.

B2   **C:** ² 推類之難。說在之³ 大小。⁴

       E: 謂四足獸，與生鳥⁵、與物，盡與大小也。此然是必然，則俱為麋⁶。

---

1.   Most, following SYR, emend 人 to 之. ACG, however, retains 人 — see his note 263, p. 348.
2.   There is an issue about the start of this C regarding the break with the previous E in the DZ (B42 in the present arrangement). The characters involved are "駉異說" — see Comment above.
3.   There is some variation in the understanding of 之. SYR considers it should be preceded by 名, WYJ by 類. JBC, following WYZ, reads it as 其, a pronoun for 類 which I have followed. ACG proposes emendation to 止.
4.   As with the start of this C, there is some uncertainty about the end concerning whether 物盡 should be included here or at the start of the following C — see ACG's note 267, p. 349.
5.   There is general acceptance of 牛馬 in place of 生鳥.
6.   Read as 迷 following WYJ (note 5, p. 548).

41 & 43: Canons & Explanations B

B1   **C:** Stopping is effected by means of classes. The explanation lies
        in sameness.

        E: Stopping: Another, on the basis of these being so, says this is
        so. I, on the basis of these not being so, call in question this
        being so. (If these are so and this is necessarily so, then all [are
        so]).[i]

B2   **C:** Making inferences about classes is difficult. The explanation
        lies in their being large and small (in scope).

        E: In speaking of four-footed animals, they are different from ox
        and horse, and different from the totality of things, being a
        larger (class than the former), and a smaller (class than the
        latter). If these being so meant that this was necessarily so, then
        all would be confused.

---

i.   This is the translation of the seven characters found prior to 為麋 in the DZ text as the
       final part of the next E — see Comment.

Comment: This C&E is also quite a problem. The text and emendations given above are largely due to BY and SYR and, among modern editors, are most completely embraced by TJF and JBC, although even between these editors there are significant variations in the punctuation of the E. Amongst other editors, notable variations in the C include, first, placement of the three characters 駟異說 at the beginning of the C, favoured initially by SYR and subsequently followed by ACG, LSL and Z&Q, although how these characters are treated differs among these commentators — i.e. SYR (followed by LSL and Z&Q) takes them as "四足牛馬異說" whereas ACG retains them as they are — see his note 265, p. 349. Second, there is the question of 之 — whether it should be emended or preceded by another character. Third, there is the matter of whether 物盡 should be included in this or the following C. In the E, there are issues concerning the provision of 推 as a head character for the E (GH, TJF), whether the final nine characters are properly placed here, and if so, how 麇 is to be understood. WFB has a complete merging of B2 and B3. It is apparent, then, that any text and translation must be rather tentative. The text followed in the translation is that given by WYJ (see particularly his note 5, p. 548) and in the CHANT. ACG's version should be consulted for an alternative which includes both the two initial and the two final contentious characters in the C.[7]

B3   C: 物盡同名。二與鬥，〔子與〕[8] 愛，食與招，白與視[9]，麗與 〔暴〕[10]，夫與履。一偏棄之，謂而固[11] 是也。說在因。

 E: 同名：俱鬥，不俱二[12]，二與鬥也。包，肝肺，子 ，愛也。 梀茅，食與招[13] 也。[14] 白馬多白，視馬不多視，白與視

---

7.   Added in some texts (e.g. TJF) on the basis of the E.
8.   Both TJF and WFB add two characters here to preserve the symmetry of the examples. " 子與" is TJF's addition.
9.   GH, followed by ACG, emends 視 to 眇.
10. 暴 is supplied here in most texts — see, for example, WYJ, note 8, p. 549.
11. Several commentators read 固 as 囚 (e.g. SYR, WYJ — see the latter's note 23, p. 550). I have followed ACG's reading.
12. Generally emended from 二.
13. This is the generally accepted emendation of 抬 — see WYJ, note 15, p. 549.
14. SYR, followed by JBC, emends 橘 to 梀, giving two words of the same sound — 梀 and 茅.

B3   C: Things "use up" the same name. (For example), "to be in two
minds" and "to contend", ["to nurture" and] "to love", "to eat"
and "to call", "being white" and "being blind", "being
beautiful" and ["being cruel"], "man" and "sandals". If one of
the pair is set aside, in naming it, it is what it inherently is. The
explanation lies in the reason/criterion.

   E: The same name: Both "contend" but not both "are in two
minds" is the example of "being in two minds" and 'to
contend". One's offspring and one's liver and lungs are related
to "nurture" and "love". *Mao* and *mao* are for "feeding" and
"calling" respectively. Most of a white horse is white; most of
a blind horse is not blind; this is white and blind. Being termed

也。¹⁵ 為麗不必麗不必，麗與暴也。¹⁶ 為非以人是不為非，若為夫勇不為夫，為履以買衣為履，夫與履也。¹⁷ 二與一亡，不與一在。偏去莫。¹⁸ 有文¹⁹ 實也，而後謂之。無文實也，則無謂也。不若敷與美。²⁰ 謂是，則是固美也。謂也，則是非美。無謂，則報也。

Comment: There are three issues with the C. First, should 物盡 be included at the start of this C or as the final part of the previous C. Opinion is divided. I have taken the former position. The second issue is whether the indicated additions should be made to complete the series of pairs. Meaning and the E seem to demand this although ACG, for example, does not make these additions. Third, should the last 12 characters be included in this C, or be treated as a separate C. I have followed LDF and ACG in taking the former position (see ACG note 271, p. 352). The E is fraught with difficulties and the version given above is quite tentative. The sense seems clearly to be about the usage of terms and their different application in different circumstances. The problems with the E are the uncertainty about the initial statement and the terse nature of the examples.

15. The two different emendations that are made in the attempt to give greater clarity to this example are 多 to 名 (WYJ) and 視 to 眇 (GH), the latter relating this example to the Xiaoqu 9 on the "scope" of terms.

16. The text given above for this example is as in early editions and is reproduced with the addition of the comma by both WYJ and WFB. I can only say that SYR's comment ("此文難通") is something of an understatement. Probably the most reasonable emendation is that proposed by ZQH which makes the text: "為麗不必麗，為暴不必暴" and makes the distinction between 暴、偶 and 麗 in the first instance, and between 暴露 and 暴虐 in the second.

17. Again there are problems with this example, not least that there is no real equivalent in the C to the first of the three statements. The modification proposed by JBC, stemming from SYR's proposals, is to make the text: "為非以人是不為非，若為夫以勇是不為夫，為履以買是不為履，非，夫與履也。" — note 8, pp. 199–200.

18. There is uncertainty about the arrangement of the preceding several characters. Some editors end the sentence at 莫, JBC framing it as a question. TJF indicates a lacuna after 莫, which WFB fills with 有.

19. Both here and in the next sentence, 文 is taken as 之 by a number of editors following SYR.

20. There are several variations in this statement. Most importantly, 敷 is interpreted as 敷陳 (e.g. JBC), or as in 皮膚 (WYJ), or as 花 (Z&Q following TJF). The latter also deletes the initial 不.

li does not necessarily mean beauty; being termed *bao* does not necessarily mean cruel. Being deemed "wrong" by others — this is not being "wrong". Being deemed "a brave man" — this is not being deemed "man". Being deemed "shoes" when linked in "buying clothes" is being "shoes" — this is man and shoes. If of two, one is lost, it is not joined with the one remaining. If the part is gone, it is not there. What is there is the entity, and afterwards one speaks of it. What is not an entity is not spoken of. It is not like "flower" and "beautiful". If one speaks of "this", then "this" is inherently beautiful. If one speaks of something else, then "this" is not beautiful. If one does not speak of it, then it is reported on.

B4   C: 不可偏去而二。説在見與倪[21]，一與二，廣與循[22]。

E: 〔?〕[23]：見不見離。一二不相盈。廣循，堅白。

Comment: This C&E continues the discussion of part and whole, and relates particularly to GSL's "hard and white" argument (GSLZ 3). Quite different views have, however, been advanced by different commentators as to how, views which depend on proposed emendations and rearrangements. Thus, WFB identifies this C&E as stating an anti-GSL position, a view which depends critically on the one emendation that is itself critical — the placement of 不 as the head character in the E. Other commentators see the C&E as supporting GSL (see e.g. QM's comments on GSLZ 3), whilst the extreme of this position is taken by ACG who considers it to be the basis for the supposed forgery of the "Jian Bai Lun" chapter in the GSLZ (GSLZ 3).

B5   C: 不能而不害。説在害。

E: 舉不[24] 重不與箴，非力之任也。為握者觭倍[25]，非智之任也。若耳目。

Comment: The text of the C is uncontroversial and the meaning also seems clear — the issue is the context. JBC equates it with *Mencius* IIIA. 4(6) where the point is that each person has a particular competency that is appropriate. The examples in the E remain somewhat unclear, in part due to textual uncertainty. In fact, influenced particularly by the final statement, most commentators take this C&E, like the previous one, to be related to GSL's "Jian Bai Lun" (GSLZ 3).

---

21. In most texts there is 倶 here, although WFB has 倶. 不兄 (used in the translation) is GH's proposed emendation.

22. Most accept YY's emendation of 循 to 修 as in the translation .

23. There is some question about the placement of 不 as a head character. The text above is that of the DZ which is followed by a number of editors (e.g. WYJ, TJF, Z&Q, JBC) and is what is translated. ACG considers 不 to be the misplaced head character (see his note 284, p. 355) whilst WFB adds it as a head character.

24. 不 is transposed by a number of editors following LQC to become the head character — see, for example, WYJ, note 32, p. 552. This is followed in the translation. ACG omits 不 in his version.

25. There is some uncertainty about this pair of characters. Whilst there is general acceptance of SYR's emendation of the character combining 角 and 頁 to 觭 giving the sense for the pair of 奇偶, referring to counters, WYJ emends to 顚蹄 whilst ACG translates the initial part of this sentence as: "Whether being deemed a complement is one-sided or double…"

B4   **C:** Even where a partial setting aside is not possible, there are two. The explanation lies in "seen and not-seen", "one and two", "length and breadth".

        E: ? : The seen and the not-seen are separate; one and two do not fill each other; length and breadth; hard and white.

B5   **C:** Not being able but not being harmful. The explanation lies in harmful.

        E: Not: Lifting a weight is not equivalent to lifting a needle, which is not the strength's responsibility. Taking counters that are grasped to be odd or even is not the intellect's responsibility. It is like ears and eyes.

B6   C: 異類不比²⁶。說在量。

E: 異²⁷：木與夜孰長？智與粟孰多？爵，親，行，賈，四者孰
貴？麋與霍孰高？(麋與霍孰霍？)²⁸ 蟬與瑟孰瑟？

Comment: The only issue in the C is the reading of 比 for the rare character
of the same form with the 冂 radical. By general consent, this is taken as 比.
The point then is that things of different classes cannot be compared in terms
of measurement in that, although the same adjective may be used, the
application is clearly different — as with the length of time and space to use
the first example. The two/three final examples present problems. ACG retains
all three — see his note 293, p. 357.

B7   C: 偏去莫加少。說在故²⁹。

E: 偏：俱一無變。

Comment: Terseness of expression in both C and E, together with variation in
the readings of 加少 and 故, obviously allow a range of interpretation. Thus,
TJF speaks of "beautiful flower", the flower remaining when "beautiful" is taken
away. MZQY reads it as a statement of physics and ACG refers back to what
is here B3. WYJ, on the other hand, refers to what is here B4, and via this to
GSL's "On Hard and White" (堅白論 — GSLZ 3). I favour WFB's interpretation.
He brackets what are here B4, B5 and B8 (his B4–6) and understands the
three as being about using 偏去 to clarify "名實通變" in the three different
situations. He relates this particular C&E to GSLZ 4.

---

26. In early texts (including the DZ) this is written with the 冂 radical (ZWDCD #3432).
    It is generally accepted as 比 or 仳 (WFB, JBC), the latter being defined in A69. See
    WYJ, note 36, p. 553 and ACG, note 291, p. 357.

27. There is some question about the placement of 異 — whether it is the final character of
    the preceding E or the head character as here. The majority of modern commentators,
    including TJF, WYJ, WFB, GH and JBC, take the latter position.

28. There is considerable variation in this example. In many texts it is duplicated but with
    霍 replacing 高 in the second instance. Many, following SYR, omit the second instance,
    and even where it is included, it may be recognised as superfluous (e.g. JBC). ACG, on
    the other hand, retains it and translates both examples. Variations within the examples
    are 霍, 鶴 or 義 (WFB) as the third character in the first and 霍 or 高 as the final character
    in the second.

29. There is general agreement that 故 should be understood as 舊 in the sense of 原來
    (JBC), i.e. what the thing was originally. ACG reads 故 here and elsewhere as "things
    as they inherently are" — see his note 294, p. 357.

B6   **C:** Different classes are not comparable. The explanation lies in measurement.

E: Difference: Of wood and night, which is the longer? Of knowledge and grain, which is the greater? Of the four things — rank, family, good conduct and price — which is the most valuable? Of the tailed deer and the crane, which is the higher? Of the cicada and the zithern, which is the more mournful?

B7   **C:** In a partial going away there is no adding or subtracting. The explanation lies in the original.

E: Part: In both being one there is no change.

B8   C: 假必誖。說在不然。

E: 假：假必非也而後假。狗假霍[30] 也，猶氏霍也。

Comment: There are several issues here. In the C there are the precise meanings of 假 and 誖. As JBC points out, the *Shuo Wen* definition ("假，非真也") seems appropriate for the former. Recent commentators use 虛假 as the modern equivalent. However, where the statement "假者，今不然也" appears in the Xiaoqu (45.2) commentators generally take 假 as 假使. I have read 誖 as "erroneous" rather than 亂 ("confusing"). ACG has a somewhat different interpretation, taking 假 as "loan-name" and 誖 as "self-contradictory". Several modern commentators (e.g. LSL, JBC) follow SYR's reading which is to take 假 as 非真 based on the *Shuo Wen*, and 誖 as 亂 which is essentially what I have done.

B9   C: 物之所以然，與所以知之，與所以使人知之；不必同。說在病。

E: 物：或傷之，然也。見之，智[31] 也。告[32] 之，使智也。

Comment: The only real issue with this C&E concerns what "不必同" refers to in the C. There are, in essence, three possibilities. The first is that the difference is between the three circumstances stated. This does appear to be stating the obvious, but ACG, who takes this position, explains why it might be important to the Later Mohists to stress the distinction. The second possibility is that the phrase refers to each individually. Thus, in the case of an illness, it may come about in different ways, its recognition may be by different means, and informing someone about it may be done in different ways. This is TJF's reading and seems the most plausible. It is particularly clearly expressed by MZQY. The third, and intermediate, position is that, whilst a thing is how it is, how it is known and how someone is informed about it may both differ. WYJ reads it like this, referring to *Zhuangzi* 13 and the discussion between Duke Huan and wheelwright Pian.

---

30. Most commentators read 霍 as 鶴.
31. ACG points out that from here on 知 tends to be replaced by 智. There is no basis on which to suppose a different meaning.
32. Emended from 吉 by WYZ and generally accepted.

B8   **C:** What is false is certainly erroneous (contradictory). The explanation lies in not being so.

E: False: False is necessarily wrong and only then is false. "Dog" is falsely taken as being "crane"; like a family name is "crane".

B9   **C:** With respect to a thing, there is how it is so, how it is known, and how to cause another to know it. These are not necessarily the same. The explanation lies in illness.

E: A thing: Someone wounding him is how it is so. Seeing it is knowing [it]. Informing them is causing [others] to know.

B10   C: 疑，說在逢，循，遇，過。

E: 疑：逢[33]為務則士，為牛廬者夏寒，逢也。舉之則輕，廢之則重，若石羽[34]，非有力也。柿[35]從削，非巧也，循[36]也。鬥者之敝也，以飲酒，若[37]以日中[38]，是不可智也，愚[39]也。智與[40]？以已為然也與？過[41]也。

Comment: This C&E on "doubt" is itself mired in doubt and obscurity, with a wide range of interpretations and puzzlement over the examples in the E. It is agreed that the subject is "doubt" or "difficulty" — 疑 in the sense of 懷疑 (JBC) or 疑難 (LSL), and that three of the four instances listed are to do with the present and the other one with the past (SYR). The problems are with the examples in the E. WFB provides a detailed and interesting analysis of the four aspects of "doubt", relating them respectively to 兩歧, 逃難, 例外 and 巧合 — see his pp. 121–124.

B11   C: 介與 ‥，或復否。說在拒[42]。

E: None

Comment: Despite its apparent simplicity, this C has given rise to quite different interpretations. There are four issues: (i) What it is that 介 refers to. (ii) How 復 should be read — possibly as 複 (see ACG, note 309, p. 362). (iii) Whether 或 should be repeated — again see ACG. (iv) Whether 拒 should be

33. Emended from 逢 by BY.
34. On the repositioning of these three characters see ACG note 305, p. 360. In the DZ they follow 非巧也.
35. Following ZHY and SYR, emended from 沛. The *Shuo Wen* definition of 柿 is: "削木札樸也。"
36. Variously written 循 (in accord with the C), 遁 (WFB), or 楯, the last being what is in the DZ.
37. Following TJF, 若 here is read as 或.
38. The emendation of 日 (in the DZ) to 日 is generally accepted (see WYJ, note 61, p. 556). 日中 is read by SYR as 巿 based on passages in the *Yi Jing* and *Zhou Li*. This is also generally accepted.
39. Most commentators emend 愚 to 遇 on the basis of conformity with the C. WFB reads this as 偶 in the sense of 偶然 — "accidental" or "fortuitous".
40. In both instances here 與 is taken to be an interrogative particle.
41. SYR's emendation from 愚 is generally accepted.
42. This character is either emended to 矩 following SYR, as accepted by many commentators (e.g. WFB, JBC), or retained in its original form as "resistance" which LSL here equates with 抵觸 in the sense of "conflict" or "contradiction".

B10 **C:** Where there is doubt the explanation lies in "coming upon"
(逢), "following" (循), "meeting with" (遇), and "being past"
(過).

E: Doubt: If one comes upon someone engaged in affairs, then
one takes him to be an officer. If one comes upon an ox in a
shelter, then one takes the summer to be cold. This is "coming
upon". If one raises it, then it is light, if one casts it away, then
it is heavy — like stone and feathers. It is not that there is
strength. A wooden writing strip follows paring. This is not
skill. This is "following". Whether the concealment of
contention is through the drinking of wine or the conduct
of business cannot be known. This is "meeting with". Is it
known? Is it through already being so? This is "being past".

B11 **C:** Combining joins ones; there is either doubling or there is not.
The explanation lies in the opposition.

E: None

retained (see, for example, WYJ, LSL), or emended to 矩 (SYR, WFB, JBC), or emended to 摳 (ACG). Clearly the reading of the C is going to depend on how these issues are resolved. Thus, some make it about "forces" (力), for example TJF and MZQY, and some about geometry, for example WFB, JBC. ACG, however, understands it as being about words, by way of a major modification of the C and the addition of an E, constructed in part from the E to B43. LSL, who groups it under Logic, does not make any attempt to specify precisely what is combined and takes the final character as 'contradiction' or 'conflict'. See also WYJ, note 69, pp. 556–557 on this last view

B12   **C:** 歐[43] 物一體也。説在俱一，惟[44] 是。

      E: 俱[45]：俱一，若牛馬四足。惟是，當牛馬。數牛數馬則牛馬二。數牛馬，則牛馬一。若數指，指五而五一。

Comment: Although textual problems clearly exist, there is a uniformity in interpretation of this C&E which it is agreed is about the issue of classes and classification. The relation to the *Zhuangzi* 33, and particularly to the GSLZ 3 and 4, is apparent.

    ** There appears to be a dislocation in the DZ text for chapter 41 (經下) in the following C which ACG places after 宇久 (see his note 322, p. 368). This makes the arrangement of the next three C&Es somewhat problematical and there is notable variation amongst editors. What follows is GH's version (adopted by JBC) for B13–B16 with the range of variations being indicated in the Comment to each of these C&Es.

---

43. 歐 is read as 區 — see, for example, ACG, note 311, p. 362.
44. The reading of 惟 as 唯 following SYR is generally accepted.
45. Among those who preserve 歐 (as 區) in the C are those who would then emend 俱 here to 區 — see JBC, note 2, p. 223.

B12   **C:** Demarcated things are one unit. The explanation lies in both being one, and specifically this [one thing].

      E: Both: Both being one. For example [both] ox and horse have four feet. Being specifically this fits [both] ox and horse. If you count oxen and you count horses, then ox and horse are two. If you count ox-horse, then ox and horse are one. It is like counting fingers; the fingers are five yet the five are one.

B13　　C: 宇或徙。[46] 説在長宇久。

E: 長[47]：宇徙而有處宇。宇南北在旦[48] 有[49] 在莫[50]，宇徙久。

Comment: Any interpretation of this C&E must remain very tentative. The key issue is whether 宇久 is included in this C as above (see also, for example, GH, JBC, Z&Q, LSL, WFB, CHANT) or not (e.g. ACG, TJF). This, in turn, determines where the break is made in the E. Thus ACG, who does not include 宇久 in the C, limits the E to the first seven characters above. There are also issues regarding how several of the characters are read — notably 或 and 長 as well as 宇 and 久 themselves. There is also the validity or otherwise of the emendations indicated in notes 47–50. On the grounds that it is reasonable to maintain consistency with A39 and A40 as regards 久 and 宇 respectively, one interpretation of the present C&E, on which the translation is based, is that change of position takes place in space and has "length" (長), but also involves "length" of time, the connection being illustrated by the linking of north and south (space) with morning and evening (time). As alternative views, those of ACG and WFB may be mentioned.

B14　　C: 不堅白。説在 (無久與宇。)[51]

E: None

Comment: The critical issues of this C&E are to do with arrangement. Nine of twelve versions examined have the same initial three characters, the exceptions being WFB who has an initial 、, and TJF and ACG who include 宇久 from what is here the preceding C, the former omitting the 不 and the latter not. The majority of versions (eight of twelve) end the C with 説在. There is an even split as to whether an E is included, both TJF and ACG including material which is here placed in the preceding E. On the subject matter see the Comment to B15.

---

46. In this opening statement most editors accept SYR's reading of 或 as 域 or 邦, although ACG takes issue with this, translating 或 here and earlier as "in some direction" — see his note 319, p. 367. There is general acceptance of the emendation of 從 (in the DZ) to 徙 as above on the basis of the E.

47. There are three versions of the head character: (i) 長 which follows the original and is retained by GH and LSL. (ii) 宇 which is used by TJF. (iii) 長宇 which JBC has.

48. Emended from 旦 following WYZ and SYR.

49. Read as 又 following WYZ and SYR.

50. Generally read as 暮 ("evening").

51. The placement of these final four characters is contentious — see Comment. The arrangement above is to be found in GH, WYJ and JBC.

B13   **C:** Space involves movement in location. The explanation lies in length in terms of both extension and duration (space and time).

E: Length: There is movement in space and there is position (rest) — (this is) space. Space is north and south at morning and also at evening — (this is) space moving in time.

B14   **C:** Not hard and white. The explanation lies in (no duration and extension).

E: None

B15   C: 堅白。説在因[52]。

E: 無[53] 堅得白，必相盈也。

Comment: As indicated in the earlier note (**, p. 480), there is considerable uncertainty regarding this and the previous C&E. The arrangement above is that given by GH, which is itself essentially followed by WYJ and JBC. The two commentators who merge B15 and B16 (WFB, LSL) do so on the basis of a very similar interpretation, although WFB particularly stresses the textual uncertainty and makes more extensive modifications than the other commentators referred to. Whilst the original terse expression in both Cs and the absence of an E for B14 add to the difficulties, I follow GH in seeing these two C&Es as statements of the GSL and Later Mohist positions respectively, with the final six characters in B14 offering an explanation of why the GSL position is wrong whilst B15 as a whole supports the Later Mohist position. It is, as JBC observes, the distinction between 離堅白 (GSL) and 盈堅白 (Later Mohists), or, in more general terms, between the separate existence of the qualities (the idealist position) and their necessary dependence on the object (the materialist position).

B16   C: 在[54] 諸其所然未然者[55]。説在於是[56] (推之)[57]。

E: 在：堯善治，自今在諸古也。自古在之今，則堯不能治也。

Comment: The problems in the C are to do with the reading of 在, the use of 諸, the word order in the last part of the first sentence, and whether the final two characters are included. Despite these difficulties, there is broad agreement as to meaning. The C&E is about making inferences regarding what is not yet so, on the basis of what is already so. The E introduces the

---

52. Read as 因依 — see JBC, p. 229.
53. 無 is read as 撫 by a number of commentators — e.g. GH, JBC (see the latter's note 2, p. 229).
54. Most modern commentators accept ZHY's reading of 在 as 察 in the sense of 考察, although ACG translates it as "locate". WFB, who transposes this C&E to his B52, emends 在 to 推 in both C and E.
55. There is variation in the final three characters of this first statement, and their order. The above proposal, which reverses the order of 者然 as found in the DZ, is usually attributed to LQC, and is accepted by a number of modern commentators (e.g. GH, JBC, ACG).
56. I have accepted LSL's reading of 是 as referring to 其所然. WFB reads it as 實. See also ACG, note 329, p. 369.
57. I have accepted WYJ's placement of these two characters at the start of B57 rather than here — see ACG, note 495, p. 429.

B15   C: Hard white. The explanation lies in interdependence.

E: Touching hard, one obtains white; they necessarily mutually fill.

B16   C: "Placing" what is not yet so in relation to what is so. The explanation lies in its being what is so (in this).

E: "Placing": [To say that] Yao was skilled at ruling is to examine the past from the perspective of the present. If one examines the present from the perspective of the past, Yao would not be able to rule.

issue of perspective, in this case temporal. Seen from the standpoint of the present, Yao was a skilled ruler in his time, but would not (necessarily) be so at the present — different times, different circumstances.

** Although, of course, all commentators offer their analysis of the following eight C&Es on optics (here B17–B24), particular mention should be made of the detailed treatment given by several authors including Graham and Sivin (G&S) in English and Hong Zhenhuan (HZH), TJF and JBC in Chinese, with diagrammatic representations. Needless to say, there are points of disagreement, even between the co-authors of the first study, related to the usual textual and interpretative problems. These will be considered in the notes.

B17   C: 景[58] 不徙[59] 。說在改為 。

E: 景 ： 光至景亡 。若在盡古息 。[60]

Comment: The main issue with this C&E is whether it is a statement in agreement with apparently similar statements in the *Zhuangzi* 33 and the *Liezi* 4, or in opposition. This largely depends on which textual emendations are accepted and the readings of the controversial final two characters of the C and final five characters of the E. I incline to the view, more or less consistent through TJF, LDF, LSL, WFB and MZQY, that this is a clarification of the common sense position and a demystification of the apparent paradox.

B18   C: 景二 ，說在重 。

E: 景 ： 二光夾一光 ，一光者景也 。

Comment: Several proposals have been made to make this C&E say more than the trivial point that two shadows mean two light sources. ACG, and subsequently G&S, read 夾 as "flank" and take the point to be that the second light does not obliterate the shadow from the first light, as might be assumed from the previous C&E. Based on HZH's analysis, I consider this C&E to mean that when two light sources illuminate one object, there are two shadows not one, the darker representing the area which the object shadows from both light sources and the lighter the area which the object shadows from each light source individually.

---

58.   This is generally accepted as 影 both here and in the following C&Es.
59.   The emendation from 從 following WYZ is generally accepted.
60.   This final statement presents problems. G&S consider it misplaced here and relate it to B14 (ACG's B13). There are issues about what stays in place and what both 盡古 and 息 mean in this context. There is quite wide acceptance of SYR's reading of 盡古 as 終古 ("forever") and 息 in the sense of "remain".

B17   **C:** A shadow does not move. The explanation lies in change taking place.

   E: A shadow: When the light arrives the shadow disappears. If it stays, it remains indefinitely.

B18   **C:** When the shadow is two the explanation lies in doubleness.

   E: The shadow: Two lights double one light and the shadow produced by one light.

B19   **C:** 景到⁶¹，在午⁶² 有端與景長。説在端。

E: 景：光之人煦若射。⁶³ 下者之人也高，高⁶⁴ 者之人也下。足蔽下光，故成景於止⁶⁵；首蔽上光，故成景於下。在遠近有端與於光，故景庫⁶⁶ 内也。

Comment: There is agreement that the C is a description of the "pinhole camera", or camera obscura, with the formation of an inverted image. In the E, there are difficulties in the initial statement which are variously dealt with but not to the point where the basic meaning is changed. The reading of 高 in the second instance as 上 and the emendation of 止 to 上 are generally accepted. The issue of 庫 in the final clause is more of a problem — for a detailed discussion with a diagram see WYJ, note 98, pp. 561–562.

B20   **C:** 景迎日。説在轉。⁶⁷

E: 景：日之光反燭人，則景在日與人之間。

Comment: The text is essentially without controversy and the meaning seems clear. 轉 is translated as "reflection", but the meaning is unaffected if the more general use of 轉 or even 博 is understood. The assumption is that a plane mirror is being referred to here and this might raise the problem of the size of the mirrors available, as discussed by G&S and leading to HZH's alternative version. It would seem, however, that any reflective surface would suffice for the proposition.

61. There is general agreement that this is to be read as 倒.
62. Again there is general agreement in that, based particularly on the *Yi Li*, 午 is taken as referring to a point of intersection, e.g. between horizontal and vertical lines, and is equated with 交午 or 交叉.
63. There are several issues in this first statement, involving characters 2–4. The most common position (and the one I have taken) is to read 之 as verbal, to accept 人 as "man", and to emend 煦 to 照. Other proposals include emending 人 to 入 (ACG), retaining 煦 in the sense of "emanate" (SYR), and emending 煦 to 照 but reversing the order of 人 照 (WYJ).
64. There is general acceptance of the reading of 高 as 上 (ZHY).
65. There is general acceptance of the emendation of 止 to 上 here although, as WYJ points out (note 97, p. 561), all the ancient editions have 止.
66. There is uncertainty about this character and hence about the whole phrase. BY initially emended 庫 to 障 with radical 53 on grounds of meaning. In fact, there are at least six suggestions: 窟 (TJF, LSL), 障 (BY, WFB), 庚 (GH), 易 (MZQY), 庫 (WYJ), and a reading in the sense of 運 (G&S).
67. This version of the C contains two emendations from the DZ text: 冃 to 日 and 博 (or 博 or 博 in other early texts) to 轉 (CYX, SYR) — see, for example, WYJ, notes 99, 100, p. 562. The emendation to 轉 is widely, but not universally, accepted — see HZH and G&S.

B19   C: The image (shadow) being inverted depends on there being an aperture at the cross-over and the image (shadow) being distant. The explanation lies in the aperture.

      E: The image (shadow): The light reaches the person shining like an arrow. The lowest [light] that reaches the person is the highest [in the image] and the highest [light] that reaches the person is the lowest [in the image]. The feet conceal the lowest light and therefore become the image (shadow) at the top. The head conceals the highest light and therefore becomes the image (shadow) at the bottom. This is because either far or near there is an aperture and in it light, therefore the image (shadow) revolves within.

B20   C: The shadow "meets" the sun. The explanation lies in reflection.

      E: The shadow: When the sun's light returns to illuminate the person, then the shadow is situated between the sun and the person.

B21   **C:** 景之小大。説在杝[68] 正[69] 遠近。

     E: 景：木杝[70]，景短大；木正，景長小。大[71] 小於木，則景大於木，非獨小也。遠近⋯。

Comment: There are several problems with this C&E which make a confident interpretation impossible. The first is uncertainty about the character given above as 杝 or 柂 — whether it refers to the object illuminated (?gnomon) or is the converse of 正, i.e. 斜. The second problem concerns the conjunctions of 短/大 and 長/小, particularly the second member of each pair, 大 and 小. Do 大 and 小 mean "more clear" and "less clear" (SYR), "wider" and "narrower" (HZH), or simply "bigger" and "smaller" (G&S), or is WYJ correct in assuming that 短 and 小 are interchangeable as are 長 and 大? The third problem is the final part of the E, which is quite possibly mutilated as G&S suggest. I have accepted the interpretations of LSL and particularly JBC, the essential features of which are that 非獨小也 indicates the converse of the preceding example whilst the situation in respect to "near" and "far" is implied but left unstated (but see JBC's diagram p. 244). WYJ offers a plausible alternative interpretation if one accepts his basic assumptions noted above. It is, however, by no means certain that the gnomon is the subject here.

** The following three Canons come between what are B13 and B14 above — the dislocation previously referred to.

---

68. This character is variously emended although it is retained by BY. Proposals include 杝 (SYR, WYJ, G&S), 施 (WFB), 柂 (LSL) and 迤 (JBC). The first seems the most appropriate given its use in the E. However written, it is seen as either referring to the object (?gnomon — see Comment), or as 斜 in contrast to 正.

69. Written in the rare variant form.

70. For the variations in this character see WYJ, note 103, p. 563.

71. 大 is here emended to either 光 (SYR) or 火 (TJF), giving essentially the same meaning.

B21   **C:** A shadow's being small or large depends on whether (the object) is oblique or upright, far or near.

   E: A shadow: When the post is oblique the shadow is short and large (broad) whereas, when the post is upright, the shadow is long and small (narrow). When the light source is smaller than the post, then the shadow is larger than the post and vice versa (and not only in the case of small). With far and near ...

B22   **C:** 臨鑒而立，景到。多而若少。説在寡區。[72]

　　　　E: 臨：正鑒，景寡[73]。貌能[74]，白黑，遠近，杝正，異[75]於光。
　　　　鑒景當俱。就去亦當俱，俱用北[76]。鑒者之臭[77]，於鑒，無所
　　　　不鑒。景之臭無數，而必過正。故同處其體俱，然鑒分[78]。

Comment: Without question this is a very problematical C&E. There are at
least three distinct views as to what is being discussed here, which, of course,
influence which characters are emended and how, the interpretation of these
and other non-emended characters, and the punctuation. The three
standpoints are, in summary, as follows:

(i) The subject is two plane mirrors placed together at different angles (e.g.
     TJF, HZH).
(ii) The subject is perspective, specifically the appearances when someone
     stands on a horizontal plane reflecting surface (G&S).
(iii) The subject is reflection at curved surfaces (MZQY).

B23   **C:** 鑑位景二[79]，一小而易，一大而正。説在中之外內。

　　　　E: 鑒：中之內，鑒者近中，則所鑒大，景亦大。遠中，則所鑒
　　　　小，景亦小，而必正。起於中，緣正而長其直也。中之外，鑒
　　　　者近中，則所鑒大，景亦大。遠中，則所鑒小，景亦小，而必
　　　　易。合於〔中緣易〕[80] 而長其直也。

72. In the C there are three characters whose readings or emendations are generally agreed:
     鑒 or 鑑 as 鏡 ("mirror"), 景 as 影 ("image", "shadow") and 到 as 倒 ("inverted",
     "reversed").
73. There is variation in the reading of 寡. "Single" (JBC, LSL), "small" and "reduced"
     (G&S) have all been proposed. SYR advocates inserting 多 before 寡.
74. This emendation of 能 to 態 (ZHY) is generally accepted.
75. LSL reads 異 in the sense of "opposite to" (i.e. in spatial terms), which I have accepted.
76. Interpreted in the sense of 背 (LSL).
77. This character is a problem. I have followed TJF's reading of 臬 for 臭. Other
     suggestions include 夏 (GH), 異 (ZQH) and 貌 (in its simpler form — WYJ) — see also
     G&S p. 131.
78. There is uncertainty about the end of this E — specifically, whether 鑒分 belongs here
     (e.g. TJF, GH) or at the start of the next E (see WYJ, note 120, p. 565. The arrangement
     above follows TJF.
79. There is doubt about the first part of this C. The DZ has: "鑑位量". The version above
     is that given by WYJ — see his note 118, p. 565.
80. Early texts (e.g. DZ) do not have these three characters. It is generally agreed that one
     to three characters are missing here, on the grounds both of meaning and of parallelism
     with the corresponding sentence for the first case. G&S are prepared only to restore 中.
     Most commonly the restoration consists of 中緣正 (e.g. TJF, WYJ). The version above
     is that of WFB.

B22 **C:** When something is near a mirror and upright, the image (shadow) is reversed. There are many yet they are like few. The explanation lies in the small surface.

E: Near: In a plane mirror the image (shadow) is small. Form and appearance, brightness and darkness, far and near, oblique and upright, are opposite to the illuminated [object]. The mirror faces and the image (shadow) doubles. In coming towards and going away there is also facing and doubling, the doubling using the "back". With respect to the mirror, its post is in the mirror and there is nothing which is not mirror. The image's (shadow's) post is without number, and necessarily exceeds the upright. Therefore, in the same place its body is double; nevertheless, the mirror separates.

B23 **C:** In a concave mirror there are two images; one is small and changed (inverted) and one is large and upright. The explanation lies in whether [the object] is outside or inside the centre [of curvature].

E: A mirror: When the object is within the centre and approaches the centre, then what is mirrored becomes larger and the image also larger. When it moves away from the centre, then what is mirrored becomes smaller and the image also smaller, yet necessarily upright. Arising at the centre is the cause of being upright and extending its vertical [height]. When the object is outside the centre and approaches the centre, then what is mirrored becomes larger and the image also larger. When it moves away from the centre, then what is mirrored becomes smaller and the image also smaller, and necessarily changed (inverted). Converging at the centre is the cause of being changed and extending its vertical [height].

Comment: Although there is widespread acceptance that this C&E is about reflection from a concave surface, in the C this reading depends on several emendations or particular interpretations as follows: (i) 位, initially emended to 立 by BY (followed by WFB), is variously emended by other commentators; 低 (TJF, LSL), 弧 (GH), 洼/窪 (G&S), 正 (ZCY), 區 (ZQH). (ii) 景 here is emended from 量 following WYZ. (iii) ⸱ is transposed here from its uncertain position at the start of the preceding C following WYJ. (iv) 易 can be retained in the sense of "changed" (e.g. JBC), or the nature of the change assumed to be inversion (倒 — e.g. WYJ). (v) 正 is emended from the Mohist character as elsewhere. There are also problems with the first half of the E, that dealing with 中之內 (i.e. the object within the focal point/centre of curvature).

B24   **C:** 鑑團，景⸱⸱⸱[81] 小一大而必正[82]。說在得[83]。

        E: 鑑：鑑者近則所鑑大，景亦大。其[84]遠，所鑑小，景亦小，而必正。景過正，故招。[85]

Comment: Although there is widespread agreement that this C&E is about reflection at a convex surface, and this would be appropriate as the last of a series of three C&Es dealing with reflection at plane, concave and convex surfaces respectively, there are clearly textual problems, particularly in the C which appears to have suffered a dislocation in the DZ text. The re-arrangement follows LDF. The DZ text is "鑑團景⸱⸱⸱⸱天而必正說在得".

---

81. A number of commentators end the C here — see, for example, LSL. This is, in fact, a point of dislocation in the DZ text as identified by LDF.

82. Among editors who continue the C, this usually involves transposition of a fragment that follows in the DZ what is the C for B63 in WYJ giving a text: "天而必正說在得". The text used above is that of LDF. The essence of this version is the addition of 小 and the emendation of 天 to ⸱大, which is accepted, for example, by G&S.

83. I have taken this somewhat controversial final character in the sense of 適宜 or 得當 following JBC.

84. Emended from 亦 in the DZ text following WYZ — see WYJ, note 128, p. 568.

85. There is doubt about these final five characters. WYJ places them in the previous E thus making the present E a relatively straightforward statement about reflection at concave surfaces. Where they are retained here, which is the case in most texts, there is a problem with 招 and possibly with 正, depending on the interpretation of 招 which I have taken in the sense of 模糊 following the modern commentators JBC and LSL.

B24   **C:** In a convex mirror the image (shadow) is in one case smaller
and in one case larger yet necessarily upright. The explanation
lies in what is appropriate.

E: [Convex] mirror: When the object is near, then what is
mirrored is large and the image is also large. When it is distant,
then what is mirrored is small and the image is also small and
necessarily upright. When the image (shadow) goes beyond
what is normal it is caused to be indistinct.

B25　C: 貞[86] 而不撓[87]。說在勝。

　　E: 負：衡木，如[88] 重焉而不撓，極[89] 勝重也。右校[90] 交繩，無加焉而撓，極不勝重也。衡[91] 加重於其一旁，必捶[92]，權重相若也。相衡則本短標長。兩加焉，重相若，則標必下，標得權也。

Comment: There are issues here pertaining to the division into particular C&Es. With respect to the C, having accepted LDF's placement of the seven characters from 大 (emended) to 得 in B25, I have taken this C (and E) to be a single C&E about weights and bars. There is, however, an apparent break in the subject matter of the E which led LQC and others (e.g. ZQH, TJF, LSL) to make what is here B25 two separate C&Es, fashioning a C for the second out of the seven characters referred to above. In doing this, there remains a significant problem with a head character for the additional C&E (e.g. TJF's B25), which is usually given as 衡. ACG's solution (and his "textual note" on pp. 387–388 provides a very detailed discussion of the issue) is to divide B25 (his B25) into two parts — B25a and B25b. The arrangement I have given is essentially that given by WYJ, WFB, LDF, GH and JBC *inter alia*. It seems clear that this C&E (or two C&Es) is about the principles of the lever, horizontal beam or steelyard in terms of moments of force, although, of course, not articulated in these terms. A precise and assuredly accurate translation is not, however, possible given the textual difficulties, both the arrangement as a whole and the emendation of several critical characters, as discussed in the notes.

86. The emendation of 貞 to 負 to bring it into accord with the E, following SYR, is widely but not universally accepted — see, for example, LDF and WYJ (note 130, p. 568).
87. Read as 橈 in the sense of 傾倒 (LSL) by most modern editors, both here and in the E.
88. Almost all modern editors follow BY's emendation of 如 to 加, although WYJ retains 如 — see his note 132, p. 568.
89. Most follow SYR in taking 極 to refer to the beam — e.g. WYJ and JBC. ACG regards it as referring to "limit", TJF and others to the beam's centre (of gravity) and MZQY to the weight placed at the end of the beam. Perhaps, however, WFB's emendation to 權 is the most satisfactory, hence my use of it in the translation.
90. As with 極, there are several quite different readings of 校. WFB emends both to 權 and this I have followed.
91. 衡 becomes the head character of the E for those who divide this C&E (e.g. TJF, LSL) which brings into focus the problem of the head character from the corresponding C. In the combined E as above, it appears to have the same role as 衡木 in the initial sentence. WYJ reads it as equivalent here to 平衡狀態 (poised or equilibrium state).
92. There is general acceptance of ZHY's reading of this as 偏下. Emendation to 垂 (e.g. JBC) seems appropriate therefore.

B25   **C:** Bearing and not inclining. The explanation lies in "being equal to".

E: Bearing: In the case of a horizontal piece of wood, if a weight is added to it and it does not incline, the counterweight "is equal to" the weight. If the point of suspension of the counterweight is moved to the right and, without adding to it, it does incline, the counterweight "is not equal to" the weight. When horizontal, if a weight is added to one of its sides, it necessarily inclines downward, the counterweight and the weight corresponding (i.e. prior to the addition). When both are horizontal, then the "root" is short and the "branch" is long. When the two are added to with equivalent weights, then the "branch" necessarily falls, the "branch" acquiring the "force".

B26   **C:** 挈與枝板。⁹³ 説在薄⁹⁴。

    E: 〔挈〕⁹⁵：挈有力也，引無力也。不心⁹⁶ 所挈之止於施也。繩制挈之也，若以錐刺之。挈，長重者下，短輕者上。上者愈得，下⁹⁷ 下者愈亡。繩直權重相若，則正⁹⁸ 矣。收，上者愈喪⁹⁹，下者愈得。上者權重盡，則遂挈。¹⁰⁰

Comment: This is another extremely problematical C&E and has been interpreted in a number of quite different ways. In view of the difficulties, it is hardly surprising that a number of disparate interpretations have been advanced and that it is not possible to embrace any one with confidence. Is the C&E, then, entirely about pulleys (e.g. JBC), or entirely about levers (WYJ), or are a number of different situations being considered (e.g. TJF, GH)? I tend towards the last position, but, given the problems, the matter must, I think, remain *sub judice*.

---

93. Most commentators, particularly following ZHY, emend the first, third and fourth of these initial four characters to give "挈與收反" (see, for example, WYJ, note 141, p. 570) which is what has been translated.
94. This is generally read in the sense of 迫 (e.g. JBC, LSL). Some, however, read it as 權 (SYR, MZQY), or actually emend it to 權 (WFB), whilst ACG retains 薄 in the sense of "curtain".
95. Most texts are without a head character. WFB supplies 挈 as here.
96. 心 was first emended to 止 by BY, who incorporated it into the previous sentence as does WYJ. Most commonly it is emended to 必 (e.g. TJF, WFB, Z&Q, LSL, JBC) which is what is accepted in the translation, or to 止 (ACG).
97. The duplication of 下 is found in the DZ but not in the 吳 manuscript. The excision of one 下 following ZHY is generally accepted — see WYJ, note 148, p. 570.
98. There is general acceptance of this emendation of 心 following BY.
99. 喪 is read as the equivalent of 亡 in the previous example.
100. This final sentence is quite problematical — see, for example, WYJ, note 151, p. 571. WFB's version reads: "上得權，重盡則墜" and is followed in the translation.

B26 **C:** Lifting and lowering (receiving) are in opposition. The explanation lies in compelling (force).

E: Lifting: Lifting up, there is force; drawing down, there is no force. It is not necessary that what raises it stops in action (is direct or oblique). The rope restrains raising it, like by an awl piercing it. In lifting, what is long and heavy descends, what is short and light ascends. What ascends increasingly gains, what descends increasingly loses. If the rope is straight and the counterweight and weight are alike, then it is in balance. In lowering, what ascends increasingly loses, what descends increasingly gains. Ascending involves the counterweight, the weight then completely falling.

B27   C: 倚者不可正。說在梯[101]。

E: 〔倚〕[102]：兩輪高，兩輪為輲，車梯也。重其前，弦其前，載弦其前，載弦其軸，而縣重於其前。是梯[103]，挈且挈則行。凡重，上弗挈，下弗收，旁弗劫，則下直。地或害之也，流[104]。梯者不得流，直也。今也廢石[105]於平地，重不下，無旁[106]也。若夫繩之引軸也，是猶自舟中引橫也。倚倍拒堅，邪[107]倚焉則不正。[108]

Comment: Clearly this is, again, a very difficult C&E. The text is replete with unusual and contentious characters and issues of placement are also significant. I have omitted detailed notes from this version. What follow are some summarising remarks. On the subject matter, there does seem to be agreement that it is about a mobile ladder which can be raised by weights and ropes/pulleys, whether for military use or otherwise. There is, however, considerable variation in how this structure is envisaged, leading to several quite different diagrams — for the simple, see e.g. GH and JBC and for the complex, see JN and ACG. As to what constitutes the C&E, there are broadly three positions. The first is as above, although with variable placement of what are here the last 10 characters. The second is to create a separate C&E about the ladder, of which the C is essentially lost, and with the 10 characters mentioned above omitted from the E (TJF, ACG). The third is to make the discussion of the ladder a part of the preceding C&E (here B26), a position taken by GH. Within whatever is taken as the text of the C&E there is an inordinate number of rare, unknown or otherwise controversial characters which are quite variously emended or interpreted so, in conclusion, one is left with a C&E of uncertain constitution which is probably about a mobile ladder of uncertain construction.

101. Emended from 刜 to (車) 梯 by SYR based on meaning and on the E.
102. There is no head character in the DZ.
103. This is BY's widely accepted emendation of the unknown graph (弟 with the 上 radical) which appears here and subsequently.
104. In the DZ 流 appears here and subsequently in a variant form (ZWDCD #17554 — see ACG, note 378, p. 393).
105. There is general acceptance of this emendation of 尺 (which appears in the DZ) following SYR.
106. See WYJ, note 167, p. 572 on the rare character (旁 with the 足 radical — ZWDCD #38592) which appears here in the DZ. He has: "依徬之徬". See also ACG, note 382, p. 393.
107. This is SYR's widely accepted emendation of the rare character (ZWDCD #38928) which appears here.
108. See WYJ, note 171, p. 573 on what is the final sentence here.

B27   **C:** What is leaning cannot be straight. The explanation is given by a ladder.

E: Leaning: Two wheels being high and two wheels being small and without spokes are [the features of] a mobile ladder. There is a weight at its front and a drawing cord at its front. You carry the drawing cord at its front, you carry the drawing cord on its wheel and suspend the weight at its front. In the case of this ladder, you lift and, moreover, when you lift, it then goes. In general, with a weight, if from above it is not lifted up, if from below it is not received, if it does not have a lateral force applied, then it goes downwards vertically. If it is slanting or something "harms" it, it is unstable. The ladder itself does not have instability — it is upright. In the present case, when the weight is placed on level ground, the weight is necessarily down, not to the side. The situation where the rope draws down on the wheel is like that where there is a horizontal drawing on a boat's centre. Leaning against, resisting, firm, ladder; if it is leaning against something, it is not upright.

B28   C: 推之必往。[109] 說在廢材[110]。

E: 堆：並石，絫石耳。夾寢者，法也。[111] 〔今也廢石於平地，〕[112] 方石去地尺，關[113] 石於其下，縣[114] 絲於其上，使適至方石，不下，柱也。膠[115] 絲[116] 去石，挈也。絲絕，引也。未變而石[117] 易，收也。

Comment: Although there are several emendations, not all identical, there is broad but not universal agreement on the meaning of the C, taking 廢 in the sense of 放置 as in B27. To erect any structure, or a pillar specifically, there must be a base or foundation (but note WYJ's version). The E is very problematical. The first sentence in particular is beset by problems as indicated in the notes, so only a very tentative version can be offered. The translation given depends particularly on TJF and ACG. There is then the problem of the seven characters referred to in note 112, which TJF alone places here. Because this placement does seem apposite, and because so much is uncertain about the previous C&E, I have included them here in parentheses. Regardless of whether this sentence is included or not, there are

109. There are two issues in this initial statement. The first is whether to accept ZCY's proposed emendation of 推 to 堆 as many commentators do (e.g. GH, TJF, ACG, LSL, JBC) or to retain 推 (see, for example, WYJ, note 179, p. 574). The second is whether to retain 往 or to emend it to 柱 (see ACG, note 388, p. 395). The version translated is: "堆之必柱". WFB has a slightly different version: "柱之必往".

110. Whilst most commentators interpret 材 in the sense of 材料, WFB emends it to 石, whereas TJF takes it to refer specifically to the stone base (石材) of a pillar, a view with which ACG concurs (see his note 389, p. 395).

111. There are many variations involving these initial 11 characters, in their placement, in their punctuation, and to a lesser degree in the characters themselves. Most editors do place them here, although WYJ has them as the final part of the preceding E. The important issues in the characters themselves are the emendation of 誰 to 堆 to conform with the C and the reading of the rare character 幷 with the 立 radical (ZWDCD #26338) as 並 in the sense indicated by ACG (see his note 390, p. 396).

112. This sentence, placed here by TJF, is included in parentheses, although it is used in the E for B27 — see Comment.

113. Variously emended to 罡 (GH, ACG), 貫 (TJF, MZQY, WYJ, LSL), or 管 (WFB). I have accepted the second, and majority, view.

114. Read as 懸 — see, for example, LSL.

115. I have retained 膠 in the sense of "attach". GH, followed by ACG, reads it as 繆 in the sense of "to tie".

116. Equated with 繩 from ZHY on.

117. There is general acceptance of 石 as the emendation of 名, although ACG retains the latter.

B28   **C:** In piling up, there must be a support. The explanation lies in placing material (a stone base).

      E: Piling up: Placing stones together [horizontally] and adding stones [vertically] is the method used for the side room and the central room. [In the present case place a stone on level ground.] A square (reference) stone is placed 1 *chi* away from the ground, a connecting stone is placed at its lower surface, and a suspending cord at its upper surface and is caused to reach to the square (reference) stone so it does not fall down, and there is a column. If the cord remains attached but the (supporting) stone is removed, this is lifting. If the cord is cut, this is drawing down. If there is no change (in the cord) yet the stone changes, this is "receiving".

apparently three things referred to: the square (reference) stone, the "connecting" (supporting) stone, and the suspending cord. There is uncertainty also in the final three sentences, although these are clearly intended to exemplify the three terms used earlier, i.e. 挈, 引 and 收. What is uncertain is quite how they do so. In any analysis the final sentence is a problem. The interpretation I have given, which is in line with the most recent commentators (MZQY, JBC, LSL), takes 變 and 易 both to mean "change", the former in respect to the cord, the latter in respect to the stone, and accepts the emendation of 名 to 石.

B29   C: 買無貴。說在反其賈[118]。

   E: 買：刀糴[119] 相為賈。刀輕則糴不貴，刀重則糴不易[120]。王刀[121] 無變，糴有變。歲變糴，則歲變刀。若鬻子。[122]

Comment: There are no significant textual issues in this C&E. The meaning is well brought out by WFB's version and discussion (pp. 139–141). In essence, goods have no intrinsic value so price is determined by the reciprocity of buying and selling. The most straightforward reading of the E is as an exemplification of the reciprocal relationship in terms of money and grain. This interpretation depends on equating 重 with 貴 and 輕 with 易 in the sense of 賤, which the majority of modern commentators do (e.g. WYJ and JBC). The particular point of the last two sentences is that even if money minted under royal regulations is intended to have a fixed value, it still cannot take into account the vagaries of grain production. In other words, both sides of the equation are ultimately subject to variation due to factors beyond human control.

---

118. The two points in the C are that 反 is given in the rare form with the "man" radical (i.e. ZWDCD #433 — on this see ACG, note 395), and that 賈 is understood as 價.

119. There is widespread acceptance of 刀 as money, following BY's equating it with 泉刀, and 糴 as grain.

120. There is some variation in the reading of 易. The most obvious interpretation is to take it as the converse of 貴 and this is what a number of commentators do (e.g. WYJ, LSL).

121. There is general acceptance of ZHY's reading of this as "royal coinage" — "王者所鑄、故曰王刀。"

122. There is broad acceptance of this statement here as indicating a bad year. ACG, however, regards it as part of the final sentence of the E of B30.

B29   C: Price does not equate with value. The explanation lies in the
reciprocal nature of price (trading).

E: Price: Money and grain are mutually related in terms of price.
If money is low (in value), then grain is not expensive,
whereas, if money is high (in value), then grain is not cheap.
The royal coinage does not change but grain does change, and,
if the year changes grain, then the year changes money. It is
like selling sons.

B30   C: 賈宜則讎[123] 。説在盡。

       E: 賈：盡也者，盡去其〔所〕[124] 以不讎也。其所以不讎去，則讎正賈也。宜不宜，正欲不欲。若敗邦鬻室嫁子。

Comment: The version of this C&E here given depends on reading 賈 as 價, emending 讎 to 售 and taking 盡 according to the clarification in the E. All these are broadly accepted. Although there is some doubt about punctuation in the E (see ACG), and what should be included in the final sentence, the meaning seems clear.

B31   C: 無説而懼。説在弗心[125] 。

       E: 無：子在軍，不必其死生。聞戰，亦不必其〔死〕[126] 生。前也不懼，今也懼。

Comment: The only textual issue in the C concerns 心 as the final character. SYR's proposed emendation seems appropriate and is generally accepted. There is some variation in interpretation of the E, but again this is not of great significance. 前 and 今 are most commonly taken to refer respectively to the two situations of simply being in the army, and of being in the army and engaged in a battle.

B32   C: 或[127] ，過名也。説在實。

       E: 或[128] ：知是之非此也，有[129] 知是之不在此也，然而謂此南北，過而以已為然。始也謂此南方，故今也謂此南方。

---

123. Since BY, there has been wide acceptance that 讎 should be read as 售 — see, for example, WYJ, note 198, p. 576. A similar reading is noted in the *Han Shu* (vol. 1, p. 2 — see note 9, p. 3).
124. Added on the grounds of parallelism following SYR.
125. There is wide acceptance of SYR's proposed emendation of 心 to 必.
126. Most modern commentators accept SYR's insertion of 死 here in line with the previous sentence.
127. From SYR on, there has been wide acceptance of 域 here and in the E for 或. In ACG's view this position is "untenable" and he reads 或 as "in one case ... in the other case" — see his p. 401. Neither GH nor WYJ make the proposed emendation. The problem of 或 also occurs elsewhere (e.g. Xiaoqu 2).
128. Again many editors accept SYR's reading of 或 as 域.
129. ZHY's reading of 有 as 又 is generally accepted.

B30   **C:** If the price is appropriate, then sell. The explanation lies in "completeness".

        E: Price: "Completeness" is to completely do away with whatever makes it not sell. If what makes it not sell is done away with, then it sells, "correcting" the price. Whether it is appropriate or not appropriate "corrects" whether (the item) is desired or not desired. It is like a defeated country where houses are sold and offspring given in marriage.

B31   **C:** If there is no explanation, there is fear. The explanation lies in not being certain.

        E: Not: If one's son is in the army, one is not certain whether he is dead or alive. If one hears of a battle, one is also not certain whether he is dead or alive. In the former case, there is no fear; in the latter case, there is fear.

B32   **C:** *Huo* (Something, someone) is a "passing" name. The explanation lies in the entity.

        E: *Huo* (Something, someone): One knows "this" is not "this" and also knows "this" is not at "this". Nevertheless, one calls "this" south or north, having passed through and taken it already to be so. At first, one called "this" the south so, at present, one calls this the south.

Comment: Whether the head character is taken as 或 or as 域, as many Chinese commentators do following SYR, this C&E is about naming. This is well brought out by WFB in relationship to GSLZ I (Mingshi Lun) and also to Hui Shi's Paradox 7. Thus two situations are defined. In the first, the name applies to a specific entity and is fixed e.g. "horse", "ox", whereas, in the second, the name is variously applied or is relative, the examples being the demonstrative pronouns 此 and 彼, and the directions north, south, east and west. For a discussion of the interpretation if 或 is retained see ACG, p. 401.

B33   C: 知知之否之足用也諄[130]。説在無以也。

   E: 智：論之，非智，無以也。

Comment: As indicated in note 130, this is a rather contentious C. Four modified versions are briefly listed below to indicate attempts to make the statement more intelligible.
   (i) LCR: "知之否之，足用也、諄。" This accepts SYR's omission of the initial 知 as displaced from B72 and also ZHY's emendation of 諄 — see his pp. 45–46.
   (ii) WYJ: "知知之不足用也、諄。" — see his note 210, p. 577.
   (iii) TJF: "知 — ‘知之’‘否’ — 之足用也諄。" — see his pp. 278–279.
   (iv) WFB: "知之否之足同也、諄。" — see his pp. 144–145.
   The translation is based on the original text apart from ZHY's emendation and is similar in meaning to that given by ACG. Despite the variety of interpretations by other commentators, most do, however, see it as a response to Confucius' views expressed in *Lunyu* II.17, and amplified in *Xunzi* 29.6 (see K, vol. 3, p. 254).

B34   C: 謂辯無勝，必不當。説在辯。

   E: 謂：所謂，非同也，則異也。同則或謂"之狗"，其或謂"之犬"也。異則或謂"之牛"，牛[131] 或謂"之馬"也。俱無勝。〔俱無勝〕[132]，是不辯也。辯也者，或謂"之是"，或謂"之非"。當者勝也。

---

130. This initial statement is somewhat problematical. The version given is what appears in the DZ and is found also in this form in JBC for example. Other options are listed in the Comment. One constant, however, is the acceptance of ZHY's emendation of 諄 to 諄.

131. I have accepted the emendation of the second 牛 proposed by both WFB and ACG on grounds of parallelism. Where 牛 is retained (as in most texts), the comma may be placed after the first 牛 (e.g. GH) or after the second 牛 (e.g. WYJ).

132. The duplication of the three preceding characters follows WFB and is included in the translation.

B33   **C:** With respect to knowing, it is fallacious (perverse) [to take] knowing something and not knowing something to be sufficient for use. The explanation lies in there not being the means.

        E: When there is knowledge, one can discuss it; when there is not knowledge, there is no means (to do so).

B34   **C:** Calling is disputation without the overcoming and certainly is not about correctness. The explanation lies in disputation.

        E: Calling: If what is called [something] is not the same, then it is different. The case of being the same, then, is one saying, "this is a dog" and the other saying, "this is a pup". The case of being different, then, is one saying, "this is an ox" and the other saying, "this is a horse". Both do not overcome. Where both do not overcome, this is not disputation. Disputation is where one says, "this is this" and the other says, "this is not [this]". The one who is correct, overcomes.

Comment: This C&E remains somewhat problematical despite there being widespread agreement on the text. The principal issue is whether it is primarily about 謂, as most modern Chinese commentators assume, or 辯, as translators have generally taken it (e.g. HM, ACG, JC). Thus, JC translates the C as: "It is said: if there is no victory in discrimination, (the discrimination itself) must be invalid." This reading ignores the role of 謂 as the head character in the E. The point, in fact, appears to be to make a contrast between 謂 and 辯. If two people say something about an entity, whether it be the same or different, if there is not the establishment of validity of one position (i.e. overcoming), it is not disputation. The reading above is facilitated by, although not dependent upon, TJF's addition of the negative in the C (he has: "説在不辯" and is followed in this by LSL). There is general agreement that the C&E, regardless of the precise interpretation, is directed at *Zhuangzi* 2 (GQF, vol. 1, p. 107) — or vice versa.

B35   **C:** 無不讓也不可。説在始[133]。

E: 無：讓者酒木[134]讓；始也，不可讓也。[135] 〔若殆於城門與於臧也。〕[136]

Comment: There are substantial problems in the text and interpretation of this C&E involving particularly the following five issues, the first in the C and the remainder in the E:

(i) Assuming 始 is emended to 殆, should the latter be read as "danger" (危殆), or "near to" (either physically or in personal terms — see JBC, note 1, p. 296)?

(ii) Should 木 be emended to 之 following WFB?

(iii) Are the examples in the E contrasting or complementary?

(iv) Should the final nine characters be placed here or elsewhere (see note 136)?

(v) How should 臧 be read?

I have taken 殆 as "near to", 臧 as a person (slave), the emendation of 木, and the placement of the contentious nine characters here, making the examples

133. There is widespread acceptance of SYR's emendation of 始 to 殆, although ACG, for example, retains the former. There is, however, variation in the understanding of 殆, some taking it as "near" (e.g. SYR, LSL) and others as "danger" (e.g. WFB, JBC).

134. WFB emends 木 to 之.

135. The quite variable punctuation of this initial sentence reflects the problems of interpretation. The reading of 殆 for 始 (see note 133) here is critical.

136. There is a problem with placement of these nine characters and, within them, regarding the interpretation of 殆 (near or danger) and of 臧 (slave or funeral). The placement here is due to SYR and is followed by others (e.g. TJF, JBC and LSL). Some (e.g. WFB, ACG) place them at the end of what is here B52. WYJ also includes them in B52, but suggests a possible placement as the otherwise missing E of B75.

B35   C: Not not (always) yielding is not permissible. The explanation
lies in proximity.

E: Not: In respect to yielding, there is that in relation to wine;
where there is proximity, it is not permissible to yield. [It is like
being near to the city gate or to *Zang*.]

in the E contrasting. WFB, who reads 殆 as "danger", refers to the views of Song Xing and Yin Wen as recorded in *Zhuangzi* 33 (GQF, vol. 4, p. 1082). Other commentators take this C&E as a statement in opposition to the Confucian position, referring to such texts as *Lun Yu* IV.13, *Mencius* IIA.6(5), and *Zuo Zhuan* Xiang 13, as well as to *Xunzi* 4.1 which has: "巨涂則讓、小途則殆。" (K, vol. 1, p. 186) translates this as: "When the roadway is broad, people yield the way; when the roadway is narrow, they are crowded together."

B36   C: 於一，有知焉，有不知焉。説在存。

   E: 於：石一也，堅白二也，而在石。故有智[137]焉，有不智焉，可。[138]

Comment: Whilst I have followed the majority in the text above (it is the DZ text without emendations), it must be said that TJF's rearrangement is attractive in terms of meaning and the development of the argument. Whichever arrangement is followed, it is clear that this and the following C&E must be seen in relation to Gongsun Long's argument about the "hard white stone" (GSLZ 3). Indeed, the second sentence of the E, apart from the final 可, is identical, possibly even a direct quote, from that essay, although ACG's views on this issue (i.e. that the GSL essay is a later forgery, and the implications of this in relation to the present C&E) must be taken into account.

137. 智 here and in the following instance is read as 知 as is often the case in this text.
138. TJF includes an additional 57 characters which comprise the first 25 (apart from the 2 head characters) and the last 32 (with transposition of 謂 and 而) of the E, given here in B37 following.

B36   C: In one [thing] there is the known in it and there is the not
known in it. The explanation lies in existing.

E: In: A stone is one [thing]; hard and white are two [things] and
are in the stone. Therefore "there is the known in it and there is
the not known in it" is permissible.

B37 C: 有指於二而不可逃。說在以二絫[139]。

E: 有指：子智是，有智是吾所先舉，〔是〕重。[140] 則子智是，而
不智吾所先舉也，是 ⠄。謂有智焉，有不智焉也。若智之，則
當指之。智告我，則我智之。兼[141] 指之，以二也。衡指之，
參直之也。若曰，"必獨指吾所舉，毋舉[142] 吾所不舉。"則
〔指〕[143] 者固不能獨指，所欲相不傳，意若未校。[144] 且其所智
是也，所不智是也，則是智是之不智也，惡得為一而謂[145]，
"有智焉，有不智焉？"

Comment: It must be said that this C&E remains quite problematical. The
difficulties particularly relate to ⠄ and 絫 (and to a lesser extent to 指) in the
C, and to the extent to which the E is a single statement amplifying the point
made in the C, or a presentation of opposing views as interpreted by ACG.
There is also the issue of how, specifically, this C&E is linked to GSL's
"Discussion of Hard and White". Also, in the E, there are the issues of whether
先 should be emended to 無 in the first sentence following SYR, and what
precisely 兼, 衡 and 獨 mean preceding 指. The argument, then, is that the
qualities "hard" and "white" cannot be separated from each other nor from the

---

139. Although this character is retained by BY in the sense of 增 (as in the *Shuo Wen*
definition), ZHY's emendation to 參 is generally accepted, although there is variation
in interpretation.

140. There are several issues in this first sentence as follows: (i) WFB makes 有 alone the
head character. (ii) 智 is generally accepted as 知, i.e. verbal. (iii) 有 is read as 又
following ZHY. (iv) 先 is retained (note ACG's reading of this as a technical term —
"a priori" — here and elsewhere — see his pp. 188–189), rather than emended to 無 (in
alternative form) following SYR — see LSL, note 4, p. 330. (v) GH's inclusion of 則
is not followed. (vi) 是 is added as the penultimate character following WFB. (vii) There
is placement here rather than in B36 following TJF — see Comment to B36.

141. There are the same issues with 兼 as with ⠄ in the C (see Comment). I have taken the
three combinations 兼指, 衡指 and 獨指 as quasi-technical terms: "combined *zhi*
(representation/pointing out)", "crosswise *zhi* (representation/pointing out)" and
"individual *zhi* (representation/pointing out)" respectively. The last then refers to a
single quality, the first to two qualities combined (e.g. hard and white) and "crosswise
zhi (representation/pointing out)" to the two qualities linked to the stone.

142. In these two characters, I have followed WFB who accepts LQC's emendation of 舉 to
指.

143. Some commentators have suggested the addition of one character here — either ⠄
(ZHY) or 指 (SYR). Along with WFB and LSL, I have accepted the latter.

144. The version given of this sentence depends on acceptance of SYR's emendation of 相
to 指 and the reading of 校 as 較 in the sense of 清楚 (JBC).

145. The reversal of 謂 and 而 follows WFB.

B37   **C:** There is *zhi* (representation, pointing out) through two and they cannot be separated. The explanation lies in taking the two and the three.

   E: There is *zhi* (representation, pointing out): If you know this and also know this which I previously raised, this is double. Then, if you know this, but do not know that which I previously raised, this is one. This is to say there is the known in it and there is the not known in it is admissible. If you know it, then it is valid to *zhi* it (represent it, point it out). If knowledge informs me, then I know it. A combined *zhi* (representation, pointing out) is through two. A "crosswise" *zhi* (representation, pointing out) is when three are met with. It is like saying what I raise is necessarily individually *zhi* (represented, pointed out) and what I do not raise is not *zhi* (represented, pointed out), so the *zhi* (representation, pointing out) is certainly not able to be individually *zhi* (represented, pointed out), and what you wish to *zhi* (represent, point out) is not put forward, so the concept is still not clear. Moreover, if what is known is this and what is not known is this, then this is known and this is not known, so how can you make it one and say: "There is the known in it, there is the not known in it?"

stone, but all are "represented" i.e. capable of independent or individual identification as qualities or entities that can be perceived separately, but are inextricably linked.

B38   C: 所知而弗能指。説在春[146]也，逃臣，狗犬，貴[147]者。

E: 所：春也，其執[148]固不可指也。逃臣，不智其處。狗犬，不智其名也。遺者，巧弗能兩也。[149]

Comment: This C&E clearly continues the discussion of 指 and its relationship to 知. Assuming, as earlier, a usage of 指 similar to that in GSL's "Zhiwu Lun", the point would seem to be that, contrary to the comprehensive nature of 指 proposed by GSL, the Later Mohists wish to claim that some "things" cannot be represented/pointed out, or are not representations/pointings out. The examples, already somewhat obscure and variable in the C, are rather more so in the E, not least due to textual uncertainty.

B39   C: 知狗而自謂不知犬，過也。説在重。

E: 智：智狗，重，智犬，則過；不重，則不過。

Comment: The C appears to be clear and without textual uncertainty. However 狗 and 犬 are rendered into English (dog/hound, whelp/dog, pup/dog, dog/dog) the point is that both are names for the one entity, i.e. "二名一實", or a "duplicated name", so to claim to know one and not know the other is a mistake. The difficulty arises with the E and has led to different emended versions and interpretations. The text given above is that of the DZ with LCR's added punctuation and what I take to be his interpretation — see his p. 55. GH also has this structure. Some commentators add 不 as the fourth character

---

146. 春 has occasioned some difficulty, with various emendations and interpretations being put forward as follows: (i) The name of a person (TJF, JBC). (ii) Emended to an old form of 冬 (ZWDCD #14088 — GH) or retained as 春 (ACG) and combined with 也 read as 蛇 to mean "winter snakes" or "spring snakes". (iii) Emended to 推 based on the *Shuo Wen* (WFB). I have left it as 春 and relied on the E for clarification — see, for example, LSL.

147. There is general acceptance of ZHY's emendation of 貴 to 遺.

148. There is widespread acceptance of ZHY's emendation of 執 to 勢.

149. This sentence remains problematical, particularly as to whether 網 or 网 is given as the penultimate character. Use of 网 stems primarily from SYR who provides an extensive note referring to *Mencius* IIB.10(7) (MZJC, vol. 14, p. 534). Whichever of the two characters is used, there are still variations in interpretation. The translation given is particularly influenced by WYJ (see his note 241, p. 581).

B38   **C:** There is that which you know but are unable to *zhi* (represent, point out). The explanation lies in spring, a runaway servant, pup/dog, what is lost.

   E: That which: In the case of spring, its state cannot be represented. In the case of a runaway servant, there is not knowing his whereabouts. In the case of pup/dog, there is not knowing its name. In the case of what is lost, despite skill, one is not able to regain (duplicate) it.

B39   **C:** To know a pup (*gou*) yet to say of yourself that you do not know a dog (*quan*) is a mistake. The explanation lies in duplication.

   E: Knowing: If to know a pup (*gou*) duplicates to know a dog (*quan*), then it is a mistake. If it does not duplicate, then it is not a mistake.

(e.g. WYJ, WFB, TJF) although there is variation in punctuation between them. The point appears to be that if "knowing a pup" does duplicate "knowing a dog", then to make the claim instanced in the C is, indeed, a mistake. If there is not such duplication, then it is not a mistake. ACG's discussion should also be examined — see his pp. 408–409.

B40   C: 通意後對。説在不知其誰謂也。

E: 通：問者曰：「子知羈¹⁵⁰ 乎？」應者曰：「羈何謂也？」彼曰：「羈，施」，則智之。若不問「羈何謂」，徑應以「弗智」，則過。且應必應問之時。若應長，應有深淺。（天常中在兵人長。）¹⁵¹

Comment: A number of modern commentators quote ZHY's paraphrase of the C which makes the meaning very clear (先通彼意，後乃對之，否則不知其何謂). There are two difficult issues in the E. The first is the unknown character written above as 羈, both where it occurs alone and also in conjunction with 施. As indicated in the notes, there are several different proposals for these characters. With regard to 羈, I have followed GH (see his p. 160 and the reference to *Zuo Zhuan* for the 7th year of Duke Zhao — LCC, vol. 5, p. 614). On 施 I have taken WYJ's suggestion that it is a name — see his note 248, p. 582. ACG makes an interesting, and quite plausible, case for treating the unknown character as an unknown word. In general, whilst there is disagreement on these characters, there is agreement that the point is about different names for the same entity. Ignorance of the meaning of one term can then be overcome by the use of the other, whilst not to enquire further, if the first term is not understood, is a mistake on the part of the listener. The second issue is the final seven characters in parentheses above — whether they should be included as the end of this E or as the initial part of the next E, and also what emendations should be made. Most commentators do include them in the present E but variably punctuated and usually with 犬 emended to 大. ACG, who retains 犬, offers this translation: "Among Heaven's constants its

---

150. There is considerable variation in the reading of this unknown character. 羸 was originally proposed by BY and is accepted by WFB, JBC and LSL. Other emendations include 羈 (TJF, GH, MZQY) and 孰 (WYJ). ACG considers the meaningless character to be intentional in the manner of Quine's "gavagai" and arbitrarily translates it as "blomes". I have followed GH's interpretation.

151. The seven characters included in parentheses are as in the DZ and have presented very considerable problems. Broadly there are three proposed readings: (i) To omit them here and place them at the start of the next E (WFB, LSL). (ii) To retain them as they are and attempt interpretation, particularly relying on CYX's analysis. (iii) To include them but with modification and emendation, interpreting the last part in relation to *Mencius* VIA. 4(3) (TJF).

B40   **C:** Understand the idea (meaning) before replying. The explanation lies in not knowing what it is he is speaking of.

        E: Understanding: The questioner asks: "Do you know the sojourner?" The one replying says: "What is the sojourner called?" The other says: "The sojourner is *Shi*." Then you know him. If you don't ask what the sojourner is called but directly respond with "I don't know", then it is a mistake. Moreover, the response must be appropriate to the question in terms of time. For example, the response may be long; the response may be profound or superficial.

presence is prolonged with man." which is not only difficult to understand in itself but also difficult to relate to the subject matter of the C. I have left them untranslated apart from offering in the Comment to B41 a version which follows the transfer and emendation suggested by WFB and LSL.

B41   C: 所存與〔存〕[152] 者，於存與孰存，駟[153] 異。說〔在主〕[154]。

E: 所：室堂，所存也。其子，存者也。據在[155] 者而問室堂，「惡可[156] 存」也。主室堂而問存者，「孰存」也。是一主存者以問所存，一主所存以問存者。

Comment: There is considerable uncertainty about this C&E which ACG describes as "badly mutilated" (see his note 429, p. 410). Considering the C, in the DZ text (所存與者於存與孰存駟異說) there is clearly the need to insert something before 者, there is doubt about 駟異, and there is a lacuna after 說. There is also the issue of how 存 is to be understood in this context. In addition, ACG suggests the emendation of 於 to 惡. The reading given above remains tentative. The E also poses problems, the first being whether the problematic seven characters discussed in the previous Comment should be included here. WFB, who does include them here, emends them to read: "人在堂中，其人與所。" which might be translated: "If a person is in a hall, there is his person and where he is", so establishing the situation about which questions are framed. Apart from this issue, the E does seem relatively straightforward.

---

152. Following ZHY, this has been restored by most modern editors based on the E.
153. 駟 is read as 四 following WYJ and JBC — see the former's note 255, p. 583. Some omit this character — for example, WFB, ACG.
154. These two characters are missing from the DZ, i.e. the "說" has been lost — see ACG, note 429, p. 410. Some recent commentators (e.g. WFB, JBC, TJF) suggest the addition of two characters: 在主 in the case of WFB & JBC, 在駐 in the case of TJF.
155. Some commentators suggest the emendation of 在 to 存 (e.g. WFB) although most retain the former.
156. WFB omits this character as superfluous. WYJ reads it as 所.

B41   **C:** Where someone is, and who it is that is there; where (in what) they are, and who they are. The four are different. The explanation [lies in what is primary].

       E: Place: The room or hall is the place where they are. His sons are those who are there. To rely on who is there and ask about the room or hall, one says: "Where (in what) are they?" To take as primary the room or hall and ask about who is there, one says: "Who is there?" In one case this is to take as evident who is there as the basis for asking where they are, and in the other case to take as evident where they are as the basis for asking who is there.

B42   **C:** 五行毋常勝。說在宜。

E: 五：合水土火火離然。[157] 火鑠金、火多也。金靡炭，金多也。合之府木，木離木。[158] 若識麋與魚之數，惟所利。[159]

Comment: As it stands this appears to be a straightforward statement of the "Five Phases" theory. The same statement (apart from 无 for 毋) appears in *Sunzi* 6 (虛實) where Ames (1993) translates it: "Thus, of the five phases (*wu xing*), none is the constant victor" — see his pp. 124, 127. FYL, quoting from the early commentator Li Shan, writes: "In Tsou Tzu's cycle of the Five Powers, each one follows that one which it cannot overcome ..." (FYL/DB, vol. 1, p. 162). It should be noted that ACG takes this C&E as expressing opposition to the theory — see his pp. 53–56 and pp. 411–412. The E certainly presents textual problems as indicated in notes 157–159. In relation to the problematic third sentence, WYJ draws attention to the *Lü Shi Chunqiu* 8/2.5 which has: "今以木擊木則拌。"

B43   **C:** 無欲惡之為益損也。說在宜。

E: 無：欲惡傷生損壽。說以少連[160]，是誰愛也。嘗多粟或者欲不有，能傷也。若酒之於人也。且智[161] 人利人，愛也。則惟智，弗治也。

---

157. There are basically three approaches to these first seven characters: (i) To make no emendations, place a comma after the first 火, read 離 as 失去, and end the sentence with 然 (e.g. WYJ). (ii) To regard them as displaced from an earlier C — see ACG, note 433, p. 411. (iii) To emend 合 to 金, the first 火 to 木, and end the sentence with 離 (e.g. TJF).

158. As with the first sentence, the DZ text is retained and 府 is taken as referring to wood as one of the "Six Treasuries of Nature" 六府 (water, fire, metal, wood, earth, grain). Other versions include those of TJF who again emends 合 to 金 and also the first two instances of 木 to 水 and 火 respectively, and of GH who emends only the first 木 (to 水) but includes 若識 in this sentence. ACG also transfers this sentence to his B11.

159. This sentence is also problematical. WFB adds a note to the effect that the example is not clear and does not include it in his analysis of the C&E. The rather free translation given relates particularly to LSL's analysis. It is part of the material transferred by ACG to B11.

160. In the translation I have followed WFB's emendation of the problematical 連 to 進. LSL, following SYR, reads it as 適 in the sense of 適中.

161. Emended in this and the following instance from the Mohist graph 知 with the 心 radical (as in C&E A6).

B42   **C:** Among the Five Phases, there is not one that constantly overcomes (all the others). The explanation lies in the appropriateness.

       E: Five: If you combine water, earth and fire, fire loses. Nevertheless, fire melts metal, fire being greater, and metal extinguishes charcoal, metal being greater. If you combine the "treasury" wood [with itself, then] wood "loses" wood. It is like distinguishing the numbers of deer and fish — it simply depends on circumstances.

B43   **C:** It is not the case that desiring and detesting are respectively beneficial and harmful. The explanation lies in being appropriate.

       E: Not: Desiring and detesting injure life and harm longevity. This is explained by reducing what is offered and liking this only. When there is a lot of grain, there may be the wish not to have it because it can also be injurious — like the effect of wine on people. Moreover, when a wise person benefits others, it is love. Then wisdom alone is not controlling.

Comment: There are no textual issues in the C. ACG discusses the relevance of this statement to the views of Yang Zhu and related Daoist concepts. The problems of the E relate particularly to whether the usual 少連 refers to the person noted for his moderation, who is spoken of in the *Li Ji* (SSJZS, vol. 5, p. 737) and *Lun Yu* XVIII.8, or not. Several modern commentators, including TJF, GH, ZCY and JBC take this to be the case. ACG argues strongly against this, not only on the basis of interpretation, but also on grammatical grounds. The sentence remains a problem. I have translated WFB's version, the key feature of which is the emendation of 連 to 進. Other problems include the reading of 知 with 心 and 治, and precisely how 愛 is to be understood. ACG takes this as "loving people", as I have done, but it is also possible that it refers to the two examples, food and wine. This is WFB's interpretation which involves several emendations of the DZ text. It is, then, basically an argument for moderation and, as he points out in his analysis, a position between Song Xing and Xun Zi (see his pp. 155–156).

B44   **C:** 損而不害。說在餘。

   E: 損：飽者去餘，適足不害。能害，飽。若傷糜之無脾也。[162] 且有損而后益智[163]者，若瘧[164]病之之[165]於瘧也。

Comment: Despite the difficulties, the meaning here does seem clear. There can be loss without there being harm if the loss involves what is superfluous. WFB states that this C&E opposes the view "損有害" and links both this and the preceding C&E to the argument in favour of moderation (節用) which he relates to Song Xing. JBC refers to *Zhuangzi* 8 (GQF, vol. 2, p. 311) and the matter of excess flesh as exemplified by webbed toes and supernumerary digits. The E appears to amplify the argument with three instances. The first is the case of eating. To stop eating when enough has been eaten and not go on

---

162. This sentence presents problems. As it stands, no sense can be made of it, particularly as an illustration of the previous sentence. One solution is to retain 糜 as "deer" and read 脾 as 髀. The example may then be related to sacrificial use (e.g. SYR, LSL), as ACG reads it that, in reference to the deer, "… removal of a part does not affect what the thing is." (his p. 415) Another suggestion (see TJF, MZQY) is to emend 糜 to 糜 (i.e. 糜粥) and retain 脾 as 脾胃. JBC accepts the first emendation but reads 脾 as 神益. The simplest solution seems to be to emend only 脾 to 髀, leaving open whether this relates to sacrificial use.

163. This is probably best regarded as superfluous and deleted (SYR). TJF reads it as 知 and transposes 益 and 知.

164. Since BY, this character, originally written here as ZWDCD #22942, has been emended to 瘧.

165. Some commentators suggest omission as an erroneous duplication (e.g. ACG) whilst some propose emendation, either to 止 (CYX) or 人 (LSL).

B44 **C:** There are instances where loss is not harmful. The explanation lies in there being excess.

E: Loss: In the case of eating one's fill, to set aside what is superfluous having eaten enough is not harmful. Eating to satiety can be harmful. It is like the injured deer being without a haunch. Moreover, there are instances of loss before there is gain. It is like the fever in a febrile illness.

to excess avoids any harm. Eating to excess is harmful, although quite how the example illustrates this remains obscure. The second example remains unclear. In the third case, what is at first damaging can later be beneficial, as in the case of a fever which may bring resolution of an illness.

B45   **C:** 知而不以五路。説在久。

     E: 智[166]：以目見，而目以火見，而火不見。惟以五路智，久不當。以目見，若以火見。[167]

Comment: Once LQC's proposal that 五路 refers to the five senses (五官) is accepted, the meaning is relatively clear, although there is some variation in the reading of 久. The point appears to be that knowledge by means of the five senses (empirical knowledge) is instantaneous, but enduring knowledge involves some process other than immediate sensation. There is variation in the punctuation of the last part of the E but this does not affect the basic point.

B46   **C:** 〔火〕[168] 必熱。説在頓[169]。

     E: 火：謂火熱也非以火之熱我有，若視日[170]。

Comment: As the notes indicate, several important characters are contentious so it is hardly surprising that interpretations vary. There is widespread agreement that 頓 should be emended but not agreement on what it should be emended to. WFB also suggests the emendation of 我 to 弗 in the E. CYX's emendation of 日 to 日 in the E is generally accepted. WFB's reading, in particular, brings this C&E into close relation with those before and after and to the issue addressed particularly in GSL's "堅白論" ('On Hard and White') about the separate perception of qualities.

166. WFB emends 智 to 知, but even without emendation it is often read as 知 (e.g. JBC). This is, of course, a recurring issue in the C&Es, but perhaps of particular relevance here. See also ACG's comment on the placement of the head character (his note 446, p. 415).
167. There are variations in the punctuation of this sentence in modern texts. That given above follows ACG.
168. 必, which is in the DZ, is either emended to 火 on the basis of the E (e.g. SYR, GH, TJF, AGC), or is retained and 火 is added as above (e.g. WFB, WYJ).
169. Few commentators retain 頓. Emendations include 視 (WFB), 純 (GH), 屯 (in the sense of 聚積 — TJF, MZQY, JBC), 睹 (SYR), and 遄 (CYX, LSL). I have used the first.
170. There is general acceptance of CYX's emendation of 日 to 日.

B45   **C:** There is knowing that is not by way of the "five roads" (five senses). The explanation lies in duration.

       E: Knowledge (knowing): Seeing is by means of the eyes and the eyes see by fire but fire does not see. If knowledge was only by way of the "five roads" (five senses), it would not relate to duration. Seeing is by means of the eyes is like seeing is by means of fire.

B46   **C:** Fire is necessarily hot. The explanation lies in seeing.

       E: Fire: Calling the fire hot is not to take the fire's heat as something I have. For example, looking at the sun.

B47   C: 知其所以不知。說在以名取。

E: 智：雜所智與所不智而問之，則必曰：「是所智也，是所不智也。」取去俱能之，是兩智之也。

Comment: There are several interpretations of this C&E, related particularly to the different versions of the first sentence of the E, to precisely how 名 and 取 are interpreted, and to whether 之 in the E refers to 名 and 取 or to 取 and 去. The most straightforward interpretation, given for example by GH and WYJ, is to take this as being about the method of asking (GH has "驗問之法") to determine what another (其) knows and does not know, which can be gauged by his ability to "name" and to "choose". Both commentators refer to the *Mozi* 47.

B48   C: 無不必待有。說在所謂。

E: 無：若無焉，則有之而后無。無天陷，則無之而無。

Comment: The C makes the contrast between the pair, "being" and "not being", which differs from the previous pair, "knowing" and "not knowing" in that the former are not interdependent. This may be taken as a counter to the Daoist position of regarding "being" and "not being" as mutually dependent (e.g. *Laozi* 2, *Zhuangzi* 2 — GQF, vol. 1, p. 79). Such an interpretation is strengthened by TJF's version. Variation in the E depends on the reading of 焉 (i.e. whether it is interpreted as a bird, as for example by TJF who refers to the *Shuo Wen* as well as *Lun Yu* IX.8 and *Mozi* 52, or as a horse, as by SYR), and whether 天陷 is accepted as "heaven falling", i.e. the Daoist example — see the dialogue between Zhuang Zhou and Hui Shi in *Zhuangzi* 33.

B47   **C:** Knowing what he knows and does not know. The explanation lies in the use of naming and choosing.

       E: Knowing: If you lump together what he knows and what he doesn't know and question him, then he has to say: "This is what I know, this is what I do not know." Choosing and discarding both make this possible; these are the two kinds of knowing something.

B48   **C:** Not being does not necessarily depend on being. The explanation lies in what is said.

       E: Not being: For example, with something not being there, then there was this and afterwards there is not. In the case of there not being "heaven falling", then this was not so (before) and is not so (now).

B49   C: 擢慮不疑。說在有無[171]。

E: 擢：疑無謂也。臧也今死，而春也得之之死也，可。[172] 〔且猶
是也。〕[173]

Comment: There are major problems with this C&E. The version given is particularly dependent on several readings or emendations that remain contentious or uncertain. These are: (i) WYJ's analysis (his note 290, p. 588) and TJF's version (his p. 203) of the first two characters of the C. (ii) The acceptance of 臧 and 春 as names and therefore the rejection of ACG's proposed emendations. (iii) The adoption of SYR's proposed emendation of 文 文 to 之 又. (iv) The inclusion of "且猶是也" in the following E. The point then becomes one about the reliability of making an inference from an established fact. It is obvious, however, that any reading must be tentative.

B50   C: 且然不可正[174]，而不害用工[175]。說在宜 (歐)[176]。

E: 且：〔且〕猶是也。且〔然〕[177] 必然，且已必已。且用工而後已
者，必用工.〔而〕[178] 後已。

Comment: The only two issues in the C are whether 正 should be emended to 止 and whether 歐 should be included in B12 rather than here. Both are accepted in the translation. ACG, who retains 正, has: "What is about to be so

---

171. TJF's transposes the final two characters of this C to B48 above and vice versa. WFB emends to 有 (又) 然. Thus, there are at least three versions: (i) 有無 (in the DZ and most common). (ii) 所謂 (TJF). (iii) 又然 (WFB).

172. This sentence is almost entirely problematical. Thus, (i) Are 臧 and 春 to be taken as names, as most commentators assume, or are ACG's emendations to be accepted? His version depends on punctuating after 無, emending 也 to 蛇 throughout, reading 臧 as "hide away", and 春 as 蠢. (ii) Is 也 to be emended as indicated (see also GH)? (iii) Should 死 be emended to 然 in both instances? (iv) Is SYR's emendation of 文 文 to 之 又 acceptable or should 文 文 be retained (see LCR)?

173. There is uncertainty about these four characters. Some editors include them here (e.g. TJF, Z&Q) whilst others have them as the initial characters of the next E — e.g. WYJ, LDF, GH. I have taken the latter position.

174. Several modern editors emend 正 to 止 (e.g. WFB, GH, TJF), or to 凵 (ZQH, accepted by JBC). In the translation the former is followed.

175. Read as 功 following SYR.

176. There is some uncertainty about the placement of this character which is, more usually, the initial character of B12. There also it raises problems — see, for example, JBC, note 1, p. 334.

177. The more usual change is to emend the second 且 to 然, as here.

178. 而 is added here following WNS and WYZ.

B49   **C:** In quoting a precedent, in general there is not doubt. The explanation lies in what is and what is not.

E: Quoting a precedent: If there is doubt it is not said. "If *Zang* has recently died and the same thing also affects *Chun*, he will also die", is permissible.

B50   **C:** What is about to be so cannot be stopped, yet there is no harm in putting forth effort. The explanation lies in what is appropriate.

E: About to be so: It is like this. What is about to be so is necessarily so. What is about to come to an end necessarily comes to an end. With regard to being about to put forth effort for something to come to an end, it is necessary to put forth the effort and afterwards it comes to an end.

is incorrigible ..." which doesn't really affect the basic argument. There is some textual uncertainty at the start of the E concerning the four characters referred to in note 173 which are included here. The DZ text has: "且猶是也且 且必然…" so the emendation/rearrangement to get to the version above is the transfer of one of the paired 且 to follow the head character and the addition of 然 or, as indicated, the addition of 且 as the second character and the emendation of the first of the paired 且 to 然. Then, taking 且 as 將來 and 已 as 完成, what is about to be so will necessarily be so, and what is going to end (be brought to completion) will necessarily end (be brought to completion). Nevertheless, this should not prevent a person from putting forth effort. WYJ suggests that this C&E exemplifies the Mohists' "spirit of constantly striving to be better" (his note 298, p. 589). Of course, this C&E must be seen in relation to the anti-Fatalist position taken in the main body of the *Mozi*. ACG (p. 420) describes the C&E as being "... remarkable in touching the issue of fatalism at a much deeper level than elsewhere in the *Mozi*." WFB, however, depending on his emendation of 是 to 時 in the E, interprets the C&E as voicing opposition to the Daoist view of "時無止".

B51   **C:** 均之絕不。說在所均。

E: 均：髮均，縣[179] 輕〔重〕[180]，而髮絕，不均也。均，其絕也莫 絕。

Comment: Despite some uncertainty about the first section of the E, there appears to be consensus on meaning here. Variations that should be noted, however, are TJF's version of the first sentence of the E ("髮。均髮。 輕而髮。") and WFB's placement as B21. The same matter is raised twice in the *Liezi* (4.13 and 5.8 — see *LZDB*, pp. 147, 172).

---

179. Read as 懸 (see, for example, JBC).
180. Added in some texts (e.g. BY, LCR, WFB, JBC) and included in the translation.

B51   C: Being balanced [determines] whether something breaks or not.
The explanation lies in what is balanced.

E: Balanced: If a hair is balanced it suspends light [or heavy
things], but, if the hair breaks, it is not balanced. Balanced is
when what might break does not break.

B52   C: 堯之義也，生[181] 於今而處於古，而異時。説在所義二。

E: 堯霍[182]：或以名視[183] 人，或以實視人。舉友富商也[184]，是以
名視人也。指是膲[185] 也，是以實視人也。堯之義也，是聲也
於今，所義之實處於古。（若殆於城門與於臧也。）[186]

Comment: The only issues in the C are whether 義 should be read as
"righteousness" or "goodness" (WFB emends 義 to 善 throughout), or as
"example" or 'model' as ACG does, and whether 生 should be emended to 聲
(WNS and others), or retained (ACG). I have taken the first option in both
instances but there is little basic difference in meaning. If Yao's righteousness
is being raised or Yao is being used as an example, he is indicated by name.
The name is raised in the present but the "entity" (reality) — i.e. Yao and his
righteousness — existed in the past. The E is more of a problem. In brief, I
have followed WYJ's reading, the essential features of which are the retention
of both 堯 and 霍 (read as 鶴) as the head characters, the emendation of the
problematic third clause to "舉堯備帝也", obviating the need for the additional
example required by ACG, and the widely accepted reading of 視 as 示. There
are, then, two examples — Yao's righteousness and crane — one of which
can only be indicated by name whereas, in the other case, there can be a
direct pointing to the entity. The final sentence remains a problem, not only in
terms of placement but also how it should be understood. The latter
particularly hinges on how 殆 and 臧 are taken — see WYJ, note 311, p. 590
and ACG, note 475, p. 422.

181. Whilst most modern commentators accept WSN's emendation of the troublesome 生 to
    聲 (e.g. GH, WYJ, MZQY, LSL), ACG retains it as "engendered", whilst TJF omits it,
    rather problematically placing the comma after 義.
182. There is variation in the initial characters of the E. Above, the DZ text is given and this
    is accepted, for example, by WYJ with 霍 being read as 鶴 (see his note 305, p. 590).
    Some commentators follow LQC in omitting 霍 (e.g. TJF, JBC). ACG retains 霍 reading
    it as 膲 in line with what follows and translating it as "meat soup". He also suggests that
    there is a lacuna between 堯 and 霍 (see his note 468, p. 422).
183. There is wide acceptance of SYR's reading of 視 as 示 — see, for example, WYJ, note
    306, p. 590.
184. This is a problematic clause — see Comment.
185. There is uncertainty about this character. Some commentators suggest 霍 as initially,
    and interpret it as a surname (e.g. LSL), some emend to 鶴 in both places (e.g. WYJ,
    JBC). ACG retains it as meaning "meat broth", whilst WFB emends it to 善.
186. This sentence is placed here in some texts — e.g. WFB, AGC.

B52   **C:** In the case of Yao's righteousness, it is heard of in the present but it is located in the past, and these are different times. The explanation lies in what is righteous being two.

        E: Yao and crane: The one is shown to people through the name; the other is shown to people through the object. When you raise Yao's perfection, this is to use the name to show people. When you point to this crane, this is to use the object to show people. In the case of Yao's righteousness, the hearing of it may be in the present, but what is righteous is located in the past. (For example, danger at the city gates and in the storehouse.)

B53   C: 狗[187]，犬也，而殺狗非殺犬也，可。説在重。

E: 狗：狗，犬也。〔而殺狗〕[188] 謂之殺犬，可。若兩髀[189]。

Comment: The key issue with this C&E is whether 不 is added to the C (giving
不可), apparently bringing the C and E into agreement. All accept that this is
the Later Mohist response to Paradox 17 of the second list in *Zhuangzi* 33
(GQF, vol. 4, p. 1106), that it must also be seen in the light of Xiaoqu 6 ("Killing
a robber is not killing a person"), that it is an example of " 名 實" (hence the
重), and that it is an issue of some importance to the Later Mohists. Although
ACG dismisses the addition of 不 as a "facile expedient", it does have some
merit. The C&E then both become straightforward refutations of the Paradox.
It seems, however, more probable that in the C the Later Mohist is
acknowledging the possibility of making the distinction, just as in the case of
"robber" and "man", although, in fact, killing a pup is killing a dog as the E
explains.

B54   C: 使殷美。説在使。(使役義。説在使。)[190]

E: 使：令使也。我使我，我不使亦使我。殷戈亦使殷，不美亦使
殷。(使：令使也：義使，義；義不使，亦義。使役：義亦使
役；不義亦使役。)[191]

Comment: All Chinese commentators take this C&E to be incomprehensible
as it stands and propose various major changes. ACG, however, retains the C
and writes: "*Shi dian mei* 'cause a hall to be beautiful' is so unidiomatic that no
commentator known to me has ever taken the sentence in this sense, but a
consideration of the Mohist's special style shows it to be acceptable" — see
ACG, note 478, p. 425. Since SYR originally proposed that all three
characters, 我, 美 and 戈 should be emended to 義 and both 殿 and 殷 to 假,
there have been various combinations of emendations. Three approaches
taken to this very problematic E are as follows:

187. It is generally agreed that a 狗 is an immature 犬 — see WYJ, notes 312 and 316, pp.
     591–592.
188. Only some editors (e.g. WYJ and WFB, the latter without 而) accept SYR's addition
     of these characters. Nonetheless, they are at least implied.
189. This character, originally written as ZWDCD #30456, is usually now emended as above,
     but 脾 (YBY) and 槐 (WYJ) have been suggested.
190. This is TJF's version of the C.
191. This is TJF's version of the E which is the one accepted by LSL and the one used for
     the translation. It depends essentially on the emendation of 殷 to 役, the emendation of
     both 美 and 我 to 義, and some modification at the start of the second sentence, including
     the omission of 戈.

B53   **C:** A pup is a dog, yet "to kill a pup is not to kill a dog", is admissible. The explanation lies in the duplication.

E: A pup: A pup is a dog. So to call killing a pup killing a dog is admissible. It is like the two buttocks.

B54   **C:** In causing a servant [to act] there is righteousness. The explanation lies in causing.

E: Causing: Ordering is causing: Righteously to cause is righteous; righteously not to cause is also righteous. There is causing to employ: Righteous also applies to causing to employ; not righteous also applies to causing to employ.

(i) TJF's version which is given in parentheses above and is followed by modern editors LSL and Z&Q. This has been used for the translation.

(ii) ACG's version which uses the DZ text with relatively minor changes. His translation is: "To command is to intend an effect. Whether I obey or not, you intend the effect on me; whether the hall becomes beautiful or not, you intend the effect on it."

(iii) WYJ simply gives the DZ text without punctuation and with the brief note "未詳" which note he also appends to the E.

B55 C: 荆[192] 之大，其沈[193] 淺也。說在具[194]。

E: 荆：沈，荆之具也。則沉淺非荆淺也。若易五之一。[195]

Comment: There is notable variation in the reading of this C&E depending particularly on how 荆 (the state of Chu or bramble), 沈 (as a dependency of Chu, as submerged, or as 沉 being the name of a marsh in Chu), 具 (see WYJ's note and ACG, note 485, p. 426), 淺 (as shallow or as weak) are understood. Obviously, any translation will depend on the positions taken on these issues. The reading given depends particularly on WYJ. WFB takes this to be about the applicability of terms (推類行辭) — i.e. 大 can apply to both 荆 the kingdom and to 沉 the marsh, but 淺 only to the latter. 具 is read as 具區 and the final example is linked to B58 (see Comment to B58). ACG reads 荆 as "bramble" making the C&E about submerging brambles. There is also the question of the final five characters. The reading given makes this comment applicable here whilst ACG transfers them to the following E — see his note 490, p. 428.

192. Of the two common uses of 荆, as "bramble", and as the state of 楚, there is general agreement among Chinese commentators that the latter is intended here. Both AF and, later, ACG read it as "bramble".

193. Whilst a number of commentators accept SYR's emendation of 沈 to 沉, the latter referring to a marsh within 楚, 沈 is retained by others, either as an ancient state later contained in 楚 (e.g. GH, LCR, WYJ — see the last's note 319, p. 592), or in its usual meaning to give the contrasting term to the following 淺.

194. See WYJ's note 320, p. 592 supporting this character here and in the E.

195. There is doubt about these final five characters, whether they should be transferred (to B57 — ACG), or, if retained, how they should be interpreted — see Comment.

B55   **C:** [Despite] Jing's (Chu's) greatness, its [dependency] Shen is weak. The explanation lies in it being a tool.

E: Jing (Chu): Shen is Jing's (Chu's) tool. Then Shen's weakness is not Jing's (Chu's) weakness. It is like changing one part of five.

B56   C: 以楹[196] 為搏[197] 於以為無知也。說在意。

E: 以：楹之搏也，見之，其於意也，不易先智。意，相也。若楹
輕於秋[198]，其於意也洋然[199]。

Comment: There is so much uncertainty about this C&E that any translation or interpretation must remain quite tentative. WFB has only "文疑從闕" in his analysis. The version above is based on acceptance of the most widely agreed upon emendations and readings, and on TJF's punctuation of the E. The analogy remains a particular problem, as does the issue of the five characters included at the end of the previous E. The example of the pillar in relation to 意 is also raised in the Daqu (44.11). Whilst several modern commentators interpret 意 in the sense of 意度 ("conjecture" — e.g. WYJ, LSL, JBC), I have translated it as "concept". For attempts to sort out what is at issue here, see WYJ, note 328, p. 593 and ACG, pp. 428–429.

B57   C: 推之[200] 意未可知。說在可用，過仵[201]。

E: 〔錐〕[202]：段[203] 椎俱事於履，可用也。成繪履過椎[204]，與成椎
過繪履，同；過仵[205] 也。

---

196. Emended from 檻 following SYR and CYX.
197. There is general acceptance of this emendation of the unknown character found in the DZ — see WYJ, note 322, p. 592 and ACG, note 487, p. 427.
198. There is general agreement that this should be read as 萩 or 楸, i.e. the catalpa — see, for example, GH.
199. Some doubt exists regarding 洋然 — see ACG's note 494, p. 428. Alternative readings include 詳 in the sense of 悉 or 盡 (WYJ), 莊 (然) (LSL), and 樣 (MZQY).
200. Both WYJ and ACG include these two characters here rather than at the end of the E for B17 — see ACG's argument in his note 495, p. 429.
201. There is notable variation in how this character is read (午 by BY, 悟 as 逆 by SYR, 伍 as "matching" by GH and ACG, 午 as 交叉 by WFB), and how the last four characters in the C are grouped — either 可"用""過"仵 or "可用""過仵".
202. Transferred from its position as the third character of the E and read as 推 to provide an otherwise absent head character following WYJ. Other commentators supply 意 — for example, GH and WFB — or leave the E without a head character.
203. There is general agreement following SYR that this is some form of "*duan*", probably best as 碬 in the sense of "stone block" — see ACG, note 498, p. 430.
204. Variably written as either 椎 or 錐 here and in the following use.
205. Emended from 仵 on the basis of the C — see WYJ, note 333, p. 594.

B56 **C:** To take the pillar to be round is in taking it to be what is not known. The explanation lies in conceptualising (conjecturing).

E: To take: In the case of the pillar's roundness, when we see it, its being in the concept doesn't change from prior knowledge. A concept is an image. For example, the pillar being lighter than catalpa [wood] — if it is as a concept, it is foolish.

B57 **C:** The concept of a hammer cannot be known beforehand. The explanation lies in its being possible to use and goes beyond matching.

E: A hammer: That hammering block and hammer both serve in [the making of] shoes is "being possible to use". Completing the decorating of shoes goes beyond the hammer and the hammer goes beyond the decorating of shoes — they are the same in this respect. This is going beyond matching.

Comment: The key features of the above version of this C&E are, with regard to the C, taking the break from B16 to occur before rather than after "推之" and reading 件 as "matching". In the E, the issues are whether there is a head character and if so what, how 段 is to be understood, and whether the emendation of the final 件 to 作 is acceptable. The resolution of these questions, and so the reading given above, depends particularly on WYJ. — see his notes 329–333, pp. 593–594.

B58   C: 一少於二而多於五。說在建住[206]。

E: 一：五有一焉；一有五焉，十二焉。

Comment: This apparently simple C&E has caused considerable puzzlement despite the absence of textual difficulties. Most commentators have taken the observations to be about 1 and 10, i.e. about the two cases of 1 being one unit and 10 being one unit. Thus, in WFB's emendation of the final part of the E, 一 and 二 refer to these two situations (i.e. 單位 and 建位). The specific relation to the abacus, which offers a satisfactory interpretation of 建位, is suggested by CYX. As ACG has pointed out, however, this kind of interpretation does present problems with the syntax of the final sentence, particularly if 十 is retained. Perhaps the simplest and most appropriate interpretation is that offered by GH, which, in essence, is to take this to be about hands and fingers. Thus, 1 finger is less than 2 fingers yet 1 hand is more than 5 fingers, i.e. it depends on whether finger or hand is given "position". Then, in the E, 5 fingers are on 1 hand, 1 hand has 5 fingers on it and there are 10 fingers on 2 hands. There is reference here to B12.

B59   C: 非半弗斱[207] 則不動。說在端[208]。

E: 非：斱半，進前取也。前則中無為半，猶端也。前後取，則端中也。斱必半，毋與非半，不可斱也。

---

206. Most commentators accept the emendation of 住 to 位 (SYR, CYX). CYX emends 建 to 立 and interprets 位 as "position", i.e. 上下左右 with respect to the abacus.

207. I have used WFB's interpretation of this character, usually given here and thrice subsequently in the E as ZWDCD #13920. In the *Yu Pian* (玉篇) this character is equated with 破 (which is BY's emendation) and in the *Guang Yun* (廣韻) with *zhuo* (ZWDCD #41859), which is ACG's emendation, making this about hoeing. Another variant is 斫 — see, for example, LSL. Several commentators, including TJF, quote YBY in equating this character with ZWDCD #16172, for which the *Shuo Wen* (說文) has, in fact, the definition 斫 as read by LSL. For a discussion of this issue see particularly WYJ, note 336, p. 594.

208. GH emends the usual 端 to 竭 both here and in the E. This does create a problem with the second 端 in the E, but does accord with the use of 竭 in *Zhuangzi* 33 — see TJF.

B58   C: One is less than two yet more than five. The explanation lies in "establishing the position".

E: One: Five has one in it; one has five in it; ten is (means) two.

B59   C: If what is not divisible in half is not divided, then there is not progression. The explanation lies in the point.

E: Not: In dividing in half, you progress taking what is in front. The front, then, is the centre of what was not halved; like a point. If you take both what is in front and what is behind, then a point is the centre. In dividing, there must be a half for, if there is not, and there is not a half, it is not possible to divide.

Comment: The two textual issues in this C&E are how to read the unknown character which occurs fourth in the C and twice again in the E, and, of lesser significance, whether 端 should be retained or emended to 竭 as suggested by GH. On the first point, the rare character (ZWDCD #13920) is usually taken as 破 (for discussion see WYJ, note 336, p. 594) although I have followed WFB's proposal to read it is as 析. ACG, however, reads it as "to hoe" — see his note 504, p. 432. GH's proposal on 端 seems unnecessary. Despite these variations the overall meaning does seem clear. There is, in fact, general agreement that this C&E is intended as a refutation of Paradox #21 of the 2nd List — *Zhuangzi* 33, GQF, vol. 4, p. 1106. The explanation considers two methods of division, the first being to take what is in front, leaving finally what was, say in the case of a line, the extreme right point, and, in the second case, taking from both in front and behind, leaving what was initially the central point. The issue is that either way one comes to an individual point.

B60　　**C:** 可無也，有之而不可去。說在嘗然。

　　E: 可：無也：已給則當給，不可無也。（久有窮，無窮。）[209]

Comment: Although there are some contentious points, particularly with the E, there is general agreement on meaning and perceived intent, accepting 無 / 有 as not-being/being. There are three issues in the E as follows: (i) The arrangement at the start is uncertain. Whilst most modern commentators make 可 the head character, WYJ has no head character. ACG (see his note 509, p. 433) remarks on a possible lacuna at the start which WFB fills with, "可：無、可無也." TJF, however, has no punctuation after 也, writing, "無也已給". (ii) Whilst most commentators accept ZHY's reading of 給 as 具 in the sense of 具備, or as 供給 (JBC), some (e.g. SYR, GH, WFB) would emend 給 to 然 in both occurrences. (iii) WFB emends 當 to 嘗. In the translation I have used WFB's version and have included the problematic final five characters in the E for B63.

---

209. There is debate about the placement of these five characters. Although some modern editors retain them in their original position (e.g. WYJ, ACG), others, indeed the majority, following SYR and ZHY, transpose them to either B62 (TJF, LSL) or B63 (GH, MZQY, JBC). These characters certainly seem misplaced here.

B60   C: Not being is admissible, but once there is being, it cannot be set
aside. The explanation lies in once being so.

E: Admissible: Not-being is admissible: Once something has
already been, then it must have been so and [its] not-being is
inadmissible.

B61   C: 正[210] 而不可擔[211] 。説在搏。

E: 正：丸[212] ，無所處而不中縣[213] ，搏也。

Comment: The reading given depends on particular emendations of several key characters which are quite contentious. Other interpretations take this C&E to be about spherical objects tending to continuous movement by rotation (e.g. WYJ, JBC), or about matters astronomical (TJF).

B62   C: 宇進無近。説在敷[214] 。

E: 宇[215] ：偏[216] 不可偏舉，宇[217] 也。進行者先敷近，後敷遠。 (久，有窮無窮。)[218]

Comment: The two textual changes in the E, on which there is broad agreement, are the reversal of the order of 偏宇 at the start to give 宇 as the head character, and the emendation of 字 to give the second 宇. This C&E must be considered in connection with the definition of "space" (宇) in A41. Some commentators (e.g. WYJ, TJF) see a relationship to Hui Shi's Paradox 9 (1st list) — "I know the world's centre. It is north of Yan and south of Yue." (*Zhuangzi* 33, GQF, vol. 4, p. 1102). Sima Biao's note on p. 1105 reads: "The distance of Yan from Yue is established yet the distance between north and south is without limit. To consider what is established from the point of view of what is without limit, then between Yan and Yue there is not, at first, a differentiation. Heaven is without direction, therefore where one is may be deemed the centre; a circle (a revolution) is without a point of origin, therefore where one is may be deemed the origin."

---

210. This is the usual emendation of the recurring Mohist character.
211. There are several proposed, and conflicting, emendations for this character. Most commonly, following particularly SYR, it is read as, or emended to, 搖 (e.g. WFB, LSL, ACG). Others read it as 定 or 靜 via 憺 (e.g. WYJ, JBC, MZQY), whilst GH reads it as 掎. TJF equates 擔 with 擔荷 which he equates in turn with 稽留 ("to detain").
212. There is general agreement for the emendation of 几 to 丸 — see, particularly, ACG, note 512, p. 435.
213. There is likewise agreement that this should be read as 懸 — see ACG, note 513, p. 435 on taking "中懸" as "to coincide with the plumbline".
214. This is generally equated with 布 in the sense of 分布 — see, for example, WYJ, note 349, p. 596.
215. The placement of 宇 as the head character is attributed to LQC. This involves reversal of the order of 偏宇 found in the DZ.
216. There is widespread agreement for the reading of 偏 as 區 in the sense of 區域.
217. Emended from the 字 found in a number of early texts.
218. The problem of the placement of these five characters was spoken of in note 209 above. In the present text they are included in the following E (B63).

B61 **C:** Regular (central) and not able to vary. The explanation lies in being spherical.

E: Regular: With a ball there is nowhere it can be placed where it does not hang from its centre because it is spherical.

B62 **C:** Going forward in space there is no near. The explanation lies in spreading out.

E: Space: When a region cannot be partially raised (demarcated), there is space. What moves forward first spreads out near and afterwards spreads out far.

B63 C: 行循[219] 以[220] 久。説在先後。

E: 行：者[221] 行者，必先近而後遠。遠脩[222] 近脩也；先後，久也。民行脩必以久也。（久有窮無窮。）[223]

Comment: There is widespread agreement on both text and interpretation for this C&E. WFB's summation seems particularly apposite — see his p. 174. He interprets it as refuting Hui Shi's Paradox 7 (1st list): "Today I go to Yue yet I arrive yesterday." (*Zhuangzi* 33, GQF, vol. 4, p. 1102), a possibility ACG entertains only to reject.

B64 C: 一法者之相與也盡〔類〕[224]，若方之相召[225] 也。説在方。

E: 一：方貌盡[226]，俱有法而異，或木或石不害其方之相合也。盡貌猶方也。物俱然。

Comment: Although there are textual variations as noted, there is agreement on meaning here. For a somewhat different translation in which 類 is not added and 貌 is retained, see ACG, p. 437. The two main points of difference are that "complete" refers to the "belonging together" in the C and the "characteristics" in the E. He also reads 俱 in the final section as "both", referring to the wood and stone squares. Nonetheless, the essential meaning is the same. A particular criterion is the basis of class membership and, provided this criterion is met, then, despite other differences, the things possessing the criterion may be joined in a class.

---

219. There is general acceptance of the emendation of 循 to 脩 following ZHY.
220. Read as 用 following WYZ.
221. There is some dispute about this character which appears here in the DZ. The variations are to omit it (CYX, GH, WFB, LSL), to emend it to 諸 in the sense of 凡 (WYJ), or to supply an additional 行 in front of it (ACG).
222. Now omitted following YY.
223. These five characters, of uncertain placement, are included in the present E — see notes 209 and 218.
224. There is variation in the final part of this initial statement. The version given, which is found in most modern texts, depends on SYR's addition of 類 to the original text — see WYJ, note 357, p. 597.
225. There is general acceptance of the emendation of 召 (and 台 in the E) to 合 following WYZ.
226. Most modern editors accept WYZ's emendation of 貌盡 to 盡類 (see WNS). TJF, however, does not and has ACG's agreement in this (see the latter's note 520, p. 437). The same applies to the second sentence.

B63   C: Travelling a distance uses (involves) duration. The explanation lies in before and after.

        E: Travelling: The one travelling is necessarily near before and far after. Far and near are distances. Before and after are durations. If people travel distances, it must involve duration. (Duration is both limited and without limit.)

B64   C: When things belong together under one criterion this completes a class — for example, the collecting together of squares. The explanation lies in "squareness".

        E: One: When squares complete a class they all have the criterion although they may be different; if some are wood and some are stone this doesn't harm their being grouped together as squares. They complete a class such as "squares". Things are all like this.

B65   C: 狂舉不可以知異。説在有 (不可)²²⁷。

E: 狂²²⁸：牛與馬惟異，以牛有齒馬有尾，説牛之非馬也，不可。是俱有，不偏有偏無有。曰：之²²⁹〔牛〕與馬不類，用牛〔有〕²³⁰角，馬無角，〔以〕²³¹是類不同也。若〔不〕舉牛有角，馬無角，以是為類之〔不〕同也，是狂舉也。²³²猶牛有齒，馬有尾。(或不非牛而非牛也，可。則或非牛或牛²³³而牛也，可。)²³⁴

Comment: There are two particular issues with the C. The first is how best to understand, and therefore translate, 狂舉. I accept, with JC (part 8, pp. 83–89) who provides a detailed analysis of the term, that it acts as a technical term, and take it to be the converse of 正舉. 舉 itself is defined in A31. JC's own "confused statement" seems too broad. LSL's modern equivalent of "胡亂舉出" seems more appropriate. ACG renders it "referring arbitrarily" — see his note 524, p. 437. The second issue is the point of division of this C from the next as considered in note 227. On this, I have accepted the arguments of those who follow ZCY but have included a translation of the other version in parentheses. There is also an issue about where to make the division in the E.

---

227. Commentators are at odds about the point of division between this and the following C. Those who have 不可 here include TJF, GH, LSL, JBC and Z&Q, the last glossing this as, "指事物有可、又有不可" (note 4, p. 522). Those who follow ZCY in making them the initial characters of the next C include WYJ, LCR, LDF and ACG. On this point, see ACG's notes 529, 531, p. 439. As a third possibility, WFB retains the two characters here but emends 可 to 有.

228. The reversal of the first two characters (the DZ has 牛狂) follows ZHY and CYX and is generally accepted — see, for example, WYJ, note 366, p. 598.

229. There is general acceptance of the emendation of 之 to 牛 — see, for example, ACG, note 526, p. 437.

230. Added following WYZ and ZCY.

231. Added by WFB.

232. This is the problem sentence, the reading of which hinges on the two instances of 不 in parentheses. The most common arrangement has the second 不 only. This does, however, present problems in interpretation, to solve which three other versions are offered as follows: (i) To include 不 in both places (WFB, followed by MZQY and JBC). (ii) To omit 不 in both places (MZS, JC). (iii) To make several emendations, i.e. 角 to 齒 in the first instance and to 尾 in the second instance, whilst leaving the second 不 (WYJ, following LQC in part). ACG translates the sentence as it appears in the DZ which is what I have done.

233. Most commentators follow SYR and CYX in excising 或牛 here.

234. The preceding 17/19 characters are most commonly found at the start of the E for B66 — see Comment.

B65   C: "Wild raisings" are inadmissible as a means of knowing differences. The explanation lies in "having" (or — in their being inadmissible).[ii]

      E: "Wild": Ox and horse are certainly different but to take "ox has incisors", "horse has tail" as an explanation of "ox is not horse" is inadmissible. These are what both have, not what one has and one does not have. If you say, "ox and horse are not of a class" on the basis of ox having horns and horse not having horns, this is the class not being the same. But if you do [not] raise, "ox has horns, horse does not have horns" as the basis for the classes not being the same, this is wild raising. It is like "ox has incisors, horse has tail". (Sometimes "not not-ox and not-ox" is admissible. Then sometimes "not-ox and ox" is admissible.)

---

ii.   Included in parentheses is the translation if "不可" is incorporated into this C.

The majority include what are the last 17/19 (depending on whether the omission of "或牛" proposed by SYR and CYX is accepted or not) characters in parentheses above in the next E. This position is exemplified by GH, TJF, LCR and ACG and is followed by the modern editors LSL and Z&Q. Some, however, include them here — for example, WYJ, WFB, CHANT. As with the C, I have given a translation in parentheses but favour the inclusion of the 17 characters in the following E. There are clearly also issues with the E. The point is, following the interpretations of WFB (apart from the transfer of the 17 characters from the next E), MZS and JC, that "wild raising" is to take as a basis for distinction of classes; something that both entities under consideration (i.e. ox and horse) have, even though, in the case of incisors and tails, there may be some specific differences in the forms of these. What is "correct raising" is then to take the presence and absence of horns as the basis for class distinction.

B66   **C:** 不可牛馬之非牛，與可之同。説在兼。

E: 或不[235] 非牛而非牛也，可。則或非牛或牛[236] 而牛也 ，可。故曰：「〈牛馬〉非牛也」，未可。〈牛馬〉牛也未可，則或可或不可。而曰：「〈牛馬〉牛也未可」，亦不可。且牛不二，馬不二，而〈牛馬〉二，則「牛不非牛」，「馬不非馬」，而「〈牛馬〉非牛非馬」，無難 。

Comment: Clearly there are problems with this C&E, predominantly in relation to its division from the preceding C&E. ACG firmly supports ZCY's division to include 不可 at the start of the present C and also includes the 17 characters added in the present text to the end of the previous E, at the start of this E (as, indeed, do most commentators, albeit with modifications). He makes the point that B65 is about "having" (有) horns and tails and not about "something admissible", and further, that the C requires 不可 to balance 可之. Clearly these are valid points but can be countered by saying that the second C&E (B66) is, in fact, specifically about a combined name, in relation, for example, to *Xunzi* 22 (XZXZ, p. 372, K, vol. 3, p. 130 and note 34, p. 338) and GSLZ 2 (白馬論), as WFB argues. On balance, the evidence appears to be in favour of ZCY and his proposed arrangement is followed in the present text.

---

235. Transferred to precede 或 making 不 the head character — see ACG, note 531, p. 439.
236. Most commentators follow SYR and CYX in excising 或牛 here.

B66 **C:** The grounds for taking "ox-horse is not ox" being inadmissible and being admissible are the same. The explanation lies in the joining (combination).

E: Not: If it is admissible that some are not ox is not ox then some are not ox and some are ox is [also] admissible. Therefore, it is never admissible to say that "ox-horse is not ox", and it is never admissible to say that "ox-horse is ox", since it is admissible of some but inadmissible of others. And to say "ox-horse is ox" is never admissible is also inadmissible. Furthermore, if ox is not two and horse is not two, but ox-horse is two then "ox is not not-ox", "horse is not not-horse", and "ox-horse is not ox and not horse" are without difficulty.[iii]

---

iii.   The problem with this translation of the final statement is the absence of 也 after the final 馬 as ACG has pointed out (note 532, p. 439). The problem with the alternative is meaning.

B67   C: 循（彼）此循（彼）此²³⁷ 與彼此同。説在異。

E: 彼：正名者彼此。彼此可：彼彼止於彼，此此止於此。彼此不
可：彼且此也。彼此亦可：彼此止於彼此。若是而彼此也，則
彼亦且此，此〔亦且彼〕也。²³⁸

Comment: Clearly there is some difficulty with the C, most commentators
being dissatisfied with, or puzzled by, 循, although it should be noted that
MZS makes a case for retaining 循 in the sense of 順 ("agree", "comply with").
Otherwise, several different attempts at resolution of this problem have been
made (note 237). There is also the issue of the apparently paradoxical
conjunction of 同 and 異. This does seem to be clarified by the idea of three
combinations of 彼 and 此 in which the two characters are the same, but their
"validity" differs. This brings the C&E into close association with GSL's "On
Names and Entities" (GSLZ 1), but essentially in agreement rather than
opposition, the conflict being with the view expressed in *Zhuangzi* 2 (GQF, vol.
1, p. 66). In the division of the E into three cases, prefigured in the C, I have
followed particularly MZS's analysis (his pp. 88–91).

237. In the DZ text the first four characters of this C are written, "循此循此", in which form
     they present a problem. Three variations have been proposed: (i) Simply to omit 循 in
     both instances (ZHY). (ii) To emend 循 to 彼 in both instances, retaining the same order
     (WFB, ACG, JBC). (iii) To emend 循 to 彼 and to change the sequence giving 彼彼此
     此 (CYX, LQC, TJF, WYJ, GH). I have followed the second option — see Comment.
238. There are several versions of what are here the final 10 characters. Early manuscripts
     have either "則彼亦且此此也" or, in the case of the Wu manuscript, "則彼亦且此
     也". In modern versions, ACG retains the Wu version, whereas a number of
     commentators retain the duplicated 此 (WFB, GH). WYJ raises the possibility of
     emending the first 此 to 止. The version above, with the addition of the three characters
     in parentheses, follows SYR and is itself followed by MZS.

B67   **C:** That this, that this and that this are the same. The explanation lies in the differences.

E: That: In the correction of names, with respect to that and this [there are three cases].

    i.   That and this are admissible: That [name] applies to that [entity] and stops at that [entity]; this [name] applies to this [entity] and stops at this [entity].

    ii.   That and this are not admissible: That [name] but this [entity].

    iii.   That-this is also admissible: That-this stops at that-this. In this case, with respect to that and this, then there is that also as well as this, this also as well as that.

B68   C: 唱和同患。說在功。[239]

E: 唱：〔唱〕[240] 無過、無所周。若粺。[241] 和無過，使也 ，不得已。唱而不和，是不學也。智少而不學，〔功〕[242] 必寡。和而不唱，是不教也。智〔多〕[243] 而不教，功適息。〔若〕[244] 使人奪人衣，罪或輕或重。使人予人酒，〔功〕[245] 或厚或薄。

Comment: Although it seems clear that this C&E is about the interrelationship between leading and following and their relative merits, there are several unresolved issues, particularly how to understand the presumed correspondence between 倡 / 和 and 教 / 學. One of the critical issues in the E is whether to add 功 where indicated or omit it where it is present. On this see particularly WYJ, note 393, pp. 601–602. A lesser issue is the initial nine characters of the E. There seems to be no objection to the addition of 唱 in the second place and no need to emend 過 to 遇 and 周 to 用 as suggested by WFB. There are questions about whether 若粺 is a misplaced gloss (as suggested by ACG), and about whether 粺 should be read as 稗 (SYR) or as 髀 (ACG). This does not affect the argument. It seems reasonable to accept the two other proposed additions as indicated (i.e. 多 and 若).

---

239. There are several issues in the C with variations in emendations and interpretation leading to somewhat different readings. Whilst there is general acceptance of 唱 as 倡 in the sense of 倡導 and 和 as 應和, there is division regarding 患, whether it should be left in its original form with the sense of 憂苦 (JBC), or 弊病 (LSL), or emended to 串 (e.g. YY, CYX, TJF, GH, AGC) in the sense of 貫穿 (MZQY). WFB emends 患 to 遇 in the sense of 偶 whilst WYJ suggests 惠. There is also a variation in the reading of 功 between 功勞 ("merit", "achievement") and 功效 ("efficacy"). Two versions often quoted which give the two basically different views are those of SYR (see WYJ, note 389, p. 601 — "言唱而不和，和而不唱，其患同") and of CYX (see TJF, p. 331).
240. Restored following, for example, ACG — see his note 539, p. 441.
241. There are several issues in these first nine characters — see Comment.
242. Added by a number of commentators (e.g.WFB, TJF, JBC) following YBY.
243. Restored on grounds of parallelism with 少 by, for example, SYR, WFB, AGC and JBC.
244. Added following ZCY.
245. 功 is added following a number of commentators (e.g. WFB, WYJ, JBC, LSL). Others add 義 (e.g. GH, TJF, MZQY).

B68   **C:** Leading and following are linked together. The explanation
lies in the merit.

E: Leading: In leading without exception, there is not what is
comprehensive — like weeds. In responding without exception, there is being directed; there is no choice. Leading but not
following — this is not to learn. If you do not learn when your
knowledge is slight, your merit must be diminished. Following
but not leading — this is not to teach. If you do not teach when
your knowledge is great, your merit comes to an end. For
example, if you cause a person to seize another's garment, the
fault in one (the perpetrator) is slight and in the other (the
instigator) is great. If you cause a person to give wine to
another, the merit in one (the instigator) is great and in the
other (the perpetrator) is slight.

B69   C: 聞所不知若所知，則兩知之。說在告。

E: 聞：在外者，所〔知也。在室者所〕不知也。[246] 或曰：「在室者
之色，若是其色」。是〔聞〕[247] 所不智，若所智也。猶白若黑
也，誰勝？[248] 若是[249] 其色也，若白者必白。今也智其色之若
白也，故智其白也。夫名以所明正所不智，不以所不智疑所
明。若以尺度所不智長。外，親智也。室中，說智也。

Comment: The C here is free of contention and the meaning seems clear.
One learns of what one does not know by hearing it linked to what one does
know. There are then, as the E concludes by saying, two ways of knowing: by
direct experience (親知) and by being informed (説知), which may require the
use of something already known.

B70   C: 以言為盡誖，誖。說在其言。

E: 以：誖不可也。之人[250] 之言可，是不誖[251]，則是有可也。之
人之言不可，以當，必不審[252]。

---

246. There are several approaches to the difficulties presented by this initial sentence of the
     E as it appears in early texts without the six characters in parentheses. One, particularly
     associated with LQC, but followed by WFB, ACG, GH and JBC for example, is to add
     these six characters. The second proposal, advocated by TJF and followed by LSL, is
     to omit 不 (see LCR for discussion). Another variant, proposed by WYJ, is to add "室
     中" following a comma after "外者". In translation I have followed the first proposal.
247. 聞 is added here by WFB and used in the translation on the grounds of meaning.
248. There are several issues with this sentence as follows: (i) How 猶 is to be read — e.g.
     "it is just as with" (ACG) or as 若 (WFB). (ii) How 若 is to be read — as 或 (WYZ,
     JBC), as 與 (SYR, WFB, LSL), as "or" (ACG). (iii) Whether GH's rather far-reaching
     emendation to "謂白若白，黑若黑也?" should be considered. In fact, this last has been
     used in the translation.
249. The two preceding characters are reversed from their usual order following LQC — see
     also LCR.
250. The emendation of 出入 to 之人 in line with the next sentence, following SYR, is
     generally accepted.
251. ACG takes these three characters to be a gloss — see his note 555, p. 445.
252. In the translation I have followed SYR's proposed emendation of 審 to 當. Many
     commentators retain 審 in the sense of 慎重, with reference to the LSCQ 6/2.2 (K&R,
     p. 160).

B69 **C:** If you hear that what you don't know is like what you do know, then you know both (the two). The explanation lies in informing.

E: Hearing: What is outside is what you know. What is in the room is what you don't know. Someone says: "The colour of what is in the room is like the colour of this." This is to hear that what you don't know is like what you do know. One says that white is like white, black is like black. It is like this is its colour; like white necessarily being white. Now you know its colour is like white, therefore you know it is white. Names are the means whereby what is not known is made clear and corrected and not the means whereby doubt is cast on what is clear. It is like using *chi* as a measurement for an unknown length. What is outside you know by direct experience; what is in the room you know by being told.

B70 **C:** To take words to be completely false is false. The explanation lies in his words.

E: To take: False equates with inadmissible. If this person's words are admissible and this is not false, then this is also admissible. If this person's words are inadmissible in terms of validity, they are certainly not valid.

Comment: The variations in the text are either generally agreed or do not affect meaning significantly. If 審 is retained in the final sentence of the E, this would read: "If this person's words are inadmissible, to take them as valid is certainly not to be prudent." On 誖 ACG writes: "*Pei (bei)* 'confused', 'fallacious' in later Mohist usage seems always to imply self-contradiction. The reference is presumably to Chuang-tzu's thesis that of anything said we may equally well say the opposite." — his note 553, p. 445.

B71   C: 惟²⁵³ 吾謂，非名也，則不可。說在反²⁵⁴。

   E: 惟²⁵⁵：謂「是霍」²⁵⁶，可。而猶之非「夫霍」也，謂「彼是」是也，不可。謂者毋惟乎其謂。彼猶惟乎其謂，則吾謂不²⁵⁷ 行。彼若不惟其謂，則〔其謂〕²⁵⁸ 不行也。

Comment: This is a very problematical C&E, as indicated in the notes. The first difficulty is with the head character. Should SYR's reading of 惟 as 唯, considered in note 253, be accepted? On this point, WYJ observes that the 吳 edition does, in fact, have 唯 — see his note 404, p. 603. ACG retains 惟 and renders it "specifically" — see his note 557, p. 446. In the E there is a question of whether 霍 should be understood as "crane" ("... the stock example of a name which can be loaned for another thing ..." — ACG, note 559, p. 446) or perhaps as the name of a person. I have left this question open. There is also the matter of whether SYR's proposal to delete 不 from the penultimate sentence should be accepted. Broadly, I have followed WYJ's reading of this C&E but note that WFB provides a relatively lucid reading, albeit one that requires a number of emendations. He takes this C&E to be about the distinction between 謂 and 名. What does seem likely is that the subject matter is related to GSLZ 1 (名實論), although exactly how is also problematical.

---

253. Following SYR, many commentators emend 惟 to 唯 in the sense of 諾 (see his note p. 473 relating it to the LSCQ 3/5.2 — K&R, p. 110), equating this with the modern 應 諾 ("agree", "respond"), for example, LSL. Some, however, retain 惟, for example, WFB and ACG, the latter reading it as "specifically". GH idiosyncratically emends 惟 to 離, also referring to the LSCQ, but this time Book 18. See LCR's discussion of this (p. 115).
254. In the DZ this is written with the 人 radical (ZWDCD #433).
255. Those who emend 惟 to 唯 in the C generally do so here also.
256. Most commentators read 霍 as 鶴 ("crane"). LSL, however, takes it to be a person's name, whilst SYR earlier proposed emendation to 虎.
257. There is division of opinion on whether SYR's proposal to delete 不 here should be accepted. Thus, WYJ does make the deletion (note 411, p. 603) whereas ACG does not.
258. Added following ACG.

B71 **C:** If the response to what I say (call it) is not the name, then it is inadmissible. The explanation lies in the converse.

E: Responding: To say this *huo* is admissible but still it is not *huo* in general. To say "that" and "this" are "this" is inadmissible. What is spoken of does not correspond to what he says. If "that" corresponds to what he says, then what I say works. If "that" does not correspond to what he says, then what the other says does not work.

B72   C: 無窮不害兼。説在盈否[259]。

E: 無：**Objection**: 南者有窮則可盡， 無窮則不可盡。有窮無窮未可智， 則可盡不可盡[260] 未可智。人之盈，之否未可智，而必[261] 人之可盡不可盡亦未可智。而必人之可盡愛也，誖。

Response: 人若不盈無[262] 窮，則人有窮也。盡有窮，無難。盈無窮，則無窮盡也。盡無[263] 窮，無難 。

Comment: This is generally accepted as a defence of the central Mohist doctrine of "universal love" with the E taking the form of an objection to the postulate of the C, followed by a response to this objection. The Objector uses Hui Shi's Paradox 6 (1st list) — "The southern region is 'without limit' yet is 'with limit'," — as the starting point of his argument which is, in essence, that there cannot be "universal love" for what is "without limit". The Responder establishes that whether people are "with limit" or "without limit", it is nevertheless possible to love them all.

---

259. There is the question of whether 知 should be the final character of this C (e.g. SYR, WFB), or the initial character of B33, in which case it is duplicated (e.g. LQC, GH, WYJ, TJF). I have taken the latter position on the grounds of sense.

260. These three characters are duplicated, presumably accidentally, in the DZ. Since BY they have been accepted as superfluous and the duplicated characters are omitted from the present text.

261. There is some doubt about 而必 here. Some regard it as misplaced from what follows and would delete it (e.g. LQC, ACG). Some emend 必 to 愛 (WFB) or to an ancient form of 愛 (ZWDCD #10644) — see TJF.

262. There is general acceptance of SYR's emendation of 先 to 無.

263. Emended from 有 or 其 — see ACG's note 571, p. 448.

B72   C: "Without limit" does not preclude (harm) "universal". The explanation lies in being filled or not.

E: Not: **Objection:** In the case of the south, if it has a limit, then it can be "exhausted"; if it has no limit, then it cannot be "exhausted". If whether it has a limit or does not have a limit can never be known, then whether it can be "exhausted" or cannot be "exhausted" can never be known. Whether people "fill" it or not can never be known, and whether people can be "exhausted" or cannot be "exhausted" also can never be known. So, of necessity, the claim that people can love exhaustively is perverse.

Response: With respect to people, if they do not "fill" what is "without limit", then people are "with limit". "Exhausting" what is "with limit" presents no difficulty. If (people) "fill" what is "without limit", then what is "without limit" is 'exhausted'. "Exhausting" what is "without limit" presents no difficulty.

B73   C: 不知其數而知其盡也。説在明[264] 者。

E: 不：**Objection:** 不[265] 智[266] 其數，惡智愛民之盡之[267] 也？
Response: 或者遺[268] 乎其問也。盡問人，則盡愛其所問。
若[269] 不智其數，而智愛之盡之也，無難。

Comment: This continues the debate about "universal love", using the analogy between "questioning" and "loving", if the emendation of 明 is accepted. It does seem that here, as with the previous E, the "Objection-Response" structure is used, although not all commentators/editors make this clear in this case. There is some ambiguity in the first sentence of the response. I have followed the simple interpretation — see, for example, JBC. The objection is that, if you do not know how many people there are, how can you claim to love them all? The response is that it is just like asking or questioning. One can claim to have asked/questioned everyone without knowing the number. It is in the response that the retention of 明 would seem to present some difficulty.

B74   C: 不知其所處，不害愛之。説在喪子者。[270]

E: None[271]

---

264. There is wide, but not universal, support for SYR's proposed emendation of 明 to 問 on the basis of the E. WFB, however, retains 明 equating it with 知.
265. Most editors follow CYX in emending 二 to 不 here, assuming there to have been a misreading of a duplication sign for 不. AGC, however, retains 二.
266. WFB emends 智 to 知 throughout the E. Whilst most editors retain 智, they read it as 知, as in a number of other instances.
267. There is general acceptance of SYR's emendation of 文 to 之 after 盡, here and in the final sentence.
268. Several modern editors equate 遺 with 遺漏 (e.g. LSL, MZQY), others with 失 (e.g. JBC).
269. I am inclined to follow WYZ"s reading of 若 as 則.
270. There is some variation in precisely how the final part of the C is interpreted. CYX equates 喪 with 出亡 ("flee", "live in exile"), LSL with 喪失 ("lose", "be deprived of"), and JBC with 逃失 or simply 亡, as does GH.
271. ACG takes the final sentence of the previous E as the E for this C&E — see his note 576, p. 450. He appears to be alone in doing this.

B73 **C:** Not knowing their number yet knowing their being "exhausted." The explanation lies in questioning.

E: Not: **Objection**: If you do not know their number, how do you know that loving the people is something that "exhausts" it?

Response: There are some who are left out in his questioning. If he exhaustively questions people, then he exhaustively loves those who are questioned. Then not to know the number, yet to know loving them "exhausts" it, is without difficulty.

B74 **C:** Not knowing their whereabouts does not preclude (harm) loving them. The explanation lies in lost sons.

E: None

Comment: This is the third of the three C&Es taken to be in defence of the Mohist doctrine of "兼愛" ("universal love"). It doesn't matter if there is no limit to the number of people, or the number is not known, or their location is not known, one can still love them all. There are minor variations in how the final three characters of the C are interpreted but these do not affect the basic meaning. ACG transfers the last sentence of the previous E to become the E for this C on the grounds that it "hardly makes sense" in B73. However, it also does not seem to make sense to talk of not knowing their number if the explanation lies in lost sons.

B75   **C:** 仁義之為外內[272] 也 ，內[273] 。説在仵顏[274] 。

   E: 仁：仁，愛也。義，利也。愛利，此也。所愛所利，彼也。愛利不相為內外，所愛利亦不相為外內。其為[275]「仁，內也」，「義，外也」；舉「愛」與「所利」也。是狂舉也。若左目出，右目入。[276]

Comment: There are three issues in the C: (i) The order of 外 and 內. (ii) How to read the second 內. (iii) How to interpret 仵顏. These points are considered in notes 272–274 below but, in summary, on the first I have followed most commentators in accepting the reversed order of 外 and 內 to make the structure equate with that put forward by Gaozi in his exchange with Mencius (particularly VIA.4). WFB retains the original order, the point then being more general — i.e. "external" and "internal" don't apply to 仁 and 義. I have followed ZQH and WYJ (among others) in reading the second 內 as 詩. I have retained 仵顏 following, for example, ACG — see his note 579, p. 451. This particularly makes sense in relation to the final sentence of the E. Whatever

---

272. The majority of modern commentators reverse the order of 外內 on the basis that it is 仁 that is 內 and 義 that is 外. In fact, "內外" is found in the 吳 manuscript.
273. What is the second 內 in early texts is variably treated. Some retain it as it is (e.g. LSL — see note 1, p. 354), some regard it as superfluous (e.g. GH), and some emend it — to 病 (WFB, JBC), to 詩 or 字 (WYJ, ZQH, ACG), or to 㐱 as 凶 (TJF).
274. There is considerable doubt about the final two characters which appear as 仵顏 in early texts. SYR proposed an emendation to 頡㬪 as in the LSCQ 6/5.3 (K&R, p. 170), which may indicate "confusion" or "disorder". WFB emends 顏 to 觭 in the sense of 奇 and offers a diagrammatic representation of the relationship between the matters discussed (see his p. 188). In view of the illustrative example at the end of the E, it seems best to retain 仵顏 — see WYJ, note 431, p. 606.
275. A number of commentators accept SYR's reading of 為 as 謂 here — e.g. WYJ, WFB, LSL.
276. There has been some debate about the final sentence. WYJ equates 出 with 外 and 入 with 內.

B75   **C:** To take benevolence as being internal and righteousness as being external is wrong. The explanation lies in matching in the face.

    E: Benevolence: Benevolence equates with love; righteousness equates with benefit. Love and benefit relate to "this" (the self); what is loved and what is benefited relate to "that" (the other). Love and benefit are neither internal nor external; what is loved and what is benefited are neither external nor internal. To say that benevolence is internal and righteousness is external and to conflate love with what is benefited are examples of "wild raising". It is like the left eye being external and the right eye being internal.

position is taken on these issues, and on some minor points in the E, there is
general agreement that the target here is the *Mencius* discussion — but see
also *Guanzi* 10.26 (SBCK, pp. 59–61).

B76   C: 學之〔無〕益也。説在誹者。[277]

E: 學也[278]，以為不知學之無益也，故告之也。是使智學之無益
也，是教也。以學為無益也，教誖。

Comment: Regardless of the textual variations indicated in notes 277 and
278, the interpretations of this C&E are essentially uniform and the meaning
seems clear. To advance the viewpoint that learning is of no benefit yet to
attempt to teach someone this is contradictory. The view itself, which clearly
the Mohists oppose, is exemplified by *Laozi* 20 which begins: "絕學無憂".

B77   C: 誹之可否，不以眾寡。説在可非。

E: 誹：論[279] 誹之可不可，以理之可誹，雖多誹，其誹是也。其
理不可非[280]，雖少誹，非也。今也謂多誹者不可，是猶以長論
短。

---

277. There are three issues regarding the C as follows: (i) Should 無 be added before 益 as
advocated by SYR? Opinion is quite divided on this. For example, among relatively
recent commentators WFB, GH and LSL favour doing so whilst WYJ, TJF, ACG, JBC
and MZQY do not. I have taken the former position. (ii) Should 誹 be emended to 誖,
again following SYR? LSL certainly agrees with this reading which does relate to the
E, but most retain 誹. (iii) What, then, is the meaning of 誹, both here and in the
subsequent two C&Es? 誹 is the subject of A30 where it is defined as "明惡". Proposals
for a modern equivalent include "非議" or "批評" (JBC), "誹謗" (MZQY) and "謗
議" (TJF). I have translated 誹 as "criticise" but think that censure or reproach is also
implied.
278. There is doubt about the initial characters here. Early texts have 學也 as above.
Variations are as follows: (i) To omit 也 (GH). (ii) To make 學也 the head characters
(JBC, LSL). (iii) To recognise a lacuna in front of 也 (ACG) and to fill it (e.g. 學也 —
WFB). (iv) To emend 也 to 他 in the sense of 彼, i.e. "the other" or "the one criticising"
(CYX, WYJ, TJF).
279. I have followed CYX in reversing the order of the first two characters in the DZ —
i.e. "論誹誹" becomes "誹：論誹" — and ACG in his reading of 論 in this context.
280. Taken as 誹 in conformity with the previous example, following WYZ and WYJ.

B76   **C:** "Learning is of no benefit." The explanation lies in the one criticising.

       E: In the case of learning, consider taking someone as not knowing that learning is without benefit and therefore teaching him [this]. This causing him to know that learning is without benefit is, in fact, teaching him. To take learning to be of no benefit yet to teach is contradictory.

B77   **C:** Whether criticism is admissible or not does not depend on whether it is much or little. The explanation lies in being admissible to negate (deny).

       E: Criticism: In sorting out whether criticism is admissible or inadmissible, if you take the principle as susceptible to criticism, then, even if the criticism is excessive, it is right. If its principle is not susceptible to criticism, even if the criticism is slight, it is wrong. Nowadays, it is said that what is much criticised is not admissible. This is like using the long to discuss the short.

Comment: The reading given above depends on taking 誹 as "criticism" and emending the first 非 to 誹. A somewhat different reading is given by ACG based on taking 誹 as "reject" or "deny" and emending the third 誹 in the E to 非 (his note 585, p. 452). A more thoroughgoing rearrangement of the E is made by WFB (p. 190). Although this contains four additional characters, these create a symmetry in the construction and obviate the problems of punctuation. What I understand WFB to be taking the E to say is that whether something is open to criticism or not depends on whether it is right in principle or not. A great amount of criticism does not invalidate something that is right in principle just as, conversely, a paucity of criticism does not confer validity on something that is wrong in principle. This is to counter the tendency to take the amount of criticism as the criterion of validity. What the "something" is, is not made explicit, although TJF is probably correct in assuming it to be philosophical doctrines in general.

B78   **C:** 非誹者，誖[281]。說在弗非。

   E: 非[282]：誹非[283]，己之誹也不非，誹非[284] 可非也。不可非也，是不非誹也。

Comment: Allowing for some variation in the reading of 誹 as discussed earlier, the meaning of this C is clear. The meaning of the E is less clear, as again evidenced by the variations, particularly in punctuation. Is it a simple statement about criticism, as I have translated it following primarily WYJ (his note 447, pp. 607–608), is it more generally about the denial of denial (e.g. ACG), or is it aimed at what are seen as the obfuscations of the Xingmingjia, as spoken of in the LSCQ 16/8.1 (K&R, pp. 400–401), which is what TJF believes? I have followed the apparently simple path, using WYJ's punctuation.

---

281. Emended from 誖 following ZHY.
282. The emendation of 不 to 非 following SYR is generally accepted.
283. There are several different arrangements of the two to four characters prior to 己 as follows: (i) That given above, found in WFB, and in WYJ and JBC, accepting SYR's emendation of 不 (note 282). (ii) 不誹，非 ... (WNS, MZQY). (iii) 非誹，非 ... (LSL). (iv) 不〔誹〕非 ... (ACG). (v) 〔不〕誹非， (GH). (vi) 非：“不非”言 ... (TJF).
284. A number of commentators (e.g. WYJ, JBC) follow WYZ in reading 非 here as 不.

B78 **C:** Negating criticism is perverse. The explanation lies in not negating.

   E: Negating: If the criticism is negatable, my criticism of it is not negatable; it is criticism inadmissible to negate. Being inadmissible to negate, this is not negatable criticism.

B79   C: 物甚[285] 不甚。説在若是。

E: 物：甚長甚短，莫長於是，莫短於是。是之是也。非是也者，莫甚於是。[286]

Comment: The above translation depends on accepting the changes at the start of the C (note 285), reading 甚 as 過度 following LSL, and following JBC's punctuation of the E. Despite the variations indicated, there is general agreement on meaning, well expressed by TJF (see his p. 346). A number of commentators stress that 是 should be read as 標準 in the sense of "standard" or "criterion".

B80   C: 取下以求上也。説在〔山〕[287] 澤。

E: 取：高下以善[288] 不善為度。不[289] 若山澤。處下善於處上，下所請[290] 上也。

Comment: There are several quite different interpretations of this C&E which are, of course, related to what emendations are made. The first, exemplified by GH and WFB, takes it to be a refutation, on grounds of common sense, of the paradoxical statements in the *Zhuangzi* 17 and 33 and *Xunzi* 3 and 22, in part at least attributable to Hui Shi, and focusing particularly on Paradox 3 of the 1st list — "Heaven and earth are low, mountain and marsh are level." The most critical emendation here is 善 to 差 in its three uses in the E. ACG, who makes none of these emendations, sees it as a Daoist statement, which, indeed, in his translation it becomes. WYJ (see particularly his note 450, p. 608), who also does not make the emendations apart from 請 to 謂, gives it an ethical interpretation which he illustrates by a quote from the *Jiazi* 9 (CSJC New Series, vol. 18, p. 528).

---

285. Uncertainty about the initial characters of the C — whether 物 is included in the previous C (BY) and whether the second character is 箕 — was cleared up to the general satisfaction by YY, ZHY and SYR.
286. Difficulties with what is here the second sentence of the E are evidenced by the variations in punctuation, the use of inverted commas (TJF), and by WFB's emendation of the third and sixth 是 to 甚 in both instances. TJF places a full-stop after 於是, as do WFB, WYJ and ACG. Others have no full-stop, but a single sentence (LSL, MZQY).
287. GH proposes the addition of 山 here.
288. Both WFB and GH emend 善 here and in the two following instances to 差.
289. Omitted by GH.
290. A number of modern commentators (e.g. GH, WFB, WYJ) emend 請 to 謂, following SYR. Others retain 請 — for example, TJF in the sense of 請求 and ACG in the sense of 精 ("essence").

B79 **C:** A thing [may be] extreme or not extreme. The explanation lies in being like "this".

   E: A thing: If it is extremely long (the longest) or extremely short (the shortest), there is nothing longer than "this", or nothing shorter than "this". In the cases of "this" being "this" or not being "this", there is nothing more extreme than "this".

B80 **C:** Choosing the low in order to seek the high. The explanation lies in [mountain and] marsh.

   E: Choosing: High and low are judged by the standards of good and bad. It is not like mountain and marsh. If being situated low is better than being situated high [then] low is what is called high.

B81 C: 是[291] 是與是同 。説在不州[292] 。

E: 不：是是，則是且是焉 。今是，〔文〕〔是〕於是而不〔是〕於是，故「是不〔文〕〔是〕」。[293] 是不〔文〕〔是〕，則是而不〔文〕〔是〕焉 。[294] 今是，不〔文〕〔是〕於是而〔文〕〔是〕於是，故「〔文〕〔是〕」與「是不〔文〕〔是〕」同説也 。[295]

Comment: What can be said of this rather perplexing C&E? Clearly the reading depends on how the C is structured and particularly on how the recurring 文 in the E, which no-one seems content to leave unaltered, is emended. Two areas where there is at least some common ground are the structure which, for example, both TJF and ACG take as two arguments and refutations (although in reverse order), and the possible relation to *Zhuangzi* 2 and to the GSLZ, particularly the "White Horse Discussion". I have followed TJF's text which involves, in the C, the emendation of the first 是 to 不 and 州 to 殊, and, in the E, the emendation of 文 in each instance to 是 and the addition of 是 where indicated in the second sentence. Following his analysis, the two pairs of statements in the E consist of an initial statement representing the Mingjia position (i.e. firstly, a white horse is a horse and secondly, white can be separate) — the common sense position — followed in each case by the Xingmingjia position, exemplified by GSL (i.e. firstly, a white horse is not a horse, and secondly, "不離白" or "守白"). Several alternative approaches may be briefly listed as follows:

---

291. There has been puzzlement over the initial duplicated 是 of early texts, as expressed by SYR. BY incorporated the first 是 in the previous C whilst a number of commentators (e.g. TJF, WFB, WYJ) emend it to 不 on the basis of the E. Others, however, retain the duplicated 是 (e.g. GH, LCR, ACG).

292. 周 is the emendation from 州 proposed, for example, by WYJ, ACG and JBC, in the sense of 周遍. Others (e.g. WFB, TJF, LCR, LSL, MZQY) take 州 to be 殊.

293. There are several variations of this second sentence which depend on the emendation of 文 as the third and the final characters and whether a character is added as the eighth character. The version above is that of TJF with 文 emended to 是 and 是 added as the eighth character. Other proposals include 止 (ACG), 之 (WFB, JBC) or 久 (GH) for 文 and 止 (ACG) or no addition (WFB) as the eighth character. The latter adds 之 as the penultimate character.

294. This is again TJF's version, depending on the emendation of 文 to 是 as the third and penultimate characters. Other commentators follow the pattern of emendation as indicated in the previous note. WFB has: "不不，則是而不之是焉", reading "不不" as 否. GH has: "是不久則是而亦久焉 。"

295. The final sentence of TJF's version again depends on the emendation of 文 to 是, others again emending to 之 (WFB), 止 (ACG), or 久 (GH).

B81   **C:** Not this and this are the same. The explanation lies in "not different".

         E: Not: (In the case of) "this-this", then there is "this" as well as "this" in it. Now in the case of "this", there is "this" in "this" and "not this" in "this", therefore "this-not this". In the case of "this-not this", then there is "this" and "not this" in it. Now in the case of "this", there is "not this" in "this" and "this" in "this", therefore "this" and "this-not this" are both said.

(i) WYJ: In the C, the emendation of the first 是 to 不 and 州 to 周, and, in the E, the consistent emendation of 文 to 之, the addition of 是 as with TJF in the second sentence, and the omission of the final 是 — see his notes 451–460, pp. 608–609, in particular, his analysis in note 460.

(ii) LCR: In the C, he retains the initial 是 but reads 州 as 殊. In the E, he consistently emends 文 to 之 and 不文 to 否之, and adds 之 in the second sentence where TJF and WYJ add 是 — see his pp. 132–134.

(iii) ACG: In the C, he retains the initial 是 but reads 州 as 周. In the E, he omits the first 是, consistently emends 文 to 止, and adds 止 in the second sentence where others add 是 (TJF, WYJ) or 之 (LCR) — see his analysis on pp. 454–457.

44: 大取

44.1   天之愛人也，薄[1] 於聖人之愛人也。其利人也，厚於聖人之利人
也。大人之愛小人也，薄於小人之愛大人也。其利小人也，厚於
小人之利大人也。

> **Comment:** Clearly the interpretation of this section depends on the reading of
> 薄. The subject is obviously love and benefit (愛 and 利), probably with
> emphasis on the distinction between the Confucian position, where the two
> are somewhat mutually exclusive with 利 being used pejoratively, and the
> Mohist position where love and benefit are inextricably linked. If 薄 is read as
> "extensive" or "all-embracing" (as many assume — see note 1 below), then
> there is identified an hierarchical arrangement of the conjunction of love and
> benefit, i.e. Heaven>sage>great man>small man, whereas, if it is read as
> "slight", the relationship is seen as antithetical and reciprocal, i.e. Heaven/
> sage, and great man/small man. I think the decisive argument for the former
> position is the usage elsewhere in the *Mozi* as indicated in note 1.

44.2   以臧[2] 為其親也而愛之，非[3] 愛其親也。以臧為其親也而利之，
非利其親也。以樂[4] 為利其子，而為其子欲之，愛其子也。以樂
為利其子，而為其子求之，非利其子也。

---

1. Two quite opposing views are taken on the reading of this character. First, there are those
   who give it its usual meaning. For example, LSL, quoting ZZR, equates it with 淡薄
   ("slight", "poor") whilst ZQH has "言天不能煦嫗之。" Second, there are those who
   read it as 博 or 溥 as, for example, in the *Doctrine of the Mean* XXXI.3 "溥博如天",
   for which Legge has, "all-embracing and vast, he is like heaven", in relation to Confucius
   (LCC, vol. 1, p. 429). The main argument for this position is that it accords with the usage
   of 博 and 厚 together elsewhere in the *Mozi* (e.g. *Mozi* 26 — 天志上) which has "愛人
   者，此為博焉，利人者，此為厚焉" in relation to Yu, Tang, Wen and Wu. This is a
   view expressed, for example, by both WYJ and TJF.
2. The majority take 臧 as "funeral", perhaps with "elaborate" implied, relying particularly
   on the *Shuo Wen*: "葬，臧也". Some, however, take it as the name of a person — for
   example, WYJ, ACG.
3. The translation depends on the omission of 非 following SYR, which most modern
   editors accept.
4. There is the same issue with 樂 as with 臧. Should it be read as "music" (音樂) as most
   commentators assume, or is it a name (e.g. WYJ)?

44: Choosing the Greater

44.1   Heaven's love of man is more all-encompassing than the sage's love of man; its benefiting man is more profound than the sage's benefiting man. The great man's love of the small man is more all-encompassing than the small man's love of the great man; the great man's benefiting the small man is more profound than the small man's benefiting the great man.

44.2   To consider an elaborate funeral as a manifestation of love for one's parents is to love one's parents. To consider an elaborate funeral as being of benefit to one's parents is not to benefit one's parents. To consider music to be of benefit to one's son and to desire it for one's son is to love one's son. To consider music to be of benefit to one's son and so seek it for one's son is not to benefit one's son.

Comment: Here interpretation depends on the reading of the two contentious characters 藏 and 樂. If they are taken as "(elaborate) funerals" and "music" respectively, the point is that, in the case of these two Mohist anathemas, such demonstrations of love ignore the necessary nexus between love and benefit in that, while they may be manifestations of the former, they do not, in fact, bring the latter, and so fail to qualify as true examples of the former. On the other hand, if both are taken as names, these sentences can be interpreted as examples of incorrect inference, as Zong has argued.[5]

44.3 於所體之中而權輕重，之謂權。權非為是也，亦[6]非為非也，權 正也。斷指以存腕[7]，利之中取大，害之中取小也。害之中取小 也[8]，〔子〕非取害也，取利也。其所取者，人之所執也。遇盜人而 斷指以免身，利也。其遇盜人，害也。斷指與斷腕，利於天下相 若，無擇也。死生利若一，無擇也。殺一人以存天下，非殺一人 以利天下也。殺己以存天下，是殺己以利天下。於事為之中而權 輕重，之謂求。求為之非也。害之中取小，求為義非為義也。

Comment: Whilst there are some minor textual issues in this section, more problematical are matters of interpretation. The first is how "於所體之中" is to be understood. There are several different readings here but I have opted to take it as referring to parts of the body.[9] The second is the reading of the sentence: "其所取者、人之所執也". I have taken this to mean that others determine what must be done i.e., the meeting with a robber is determined by another. Broadly, I have followed WFB's interpretation (although not his text) which makes the key distinction that between 所體 / 權 and 事 / 求. In the first case, the considerations are essentially practical. It is a matter of "weighing up" what is best. Meeting a robber is, at least to some extent, beyond one's control. If, in dealing with the adverse situation, one can escape with only the loss of a finger rather than the whole hand, one has "chosen the greater" in terms of benefit, and the converse in terms of harm. By contrast, in the conduct of one's affairs, matters which might be taken to be under one's control, there is an ethical element signalled by "seeking". The sentence about dying and living does present some problems in understanding. Some take it

5. Zong (2000), p. 210.
6. Following SYR, the emendation to 亦 here from 非 is generally accepted.
7. This is the generally accepted emendation, since BY, of the unidentified character or ZWDCD #12737 which is found in early editions.
8. 也 here should be deleted or emended to 子 and transferred to the next clause — see, for example, WYJ, note 14, p. 619, ACG, note 34, p. 253.
9. For a fuller discussion see Johnston (2000), note 19, p. 401.

44.3   With respect to what are parts [of the body], there is the weighing of light and heavy. This is called "weighing". "Weighing" is not about right and wrong. It is about the "weighing" being correct (i.e. making the correct choice). In terms of benefit, cutting off a finger to preserve the hand is to choose the greater [benefit]; in terms of harm, it is to choose the lesser [harm]. In terms of harm, choosing the lesser is not to choose harm, but to choose benefit. What is chosen is controlled by others. In meeting a robber, to cut off a finger to spare the (whole) body is a benefit. Meeting a robber is the harm. Cutting off a finger and cutting off a hand are alike in terms of benefit to the world; there is no choosing. Dying and living, in terms of benefit, are as one; there is no choosing. If killing another person will preserve the world, it is wrong to kill another person to benefit the world. If killing oneself might preserve the world, it is right to kill oneself to benefit the world. With respect to the conduct of affairs, there is a weighing up of light and heavy. This is called "seeking". "Seeking" *is* about right and wrong. In situations where the lesser harm is chosen, the "seeking" may be righteous or it may not be righteous.

to mean that there is no real choice in that death is shunned and life is chosen inevitably, but clearly there are situations in which this might not be the case. WYJ sees it as a statement of the "spirit of sacrifice" of the Mohists, referring also to both the *Mencius* and the *Zhuangzi.*[10]

44.4　為暴人語天之[11] 為是也[12]？而性為暴人，歌天之為非也。諸陳執[13] 既有所為，而我為之陳執， 執[14] 之所為，因吾所為也。若陳執未有所為，而我為之陳執 ，陳執因吾所為也。

Comment: This is a problematic section. The version given is dependant particularly on CYX's reading of "天之" as "天志" and his interpretation of "陳執". ZQH modifies the first two sentences to read: "為暴人語天之〔志〕為是也而惟。為暴人歌天之〔志〕為非也而惟。" He then transposes the first sentence of 44.5 below as: "為暴人謂天之〔志〕以人非為是也而惟。" which makes the whole statement seem to claim, in an unremarkable way, a significant role for the "will of Heaven", here in the specific case of the tyrannical or cruel ruler. ZQH speaks of a "usurper". In TJF's interpretation, the meaning is that a person's actions are not the ineluctable consequences of the will of Heaven, but are directly attributable to that person's nature and this, in turn, is not immutable, but is susceptible to change through environmental influences. This is, then, an argument against a significant role for the will of Heaven in determining human conduct, which has an important bearing on the issue of whether or not Mozi is a utilitarian, and for the influence of environmental factors on moral development, the kind of argument advanced elsewhere in the *Mozi.* It must be said that this is a very contentious passage.

10. The references are, respectively: *Mencius* VIIA.26(2) and *Zhuangzi* 2 (GQF, vol. 1, p. 96). Watson (1968) offers the following translation of the relevant statement in the latter, which is on the topic of the "perfect man": "Even life and death have no effect on him, much less the rules of profit and loss." See also *Mozi* 16 which has: "The weighing of life and death cannot be known."

11. There is widespread, although not universal, acceptance of CYX's reading of 之 as 志, both here and subsequently.

12. 也 here is read as 邪 making this a question in the version above, following WYJ.

13. A number of modern commentators accept CYX's analysis of this problematic phrase. He writes: "諸陳執者，人之所執不一也，如執無鬼，執有命，執厚葬久喪，與夫攻伐并兼音樂人之有所執而不化也久矣。是陳執也。墨子節用節葬非攻非命非樂之說，亦陳執也。" (MZJC, vol. 17, p. 193). See also WYJ, notes 27 to 33, pp. 620–622.

14. There are several variations here: (i) 執，執 as above — e.g. LSL, MZQY. (ii) 〔之，陳〕執執 — WYJ. (iii) 執；執 — TJF. (iv) 陳執，陳執 — WFB. (v) Omission of 執之所為 and reversal of 因 and 吾 — ZQH.

44.4   Is it right to speak of the will of Heaven with respect to the tyrant? It is his nature to be a tyrant. To attribute this to the will of Heaven is wrong. If the various long-established beliefs have already had their effects and I act in accordance with these effects, [then] it is the effects of these beliefs that cause me to act as I do. If the various long-established beliefs have not had effects, yet I act in accordance with these beliefs, then in terms of the long-established beliefs, it is through me that there are effects.

44.5   暴人為[15]：「我為天之〔志〕」以人非為是也，而性不可正而正之。
利之中取大，非不得已也。害之中取小，不得已也。所未有而取
焉，是利之中取大也。於所既有而棄焉，是害之中取小也。

> **Comment:** There are several issues with this short passage. First, there is its
> context, in particular whether the initial sentence should be retained in this
> position (as in the DZ) or transferred to follow the earlier statement about the
> "暴人" (see ZQH and Comment to 44.4 above). Then there is the validity of the
> reading of "天之" as "天志", as in the previous section, and third, whether the
> reading of 為 as 謂 in the opening sentence should be accepted.

44.6   義可厚，厚之。義可薄，薄之。〔之〕[16]謂倫列[17]。德行，君上，
老長，親戚[18]，此皆所厚也。為長厚，不為幼薄。親厚，厚；親
薄，薄；親至，薄不至。義，厚親不稱[19]行而顧[20]行。

> **Comment:** In the interpretation of this section there are three characters or
> phrases which present some difficulty. First, there is 義 which I have here
> translated as "duty" rather than the more usual "righteousness", being
> influenced by context and the suggestions of several modern commentators.
> Second, 薄 presents a problem, again used in the 厚 / 薄 conjunction. Here,
> however, unlike in 44.1, the reading as "extensive" or "all-embracing" seems
> inappropriate. Third, there is the matter of 倫列 which I have translated as
> "proper sequence". An alternative is "without difference of degree" (see TJF
> and *Mencius* IIIA.5(3)). It is of interest to note that the ZWDCD gives the latter
> interpretation to this term using the present passage as exemplification (vol. 1,
> p. 1101). Influenced by ZQH, who prefaces his section containing these
> statements with the "wandering fragment", "These are the Mohist's words", I
> have taken it to be both a statement of Mohist views and a defence against
> Mencius' attack through the acknowledgement of what Hansen terms "thick"
> and "thin" (terms I have used in the translation) responsibilities within the

---

15. 為 is read as 謂 — see, for example, Z&Q.
16. Added by SYR and some later commentators but not, for example, by CYX or MZQY
    — see WYJ, note 35, p. 622.
17. Most modern commentators accept SYR's interpretation of the term 倫列 (WFB and TJF
    put it in inverted commas), based on equating 倫 with 等, following a passage in the
    Zhanguoce, and 列 with 等比, in accordance with a passage in the *Li Ji*. LSL, who
    follows SYR, has: "…即平等對待。" WFB equates 倫列 with 差等.
18. The reading of 親戚 as "parents" here follows CYX.
19. On 稱, CYX has: "稱，審量也。"
20. Most modern commentators follow SYR in emending 顧 to 類 (e.g. WFB, WYJ, LSL).
    Some, however, retain 顧 (e.g. TJF, MZQY).

44.5 The tyrant says: "I am the will of Heaven" which is to take what people condemn and deem it right, and a nature that cannot be corrected and correct it. In choosing the greater from what is beneficial, there is an alternative. In choosing the lesser from what is harmful, there is no alternative. Choosing what one does not yet have is to choose the greater from what is beneficial. Casting aside what one already has is to choose the lesser from what is harmful.

44.6 If, according to duty, it is permissible to love [someone] "thickly", then love them "thickly". If, according to duty, it is permissible to love [someone] "thinly", then love them "thinly". This is to speak of "proper sequence". Virtuous rulers, elders and parents all are those one should love "thickly". [However], loving one's elders "thickly" does not entail loving those who are young "thinly". If relations are close they should be loved "thickly"; if they are distant they should be loved "thinly". One should be on close terms with one's parents whereas, with respect to those other than parents, one may love "thinly". It is in accord with principle to love one's parents "thickly". One must look closely at their conduct, but hope only to see virtues.

framework of universal love.[21] It cannot be claimed, however, that the difficulties have been resolved.

44.7   為天下厚禹，〔非〕[22] 為禹也。為天下厚愛禹，乃為禹之愛人[23]
也。厚禹之〔為〕[24] 加於天下，而厚禹不加於天下。若惡盜之為加
於天下，而惡盜不加於天下。愛人不外己；己在所愛之中。己在
所愛，愛加於己。倫列之愛己，愛人也。

Comment: Clearly there are problems in the first two sentences. On the grounds of meaning I have followed WYJ in adding 非 in the first sentence although he is something of a lone voice. I have also accepted SYR's reversal of "人愛", but not TJF's transposition from before 愛 in the second sentence to after the second 禹 in the first sentence. The correct rendering of 厚 is also something of a problem — again I have used "thickly" but also "esteem" in two instances — and I also have some disquiet about "proper sequence" for 倫列 in this context. As this was the translation in the preceding section, consistency demands its use here also. In a previous translation, I used "without distinction", which is TJF's reading, and I offer this again in parentheses above. These difficulties notwithstanding, it does seem that this section continues the discussion of the love/benefit nexus and makes two separate points. The first, which is based on the contrast between Yu as the paradigm of the virtuous man and a robber as the paradigm of the evil man, is that it is because of their actions that people are held in esteem or reviled. There is no ground for a specific response to the "undefined" person. It is people's actions that "define" them. The second point is that the self should be included in the scope of those who are loved, which would seem to be a prerequisite for truly universal love. This is, however, an important point for the Mohist to make explicit.

--- --- --- --- ---

21. Hansen (1992), p. 248. The reference to the *Mencius* is IIIB.9(9).
22. 非 is added here by WYJ on grounds of meaning — see his note 44, p. 623.
23. In the DZ there is "人愛", an order retained by TJF. Most modern commentators accept the reversal proposed by SYR to give "愛人" as above.
24. There is general acceptance of SYR's addition of 為 here in parallel with the next example.

44.7   To [love] Yu "thickly" for the sake of the world is not for the sake of his being Yu. To love Yu "thickly" for the sake of the world is, in fact, for the sake of Yu's love of man. To hold Yu in esteem for what he does "adds to" the world, whereas to hold Yu in esteem (as an individual) does not "add to" the world. Likewise, to abominate a robber for what he does "adds to" the world, whereas to abominate a robber (as an individual) does not "add to" the world. The love of mankind does not exclude the self, for the self lies within that which is loved. If the self lies within that which is loved, then love "adds to" the self. There is "proper sequence" in love of the self and love of mankind. (or — Love of the self and love of mankind are without distinction.)

44.8   聖人惡疾病，不惡危難。正體不動。[25] 欲人之利也，非惡人之害[26] 也。聖人不為其室 (臧之故在於臧)[27]。聖人不得為子之事。聖人之法，「死亡親」，為天下也。厚親，分也。以死，亡之，體渴興利。有厚薄而毋倫列之興利，為己。

Comment: Apart from the specific textual difficulties, the problem with this section is how to relate it to what has been said, with apparent acceptance, about gradations of love. The initial statements seem unexceptionable. The sage's attitude to disease and danger is determined only by the extent to which such vicissitudes impede him in his bringing of benefit to the people. He sets aside personal concerns, his own dwelling (echoes of Yu again here), his sons, and mourning for his parents, again because such things would interfere with his purpose. The problem comes when the argument turns to the opposite — that is, according special consideration to parents and accepting "proper sequence". This is identified as acting for the self. How this problem can be resolved without major textual changes is not clear. Even taking the earlier statements to be about the Confucian position, as some commentators do, is quite unsatisfactory in that it leaves the Mohist without a response to Mencius' challenge.

---

25. This is a difficult sentence. ZCY begins his long note with: "四字義其精微". On the recurring problem of 體, LSL has: "正體，指正其身" whilst WYJ has: "正體指感官言，不動指心言。" TJF places a comma after the first two characters. My translation, a somewhat free one, relies on these commentators. I have followed CYX in reading 惡 in the sense of 畏.
26. On the reading of 愛 for 害 here (included in the translation), see WYJ, note 52, p. 624.
27. These six characters have caused considerable puzzlement, although most editors retain them here. Then, by reading 臧 as 藏, for example following LSL, as 貨藏 in the first instance and 庫藏 or 國庫 in the second, and by ignoring the problem of 故, they take the statement to indicate that the sage does not store up goods for his own family, but in the national interest. I have, however, omitted them from this translation (ZQH also omits them). For an alternative reading, translating 臧 as a name, see ACG, p. 257.

44.8   The sage dreads disease and decay but does not dread danger and
difficulty. He maintains the integrity of his body and the resolve of
his heart. [He] desires the people's benefit: he does not dislike the
people's love. The sage does not consider his own dwelling. The
sage does not concern himself with the affairs of the son. The
sage's model (method) is to turn his mind from his parents on their
death for the sake of the world. To treat parents "thickly" is
divisive. By turning his mind from them after their death his whole
endeavour is to bring benefit [to the world]. When there is "thick"
and "thin" and not "proper sequence" (or — "no difference of
degree") in bringing about benefit, this is for the self.

44.9[28]   語經：語經者*，非白馬馬*。執駒馬*說求之，〔有〕*無*說非
也。殺*狗*之無*犬*，非也。[29] 三物必具，然後足以生。[30] 臧之
愛己，非為愛己之人也。厚〔人〕*不外己。愛無厚薄，譽*己，非
賢也。義，利；不義，害。志功為辯。[31] 有友*於秦馬，有友*於
馬也；知*來者之馬也。[32] (* indicates emended characters — see
notes)

---

28. In early texts, this section comprises 84 characters; modern editions of the complete *Mozi* (e.g., WYJ, LYS, LSL, Z&Q and MBJ) also have 84/85 characters. All would agree that the original text is incomprehensible, so a variety of emendations and transfers have been proposed. In the interests of clarity I shall divide the section into four parts, comprising 26, 9, 33 and 16 characters respectively, and deal with each of these in order in the following four notes. The same division is used by LYS.

29. On this particularly difficult statement, WYJ writes: "自 ‘語經’以下 二十六字，文有錯偽，其義未詳。" Several editors transfer it. Thus, TJF and ACG each make it the opening of a separate section with 語經 as the title. WFB and ZQH transfer the 26 characters, together with the following 9 characters, to 44.20 in the present text. Those who leave the characters here quote SYR: "語經者，言語之常經也。" Regardless of context, emendations are necessary. The emended characters are as follows: (i) 者 from 也 — widely accepted. (ii) 馬 from 焉 — widely accepted. (iii) 有 is added by SYR but not generally accepted. (iv) 無 from 舞 — widely accepted. (v) 殺 or 謂 from 魚 — widely accepted. (vi) 狗 and/or 犬 from 大 — widely accepted.

30. Placement is the issue here. What are the "three things"? On the reading above, they are the three "arguments" tersely referred to, all of which are of particular importance to the Later Mohists and the School of Names. For the transfer by WFB and ZQH see 44.20. For ACG, the three things are "love", "thought" and "benefit" — LMLES, pp. 246–248.

31. There is wide acceptance of SYR's addition of 人. The reading of 譽 for 舉 is also due to SYR and accepted by a number of later editors. LSL has 舉, reading it as 謀 on the basis of the LSCQ 10/4.2 which has: "不足與舉". The punctuation given for the five characters "義利不義害" is that of WFB which I think brings out the intended meaning. ZQH makes the final four characters the start of a separate section.

32. Quite apart from issues of placement, there are significant problems with the text of this short statement, as follows: (i) Should 有有於 stand, as argued by ACG, who takes "有有於X" in the sense of "have some X", or should one 有 in both of the first two clauses be emended to 又 (LSL), to 友 (SYR), to 囿 (WYJ), or to 乘 (WFB)? (ii) Should 秦 be retained as the name of the state, or emended to 來 as the name of a kind of horse, as suggested by ZQH? (iii) Is the reading of 知 for 智 acceptable? (iv) Should 來 in the final clause be retained in its usual sense (ZCY), read as the name of a kind of horse as above (ZQH), or emended to 乘 (WFB)? I have opted for SYR's emendation of the second 有 to 友 in the first case, for the retention of 秦 in the second, for the reading of 知 as 智 in the third, and for the retention of 來 in its usual sense in the fourth, all on the grounds of meaning.

44.9   With respect to language, there are constant rules. (These include) negating the "white horse/horse" (argument), not saying that "in seeking a horse one may direct attention to a foal" is wrong, and negating (the argument) that killing a pup is not killing a dog. These three things must be set out and then there is enough for life. Zang's loving himself does not make him a self-loving person. "Thick" does not exclude the self. Love is without distinction between "thick" and "thin". To praise oneself is not being worthy. Righteousness equates with benefit; non-righteousness equates with harm. The intention and the outcome are to be distinguished. To have a friend on a *Qin* horse is to have a friend on a horse. One knows that what has come is a horse.

Comment: This is arguably the most corrupt section of text in the whole Daqu. The issues are both textual and contextual. The former have been dealt with relatively completely in the notes, and the latter considered more briefly. I have opted to retain the 84/85 characters in the position in which they are found both in early texts and in standard modern texts of the complete *Mozi*. It must be acknowledged, however, that there are more or less good arguments for proposing an alternative placement, offered notably by TJF, ACG, WFB and ZQH.

44.10   〔凡學愛人〕³³。愛眾眾³⁴ 世³⁵ 與愛寡世相若。³⁶ 兼愛之有³⁷ 相若。
愛尚³⁸ 世與愛後世，一若今世之人也³⁹。〔人之〕鬼，非人也。兄
之鬼，兄也。⁴⁰ 天下之利驩⁴¹。聖人有愛而無利，儒者⁴² 之言
也；乃客之言也⁴³。天下無人⁴⁴，子墨子之言也猶在。⁴⁵

Comment: There are issues with all the sentences in this section. Nevertheless, it does appear to be a relatively unadorned statement of the Mohist position on universal love contrasted with the Confucian separation of benefit from love. The final three sentences pose the greatest problem. ZQH takes the Mohist's words to be "the world is not benevolence", which may be seen as a rebuttal of the Confucian statement "benevolence is humanity"

---

33. The placement of the preceding four characters here, attributable to WYZ, is accepted by a number of editors (e.g. WYJ, ZCY, LSL), but certainly not by all.
34. Generally accepted as superfluous following SYR.
35. 世 is read as 也 here and in its immediately subsequent use by BY.
36. The form of this sentence, with the second 眾 omitted and 世 retained, is due to SYR and is accepted by most modern editors (e.g. WFB, TJF, MZQY, MBJ, LSL).
37. Most commentators accept SYR's emendation of 有 to 又 although ZQH argues against this.
38. There is general acceptance of the reading of 尚 as 上.
39. Following WYZ's rearrangement of the original "今之世人也".
40. The addition of 人之 to the start of this sentence as it appears in the DZ is due to WYZ and is generally accepted. WYJ transfers this statement to what is 44.19 below — see his note 170, p. 639. The same statement also appears in 45.9.
41. There is some debate about 驩 — see WYJ, note 73, p. 626.
42. 儒者 is SYR's widely accepted emendation of 悅日 — see, for example, WYJ, note 74, p. 626. ACG, however, retains 悅 in the sense of 現 — see his note 21, p. 247.
43. ZCY takes this clause to be a later gloss.
44. Several modern editors (e.g. WYJ, LSL) quote SYR's note on this problematic clause: "無人即兼愛之義，言人己兩忘，則視人如己矣。"
45. There is a divergence of view on 猶在 as to whether the two characters should be retained here. I have followed TJF and ACG in doing so.

44.10 Everywhere study the love of people. The love of many generations and the love of few generations are the same. In universal love it is also the same. The love of former generations and the love of future generations are the same as the love of the present generation. A person's spirit is not the person. An older brother's spirit is the older brother. The world's benefit is pleasing. For the sage there is love and not benefit. These are Confucian words; that is to say, a stranger's words. Even if the world had no people, the words of Master Mo Zi would still remain.

found in the *Doctrine of the Mean* XX.5. TJF's version, which includes the problematic 'wandering fragment' (猶住), would read: "In the world there are no men (to continue his teaching), yet Master Mo's words are still preserved." In ACG's version, in which SYR's emendation of 倪日 to 儒者 is not accepted, there is no mention of Confucianism. In general, the equating of benefit and happiness, also seen in Canon A26, is in accord with a utilitarian ethics.

44.11[46] 不得已而欲之，非欲之 (非欲之)[47] 也。〔專殺臧〕[48]，非殺臧也，專殺盜，非殺盜也。(凡學愛人。)[49] 小圜之圜，與大圜之圜同。[50] 不至尺之不至也，與不至千里之不至不異。其不至同者，遠近之謂也。是璜也，是玉也。[51]〔意璜，非意玉也。意是璜之玉也。是楹也，是木也。〕意楹，非意木也。意是楹之木也。意人之指[52] 也，非意人也。意獲也，乃意禽也。

Comment: There are numerous difficulties with this section. I shall consider each sentence/claim in order as below:

1. Should the first sentence be retained here or be placed elsewhere as WFB proposes? This depends in part on what is made of the next two sentences.

---

46. Some editors start this section with 猶住 rather than include them in the previous section or move them elsewhere. WFB starts this section with: "凡學愛人".

47. These three duplicated characters are generally removed in modern editions following SYR — see WYJ, note 79, p. 627.

48. Added on the grounds of parallelism and meaning following WYZ.

49. This is the DZ placement of these four problematical characters which, in the present text, have been transferred to the start of the previous section. I can find no modern commentator who is satisfied with their placement here.

50. There are several problems with the following two sentences, the main ones being: (i) SYR's emendation of the original 方 to 不. Although many commentators accept this, it does demand some subsequent changes. TJF regards 方 as the start of a statement, the remainder of which is missing, but which is similar or identical to that in the LSCQ 25/ 2.1: "小方、大方之類也" (K&R, p. 627). ACG also retains 方 (ii) ZCY argues to retain 方 which favours the omission of 〔不〕至 in the first two instances. (iii) Should SYR's emendation of 錘 to 千里 be accepted? (iv) Should WFB's rearrangement of these two sentences (see his p. 414) be accepted?

51. The characters in parentheses are those added by CYX whose version is followed in the translation.

52. In most editions, the order of these characters is, 指之人. The reversal used above follows WYZ. ACG, who retains the first form, glosses the whole clause as: "visualise the finger as being the man."

44.11   To have no alternative to desiring something is not to desire it. [To take it upon oneself to kill Zang] is not to kill Zang. To take it upon oneself to kill a robber is not to kill a robber. The "circle" of a "small circle" and the "circle" of a "large circle" are the same. The "not reaching" of "not reaching a *chi*' and the "not reaching" of "not reaching a thousand *li*" are not different. That their 'not reaching' is the same is that far and near are being spoken of. This *huang* (jade ornament) is this jade, but thinking of the *huang* is not thinking of jade. It is thinking of this *huang's* jade. This pillar is this wood, but thinking of a pillar is not thinking of wood. It is thinking of this pillar's wood. Thinking of a person's finger is not thinking of a person. Thinking of the catch of the hunt is, however, thinking of animals.

2. What can be made of the next two sentences which are essentially incomprehensible without emendation? I have followed WYZ's addition of "專殺臧" at the start of the first sentence, reading 專 as 欲 to give a meaning which does relate to the opening statement. If 專 is retained it may be read as "only", "singly", or perhaps best, "to act on one's own responsibility" or "take it upon oneself" (see *Mencius* VIB.7(3), LCC, vol. 2, p. 437). ACG's suggestion, which has obvious merit, is that the start of the sentence is missing — see his p. 251.

3. The next four characters certainly seem out of place. Their transfer is generally accepted.

4. The claim about the circle seems unexceptionable, the term "circle" having the same meaning in both instances. By contrast, the term "not reaching" has different connotations in the two instances. There are, however, textual difficulties with the second case which must be taken into consideration.

5. As they stand, the next pair of statements are not obviously connected. In the first, all that is said is that the *huang* is jade — a completely trivial claim. In the second, the point is that if someone thinks of a wooden pillar, they do not think of wood in general, but specifically of the wood of the pillar. CYX's emendation, which I have accepted, gives the statement some substance, bringing the two into line, as do the modifications of WFB and ZQH, albeit in different ways.

6. The aim of the final two statements, particularly if WYZ's reversal is adopted as above, is to make a point about the part/whole relationship.

44.12 志功，不可以相從也。〔凡譽—愛人〕利人也，為其人也；富人，非為其人也，有為也，以富人富人也。[53] 治人有為鬼焉。為賞譽利一人，非為賞譽利人也，亦不至無賞譽[54] 於人。智親之一一利，未為孝也，亦不至於智不為己之利於親也。

---

53. This sentence as it appears in the DZ and other early editions is, in effect, incomprehensible. Numerous emendations and rearrangements have been made to extract meaning from it. I have followed TJF's version, the key features of which are: (i) The placement of 凡譽 at the start. (ii) The addition of 愛人 before 利 人. (iii) The retention of the duplicated 富人. (iv) The punctuation. An alternative version, which involves a greater degree of modification, is that of WFB.

54. There is general acceptance of SYR's replacement of 貴, found in early texts, with 賞 譽.

44.12   Intention and outcome may not follow each other. In general, what
is praised is loving people and benefiting people for the sake of
their being people. Enriching people is not for the sake of their
being people. In terms of "for the sake of", it is by enriching
people that one enriches people. Bringing order to people is for the
sake of ghosts. To consider reward and praise to be of benefit to
one person is not to consider reward and praise to be of benefit to
mankind, but it also does not mean that one does not reward and
praise one person. To know a parent is one (person) and to benefit
(the parent) is not to be filial, but it also does not go so far as to
mean that one does not know that being filial is to benefit one's
parents.

Comment: Although the meaning of the first sentence seems clear enough, its placement has occasioned some difficulty. There is considerable doubt too about the following sentence (or sentences, depending on punctuation). The translation follows TJF's version which includes the idiosyncratic addition of "凡譽一愛人" at the start. The short statement about ghosts accords with the general tenor of *Mozi* 31, and specifically the following: "In this case, the reason the ancient sage kings brought order to the empire was certainly that they put ghosts and spirits first, and people second."[55] The rather free translation of the final two sentences follows ZQH.

44.13   智是之[56]世之有盜也，盡愛是世。智是室之有盜也，不盡〔惡〕[57] 是室也。智其一人之盜也，不盡〔惡〕是二人。雖其一人之盜，苟 不智其所在，盡惡其弱[58] 也[59] ？

Comment: There are several textual emendations in this short section which are either generally agreed upon, or, in respect to which, variations do not affect meaning. The version above predominantly follows SYR's changes with the addition of WYJ's framing of the last sentence as a question. The argument is one of particular importance to the Mohist. If one embraces "universal love", what is one's position vis-à-vis robbers? Three cases are considered; the world, a household, and a pair of men. ZQH's view, reflected in his textual emendations, appears to be that despite the presence of men whom it is appropriate to dislike within each group, it is still possible to love the group as a whole regardless of size. TJF, with somewhat different emendations, takes the view that it is a question of dilution in that, in the world, the proportion of robbers is small so one can love the world whereas, in the smaller groupings, the proportion is larger so loving completely may not be appropriate.

---

55. See *Mozi* 31.10.
56. There is general agreement following SYR that 之 should be omitted here.
57. 惡 is added here and in the following sentence by SYR and by the majority of subsequent commentators.
58. Many commentators, following SYR, emend 弱 to 朋 which is used in the translation.
59. I have followed WYJ in reading 也 here as 耶, making this final sentence a question.

44.13 One may know that in this world there are robbers, but still have complete love for this world. One may know that in this household there is a robber, but not have complete hatred for this household. One may know that of two men one is a robber, but not have complete hatred for these two men. Although one of the men is a robber, if one does not know which one it is, can one have complete hatred for the associate?

44.14 諸聖人所先為人[60]。欲名實名實不必名[61]。苟是石也白，敗[62] 是石
也，盡與白同。是石也雖[63] 大，不與大同。是有便[64] 謂焉也。以
形貌命者，必智是之某也，焉[65] 智某也。不可以形貌命者，雖不
智是之某也，智某可也。諸以居運命者，苟入[66] 於其中者，皆是
也。去之，因非也。諸以居運命者，若鄉里齊荊者，皆是。諸以
形貌命者，若山丘室廟者，皆是也。[67]

Comment: This is a very contentious, but critical, section. Essentially, there
have been four different approaches to it as follows:

1. To make the issue of the correspondence of names and objects — of
    course, of central importance to the Later Mohist — the primary task of the
    sage. This is the position I have taken following, in particular, ZQH and
    LSL.

2. To treat the sage's primary responsibility as separate from the issue of
    names and objects, defining it rather as acting for the general good, as
    opposed to being guided by self-interest. This is WYJ's interpretation,
    citing the *Yanzi Chunqiu* and the *Han Feizi*.[68]

3. To read 名 and 實 as "reputation" and "practice" respectively, in the sense
    used, for example, in Mencius: "Ch'un-yü K'un said, 'He who puts
    reputation and real achievement first is a man who tries to benefit others
    ...'."[69] This is the position taken by both TJF and LQC. TJF then retains the
    first two sentences in his version of the "Daqu" and places the rest of the
    section in his 語經 ("Rules of Language").

---

60. See Comment on the issue of whether this should be considered as separate from what
     follows or not.
61. ZQH has the following arrangement of these two sentences: "諸聖人所先為，必效名
     實。名實不必合。" — see MZJC, vol. 29, p. 262. This is what is translated above and
     is also found in the recent editions of LSL and Z&Q. The variations are numerous as
     discussed under Comment.
62. Emended to 取 by SYR and ZQH, or read as 毀 (MZQY) or 壞 (WYW) in the sense of
     毀壞 or 破損.
63. There is widespread acceptance of SYR's emendation of 唯 to 雖 here and in the
     following instance.
64. SYR has the following note: "使、疑當為使" which most accept, although some retain
     使 in the sense of 便宜 or 便于 (ZCY, LSL).
65. Most recent commentators accept SYR's reading of 焉 as 乃 here.
66. There is general acceptance of SYR's emendation of 人 to 入.
67. As with the start, there is also some doubt about the end of this section. Whilst the
     majority of editors end it as above, others (e.g. WFB and YTY) have different versions.
68. The references in the SBCK are vol. 14, YZCQ, p. 29 and vol. 18, HFZ, p. 89.
69. *Mencius* VIB.6(1) transl. after Lau, p. 271.

44.14 The primary task for all sages must be to establish the correspondence of names and entities. Names and entities are not necessarily in accord. If this stone is white, and you break this stone up, its whiteness is the same throughout. [If] this stone is large, the same does not apply to its largeness. This is the ordinary way of speaking about it. With things named on the basis of form and appearance, one must know it is this sort of object (entity) and then one knows what it is. With things that cannot be named on the basis of form and appearance, although one does not know it is this sort of object (entity), it is still possible to know it. With all things named on the basis of dwelling in or departing from, if there is entry into them, they are all this, and if there is departure from them, they are not this. For example, district, village and the kingdoms of Qi and Jing are all things named on the basis of dwelling in or departing from, whilst mountains, hills, houses and temples are all things named on the basis of form and appearance.

4. To make the terms "name" and "object" ("entity") the title of a separate, hybrid treatise, which is what ACG has done, omitting any reference to the sage's tasks.

What I have done in the translation above is to relate the first sentence to the rest of the section (as in point 1 above), and then followed SYR's five widely (but not universally) accepted emendations as detailed in notes 62–66.

44.15　智與意異。[70] 重同，其同[71]，連同、同類之同，同名之同，同根之同[72]，丘[73] 同，鮒[74] 同，是之同、然之同，有非之異，有不然之異。[75] 有其異也，為其同也，為其同也異。[76] 一曰乃是而然，二曰乃〔不〕[77] 是而不然，三曰遷，四曰強。

Comment: The first issue with this section is the placement of what are here the first four characters. It could be maintained that they are out of place with respect to the argument, although that depends on their reading. In the immediately following enumeration of ten bases of sameness, there are both questions of order and questions of emendation or interpretation of individual characters. On the matter of order, ACG argues forcefully for the retention of the original order on the grounds that the list is really of eight kinds of sameness divided into two groups, taking the fifth and tenth phrases as summarising the respective groups. In the translation, I have changed the order to accord with that proposed by SYR, TJF and ZQH. This is for two reasons. The first, and less important, is that of structure. The second, and more significant, is that it allows the grouping of statements on 是 / 非 and 然 / 不然. The next statement presents considerable difficulty. Because I think

---

70. The placement of the preceding four characters varies. Several modern editors (e.g. WFB, TJF, ZQH, ACG) do not have them here.

71. There is general acceptance of SYR's reading of 具 as 俱.

72. There is some question about the placement of these four characters. In the DZ they follow the next ten characters, a position which a number of editors retain — see particularly ACG. I have followed SYR who places them here, as do TJF and ZQH.

73. BY gives this as the variant of 邱 which SYR, who refers to another variant (ZWDCD #28) reads as 區. WYJ quotes SYR as follows:"丘與區通，謂同區域而處。"

74. There is general acceptance of SYR's emendation of 鮒 to 附 which LSL glosses as "互相依附".

75. To this point there is, apart from the specific character emendations, relative uniformity in the various texts. The sentence that follows is, however, very problematic. In the translation I have followed WFB's modified version which seems to make sense. This reads:"有其異也，為其同也，其同也、為其異也；異。"

76. The placement of this final sentence varies — see Comment.

77. TJF appears to be alone in adding 不 here. This is followed in the translation.

44.15   Knowing and conceptualising are different. There is the sameness of duplication (two names for the same entity). There is the sameness of being together (agreement). There is the sameness of being connected (components of one body). There is the sameness of the same class. There is the sameness of the same name. There is the sameness of the same root (origin). There is sameness related to region (place). There is the sameness of inter-dependence. There is the sameness of *shi* (是 — the same in reality) and the sameness of *ran* (然 — the subjective impression of sameness). There is the difference denoted by *fei* (非 — different in reality) and the difference denoted by *bu ran* (不然 — the subjective impression of difference). There are instances of something's difference being taken as its sameness, and of something's sameness being taken as its difference; these are different.[i] The first is said to be *shi* and *ran* (是 and 然 — so objectively and subjectively). The second is said to be *bu shi* and *bu ran* (不是 and 不然 — not so objectively and not so subjectively). The third is said to be *qian* (遷 — a transformation or change). The fourth is said to be *qiang* (強 — a forced analogy).

---

i.   This sentence follows WFB. In his own notes he gives his interpretation as: "…異之中有同，同之中有異。" — "… in difference there is sameness; in sameness there is difference."

it makes the point intended, I have followed WFB's version in the translation. In no small part, the problems relate to context, particularly with respect to what follows. The section as given above concludes with a summary of four situations, the first two desirable but the second two not so. In the first two instances, things that are objectively the same or objectively different are recognised as being so by the perceiving subject. In the second two instances, there is failure of the objective and subjective to coincide in either direction, for which specific terms are offered.

44.16   子[78] 深其深，淺其淺，益其益，尊[79] 其尊。察次山[80] 比，因至優指。復次，察聲端名，因請[81] 復正。

Comment: Of the three sentences in this short section, the translation of the first depends on understanding 子 as referring to 墨子 as many commentators do, and accepting YY's emendation of 尊 as, again, most commentators do. The meaning then becomes clear, but the context remains a problem. I am inclined to favour WFB's placement as the concluding statement of the preceding section. The translation of the second and third sentences presents greater difficulties. That given above is based on the emendations and interpretations of CYX and TJF which are also followed, for example, by LSL.

44.17   〔正〕[82] 夫辭惡者，人右[83] 以其請[84] 得焉。諸所遭執，而欲惡生者，人不必以其請得焉。

Comment: There are problems with these two sentences involving both text and context. I have isolated it here to draw attention to the difficulties and have offered what is, at best, a tentative translation which depends on starting with

---

78. A number of commentators (e.g. WYJ, TJF, LSL, LYS) take this to refer to Mo Zi's doctrines.
79. There is general acceptance of YY's proposal that 尊 should be emended to the uncommon character of the same sound (ZWDCD #2211) in the sense of 減 — see, for example, LSL.
80. Read as 由 following, for example, TJF.
81. Read as 情 following SYR.
82. It is debatable whether this character is the first character of this sentence or the last character of the last sentence of the preceding section, and, if the former, whether it should be emended to 匹 as suggested by SYR and accepted by a number of later commentators.
83. There is general dissatisfaction with 右 here, although WFB for one leaves it. The majority emend it to 有, possibly in the sense of 或, following SYR. There may be a case for emendation to 必 to parallel the following statement. ZQH emends 右 to 可.
84. There is widespread agreement that 請 should be read as 情.

44.16 With respect to Master Mo's doctrines, look deeply into what is deep and superficially at what is superficial. Increase what should be increased; decrease what should be decreased. Examine sequence by means of comparison; as a consequence, one comes to many manifestations. Next, examine sounds for the origin of names; as a consequence, the reality is again made correct.

44.17 If a man avoids what he dislikes, others are able to ascertain his feelings. In the case of all who meet with life's vicissitudes, and in whom likes and dislikes arise, others are not necessarily able to ascertain their feelings.

正 read as 匹 (SYR), reading 辭 as a verb, emending 請 to 情, and taking 欲 and 惡 as "opposites". I shall briefly enumerate some of the other versions and interpretations below:

1. WFB: This section is joined with the last two sentences of the previous section, the whole being followed by the comment given in the Comment to the previous section.

2. ZQH: This section is placed in his final section which begins with "志功不可以相從也" followed by the sentences on tyrants, then these sentences, then "志功為辭", followed by the list of four which completes 44.15 above.

3. ACG: To make this section part of his separate treatise "Expounding the Canons" where it is contained in #2 which begins with what is here 44.8 — see LMLES, pp. 246–248.

4. TJF: He has this as a separate statement in his Daqu following the first sentence of the previous section, the two intervening sections being included in his '語經'.

5. Z&Q: They essentially follow SYR and quote him as follows: "正：孫詒讓：'當為"匹"。'正夫、即匹夫。辭惡：孫詒讓注：'此以訟獄為喻也。辭惡，謂不受惡。言匹夫雖賤，而不肯受屈，必欲自明其志，則可以得其情實。'" (note 19, p. 664).

6. WYJ: He makes substantial changes to the initial statement and also adds the first sentence of the next section to this section. He has a detailed note (note 143, p. 635) which begins: "此言觀察事物，不僅如上文繫於用以觀察之方法，尤繫於能觀察之本身。觀察事物，欲得其真實，須觀者本身正其欲惡。欲惡正者，常能得是非利害之情。凡於外物有所遭遇執箸而欲惡生者，則不必得是非利害之情，因心有所偏蔽也。" He gives references to a number of what he sees as related passages including, particularly, the *Xunzi* 21 (21/7b, K, vol. 3, p. 107).

44.18　聖人之拊潰[85]也，仁而無利愛。利愛生於慮。昔者之慮也，非今日之慮也。昔者之愛人也，非今之愛人也。愛獲[86]之愛人也，生於慮獲之利。慮獲之利，非慮臧之利也。而愛臧之愛人也，乃愛

---

85. There are issues with these two characters which appear in the DZ as 拊 and the unknown character consisting of 賈 with the 水 radical. BY was initially responsible for the reading of 拊 as 附 whilst CYX suggests 撫 and has the following note: "拊與撫同，撫覆者，天下皆在含育之中也" (MZJC, vol. 17, p. 200). TJF and others proposed 潰 for the unknown character and this is used above.

86. Here and following, both 獲 and 臧 are generally accepted as names to indicate different people.

44.18   The nurturing of the sage is based on benevolence and not on benefit and love. Benefit and love arise from "consideration". The "consideration" of former times is not the "consideration" of the present day. Love of *Huo* as loving another arises from

獲之愛人也。去其愛而天下利，弗能去也。昔之知墻，非今日之知墻也[87]。貴為天子，其利人不厚於正夫[88]。二子事親，或遇熟，或遇凶，其親也相若，非彼其行益也，非加也[89]。外埶[90]無能厚吾利者。藉臧[91]也死，而天下害，吾特[92]養臧也萬倍，吾愛臧也不加厚。

Comment: In this section, the problems again involve both text and context. Considering the latter first, of the five recent editions of the complete *Mozi* consulted, two have it separate from, but immediately following, the two previous sections in the present text (MZQY/Z&Q, LSL), whilst three have it more (LYS, MBJ) or less (WYJ) with the previous two sections. Other editors, however, treat it quite differently. On the issues of text, the main questions concern first, the two characters given as 拊 / 附 and 瀆 in the opening sentence; second, the reading of 慮; and third, the problem of 牆 or 嗇 (or something else). On the first, the reading of 撫養 suggested by LSL seems appropriate. On the second, the interpretation of 慮 must take into account the definition in C&E A4 where it is equated with 求. On the third, YY's proposed emendation of 牆 to 嗇, although widely accepted, does seem slightly contrary to context, making WFB's emendation of 知 and 牆 / 嗇 to 利 and 臧 in both instances, an attractive alternative. In general, this section returns to the issues addressed at length in the first sections of the Daqu: the relationship between love and benefit; the Mohist definition of "seeking" (depending on how 慮 an 求 are related); the independence of one's endeavours in these areas to changes of external circumstances; and, somewhat obliquely, the matter of choosing in relation to benefit and harm. In this respect, one might note again ZQH's placement of this section at the start of the Daqu.

---

87. There is variation in the reading of this statement. WYJ, who cites SSX's proposed emendation of 墻 to 臧, dismisses it as "未詳" — see his note 150, p. 637. Others, including the modern editors LSL, MBJ and Z&Q, accept YY's proposed emendation of 墻 to 嗇 which is what is followed in the translation.
88. The emendation of 正夫 to 匹夫 due to SYR is followed in the translation.
89. There is some question about the placement of these three characters — see WYJ, note 152, p. 637.
90. There is some variation in this character given as above in the DZ. WYJ has 埶 and adds the note "'埶'舊本作'熟'。" and adds BY's note as follows:"言歲埶，歲凶。" Some emend 埶 to 勢 (e.g. WFB) or read it in this sense (e.g. Z&Q), the latter taking 外勢 in the sense of "the force of external things" — see their note 7, p. 665.
91. Taken as 臧 as elsewhere in the passage.
92. Read as 持.

"considering" *Huo's* benefit and not from "considering" *Zang's* benefit. Yet loving *Zang* as loving another is the same as loving *Huo* as loving another. If doing away with loving them brings benefit to the world can one not do away with it?[ii] The knowledge of frugality in former times was not like that of the present day. The Son of Heaven may be rich, but in his bringing benefit to the people, he is not more generous than the ordinary man. [Suppose there are] two sons serving their parents. One may meet with a good year and the other a bad year yet, in benefiting their parents, they are the same. It is not that the former's benefiting is increased (by the good year) and the latter's diminished (by the bad year). External circumstances cannot determine the generosity of their benefiting. If the death of *Zang* were to bring harm to the world, although I might support and nurture *Zang* ten thousand fold, my love for him would not be any greater.

---

ii.   Two ways of giving this sentence the force it seems to require are to phrase it as a (rhetorical) question as above (following WFB) or to add 不 to again give a question.

44.19　長人之異短人之同[93]，其貌同者也，故同。指之人也與首之人也
異。人之體，非一貌者也，故異。[94] 將劍與挺劍異[95]，劍以形貌
命者也，其形不一，故異。楊木之木與桃木之木也同。諸非以舉
量數命者，敗之盡是也。[96] 故 一人指，非一人也。是一人之指，
乃是一人也。(故一指非一人也。一人之指乃是一人也。)[97] 方之
一面，非方也。方木之面，方木也。

Comment: On the surface, and accepting the various emendations
proposed, this section seems to signal a return to the issues of sameness and
difference and their relation to naming, addressed in 44.11. Things named on
the basis of form and appearance, providing they conform to the essential
requirements of the class, can be subsumed under the class name, e.g.
swords and men, despite their wide variation in actual appearance. The
remaining examples are, however, an odd assortment. Even with respect to
men and swords, the argument depends on several critical textual
emendations and word interpretations. The statement apparently about the
wood of the two types of tree might, in fact, be about the word "tree" in the two
descriptions and belong with similar observations about circles and
distances, to which it is placed in apposition by ZQH in his section 5. Likewise,
the variably placed statement about the uniformity of some properties within
an object may be more appropriately read in conjunction with the discussion
of large and white in 44.14 above. The two separate claims involving 指 are
bedevilled not only by the uncertainty surrounding this word itself, but also the
reading of the phrase "指之人". In the first instance, I have accepted WYZ's
reversal of the nouns and, in the second instance, I have equated the usage
of 指 with that in GSLZ 5, as suggested by WYJ. The argument about the cube
of wood is clarified by CYX as follows: "In establishing a cube there are

---

93. YY has proposed two emendations to this clause: The first is 與 from 異 and is widely
accepted; the second is 也 from 之 and is less widely accepted.
94. The problem with this phrase is the somewhat odd construction seen in "指之人" and
"首之人". As in 44.11, the simplest approach is to reverse the positions of the nouns in
each case, as WYZ suggested there. This is done by LSL and Z&Q, for example, and is
followed in the translation.
95. There are divergent views on whether 將 and 挺 refer to types of sword (see, for example,
ZQH, ACG), or actions with a sword — 扶 and 扙 — see particularly SYR and LSL.
I have taken the first position.
96. In this sentence, SYR and a number of commentators following him, read 敗 as 取.
Others, including ZCY who refers to the LSCQ 14/4.2, read 敗 as 破 or 析開 (LSL).
97. This is WYZ's version, accepted by a number of commentators. CYX and ZCY simply
omit the first 人. There is an important issue here relating to the problematic character
指.

44.19   A tall man and a short man are the same; their appearance is the same, therefore they are the same. A man's head and a man's finger are different. (The parts of) a man's body are not of one appearance, therefore they are different. A *jiang* sword and a *ting* sword are different. Swords are named according to form and appearance. Their form is not the same, therefore they are different. The wood of the willow tree and the wood of the peach tree are the same. With respect to all things which are not named on the basis of measurement and number, when broken up they are completely uniform, therefore they are the same. One man's *zhi* (representation, manifestation, attributes) are not the man himself, yet this one (particular) man's *zhi* (representation, manifestation, attributes) is, in fact, this one (particular) man. One surface of a cube is not a cube. A cube of wood's surface is a cube of wood.

altogether six surfaces. One surface is not sufficient for it to be deemed a cube (but) if the cube is of wood then, from seeing one surface, it is possible to know the rest." The probable relationship to the previous statement is that one need only see a part of something, under some circumstances, to be able to infer that it is that thing.

44.20 〔夫辭〕[98] 以故[99] 生，以理長，以類行者也[100]。立辭而不明於其〔故〕[101] 所生，忘[102] 也。今[103] 人非道無所行，雖[104] 有強股肱，而不明於道，其困也可立而待也。夫辭以類行者也，立辭而不明於其類，則必困矣[105]。

Comment: This is an important section although there are problems in relation to both placement and "structure", and also interpretation of the key terms, specifically, 辭, 故, 理, 類 and 道. Considering the former, the issues concern how the section starts, how it ends, where (i.e. in relation to what) it is placed, and the matter of the nine characters beginning 三物 which are given earlier in 44.9. Clearly, interpretation will depend on the "structural" arrangement decided upon and especially on context. There is, in fact, no compelling evidence which would lead someone to adopt any particular one of the proposals advanced. All have their merits, but, if one focuses on what is actually being claimed, it does seem that, if 夫辭 are accepted as being the opening characters, three claims are being made about 辭 — that they arise through 故, are extended or develop through 理, and are put into action on the basis of 類. The question then becomes precisely what these terms signify in this context. Here again opinions differ. They do, however, appear to be general claims, and the following three sentences contain some elaboration of these claims, as WFB has made explicit. Whether the three claims are the "三物" is another matter. Indeed, I am unable to persuade myself of any clear evidence regarding context and so favour the placement of the nine characters in the earlier section where they are found in earlier texts.

98. Opinion is divided on these two characters; whether they do not occur here (e.g. DZ, BY, WKY, YTY), or do occur here, and, if the latter, whether by "external" transfer (e.g. WYJ, SYR) or by "internal" transfer (TJF).
99. The precise meaning of 故 here is something of an issue — see Comment.
100. I have followed the transposition of 也 and 者 proposed by SYR and CYX.
101. TJF transfers 故 from the end of this section to here. It is usually incorporated into the next section as the opening character, although there are difficulties with this.
102. Generally read as or emended to 妄 — see, for example, SYR.
103. Some commentators indicate that 今 should be read as 假使 (e.g. LYS, Z&Q). I have followed this.
104. The emendation of 唯 to 雖 following SYR is generally accepted.
105. Emended to 也 by WFB.

44.20   Words (statements, propositions) originate from causes, grow according to reasons (principles, patterns), and proceed according to similarities (kinds, classes). To put forward words (statements, propositions) without a clear understanding of the causes from which they arise is foolish. If people do not follow the road (comply with principles), there is no way forward. Although there may be strength in the limbs, if there is no clear understanding of the road (principles), then obstacles may arise to halt progress. If words (statements, propositions) are set up without there being clarity about similarities (kinds, classes), for sure there will be difficulty.

44.21   1. 故[106] 浸淫之辭。其類在於[107] 鼓栗[108]。

2. 聖人也，為天下也，其類在於[109] 追迷。

3. 或壽或卒，其利天下也指[110] 若，其類在譽石[111]。

4. 一日而百萬生，愛不加厚，其類在惡害。

5. 愛二世[112] 有厚薄，而愛二世相若，其類在蛇文[113]。

6. 愛之相若，擇而殺其一人，其類在阬[114] 下之鼠。

7. 小仁與大仁，行厚相若，其類在申凡[115]。

8. 〔凡〕[116] 興利除害也，其類在漏雍[117]。

---

106. I have accepted the readings of TJF and ACG who both include 故 in the previous section, albeit in different places.

107. 於 is present here in the DZ but omitted in most modern texts following BY. WYJ, however, retains it — see his note 178, p. 640.

108. The meaning of 鼓栗 remains obscure. Indeed, WYJ has "未詳". I originally took it to refer to the smelting of metal (see TJF), but now accept LSL's reading as "危言聳聽". This would be in keeping with WFB's relating this statement to the apparently paradoxical statements about white horses and foals.

109. Unlike the case of the previous statement, all editors retain 於 here, although it does not appear in subsequent statements in this section.

110. There is general acceptance of SSX's reading of 指 as 恉 here.

111. In interpreting this final phrase (in the DZ as above — 譽石), some commentators follow BY in emending 石 to 名 (e.g. LSL who has: "即名稱於世"), whilst others follow WKY in emending 譽 to 礜.

112. There are differing views on 二世. Thus WYJ suggests that it is a reference to "眾眾世" and "寡世" of 44.10 whilst SYR, followed by LSL, offers the view that "尚世" and "後世", also from 44.10, are indicated. WYJ raises the possibility of adding "今世" and emending 二 to 三.

113. I have followed TJF in reading 文 as 交. Most editors retain 文, including CYX who has the following note: "二世即前文所謂尚世後世也蛇文蛇之有文者蛇有大小而文相若以喻愛有厚薄而愛相若也。"

114. There is an issue here between 坑 / 阬 and 阮 — see Z&Q, p. 669, note 14. In the translation I have followed particularly LSL who has this note: "阬下之鼠，洞中之鼠，人皆欲殺，故取為喻。阬，虛。"

115. There is considerable variation in these two final characters. ZQH has 巾凡, the point being that the value of something does not depend on whether it is great or small, or on external circumstances.

116. Some editors (e.g. LSL) place 凡 here rather than at the end of the previous sentence.

117. The main difference among modern commentators with respect to these final two characters is that some follow WYZ and read 雍 as 甕, whilst others follow CYX who has: "漏潰也雍與甕同塞也。"

44.21 1. Words (statements, propositions) gradually soak in; the analogy lies in the making of startling claims.

2. The sage acts for the sake of the world; the analogy lies in overcoming doubt.

3. One person may live long, another may die [young], yet their benefiting the world may be the same; the analogy lies in praising the name.

4. In the space of one day a million things come forth, yet love is not, thereby, more profound: the analogy lies in the abhorrence of harm.

5. In the love for the two ages there is the "thick" and the "thin", yet the love for the two ages is the same; the analogy lies in snakes intertwined.

6. Although all are loved equally, one man may be selected and killed; the analogy lies in a rat in a hole.

7. Small benevolence and great benevolence — in action their "weight" is the same; the analogy lies in the towel and the table.

8. Promote benefit and do away with harm; the analogy lies in stopping a leak.

9. 厚親不稱行而類行，其類在江上井。

10. 不為己之可學[118]也，其類在獵走。

11. 愛人非為譽也，其類在逆旅。

12. 愛人之親若愛其親，其類在官苟[119]。

13. 兼愛相若，一愛相若，一愛相若[120]，其類在死也[121]。

Comment: The "standard" version of the Daqu (*Mozi* 44) concludes with this series of 13 statements, each of which ends with the phrase, "其類在 (於) X" ("the analogy lies in x"). The placement of this section, if indeed it is to be treated as a separate section, is quite variable. Thus some modern editors join it with what is here the preceding section (e.g. Z&Q, LSL) and, in fact, the transition between the two is uncertain, specifically with respect to the problematic character 故. TJF makes these 13 statements a separate section apart from his version of the Daqu, whilst both WFB and ZQH attach them to the very contentious section including 語經 (here 44.9), albeit in different ways. ACG takes the 13 statements as the basis of his separate "treatise" *Expounding the Canons* (see his pp. 243–259) and lists the 13 together as an appendix to that "treatise". Turning to the statements themselves, the first is something of an "odd man out" both in subject matter (although there are textual issues here) and in containing (variably) the preposition 於 in the analogy, although it does share this feature with the second statement. Certainly the other 12 statements pertain to matters dealt with elsewhere in the Daqu whilst the last 11 are all on ethical matters, reiterating some of the key points made earlier; to wit, the importance of (universal) love and its relationship to benefit; the somewhat equivocal stance on whether there are, in fact, permissible gradations of love; the promotion of benefit and the eschewing of harm; that love and benefit are independent of external

---

118. SYR suggests the emendation of 學 to 譽 but ZQH for one specifically disagrees. In fact, most editors retain 學.

119. Several modern commentators (e.g. TJF, LSL) follow CYX in reading 苟 as 佢 in the sense of "earnest" or "diligent".

120. Most, but not all (e.g. TJF is an exception), accept SYR's omission of the duplicated four characters.

121. There is variation in these two final characters and hence in the interpretation of the analogy. The majority of editors retain the original "死也" (e.g. ZCY), others have "死蛇" (some with the second character in the unusual simpler form — see ZWDCD #33629), whilst TJF has "宛也". "Killing the snake" is seen as a reference to Sunshu Ao's killing of the double-headed serpent for the general good — see, for example, MZQY. TJF takes the analogy to indicate a coiling around in continuity representing universal love as being without limit.

9. In loving one's parents "thickly", do not consider their conduct but who they are; the analogy lies in the well above the river.

10. One may learn not to be selfish; the analogy lies in the hunter's pursuit.

11. The love of man is not about being praised; the analogy lies in the innkeeper.

12. Love for others' parents is like love for one's own parents; the analogy lies in the concern for the general good.

13. Universal love is alike; the one love is alike. The one love is alike; the analogy lies in dying (killing the snake).

circumstances; that goodness may be acquired; and finally, that the evil person may be singled out and punished without invalidating the principle of universal love. How helpful the analogies are varies; some are obvious, some are illuminating, and some are incomprehensible.

45: 小取

45.1 夫辯者，將以明是非之分，審治亂之紀，明同異之處，察名實之
理，處利害，決嫌疑。焉[1] 摹略萬物之然，論求群言之比。以名
舉實，以辭抒意，以說出故，以類取，以類予。有諸己不非諸
人，無諸己不求諸人。[2]

Comment: The only real textual issue is the placement of 焉, although several
characters are open to different interpretations, not least 辯 itself. There has
been an on-going debate both as to meaning in Chinese and the most
appropriate rendering in translation.[3] A brief definition is given in the C for A75:
"辯、爭彼也。" Clearly the scope is wider here, although the core meaning —
the resolution of binary issues and the identification of the true and false — is
retained. In fact, extended discussion of the meaning of 辯 with respect to the
Xiaoqu specifically, and to the Later Mohists more generally, is somewhat
superfluous as a detailed definition is precisely what is offered here.

---

1. There is some variation in the placement of 焉, either at the start of this sentence (e.g.
   TJF, ACG — as 乃 according to the former), or at the end of the preceding sentence
   (e.g. WYJ).
2. The translation of this somewhat enigmatic statement depends particularly on the reading
   of 諸 in each of the four instances. ZYZ, in his modern version, has: "自己所不贊同的
   論點，也不應要求別人去堅持。"
3. See, for example, Chong (1999), Sun Zhongyuan (1998), p. 202ff and ZYZ, p. 79ff.

45: Choosing the Lesser

45.1   Disputation is about making clear the distinction between right and wrong (true and false), and investigating the pattern of order and disorder. It is about clarifying instances of sameness and difference, examining the principles of name and entity, determining what is beneficial and harmful, and resolving what is doubtful and uncertain. With it, there is enquiry and investigation into how the ten thousand things are; there is discussion and analysis of the kinds of the many words. Names are the means of "picking out" entities; words are the means of expressing concepts; explanations are the means of bringing out causes. Through kinds (classes) choices are made; through kinds (classes) inferences are drawn. What one has in oneself, one does not criticise in others; what one does not have in oneself, one does not demand of others.

45.2   或也者，不盡也。⁴假者，今不然也。效者，為之法也。所效
者，所以為之法也。故⁵中效，則是也。不中效，則非也。此效
也。辟⁶也者，舉他⁷物而以明之也。侔也者，比辭而俱行也。援
也者，曰：子然，我奚獨不可以然也？推也者，以其所不取之，
同於其所取者，予之也。是猶謂「他者同」也，吾豈謂「他者異」
也。⁸

Comment: The only textual issues of note in this section are whether, in
several cases, 也 should be emended to 他, and whether the final 效 should
be emended to 故 as advocated by TJF. The real problems are, first, the
interpretation of the terms themselves. These include the question of whether
故 is to be read simply as "therefore" or is itself a term, and, second, whether
the seven or eight terms (depending on the inclusion of 故 or otherwise) are
equivalent in the sense of being "seven ways of establishing a statement"⁹ or
whether there is a division, either 3/4 (WFB) or 2-3/5 (TJF). The continuity of
argument and the correspondence of enumerations is probably best
preserved by the 3/4 division proposed by WFB. In this case, the four terms
specifically identified as methods of reasoning are 譬 (comparing), 侔
(equating), 援 (citing, drawing an analogy), and 推 (inferring).

---

4.   There are two issues with this first statement The greater uncertainty concerns 或, about
     which there are four positions as follows: (i) 或 is related to 域 in the sense of "part" (部
     分) — see, for example, WFB, ACG. (ii) 或 is equated with "doubt" (疑) following the
     Yi Jing 易經 which has "或之者疑之也" (SSJZS, vol. 1, p. 17) — see TJF. The MZQY
     has simply "或，通惑". (iii) 或 is equated with 或然 in the sense of "probable" (ZYZ).
     (iv) The use of 或 is related to the E of B34 which has: "辯也者，或謂之是，或謂之
     非。當者勝也。" There is also the issue of 盡 which a number of commentators relate
     to the C for A43 — "盡，莫不然也". This is itself a rather controversial C&E.
5.   Some take 故 as a term like 或, 假 and 效. Thus HS writes: "欲明此段，須知效、法、
     故，三字皆墨家名學之術語" — MZJC, vol. 21, p. 6. TJF strongly supports this view
     and emends the final 效 to 故. An alternative is to read 故 as 所以 (ZYZ). WFB has: "故
     為承上詞，今人有以故作大故小故解者，非是" — p. 443. I have accepted the latter
     view.
6.   There is general acceptance of BY's suggestion that 辟 be read as 譬.
7.   Emended from 也 following SYR and others.
8.   This version of the final sentence follows LSL. Most commentators make the
     emendation of 也 to 他 in both instances. ACG, however, retains 也, identifying 也者
     as a "quotation device" and taking what is quoted to be the initial three characters of each
     clause. The DZ text has: "是猶謂也者同也吾豈謂也者異也".
9.   See, for example, FYL (trans. Bodde), vol. 1, p. 259.

45.2   "To doubt (to consider possible)" is about what is not complete.
"To suppose" is about what is presently not so. "To liken to" is
about taking something as a model. That which is likened to is
what is taken as the model. Therefore, if there is correspondence
in the likening, then it is so, and, if there is not correspondence in
the likening, then it is not so. This is what "likening to" is.
"Comparing" is putting forward one thing to make another thing
clear. "Equating" is taking one term to be equivalent to another.
"Drawing an analogy" is to say: "If this is so why should I be the
only one for whom it is not so?" "Inferring" is to take what has not
been ascertained and identify it with what has been ascertained,
and so make a judgement. This is like saying: "The other is the
same" so how can I say: "The other is different"?

45.3   夫物有以同而不率遂同。辭之侔也，有所至而正[10]。其然也，有所以然也。〔其然也〕[11]同，其所以然不必同。其取之也，有〔所〕[12]以取之。其取之也同，其所以取之不必同。是故辟，侔，援，推之辭，行而異，轉而危，遠而失，流而離本，則不可不審也，不可常用也。故言多方，殊類異故，則不可遍觀也。

Comment: There is broad agreement that this section is, in effect, a listing of possible pitfalls in the application of the four methods outlined in the previous section – comparing (譬), equating (侔), drawing an analogy (援), and inferring (推). Thus, in summary, although in things compared there are, necessarily, points of identity, the entities are not strictly identical so the comparison may break down. In equating terms, similarity of form clearly does not guarantee security of conclusion. In recognising identical outcomes (existing states), one cannot infer identity of causes, and in making inferences there are difficulties insofar as inferences may be accepted without the reasons for acceptance being the same. The sources of these several problems are then identified, first in the list of four 3-character phrases, and second, in the final sentence.

45.4   夫物或乃是而然，或是而不然，〔或不是而然〕[13]，或一周[14]而一不周，或一是而一 (不是也不可常用也故言多方殊類異故則不可偏觀也)[15] 非也。

Comment: There are significant textual difficulties with this section as indicated in notes 13–15. Nevertheless, there is broad agreement on how the section is to be understood. TJF, in particular, focuses on these five propositions as being individually exemplified in the five remaining sections (45.5–9). In fact, TJF makes what is here 45.4 the initial statement of the Xiaoqu which, in his arrangement, becomes in its entirety the list of propositions and their subsequent exemplification.

---

10. There is variation in how 正 is read — for example, as 正確 or as 止. To quote WYJ: "言比辭俱行，其正確有一定限度。"
11. It is generally accepted that the preceding three characters should be added on grounds of parallelism following particularly WYZ.
12. 所 is added to modern texts following WYZ.
13. A number of modern editors add these five characters here, for example TJF, WYJ, ACG, ZYZ. It is a modification probably first proposed by HS.
14. There is general acceptance of 周 for 害 here and in the following sentence, the former in the sense of 周遍 or 普遍 (MZQY).
15. It is generally accepted (following WYZ) that the 22 characters in parentheses which appear in the DZ text are an erroneous duplication, although the initial "不是" might be displaced from the presumed missing example considered in note 13 — see, for example, WYJ, notes 37–39, p. 651 and ACG, notes 630, 631, p. 485.

45.3   With respect to things, there is that by which they are the same yet not completely the same (i.e. 譬). In equating terms, there is a proper limit to be reached (i.e. 侔). (With things), there is their being so and there is how they come to be so. In their being so, they may be the same but how they come to be so is not necessarily the same (i.e. 援). (With things), there is their being chosen and there is that by which they are chosen. In their being chosen, they may be the same but in that by which they are chosen, they are not necessarily the same (i.e. 推). For this reason, with the terms comparing, equating, drawing an analogy, and inferring, (there may be respectively) differences as they proceed, dangers as they change, failure as they go too far, and "slippage" as they leave their base, so then one must be careful and cannot expect constancy of use. Thus, if saying something has many methods, and different classes have different reasons, then it is not possible to take a prejudiced viewpoint.[i]

45.4   With respect to things (the following apply):

1. Sometimes a thing is so if it is this.

2. Sometimes a thing is not so if it is this.

3. Sometimes a thing is so if it is not this.

4. Sometimes a thing is general (in one case) but is not general (in another case).

5. Sometimes a thing is so (in one case) but not so (in another case).

---

i.   TJF gives a somewhat different reading of these last two sentences based on several textual emendations and a rearrangement involving the placement of "不可不審也" — see his pp. 442–447.

45.5 白馬，馬也。乘白馬，乘馬也。驪馬，馬也。乘驪馬，乘馬也。
獲，人也。愛獲，愛人也。臧，人也。愛臧，愛人也。此乃是而
然者也。[16]

> **Comment:** This brief section illustrates the first case listed in 45.4 with two
> examples, each duplicated. It should be noted that the pairs differ somewhat
> in that both members of the first pair have a qualifying adjective preceding the
> initial substantive. While there are obvious elements of the Later Mohist
> opposition to the arguments of Gongsun Long, the main purpose is to
> establish this form of proposition in contrast to what follows, which has critical
> ethical connotations for the Mohists.

45.6 獲之親[17]，人也。獲事[18] 其親，非事人也。其弟，美人也。愛
弟，非愛美人也。車，木也。乘車，非乘木也。船，木也。人
〔入／乘〕[19] 船，非人〔入／乘〕木也。盜人[20]，人也。多盜，非多人
也。無盜，非無人也。奚以明之？惡多盜，非惡多人也。欲無
盜，非欲無人也。世相與共是之。若[21] 若是，則雖盜人人也，愛
盜非愛人也，不愛盜非不愛人也，殺盜人非殺人也，無難 (盜無
難)[22] 矣。此與彼同類。世有彼而不自非也，墨者有此而非之。無

---

16. From the earliest modern commentators (e.g. BY, SYR) on, 驪 has been taken as "black"
    and both 獲 and 臧 as the names of servants (奴婢).
17. There is general acceptance of WYZ's emendation of 視 to 親 on the basis of the
    following clause.
18. 事 is commonly accepted as having the general meaning of 侍奉 or 服侍 ("to serve").
    ACG suggests a more specific meaning in the following "事人" of "be in service to a
    lord, be married to a husband" (his note 633, p. 487).
19. There is agreement on the need to emend 人 here, either to 入 (e.g. HS, TJF, WFB, ZYZ)
    or to 乘 in line with the previous example (e.g. BY, WYJ).
20. A number of commentators, following particularly SYR, regard the 人 immediately after
    盜, both here and subsequently, as superfluous and so omit it (e.g. TJF, ZYZ, WFB).
    Others retain it in both places (e.g. WYJ, LSL, HS).
21. One 若 is regarded as superfluous (e.g. WFB).
22. All agree on the excision of these three characters — see, for example, ACG, note 636,
    p. 487.

45.5 A white horse is a horse. To ride a white horse is to ride a horse. A black horse is a horse. To ride a black horse is to ride a horse. *Huo* is a person. To love *Huo* is to love a person. *Zang* is a person. To love *Zang* is to love a person. These are examples of there being this and it is so.

45.6 *Huo's* parents are people. *Huo's* serving his parents is not serving people. His younger brother is a beautiful person. Loving a younger brother is not loving a beautiful person. A cart is wood. Riding a cart is not riding wood. A boat is wood. Boarding a boat is not boarding wood. A robber is a person. Many robbers are not many people. Not being a robber isn't not being a person. How can this be made clear? To dislike many robbers is not to dislike many people. To wish there were no robbers is not to wish there were no people. The world is united in its agreement that this is so. If it is thus, then although (one says): "A robber is a person. Loving a robber is not loving a person. Not loving a robber isn't not loving a person. Killing a robber is not killing a person", there is no difficulty. This and that are both of the same class. Nevertheless,

也故焉²³，所謂內膠外閉，與心毋空乎，內膠而不解也。²⁴ 此乃是而不然²⁵ 者也。

Comment: This section presents examples of the second case (是而不然) in contrast to the previous section. Despite the identity of the form of the argument, the conclusion may be either true (然) or false (不然). The two cases may be set out as below:

Case I   Premise 1: *Huo* is a person.
Premise 2: What is loved is *Huo*.
Conclusion: What is loved is a person.

Case II   Premise 1: *Huo's* parents are people.
Premise 2: What *Huo* serves are his parents.
Conclusion: What *Huo* serves are people.

Whilst all would accept the first and, of course, from the logical point of view the second too seems irrefutable, still it could be challenged at an interpretative level, i.e. that what *Huo* serves are his parents *qua* parents not his parents *qua* people. HS attempts to dissolve the problem by a piece of linguistic sleight of hand, reading 非 as 異於 (different from) rather than 不是 (is not). Does the Mohist position hold up, at least sufficiently to provide support for the argument for universal love and defence for the punishment of robbers despite their being people, or is it a piece of sophistry, as Xun Zi would claim?²⁶ No one can deny that there are some, perhaps ultimately indefinable, differences between killing a robber and killing a person (assuming the person in question is not a robber), just as there is a difference between killing a pup and killing a dog, although all would accept that a pup is a dog, insofar as pup is a sub-class of the larger class, dog, just as robber is a sub-class of the larger class, people. It is notable, however, that the ethical connotations present in the second instance are not present in the first. Thus, one might conclude that while the Mohist defence is not secure on logical grounds, in practice it can be justified by awareness of the nuances that escape the strictly logical formulation and that such nuances have a wider range than just the group of Mohist ethical formulations.

---

23. There are variations in these four characters which may be written, "無也故焉" or "無故也焉" or "無故焉也".
24. There are several issues with this statement as follows: (i) Whether it follows a comma or a full-stop. (ii) Whether the next comma follows 閉 or 與. (iii) If 與 should be read as 歟. (iv) If 空 should be read as 孔. (v) Whether the comma is before or after the second 內. (vi) Whether the final nine characters (毋 to 也) are, in fact, a gloss, as proposed by TJF who has them in parentheses — a suggestion accepted by ACG. WYJ paraphrases the initial part of the statement with "謂內固執而外閉拒".
25. Emended from 殺 following BY — an emendation accepted by all modern editors.
26. *Xunzi* 22.3a — see Knoblock, vol. 3, p. 131 and note 48, p. 339.

the people of the world believe that and consider themselves not mistaken, whereas the Mohists believe this and all consider them mistaken. This is without reason and may be spoken of as being fixed with respect to what is within and unreceptive to what is without (i.e. as having a closed mind that is not susceptible to change). These are instances of something being this and it not being so.

45.7 夫且讀書，非讀書也。好讀書，(好) 讀書也。[27] 且鬥雞，非雞
也。好鬥雞，好雞也。[28] 且入井，非入井也。止且入井，止入井
也。且出門，非出門也。止且出門，止出門也。[29] 若若[30] 是，(且
天非天也壽天也)[31]〔執〕[32] 有命，非命也。非執有命，非命也，
無難矣。此與彼同〔類〕[33]。世有彼而不自非也，墨者有此而罪[34]
非之。無也故焉[35]，所謂內膠外閉，與心毋空乎，內膠而不解
也。此乃不是而然者也。[36]

---

27. All commentators since SYR emend this initial statement which appears in the DZ (and in BY's text) as: "且夫讀書非好書也". Almost all reverse the order of 且 and 夫 and take the former as 將 (e.g. LSL), 將要 (e.g. MZQY), or 將然未然 (e.g. ZYZ), and then either "書也，好讀書" (e.g. HS, WYJ, ACG), or these five characters preceded by 讀 (e.g. SYR, TJF, LSL), or by 好 (e.g. WFB). ZCY, however, emends the final 好 to 讀. It is this version that is followed in the translation.

28. There are also variations in this second statement which appears in the DZ as: "且鬥雞非雞也好鬥雞好雞也". BY makes no emendations but adds the note "言人使之鬥" after the first 也. Likewise, SYR, HS, WYJ and WYW make no emendations. ACG alone argues for the omission of the initial 且. Other commentators add a 鬥 either before (TJF, ZYZ) or after (LSL) the second 雞 whilst WFB adds 好 before it. ZCY emends the final 好, this time to 鬥, his text again being used for the translation.

29. Some editors add the six characters "世相與共是之" here in conformity with the same argument structure as in the previous section.

30. One 若 is regarded as superfluous as in the previous section (e.g. WFB).

31. The eight characters in parentheses are those that appear in early editions (e.g. DZ, BY). BY makes no attempt at explanation although ZCY does without modification of the text. All other modern commentators regard the statement as unintelligible in this form. Most accept SYR's proposal to add a further 天 after 壽 giving: "且天，非天也；壽天，天也。" This still presents problems of comprehension. More satisfactory is TJF's version: "且天，非天也；壽，非天也。" More radical is TJY's version: "且天 非天也；止 且天止天也。" More radical still is HS's proposal: "且 `天壽有命` 非 `命` 也；非 `執 有命` 非 `命` 也。"

32. Added by WYJ on the basis of the following sentence.

33. 類 is added by most commentators following BY.

34. Most commentators agree that 罪 is wrong here. It is usually either omitted (e.g. LSL) or emended to 眾 following WYZ.

35. As in the previous section, these four characters are invariably modified. In fact, BY has a different structure (無故焉也) which he suggests should be brought into conformity with the previous section. The usual form in modern editions is: "無也故焉" as above.

36. There are important issues with this final sentence which appears in the DZ and in BY as: "此乃是而然者也". A number of commentators follow WYZ and SYR in adding 不 before 然, making the statement identical with that in the previous section (e.g. WFB, LSL, MZQY). Others, however, place the additional 不 before 是 as above (e.g. ZCY, TJF, WYJ, ZYZ, ACG) which brings this section into line with the enumeration in 45.4.

45.7   Being about to read a book is not reading a book. Liking to read a book is reading a book. Being about to fight a cock is not fighting a cock. Liking to fight a cock is fighting a cock. Being about to enter a well is not entering a well. To stop being about to enter a well is to stop entering a well. Being about to go out a door is not going out a door. To stop being about to go out a door is to stop going out a door. If it is thus (then one may say): "Being about to die young is not dying young; longevity is not dying young." To consider there to be Fate does not mean there is Fate and "to reject fatalism is to reject Fate" is without difficulty. This and that are of the same class. The people of the world believe that and do not consider themselves mistaken, whereas the Mohists believe this and all consider them mistaken. This is without reason and may be spoken of as being fixed with respect to what is within and unreceptive to what is without (i.e. as having a closed mind that is not susceptible to change). These are examples of a thing being so if it is not this.

Comment: This is a very problematic section. There are significant textual concerns with 4 of the 15 sentences of the text. In addition, there are issues with the sentence "此與彼同類" concerning what 此 and 彼 refer to, and whether the addition of 類 is warranted. With respect to the translation, I have followed ZCY's version of the second and fourth sentences, TJF's version of the very contentious sentence on dying young, and the version of the final sentence which brings it into line with the third proposition of 45.4, itself a matter of dispute. There is, nonetheless, widespread acceptance of the view that this section is a statement against fatalism, anti-fatalism being one of the main planks of the Mohist construction and important in the Ru-Mo opposition.[37] The argument takes the form of demonstrating two parallel phrases or propositions, the first of which is "not so" and the second of which is "so". What is not clear is precisely how the two paired propositions under scrutiny equate with the preceding four examples to establish the argument if, indeed, it is one argument (i.e. a denial of fate) or two, as ACG suggests.[38]

45.8   愛人，待周[39]愛人，而後為愛人。不愛人，不待周不愛人。不失[40]周愛，因為不愛人矣。乘馬，〔不〕[41]待周乘馬，然後為乘馬也。有乘於馬，因為乘馬矣。逮至不乘馬，待周不乘馬，而後〔為〕[42]不乘馬。（而後不乘馬。）[43]此一周而一不周者也。

Comment: This section, which deals with the fourth of the five propositions in 45.4, is free of significant textual problems and is also relatively clear in meaning. It characterises two situations which are susceptible of grammatically identical descriptions. The Mohist point is that this grammatical identity obscures important differences, important, that is, to another central Mohist tenet, the possibility and desirability of universal love. In the first case, loving people, to satisfy the requirements of the description, one needs to love all people all the time, i.e. universal love. Failing to love even one person at any time invalidates the description. In the second case, riding horses, to satisfy

37. See, for example, HS's analysis (MZJC, vol. 21, pp. 23–24) where he refers to the *Mozi* 48.
38. See ACG, LMLES, pp. 490–491.
39. 周 is taken in the sense of 遍 and equated with the modern 全部 or 所有. ZYZ writes that 周 is a logical "詞項周延" (p. 88). LSL equates 周 with 完全.
40. 失 is omitted in most modern texts. WYJ makes a case for emendation to 先 whilst TJF replaces 不 with 有失.
41. The addition of 不 (lacking in early texts such as the DZ) was proposed by WYZ and is generally accepted.
42. The addition of 為, due to WYZ, is generally accepted.
43. The repetition of these five characters is regarded as an error and they are omitted in all modern texts.

45.8 Love of people depends upon a generalised love of people and subsequently there is love of people. Not loving a person does not depend on a generalised not loving of people. There is loss of generalised love and, for this reason, there is not loving a person. Riding horses does not depend on a generalised riding of horses for there subsequently to be riding horses. There is riding a horse and, for this reason, there is riding horses. When it comes to not riding horses, this does not depend on a generalised not riding horses for there subsequently to be not riding horses. This is an instance of one generalised and one not generalised.

the requirements, one need only ride some horse(s) some of the time whereas the conditions for non-applicability require not riding any horse at any time. Thus, in these two parallel phrases with essentially identical structures, one is generalised and one is not.

45.9   居於國，則為居國。有一宅於國，而不為有國。桃之實，桃也。棘之實，非棘也。問人之病，問人也。惡人之病，非惡人也。人之鬼，非人也。兄之鬼，兄也。祭〔人〕[44]之鬼，非祭人也。祭兄之鬼，乃祭兄也。之馬之目眇[45]，則為[46]之馬眇。之馬之目大，而不謂之馬大。之牛之毛黃，則謂之牛黃。之牛之毛眾，而不謂之牛眾。一馬，馬也。二馬，馬也。馬四足者，一馬而四足也，非兩馬而四足也。一〔白〕馬，馬也。[47]馬或白[48]者，二馬而或白也，非一馬而或白。此乃一是而一非者也。

Comment: This final section differs in several respects from those preceding it. ZYZ describes it as being about the limits and principles of use of natural language. First, there is no obvious attempt to buttress any particular Mohist doctrine. Second, the examples are quite diverse, and third, it does not seem to correlate as well as the other sections with the listing of potential errors and the application of the terms in 45.3 and 45.4. Whatever the relationship of this section to those preceding it, it does seem relatively straightforward with respect to the examples, all six of which are subsumed under the heading of "one is, one is not". The first depends on the possibility of giving a verb an adjectival role in the first example but not being able to do so in the second. The second is simply a matter of usage; the fruit of the peach tree is the peach but the fruit of the *ji* tree is not the *ji* but the *zao*. The third is about the "scope" of verbs in relation to direct and indirect objects and transitive and intransitive forms. In the fourth example, TJF's explanation hinges on the fact that after a man's death, necessary for the "existence" of his spirit, he can no longer be

---

44. This character, absent, for example, from the DZ, was added by WYZ and is present in all modern texts.
45. Written as 盼 in early texts and equated with 視 by LSL. In most modern editions 盼 is emended to 眇 — see, for example, ZCY.
46. There is general acceptance of BY's reading of 為 here as 謂 to bring this clause into conformity with those that follow.
47. Most modern commentators accept WYZ's suggestion that this repeated statement be omitted. TJF, however, retains it and emends ‧ to 白 as in parentheses above. WFB retains the four characters and adds "‧馬、馬也" here also.
48. There is general acceptance of BY's emendation of 白 to 白.

45.9   If someone lives in a kingdom then it becomes a 'lived-in' kingdom. If there is one dwelling in a kingdom it does not become a "there is" kingdom. The fruit of the peach tree is the peach; the fruit of the *ji* tree is not the *ji*. To ask about a person's illness is to ask about the person; to dislike a person's illness is not to dislike the person. A person's spirit is not the person; an older brother's spirit is the older brother. To sacrifice to a person's spirit is not to sacrifice to the person; to sacrifice to the older brother's spirit is, in fact, to sacrifice to the older brother. If this horse's eyes are blind, one calls it a blind horse. If this horse's eyes are large, one does not call it a large horse. If this ox's hairs are yellow, one calls it a yellow ox. If this ox's hairs are many, one does not call it many oxen. One horse is "horse". Two horses are "horse". With respect to a horse and four legs, there is one horse and four legs, not two horses and four legs. A white horse is a horse. With respect to some horses being white, there are (at least) two horses and some are (one is) white, not one horse and some are (one is) white. These, then, are instances of one being so and one not being so.

deemed a man, whereas the spirit of the older brother is linked only to that brother, so the two can be equated, this being particularly relevant in sacrificing to the spirit. The fifth example is about the scope of descriptive terms; if a horse's eyes are blind or an ox's hair is yellow they can be called, respectively, a blind horse and a yellow ox. The descriptive terms "large" and "many" cannot have the same dual application to part and whole. In the final example, TJF sees the distinction simply as one between singular and plural, a distinction which is often not explicit in written Chinese. ACG, however, writes that the distinction "... is not between singular and plural, but between distributive and collective, which is not exhibited by Indo-European number. ..."[49] The example clearly also has relevance to Gongsun Long's "white horse" argument and the Mohist response to this.

49. See ACG, LMLES p. 493.

PART *IV*

The Dialogues

46: 耕柱

46.1   子墨子怒耕柱子，耕柱子曰：「我毋俞[1]於人乎？」子墨子曰：「我將上大行[2]，駕驥與羊[3]，子將誰敺？」耕柱子曰：「將敺驥也。」子墨子曰：「何故敺驥也？」耕柱子曰：「驥足以責。」子墨子曰：「我亦以子為足以責。」

46.2   巫馬子謂子墨子曰：「鬼神孰與聖人明智？」子墨子曰：「鬼神之明智於聖人，猶聰耳明目之與聾瞽也。昔者夏后開使蜚廉折金於山川，而陶鑄之於崑吾，是使翁難雉乙卜於白若之龜[4]，曰：『鼎

---

1.   On 毋俞, LYS has: "毋與不同，俞讀為愈，勝的意思。"

2.   大行 is taken to be 太行山, a mountain in present-day Henan.

3.   There is general acceptance of WYZ's reading of 牛 for 羊.

4.   There is considerable uncertainty about this sentence, not only concerning the name of the person (see note iv below), but also the term *bairuo* 白若 — see WYJ, note 15, pp. 665–667 for a detailed discussion. The translation follows Z&Q's analysis.

46: Geng Zhu

46.1   Master Mo Zi was angry with Geng Zhu Zi[i].

Geng Zhu Zi asked: "Do I not surpass [other] men?"

Master Mo Zi [in turn] asked: "If I were about to ascend Taihang Mountain and I yoked a thoroughbred horse and an ox [to my cart], which one would I urge on?"

Geng Zhu Zi replied: "You would urge on the thoroughbred horse."

Master Mo Zi asked: "And why would I urge on the thoroughbred horse?"

Geng Zhu Zi replied: "Because the thoroughbred horse is up to the task."

Master Mo Zi said: "I also take you to be up to the task."

46.2   Wu Ma Zi[ii] spoke to Master Mo Zi saying: "Which are more perspicacious and wise — ghosts and spirits, or sages?"

Master Mo Zi said: "Comparing the perspicacity and wisdom of ghosts and spirits to that of the sages is like comparing those with sharp hearing and clear sight to those who are deaf and blind. Formerly, the Xia king, Kai (Qi) sent Fei Lian to search for metals in the mountains and rivers, and to cast tripods (*ding*) at Kun Wu.[iii] He also ordered Wengnan Yi[iv] to prognosticate from

---

i.   Other than accepting SYR's supposition that he was a disciple of Mo Zi, nothing is known of Geng Zhu Zi. Some texts have 桂 rather than 柱 in the name — see WYJ, note 1, p. 661.

ii. BY speculates that Wu Ma Zi 巫馬子 is Wu Maqi 巫馬期, a disciple of Confucius, or one of his descendants.

iii. This is a reference to Yu's son Qi 啟, traditional dates 2197–2188 BC, the name being changed due to a Han taboo. 后 is read as 王 (Z&Q). Fei Lian 蜚廉 was a minister in his service. Kun Wu 崑吾 is a mountain in what is now Henan province.

iv. 雉 is taken to be an erroneous duplication of 難. The man in question was a diviner in the service of 夏王 — see Z&Q, note 13, p. 685.

成，三[5]足而方，不炊而自烹，不舉而自臧，不遷而自行，以祭於崑吾之虛[6]，上鄉[7]。』乙又言兆之由[8]，曰：『饗矣！逢逢[9]白雲，一南一北，一西一東，九鼎既成，遷於三國。』夏后氏失之，殷人受之，殷人失之，周人受之。夏后、殷、周之相受也，數百歲矣。使聖人聚其良臣與其桀相而謀，豈能智數百歲之後哉！而鬼神智[10]之。是故曰，鬼神之明智於聖人也，猶聰耳明目之與聾瞽也。」

46.3   治徒娛、縣子碩問於子墨子曰：「為義孰為大務？」子墨子曰：「譬若築牆然，能築者築，能實壤者實壤，能欣[11]者欣，然後牆成也。為義猶是也。能談辯者談辯，能說書者說書，能從事者從事，然後義事成也。」

---

5. 三 here is taken to be an error and should read 四 (see, for example, LYS, LSL).
6. 虛 is read as 墟 — see LYS, Z&Q.
7. Following BY, 上鄉 is taken as 尚饗, a formal conclusion to an offering.
8. On this clause, LYS has: "乙應作已，由與繇通，卦兆的占辭。是說已經卜過，又把卦兆上面的占辭說出來。" — see his note 10, p. 325. WYJ has 卜人 rather than 乙又 as the initial two characters — see his note 23, p. 669.
9. Read as 逢逢 — see, for example, LYS, Z&Q.
10. 智 is read as 知 both here and in the following sentence.
11. Following WYZ, 欣 is read 睎 in the sense 測量.

the *bairuo* tortoise. The diviner said: 'The tripods (*ding*) when complete will have four legs and be square. They will cook by themselves without fire. Without lifting, they will store themselves. They will move themselves without being moved. Use them for sacrifice at Kun Wu and let the Gods receive the offering.' Having made an interpretation of the lines, he also said: 'The Gods receive the offering. Profuse are the white clouds. At one time they are in the south, at one time in the north, at one time in the west, at one time in the east. The nine tripods (*ding*) are already complete and will pass from one to the other among the three countries.' [Subsequently] the Xia King's clan lost them and the Yin (Shang) founder received them. The Yin lost them and the Zhou founder received them. This transmission between the Xia King, Yin and Zhou occupied several hundred years. Even if a sage gathered together his good officials and excellent ministers and planned, how can he know what will transpire after several hundred years? Yet ghosts and spirits know! This is why I say that the perspicacity and wisdom of ghosts and spirits when compared to sages are like sharp hearing and keen sight when compared to deafness and blindness."

46.3   Zhi Tuyu and Xian Zishuo[v] questioned Master Mo Zi, saying: "In practising righteousness, what is the most important aspect?"

Master Mo Zi said: "It is like building a wall. Those who are able to compact the earth should compact it; those who are able to carry the earth should carry it; those who are able to do the survey should do it. Then the wall will be completed. Practising righteousness is like this. When those who are able to dispute, dispute; when those who are able to explain the writings, explain them; when those who are able to conduct affairs, conduct them — then righteousness will be complete."

---

v.   These two men are assumed to have been disciples of Mo Zi (SYR). Nothing is known of them, although WYJ draws attention to a Xian Zishi 縣子石, mentioned in the LSCQ 4/3.2 as a student of Mo Zi.

46.4 巫馬子謂子墨子曰:「子兼愛天下,未云[12]利也。我不愛天下,未云賊也。功皆未至,子何獨自是而非我哉?」子墨子曰:「今有燎者於此,一人奉水將灌之,一人摻火將益之。功皆未至,子何貴[13]於二人?」巫馬子曰:「我是彼奉水者之意,而非夫摻火者之意。」子墨子曰:「吾亦是吾意,而非子之意也。」

46.5 子墨子游荊耕柱子於楚。[14]二三子過之,食之三升,客之不厚。二三子復於子墨子曰:「耕柱子處楚無益矣。二三子過之,食之三升,客之不厚。」子墨子曰:「未可智也。」毋幾何而遺十金於子墨子曰:「後生不敢死[15],有十金於此,願夫子之用也。」子墨子曰:「果未可智也。」

46.6 巫馬子謂子墨子曰:「子之為義也,人不見而耶,鬼而不見而富,而子為之,有狂疾!」[16]子墨子曰:「今使子有二臣於此,其

---

12. I have followed some modern editors (LSL, Z&Q) in accepting YY's reading of 云 as 有.

13. 貴 here is read as 贊揚 or 贊賞 (Z&Q).

14. There are two points in this sentence: (i) On 游, BY has: "謂游揚其名而使之仕。" (ii) Following WYZ, 荊 is regarded as superfluous.

15. In this clause, 後生 is understood as 弟子 (SYR). On "不敢死" there are differing views. WYJ reads 死 as 私 and has: "猶言不敢據為私有也。" Alternatively, LYS has: "是一種客氣語,好比古人寫信自稱'死罪死罪'一樣。" — see his note 8, p. 328. I have followed the former.

16. In this sentence, 而 in both instances is taken as 你, 耶 is read as 服 (WYZ), and 富 as 福. WYJ has a slightly different text — see his notes 47 and 48, p. 673.

46.4   Wu Ma Zi spoke to Master Mo Zi saying: "You practise universal love for all under Heaven but as yet there is no benefit. I do not practise universal love for all under Heaven but as yet there is no harm. In both instances, nothing has yet been achieved so how can you claim that you alone are right and I am wrong?"

Master Mo Zi said: "Suppose now someone lights a fire and one man is bringing water which he will pour on it and another is gathering fuel with which he will increase it. In both instances nothing has yet been achieved so which of the two men do you commend?"

Wu Ma Zi said: "I regard the intention of the one who is bringing water as right and that of the one who is gathering fuel as wrong."

Master Mo Zi said: "I also regard my intention as right and your intention as wrong."

46.5   Master Mo Zi recommended Geng Zhu Zi for office in Chu. Several of the Master's disciples visited Geng Zhu Zi who gave them only three *sheng* [of rice] to eat and entertained them in meagre fashion.

The disciples returned and said to Master Mo Zi: "Geng Zhu Zi's position in Chu does not benefit him. When several of us visited him, he gave us only three *sheng* [of rice] to eat and entertained us in meagre fashion."

Master Mo Zi said: "One cannot yet tell."

A little while later [Geng Zhu Zi] sent 10 *chin* of gold to Mo Zi, saying: "I, your disciple, dare not keep this for myself. Here are 10 *chin* of gold which, Sir, I wish you to use."

Master Mo Zi said: "As I thought, it was too soon to tell."

46.6   Wu Ma Zi spoke to Master Mo Zi saying: "You, Sir, practise righteousness but I don't see people submitting to you and I don't see ghosts blessing you. Still you practise it. You must be mad!"

一人者見子從事，不見子則不從事；其一人者見子亦從事，不見
子亦從事。子誰貴於此二人？」巫馬子曰：「我貴其見我亦從事，
不見我亦從事者。」子墨子曰：「然則，是子亦貴有狂疾也。」

46.7　子夏子徒問於子墨子曰：「君子有鬥乎？」子墨子曰：「君子無
鬥。」子夏之徒曰：「狗豨猶有鬥，惡有士而無鬥矣？」子墨子曰：
「傷矣哉！言則稱於湯文，行則譬於狗豨，傷矣哉！」

46.8　巫馬子謂子墨子曰：「舍今之人而譽先王，是譽槁骨也。譬若匠
人然，智槁木也，而不智生木。」子墨子曰：「天下之所以生者，
以先王之道教也。今譽先王，是譽天下之所以生也。可譽而不
譽，非仁也。」

46.9　子墨子曰：「和氏之璧，隋侯之珠，三棘六異，此諸侯之所謂良
寶也。可以富國家，眾人民，治刑政，安社稷乎？曰不可。所謂

Master Mo Zi said: "Suppose now there were two officials — one who carried out his duties when he saw you, but not when he did not see you, and one who carried out his duties whether he saw you or not. Which of these two men would you value?"

Wu Ma Zi replied: "I would value the one who carried out his duties whether he saw me or not."

Master Mo Zi said: "In that case, then, you would also be valuing one who is mad!"

46.7   A follower of Zi Xia[vi] questioned Master Mo Zi saying: "Is there contention among gentlemen?"

Master Mo Zi replied: "There is no contention among gentlemen."

Zi Xia's follower said: "There is contention among dogs and swine so how is it that there is no contention among officers?"

Master Mo Zi said: "What a shame! With words you praise Tang and Wen, but in regard to actions, you make comparison to dogs and swine. What a shame!"

46.8   Wu Ma Zi spoke to Master Mo Zi saying: "To set aside men of the present and praise former kings is to praise old bones. It is like a carpenter knowing only rotten wood and not knowing living wood."

Master Mo Zi said: "The way the world survives is through the doctrines and teachings of the former kings. Now to praise the former kings is to praise the means whereby the world survives. Not to praise what may be praised is not benevolent."

46.9   Master Mo Zi said: "He Shi's jade, Marquis Sui's pearl, and the nine tripods (*ding*) are what the feudal lords spoke of as precious treasures.[vii] [But] can they enrich the country, make the people

---

vi.   This is Bu Shang 卜商, one of the most renowned of the Confucian disciples — see, for example, *Lun Yu* I.7.

vii. For the story of He Shi's 和氏 jade, see *Han Feizi* 43. For that of Marquis Sui's 隋公 pearl, see *Huainanzi* 6. "三棘六異" refers to the "nine *ding*". 棘 is read as 翮 and 異 as 翼. SYR has: "棘同翮，異同翼，亦謂九鼎也。"

貴良寶者，為其可以利〔民〕[17]也。而和氏之璧、隋侯之珠、三棘六異不可以利人，是非天下之良寶也。今用義為政於國家，人民必眾，刑政必治，社稷必安。所為[18]貴良寶者，可以利民也，而義可以利人，故曰，義天下之良寶也。」

46.10 葉公子高問政於仲尼曰：「善為政者若之何？」仲尼對曰：「善為政者，遠者近之，而舊者新之[19]。」子墨子聞之曰：「葉公子高未得其問也，仲尼亦未得其所以對也。葉公子高豈不知善為政者之遠者近也[20]，而舊者新是[21]哉？問所以為之若之何也。不以人之所不智告人，以所智告之，故葉公子高未得其問也，仲尼亦未得其所以對也。」

---

17. Inserted by WYJ on the basis of the second clause in the final sentence.
18. 為 is taken as 謂 (Z&Q).
19. On this clause, SYR has: "言待故舊如新，無厭怠也。"
20. As BY points out, 也 should be taken as 之 in conformity with the rest of the passage.
21. 是 is taken as 之 (SSX).

numerous, bring order to government, and bring peace to the nation? I say they cannot. Something is spoken of as being valued as an excellent treasure because it can benefit the people. But He Shi's jade, Marquis Sui's pearl, and the nine tripods (*ding*) cannot benefit people, so, in terms of the world, they are not excellent treasures. Now if righteousness is used in governing the country, the people will certainly be numerous, government will certainly be well ordered, and the nation will certainly be at peace. That which is said to be valued as an excellent treasure is that which can benefit the people. And righteousness can be of benefit to the people. Therefore, I say that righteousness is the world's excellent treasure."

46.10 The Duke of She, Zi Gao[viii] asked Confucius about government saying: "What constitutes skill in governing?"

Confucius replied: "Good government consists of becoming close to those who are distant and treating old friendships like new ones."[ix]

Master Mo Zi, on hearing this, said: "The Duke of She, Zi Gao did not hit on the right question so Confucius, in turn, did not find the way to answer him. How could it be that the Duke of She, Zi Gao did not know that skill in government consisted of bringing near those who are distant and treating old friendships as new? His question should have been how to do this. It was a case, then, not of telling him something he did not know, but of telling him what he already knew. That is why I say that the Duke of She, Zi Gao was not able to ask the right question so Confucius was also not able to frame the right reply."

---

viii. Zi Gao (名 – 諸梁) was a great officer of Chu in the Spring and Autumn Period.

ix. A similar exchange is to be found in the *Lun Yu* XIII.16 where the response is "近者説，遠者來", whilst in the *Han Feizi* 161 〈難三〉 there is: "政在悦近而來遠。" A detailed note is given in the *Xinyi Han Feizi*, p. 593.

46.11   子墨子謂魯陽文君曰:「大國之攻小國,譬猶童子之為馬也。童
子之為馬,足用而勞。今大國之攻小國也,攻者農夫不得耕,婦
人不得織,以守為事。攻人者亦農夫不得耕,婦人不得織,以攻
為事。故大國之攻小國也,譬猶童子之為馬也。」

46.12   子墨子曰:「言足以復行者,常之;不足以舉行者,勿常。不足
以舉行而常之,此蕩口也。」

46.13   子墨子使管黔敖游高石子於衛。衛君致祿甚厚,設之於卿。高石
子三朝必盡言,而言無行者。去而之齊,見子墨子曰:「衛君以
夫子之故,致祿甚厚,設我於卿。石三朝必盡言,而言無行,是
以去之也。衛君無乃以石為狂乎?」子墨子曰:「去之苟道,受狂

46.11 Master Mo Zi spoke to Prince Wen of Luyang,[x] saying: "A large state attacking a small state is like a young boy [playing at] being a horse. When he [plays at] being a horse, he tires out his legs. Now, when a large state attacks a small state, the farmers in the state that is being attacked cannot plough and the women cannot weave because they are occupied with defence. And in the case of those who are attacking, the farmers also cannot plough and the women cannot weave because they are occupied with attack. Therefore, a large state attacking a small state is like a young boy [playing at] being a horse."

46.12 Master Mo Zi said: "Words that are good enough to be put into practice, use frequently. [Words] that are not good enough to be put into practice, do not use frequently. Words that are not good enough to be put into practice, yet are frequently used, are a waste of breath."

46.13 Master Mo Zi sent Guan Qian'ao to promote Gao Shi Zi in Wei.[xi] The Prince of Wei gave him a substantial salary and established him among the high officials. Gao Shi Zi entered the court three times and certainly gave completely of his counsels, but his words were not put into action. He left and went to Qi. There he saw Master Mo Zi to whom he said: "Because of you the Prince of Wei gave me a substantial salary and ranked me with the high officials. I went to the court on three occasions and certainly gave completely of my counsels, but my words were not put into action. That is why I left. Would the Prince of Wei take me to be mad?"

---

x. A descendant of King Ping 平王 of Chu. Luyang was in what is now Henan province — see Z&Q's detailed note (note 7, p. 693).

xi. Both men, Guan Qian'ao 管黔敖 and Gao Shi Zi 高石子 were disciples of Mo Zi. Nothing else is known about them. BY suggests 敖 rather than 敖 in the first case and SYR agrees.

何傷！古者周公旦非關叔，辭三公東處於商蓋，人皆謂之狂。後世稱其德，揚其名，至今不息。且翟聞之為義非避毀就譽，去之苟道，受狂何傷！」高石子曰：「石去之，焉敢不道也。昔者夫子有言曰：『天下無道，仁士不處厚焉』。今衛君無道，而貪其祿爵，則是我為苟啗人食也[22]。」子墨子說，而召子禽子曰：「姑聽此乎！夫倍義而鄉祿者，我常聞之矣。倍祿而鄉義者，於高石子焉見之也。」

46.14 子墨子曰：「世俗之君子，貧而謂之富，則怒，無義而謂之有義，則喜，豈不悖哉！」

---

22. According to SYR, "苟啗人食也" should read "苟啗人食也". This is accepted by modern commentators.

Master Mo Zi said: "Leaving was in accord with the Way — what harm is there in being thought mad? In ancient times, Duke Dan of Zhou opposed Guan Shu.[xii] He resigned from his position as one of the Three Dukes (*San Gong*) and went east to dwell in Shangyan.[xiii] Everyone said he was mad. Yet later generations extolled his virtue, and praise for his name has extended unceasing to the present time. Moreover, I have heard that being righteous does not involve avoiding censure and seeking praise. So leaving was in accord with the Way. What harm is there in being thought mad?"

Gao Shi Zi said: "I, Shi, left. How could I dare not to follow the Way? Formerly you, Master, said these words: 'If the world is without the Way, benevolent officers should not accept a substantial salary.' Now the Prince of Wei is without the Way, so if I were to desire salary and position from him, this would be merely taking the food from the people."

Master Mo Zi was pleased and summoned Master Qin Zi[xiv] saying: "Now I have heard this! I have often heard of those who turn their backs on righteousness and turn towards salary. But turning one's back on salary and turning towards righteousness, I have seen only in Gao Shi Zi."

46.14   Master Mo Zi said: "It is customary among gentlemen that if you say they are rich when they are poor, they become indignant. But if you say they are righteous when they are not, they are pleased. Is this not perverse?"

---

xii. Most commentators would emend 關 to 管, taking Guan Shu 管叔 as the third son of Wen Wang and younger brother of Wu Wang, whilst Dan 旦, the renowned Duke of Zhou, was the fourth son of Wen Wang. Guan Shu led an uprising to seize the succession after the death of Wu Wang but was defeated by the Duke of Zhou. Regarding the place name, the emendation of 蓋 to 奄 follows BY.

xiii. The 三公, established in Zhou times, are described by Hucker (#4871) as "... the three paramount aides to the ruler ... [who] held the highest possible ranks in the officialdom."

xiv. This is Qin Guli 禽滑釐, one of Mo Zi's foremost disciples.

46.15[23] 公孟子曰:「先人有則三[24]而已矣。」子墨子曰:「孰先人而曰有則三而已矣?子未智人之先有[25]。」

46.16 後生有反子墨子而反者:[26]「我豈有罪哉?吾反後。」子墨子曰:「是猶三軍北[27],失後之人求賞也。」

46.17 公孟子曰:「君子不作,術而已。」[28] 子墨子曰:「不然,人之其不君子者,古之善者不誅,今也善者不作。[29] 其次不君子者,古之善者不遂,己有善則作之,欲善之自己出也。今誅而不作,是無所異於不好遂而作者矣。吾以為古之善者則誅之,今之善者則作之,欲善之益多也。」

46.18 巫馬子謂子墨子曰:「我與子異,我不能兼愛。我愛鄒人於越人,愛魯人於鄒人,愛我鄉人於魯人,愛我家人於鄉人,愛我親於我家人,愛我身於吾親,以為近我也。擊我則疾,擊彼則不疾於我,我何故疾者之不拂,而不疾者之拂?故有我有殺彼以我,無殺我以利。」[30]

---

23. First, there is doubt about the placement and completeness of this fragment — see SSX. Second, it is not clear who Gongmeng 公孟, taken to be a double surname (see ZWDCD, vol. 1, p. 1478), was, apart from the probability that he was a Confucian — see *Mozi* 48 which is titled after him.

24. ZCY considers the "three principles" 則三 to be "heaven" 天, "earth" 地 and "people" 人.

25. There is uncertainty about the end of this sentence. WYJ has "後生" here rather than at the start of the next section — see his note 91, p. 679.

26. There is general acceptance of the reading of the first 反 as 背版 and the second as 返 or 歸, and also of the addition of 日 after 者 — see WYJ, notes 92, 93, p. 679. 後生 here is taken as "disciples".

27. On 北, Z&Q have: "北:敗北,打敗仗。" — see their note 5, p. 698.

28. In this sentence 作 is read as 做 and 術 as 述. It is taken to be a reference to the *Lun Yu* VII.1: "子曰,述而不作,信而好古,竊比於我老彭。" — see LCC, vol. 1, p. 195.

29. The reading of this rather problematic sentence depends on taking 其 as 綦 or 甚 (SSX), 誅 as 述 (BY), and 也 as 之 (SYR).

30. According to YY, this sentence should read: "故我有殺彼以利我,無殺我以利彼。" I have followed this in the translation.

46.15 Gongmeng Zi said: "The first people had three principles and that was all."

Master Mo Zi asked: "Who were the first people you say had three principles only? You will never know what the first people had."

46.16 Among the disciples there was one who forsook Master Mo Zi but later returned, saying: "How am I at fault? I did later return."

Master Mo Zi said: "This is like the three armies being defeated and those who have lagged behind or lost their way seeking reward."

46.17 Gongmeng Zi said: "The gentleman is not a creator. He is a transmitter, and that is all."

Master Mo Zi replied: "Not so. Those men who are the most ungentlemanly did not transmit what was good in the past and do not do what is good in the present. Those who are the next most ungentlemanly do not transmit what was good in the past, but, if they themselves possess goodness, then they reveal it in the hope that it will redound to their credit. Now there is no difference between transmitting but not doing, and not wanting to transmit yet doing. In my view, if something was good in the past, then transmit it. And if something is good in the present, then do it in the hope that the good will be greatly increased."

46.18 Wu Ma Zi spoke to Master Mo Zi, saying: "I am different from you. I am not able to love universally. I love the people of Zou more than I love the people of Yue. I love the people of Lu more than I love the people of Zou. I love the people of my district more than I love the people of Lu. I love the people of my family more than I love the people of my district. I love my parents more than I love the people of my family. I love myself more than I love my parents, based on the closeness to myself. If another strikes me, I feel the pain, but if I strike another, the pain is not mine. Why, then, should I not prefer the pain of striking another to the pain of being struck myself? This is the reason why I would kill another to benefit myself rather than be killed myself to benefit another."

46.19 子墨子曰:「子之義將匿邪,意將以告人乎?」巫馬子曰:「我何故
匿我義?吾將以告人。」子墨子曰:「然則,一人說子,一人欲殺
子以利己;十人說子,十人欲殺子以利己;天下說子,天下欲殺
子以利己。一人不說子,一人欲殺子,以子為施不祥言者也;十
人不說子,十人欲殺子,以子為施不祥言者也;天下不說子,天
下欲殺子,以子為施不祥言者也。說子亦欲殺子,不說子亦欲殺
子,是所謂經者口也,殺常之身者也。[31]」子墨子曰:「子之言惡
利也?若無所利而不言[32],是蕩口也。」

46.20 子墨子謂魯陽文君曰:「今有一[33]人於此,羊牛犓豢[34],維人[35]但
割[36]而和之,食之不可勝食也。見人之作餅,則還然竊之,曰:
『舍[37]余食。』不知日月[38]安不足乎,其有竊疾乎?」魯陽文君曰:
「有竊疾也。」子墨子曰:「楚四竟[39]之田,曠蕪而不可勝辟,呼

---

31. In this sentence 經 is read as 到, 常 as 事 (SYR), and 之 as 至. WYJ offers a slightly
    different reading, stating: "猶言輕率之口,殺常全身者也。" — see his note 112,
    p. 681.
32. Following SYR, 不言 is taken to be 必言.
33. WYJ considers 一 here to be superfluous.
34. Typically written with the 牛 radical (ZWDCD #20664).
35. On the emendation of 雍 to 維 following BY and SYR see WYJ, note 118, p. 682. 維
    人 is taken as 饔人 (BY).
36. Following BY, 但割 is read as 袒割.
37. 舍 is taken as 予 (SYR).
38. 日月 is read as 耳目 (SYR).
39. Here 竟 is understood as 境 (e.g. Z&Q).

46.19   Master Mo Zi said: "Is your way of thinking to be kept secret or is it to be told to others?"

Wu Ma Zi replied: "Why should I keep my way of thinking a secret? I shall tell others."

Master Mo Zi said: "In that case, then, if one person agrees with you, one person will want to kill you to benefit himself. If ten people agree with you, ten people will want to kill you to benefit themselves. If [everyone in] the world agrees with you, [then everyone in] the world will want to kill you to benefit themselves. If one person does not agree with you, one person will want to kill you, taking you to be a person who disseminates evil words. If ten people do not agree with you, ten people will want to kill you, taking you to be a person who disseminates evil words. If [everyone in] the world does not agree with you, [then everyone in] the world will want to kill you, taking you to be a person who disseminates evil words. So not only those who agree with you will want to kill you, but also those who do not agree with you will want to kill you. This is to say that what brings about the killing is the mouth, but the matter of the killing concerns the person."

Master Mo Zi said: "What benefit is there in your words? If you must speak although you have nothing of benefit to say, you are wasting your breath."

46.20   Master Mo Zi spoke to Prince Wen of Luyang, saying: "Now suppose there is this person who cannot consume all the food from grain-fed sheep and oxen that his kitchen-master skins and cuts, and prepares for him, yet, when he sees someone else preparing cakes, he suddenly seizes them saying, 'Give them to me to eat'. Do you not know whether this is a case of his not being satisfied with what he has to eat, or of him being a pathological thief?"

Prince Wen of Luyang replied: "He is [obviously] a pathological thief."

Master Mo Zi said: "Chu had fields extending to its four borders that were overgrown and neglected and could not be opened up.

虛[40] 數千、不可勝〔用〕[41]，兒宋、鄭之閒邑[42]，則還然竊之，此與彼異乎？」魯陽文君曰：「是猶彼也，實有竊疾也。」

46.21　子墨子曰：「季孫紹與孟伯常治魯國之政，不能相信，而祝於叢社，曰：『苟[43]使我和』。是猶弇其目，而祝於叢社，曰[44]：『苟使我皆視』。豈不繆哉！」

46.22　子墨子謂駱滑氂曰：「吾聞子好勇。」駱滑氂曰：「然，我聞其鄉有勇士焉，吾必從而殺之。」子墨子曰：「天下莫不欲與其所好，度其所惡[45]。今子聞其鄉有勇士焉，必從而殺之，是非好勇也，是惡勇也。」

---

40. 呼虛 is SYR's emendation for the rare character 乎 with the 言 radical (ZWDCD #36210) followed by 霝.
41. Added following BY.
42. On 閒邑, Z&Q have: "空邑、空地。" which I have followed.
43. 苟 here and subsequently is read as 尚 (WYZ).
44. 曰 is YY's emendation of 也.
45. There are two proposed emendation in this sentence: 興 for 與 (WYZ) and 廢 for 度 (Z&Q).

And it had vacant land to the extent of several thousand [*mu*] that could not be completely used. Yet, when it saw the unoccupied regions of Song and Zheng, it suddenly seized them. How is this different from the first case?"

Prince Wen of Luyang replied: "This is just like the other. It is truly pathological theft."

46.21 Master Mo Zi said: "Jisun Shao and Meng Bochang[xv] jointly conducted the government of the state of Lu but were unable to trust each other, so they swore an oath at the temple altar saying, 'Cause us to be harmonious'. This is like people covering their eyes and swearing an oath at the temple altar saying, 'Cause us to see everything'. Is this not absurd!"

46.22 Master Mo Zi spoke to Luo Guli,[xvi] saying: "I hear you love bravery."

Luo Guli replied: "That is so. Whenever I hear there is a district that has a brave knight in it, I must follow and kill him."

Master Mo Zi said: "In the world, there is no-one who does not wish to foster what he loves and discard what he hates. Now when you hear there is a district with a brave knight in it, you must follow and kill him. This is not loving bravery; this is hating bravery."

---

xv. Nothing significant is known about these two men, Jisun Shao 季孫紹 and Meng Bochang 孟伯常. Commentators take them to be descendants of Ji Kangzi and Meng Wubo respectively and contemporaries of Mo Zi.

xvi. Luo Guli 駱滑釐 is said to have been a disciple of Mo Zi.

47: 貴義

47.1 子墨子曰：「萬事莫貴於義。今謂人曰『予子冠履，而斷子之手足，子為之乎？』必不為，何故？則冠履不若手足之貴也。又曰『予子天下而殺子之身，子為之乎？』必不為，何故？則天下不若身之貴也。爭一言以相殺，是貴義¹於其身也。故曰，萬事莫貴於義。」

47.2 子墨子自魯之齊，即過故人²，謂子墨子曰：「今天下莫為義，子獨自苦而為義，子不若已。」子墨子曰：「今有人於此，有子十人，一人耕而九人處，則耕者不可以不益急矣。何故？則食者眾，而耕者寡也。今天下莫為義，則子如³勸我者也，何故止我？」

47.3 子墨子南游於楚，見楚獻惠王。獻惠王以老辭，使穆賀見子墨子⁴。子墨子說穆賀，穆賀大說，謂子墨子曰：「子之言則成善矣！而君王，天下之大王也，毋乃曰『賤人之所為』，而不用乎？」

---

1. SYR suggests transposing 貴 and 義 in this sentence.
2. The opening 11 characters of this section follow WYJ's text, the distinctive features of which are the transposition of 即 and 齊 and the addition of 之 before the latter — see his note 4, p. 690.
3. Following WYZ, 如 is taken as 宜 in the sense of 應該.
4. There are significant textual issues with this sentence involving particularly the character 獻 — see BY's note (MZJC, vol. 8, p. 314) and WYJ's detailed discussion (his note 10, p. 691). The translation follows WYJ's text. Mu He 穆賀 was a high official of Chu.

47: Valuing Righteousness

47.1   Master Mo Zi said: "Of the ten thousand things, there is none more valuable than righteousness. Nowadays, if you speak to someone and say, 'I shall give you a cap and shoes but I shall cut off your hands and feet — is this acceptable?' It is certainly not acceptable. And for what reason? Because caps and shoes are not like hands and feet in terms of value. Again, if you say, 'I shall give you the world but I shall kill you as a person — is this acceptable?' It is certainly not acceptable. And for what reason? Because the world is not like one's own person in terms of value. [Still], people contend over a single word (i.e. *yi*) and kill each other, which means that righteousness is more valuable than one's own person. This is why I say that, of the ten thousand things, there is none more valuable than righteousness."

47.2   Master Mo Zi was going from Lu to Qi when he passed an old friend who spoke to him, saying: "Nowadays, no-one in the world is righteous. You are only inflicting pain on yourself by being righteous. Better that you stop."

Master Mo Zi said: "Now suppose there was a man here who had ten sons, one of whom ploughed while the other nine stayed at home. The one who ploughed could not help but work with increased urgency. Why is this? It is because those who eat are many, but those who plough are few. Nowadays, no-one in the world is righteous so you should be encouraging me. Why would you stop me?"

47.3   Master Mo Zi travelled south to Chu to present a document to King Hui but King Hui declined [to see him] on the grounds of age. [Instead] he sent Mu He to receive Master Mo Zi. Master Mo Zi spoke to Mu He and Mu He was greatly pleased. He addressed Master Mo Zi saying: "Your words, Sir, are truly excellent but our ruler is a great king in the world. Would he not say, 'This is what a lowly man would do', and not make use of it?"

子墨子曰：「唯其可行。譬若藥然，草之本[5]，天子食之以順其疾，豈曰『一草之本』而不食哉？今農夫入其稅於大人，大人為酒醴粢盛，以祭上帝鬼神，豈曰『賤人之所為』，而不享哉？故雖賤人也，上比之農，下比之藥，曾不若一草之本乎？且主君亦嘗聞湯之說乎？昔者湯將往見伊尹，令彭氏[6]之子御。彭氏之子半道而問曰『君將何之？』湯曰：『將往見伊尹。』彭氏之子曰：『伊尹天下之賤人也。若君欲見之，亦令召問焉，彼受賜矣。』湯曰：『非女所知也。今有藥此，食之則耳加聰，目加明，則吾必說而強食之。今夫伊尹之於我國也，譬之良醫善藥也。而子不欲我見伊尹，是子不欲吾善也。』因下彭氏之子，不使御。彼苟然，然後可也[7]。」

47.4   子墨子曰：「凡言凡動，利於天鬼百姓者為之；凡言凡動，害於天鬼百姓者舍之；凡言凡動，合於三代聖王堯舜禹湯文武者為

---

5. Following SSX, 一 is added before 草. 本 is taken as 根.
6. I have taken 彭 as a surname. On 彭氏 see ZWDCD #10231 (10), vol. 3, p. 1542.
7. There is textual uncertainty regarding this sentence. Amongst modern editors there is general acceptance of CYX's interpretation: "言惠王誠能如湯然後可用。"

Master Mo Zi said: "It is simply a question of efficacy. It is like the case of a medicine. It may be the root of one herb yet the Son of Heaven will eat it to cure his sickness. Does he say, 'This is [just] the root of one herb' and not eat it? Now the farmer pays his taxes to the great officer, and the great officer makes sweet wine and millet for sacrifices to the Supreme Lord and to ghosts and spirits. Does he say, 'This was made by a lowly man' and so not use it? Therefore, although the man may be lowly, above, he is comparable to the farmer and below, he is comparable to a medicine, so is he not ultimately like the root of one herb? Moreover, has the ruler also not previously heard the story of Tang? Formerly, Tang was about to go to see Yi Yin.[i] He ordered the son of the Peng family to drive the chariot. They were halfway along the road when the son of the Peng family asked: 'Where is your lordship going?' Tang replied: 'I am on my way to see Yi Yin.' The son of the Peng family said: 'Yi Yin is a lowly person in the world. If your lordship wishes to see him just send him a summons and he will take it as an honour.' Tang replied: 'This is not something you know about. Suppose now there was this medicine which, if I ate it, would make my hearing more acute and my vision sharper. Then I would certainly be happy to force myself to eat it. Now with respect to my country, Yi Yin is like a good doctor or an excellent medicine. Your not wishing me to go to see Yi Yin is tantamount to your not wishing me to become good.' As a result, he dismissed the son of the Peng family and did not allow him to drive the chariot. If that man (i.e. your ruler) were [like Tang], then he would be able [to accept the advice of a lowly person]."

47.4 Master Mo Zi said: "Any statements, any actions that are beneficial to Heaven, to ghosts, or to the ordinary people should be put into effect. Any statements, any actions that are harmful to Heaven, to ghosts, or to the ordinary people should be set aside. Any statements, any actions that are in accord with the sage kings of the Three Dynasties, Yao, Shun, Yu, Tang, Wen and Wu should

---

i.   Yi Yin 伊尹 was a renowned minister of state under Tang who was, so the story goes, summoned five times before he agreed to serve.

之；凡言凡動，合於三代暴王桀紂幽厲者舍之。」

47.5　子墨子曰：「言足以遷行者，常之；不足以遷行者，勿常。不足以遷行而常之，是蕩口也。」

47.6　子墨子曰：「必去六辟[8]，嘿則思，言則誨，動則事。使三者代御，必為聖人。必去喜，去怒，去樂，去悲，去愛，〔去惡〕[9]，而用仁義。手足口鼻耳〔目〕[10]，從事於義，必為聖人。」

47.7　子墨子謂二三子曰：「為義而不能，必無排[11]其道。譬若匠人之斲而不能，無排其繩。」

47.8　子墨子曰：「世之君子，使之為一犬一彘之宰，不能則辭之；使為一國之相，不能而為之。豈不悖哉！」

47.9　子墨子曰：「今瞽曰『鉅[12]者白也，黔者黑也。』雖明目者無以易之。兼白黑，使瞽取焉，不能知也。故我曰瞽不知白黑者，非以其名也，以其取也。今天下之君子之名仁也，雖禹湯無以易之。

8.　辟 is read as 僻 in the sense of 偏好. The 六辟 ("six partialities") are listed in the next sentence. Some editors (e.g. WYJ) transpose this statement to the start of that sentence.
9.　There is general acceptance of the addition of 去惡 here to complete the six (YY).
10.　Supplied following SYR.
11.　Some editors (e.g. LSL) follow BY's reading of 排 as 𢫾 in the sense of 背離.
12.　Editors generally follow YY in emending 鉅 to 皚.

be put into effect. Any statements, any actions that are in accord with the tyrannical kings of the Three Dynasties, Jie, Zhou, You and Li should be set aside."

47.5 Master Mo Zi said: "Words that are enough to change conduct (for the better) should be spoken frequently. Words that are not enough to change conduct (for the better) should not be spoken frequently. If words that are not enough to change conduct (for the better) are spoken frequently, this is a waste of breath."

47.6 Master Mo Zi said: "It is necessary to do away with the six partialities. When silent, one should be thinking; when speaking, one should be instructing; when acting, one should devote oneself to affairs. If one employs these three [rules] in turn, one will certainly become a sage. One must do away with pleasure, do away with anger, do away with joy, do away with sorrow, do away with love, [do away with hate] and make use of benevolence and righteousness. When hands, feet, mouth, nose, ears and [eyes] are devoted to affairs through righteousness, one will certainly become a sage."

47.7 Master Mo Zi spoke to two or three disciples, saying: "Even if one is not able to achieve righteousness, one must not abandon one's Way, just as the carpenter who is not able to cut [straight] does not abandon his line."

47.8 Master Mo Zi said: "With gentlemen of the age, if you ask them to be butchers for a dog or a pig and they do not have the ability to do it, then they decline it. If you ask them to be ministers of a state, although they do not have the ability, they do it. How is this not perverse!"

47.9 Master Mo Zi said: "Now a blind person says, 'What is white is light, what is black is dark'. Even those who are keen-sighted have no way of changing this. [But if you] mix together white and black [objects] and ask a blind person to select, they are not able to know. Therefore, when I say that the blind person does not know white and black, this does not refer to their naming, but to their choosing. Now the way the gentlemen of the world name

兼仁與不仁，而使天下之君子取焉，不能知也。故我曰天下之君子不知仁者，非以其名也，亦以其取也。」

47.10   子墨子曰：「今士之用身，不若商人之用一布[13]之慎也。商人用一布布[14]，不敢繼苟而讎焉[15]，必擇良者。今士之用身則不然，意之所欲則為之，厚者入刑罰，薄者被毀醜，則士之用身不若商人之用一布之慎也。」

47.11   子墨子曰：「世之君子欲其義之成，而助之修其身則慍，是猶欲其牆之成，而人助之築則慍也。豈不悖哉。」

47.12   子墨子曰：「古者聖王，欲傳其道於後世，是故書之竹帛，鏤之金石，傳遺後世子孫，欲後世子孫法之也。今聞先王之遺[16]而不為，是廢先王之傳也。」

47.13   子墨子南遊使衛，關中載書甚多[17]。弦唐子見而怪之曰：「吾夫子教公尚過曰『揣曲直而已』。今夫子載書甚多。何有也？」子墨子

13. I have followed modern editors in taking 布 as "古代的錢幣" (e.g. Z&Q).
14. The second 布 is taken as 市 in the sense of 買物 (SYR).
15. In this clause, 繼 is regarded as superfluous, 苟 is taken as 隨便, and 讎 is read as 售.
16. 遺 is read as 道 here following WYZ.
17. Most commentators accept BY's reading of 關 as 扃. For further details of the structural issues and other references to Mo Zi's carrying about of books, see WYJ, note 55, p. 696.

benevolence, even Yu and Tang would have no means of changing. [But if you] mix together the benevolent and the non-benevolent and ask the gentlemen of the world to choose, they are not able to know. Therefore, when I say that the gentlemen of the world do not know benevolence, this does not refer to their naming. It too refers to their choosing."

47.10 Master Mo Zi said: "Nowadays, officers are not prudent in using themselves the way merchants are in using money. When a merchant spends money on buying something, he does not dare to be careless in his buying. He certainly selects what is good. Nowadays, officers are not like this in using themselves. If they think of something they wish to do, then they do it. In severe cases they suffer penalties and punishment; in minor cases they are criticised and reviled. So officers are not prudent in using themselves like merchants are in using money."

47.11 Master Mo Zi said: "Gentlemen of the age wish their righteousness to be complete, but if you help them cultivate themselves, they become indignant. This is like wishing to complete a wall, but becoming indignant if someone helps you build it. How is this not perverse!"

47.12 Master Mo Zi said: "The sage kings of ancient times wished to hand down their Way to later generations. For this reason, they recorded it on bamboo and silk and carved it on metal and stone to transmit and hand it down to their descendants of later generations, wishing these descendants to use it as a model. Now we hear of the Way of former kings, but we do not put it into practice. This is to discard the transmission of former kings."

47.13 When Master Mo Zi was travelling south to serve in Wei, he carried many books in his wagon. Xian Tangzi, seeing this, was surprised and said: "You, sir, have taught Gongshang Guo saying, 'Evaluate the crooked and the straight and that is all'.[ii] Now you carry about many books. Why is this?"

---

ii. Little is known of the two men spoken of here. Both are taken to be disciples of Mo Di. Xian Tangzi 弦唐子 also appears in *Mozi* 49 whilst there is record of an exchange between Mo Zi and Gongshang Guo 公尚國 in the *Lü Shi Chunqiu* 19/2.3.

曰：「昔者周公旦朝讀書百篇，夕見漆[18]十士。故周公旦佐相天子，其脩至於今。翟上無君上之事，下無耕農之難，吾安敢廢此？翟聞之『同歸之物，信有誤者』。然而民聽不鈞，是以書多也。今若過之心者，數逆於精微，同歸之物，既已知其要矣，是以不教以書也。而子何怪焉？」

47.14 子墨子謂公良桓子曰：「衛小國也，處於齊晉之間，猶貧家之處於富家之間也。貧家而學富家之衣食多用，則速亡必矣。今簡[19]子之家，飾車數百乘，馬食菽粟者數百匹，婦人衣文繡者數百人，吾[20]取飾車，食馬之費，與繡衣之財以畜士，必千人有餘。若有患難，則使〔數〕[21]百人盛處於前，數百於後，與婦人數百人處前後，孰安？吾以為不若畜士之安也。」

---

18. Following BY, 漆 is read as 亡.
19. 簡 is read as 閒 in the sense of 察看 following SYR.
20. Not all commentators accept YY's proposed emendation of 吾 to 若.
21. On this suggested addition see WYJ, note 72, p. 698.

Master Mo Zi replied: "In former times, Dan, the Duke of Zhou, read a hundred *pian* of books in the morning and received seventy officers in the evening. Therefore, the Duke of Zhou, Dan's, assistance to the son of Heaven and his cultivation have reached to the present day. I have no prince to serve above, nor any ploughing and farming to contend with below. How do I dare to set these [books] aside? I have heard this — 'Principles may have the one path, but it is difficult to avoid errors on the way.'[iii] This being so, what the people hear is not uniform. That is why I have so many books. Now when one has gone over things in one's mind and has considered them in fine detail, one understands that the essential elements of the principles form a single path. When this is achieved, one does not learn through books. Why do you find this so strange?"

47.14 Master Mo Zi spoke to Gongliang Huan Zi[iv] saying: "Wei is a small country situated between Qi and Jin. It is like a poor household situated between rich households. If a household is poor yet imitates the great consumption of clothes and food of a rich household, then its quick destruction is certain. Now, when I look at your household, there are several hundred decorated carriages, several hundred fine, grain-fed horses, and several hundred women with elegant and embroidered clothes. If I were to take the money wasted on decorated carriages and fine horses, and the wealth invested in embroidered clothes, to gather knights-errant, I would certainly have a thousand men or more. If, then, there was some misfortune or difficulty and I positioned a hundred men at the front and several hundred men at the rear, or I positioned several hundred women front and rear, which is the more secure? I think the latter would not compare in terms of security to the collected knights-errant."

---

iii. This is a rather free rendering of the obscure statement: "同歸之物，信有誤者。" It follows SYR's commentary with reference to the *Changes* "繫辭", SSJZS, vol. 1, p. 169: "天下同歸而殊塗。"

iv. Gongliang Huan Zi 公良桓子 has been regarded as a great officer of Wei by all commentators following SYR but there is no biographical information about him.

47.15 子墨子仕人於衛，所仕者至而反。子墨子曰：「何故反？」對曰：「與我言而不當。曰，『待女以千盆』。授我五百盆，故去之也。」子墨子曰：「授子過千盆，則子去之乎？」對曰：「不去。」子墨子曰：「然則，非為其不審也，為其寡也。」

47.16 子墨子曰：「世俗之君子，視義士不若負粟者。今有人於此，負粟息於路側，欲起而不能，君子見之，無長少貴賤，必起之，何故也？曰義也。今為義之君子，奉承先生之道以語之，縱不說而行，又從而非毀之。則是世俗之君子之視義士也，不若視負粟者也。」

47.17 子墨子曰：「商人之四方，市賈信徙[22]，雖有關梁之難，盜賊之危，必為之。今士坐而言義，無關梁之難，盜賊之危，此為信徙，不可勝計，然而不為。則士之計利不若商人之察也。」

---

22. In this problematic clause, 市 is read as 買賣, 賈 as 價, and 信徙 as 倍徙 following BY with reference to *Mencius* IIIA.4(18) — LCC, vol. 2, p. 256.

47.15 Master Mo Zi recommended someone for office in Wei. The man he recommended went and returned. Master Mo Zi asked: "Why have you returned?"

The man replied: "[The prince] spoke with me but not properly. He said, 'I shall give you 1000 *pen*', but I received only 500 *pen*. That is why I left."

Master Mo Zi asked: "If he had given you more than 1000 *pen*, would you have left?"

The man replied: "I would not have left."

Master Mo Zi said: "In that case, then, it was not his failure to keep his word. It was his parsimony."

47.16 Master Mo Zi said: "It is characteristic of the age that the gentleman does not look on a righteous officer like he does on a grain carrier. Now suppose there was a man here, a grain carrier, resting at the side of the road, who wanted to rise but was unable to, and a gentleman saw him. Whether he was old or young, rich or poor, [the gentleman] would certainly help him rise. Why is this? I say it is [because of] righteousness. Nowadays, if a gentleman, in being righteous, carries on the Way of former kings and speaks about it, not only are others not happy to put it into practice, but they even criticise it. This, then, is what I mean by saying that it is characteristic of the age that a gentleman does not look on a righteous officer like he does on a grain carrier."

47.17 Master Mo Zi said: "Merchants travel in the four directions looking to make a twofold or fivefold profit in their trading. Even if there are the difficulties of barriers and bridges, and the dangers of thieves and robbers, they must do this. Nowadays, officers sit and discuss righteousness and have no difficulties with barriers and bridges, and no danger from thieves and robbers. In this, the benefit would not only be twofold or fivefold, but would be beyond calculation. Nevertheless, they do not practise it. Thus officers, in calculating what is profitable, do not examine [the matter] like merchants."

47.18　子墨子北之齊，遇日者[23]。日者曰：「帝以今日殺黑龍於北方，而
先生之色黑，不可以北。」子墨子不聽，遂北，至淄水，不遂而
反焉。日者曰：「我謂先生不可以北。」子墨子曰：「南之人不得
北，北之人不得南，其色有黑者，有白者，何故皆不遂也？且帝
以甲乙殺青龍於東方，以丙丁殺赤龍於南方，以庚辛殺白龍於西
方，以壬癸殺黑龍於北方，〔以戊己殺黃龍於中方〕[24]，若用子之
言，則是禁天下之行者也。是圍心而虛天下也，子之言不可用
也。」

47.19　子墨子曰：「吾言足用矣，舍言革思者，是猶舍獲而拾[25] 粟也，以
其言非吾言者，是猶以卵投石也，盡天下之卵，其石猶是也，不
可毀也。」

---

23. For 日者, here translated as "soothsayer", see *Shi Ji* 127 〈日者列傳〉 where at the start
    of the chapter this passage from the *Mozi* is quoted as an explanatory note — vol. 10,
    p. 3215.
24. This final instance is added by BY — see WYJ, note 93, p. 701 and YPM, notes 1 and
    2, p. 229.
25. 拾 is used for the variant of 麇 *(jun)* — ZWDCD #13257.

47.18 When Master Mo Zi was travelling north to Qi he met a soothsayer. The soothsayer said: "The Supreme Being on this day kills the black dragon in the Northern Region so, since you, Sir, have a dark countenance, you may not go north." Master Mo Zi did not listen and continued north, but when he reached the Zi Waters[v] he ran into difficulty and returned. The soothsayer said: "I told you, Sir, that you could not go north."

Master Mo Zi said: "People to the south can't reach the north and people to the north can't reach the south.[vi] In terms of complexion, there are some who are dark and some who are fair. Why is it that they all cannot proceed? Moreover, the Supreme Being, on the days of *jia* and *yi*, kills the green dragon in the Eastern Region, on the days of *bing* and *ding* kills the red dragon in the Southern Region, on the days of *geng* and *xin*, kills the white dragon in the Western Region, on the days of *ren* and *gui*, kills the black dragon in the Northern Region, [and on the days of *wu* and *ji* kills the yellow dragon in the Central Region]. If, Sir, we use your words, then this prohibits all travel in the world. This runs counter to people's minds and 'empties' the world, so your words cannot be used."

47.19 Master Mo Zi said: "My words are sufficient for use. One who casts aside my words and changes my ideas is like one who casts aside the harvest and picks up grains. To use one's own words to negate my words is like throwing eggs against a rock. Even if one uses all the eggs in the world, the rock remains as it is and cannot be destroyed."

---

v. The Zi Waters 淄水 were in what is present-day Shandong.

vi. Modern editors relate the north and south here to the Zi Waters.

48: 公孟

48.1 公孟子謂子墨子曰：「君子共己[1]以待，問焉則言，不問焉則止。譬若鐘然，扣則鳴，不扣則不鳴。」子墨子曰：「是言有三物焉。子乃今知其一耳也[2]，又未知其所謂也。若大人行淫暴於國家，進而諫，則謂之不遜，因左右而獻諫，則謂之言議。此君子之所疑惑也。若大人為政，將因於國家之難，譬若機之將發也然[3]，君子之必以諫，然而大人之利[4]，若此者，雖不扣必鳴者也。若大人舉不義之異行，雖得大巧之經，可行於軍旅之事，欲攻伐無罪之國，有之也，君得之，則必用之矣。以廣辟土地，著稅偽材[5]，出必見辱，所攻者不利，而攻者亦不利，是兩不利也。若此者，雖不扣必鳴者也。且子曰：『君子共己待，問焉則言，不問焉則

---

1. There is general acceptance of SYR's reading of 共己 as 拱己.
2. There are several issues with this clause, the most notable being the emendation of 身 to 耳 following WYZ. For a detailed discussion see WYJ, note 5, p. 710.
3. The reading of this phrase follows LSL.
4. Some commentators think there is a lacuna here — see, for example, YPM. The reading above follows WYJ and Z&Q.
5. The original text for this clause is as above: "著稅偽材". Following proposals by BY and SYR, this is emended to read what is equivalent to: "籍斂貨財".

48: Gongmeng

48.1 Gongmeng Zi[i] spoke to Master Mo Zi saying: "A gentleman folds his hands and waits. If he is questioned, then he speaks. If he is not questioned, then he desists. He is like a bell. If it is struck, then it sounds; if not struck, then it does not sound."

Master Mo Zi said: "To this, I say there are three conditions.[ii] You, Sir, know only of one, so you do not yet know what is being said. If a great officer behaves in a dissolute and cruel way in the state, to come forward to remonstrate is called not being humble. To remonstrate through those on either side is called privately criticising. For the gentleman this is a perplexing matter. Now if the great officer who is governing is about to encounter some difficulty in the state, just like an arrow that flies from a bow, the gentleman must come forward to remonstrate, and so be of benefit to the great officer. In this case, even if he is not struck, he must sound. Suppose a great officer undertakes some unusual enterprise that is not righteous. For example, suppose he acquires some ingenious device which can be employed in military matters and wishes to attack some unoffending state with it. If he has acquired it, he will certainly use it as a means of extending his territory and land, and illegally extorting goods and wealth. In going forth there is, however, unquestionably disgrace, and there is no benefit either to the one attacked or to the one attacking — that is, neither benefits. In such a case, although not struck, one should certainly sound. Moreover, you say, 'A gentleman will fold his hands and

---

i. There is some uncertainty as to who Gongmeng (taken as a double surname) was — possibly Gong Mingyi 公明儀. What is agreed is that he was a Confucian and may have been a disciple of Zeng Zi 曾子. See WYJ, note 1, p. 709 for a detailed discussion of this matter.

ii. Following WYZ, the three conditions are taken to refer to the second part of the preceding phrase, i.e. "not striking so not sounding". The other two are "although not striking yet necessarily sounding" and "striking yet not sounding" — see, for example, LSL, p. 409.

止。譬若鐘然，扣則鳴，不扣則不鳴。』今未有扣，子而言，是子之謂不扣而鳴邪？是子之所謂非君子邪？」

48.2   公孟子謂子墨子曰：「實為善人，孰不知？譬若良玉[6]，處而不出有餘糈[7]。譬若美女，處而不出，人爭求之。行而自衒，人莫之取也。今子遍從人而說之，何其勞也？」子墨子曰：「今夫世亂，求美女者眾，美女雖不出，人多求之。今求善者寡，不強說人，人莫之知也。且有二生，於此善筮，一行為人筮者，一處而不出者。行為人筮者與處而不出者，其糈孰多？」公孟子曰：「行為人筮者其糈多。」子墨子曰：「仁義鈞。行說人者，其功善亦多，何故不行說人也！」

48.3   公孟子戴章甫[8]、搢忽[9]、儒服，而以見子墨子曰：「君子服然後行乎？其行然後服乎？」子墨子曰：「行不在服。」公孟子曰：「何以

---

6. Commentators follow SYR in reading 玉 as 巫, or 筮, in accord with what follows.

7. 糈 is taken as 糧食 (LSL). WYJ emends to 精 — see his note 24, pp. 712–713.

8. On the emendation of the 義 of early texts to 戴 and the reference to 章甫 in the *Li Ji* see WYJ, notes 26 and 27, p. 713.

9. 搢忽 is read as 搢笏〔於紳〕with 搢 in the sense of 插.

wait. If he is asked, then he speaks; if he is not asked, then he desists. He is like a bell. If it is struck, then it sounds; if it is not struck, then it does not sound.' Now you have not yet been struck yet you speak. Isn't this what you call sounding without being struck? Isn't this what you call not being a gentleman?"

48.2 Gongmeng Zi spoke to Master Mo Zi, saying: "Is there a person who is genuinely good, but is not known? Like, for example, a prognosticator who stays at home and does not go out, but has an abundance of grain. Like, for example, a beautiful maiden who stays at home and does not go out, but has men contending to win her. If, however, she goes out and displays herself, men will not seek her. Now you go about everywhere offering your theories. Is it not a great trouble!"

Master Mo Zi replied: "Now is an age of disorder. Those who seek beautiful maidens are many, so even if a beautiful maiden does not go out, there are still many who seek her. But now those who seek goodness are few. If there are not men who take the trouble to go about exhorting them, people will not know about it. Moreover, suppose there are two people, both of whom are good at prognostication, but one goes out and prognosticates for people whilst the other stays at home and does not go out. Of the one who goes out and prognosticates for people and the one who stays at home and does not go out, who will have the more grain?"

Gongmeng Zi answered: "The one who goes about prognosticating for people will have the more grain."

Master Mo Zi said: "It is the same with benevolence and righteousness. The one who travels about speaking to people will also have much greater merit. So why not go about speaking to people?"

48.3 Gongmeng Zi, having donned his ceremonial cap, stuck the official tablet [into his girdle], put on a scholar's robes, went to see Master Mo Zi, and asked: "Does a gentleman attire himself and afterwards act or does he act and afterwards attire himself?"

Master Mo Zi replied: "Actions have nothing to do with attire."

知其然也？」子墨子曰：「昔者齊桓公高冠博帶，金劍木盾，以治其國，其國治。昔者晉文公大布之衣，牂羊之裘，韋以帶劍，以治其國，其國治。昔者楚莊王鮮冠組纓，絳衣博袍，以治其國，其國治。昔者越王勾踐剪髮文身，以治其國，其國治。此四君者，其服不同，其行猶一也。翟以是知行之不在服也。」公孟子曰：「善！吾聞之曰：『宿善者不祥』。請舍忽，易章甫，復見夫子可乎？」子墨子曰：「請因以相見也。若必將舍忽，易章甫，而後相見，然則行果在服也。」

Gongmeng Zi asked: "How do you know this to be so?"

Master Mo Zi answered: "Formerly, Duke Huan of Qi, wearing a high cap and broad girdle, and [carrying] a gold sword and wooden shield, brought order to his country and his country was well governed.[iii] Formerly, Duke Wen of Jin, wearing clothes of coarse cloth and a sheepskin cloak, and [carrying] a sword in a leather belt, brought order to his country and his country was well governed.[iv] Formerly, King Zhuang of Chu, wearing a brightly coloured cap with silk ribbons attached and a large robe, brought order to his kingdom and his kingdom was well governed.[v] Formerly, the Yue king, Gou Jian, having cut his hair short and decorated his body, brought order to his kingdom and his kingdom was well governed.[vi] In the case of these four rulers, although in attire they were different, in actions they were as one. This is how I know that actions have nothing to do with attire."

Gongmeng Zi said: "Ah goodness! I have heard it said that the one who ceases from goodness is not fortunate. May I ask if it is possible to put aside the official tablet, change the ceremonial cap, and visit you again?"

Master Mo Zi answered: "You ask how we should meet. If you must put aside the official tablet, change the ceremonial cap, and afterwards meet, this then is action being a result of attire."

---

iii. Qi Huan Gong 齊桓公 (ruled 685–643 BC), also known as Xiao Bo 小白 was, with the assistance of his renowned minister Guan Zhong 管仲, an effective ruler of his country, at least until his final years. There is some doubt about 木盾. SYR has a note to the effect that a shield was not part of ceremonial dress and raises the question of whether a tablet (笏) is meant, although, as he points out, a wooden tablet would not be associated with high rank.

iv. Jin Wen Gong 晉文公 (ruled 636–628 BC), also known as Chong'er 重耳, survived an attempt on his life instigated by his father's concubine in 654 BC and subsequently returned to become a powerful and effective ruler.

v. Chu Zhuang Wang 楚莊王 (ruled 613–591 BC) was one of the Five Lords-Protector — LSCQ 2/4.2.

vi. Yue Wang Gou Jian 越王勾踐 (ruled ca 496–465 BC). He was defeated in battle by the Wu army under Fu Chai, having attacked that state, but subsequently reversed that defeat and returned to become an effective ruler.

48.4   公孟子曰：「君子必古言服，然後仁。」子墨子曰：「昔者商王紂、
卿士費仲，為天下之暴人。箕子、微子為天下之聖人。此同言而
或仁〔或〕[10] 不仁也。周公旦為天下〔之〕聖人，關叔為天下之暴
人。此同服或仁或不仁。然則不在古服與古言矣。且子法周而未
法夏也，子之古非古也。」

48.5   公孟子謂子墨子曰：「昔者聖王之列也，上聖立為天子，其次立
為卿、大夫。今孔子博於《詩》《書》，察於禮樂[11]，詳於萬物，若
使孔子當聖王，則豈不以孔子為天子哉？」子墨子曰：「夫知者，
必尊天事鬼，愛人節用，合焉為知矣。今子曰：『孔子博於《詩》
《書》，察於禮樂，詳於萬物』，而曰可以為天子，是數人之齒[12]，

---

10. The addition of 或 here and 之 in the next clause follow WYJ.
11. Some editors take 詩, 書, 禮 and 樂 all to refer to books, i.e. the relevant classics (e.g.
     LSL), some to the practices and not to books specifically (e.g. LYS), and some take the
     first two only to be books, as above (e.g. WYJ, Z&Q). LYS replaces 樂 with 義.
12. The "teeth" here are marks on a piece of wood — 契齒. This explanation stems from YY.
     See also the *Liezi* 8.

48.4 Gongmeng Zi said: "A gentleman must be ancient in speech and attire, and afterwards he is benevolent."

Master Mo Zi replied: "In former times, the Shang king, Zhou and Chief Minister Fei Zhong were tyrants of the world. [On the other hand] Ji Zi and Wei Zi were sages of the world. This is a case of having the same speech, but some being benevolent and some not being benevolent.[vii] Dan, the Duke of Zhou was a sage of the world [whereas] Guan Shu was a tyrant of the world.[viii] This is a case of having the same attire, but one being benevolent and one not being benevolent. This being so, [benevolence] does not lie in ancient attire and ancient words. Moreover, you take Zhou as the model and not Xia as the model,[ix] so your 'ancient' is not ancient."

48.5 Gongmeng Zi spoke to Master Mo Zi, saying: "In former times, the sage kings, in establishing rank, gave the highest sage the position of Son of Heaven, and gave the next in order positions as ministers and great officers. Now Confucius had a wide knowledge of the *Odes* and the *Documents*. He had looked carefully into the rites and music, and had a clear understanding of the ten thousand things. If Confucius was properly a sage king, then how was he not made the Son of Heaven?"

Master Mo Zi said: "In the case of the wise man, he must certainly honour Heaven and serve the ghosts, love people and show moderation in use, combining these things in being wise. Now you say, 'Confucius had a wide knowledge of the *Odes* and the *Documents*, had looked carefully into rites and music, and had a

---

vii. Zhou 紂 was the last ruler of the Shang/Yin dynasty and was notorious for his cruelty and depravity. Fei Gong 費仲 was chief minister to Zhou. Viscount Ji 箕子 was a leading noble at the time of Zhou and one of his uncles. He was imprisoned for protesting against Zhou's excesses. Viscount Wei 微子 was also a relative of Zhou and opposed his conduct, going into voluntary exile.

viii. The Duke of Zhou, Dan 周公旦 was the fourth son of Wen Wang and counsellor to Wu Wang. He was renowned for his wisdom and rectitude. Guan Shu 關叔 is taken to be Guan Shu Xian 管叔鮮, the third son of Wen Wang, who was enfeoffed with Xian in 1122 BC and who plotted (unsuccessfully due to the Duke of Zhou) to seize the throne on the death of Wu Wang.

ix. The Zhou 周 dynasty extended from 1122 to 255 BC, the Xia 夏 from 2205 to 1766 BC.

而以為富。」公孟子曰:「貧富壽夭,齰[13]然在天,不可損益。」又
曰:「君子必學。」子墨子曰:「教人學而執有命,是猶命人葆[14]而
去其冠也。」

48.6 公孟子謂子墨子曰:「有義不義,無祥不祥。」子墨子曰:「古聖王
皆以鬼神為神明,而[15]為禍福,執有祥不祥,是以政治而國安
也,自桀紂以下,皆以鬼神為不神明,不能為禍福,執無祥不
祥,是以政亂而國危也。故先王之書,《子亦》有之曰:『其傲也,
出於子,不祥。』[16]此言為不善之有罰,為善之有賞。」

48.7 子墨子謂公孟子曰:「喪禮,君與父母、妻、後子死,三年喪
服;伯父、叔父、兄弟期;族人五月;姑、姊、舅、甥皆有數月

---

13. There are different views on the character 齰. BY takes it as 錯 or 措 in the sense of 措
    置 — "arranged by heaven". CYX takes it as 鑿 and equates it with 確然 as above.
14. There is wide acceptance of BY's note: "葆,言包裹其髮。"
15. 而 here is taken as 能 following BY.
16. The majority of modern commentators take this chapter title to be 箕子 (Viscount Ji) and
    the chapter to be a lost part of the 書經. WYJ takes a different view and this is what is
    followed above — see his note 57, p. 718.

clear understanding of the ten thousand things' and you say he can be taken to be the Son of Heaven. This is like counting a person's 'teeth' to determine his wealth."

Gongmeng Zi said: "Poverty and wealth, longevity and early death, truly lie with Heaven, and cannot be decreased or increased." He also said: "A gentleman must study."

Master Mo Zi said: "To teach a person to study and to hold that there is Fate is like telling him to bind up his hair, but do away with his cap."

48.6   Gongmeng Zi spoke to Master Mo Zi, saying: "There is righteousness and there is unrighteousness. There is not good fortune and bad fortune."ˣ

Master Mo Zi said: "The ancient sage kings all considered the ghosts and spirits to be divine and all-seeing, to be able to dispense calamity and blessing, and to have control of good fortune and bad fortune. This was how they brought order to the government and peace to the country. From Jie and Zhou onwards, all considered the ghosts and spirits not to be divine and all-seeing, not to be able to dispense calamity and blessing, and not to have control of good fortune and bad fortune. This was how they brought disorder to the government and danger to the country. Therefore, the historical writing of the former kings, the *Zi Yi*, has this to say: 'If you manifest pride you will not have good fortune.' This is to say that when something is done that is bad there will be punishment, and when something is done that is good there will be reward."

48.7   Master Mo Zi spoke to Gongmeng Zi, saying: "With regard to mourning rites, when the ruler, father or mother, wife, or eldest son die, there is mourning for three years. In the case of a father's older or younger brothers, or [one's own] older or younger brothers, the period is one year. For members of one's clan, it is

---

x.   All modern editors feel the need to clarify this terse statement (not surprisingly!). The point appears to be that people can certainly be righteous or not, but their being fortunate or not does not depend on their being righteous or not, and the spirits and gods responding to this — see, for example, Z&Q, p. 733.

之喪。或以不喪之間，誦詩三百，弦詩三百，歌詩三百，舞詩三百。若用子之言，則君子何日以聽治？庶人何日以從事？」

48.8　公孟子曰：「國亂則治之，國治則為禮樂。國治[17] 則從事，國富則為禮樂。」子墨子曰：「國之治。治之廢，則國之治亦廢[18]。國之富也，從事，故富也。從事廢，則國之富亦廢。故雖治國，勸之無饜，然後可也。今子曰『國治，則為禮樂，亂則治之』。是譬猶噎[19] 而穿井也，死而求醫也。古者三代暴王桀紂幽厲，薦為聲樂，不顧其民，是以身為刑僇，國為戾虛者，皆從此道也。」

---

17. Following WNS, 治 is read as 貧.
18. The translation of this statement follows WHB's emended text which reads: "國之治也，聽治，故治也；聽治廢，則國之治亦廢。"
19. Following YY, 噎 is read as 渴.

five months. Paternal aunts, older sisters, maternal uncles and a sister's children all have several months of mourning. Some use the periods between mourning to recite the three hundred odes, to play the three hundred odes on stringed instruments, to sing the three hundred odes, or to dance to the three hundred odes.[xi] If your words are used, then how can the gentleman attend to the day-to-day business of government? How can the ordinary people attend to their day-to-day affairs?"

48.8   Gongmeng Zi said: "If the country is in disorder, then it should be brought to order. If the country is well ordered, then rites and music should be practised. If the country is poor, then affairs should be attended to. If the country is rich, then rites and music should be practised."

Master Mo Zi said: "If a country is well ordered, there is attention to order and so it is well ordered. If attention to order is done away with, then the order of a country is also done away with. If a country is rich, there has been attention to affairs — this is why it is rich. If attention to affairs is done away with, then a country's wealth is also done away with. Therefore, although a country is well ordered, it is unceasing diligence that makes this possible. Now you say, 'If the country is well ordered, then practise rites and music and, if it is in disorder, then bring it to order.' This is like saying that if someone is parched he should dig a well, or if someone has died a doctor should be sought. In ancient times, the tyrannical rulers of the Three Dynasties, Jie, Zhou, You and Li[xii] took delight in music and did not look to their people. This is why they themselves were punished and killed, in the country there were no descendants and the houses were empty.[xiii] In all instances, it was from following this road."

---

xi. These are taken to be the 305 poems of the *Shi Jing* 詩經.

xii. The Xia (Jie 桀), Shang/Yin (Zhou 紂), and Zhou (You 幽 and Li 厲).

xiii. This follows LYS's interpretation and a similar passage in the *Zhuangzi* 4 (GQF, vol. 1, p. 139).

48.9   公孟子曰：「無鬼神。」又曰：「君子必學祭祀[20]。」子墨子曰：「執
無鬼而學祭禮，是猶無客而學客禮也，是猶無魚而為魚罟也。」

48.10   公孟子謂子墨子曰：「子以三年之喪為非，子之三日[21]之喪亦非
也。」子墨子曰：「子以三年之喪非三日之喪，是猶裸謂撅者不恭
也。」

48.11   公孟子謂子墨子曰：「知有賢[22]於人，則可謂知乎？」子墨子曰：
「愚之知有以賢於人，而愚豈可為知矣哉？」

48.12   公孟子曰：「三年之喪，學吾[23]之慕父母。」子墨子曰：「夫嬰兒子
之知，獨慕父母而已。父母不可得也，然號而不止，此其故何
也？即愚之至也。然則儒者之知，豈有以賢於嬰兒子哉？」

48.13   子墨子問於儒者曰[24]：「何故為樂？」曰：「樂以為樂也。」子墨子

---

20. Following BY, 禮 is read for 祀 in conformity with what follows.
21. The change from days 日 to months 月 here and in the following sentence is based on
    the passage in the *Han Feizi* 1 on Mo Zi's views.
22. 賢 here and in the following sentence is taken in the sense of 超過 or 勝過 (see, for
    example, Z&Q).
23. Following YY, 子 is understood after 吾.
24. I have transposed 曰 from its position after 子墨子 following SSX.

48.9 Gongmeng Zi said: "There are no ghosts and spirits." He also said: "A gentleman must study sacrifices and rituals."

Master Mo Zi said: "To hold that there are no ghosts, yet to study sacrifices and rituals is like having no guests, but studying the ceremonies for guests. It is like there being no fish, but making a fish-net."

48.10 Gongmeng Zi spoke to Master Mo Zi, saying: "You consider three years of mourning to be wrong. Your three months of mourning is also wrong."

Master Mo Zi said: "You accept three years of mourning, but you condemn three months of mourning. This is like someone who has stripped naked saying a person who has just lifted his garments is not respectful."

48.11 Gongmeng Zi spoke to Master Mo Zi, saying: "If one man's knowledge surpasses that of another man, can he then be said to be knowledgeable?"

Master Mo Zi replied: "A fool's knowledge may surpass that of another man, but how can a fool be deemed knowledgeable?"

48.12 Gongmeng Zi said: "Three years of mourning teaches my son of my affection for my parents."

Master Mo Zi said: "A baby boy's knowledge is such that he just loves his father and mother and that is all. If he cannot have his father and mother, he will cry and not stop. What is the reason for this? It is because his foolishness is extreme. If this is so, then how is the knowledge of a Confucian greater than that of a baby boy?"

48.13 Master Mo Zi questioned a Confucian, asking him: "Why make music?"

[The Confucian] replied: "Music is for the purpose of music."[xiv]

---

xiv. I am indebted to the anonymous reader who kindly drew my attention to the opening sentence of *Xunzi* 20 ("夫樂者，樂也" translated by Knoblock as "Music is joy") as exemplifying a Confucian play on words deliberately overlooked by the Mohist writer of the present passage.

曰：「子未我應也。今我問曰：『何故為室？』曰：『冬避寒焉，夏避暑焉，室²⁵以為男女之別也。』則子告我為室之故矣。今我問曰：『何故為樂？』曰：『樂以為樂也』。是猶曰：『何故為室？』曰：『室以為室也』。」

48.14 子墨子謂程子曰：「儒之道足以喪天下者，四政焉。儒以天為不明，以鬼為不神，天鬼不說，此足以喪天下。又厚葬久喪，重為棺槨，多為衣衾，送死若徙，三年哭泣，扶後起，杖後行，耳無聞，目無見，此足以喪天下。又弦歌鼓舞，習為聲樂，此足以喪天下。又以命為有，貧富壽夭，治亂安危有極矣，不可損益也，為上者行之，必不聽治矣；為下者行之，必不從事矣，此足以喪天下。」程子曰：「甚矣！先生之毀儒也。」子墨子曰：「儒固無此若四政者，而我言之，則是毀也。今儒固有此四政者，而我言之，則非毀也，告聞也。」程子無辭而出。子墨子曰：「迷之！」

---

25. YY suggests emendation of 室 to 且.

Master Mo Zi said: "You have not yet answered my question. If I ask you, 'Why make a house?' and you say, 'To keep out the cold in winter and the heat in summer, and also to maintain a separation between men and women', then this is telling me what a house is for. Now, when I ask you 'Why make music?', you say, 'Music is for the purpose of music'. This is like saying, when I ask 'Why make a house?', that 'A house is for the purpose of a house'."

48.14 Master Mo Zi spoke to Cheng Zi,[xv] saying: "The Way of Confucianism has four principles which are enough to destroy all under Heaven. Confucians take Heaven not to be all-seeing and they take ghosts not to be divine. Thus they arouse displeasure in Heaven and ghosts. This is enough to destroy all under Heaven. They also have substantial funerals and prolonged mourning, give importance to the making of inner and outer coffins, make many burial garments, and have funeral processions which are like moving house. For three years there is crying and weeping. They need support to rise and a staff to walk. Their ears cannot hear and their eyes cannot see. This is enough to destroy all under Heaven. They also have stringed instruments and songs, drums and dances, and they practise making the sounds of music. This is enough to destroy all under Heaven. They also consider there to be Fate, such that poverty and riches, longevity and dying young, order and disorder, and safety and danger are predetermined and cannot be reduced or increased. If those above practise this, they will certainly not attend to government. If those below practise this, they will certainly not carry out their business. This is enough to destroy all under Heaven."

Cheng Zi said: "It is too much, your slander of the Confucians."

Master Mo Zi said: "If the Confucians do not have these four principles but I say they do, then this is slander. Now the Confucians certainly do have these four principles, so my saying so is not, then, slander. It is informing the listener."

Cheng Zi had no reply and went out.

---

xv. Cheng Fan 程繁 is thought to have been a student of both Mohism and Confucianism — see *Mozi* 7 〈三辯〉 which is entirely a dialogue between Mo Zi and Cheng Zi.

反，後坐²⁶，進復曰：「鄉者先生之言有可聞者焉，若先生之言，則是不譽禹，不毀桀紂也。」子墨子曰：「不然，夫應孰辭，稱議而為之，敏也²⁷。厚攻則厚吾²⁸，薄攻則薄吾。應孰辭而稱議，是猶荷轅而擊蛾也。」

48.15   子墨子與程子辯，稱於孔子。程子曰：「非儒，何故稱於孔子也？」子墨子曰：「是亦當而不可易者也。今鳥聞熱旱之憂則高，魚聞熱旱之憂則下，當此雖禹湯為之謀，必不能易矣。鳥魚可謂愚矣，禹湯猶云因焉²⁹。今翟曾無稱於孔子乎？」

48.16³⁰   有游於子墨子之門者，身體強良，思慮徇³¹通，欲使隨而學。子墨子曰：「姑學乎，吾將仕子。」勸於善言而學。其³²年，而責仕

---

26. The preceding five characters follow SYR: 還 is read for the otherwise perplexing 迷 (SYR), 返 for 反, and 復 for 後 (WNS). WYJ, however, follows Qiu Shan 秋山 in emending 迷 to 逆.

27. There is some uncertainty about this sentence. Commentators generally accept 熟 for 孰, understanding 熟辭 as 普通語言. SYR adds 不 before 稱議. This gives the reading above.

28. Following WYZ, 御 is read for 吾.

29. In this clause, 云 is read as 或 (WNS) and 因 is taken as 因循 (e.g. Z&Q).

30. In WYJ's text, what above are sections 48.18 and 48.19 precede sections 48.16 and 48. 17.

31. Modern editors accept SYR's emendation of 徇 in the phrase 徇通 to 徇, citing the 《說文》 in equating this with 疾.

32. 其 is taken as 期 — see, for example, Z&Q.

Master Mo Zi called: "Come back!" whereupon he returned and sat down again.

Cheng Zi then continued, saying: "What you, Sir, have just said is open to criticism for, according to your statements, there should be no praise for Yu and no blame for Jie and Zhou."[xvi]

Master Mo Zi said: "Not so. In responding to ordinary statements, there is no need for complex debate, thinking it clever. If there is a substantial attack, then there should be a substantial defence. If there is a slight attack, then there should be a slight defence. To respond to ordinary statements with elaborate debate is like using a cart-shaft to strike an ant."

48.15 Master Mo Zi and Cheng Zi were debating the issue of praise for Confucius. Cheng Zi asked: "You are not a Confucian so why do you praise Confucius?"

Master Mo Zi replied: "Because there is what is right and this cannot be changed. Now when a bird becomes aware of the problems of heat and drought, then it flies high. When a fish becomes aware of the problems of heat and drought, then it dives deep. The appropriateness of this is something even the stratagems of Yu and Tang certainly cannot change. Birds and fish may be said to be unintelligent yet Yu and Tang would, in some instances, still follow them. Now why should I never praise Confucius?"

48.16 There was a man who travelled to Master Mo Zi's school. He was strong in body and sharp in mind, and the Master wanted him to stay and study.

Master Mo Zi said: "If you study for a while, I shall make you an official."

The man was persuaded by these fine words and became a student. After a full year had passed, he demanded an official position from Master Mo Zi.

---

xvi. Yu 禹 was the founder of the Xia dynasty whilst Jie 桀 and Zhou 紂 were the paradigmatic evil rulers responsible for the downfall of the Xia and Yin dynasties respectively.

於子墨子。子墨子曰:「不仕子,子亦聞夫魯語乎?魯有昆弟五人者,其父死,其長子嗜酒而不葬,其四弟曰:『子與我葬,當為子沽酒。』勸於善言而葬。已葬,而責酒於其四弟。四弟曰:『吾末[33]予子酒矣,子葬子父,我葬吾父,豈獨吾父哉?子不葬,則人將笑子,故勸子葬也。』今子為義,我亦為義,豈獨我義也哉?子不學,則人將笑子,故勸子於學。」

48.17 有游於子墨子之門者,子墨子曰:「盍學乎?」對曰:「吾族人無學者。」子墨子曰:「不然。夫好美者,豈曰吾族人莫之好,故不好哉?夫欲富貴者,豈曰我族人莫之欲,故不欲哉?好美、欲富貴者,不視人猶強為之。夫義,天下之大器也。何以視人必[34]強為之。」

48.18 有游於子墨子之門者,謂子墨子曰:「先生以鬼神為明知,能為禍福[35],為善者福之[36],為暴者禍之。今吾事先生久矣,而福不至,意者先生之言有不善乎?鬼神不明乎?我何故不得福也?」

---

33. The emendation of 未 to 末 is generally accepted.
34. SYR transposes 必 placing it before 視人. This is followed in the translation.
35. This clause follows WYJ's text omitting as superfluous 人哉 which appears before 福 in some texts — see his note 112, p. 725.
36. In this clause, 者 and 福 are emendations of 之 and 富 respectively — see WYJ, note 115, p. 725 where a similar passage from the *Guanzi* is cited.

Master Mo Zi said: "I haven't got you an official position. But have you not heard the story of the men of Lu? In Lu, there were five brothers. Their father died, but the older brother loved wine and would not attend to the funeral. His four younger brothers told him that if he carried out the funeral for them they would definitely buy him wine. He was persuaded by these fine words and carried out the funeral. After the funeral, he demanded wine from his four younger brothers. But the four younger brothers said to him: 'We will not give you wine. You buried your father and we buried our father. Was he only our father? If you had not buried him, people would have laughed at you. Therefore, we persuaded you to bury him.' Now you are righteous and I am also righteous. Am I the only one who is righteous? If you had not studied, people would have laughed at you. Therefore, I persuaded you to study."

48.17   There was a man who travelled to Master Mo Zi's school.

Master Mo Zi asked: "Why do you not study?"

The man replied: "My clansmen do not study."

Master Mo Zi said: "That doesn't matter. Does someone who loves beauty say, 'My clansmen do not love beauty so I will not love it?' Does someone who desires wealth and riches say, 'My clansmen do not desire wealth and riches so I will not desire them?' Those who love beauty, those who desire wealth and riches, do not take into account others' views but are still strong in doing these things. Now righteousness is the 'great instrument' of the world. Why must one look to the views of others to be strong in practising it."

48.18   There was a man who travelled to Master Mo Zi's school and spoke to Master Mo Zi, saying: "You, Sir, consider ghosts and spirits to be all-seeing and knowing, and to be able to bring about bad fortune and good fortune. If someone is good, they bring him good fortune; if someone is evil, they bring him bad fortune. Now I have served you for a long time yet good fortune has not come. Does this mean that your words are not right, that ghosts and spirits are not all-seeing? Why is it that I have not obtained good fortune?"

子墨子曰:「雖子不得福,吾言何遽[37]不善?而鬼神何遽不明?子亦聞乎匿徒之刑之有刑乎?[38]」對曰:「未之得聞也。」

48.19   子墨子曰:「今人有於此,什子,子能什譽之,而一自譽乎?」對曰:「不能。」「有人於此,百子,子能終身譽其善,而子無一乎?」對曰:「不能。」子墨子曰:「匿一人者猶有罪,今子所匿者若此其多,將有厚罪者也,何福之求?」

48.20   子墨子有疾,跌鼻進而問曰:「先生以鬼神為明[39],能為禍福,為善者賞之,為不善者罰之。今先生聖人也,何故有疾?意者先生之言有不善乎?鬼神不明知乎?」子墨子曰:「雖使我有病,〔吾言何遽不善而鬼神〕[40]何遽不明?人之所得於病者多方,有得之寒暑,有得之勞苦,百門而閉一門焉,則盜何遽無從入?」

---

37. WYZ's reading of 何遽 as 何 is followed, both here and subsequently.
38. SYR's rearrangement of "匿徒之刑之有刑" to "匿刑徒之有刑" is followed.
39. "All-seeing" is the translation of 明 in this context — see *Mozi* 31.
40. On these nine added characters see WYJ, note 126, p. 727.

Master Mo Zi said: "Although you have not obtained good fortune, how does that make my words not right, or ghosts and spirits not all-seeing? Have you not also heard that a hidden crime is nonetheless a crime?"

The man replied: "I have never heard that."

48.19 Master Mo Zi said: "Suppose there is this man who is ten times greater than you.[xvii] Are you able to praise him ten times, but praise yourself only once?"

He replied: "I am unable to."

Master Mo Zi said: "Suppose there is this man who is a hundred times greater than you. Are you able, through your whole life, to praise his goodness, but not praise yourself even once?"

He replied: "I am unable to."

Master Mo Zi said: "To conceal one person is still a fault. Now what you conceal is much more than this so there will be a much greater fault. How is it you seek good fortune?"

48.20 Master Mo Zi was sick. Die Bi[xviii] approached and questioned him, saying: "Sir, you take ghosts and spirits to be all-seeing, to be able to bring about ill-fortune and good fortune, to reward those who do good and to punish those who do bad. Now you, Sir, are a sage, so how is it you are sick? Does it mean that there is in your words what is not good, or that ghosts and spirits do not see and know [all]?"

Master Mo Zi replied: "Although I am caused to be sick, how does this mean that my words are all of a sudden not good or that ghosts and spirits are, all of a sudden, not all-seeing? There are many ways in which people can become sick. They can suffer from cold or heat. They can suffer from strain or fatigue. If there are a hundred gates and only one is shut, then how, all of a sudden, can a robber not enter?"

---

xvii. It is not actually specified in what aspect the difference lies. SYR takes it to be worthiness 賢, writing: "言其賢過子什倍，下云百子同。"

xviii. Die Bi 跌鼻 is said to have been a disciple of Mo Zi. Nothing else seems to be known about him. There is some doubt about the first character — see WYJ, note 124, p. 727.

48.21   二三子有復[41] 於子墨子學射者，子墨子曰：「不可，夫知者必量其
力所能至而從事焉，國士戰且扶人，猶不可及也，今子非國士
也，豈能成學又成射哉？」

48.22   二三子復於子墨子曰：「告子曰：『言義而行甚惡。』請棄之。」子
墨子曰：「不可，稱我言以毀我行，愈於亡[42]，有人於此，翟甚不
仁，尊天，事鬼，愛人，甚不仁[43]，猶愈於亡也。今告子言談甚
辯，言仁義而不吾毀，告子毀猶愈亡也。」

48.23   二三子復於子墨子曰：「告子勝為仁。」子墨子曰：「未必然也！告
子為仁，譬猶跂以為長，隱[44] 以為廣，不可久也。」

48.24   告子謂子墨子曰：「我[45] 治國為政。」子墨子曰：「政者，口言之，
身必行之。今子口言之，而身不行，是子之身亂也。子不能治子
之身，惡能治國政？子姑亡，子之身亂之矣。」

---

41. 復 is understood as 告 both here and in the following two sections — see, for example,
Z&Q.
42. In this recurring phrase, 愈 is read as 勝 and 亡 as 無 (Z&Q).
43. There is some uncertainty about this list, particularly the duplication of "甚不仁". LSL
suggests emending 仁 to 愛 in the first instance.
44. There is some question about the meaning of 隱 here. BY equates it with 偃.
45. 能 is understood after 我 — see, for example, Z&Q.

48.21 Several disciples informed Master Mo Zi that they were studying archery.

Master Mo Zi said: "It is not possible. Those who are wise certainly measure their strength in terms of what they are able to do, and act accordingly. Even officers of the state cannot both fight and help people. Now you are not yet officers of the state so how can you become both scholars and archers?"

48.22 Several disciples informed Master Mo Zi, saying: "Gao Zi[xix] says that your talk is of righteousness but your conduct is very evil. We ask you to cast him off."

Master Mo Zi said: "It is not possible. If he praises my words in the course of criticising my conduct, it is better than nothing. Suppose there is a person [who says] that I am very non-benevolent, [but] that I revere Heaven, serve ghosts, and love people. [Although he says] I am very non-benevolent, it is still better than nothing. Now Gao Zi's discourse is very eloquent when he speaks of benevolence and righteousness, but not when he slanders me. So Gao Zi's slander is better than nothing."

48.23 Several disciples informed Master Mo Zi, saying: "Gao Zi is very diligent about being benevolent."

Master Mo Zi said: "That is not necessarily the case. Gao Zi's being benevolent is like someone standing on tip-toes to be tall, or spreading himself out to be broad. It can't last long."

48.24 Gao Zi spoke to Master Mo Zi, saying: "I am able to bring order to the country in the conduct of government."

Master Mo Zi responded: "In the case of one who governs, what his mouth says, he himself must do. Now what your mouth says, you yourself do not do. This represents disorder in yourself. You are not able to bring order to yourself, so how are you able to bring order to the country in governing? So you had best not say anything for the moment, for while you yourself are in disorder, you won't be able to do what you say."[xx]

---

xix. The consensus is that this is not the Gao Zi 告子 that features in *Mencius* Book VI.

xx. The translation of this final sentence follows LSL, particularly in reading 亡 as 無.

49: 魯問

49.1 魯君謂子墨子曰:「吾恐齊之攻我也,可救乎?」子墨子曰:「可。昔者三代之聖王禹湯文武,百里之諸侯也,說忠行義,取天下。三代之暴王桀紂幽厲,讎怨[1]行暴,失天下。吾願主君,之上者尊天事鬼,下者愛利百姓,厚為皮幣,卑辭令,亟遍禮四鄰諸侯,敺國而以事齊,患可救也。非此,顧無可為者[2]。」

49.2 齊將伐魯。子墨子謂項子牛曰:「伐魯,齊之大過也。昔者吳王東伐越,棲諸會稽,西伐楚,葆昭王於隨。北伐齊,取國子以歸

---

1. 怨 is read as 忠 following YY.
2. In this sentence, 顧 is read as 固 (e.g. WYJ, LYS) — see WYJ, note 5, pp. 741–742 on the sentence as a whole.

49: Lu's Questions

49.1 The ruler of Lu[i] spoke to Master Mo Zi saying: "I fear that Qi will attack me. Can I be saved?"

Master Mo Zi replied: "You can be. In former times, the sage kings of the Three Dynasties, Yu, Tang, Wen and Wu were feudal lords over one hundred *li*, but because they loved loyalty and practised righteousness, they gained all under Heaven. The tyrannical kings of the Three Dynasties, Jie, Zhou, You and Li, because they were inimical to loyalty and practised cruelty, lost all under Heaven. I would wish your lordship to respect Heaven and serve ghosts above, and to love and bring benefit to the ordinary people below; to be generous with skins and silk (gifts); to be humble in issuing commands; to give urgent attention to ceremonial matters involving the feudal lords on all sides; to urge the state to serve Qi. Then disaster can be averted. Apart from this, there is assuredly nothing else you can do."

49.2 Qi was about to attack Lu. Master Mo Zi spoke to Xiang Ziniu[ii] saying: "To attack Lu is a great mistake for Qi. In former times, the King of Wu attacked Yue to the east [whose army] ran into difficulties at Guiji.[iii] To the west, he attacked Chu. Under concealment, Zhao Wang fled to Sui.[iv] To the north, he attacked

---

i.   SYR takes this to be Duke Mu 穆公.
ii.   Xiang Ziniu 項子牛 is said to have been a Qi general under Tian He 田和. WYJ suggests he is the same as the 牛子 referred to in the *Huainanzi* 18.
iii. Reference to the attack by Fu Chai 夫差 on the Yue forces under Gou Jian 勾踐. The latter's forces were surrounded at Guiji. Although initially successful, Fu Chai was subsequently defeated and committed suicide. The phrase "越王勾踐棲於會稽之上" appears in the *Guo Yu* under Yue. See also *Mozi* 18.
iv.   The Wu king on this occasion was Fu Chai's father Helü 闔廬. Sui 隨 was a small state adjacent to Chu. For this event see the ZZ for the 4th year of Duke Ding (LCC, vol. 5, p. 752).

於吳[3]。諸侯報其讎，百姓苦其勞，而弗為用，是以國為虛戾，身為刑戮也。昔者智伯伐范氏與中行氏，兼三晉之地，諸侯報其讎，百姓苦其勞，而弗為用，是以國為虛戾，身為刑戮用是[4]也。故大國之攻小國也，是交相賊也，過必反於國。」

49.3   子墨子見齊大王曰：「今有刀於此，試之人頭，倅[5]然斷之，可謂利乎？」大王曰：「利。」子墨子曰：「多試之人頭，倅然斷之，可謂利乎？」大王曰：「利。」子墨子曰：「刀則利矣，孰將受其不祥？」大王曰：「刀受其利，試者受其不祥。」子墨子曰：「并國覆

3. In relation to this clause see the ZZ for the 11th year of Duke Ai (LCC, vol. 5, p. 823) where 國子 is mentioned. WYJ adds 太 to give "國太子" — see his note 9, p. 742.

4. Some commentators (e.g. Z&Q) take the two characters 用是 to be superfluous — see WYJ's discussion of this in his note 12, pp. 742–743.

5. 猝 (突然) is read for 倅.

Qi and, having seized Guo Zi, returned to Wu.[v] The feudal lords took revenge on their enemy, and the ordinary people met with suffering and hardship, and could not be of use. For this reason, the state became wasted and depopulated and he himself was punished and killed.[vi] In former times, Zhi Bo attacked the houses of Fan and Zhonghang and combined the lands of the *San Jin*.[vii] The feudal lords took revenge on their enemy, and the ordinary people met with suffering and hardship, and could not be of use. For this reason, the state became wasted and depopulated and he himself was punished and killed. Therefore, in the case of a large state attacking a small state, both will suffer injury and the fault will certainly return to the (perpetrating) state."

49.3   Master Mo Zi saw the great King of Qi[viii] and said: "Now suppose there was this sword which, when you tried it on a man's head, swiftly cut it off. Could it be spoken of as sharp?"

The great King replied: "It would be sharp."

Master Mo Zi asked: "If you tried it on many men's heads and it swiftly cut them off, could it be spoken of as sharp?"

The great King replied: "It would be sharp."

Master Mo Zi asked: "If the sword, then, is sharp, who is it that will receive its bad fortune?"

The great King replied: "The sword receives its sharpness. The one who tries it receives its bad fortune."

Master Mo Zi asked: "If you annex states and overthrow armies, if you plunder and kill the common people, who will receive the bad fortune of this?"

---

v.   This is again Fu Chai. Guo Zi 國子 is considered to be Guo Shu 國書, a Qi general — see the SAA for the 11th year of Duke Ai (LCC, vol. 5, p. 821).

vi.   Fu Chai eventually committed suicide.

vii.   The *San Jin* 三晉 refers to the houses (and later the states of) Zhao 趙, Han 韓, and Wei 魏. These events are described in detail in *Mozi* 18.

viii.   This is thought to be a reference to Tian He 田和 who seized power in Qi in 404 BC and took the title of 太王.

軍，賊殺[6]百姓，孰將受其不祥？」大王俯仰而思之曰：「我受其
不祥。」

49.4 魯陽文君將攻鄭。子墨子聞而止之，謂〔魯〕陽文君曰：「今使魯四
境之內，大都攻其小都，大家伐其小家，殺其人民，取其牛馬狗
豕布帛米粟貨財，則何若？」魯陽文君曰：「魯四境之內，皆寡人
之臣也。今大都攻其小都，大家伐其小家，奪之貨財，則寡人必
將厚罰之。」子墨子曰：「夫天之兼有天下也，亦猶君之有四境之
內也。今舉兵將以攻鄭，天誅其不至乎？」魯陽文君曰：「先生何
止我攻鄭也？我攻鄭，順於天之志。鄭人三世殺其父，天加誅
焉，使三年不全。我將助天誅也。」子墨子曰：「鄭人三世殺其父
而天加誅焉，使三年不全。天誅足矣，今又舉兵將以攻鄭，曰
『吾攻鄭也，順於天之志。』譬有人於此，其子強梁不材，故其父

---

6.   This is the generally accepted emendation of 敖 following BY.

The great King looked up and down and pondered the matter before replying: "I will receive the bad fortune of this."

49.4 Prince Wen of Luyang[ix] was about to attack Zheng when Master Mo Zi heard about it and stopped him, saying to the Prince: "Now suppose that within the four borders of Lu the great cities attacked the small cities and the great families attacked the small families, killing the people and taking their oxen, horses, dogs, pigs, cloth, silk, rice, millet, goods and valuables — then what would happen?"

Prince Wen of Luyang replied: "Within the four boundaries of Lu, all are my subjects. If now the great cities attack the small cities and the great families attack the small families, seizing their goods and valuables, then I will certainly punish them severely."

Master Mo Zi said: "Heaven possesses all that is beneath it, just as you possess all that is within the four boundaries [of your state]. Now if you raise an army with the intention of attacking Zheng will Heaven not visit its punishment on you?"

Prince Wen of Luyang asked: "Why do you stop me from attacking Zheng? In attacking Zheng I am merely complying with the will of Heaven. For three generations the people of Zheng have killed their prince and Heaven has intensified its punishment, so for three years they have not prospered. I shall be helping Heaven punish them."

Master Mo Zi said: "For three generations the people of Zheng have killed their prince and Heaven has intensified its punishment, causing them not to prosper for three years. Heaven's punishment is sufficient. Now you also raise an army, intending to attack Zheng, saying: 'My attacking Zheng is merely complying with the will of Heaven.' This is like there being a man whose son is violent and worthless so he beats him, and then his neighbour's

---

ix. Luyang is a place name. Luyang Wen Jun 魯陽文君 is taken to be Luyang Wen Zi, a descendant of King Ping 平王 of Chu and the son of Sima Ziqi 司馬子期, and is possibly Gongsun Kuan 公孫寬 who was enfeoffed with territory on the southern side of Lu mountain.

笞之,其鄰家之父舉木而擊之,曰『吾擊之也,順於其父之志』,
則豈不悖哉?」

49.5   子墨子謂魯陽文君曰:「攻其鄰國,殺其民人,取其牛馬、粟
米、貨財,則書之於竹帛,鏤之於金石,以為銘於鐘鼎,傳遺後
世子孫曰:『莫若我多。』[7] 今賤人也,亦攻其鄰家,殺其人民,
取其狗豕食糧衣裘,亦書之〔於〕竹帛,以為銘於席豆[8],以遺後世
子孫曰:『莫若我多。』其可乎?」魯陽文君曰:「然吾以子之言觀
之,則天下之所謂可者,未必然也。」

49.6   子墨子為[9]魯陽文君曰:「世俗之君子,皆知小物而不知大物。今
有人於此,竊一犬一彘則謂之不仁。竊一國一都則以為義。譬猶
小視白謂之白,大視白則謂之黑。是故世俗之君子,知小物而不
知大物者,此若言之謂也。」

49.7   魯陽文君語子墨子曰:「楚之南有啖人之國者橋[10],其國之長子
生,則解而食之,謂之宜弟[11]。美,則以遺其君,君喜則賞其

---

7.   See WYJ's detailed note on this phrase — note 29, p. 745.
8.   On this phrase LYS has the following note: "席豆:几席和籩豆,豆是食器" — see his
     note 1, p. 375.
9.   By general agreement, 為 is taken as 謂 — see, for example, Z&Q.
10. There is some uncertainty about this character. I have taken it as a place name as
     proposed, for example, by LYS and Z&Q. WYJ has 焉 here — see his note 37, p. 746.
11. In this sentence, Gu Qianli's 顧千里 emendation of 鮮 to 解 (based on *Mozi* 25〈節葬
     下〉and adopted, for example, by LYS, Z&Q), and Z&Q's reading of 宜 as 保護 are
     followed.

father takes up a cudgel and also beats him, saying that his beating him is merely complying with the will of the father. How is this not perverse?"

49.5   Master Mo Zi spoke to Prince Wen of Luyang, saying: "Suppose [a prince] attacked his neighbouring states, killed their people, took their oxen and horses, rice and millet, goods and valuables, and then recorded it on bamboo and silk, engraved it on metal and stone, and thought to carve it on bells and tripods (*ding*) to transmit it to his sons and grandsons of later generations, saying, 'No-one has as much as I have.' Then the petty man will also attack his neighbouring houses, killing their people, taking their dogs and pigs, food and grain, clothes and furs, and also record it on bamboo and silk, and think to carve it into tables and bowls in order to hand it down to his sons and grandsons of later generations, saying, 'No-one has as much as I have.' Is this permissible?"

Prince Wen of Luyang replied: "Indeed, when I look at things in the light of your words, then what the world speaks of as permissible is certainly not so."

49.6   Master Mo Zi spoke to Prince Wen of Luyang saying: "Gentlemen of the world all know about small things, but not about great things. Now, if a man were to steal a dog or a pig, they would say he was not benevolent, whereas, if he were to steal a state or a city, they would take him to be righteous. This is like seeing a small expanse of white and calling it white, but seeing a great expanse of white and calling it black. This is why I have uttered words such as these — that gentlemen of the world know about small things, but not about great things."

49.7   Prince Wen of Luyang spoke to Master Mo Zi, saying: "To the south of Chu there is the country, Qiao, in which the eating of people occurs.[x] In that country, when the first son is born, he is eaten alive. This is said to be a protection for younger brothers. If

---

x.   See also *Mozi* 25. YPM assumes that the same tribe is being referred to although the description of the practice is somewhat different.

父。豈不惡俗哉？」子墨子曰：「雖中國之俗，亦猶是也。殺其父而賞其子，何以異食其子而賞其父者哉？苟不用仁義，何以非夷人食其子也？」

49.8 魯君之嬖人死，魯君[12]為之誄。魯人因說而用之。子墨子聞之曰：「誄者，道死人之志也，今因說而用之，是猶以來首從服也。」[13]

49.9 魯陽文君謂子墨子曰：「有語我以忠臣者，令之俯則俯，令之仰則仰，處則靜，呼則應，可謂忠臣乎？」子墨子曰：「令之俯則俯，令之仰則仰，是似景[14]也。處則靜，呼則應，是似響[15]也。君將何得於景與響哉？若以翟之所謂忠臣者，上有過則微之以諫，己有善，則訪之上，而無敢以告。外匡其邪，而入其善，尚同而無下比，是以美善在上，而怨讎在下，安樂在上，而憂慼在臣。此翟之所謂忠臣者也。」

---

12. There is general acceptance of SSX's reading of 人 for 君 here, and the converse at the start of the next sentence.
13. There is considerable doubt about this concluding simile. Most commentators follow SYR's emendation of 來 to 狸 and read 服 as 服馬, but this is not the only interpretation — see, for example, WYJ and LYS.
14. 似景 is read as 像影子 (Z&Q).
15. 響 is understood as 回聲 (Z&Q).

he tastes good, then he is offered to the prince and if the prince is pleased, he rewards the father. How is this not an evil custom?"

Master Mo Zi replied: "Even in the customs of the central kingdom itself there is also something like this. For how is killing the father and rewarding the son different from eating the son and rewarding the father? If benevolence and righteousness are not practised, how can there be censure of the barbarians for eating their sons?"

49.8 When the Prince of Lu's favourite concubine died a man of Lu wrote a eulogy for her. And because the Prince of Lu was pleased, he employed the man. Master Mo Zi heard about this and said: "A eulogy is for speaking favourably of the will of the dead person. Now because [the prince] is pleased, to employ the person is like taking a fox to lead a team of horses."

49.9 Prince Wen of Luyang spoke to Mo Zi, saying: "Suppose someone told me of a loyal official who, if you ordered him to bow down, bowed down, and if you ordered him to look up, looked up; who, staying there, was quiet, but if called, responded. Could he be called a loyal official?"

Master Mo Zi said: "If you order him to bow down and he bows down, and if you order him to look up and he looks up, he is like a shadow. If staying there, he is quiet, but if called he responds, he is like an echo. What can a prince get from a shadow or an echo? What I have to say about a loyal minister is this. If the one above is at fault, then he should await the appropriate time and censure him. If he himself has something of value, then he should discuss it with the one above, but not with others generally. He should correct any heterodoxy and follow the path of goodness. He should make himself like the one above and not follow those below. In this way, beauty and goodness will lie with the one above and resentment and enmity with those below. Peace and happiness will lie with the one above and grief and sorrow with the officials. This is what I call a loyal official."

49.10 魯君謂子墨子曰:「我有二子。一人者好學,一人者好分人財,孰以為太子而可?」子墨子曰:「未可知也,或所為賞與[16]為是也。釣者之恭,非為魚賜也[17];餌鼠以蟲[18],非愛之也。吾願主君之合其志功而觀焉。」

49.11 魯人有因子墨子而學其子者。其子戰而死,其父讓子墨子。子墨子曰:「子欲學子之子,今學成矣,戰而死,而子慍,而猶欲糶,糶讎,則慍也。豈不費哉?」[19]

49.12 魯之南鄙人,有吳慮者,冬陶夏耕,自比於舜。子墨子聞而見之。吳慮謂子墨子〔曰〕[20]:「義耳義耳,焉用言之哉?」子墨子曰:「子之所謂義者,亦有力以勞人,有財以分人乎?」吳慮曰:「有。」子墨子曰:「翟嘗計之矣,翟慮耕而食天下之人矣,盛,然後當一農之耕[21],分諸天下,不能人得一升粟。籍而以為得一升

---

16. There is general acceptance of 譽 for 與 here.
17. In this sentence, 釣 is read for 魡 whilst Z&Q have the following note on 恭: "指釣魚者躬身釣魚。"
18. SYR reads 蠱 for 蟲, the former being, "有毒食物".
19. There are three points in this statement as follows: (i) 糶 and 糶 are taken as "賣出糧食". (ii) 讎 is read as 售。 (iii) 費 is read as 悖 — see, for example, Z&Q.
20. Added following WYJ.
21. On "盛然後當一農之耕" SYR has: "此云極盛,不過當一農之耕也。"

49.10   The Prince of Lu spoke to Master Mo Zi, saying: "I have two sons. One loves learning and the other loves dividing wealth among people. Which one should I make my successor?"

Master Mo Zi replied: "It is impossible to know. It may be that they do what they do for reward and praise. The fisherman's bait is not a gift to the fish. Luring a mouse with a bait is not through love of the mouse. I wish the prince to take into account both their intention and achievement, and look at the matter."   .

49.11   There was a man from Lu who sent his son to study with Master Mo Zi. His son died in battle and the father was angry with Master Mo Zi.

Master Mo Zi said: "You wished your son to study with me. Now, his studies complete, he fights in a battle and dies, and you are angry with me. This is like wishing to sell grain and being angry when it is sold. How is this not perverse?"

49.12   There was a rustic who lived in the south of Lu, a certain Wu Lü. Making pottery in the winter and farming in the summer, he compared himself to Shun. Master Mo Zi heard about this and went to see him.

Wu Lü said to Master Mo Zi: "Ah righteousness, righteousness! What is the use of talking about it?"

Master Mo Zi asked: "Is what you call righteousness also having the strength to help people and the resources to divide among people?"

Wu Lü answered: "It is."

Master Mo Zi said: "I have already thought about this. I considered taking up farming to feed the people of the world, but at the most I would only achieve the output of one farmer. If this were to be divided within the world, each person would not be able to get even one *sheng* of grain. It can be readily seen that even if they were to get one *sheng* of grain, this would not be able to

粟，其不能飽天下之飢者，既可睹矣。翟慮織而衣天下之人矣，
盛，然後當一婦人之織，分諸天下，不能人得尺布。籍而以為得
尺布，其不能暖天下之寒者，既可睹矣。翟慮被堅執銳救諸侯之
患，盛，然後當一夫之戰，一夫之戰其不御三軍，既可睹矣。翟
以為不若誦先王之道，而求其說，通聖人之言，而察其辭，上說
王公大人，次匹夫徒步之士[22]。王公大人用吾言，國必治；匹夫
徒步之士用吾言，行必修。故翟以為雖不耕而食飢，不織而衣
寒，功賢於耕而食之，織而衣之者也。故翟以為雖不耕織乎，而
功賢於耕織也。」

49.13 吳慮謂子墨子曰：「義耳義耳，焉用言之哉？」子墨子曰：「籍設而
天下不知耕，教人耕，與不教人耕而獨耕者，其功孰多？」吳慮
曰：「教人耕者其功多。」子墨子曰：「籍設而攻不義之國，鼓而使

---

22. In this clause, 說 is understood following 次 (Z&Q). On "徒步之士", LSL has: "沒有
車坐的人，指普通平民。"

satisfy those in the world who were hungry. I considered taking up weaving to make clothes for the people of the world, but, at the most, I would only achieve the output of one weaving woman. If this were to be divided within the world, each person would not be able to get even one *chi* of cloth. It can readily be seen that this would not be able to bring warmth to those in the world who were cold. I considered taking up shield and sword to save the feudal lords from calamity, but, at the most, I would only have the effect of a single soldier. It can readily be seen that a single soldier cannot resist the 'three armies'. I think nothing equals understanding the Way of former kings and seeking their concepts; understanding the words of the sages and examining their statements. Nothing equals spreading these words among kings, dukes and great officers above, and next among the ordinary people. If kings, dukes and great officers make use of my words, countries will certainly be well ordered. If the ordinary people make use of my words, conduct will certainly be regulated. Therefore, I think that although I do not plough and provide food for the hungry, although I do not weave and provide clothes for the cold, nevertheless my achievement is more worthy than those who do plough and provide food and those who do weave and provide clothes. That is, I think that although I do not plough and weave, still my achievement is more worthy than if I did plough and weave."

49.13   Wu Lü spoke to Master Mo Zi, saying: "Ah righteousness, righteousness! What is the use of talking about it?"

Master Mo Zi asked: "Suppose there was no knowledge of ploughing in the world. Of one who teaches people to plough and one who does not teach people to plough, but only ploughs himself, whose merit is the greater?"

Wu Lü replied: "The one who teaches people to plough has the greater merit."

Master Mo Zi asked: "Suppose there was an attack on a country that was not righteous. Of one who beats the drum and causes the multitude to go into battle and one who does not beat the drum and

眾進戰，與不鼓而使眾進戰，而獨進戰者，其功孰多？」吳慮
曰：「鼓而進眾者其功多。」子墨子曰：「天下匹夫徒步之士，少知
義而教天下以義者，功亦多，何故弗言也？若得鼓而進於義，則
吾義豈不益進哉？」

49.14 子墨子游公尚過於越。公尚過說越王，越王大說，謂公尚過曰：
「先生苟能使子墨子〔至〕於越而教寡人²³，請裂故吳之地，方五百
里，以封子墨子。」公尚過許諾。遂為公尚過束車五十乘，以迎
子墨子於魯，曰：「吾以夫子之道說越王，越王大說，謂過曰：
『苟能使子墨子至於越而教寡人，請裂故吳之地，方五百里，以
封子』。」子墨子謂公尚過曰：「子觀越王之志何若？意越王將聽吾
言，用我道，則翟將往，量腹而食，度身而衣，自比於群臣，奚

---

23. There are some variations in this clause — see WYJ's text and his note 85, p. 752.

cause the multitude to go into battle, but only goes into battle himself, whose merit is the greater?"

Wu Lü replied: "The one who beats the drum and brings about the advance has the greater merit."

Master Mo Zi said: "Among the ordinary people of the world, there are few who know righteousness, so the one who teaches the world righteousness also has great merit. Why would you deny this? If I were to take a drum and beat it to advance righteousness, then how is my righteousness not further advanced?"

49.14   Master Mo Zi recommended Gongshang Guo to Yue.[xi] Gongshang Guo addressed the Yue king[xii] who was greatly pleased, and spoke to Gongshang Guo, saying: "If you are able to get Master Mo Zi to come to Yue and teach me, I shall divide off a part of what was formerly Wu, to the size of five hundred *li* square, and enfeoff him with it."

Gongshang Guo agreed. Subsequently, he took fifty wagons to Lu to receive Master Mo Zi and said: "When I spoke to the Yue king about your Way he was greatly pleased and told me that if I was able to bring Master Mo Zi to Yue to teach him, he would divide off a part of what was formerly Wu, to the size of five hundred *li* square, and enfeoff you."

Master Mo Zi spoke to Gongshang Guo, saying: "What did you make of the Yue king's intentions? If you think the Yue king will listen to my words and will use my Way, then I shall go. But I shall require only enough food to fill my belly and only enough clothing to cover my body, and I shall regard myself as an equal with the crowd of officials. What would I be able to do with enfeoffment?

---

xi.   Gongshang Guo 公尚過 was a disciple of Mo Zi. Commentators are agreed in reading 游 as 游揚 or 推薦 — see, for example, LSL, Z&Q, LYS. Another version of this anecdote is to be found in the LSCQ 19/2.3.

xii. This is taken to be Gou Jian 勾踐 after he had defeated Wu.

能以封為哉？抑越不聽吾言，不用吾道，而吾往焉，則是我以義糶也。鈞之糶，亦於中國耳，何必於越哉？」

49.15　子墨子游，魏越曰：「既得見四方之君子，則將先語？」子墨子曰：「凡入國，必擇務而從事焉。國家昏亂，則語之尚賢、尚同；國家貧，則語之節用節葬；國家喜音湛湎[24]，則語之非樂、非命；國家淫僻無禮，則語之尊天事鬼；國家務奪侵凌，即語之兼愛、非攻。故曰擇務而從事焉。」

49.16　子墨子〔曰〕出曹公子而於宋[25]，三年而反，睹子墨子曰：「始吾游於子之門，短褐之衣，藜藿之羹，朝得之，則夕弗得，〔弗得〕祭祀鬼神[26]。今而以夫子之教[27]，家厚於始也。有[28]家厚，謹祭祀鬼神。然而人徒多死，六畜不蕃，身湛於病，吾未知夫子之道之可

---

24. The preceding four characters are read as: "喜音沉迷" — see, for example, Z&Q.
25. In this opening clause, 曰 is added after 子墨子 (SSX), 出 is read as 士 (YY), and 而 is regarded as superfluous (e.g. Z&Q).
26. There is general acceptance of the addition of 弗得 before 祭 following SYR — see WYJ, note 108, p. 755.
27. I have followed YY in reading 故 for 教.
28. Following WHB, 以 (as 因為) is read for 有.

If the Yue king won't listen to my words and won't use my Way and I still go, then I would be treating righteousness like grain to sell. If I make it like grain to sell, I could just as well do this in the central kingdom. Why would I need to go to Yue?"

49.15 Master Mo Zi was going to travel. Wei Yue[xiii] asked: "When you get to see the gentlemen of the four regions, what will be the first thing you speak about?"

Master Mo Zi replied: "Whenever one enters a country, one must pick out what is fundamental and devote one's attention to it. If the country is disordered and confused, then one speaks about exalting worthiness and exalting unity.[xiv] If the country is poor, then one speaks about moderation in use and moderation in funerals. If the country has a liking for music and depravity, then one speaks about condemnation of music and rejection of Fate. If the country has fallen into licentiousness and lacks propriety, then one speaks about honouring Heaven and serving ghosts. If the country is dedicated to invasion and oppression, then one speaks about universal love and condemning aggression. Therefore I say, pick out what is fundamental and devote one's attention to it."

49.16 Master Mo Zi recommended Cao Gongzi to Song.[xv] After three years he returned. He saw Master Mo Zi and said: "When I first joined your school I wore a short jacket and ate soup made from wild plants. Moreover, if I had this in the morning, then I did not have it in the evening, and I had nothing to offer in sacrifice to the ghosts and spirits. Now, because of you, my family is better off than before. And because my family is better off, I can give my attention to the sacrifices to the ghosts and spirits. Nevertheless, many of my family have died, the six animals are not flourishing, and I myself have become ill. I do not know if your Way can be used."

---

xiii. Wei Yue 魏越 is thought to have been a disciple of Mo Zi.

xiv. In the five situations listed, Mo Zi refers in pairs to the 10 chapters detailing the "core" doctrines.

xv. Cao Gongzi 曹公子 is thought to have been a disciple of Mo Zi.

用也。」子墨子曰:「不然!夫鬼神之所欲於人者多,欲人之處高爵祿則以讓賢也,多財則以分貧也。夫鬼神豈唯擢季拑肺之為欲哉[29]?今子處高爵祿而不以讓賢,一不祥也;多則而不以分貧,二不祥也。今子事鬼神唯祭而已矣,而曰:『病何自至哉?』是猶百門而閉一門焉,曰:『盜何從入?』若是而求福於有怪之鬼[30],豈可哉?」

49.17 魯祝以一豚祭,而求百福於鬼神。子墨子聞之曰:「是不可,今施人薄而望人厚,則人唯恐其有賜於己也。今以一豚祭,而求百福於鬼神,〔鬼神〕[31]唯恐其以牛羊祀也。古者聖王事鬼神,祭而已矣。今以豚祭而求百福,則其富不如其貧也。」

49.18 彭輕生子曰:「往者可知,來者不可知。」子墨子曰:「籍設而親在百里之外,則遇難焉,期以一日也,及之則生,不及則死。今有

---

29. There are several issues in this sentence as follows: (i) 擢 is read as 攫 (SYR). (ii) 季 is read as 黍 (WYZ). (iii) 拑 is read as 持. (iv) 肺 ("lungs") are taken to be this part of the animal used for sacrifice, with reference to the *Yi Li* 儀禮.
30. LYS would emend "有怪之鬼" to "有靈之鬼神".
31. Following modern commentators, 鬼神 is added before 唯 — see, for example, Z&Q.

Master Mo Zi said: "Not so. What the ghosts and spirits desire of a man is much. They desire him, when he holds a high position and emolument, to yield it to the worthy, and when he has much wealth, to distribute it to the poor. How could it be that the ghosts and spirits only desire to snatch away grain and seize lungs? Now you have occupied a high position with emolument, but have not yielded it to the worthy. This is the first misfortune. You have much, but you have not used it to distribute to the poor. This is the second misfortune. Now you serve the ghosts and spirits by sacrifice and that is all. And yet you say, 'Where is my sickness coming from?' This is like having a hundred gates, closing one, and then saying, 'How did the robber enter?' To be like this and yet seek good fortune from the ghosts and spirits — how is this possible?"

49.17   In Lu, the person responsible for sacrifice offered one pig in sacrifice and sought a hundred blessings from the ghosts and spirits.

When Master Mo Zi heard this, he said: "This is not permissible. To give a person little and ask from that person much would only make the person fearful of offerings from you. So if you sacrifice with one pig and yet seek a hundred blessings from the ghosts and spirits, the ghosts and spirits will only be fearful of your sacrifice of oxen and sheep. In ancient times, the sage kings served the ghosts and spirits by sacrifice and that is all. Now it would be better to be poor than to become rich by sacrificing one pig and seeking a hundred blessings."

49.18   Master Peng Qingsheng[xvi] said: "What has gone can be known; what is to come cannot be known."

Master Mo Zi asked: "Suppose your parents encountered difficulty when they were a hundred *li* away and there was a limit of one day. If you reached them, they would live. If you did not

---

xvi. Nothing seems to be known of 彭輕生 子. SYR takes him to be a disciple of Mo Zi.

固車良馬於此，又有奴馬四隅之輪於此，使子擇焉，子將何乘？」
對曰：「乘良馬固車，可以速至。」子墨子曰：「焉在矣來！³²」

49.19　孟山譽王子閭曰：「昔白公之禍，執王子閭斧鉞鉤要，直兵當
心，謂之曰：『為王則生，不為王則死。』王子閭曰：『何其侮我
也！殺我親而喜我以楚國，我得天下而不義，不為也，又況於楚
國乎？』遂而不為。王子閭豈不仁哉？」子墨子曰：「難則難矣，然
而未仁也。若以王為無道，則何故不受而治也？若以白公為不
義，何故不受王，誅白公然而反王？故曰難則難矣，然而未仁
也。」

---

32. There is general agreement that "焉在矣來" should read "焉在不知來" — see, for
    example, LYS.

reach them, they would die. Now if, on one side, there was a strong cart and an excellent horse, and, on the other side, there was a worn-out old horse and a cart with wheels at the four corners, and you had to make a choice, which one would you make use of?"

He replied: "I would make use of the excellent horse and the strong cart so I could arrive quickly."

Master Mo Zi said: "How is there not knowledge of what is to come?"

49.19 Meng Shan praised King Zi Lü,[xvii] saying: "Formerly, during Bo Gong's insurrection, he seized King Zi Lü, attached a battle-axe to his waist and directed a sword straight at his heart. He then spoke to him, saying, 'If you become king then you live; if you do not become king then you die.' King Zi Lü replied, 'Why do you insult me? You killed my family members and now you tempt me with the kingdom of Chu. If I were to get the whole world and it were not righteous, I would not do it. How much more is this the case with regard to Chu?' And he didn't do it. How was King Zi Lü not benevolent?"

Master Mo Zi said: "There was a difficulty and he overcame it. Nevertheless, he was not benevolent. If he thought the King was without the Way, then why did he not accept the offer and bring about order? If he thought Bo Gong was not righteous, why did he not accept the kingship, put Bo Gong to death, and then return to rule? This is why I say that meeting a difficulty and overcoming it is something, but it is not benevolence."

---

xvii. Meng Shan 孟山 was a disciple of Mo Zi. Zi Lü 子閭 (名啟) was a son of King Ping of Chu 楚平王. Bo Gong 白公 (名勝) was a descendant of the same king. The events referred to are recorded in the ZZ for the 16th year of Duke Ai 哀公, i.e. 480 BC — see LCC, vol. 5, p. 845. Zi Xi 子西 and Zi Qi 子期 were older brothers of Zi Lü who were killed by Bo Gong — i.e. the "family members".

49.20 子墨子使勝綽事項子牛。項子牛三侵魯地，而勝綽三從。子墨子
聞之，使高孫子請而退之，曰：「我使綽也，將以濟驕而正嬖
也。今綽也祿厚而諼夫子，夫子三侵魯，而綽三從，是鼓鞭於馬
靳也。翟聞之：『言義而弗行，是犯明也。』綽非弗之知也，祿勝
義也。」

49.21 昔者楚人與越人舟戰於江。楚人順流而進，迎流而退，見利而
進，見不利則其退難。越人迎流而進，順流而退，見利而進，見
不利則其退速。越人因此若埶[33]，亟敗楚人。公輸子自魯南游
楚，焉[34] 始為舟戰之器，作為鉤強之備[35]，退者鉤之，進者強
之，量其鉤強之長[36]，而製為之兵。楚之兵節，越之兵不節，楚
人因此若埶，亟敗越人。公輸子善其巧，以語子墨子曰：「我舟
戰有鉤強，不知子之義亦有鉤強乎？」子墨子曰：「我義之鉤強，

---

33. Commentators agree that 若 should be read as 此 and 埶 as 勢, making the phrase, in modern terms, "因就是此勢". I have rendered 勢 simply as "circumstances" although a deeper meaning might be indicated.

34. 焉 here is read in the sense of 乃 or 于是.

35. Most commentators — see, for example, LSL, Z&Q — read 強 as 鑲, quoting the 《說文解字》徐鍇注 as follows: "古兵有鉤有鑲，引來曰鉤，推去曰鑲." LYS, however, reads 強 as 拒 whilst YPM has "rams". The following discussion makes a grappling device the more appropriate.

36. See SYR for an alternative version of this and the following clause.

49.20   Master Mo Zi sent Sheng Chuo to serve Xiang Ziniu.[xviii] Three times, Xiang Ziniu invaded the territory of Lu and three times, Sheng Chuo accompanied him. Master Mo Zi heard about this and sent Gao Sunzi to request that he be withdrawn.[xix] He said: "I sent Chuo so that he would stop arrogance and rectify depravity. Now Chuo receives a high salary yet he deceives his master. Three times his master invaded Lu and three times Chuo accompanied him. This is to whip a horse with its martingale. I have heard this — 'To speak of righteousness but not practise it is to commit an offence knowingly.' It is not that Chuo did not know this. It is that salary triumphed over righteousness."

49.21   Formerly, the people of Chu and the people of Yue fought a naval battle on the Jiang (Yangtze). The people of Chu went with the current when advancing, but against the current when retreating. When they saw an advantage, they advanced. But when they saw a disadvantage, their retreat was difficult. The people of Yue went against the current when advancing, but went with the current when retreating. When they saw an advantage, they advanced. But when they saw a disadvantage, their retreat was swift. Because of these circumstances, the people of Yue inflicted a crushing defeat on the people of Chu. Gongshu Zi[xx] travelled south from Lu to Chu and immediately began making implements for naval warfare, undertaking the preparation of hooks and clamps. The hooks were for times of retreat and the clamps were for times of advance. The lengths of the hooks and clamps were made to be in accord with their weapons. The Chu weapons were standardised whereas those of the Yue were not. Because of these circumstances, the people of Chu inflicted a crushing defeat on the people of Yue. Gongshu Zi was very pleased with his skill and spoke to Master Mo Zi saying: "For naval battles I have hooks and clamps. I do not know if your righteousness also has hooks and clamps."

---

xviii.   Sheng Chuo 勝綽 was a disciple of Mo Zi. Xiang Ziniu 項子牛 was the Qi general referred to in *Mozi* 49.2.

xix.   Gao Sunzi 高孫子 was another disciple of Mo Zi. His mission was to bring Sheng Chuo back.

xx.   This is Gongshu Pan/Ban 公輸盤/般 who is featured in the next dialogue (*Mozi* 50). Some think he was the son of Duke Zhao 昭公 of Lu.

賢於子舟戰之鉤強。我鉤強，我鉤之以愛，揣[37] 之以恭。弗鉤以
愛，則不親；弗揣以恭，則速狎；狎而不親則速離。故交相愛，
交相恭，猶若相利也。今子鉤而止人，人亦鉤而止子；子強而距
人，人亦強而距子，交相鉤，交相強，猶若相害也。故我義之鉤
強，賢子舟戰之鉤強。」

49.22 公輸子削竹木以為鵲[38]，成而飛之，三日不下，公輸子自以為至
巧。子墨子謂公輸子曰：「子之為鵲也，不如匠[39] 之為車轄，須臾
劉[40] 三寸之木，而任五十石之重。故所為[41] 功，利於人謂之巧，
不利於人謂之拙。」

49.23 公輸子謂子墨子曰：「吾未得見之時，我欲得宋，自我得見之
後，予我宋而不義，我不為。」子墨子曰：「翟之未得見之時也，
子欲得宋，自翟得見子之後，予子宋而不義，子弗為，是我予子
宋也。子務為義，翟又將予子天下。」

---

37. There is general acceptance of the emendation of 揣 to 鑲 both here and in the following
     sentence.
38. 鵲 is used here and subsequently for the character with radical #172 (ZWDCD #43007).
39. 翟 referring to Mo Zi himself is generally read here rather than 匠 — see WYJ, note 162,
     p. 762. YPM has "carpenter". The point is the same either way.
40. There is general acceptance of WNS's reading of 斷 (斫) for 劉 here.
41. Modern commentators such as LSL and Z&Q read 謂 for 為 here.

Master Mo Zi replied: "The hooks and clamps of my righteousness have a greater worthiness than your hooks and clamps for naval battles. [To speak of] my hooks and clamps, I hook by means of love and I clamp by means of respect. If there is no hook through love, then there is not closeness. If there is no clamp through respect, then there is quickly disrespect. If there is disrespect and not closeness, then there is quickly separation. Therefore, exchange of mutual love and mutual respect is like mutual benefit. Now if you hook people and stop them, people will also hook you and stop you. If you clamp people and oppose them, people will also clamp you and oppose you. So exchange of mutual hooking and mutual clamping is like mutual harm. Therefore, the hooks and clamps of my righteousness are more worthy than your hooks and clamps for naval battles."

49.22 Gongshu Zi carved some bamboo to make a bird. When it was completed, he flew it. For three days, it did not come down. Gongshu Zi took himself to be supremely skilful. Master Mo Zi spoke to Gongshu Zi saying: "Your making a bird is not like my making the linch-pin of a cart wheel. In a few moments, I can carve a three *cun* piece of wood and it will bear a weight of 50 *dan*. Therefore, in terms of what is called an achievement, what is of benefit to people is spoken of as skilful, whereas what is not of benefit to people is spoken of as unskilful."

49.23 Gongshu Zi spoke to Master Mo Zi saying: "In the time when I had not yet seen you, I wished to take Song. After having seen you, even if Song were to be given to me, if this was not righteous, I would not do it."

Master Mo Zi said: "In the time before you had seen me, you wished to take Song, but after having seen me, even if Song were to be given to you, if this was not righteous, you would not do it. This is my giving you Song. If you take righteousness to be fundamental, I shall also give you the world."

50: 公輸[1]

50.1   公輸盤為楚造雲梯之械，成將以攻宋。子墨子聞之，起於齊，行
十日十夜而至於郢，見公輸盤。公輸盤曰：「夫子何命焉為？」子
墨子曰：「北方有侮臣[2]，願藉子殺之。」公輸盤不說。子墨子曰：
「請獻十金。」公輸盤曰：「吾義固不殺人。」子墨子起，再拜曰：
「請說之。吾從北方聞子為梯，將以攻宋。宋何罪之有？荊國有
餘於地，而不足於民，殺所不足，而爭所有餘，不可為智。宋無
罪而攻之，不可謂仁。知而不爭，不可謂忠。爭而不得，不可謂
強。義不殺少而殺眾，不可謂知類。」公輸盤服。子墨子曰：

---

1.   The events recounted in this chapter appear in a somewhat shorter form in the LSCQ 21/
     5.2.
2.   者 is taken to have dropped out here.

50: Gongshu

50.1   Gongshu Pan[i] constructed cloud ladder equipment for Chu and, having completed it, was about to use it to attack Song. When Master Mo Zi heard of this, he set out from Qi and travelled for ten days and ten nights to reach Ying[ii] where he met with Gongshu Pan.

Gongshu Pan said: "Master, what do you instruct me to do?"

Master Mo Zi replied: "In the northern region, there is one who has insulted me. I wish to make use of you to kill him."

Gongshu Pan was not happy.

Master Mo Zi said: "Let me offer you ten pieces of gold (10 *jin*)."

Gongshu Pan responded: "My righteousness is strong — I do not kill people."

Master Mo Zi rose and bowed, saying: "Allow me to explain. From the northern region, I heard that you were making cloud ladders and were about to attack Song. What crime is Song guilty of? The kingdom of Jing (Chu) has an excess of land but not enough people. To kill what there is not enough of in the struggle for what there is an excess of cannot be wise. To attack Song when it has committed no crime cannot be said to be benevolent. To know and not contend cannot be said to be loyal. To contend and not be successful cannot be said to be strong. To take as righteous not killing a few, yet to kill many cannot be called an understanding of analogy."

---

i.   Written here 公輸盤 (Gongshu Pan), this is presumably the same person as 公輸般 (or 班 — Gongshu Ban), or 公輸子, referred to in various texts, for example, *Mencius* IVA. 1(1) where Legge describes him as a "... celebrated mechanist of Lu of the times of Confucius" and "the tutelary spirit of carpenters". See WYJ's detailed note 1, p. 765.

ii. The capital of Chu.

「然，乎不已乎？」[3] 公輸盤曰：「不可。吾既已言之王矣。」子墨子曰：「胡不見我於王？」公輸盤曰：「諾。」

50.2　子墨子見王曰：「今有人於此，舍其文軒，鄰有敝輿，而欲竊之；舍其錦繡，鄰有短褐，而欲竊之；舍其粱肉，鄰有糠糟，而欲竊之。此為何若人？」王曰：「必為竊疾矣。」子墨子曰：「荊之地，方五千里，宋〔之地〕[4]，方五百里，此猶文軒之與敝輿也；荊有雲夢，犀兕麋鹿滿之，江漢之魚鱉黿鼉為天下富，宋所為[5]無雉兔狐狸[6]者也，此猶粱肉之與糠糟也；荊有長松、文梓、梗枏、豫章，[7] 宋無長木，此猶錦繡之與短褐也。臣以三事之攻宋也[8]，為與此同類，臣見大王之必傷義而不得[9]。」王曰：「善哉！雖然，公輸盤為我為雲梯，必取宋。」

---

3. In this sentence, there is general agreement that the first 乎 should be read as 胡 (WNS) and 已 as 止.
4. Supplied on the basis of other texts — see WYJ, note 22, p. 769.
5. Most commentators read 為 as 謂.
6. Some commentators follow WNS in emending 狐狸 to 鮒魚 on the grounds of the nature of the comparison.
7. There is some uncertainty about the listing of the trees, particularly the fourth, for which the unemended text has 豫章. I have followed the reading of Z&Q which includes taking 豫章 as 樟樹.
8. There is considerable variation in the reading of this sentence, hinging on what is made of 三事. BY (followed by WYJ) would emend this to 王吏 and SYR to 三吏. CYX retains 三事, taking them as the "three matters" previously referred to. Perhaps the simplest solution, and the one followed in the translation, is the reading of 王事 (Gu Qianli, cited by Z&Q, note 12, p. 780).
9. These 11 characters were added by BY and are included in modern editions such as Z&Q.

Gongshu Pan conceded.

Master Mo Zi said: "This being so, why do you not stop?"

Gongshu Pan replied: "I cannot. I have already spoken of it to the king."[iii]

Master Mo Zi said: "Why not let me meet with the king."

Gongshu Pan agreed.

50.2 Master Mo Zi met with the king and said: "Suppose now there is a man who casts aside his own decorated sedan and wishes to steal a broken-down carriage which his neighbour has; who casts aside his own embroidered coat and wishes to steal a short jacket of coarse cloth which his neighbour has; who casts aside his own grain and meat and wishes to steal chaff and dregs which his neighbour has. What sort of man would this be?"

The king replied: "He would certainly be a pathological thief."

Master Mo Zi said: "The land of Jing (Chu) is five thousand *li* square whereas the land of Song is five hundred *li* square. They are, in comparison, like a decorated sedan and a broken-down carriage. Jing has Yunmeng Park. Rhinoceroses and various kinds of deer fill it. The fish, turtles and alligators in the Yangtze and Han Rivers are the most abundant in the world. Song, it is said, does not even have pheasants, hares or foxes. It is like comparing grain and meat with dregs and husks. Jing has tall pines, elegant catalpas, cedars and camphor-laurels. Song has no tall trees. It is like comparing a garment that is embroidered and ornamented with one that is short and of coarse cloth. I take the King's business in attacking Song to be in the same class as these things. In my view, the great King will certainly damage righteousness, but will not achieve anything."

The King replied: "That is all very well. However, Gongshu Pan has already prepared the cloud ladders for me so I must take Song."

---

iii. SYR suggests that the protagonists in this case were King Hui of Chu 楚惠王 and Duke Zhao of Song 宋昭公.

50.3 於是見公輸盤，子墨子解帶為城，以牒[10]為械，公輸盤九設攻城
之機變，子墨子九距[11]之，公輸盤之攻械盡，子墨子之守圉有
餘。公輸盤詘[12]而曰：「吾知所以距子矣，吾不言。」子墨子亦
曰：「吾知子之所以距我，吾不言。」楚王問其故。子墨子曰：「公
輸子之意，不過欲殺臣。殺臣，宋莫能守，可攻也。然臣之弟子
禽滑釐等三百人，已持臣守圉之器，在宋城上而待楚寇矣。雖殺
臣，不能絕也。」楚王曰：「善哉！吾請無攻宋矣。」

50.4 子墨子歸，過宋天雨，庇其閭中，守閭者不內也。故曰：「治於
神者[13]，眾人不知其功，爭於明者，眾人知之。」

51: 闕

10. Some texts have this character with the 爿 radical (ZWDCD #20242). LSL has: "牒‘楪’
     的假借字。即筷子。" — see his note 1, p. 446.
11. 距 is taken as 拒 (Z&Q).
12. The reading of 詘 as 屈 is generally accepted.
13. The terse phrase "治於神者" is somewhat ambiguous. I take it to refer to someone, like
     Mo Zi in this instance, who resolves or prevents conflict by working privately on the
     "spirit" of those involved, as opposed to someone who engages in open battle. LYS has:
     "是說墨子救了宋，不會告人，只有神知道" — see his note 4, p. 395.

50.3   Thereupon he (Mo Zi) went to see Gongshu Pan. Master Mo Zi took off his belt and made it a city wall. With little sticks he made weapons. Gongshu Pan devised nine different strategies for attacking the city, but nine times Master Mo Zi repulsed him. Gongshu Pan used all his machines for attack, whereas Master Mo Zi's methods of defence were by no means exhausted. Gongshu Pan submitted, but said: "I know how I can oppose you but I will not say."

Master Mo Zi also said: "I know the way in which you would oppose me but I will not say."

The King of Chu asked him his reason.

Master Mo Zi said: "Gongshu Zi's idea is just to have me killed, [thinking that] if I am killed, Song would not be able to defend itself and could be [successfully] attacked. However, my disciple Qin Guli and three hundred such men have already prepared my machines of defence and are on the walls of Song awaiting the attack from Chu. Although you kill me, you will not be able to overcome [their defence]."

The King said: "Good! I now wish not to attack Song."

50.4   Master Mo Zi returned. As he was passing through Song it rained heavily. He sought shelter at the gate but the gatekeeper would not let him enter. [Mo Zi] said: "In the case of those who bring order to the spirit, the multitude do not know of their achievement. In the case of those who contend in clear view, the multitude do know."

51: Lost

PART *V*

Defence of a City

Introduction

These chapters, that is the eleven extant chapters on the personnel, equipment and strategies to be used in the defence of a city (*Mozi* 52–71), are beset with the same textual problems as the "dialectical" chapters. Yates, in his 1980 thesis devoted to this material, speaks of the text suffering "… dismemberment and massive transpositions and losses of sections", surmising that there should at least be the twelve chapters corresponding to the twelve techniques which Mo Zi's disciple Qin Guli lists in his opening question in chapter 52. In fact, only six of the twelve are represented and some of these have clearly lost material. Although the magnitude of the problem is very similar in the "dialectical" and defence sections, its nature is somewhat different. There are again many unknown characters but in these chapters a significant number are related to unknown pieces of equipment or weapons. In addition, however, there are many lacunae which are not a feature of the "dialectical" chapters. Simple errors of copying are again a feature as are the dislocation and duplication of substantial fragments. On the positive side, there are not the specific problems due to the particular arrangement of the Canons and Explanations, and the material itself is less complex, being basically descriptive, so if the text is reliable, interpretation is likely to be relatively straightforward.

The text given below follows that found in the modern editions of Li Shenglong and of Zhou Caizhu and Qi Ruiduan. Both editions follow Sun Yirang whose text has some rearrangements of the *Daoist Patrology* (DZ) text involving chapters 52, 62 and 71. These are detailed in the Comments preceding the relevant chapters below. The text given by Wu Yujiang has several points of difference from the text used, particularly regarding the order of material in chapter 52 and the transfer of some material from that chapter to chapter 70. Again, the differences are noted in the Comments. There have been two major attempts at reconstruction of these chapters — that of Cen Zhongmian, first published in 1958, and that of Yates, particularly in his 1980 thesis. The changes proposed by these authors have been detailed in the Comments. Finally, in an effort to keep the number of footnotes within reasonable limits, I have not referred to all the suggested emendations and interpretations of the DZ text. For those interested in greater detail the studies of Wu Yujiang, Cen Zhongmian and Yates are recommended, although unfortunately the last is only available as an unpublished thesis.

Six of the eleven chapters on "Defence of a City" in this section (Chapters 52, 53, 56, 62, 63 and 71) begin with a question posed by Qin Guli to which Mo Zi responds. Two of these six chapters (Chapters 52 and 71) also have a statement by Mo Zi, introduced with "墨子曰", as the final or penultimate section. In these six chapters, two modern editors (LSL and Z&Q) include all the sections following the initial exchange in quotation marks as a continuation of Mo Zi's reply. In view of the overall textual uncertainty, I have chosen not to do this although clearly they may be read as such.

52: 備城門[1]

Comment: In terms of the DZ text, this is the first of the two composite chapters, 62 below is the other, there being a bi-directional interchange of material between these chapters. In the present text, which follows that of the modern editions of LSL and Z&Q, these in turn being based on SYR, there are 29 sections. In summary, 52.1 corresponds to the opening of DZ 52, 52.2 is also from DZ 52 but later in that chapter (between 52.19 and 52.20), 52.3 and 52.4 are also part of the rearranged order whilst the latter ends with 52 characters from DZ 62. Sections 52.5–11 all comprise material from DZ 62. The remaining sections (52.12–29) all consist of material from DZ 52 although there is the addition of material from DZ 71 in 52.21 and also, between the text of 52.24 and 52.25, the DZ 52 contains material which is transferred to chapter 62 in the present text. WYJ does not make the transfer of the later material from DZ 52 to form what below is 52.2 and, in fact, his order overall is somewhat different. In addition, he has what below are 52.20 and 52.21 as part of paragraph 6 of his chapter 70. The arrangements of CZM and RDSY/T are considered in the Comment to each section below.

52.1 禽滑釐問於子墨子曰:「由聖人之言,鳳鳥之不出[2],諸侯畔殷周之國[3],甲兵方起於天下,大攻小,強執弱,吾欲守小國,為之奈何?」子墨子曰:「何攻之守?」禽滑釐對曰:「今之世常所以攻者:臨、鉤、衝、梯、堙、水、穴、突、空洞、蟻傅、轒轀、軒車,敢[4]問守此十二者奈何?」子墨子曰:「我城池修,守器具,推[5]粟足,上下相親,又得四鄰諸侯之救,此所以持也。且守者雖善,〔而君不用之〕[6],則〔猶〕[7]若不可以守也。若君用之守者,

---

1. There is a slight question about the title. AF takes it to be "the city gates" that are being referred to. In fact, 城 is used variably as "city" and "city wall". RDSY/T entitles this opening chapter "Fortifications, Weapons and Machines".
2. BY takes this to be a reference to the *Lun Yu* IX.8.
3. I have followed CZM in reading 殷周 as 王周. Others (e.g. RDSY/SC) take 殷 as a kingdom — see Z&Q, note 3, p. 789.
4. Emended from 服 — see WYJ, note 17, p. 788.
5. 推 is taken to be an error for 樵 here, following SYR.
6. These five characters are added by Lu Wenchao and included in the translation — see Z&Q, note 7, p. 790.
7. Added by modern editors to parallel the following sentence.

52: Preparing the Wall and Gates

52.1   Qin Guli[i] questioned Master Mo Zi, saying: "According to the Sage's words, when the phoenix did not come forth, the feudal lords rebelled against the King of Zhou. Weapons and armies (warfare) then arose in the world, the large attacked the small, and the strong seized the weak. If I wished to defend a small state, how would I go about it?"

Master Mo Zi asked: "Defence against what kind of attack?"

Qin Guli replied, saying: "The [methods of] attack in frequent use at the present time are: approachers (*lin*), hooks (*gou*), battering rams (*chong*), ladders (*ti*), mounds (*yin*), water (*shui*), tunnels (*xue*), sudden attacks (*tu*), *kongdong*,[ii] ant approach (massed infantry assault — *yifu*), tanks (*fenwen*), and high carts (*xuan-che*).[iii] May I ask about defence against these twelve things?"

Master Mo Zi said: "My city walls and moats would be in good repair, the instruments of defence prepared, fuel and grain would be sufficient, superiors and inferiors would be well disposed towards each other, and I would get help from the neighbouring feudal lords on the four sides. This is how [my defence] would be managed. Furthermore, if, although the Defender is skilful, the ruler does not use him, then it remains impossible to mount a

---

i.   A noted disciple of Mo Zi — see, for example, *Mozi* 50 where he is mentioned in relation to military matters, as he is in several of the following chapters. He is also referred to in *Zhuangzi* 33 and the *Lü Shi Chunqiu* 2/4.3.

ii.   It remains a puzzle what this method is. RDSY/SC writes: "Absolutely nothing is known of the ninth machine or technique in Chhin Ku-li's list in *Mo Tzu, khung-tung*, which literally means 'empty cave', for not one example of its use can be found in any ancient historical source." He takes it possibly to be "... some kind of scaling assault on the city walls allusive to the Emperor's (i.e. the Yellow Emperor) mythical climb" — see p. 419. Z&Q, following SYR, take it to be a form of tunnelling, writing: "近似於穴城之法。"

iii. For a detailed and informative discussion of all 12 methods see RDSY/SC, pp. 413–485. I have, predominantly, followed his terms for the twelve types of attack.

又必能乎守者，不能而君用之，則猶若不可以守也。然則守者必
善而君尊用之，然後可以守也。」

Comment: This is generally accepted as the introductory passage to the
chapters on methods of defence. The assumption is that the twelve methods
listed here were, in the following chapters, each dealt with individually but that
a number of these chapters are now lost and material from those extant has,
in a number of cases, been displaced. Specifically, *lin, ti, shui, tu, xue* and *yifu*
remain but *gou, chong, yin, kongtong, fenwen* and *xuanche* no longer have a
chapter to themselves although they are mentioned in the remaining material.
On the question of arrangement, 52.1 above corresponds to RDSY/T's
fragments 1a and 1b and to CZM's #1–4 and #6, his #5 being what is here
52.2.

52.2   凡守圍[8]城之法，〔城〕[9]厚以[10]高，壕池深以廣，樓撕楯[11]，守備
繕利，薪食足以支三月以上，人眾以選[12]，吏民和，大臣有功勞
於上者多，主信以義，萬民樂之無窮。不然，父母墳墓在焉；不
然，山林草澤之饒足利；不然，地形之難攻而易守也；不然，則
有深怨於適而有大功於上；不然，則賞明可信而罰嚴足畏也。此
十四者具，則民亦不宜[13]上矣。然後城可守。十四者無一，則雖
善者不能守矣。

Comment: Because it continues the general discussion, this section is placed
here by SYR and ZCY and, following them, by modern editors LSL, MBJ and
Z&Q. CZM also has it at the start, inserted in 52.1. RDSY/T, however, leaves
it in its later position where it occurs in the DZ (his fragments 20 & 21), as do
WYJ and CHANT. The major part of this section is also found in the *Guanzi* 44
(see Rickett, vol. 2, pp. 140–142 and also RDSY/T, pp. 184–185). There is
some doubt about the recurring "不然". RDSY/T has "if that is not so" whilst
Rickett has "otherwise". In view of what follows I have settled for "apart from
these" indicating the initial list of requirements to which these five additional
ones must be added.

8.   I have retained 圍 although SYR suggests it should be emended to 圉 and read in the
     sense of 御 — see RDSY/T, note 378, p. 186.
9.   Added by CZM.
10. 以 is read as 而 here and in the following sentence (see Z&Q).
11. I have followed HYX and SYR in their proposed emendations of this clause. RDSY/T
     takes this to be a type of tower (see his note 383, p. 187). SYR takes 楯 in the sense of
     脩.
12. YTY equates 選 with 練.
13. Modern editors such as LSL and Z&Q accept CZM's reading of 宜 as 疑.

successful defence. If the ruler does use the Defender, he must also be capable in defence. If he is not capable and the ruler uses him, then it remains impossible to mount a successful defence. So, then, the Defender must be skilful and the ruler must respect and use him. Only then can there be a [successful] defence."

52.2 In general, the methods of defending a besieged city involve walls that are thick and high, moats and ditches that are deep and wide, towers and parapets that are in good repair, defensive preparations that are appropriate and advantageous (weapons that are well maintained and effective in use),[iv] fuel and food supplies that are sufficient for more than three months, a populace that is capable, officers and people in harmony, many high officials of meritorious service to the ruler, a ruler who himself is trustworthy and righteous, and people who are happy to defend to the end. Apart from these, the ancestral graves of the defenders should be there. Apart from these, the mountains, forests, grasslands and marshes should be abundant and sufficient to be of benefit. Apart from these, the topography of the land should be such that it is difficult to attack and easy to defend. Apart from these, there should be deep enmity towards the foe and extraordinary service towards the ruler. Apart from these, the ruler's rewards should be clearly understood and trustworthy whilst his punishments should be sufficiently severe to be intimidating. If these fourteen conditions are all met, then the people will also not harbour doubt towards the ruler. Subsequently, there can be successful defence of the city. If [any] one of these fourteen is lacking, then, although the one responsible for defence is skilful, he cannot effectively defend [the city].

---

iv. This is Z&Q's understanding of this clause.

52.3   故凡守城之法，備城門，為縣門[14]沈機[15]，長二丈，廣八尺，為
之兩相如[16]。門扇數令相接三寸，施上扇上，無過二寸。塹中深
丈五，廣比扇，塹長以力為度，塹之末為之縣，可容一人所。客
至，諸門戶皆令鑿而慕孔。孔之[17]，各為二幕二，一鑿而繫繩，
長四尺。城四面四隅，皆為高〔樓〕磨撕[18]，使重室子居其上，候
適，視其態狀，與其進左右所移處，失候斬。

Comment: The arrangement of this section again follows SYR and is adopted
by modern editors LSL, MBJ and Z&Q. CZM and WYJ end the section at "長
四尺" and RDSY/T at "可容一人所". In these three cases what follows is here
52.12. The remainder of 52.3 above is included by RDSY/T in his fragment 9,
by WYJ (and CHANT) as the start of 52, para 13, and by CZM as #52.64.

52.4   敵人為穴而來，我亟使穴師選本，迎而穴之，為之且內弩[19]以應
之。[20]民室杙木瓦石，可以蓋城之備者，盡上之。[21]不從令者

---

14. In the *Zuo Zhuan* for the 10th year of Duke Xiang 襄公 there is mention of such gates
    which Legge translates as "portcullis gates" — see LCC, vol. 5, p. 442. Kong Yingda
    has this note: "縣門者，編版廣長如門，施關機，以縣門上，有寇則發機而下之。"
    See also RDSY/SC, pp. 347–351.
15. Here 沈 is read as 下 and 機 as 機關. For other views on 沈 see RDSY/T, note 29, pp.
    74–75.
16. SYR has this note: "謂門左右兩扇同度。"
17. These two characters, written as 攻之 in some texts, are taken to be superfluous
    following SSX.
18. In this clause, 樓 is added following YY.There are doubts, as previously, about 撕. I have
    taken it as a kind of railing or parapet following HYX and Z&Q. RDSY/T calls it a "*li-
    ssu*" being a kind of tower — see his note 220, pp. 134–135.
19. It may be that 內弩 is a special form of bow for use in the confined space of a tunnel
    — see SYR, RDSY/T.
20. In this sentence, 本 is read as 上 (WNS) and 且 as 具 (BY) in the sense of 準備.
21. In this sentence, 杙 is emended to 材 and 蓋 to 益 (WYZ).

52.3 Therefore, in general, with the methods of defending a city, city gates are prepared that are "hanging gates" (portcullis gates), with a mechanism for raising and lowering them. They should be 2 *zhang* high and 8 *chi* wide,ᵛ and consist of two equal leaves. The two leaves of the gate should overlap by 3 *cun* and there should be a covering of earth on each leaf not exceeding 2 *cun*. A trench should be dug 1 *zhang* 5 *chi* deep in the middle, with a width comparable to the width of the gate leaves. The length of the trench is determined by the strength of those digging it. At the head of the trench there should be a sluice gate and a place which can hold one man. When the enemy comes, there is an order to bore holes in both gate leaves and to cover the holes. Each gate leaf should have two holes and two covers, to one of which is attached a rope of 4 *chi* in length. At all four sides and four corners of the city, make high towers and parapets and depute the scions of noble houses to live in them. There they should await the enemy, observe the enemy's appearance, and the movements of the enemy advance. Those who fail to wait should be executed.

52.4 If the enemy makes tunnels and approaches through them, we urgently send the tunnel master to select officers to meet the enemy within the tunnels. We make them, moreover, short bows to meet them with. The materials of people's houses — wood, tiles and stones — can be added to the resources for the city's defence and are completely transported to it. Those who do not comply

---

v. Measurements of length are given throughout using the Chinese terms — 1 *cun* 寸 = 1 inch (23.1mm); 1 *chi* 尺 = 10 *cun*; 1 *zhang* 丈 = 10 *chi*; 1 *bu* 步 = 6 *chi*; 1 *li* 里 = 180 *zhang*. Also 10 *fen* 分 = 1 *cun*.

斬。²² 昔築，七尺一居屬，五步一壘，五築有錈。長斧，柄長八尺。十步一長鎩，柄長八尺。十步一鬥長椎，柄長六尺，頭長尺，斧其兩端。三步一大鋌，前長尺，蚤長五寸。兩鋌交之置如平，不如平不利，兌其兩末。穴隊若衝隊，必審如攻隊之廣狹，而令邪穿其穴，令其廣必夷客隊。²³

Comment: This is a very problematical section. For brief consideration, I shall divide it into four sub-sections.

i.   Sentence 1: This may be, as RDSY/T suggests, misplaced from the chapter on tunnelling (*Mozi* 62). He has it in that chapter as his fragment 40. Both CZM and WYJ retain it in the present chapter but later — CZM as #65, WYJ in para. 13.

ii.   Sentences 2 and 3: Both CZM (#52.66) and WYJ (52, para 13) have these following the first sentence.

iii.   Sentences 4–9: RDSY/T has the first four of these six sentences separate from the last two sentences as fragments 10 and 16 respectively. He describes the first fragment as a list of "… agricultural implements which could be used not only to repair the walls but also as weapons to fend off the enemy" (p. 137). What the implements actually are is itself uncertain. There are significant problems with the six sentences as indicated in note 22.

iv.   Sentence 10: The topic is again tunnelling and RDSY/T also moves this to *Mozi* 62 as his fragment 41.

52.5   疏束樹木，令足以為柴摶，毋前面樹，長丈七尺一，以為外面，以柴摶從橫施之，外面以強塗，毋令土²⁴漏。令其廣厚，能任三丈五尺之城以上。以柴木土稍杜之，以急²⁵為故。前面之長短，

---

22. The following six sentences are very problematical. Characters in question are: (i) 昔 in sentence 1 — whether it should be emended to 皆 (BY), 夕 (YTY), or 甬 (RDSY/T). (ii) 築 — whether it is a general term or a specific implement. (iii) Whether 居屬 should be taken as 鋸钃 indicating two implements (e.g. saw and chopper — RDSY/T) or as both indicating 鋤 (hoe — e.g. LSL). (iv) Whether 錈 should be taken as 夷 indicating a kind of scythe (SYR). (v) Whether 鬥 is superfluous (e.g. WSN) or should be emended to 斲 (BY). (vi) Whether 椎 should be retained as "hammer" or read as 錐 "awl" (SYR). (vii) Whether the second 斧 should be emended to 銳 (SYR). (viii) 鋌 is taken to be a lance (矛) following CZM. There is also the issue of punctuation throughout and particularly whether the full-stop occurs before or after "三步一".

23. In this statement, 隊 is taken as 隧道, 如 as 知 (SYR), and 邪 as 斜.

24. 土 is taken as 上 following SYR.

25. Taken as 堅 following CZM.

with the command are executed. [Prepare] all the construction [implements]. Every 7 *chi* have one hoe. Every 5 *bu* have one basket for carrying earth. For every five constructions have one iron hoe and one long axe with a handle 8 *chi* in length. Every 10 *bu* have one sickle with a handle 8 *chi* in length. Every 10 *bu* have one chopper and one long awl with a handle 6 *chi* in length and a head 1 *chi* in length. Sharpen the two points with an axe. Every 3 *bu* have one large lance (*ting*) 1 *chi* long and sharpened at the end for 5 *cun*. Two lances can be joined together and placed flat. If they are not placed flat, they are not convenient to use. The two ends of each lance are sharpened. If underground tunnels are used to counter underground tunnels, careful attention must be given to knowing the width or narrowness of the enemy's underground tunnels. Orders must be given to make one's own tunnels at an angle to the enemy tunnels and at the same level.

52.5   Pieces of wood are gathered together sufficient to make bundles of brushwood with no pieces protruding from the ends of the bundles. A piece of wood 1 *zhang* 7 *chi* long is placed on the outside [of the bundles] and the bundles of brushwood are bound together and piled up crosswise. The outside is covered with a strong coating of earth that doesn't allow leakage in from above. Let the width and thickness of the bundles be such that they are able to provide protection for a wall more than 3 *zhang* 5 *chi* high. Use brushwood, wood and earth to add somewhat to the barrier,

豫蚤接之，令能任塗，足以為堞，善塗其外，令毋可燒拔也。

Comment: This section is about a single item in the defensive armamentarium — the 柴搏 or "brushwood tie" as RDSY/T calls it. Its preparation is described and to some extent its use. This section occurs later in the rearranged texts — as #52.73 in CZM, as fragment 17 in RDSY/T. It comprises paragraph 18, sentences 4–6 in WYJ and paragraph 19, sentences 4–6 in CHANT.

52.6 大城丈五為閨門，廣四尺。

為郭門，郭門在外，為衡，以兩木當門，鑿其木維敷上堞。

為斬縣梁，令[26]穿，斷城以扳橋，邪穿外，以板次之[27]，倚殺[28] 如城報。城內有傅壤[29]，因以內壤為外。鑿其間，深丈五尺，室[30] 以樵，可燒之以待適。

令耳[31]屬城，為再重樓。下鑿城外堞內深丈五，廣丈二。樓若令耳，皆令有力者主敵，善射者主發，佐皆廣矢[32]。

Comment: This is a somewhat heterogeneous section as given here, describing at least four separate things: (i) Small gates in the wall. (ii) The structure of outer wall (*guo*) gates. (iii) The building of a suspension bridge over the moat and other defensive constructions inside the moat. (iv) The *ling-er*, taken here to be a type of tower. There is considerable doubt about what is being described in case (iii), particularly on the issue of 堞 or 壤, and also uncertainty about what a *ling'er* is. With regard to order, RDSY/T has this as part of his fragment 18, CZM as his #52.74 where it is combined with 52.7 following, and WYJ as part of his 52, para 19.

---

26. 令 is used for the unusual character (ZWDCD #40722) which appears here — see, for example, Z&Q.
27. CZM has the following note on this clause: "板橋长木達地，則再以板接之。"
28. The interpretation of this clause depends on SYR's proposal to read "倚殺" as "邪殺" and 報 as 執.
29. Both here and subsequently, 壤 is taken as 堞 (SSX). RDSY/T suggests emendation to 壕 envisaging a double moat system — see his note 308, p. 168.
30. Read as 窒 following SYR.
31. "令耳" presents a problem. The consensus is that it is a name, possibly descriptive of appearance as suggested in the text itself. CZM, who is of this view, says of the subsection as a whole: "語多難解".
32. The translation follows SYR's proposed emendation of these four characters to "佐以廣矢".

the objective being strength. Over the extent of the outer surface make preparation beforehand so that the surface can bear the smeared-on material and is sufficient to act as a parapet. Coat the outer surface well so it can't be burnt or pulled up.

52.6 In the large wall, there should be small gates 1 *zhang* 5 *chi* high and 4 *che* wide.[vi]

Make outer wall gates (*guomen*). On the outer aspect of the outer wall gates make a horizontal bar of two pieces of wood matching the gate. Drill holes in the pieces of wood through which a rope is threaded and then led up to the battlements.

Across the moat build a suspended bridge to allow crossing into the city by means of the wooden bridge which has a slope to the outside of the wall and can be added to with additional timber. The angle of inclination is determined by the form of the wall. Within the wall have a supplementary parapet. Rely on the inner parapet in making the outer parapet. Between the two parapets dig a trench 1 *zhang* 5 *chi* deep where an obstruction can be established using sharp stakes. Fire can be set there to meet the enemy.

Near the wall should be built *ling'er* towers which have two levels. At the lower level, outside the wall and between it and the parapets, dig a trench measuring 1 *zhang* 5 *chi* deep and 1 *zhang* 2 *chi* wide. The appearance of the tower is like *ling'er*. [From these *ling'er* towers] strong, able-bodied men are sent forth to confront the enemy. Skilled archers are responsible for firing arrows and should be provided with sharp arrows.

---

vi. RDSY/T takes these measurements to apply to the individual leaves.

52.7　治裾。諸延堞，高六尺，部廣四尺，皆為兵弩簡格。[33] 轉射機，機長六尺，狸一尺。[34] 兩材合而為之輻[35]，輻長二尺，中鑿夫之為道臂[36]，臂長至桓[37]。二十步一，令善射之者佐[38]，一人皆勿離。

Comment: There are clearly problems with this section. If it is accepted that 裾 is a form of fence, the first issue is whether the final clause of the second sentence is describing some support structure in the fence for the "revolving shooting machine" as RDSY/T assumes, or whether two separate matters are being considered — i.e. a protective fence and a "revolving shooting machine". This is the position taken by LSL, for example, and is the one I have followed. The translation of the final sentence is also somewhat uncertain. This section continues RDSY/T's fragment 18 whilst CZM has the first two sentences (as given above) as the final part of his #52.74 and takes the rest of 52.7 (i.e. that concerning the 轉射機 and its 輻) as a separate section (#52. 75) which has encouraged me to take the view expressed above.

52.8　城上百步一樓，樓四植[39]，植皆為通臺[40]，下高丈，上九尺，廣、喪[41] 各丈六尺，皆為寧[42]。

---

33. This first statement (two sentences) is quite problematical. I have followed CZM (as does RDSY/T) in placing a full stop after 裾. On 裾, RDSY/T says: "The interpretation of *ju* as the name of a picket fence is undoubtedly correct." LSL equates it with 藩籬 which I have followed. 治 is read as 置. 諸 then becomes part of the next sentence. The reading of 部 is also uncertain. SYR has this note: "謂城堞間守者所居立之分域" whilst YTY suggests emending it to 培 as a mound or banked-up earth. With respect to "簡格", there is general acceptance of BY's reading of 簡 as 闌. CZM has: "闌，格之義同為'阻'。"
34. Following YTY, the "轉射機" is taken as some sort of device capable of firing arrows in any chosen direction. As elsewhere, 狸 is taken as 埋.
35. 輻 is clearly not intended here in its usual sense ("sleeping car", "hearse"). SYR suggests it should be read as 車 + 宛 (ZWDCD #39215) which the《說文》defines as "大車後壓也". Presumably, then, the idea is to stabilise the "轉射機".
36. In this clause, 夫 is read as 膚 (CZM) and 道臂 as 通臂 (SYR).
37. There is some uncertainty about 桓. For example, Z&Q see it as a mistake for 垣 whilst LSL takes it in the sense of "貞木". I have followed the latter.
38. There is agreement that this clause should be rearranged to read: "令善射者佐之".
39. Following SYR, 四植 is read as 四楹.
40. This character, with the 石 radical added (ZWDCD #25048), is taken to indicate the foundation stone of the pillar.
41. As elsewhere, 喪 is taken as 㡿 in the sense of 長 (WNS).
42. There are several opinions on 寧 as follows: CZM takes it as 文 in the sense of 門 (followed by Z&Q); YTY takes it as 櫺 in the sense of 窗戶 (followed by LSL); BY reads it as 宁.

52.7   Set up a bamboo fence. In all cases extend it to join the parapet. Make it 6 *chi* high with spaces 4 *chi* wide where all those armed with crossbows can take their positions. There should be "revolving shooting machines" which are 6 *chi* high and buried in the ground 1 *chi*. Two pieces of wood joined together are used to make protective shields (*wen*) which are 2 *chi* long. Through the centres of these drill a hole to accommodate a connecting arm straight against the wall. Every 20 *bu*, there should be one of these (i.e. a "revolving shooting machine" plus its protective shields). [Put someone in charge of it and] order skilled archers to assist him. Not one person is allowed to leave his post.

52.8   On the wall, every 100 *bu*, there should be a tower having four pillars. All the pillars should have a connecting foundation. The lower (level of the tower) should be 1 *zhang* high and the upper (level) 9 *chi*. Each should be 1 *zhang* 6 *chi* in width and length, and all should have a door.

三十步一突[43]，九尺，廣十尺，高八尺，鑿廣三尺，表[44]二尺，
為寧。

城上為攢火[45]，夫長以城高下為度，置火其末。

Comment: In this section, which CZM has as three separate fragments #52.76–78, three things on the wall are described. Whilst the first is clearly a tower characterised by four supporting pillars which are connected, there is some doubt about the other two — 突 and 攢火. RDSY/T, who includes this section in his fragment 18, calls them "sally ports" and "fire javelins" respectively. In WYJ this section is the first part of 52, para 20.

52.9　城上九尺一弩、一戟、一椎、一斧、一艾[46]，皆積參石[47]，蒺藜。

渠[48]長丈六尺，[49]夫[50]長丈二尺，臂長六尺，其狸[51]者三尺，樹渠毋傅堞五寸。

藉幕[52]長八尺，廣七尺，其木也廣五尺，中藉幕為之橋，索其端。適攻，令一人下上之，勿離。

城上二十步一藉車，當隊者不用此數。

城上三十步一壟灶[53]。

---

43. As with 寧, there are differing views on 突. YTY (and LSL) take it as 窗寫 whilst CZM (and Z&Q) take it as 洞道 which I have translated as "connecting passage". RDSY/T calls them "sally ports" — see his note 329, p. 173.
44. Following WNS, 表 (like 喪) is read as 袤 in the sense of 長.
45. On the different readings of 攢火 see RDSY/T, note 333, pp. 173–174. I have used his translation as "fire javelin".
46. 艾 is taken as 刈. Z&Q have: "艾：通'刈'，割刀一類的兵器。"
47. Following HY, 參石 is taken as 礛石.
48. SYR has this note on 渠: "此渠乃守械，以金木為之。"
49. Modern commentators (e.g. LSL, Z&Q) accept WYZ's suggestion that this be made consistent with the description in *Mozi* 71 and read: "渠長丈五尺，廣丈六尺。" I have followed this.
50. Read as 膚 or 跗.
51. Read as 埋.
52. Following CZM, 莫 here and 苴 subsequently are emended to 幕 to give 藉幕 in both instances which CZM equates with 遮幕.
53. BY's proposal for the rare character (ZWDCD #4641) is followed. Other suggestions include 壟 and 聾. It is not clear what, precisely, is being described. It may be some kind of brazier for illumination — see RDSY/T, note 360, p. 180 and Z&Q, note 12, p. 801.

Every 30 *bu*, there should be a connecting passage (*tu*) 9 *chi* long, 10 *chi* wide and 8 *chi* high. A door should be cut in the connecting passage 3 *chi* wide and 2 *chi* long.

On the wall, there should be fire javelins of a length commensurate with the height of the wall and which can be lit at the tip.

52.9   On the wall, at intervals of 9 *chi*, there is placed one crossbow, one halberd, one bludgeon, one axe and one hacker. In all cases, pile up "thunder stones" and caltrops.

Qu shields [are made], being 1 *zhang* 5 *chi* high and 1 *zhang* 6 *chi* wide. Their poles should be 1 *zhang* 2 *chi* high and their limbs 6 *chi* high. They are buried to a depth of 3 *chi* with the wooden shield no nearer than 5 *cun* to the parapet.

Screens are 8 *chi* high and 7 *chi* wide. The thickness of the wood is 5 *chi* and, in the middle of the screen, a "bridge" is made with a rope attached to the ends. When the enemy approaches, one man is delegated to raise and lower this and not to leave his post.

On the wall, every 20 *bu*, there should be one trebuchet (*jiche*). When the enemy approaches by tunnelling do not use this number.

On the wall, every 30 *bu*, there should be one movable furnace.

Comment: This section, as here constituted, comprises a list of things to be available on the wall. The list includes weapons of various sorts, shields and screens, and stoves or furnaces. The *jiche* or trebuchet which is considered in greater detail elsewhere (52.26) is briefly mentioned. This section corresponds to the last part of RDSY/T's fragment 18 and the first part of fragment 19 whilst CZM to some degree separates the components of the list in his sections #52.80–83.

52.10   持水者必以布麻斗[54]、革盆、十步一。柄長八尺，斗大容二斗以上到三斗。敝裕，新布長六尺，中拙柄，長丈，十步一，必以大繩為箭。

城上十步一銚。

水缶[55]，容三石以上，小大相雜。盆、蠡各二財。

為卒乾飯，人二斗，以備陰雨，面使積燥處。令使守為城內堞外行餐。

Comment: This section considers water-holding utensils and food rations as well as making brief mention of shovels. It continues RDSY/T's fragment 19 whilst CZM divides it into five sections (#52.84–88). WYJ has it as part of his 52, para 21.

52.11   置器備，殺沙礫鐵，皆為壞斗。令陶者為薄缶，大容一斗以上至二斗，即用取，三祕合束。

堅為斗[56] 城上隔。棧高丈二，剡其一末。[57]

為閨門，閨門兩扇，令可以各自閉也。

---

54. The interpretation of the first part of this statement is based on SYR's analysis which is as follows: "蓋以布為器，加以油漆，可以抱水者。'斗'即'枓'之借字，《說文》木部云'枓，勺也'。" The emendation of 傳火 to 持水 follows WNS — see WYJ, note 337, p. 828.

55. Usually found in the rare equivalent form — ZWDCD #28750.

56. There is variation in the placement of these three characters. The arrangement above follows Z&Q.

57. Apart from the first three characters, there are several issues in this statement as follows: (i) According to SYR, 斗 should be read as 弋. (ii) On 弋, CZM has: "弋猶繳，繞也。" (iii) 棧 is taken as 小木樁 — see Z&Q who include SYR's note.

52.10   The utensils for holding water must have a ladle of lacquered hemp and should be made of hide. There should be one (such utensil) every 10 *bu*. The handle should be 8 *chi* long and the ladle should have a capacity of 2 to 3 *dou*.[vii]

Old or new hemp, 6 *chi* in length, is used (to fashion the handle). The middle of the handle is curved and it should be 1 *zhang* long. There should be one every 10 *bu* and there must be a large rope binding them.

On the wall, every 10 *bu* there should be one shovel.

There should be earthenware pots for water with capacities of 3 *dan* and upwards, the small and the large [pots] being mixed together. And there should be hide basins and calabashes as two additional utensils.

For the soldiers, there should be dried food, 2 *dou* per man. This should be prepared and protected from rain, and stored in a dry place. At the appropriate time, the defenders should be sent to a place between the inner and outer parapets to eat.

52.11   Utensils should be set up and prepared for scattering sand, small stones and pieces of iron. They should all be of rough earthenware in construction. Potters should be directed to make a small number of them with the biggest being able to hold 1 to 2 *dou*. When the time comes to use them, they should be bound together with rope.

Tightly bound stakes are placed at certain points on the wall and levelled off at a height of 1 *zhang* 2 (*chi*). These are sharpened at one end.

Make small doors with two leaves which can be opened and closed independently.

---

vii. As with length, the Chinese terms are retained for volumes — 1 *sheng* 升 = 199.7cc; 1 *dou* 斗 = 10 *sheng*; 1 *dan* 石 = 10 *dou*.

救闉[58] 池者，以火與爭，鼓橐[59]，馮埴[60] 外內，以柴為燔。

靈丁[61]，三丈一，火耳[62] 施之。十步一人。居柴內弩，弩半，為狗犀者環之。[63] 牆七步而一。[64]

Comment: This is a rather problematic section both in constitution and in placement. The placement here is that of SYR and is followed by modern editors LSL, MBJ and Z&Q. Both CZM and WYJ have these sentences later in chapter 52, the former as eight parts (his #52.89–96) and the latter as his 52, para 21. RDSY/T makes a significant rearrangement. What is the first sentence in 52.11 above, he has as the conclusion of his fragment 19 (i.e. part of chapter 52) whereas the remainder of the section above he joins with what is here 52.27 to give two fragments (his fragments 30 and 31) which he suggests might be from a lost chapter on 堙 which he calls "mounding in the moat". The evidence for such a rearrangement is rather tenuous, not least because it is dependent on the reading of 闉 as 堙 which is not universally accepted. In addition, there are textual issues as indicated in the notes.

58. There is uncertainty about 闉. Z&Q define it thus: "古代甕城的門" — and this is how I have taken it in the translation. BY, however, equates it with 堙 in the sense of 塞 so what is being relieved is the 池 only. LSL follows this interpretation.

59. 橐 is read as 風箱 following, for example, LSL.

60. Here 馮 is read as 憑 (see Z&Q) whilst 埴 is taken as 垣 (following SYR).

61. On 靈丁, CZM has: "其實乃瓴甋之音轉". See also RDSY/T, note 31, p. 233 who gives five possibilities before coming down in favour of a kind of fortification, and Z&Q (note 13, p. 804).

62. Following SYR, "火耳" is taken as "犬牙".

63. There are several issues and points of disagreement in this difficult sentence which are set out in detail in RDSY/T's note 33, pp. 233–234. I have broadly followed his interpretation but see also CZM for an alternative.

64. I have accepted Z&Q's comment that these five characters are part of an incomplete statement and are meaningless as they stand.

To relieve the city gate and the moat, use flaming torches in fighting. Bring in bellows. In addition, use brushwood to make a barrier between the outer and inner parapets.

Wide-bellied flasks (*lingding*) are placed at intervals of 3 *zhang*. And interdigitating "dog's teeth" are set up. One man is stationed every 10 *bu* within the brushwood [barrier], armed with a crossbow. Having prepared stakes (*gouxi*), [use them] to surround him.

52.12 救車火，為煙矢射火城門上，鑿扇上為棧，塗之，持水麻斗，革
盆救之[65]。門扇薄植，皆鑿半尺，一寸一涿弋，弋長二寸，見一
寸，相去七寸，厚塗之以備火。城門上所鑿以救門火者，各一垂
水，容三石以上，小大相雜。[66]

門植關必環鋼，以鋼金若鐵鍱之。[67] 門關再重，鍱之以鐵，必
堅。梳關，關二尺，梳關一覓，封以守印，時令人行貌封，及視
關入桓淺深。門者皆無得挾斧、斤、鑿、鋸、椎。

Comment: On sequence, several commentators change the position of this
section from here, where SYR and those modern editors who follow him (e.g.
LSL, MBJ, Z&Q) have it. In all cases, it is moved forward — WYJ, 52, paras 3
& 4, CZM #52.9 and #52.10, RDSY/T fragments 5 & 6 (part) where it follows
what is 52.4 above (more or less, depending on what changes are made in
that section). On subject matter, it is about the protection of gates from attack
by fire. I have taken the delivery of fire to be by flaming arrows (following, for
example, Z&Q) although RDSY/T speaks of "fire carriers". This depends on
how 車 is read — see note 65.

52.13 城上二步一渠，渠立程[68]，丈三尺，冠[69]長十丈，辟[70]長六尺。
二步一苔[71]，廣九尺，袤[72]十二尺。

二步置連梃[73]，長斧，長椎各一物；槍二十枚，周置二步中。

---

65. There are three issues in this first sentence: (i) Whether 車 should be emended to 薰
    (SYR, CZM) or to 載 (RDSY/T). (ii) Whether 煙 should be emended to 熛 (SYR) —
    Z&Q have this gloss on 煙矢: "帶火的箭矢" which I have followed. (iii) Whether 棧
    should be retained as "balcony" (RDSY/T) or read as 杙 ("post" or "stake" — SYR).
66. There is some doubt about this sentence. LSL, citing WNS and YTY, suggests that the
    first 10 characters may be misplaced. If this is so, it makes the remainder hard to
    understand. As it is, the reading given depends on two generally accepted emendations
    — 垂 to 甀 like 罋 and 火 to 容 (WNS).
67. In this sentence, the following emendations and readings are accepted: (i) 關 as 門門.
    (ii) 環鋼 as 穩固 (Z&Q). (iii) 鋼金 as 固金 (CZM).
68. Following SYR, 程 is taken as 桯 which he describes as "即渠之楨".
69. On 冠, SYR has this note: "冠，蓋渠之首。"
70. 辟 is taken as 臂, on which SYR has: "其橫出木也。"
71. CZM has this note on 苔: "苔即笘，係用竹草編織之物，可遮障敵矢。"
72. There is general agreement that 袤 should be read as 長 (e.g. LSL, Z&Q).
73. I have used RDSY's term "linked flail" for 連梃 — see his note 83, p. 97 (RDSY/T).
    See also CZM and Z&Q for helpful notes.

52.12 In seeking relief from attack by fire delivered by flaming arrows shot at the gates in the wall, drill [holes] above the leaves of the doors, make posts and cover them with earth. Prepare hempen ladles and hide buckets to contain water for relief. The door leaves, the door surrounds and the bars supporting the doors all have holes drilled in them to a depth of 1/2 *chi*. Every 1 *cun*, knock in one peg which is 2 *cun* in length and projects 1 *cun*. These [pegs] should be 7 *cun* apart and covered thickly with earth as a preparation against fire. Above the gates in the wall, holes are excavated for relief from fire, each one holding a container of water with a capacity of 3 *dan* or greater, with small and large containers mixed together. The gate bar and lever must be made strong by plating them with a strong metal like iron. The gate bolts should be double and coated with iron for they must be strong. The locking bar should be 2 *chi* long and there should be one lock. It is sealed by means of the Defender's seal. From time to time, men are sent to check whether the seal has been moved, and the depth of insertion of the bar into the supporting pillars. All those responsible for the gate are prohibited from carrying axes of any sort, chisels, saws or hammers.

52.13 On the wall, every 2 *bu*, there should be one *qu* shield with an upright pole 1 *zhang* 3 *chi* long. The top of the shield should be 10 *zhang* in length and its transverse arms 6 *chi* long. Every 2 *bu* there should be one protective screen (*da*) which is 9 *chi* wide and 12 *chi* high.

Every 2 *bu* place a linked flail (*lianting*), a long axe and a long hammer — one of each — and twenty javelins, these being spread over every 2 *bu*.

二步一木弩，必射五十步以上，及多為矢，節[74]毋以竹箭，
楛[75]、桃[76]、柘[77]、榆，可。蓋求齊鐵夫[78]，播[79]以射衝[80]及櫳
樅[81]。

二步積石，石重千[82]鈞以上者，五百枚。毋百，以亢[83]疾犂、
壁，皆可善方。[84]

二步積苙[85]，大一圍，長丈，二十枚。

Comment: In this continuing catalogue of implements and devices to be
placed on the wall, whether the preceding section is placed earlier (RDSY/T
includes it as part of his long fragment 6) or here, this and the following
sections are continuous. I have subdivided the list according to distance — 2
bu (52.13), 5–30 *bu* (52.14), 50 *bu* (52.15), and 100–200 *bu* (52.16). On the
devices considered in the present section, as RDSY points out, the *qu* shield
and *da* screen were very important components of the defensive apparatus —
see RDSY/SC, pp. 405–409 where there are diagrams of both. Also, on
'caltrops', RDSY/T writes: "Tribulus terrestris (caltrop) is a plant with sharp
spikes. It is unclear whether the Mohist is advocating the use of the plant itself
or wooden or iron spikes known also as 'caltrops'. The device was used
throughout Chinese history as an effective means to halt or slow either an
infantry or cavalry advance." — note 102, p. 100.

---

74. 節 is taken as 即 in the sense of 即使.
75. This tree is described in the ZWDCD #15505 where there are several references to its
    use for arrows.
76. SYR's emendation from 趙.
77. An emendation from the unknown character following SYR and Z&Q.
78. There are major emendations to this clause due mainly to SYR. These are: 蓋 to 益, 齊
    to 齏, and 夫 to 矢.
79. There is general acceptance of the reading of 布 in the sense of 分布 for 播.
80. This is the emendation proposed by BY and WNS for the unusual character ZWDCD
    #34888. 衝 is given in its earlier form (ZWDCD #34904). LSL has this note: "'射衝'
    當是一個詞，指設有木弩的通道。"
81. On *longcong* 櫳樅, CZM has: "櫳樅者用以窺伺之建築物。" See 52.16 for further
    description.
82. Emended from 中 following BY — see WYJ, note 83, p. 796. I have followed SYR in
    taking 千 as 十. See also Z&Q, note 1, p. 809.
83. Based on the《周禮 · 馬質》, 亢 is read as 禦.
84. There are two versions of this sentence. In the first, 白 is read as 石 and the situation is
    one in which stones are not available. In the second, following Lu Wenshao, 下 is added
    to give "毋下百" which is made part of the preceding sentence — i.e. ideally there
    should be 500 stones but not less than 100. See RDSY/T, notes 100 and 101, p. 100.
85. According to SYR, 苙 should be read as 苣.

Every 2 *bu* there should be one wooden crossbow which must be able to fire [an arrow] 50 *bu* or more. As well, there should be many arrows. If these are not of bamboo, [then wood from] the *hu*, the peach, the *zhe* or the elm will do.[viii] There should also be added a substantial collection of iron arrows which are distributed between the firing areas and the watchtowers (*longcong*).

Every 2 *bu* pile up stones, each stone weighing 10 *jun* or more, there being 500 stones. If there are no stones, use caltrops and tiles to withstand [the enemy]. Both of these can be good methods.

Every 2 *bu* have piles of reed torches, 1 *wei* (span) in size and 1 *zhang* long, 20 in all.

viii. On these timbers see RDSY/T, note 89, p. 98.

52.14 五步一罌，盛水有奚〔蠡〕⁸⁶，奚蠡大容一斗。

五步積狗屍五百枚，狗屍⁸⁷長三尺，喪以弟，瓮其端，堅約
弋。⁸⁸

十步積摶。大二圍以上，長八尺者二十枚。

二十五步一灶，灶有鐵鬵⁸⁹，容石以上者一，戒⁹⁰以為湯。及持
沙，毋下千石。

三十步置坐堠樓⁹¹；樓出於堞四尺，廣三尺，長⁹²四尺，板周三
面，密傅⁹³之，夏蓋其上。⁹⁴

Comment: This is a miscellaneous group of items — water containers,
firewood, furnaces, weapons (darts — although there is some question about
goushi), and a type of tower. RDSY/T provides a list of the different types of
tower described, identifying six in all — see his pp. 89–90. The *houlou* he calls
a "tower for sitting and watching".

52.15 五十步一藉車，藉車必為鐵纂⁹⁵。

五十步一井屏⁹⁶，周垣之，高八尺。

五十步一方⁹⁷，方尚必為關籥守之。

五十步積薪，毋下三百石，善蒙塗，毋令外火能傷也。

---

86. Added by WNS.
87. There are several views on what a 狗屍 "dog corpse" is. I have followed RDSY/T in
    taking it to be a form of "dart" — see his note 107, p. 101.
88. In this clause, 約 is read as 束 and 弋 is taken as 繳 or 繞 as elsewhere (CZM).
89. 鬵 is SYR's emendation of the variant of 鐂 (see ZWDCD #41797). The ZWDCD has
    a picture of a *qian* 鬵 — see vol. 10, p. 546.
90. 戒 here is read as 備 (Z&Q).
91. 堠 is BY's emendation of 侯. He has the following note:《通典 · 守拒法》有云：'御
    敵上建堠樓，以版跳出為櫓，與四外烽戍晝夜瞻覘'。"
92. Emended from 廣 following YY.
93. On 傅, SSX has: "傅，即塗也，所以防火。"
94. According to SSX, to protect against the sun.
95. On 纂, BY has: "説文云：'纂，治車軸也'。"
96. Following SYR, this is taken as 屏廁.
97. There is some variation in how 方 is understood. BY takes it as 房 whereas SYR takes
    it as 戸. I have followed the latter.

52.14   Every 5 *bu* there should be an earthenware water jar with a ladle to hold water which, in capacity, should contain 1 *dou* of water.

Every 5 *bu* there should be a pile of darts (*goushi*), 500 in all. The darts should be 3 *chi* long and covered over with rushes. The ends are sharpened and they are securely bound to a small wooden stake.

Every 10 *bu* there should be a pile of firewood, each pile being greater than 2 *wei* (spans) in circumference and 8 *chi* long, 20 piles in all.

Every 25 *bu* there should be one furnace with each furnace having an iron pot (*qian*) and each pot a capacity of greater than 1 *dan*. These can be used to prepare boiling water. As well, prepare sand — not less than 1000 *dan*.[ix]

Every 30 *bu* set up one observation tower (*houlou*), extending 4 *chi* beyond the parapet, 3 *chi* in width, and 4 *chi* long. It should be surrounded by wooden planking on three sides. Mud is used to conceal it, and in summer it is covered to protect it above.

52.15   Every 50 *bu* there should be one trebuchet (*jiche*). The axle of the trebuchet must be of iron.

Every 50 *bu* there should be a protected latrine completely surrounded by a wall 8 *chi* high.

Every 50 *bu* there should be a door. The door must have a locking mechanism above to defend it.

Every 50 *bu* there should be a pile of firewood of not less than 300 *dan*. It should be well covered with mud so fire from without cannot damage it.

---

ix.   The equivalences for the terms for weight are as follows: 1 *jin* 斤 = 244g; 1 *jun* 鈞 = 30 *jin*; 1 *dan* 石 = 4 *jun*.

Comment: Again, at 50 *bu*, there is something of a miscellany. A detailed description of the trebuchet including diagrams is given in RDSY/SC, pp. 203–231 and see also 52.26. It is not altogether clear what the "door" is. RDSY/T has "room".

52.16   百步一櫳樅[98]，起地高五丈，三層，下廣前面八尺，後十三尺，
其上稱議衰殺之[99]。

百步一木樓，樓廣前面九尺，高七尺，樓輣居坫[100]，出城十二
尺。

百步一井，井十甕，以木為繫連[101]，水器容四斗至六斗者百。

百步一積雜秆，大二圍以上者五十枚。

百步為櫓，櫓廣四尺，高八尺。為衝術[102]。

百步為幽殯[103]，廣三尺高四尺者千[104]。

二百步一立樓，城中廣二丈五尺二[105]，長二丈，出樞[106]五尺。

Comment: This completes the four sections with a recurring format listing various items under the heading of the frequency of occurrence, although similar descriptions are interspersed throughout the chapter. There are several quite obscure phrases or clauses as indicated in notes 98–106 inclusive. In these instances, the translation must be considered provisional. The *longcong* or watchtower is considered in RDSY/T's list referred to in the Comment to 52.14 whilst the *lu* shield is given detailed consideration in his note 138, pp. 108–109.

---

98. RDSY/T calls this a watchtower. Z&Q give the following modern equivalent: "每百步建一窺視敵人的建築物…"
99. This final phrase is incomprehensible as it stands. Following CZM, 議 is read as 宜 and 衰殺 as 減少. Z&Q have this note: "此句意思是酌度其適宜而逐漸減小。"
100. This is a very problematic phrase with the second and fourth characters unknown. Various suggestions are considered in detail by RDSY/T (note 132, pp. 106–108). I have settled for the combination of emendations proposed by SYR and BY.
101. There is uncertainty about 繫連. Some (e.g. RDSY/T, MBJ) follow SYR in taking this to be a reference to the "well-sweep" but this seems out of context here. Z&Q in their modern paraphrase have: "甕繫在木桿上。"
102. On "衝術", several modern editors quote SYR who has: "衝術，即上文之衝隊，隊，術一聲之轉。" LSL adds: "隊：通隧。"
103. The character usually found here is an ancient form of 殯 as above. See ZWDCD #30669 and #42831 as well as SYR and Z&Q, note 8, p. 813.
104. According to SYR 千 should either be emended to 一 or omitted.
105. There is general agreement that 二 should be omitted.
106. On 樞, SYR has: "'樞'疑當作'拒'，謂立樓之橫距，出堞外者五尺。"

52.16   Every 100 *bu* have 1 watchtower which rises from the ground 5 *zhang*. It should have three levels. Its width at the bottom should be 8 *chi* at the front and 13 *chi* at the book. As it gets higher, it should become narrower according to circumstances.

Every 100 *bu* have a wooden tower. The width of the tower should be 9 *chi* across the front surface and its height 7 *chi*. The tower's chimney and screen are to be 12 *chi* away from the wall.

Every 100 *bu* have one well. Each well should have 10 water containers which are attached to a wooden post. The capacity of the water containers should range from 4 to 6 *dou* [and there should be] a hundred [of them].

Every 100 *bu* there should be one pile of straw of different lengths — fifty bundles of a circumference greater than 2 *wei* (spans).

Every 100 *bu* there should be a *lu* shield. The *lu* shield should be 4 *chi* wide and 8 *chi* high. They are for approaching the enemy in tunnels.

Every 100 *bu* there should be a concealed drain, 3 *chi* wide and 4 *chi* deep.

Every 200 *bu* there should be one standing tower (*lilou*). The part within the wall should be 2 *zhang* 5 *chi* high whilst the part that projects crosswise should be 5 *chi*.[x]

---

x.   I am uncertain about this sentence. For an alternative reading see RDSY/T.

52.17 城上廣三步到四步，乃可以為使鬥。俾倪廣三尺，高二尺五寸。
陛[107] 高二尺五〔寸〕，廣長各三尺，遠[108] 廣各六尺。城上四隅童
異[109] 高五尺，四尉[110] 舍焉。

城上七尺一渠，長丈五尺，貍[111] 三尺，去堞五寸，夫[112] 長丈二
尺，臂長六尺。半植一鑿，內後長五寸[113]。夫兩鑿，渠夫前端下
堞四寸而適。貍渠，鑿坎[114]，覆以瓦，冬日以馬夫寒[115]，皆待
命，若以瓦為坎。

城上千步一表[116]，長丈，棄水者操表搖之。五十步一廁，與下同
圂。之廁者，不得操。

Comment: On sequence, RDSY/T has the first four sentences as part of his
fragment 6 whilst CZM has them as his #52.33–#52.36. The rest of the section
corresponds to RDSY/T's fragment 7 and to CZM's #52.37–#52.39. Once
again, there is something of a miscellany of items but the most clearly
described is the *qu* shield. This has already been described in slightly
different terms in 52.9. It was a most important component of the defensive
armamentarium, as RDSY/SC points out. He provides a detailed description
including a diagram on pp. 405–407.

52.18 城上三十步一藉車，當隊者不用。[117]

---

107. Here 陛 is read as 階 in the sense of 臺階 ["steps", "ascent"].
108. There is general acceptance of SYR's emendation of 遠 to 道.
109. I have followed LSL here in reading 童 as 小 and 異 as 廙, defined by the 《說文》 "行
     屋".
110. I have taken 尉 in the general sense, i.e. the four men each responsible for one section
     of the wall. "四尉" later became an official designation, but not related to defence
     against military attack — see Hucker #7657 and #5807.
111. As elsewhere, 貍 is taken as 埋.
112. 夫 here is read as 膚, which Z&Y glosses as "指露出部分".
113. SYR has the following note on these five characters: "疑當作'內徑寸'，此'徑'誤為
     '後'，又衍'長'字，遂不可通。"
114. In relation to the rather puzzling four characters, YTY has: "樹渠之地坎。"
115. 夫 here is read as 矢 in the sense of 屎 and 寒 is read as 塞 (SYR, Z&Q).
116. In this clause, I have followed SYR in emending 干 to 十 and YTY in reading 表 as 柱.
117. There are three issues with this statement. First, elsewhere *jiche* (trebuchets) are placed
     every 20 or 50 *bu*. Second, there is the question of whether 隊 should be taken as 隧 (隧
     道) as, for example, CZM and Z&Q propose. RDSY/T thinks not — see his note 169,
     p. 122. Third, there is SYR's suggestion of the addition of 此數 after 用 which most
     commentators accept.

52.17   The top of the wall should be 3 to 4 *bu* wide to allow fighting to take place on it. On it there should be a small wall with holes for observation (embrasure) and this should be 3 *chi* wide and 2 *chi* 5 *cun* high. The steps should be 2 *chi* 5 *cun* high and their width and length should both be 3 *chi*. The width of the ascent should, in each case, be 6 *chi*. On the four corners of the wall there should be small dwellings 5 *chi* in height where the four commandants reside.

On the wall, every 7 *chi*, there should be one *qu* shield, 1 *zhang* 5 *chi* long and buried to a depth of 3 *chi*. It should extend beyond the parapet for 5 *cun* [so] the exposed part is 1 *zhang* 2 *chi* long and the [horizontal] arms are 6 *chi* long. In the middle of the wooden surface a hole is drilled with an internal diameter of 5 *cun*. Drill a second hole. The front end of the shield should be lower than the parapet by 4 *cun*, this being appropriate. Drill the *qu* shield and excavate a hole, then cover it with tiles. On winter days, block it with horse dung. Then await orders for its use. Alternatively, use tiles to make the pit.

On the wall, every 10 *bu*, there should be one post 1 *zhang* in length. In the case of those hurling water, they grasp the post to throw it. Every 50 *bu* there should be a latrine. The latrines on or below the wall are places for the accumulation of filth. Those entering a latrine should not be carrying anything.

52.18   On the wall, every 30 *bu*, there should be one trebuchet. When confronting tunnelling, do not use this number.

城上五十步一道陛，高二尺五寸，長十步。城上五十步一樓撕[118]，撕勇勇必重。[119]

土樓[120]百步一，外門發樓[121]，左右渠[122]之。為樓加藉幕，棧上出之以救外。[123]

城上皆毋得有室，若也可依匿者，盡除去之。

城下州道內，百步一積薪[124]，毋下三千[125]石以上，善塗之。

城上十人一什長，屬一吏士，一帛尉[126]。

百步一亭，高垣丈四尺，厚四尺，為閨門兩扇，令各可以自閉。〔亭一尉〕[127]，尉必取有重厚忠信可任事者。

Comment: In terms of sequence, 52.18 corresponds to CZM's #52.40–#52.47, to the major part of RDSY/T's fragment 8, and in WYJ to the second half of 52, para 10 and all of 52, para 11. There are several points of contention as follows: (i) In the first statement, whether 隊 is retained as (battle-) line or taken to indicate tunnelling (as 隧道). (ii) Whether *kongyong* is, in fact, the name of a tower as RDSY/T suggests. (iii) In the third statement, whether SYR is right in taking this to be a description of a suspended door or whether it is, in reality, some kind of shooting tower as proposed by RDSY/T. (iv) The amount of firewood — 3000 *dan* does seem an awful lot! (v) Whether the first sentence of 52.19 should be included in this section — although this is a minor issue.

118. This is SYR's emendation. See also Z&Q, note 2, p. 816.

119. Following SSX, 勇 should read 樓. SYR proposes this version: "樓撕必再重". RDSY/T suggests that *kongyong* is the name of a type of tower and retains it in a transliterated form.

120. I have followed CZM in reading 土樓 as 木樓.

121. On 發樓, SYR has: "疑亦為縣門也".

122. According to SSX, 渠 should be emended to 斬.

123. There is some doubt about this clause. I have followed Z&Q's reading which includes CZM's taking of 棧 as 橋道.

124. See WYJ, note 156, p. 806 on the emendation of 藉 to 薪.

125. 千 here may be a mistake for 百 — see RDSY/T, note 179, p. 124.

126. On 帛尉, SYR has: "疑當云'百人一百尉'。" Several commentators suggest emending 帛 to 亭 — see, for example, LSL, note 3, p. 476.

127. These three characters, present in the DZ (and SYR), are not included in all texts. I have followed CZM and LSL in including them. The latter has this note: "上文說'五步一亭'，知亭尉即是百長。"

On the wall, every 50 *bu*, there should be one set of steps (staircase). The height (of the steps) should be 2 *chi* 5 *cun* and the length (overall) 10 *bu*. On the wall, every 50 *bu*, there should be one small tower and this must have two levels.

There should be one wooden tower every 100 *bu* with an external suspended door. On either side there should be a pit. A screen should be added to the tower and there should be a wooden walkway for the purpose of rescue from the outside.

On the wall, there should be no other buildings at all. Certainly, any building in which people can conceal themselves must be completely removed.

Placed in a circle around the wall at 100 *bu* intervals, there should be collections of firewood, each collection being not less than 3000 (?300) *dan* or greater, with earth used to seal them up.

On the wall, every 10 men should have a file leader (platoon commander), the file leaders should be under a subordinate officer and there should be one post captain.

Every 100 *bu* there should be one post (*ting*). The height of the walls should be 1 *zhang* 4 *chi* and the thickness 4 *chi*. The doors should have two leaves which can be opened and closed independently. Each post should have one commander (captain). Those chosen for this position must be reliable and trustworthy men who can bear the responsibility.

52.19 二舍共一井爨，灰、康、枇[128]、杯馬矢，皆謹收藏之。[129]

城上之備：渠譫[130]、藉車、行棧、行樓、到，頡皋、連梃、長斧、長椎、長茲、距、飛衝、縣〔 〕[131]，批屈[132]。樓五十步一。堞下為爵穴，三尺而一。為薪皋，二圍長四尺半必有潔。[133]

瓦石：重二升[134]以上，城上沙，五十步一積。灶置鐵鬵[135]焉，與沙同處。

木大二圍，長丈二尺以上，善耿其本，名曰長從，五十步三十[136]。木橋長三丈，毋下五十。復使卒急為壘壁，以蓋瓦復之。

用瓦木罌，容十升[137]以上者，五十步而十，盛水，且用之。五十二者十步而二。[138]

Comment: This is another miscellaneous collection of things that should be on the wall. It corresponds to CZM #52.48–#52.57, the major part of RDSY/T fragment 9, the rest of which corresponds to what is here the final statement in 52.3, and WYJ 52, para 12. The points of particular interest or uncertainty are, in sequence, as follows: (i) On 舍, CZM has "孫云，舍即什長及尉所居。" (ii) In the list of "things prepared", the main problem is *piqu* — what this might be. (iii) The question of whether, with 薪皋, well-sweeps are being referred to

---

128. More usually written with the 米 radical — ZWDCD #27473.
129. The reading of this statement depends on several emendations and interpretations as follows: (i) SYR takes the "two lodgings" to be those of the 什長 and the 百尉. (ii) Taking 康 as 糠. (iii) Taking 杯 as 稃 (SYR). (iv) Taking 矢 as 屎.
130. Following WNS and SYR, Z&Q take this as 帷幔 — see their note 5, p. 818.
131. I have followed SYR's suggestion of 梁 for the lacuna.
132. It is quite unclear what a *piqu* 批屈 is, or even if it is one thing. Thus, YTY takes *pi* 批 to be some sort of striking weapon and punctuates with 屈 as the start of the next sentence. Like RDSY/T, I have simply transliterated it as a two-component term — see his detailed note 203, pp. 131–132.
133. The punctuation of the preceding 26 characters is uncertain. As given above, the final sentence is rather problematical, particularly the last three characters — see Comment.
134. Emended to 斤 following WNS — see WYJ, note 186, pp. 809–810.
135. See 52.14, note 89 above.
136. This is a problem sentence. My translation of it is based on Z&Q who accept SYR's equating of "長從" with "櫳樅" — he has: "疑與上文櫳樅義同". On *longcong*, Z&Q have: "用以窺伺敵人的建築物。" Also, and again on the basis of what has gone before, 三十 is emended to 一.
137. Read as 斗 following SYR.
138. According to SYR, this sentence should read: "五斗以上者，十步而二。"

52.19   Two lodgings should share one well and one furnace. Ashes, chaff, grain husks and horse dung are all carefully collected and stored.

On the wall, the things that are prepared are as follows: shielding screens (shields and screens), trebuchets, trestle bridges, moveable towers, chopping tools, well-sweeps, linked flails, long axes, long hammers, long hoes, rams, attack carts (flying battering-rams), suspended bridges and *piqu*. There should be one tower every 50 *bu*. Below the parapet make holes, one every 3 *chi*. Make well-sweeps with a circumference of 4 $\frac{1}{2}$ *chi* such that they can be moved by the strength of one man.

Have tiles and stones to a weight greater than 2 *jin*.

On the wall, there should be sand, one pile every 50 *bu*. A furnace is set up with an iron vessel on it and with the sand in the same place.

Pieces of timber of 2 *wei* in circumference and of lengths greater than 1 *zhang* 2 *chi* are skilfully joined together [to make] what is called a watchtower. Every 50 *bu* there should be one.

There should be wooden bridges 3 *zhang* in length, and not less than 50 of these. They can be used to send men for urgent construction of a breastwork which is covered with tiles.

Use earthenware or wood to make pitchers which have a capacity of 10 *dou* or more. There should be ten of these every 50 *bu*. Fill them with water in readiness for use. [Also], every 10 *bu* there should be two pitchers with a capacity of 5 *dou* or more.

(see, for example, Z&Q), or some kind of torch (e.g. RDSY/T), or even two separate things (CZM), and what the final part of this statement indicates. (iv) There is the issue of what *longcong* are. My reading essentially follows SYR. RDSY/T, however, takes these to be spears of some sort and retains 三十一 i.e. 30 every 50 *bu*.

52.20   城下里中家人，各葆其左右前後，如城上。城小人眾，葆離鄉老弱國中及也[139] 大城。

寇至，度必攻，主人先削城編[140]，唯勿燒。寇在城下，時換吏卒署，而毋換其養，養毋得上城。寇在城下，收諸盆甕，耕[141] 積之城下，百步一積，積五百。

城門內不得有室，為周官桓吏，四尺為倪。行棧內閈[142]，二關一堞。[143]

除城場[144] 外，去池百步，牆垣樹木小大俱壞伐，除去之。寇所從來若昵道，傒[145] 近，若城場，皆為扈樓，立竹箭天[146] 中。

Comment: This section which, as constituted above, comprises a miscellaneous series of quite clear instructions is placed here in SYR's text and in the modern editions of LSL, MBJ and Z&Q, although divided into subsections corresponding to the paragraphs above. CZM, WYJ and RDSY/T, however, all make significant changes as summarised below:

i.   CZM: 52.20 above is transferred to chapter 70 as his #70.28–#70.34. 52.21 below is transferred to chapter 70 as his #70.35 apart from the final character 守 which he makes the start of his #70.36. In the present text this is 70.19.

ii. WYJ: Both 52.20 and 52.21 are transferred to chapter 70 as the bulk of his 70, para 6 interposed between what in the present text are 70.18 and 70.19.

---

139. 也 here is read as 他 in the sense of 其他.
140. On this clause, SYR has: "此蓋言先除附城室廬。"
141. There is general acceptance of BY's reading of 耕 as 構 or 搆.
142. There is general agreement that 閈 should be emended to 閉.
143. There are several issues in these two sentences apart from the emendation suggested in the previous note. In the translation, I have followed LSL — see his notes 1–4, p. 480.
144. Following SYR, 場 is taken as 道.
145. Again following SYR, 係 is read as 蹊.
146. There is general acceptance of the emendation of 天 to 水.

52.20 Family members who live in the wards below the wall are each required to protect those to their left and right, front and rear, just like those on the wall. When the city is small but the people are many, for protection send those who are old and frail to the capital as well as to other large cities.

When the enemy comes, and it is judged that they must attack, the commander [of the defence] first [orders the] destruction of the dwellings near to the wall, but not that they be burned. When the enemy is below the wall, he should change the duties of the officers and soldiers at the appropriate times but not change their support personnel. The support personnel must not be on the wall.

When the enemy is below (outside) the wall, there should be a collection of all bowls and jars which are then piled beneath the wall. Have one pile every 100 *bu* with five hundred items per pile.

Within the gate of the wall there must not be houses. The housing for senior officers responsible for defence must be closely guarded and places must be established for the support staff. The buildings should have parapets 4 *chi* high. The main gate should always be closed, with two men to defend the gate and one man for each parapet.

The road outside the city should be kept clear and, in the area for 100 *bu* beyond the moat, walls and trees, whether large or small, should be destroyed or cut down and then done away with. On the routes by which the enemy might approach, whether the main road or other thoroughfares, there should be large towers, and bamboo arrows should be set up in the water [of the moat].

iii. RDSY/T: Fragment 92 ends with the first sentence of what in the present text is the first sentence of 70.20. Fragment 93 contains all of 52.20 and the first sentence of 52.21 minus the final character (先 / 失). Fragment 94 then continues with the remainder of what is 70.20 below.

52.21 守堂下為大樓，高臨城，堂下周散。道中應客，客待見，時召三老在葆[147]宮中者，與計事得先[148]。行德計謀合[149]，乃入葆。葆入守，無行城，無離舍。諸守者，審知卑城淺池，而錯守焉。晨暮卒歌[150]以為度，用人少易守。[151]

Comment: This section is also involved in the transfer to chapter 70 by some editors – see Comment to the previous section. CZM makes this section his #70.35, WYJ includes it in his 70, para 6, whilst RDSY/T has the first sentence only combined with the previous section as his fragment 93.

52.22 守法：五十步丈夫十人，丁女二十人，老小十人，計之五十步四十人。城下樓卒，率一步一人，二十步二十人[152]。城小大以此率之，乃足以守圍[153]。

Comment: This and the following two sections are treated as a single fragment by RDSY/T (fragment 51), as two paragraphs by WYJ (52, paras 16, 17) and as four sections by CZM (#52.67–70). RDSY/T, however, believes these sections to be misplaced in chapter 52 and raises the possibility of their origin from chapter 70 (see his p. 344). I have chosen to treat them as three sections in line with modern Chinese editions (LSL, MBJ, Z&Q). In the first, "守法" is taken as a heading which applies either to this section alone or to all three sections — i.e. up to the final statement of 52.24. The present section is clear and is about the numbers of defenders to be present on the wall.

---

147. As elsewhere in this chapter, 葆 is taken as 保.
148. There is general agreement that 先 here should be read as 失.
149. In this clause, 德 is emended to 得. SYR has this note: "謂所行既得，計謀又相合，乃聽其入葆城也 。"
150. Following SYR, 歌 is taken as 鼓.
151. The preceding 43 characters are transferred from DZ 71 — see SYR, pp. 739–740.
152. On the emendations proposed for this sentence see WYJ's detailed note 240, p. 817.
153. Emended from 圍 following WNS — see WYJ, note 241, p. 817.

52.21   Below the Defender's hall, construct a large tower which is high and near the wall and has free access on all sides below the building. If visitors come, they are met in the middle of the road. And the visitors must wait to be seen. At the appropriate time, three elders are summoned to the defence headquarters to take part in the planning for the outcome (success or failure). When their policies are to be used and the plans and stratagems are in accord, then they enter the defence area. Having entered the defence area, they are not allowed to go onto the wall, nor to leave their dwellings. Those of the defenders who have a good knowledge of the height of the wall and the depth of the moat set up the defence. Morning and evening, the drum is sounded to stir on [the defenders]. Young men are used for ease of defence.

52.22   Methods of defence: Every 50 *bu* there should be ten able-bodied young men, twenty able-bodied young women, and ten old people and children, giving a total of forty people every 50 *bu*. With respect to soldiers for the towers below the wall, there should be uniformly one every *bu*, so, for 20 *bu*, there are twenty men. Whether the city is large or small, if this is taken as the standard, it will be enough to defend a besieged [city].

52.23 客馮面而蛾傅之[154]，主人則先之知，主人利，客適[155]。客攻以
遂[156]，十萬物[157]之眾，攻無過四[158]隊者，上術廣五百步，中術
三百步，下術五十步。諸不盡百五步[159]者，主人利而客病。廣五
百步之隊，丈夫千人，丁女子二千人，老小千人，凡四千人，而
足以應之，此守術之數也。使老小不事者，守於城上不當術者。

Comment: This is treated as two sections by CZM who takes the first
sentence as one section (#52.68) and the remainder as the other section (#52.
69). There is some merit in this since two different forms of attack are
apparently being considered — the ant approach (mass infantry assault) and
the single line attack in waves.

52.24 城持[160]出必為明填[161]，令吏民皆智知[162]之。從一[163]人百人以
上，持出不操填章，從人非其故人[164]，乃其積[165]章也，千人之將
以上止之，勿令得行。行及吏卒從之，皆斬，具以聞於上[166]。此
守城之重禁之。夫姦之所生也，不可不審也。

Comment: This is CZM's #52.70 and is given as a separate paragraph by
WYJ (52, para 17). RDSY/T comments on this, which is the fourth paragraph
in his fragment 51, that it "... perhaps belongs to a separate fragment, (and)
gives the procedure to be followed when the Mohist Defender and his retinue
leave the town or city after the successful defence." (p. 344)

---

154. In this clause, 客 is taken as 敵人, 馮 is read as 憑, 面 taken as 四面 and 蛾傅 rendered
     "ant approach" as considered in chapter 63.
155. In line with what follows, SYR suggests 客適 should be 客病. 病 is taken as 不利
     (Z&Q).
156. On 遂, CZM has: "遂猶令言隊伍展開線。"
157. 物 is regarded as superfluous.
158. See RDSY/T, note 176, p. 347 on the possible emendation of 四 to 三.
159. Following SYR, 百五步 is corrected to 百五十步.
160. Following SYR, 持 is taken as 將.
161. Following SYR, 填 is taken as 旗.
162. One of the two preceding characters is regarded as superfluous. 智, if it is retained, is
     read as 知.
163. 一人 is taken as 十人 (SYR).
164. 故人 is taken as 部屬.
165. As with 填, 積 is taken as 旗.
166. Here 聞 is understood as 報告 and 上 as 上司.

52.23   When the enemy relies on the "ant approach" (mass infantry assault) from four sides, if the leader of the defence knows this beforehand, it is to his advantage and the enemy's disadvantage. If the enemy attacks in lines, and the number is one hundred thousand, then the attack does not exceed four lines. At the most, the width of the front is 500 *bu*, whilst the intermediate front is 300 *bu* and the smallest front is 50 *bu*. When it does not exceed 150 *bu*, then the leader of the defence is at an advantage and the enemy is at a disadvantage. In the case of a 500 *bu* front, use one thousand able-bodied men, two thousand able-bodied women, and one thousand old people and children, giving four thousand in all, which is sufficient to meet them. These are the numbers for defending against a front. And let the old people and children who do not serve [at the front itself], defend on the wall but not face the front.

52.24   When a city's general goes forth, he must have a clear signal flag to let the officers and people all know of it. When he has a retinue of anything from ten men to over a hundred men, or if a general goes forth but does not carry a signal flag, or if the retinue is not composed of his own troops, or does not have a signal flag, the general leading a thousand men or more stops him and does not let him proceed. If he does go forth, and officers and soldiers follow him, they are all beheaded. All this is made known to the commander. These are important prohibitions in the defence of a city. That traitorous elements may arise is something that must be given careful attention.

52.25 城上為爵穴，下堞三尺，廣其外[167]，五步一。爵穴大容苣[168]，高
者六尺，下者三尺，疏數自適為之[169]。塞[170]外塹，去格七尺，為
縣梁。城狹[171]陝不可塹者，勿塹。城上三十步一聾[172]灶。人擅
苣長五節[173]。寇在城下，聞鼓音，燔苣，復鼓，內苣爵穴中，照
外。

Comment: In terms of arrangement, this section corresponds to RDSY/T's
fragment 11. CZM divides it into four parts and has a slightly different order.
His #52.97 includes sentences 1 and 2 describing the torch-holes or "goblets"
previously mentioned in 52.19 above. His #52.98 includes sentences 5 and 6
keeping the subject of torches together. His #52.99 includes sentences 3 and
4 on the topic of ditches. His #52.100 is the brief sentence on the movable
furnaces which is found in the same form in 52.9 above.

52.26 諸藉車皆鐵什[174]，藉車之柱長丈七尺，其狸[175]者四尺，夫[176]長
三丈以上，至三丈五尺，馬頰[177]長二尺八寸，試藉車之力而為之
困[178]，失[179]四分之三在上。

藉車，夫長三尺[180]，四之三[181]在上，馬頰在三分中。馬頰長二尺
八寸，夫長二十四尺，以下不用。治困以大車輪。[182]藉車桓長丈
二尺半[183]，諸藉車皆鐵什。復車者在之。[184]

---

167. On "廣其外" SSX has: "此言爵穴之法，廣外則狹內，令下毋兒上，上兒下也。"
168. Taken as 苣 (WYZ).
169. On this clause, Z&Q have: "疏數：指爵穴的疏密度。自：為'視'之誤。"
170. There is general acceptance of SYR's proposed emendation of 塞 to 穿.
171. Following WYZ, 狹 replaces the unknown character usually found here.
172. This character is variously written in different texts — see RDSY/T, note 360, p. 180.
173. In this clause, 擅 is taken as 撣 and 節 as 尺 (SYR).
174. There is broad agreement that 鐵什 should read 鐵鍱 — see, for example, Z&Q.
175. Understood as 埋 in this and related passages.
176. 夫 here and in the following sentence is taken as 膚.
177. On the *majia* 馬頰 CZM has: "依下文則藉車係用投擲損害敵人之物，似藉膚之彈
      力，將損害品擲向城下來。"
178. Following Z&Q, 困 is read as 梱 in the sense of 款.
179. Read as 夫 following SYR.
180. 尺 here should be emended to 丈 (SYR).
181. "四之三" should read "四之三".
182. There is uncertainty about the precise meaning of this sentence.
183. In translating this clause I have followed Z&Q — see their note 9, p. 827.
184. SYR's proposed emendations — 復 to 後 and 在 to 左 in the sense of 佐 — are accepted.

52.25   On the wall, "goblets" are excavated, 3 *chi* below the parapets. They are wide at the opening and narrow within, and there should be one every 5 *bu*. A "goblet" can contain a flaming reed torch. The highest "goblets" are at a height of 6 *chi* and the lowest at 3 *chi*. The spacing is determined by the requirement of seeing what is going on. Outside the wall, a ditch is dug at a distance of 7 *chi* from the wall and there is a suspended bridge (drawbridge). If the area outside the wall is too narrow and a ditch cannot be dug, do not have a ditch. On the wall, every 30 *bu* there should be one movable furnace (*longzao*) and each person grasps a torch 5 *chi* in length. If the enemy is outside the wall, when the sound of the drum is heard, the torches are lit. When the drum sounds a second time, the torches are placed in the "goblets" and illuminate the outside.

52.26   The various trebuchets all have iron bands, their pillars are 1 *zhang* 7 *chi* long, and they are buried to a depth of 4 *chi*. Their [throwing] arms are greater than 3 *zhang* and up to 3 *zhang* 5 *chi*. Their slings (*majia*) are 2 *chi* 8 *cun* long. The trebuchets's strength is tested using a wooden bar [to strike against]. Three quarters of the arm [of the trebuchets] lie above [the pivot].

In the case of the trebuchets, the arm is 3 *zhang* in length and three parts in four are above [the pivot]. The sling is situated in the centre of the exposed three quarters. The sling must be 2 *chi* 8 *cun* in length. The arm should be 24 *chi* in length. Less than this it is of no use. Control (?construct) the pivot with large cart wheels. The trebuchets's posts are 1 *zhang* 2$\frac{1}{2}$ *chi* in length. Every trebuchet has iron bands. Behind there is a supporting cart.

Comment: This section comprises two essentially identical descriptions of the *jiche* or trebuchet. CZM has them as a single section as above (#52.101) whilst RDSY/T has two separate fragments (12 and 13). For a detailed description of this device through history see RDSY/SC, pp. 203–230, particularly, in the present context, pp. 207–209. In the descriptions above, there is uncertainty about the final sentence.

52.27 寇闉池來[185]，為作水甬[186]，深四尺，堅慕貍之，十尺一，覆以瓦而待令。以木大圍長二尺四分而早[187]鑿之，置炭火其中而合慕之，而以藉車投之。為疾犂投，長二尺五寸，大二圍以上。涿弋[188]，弋長七寸，弋間六寸，剡其末。[189] 狗走[190]，廣七寸，長尺八寸，蚤長四寸，犬耳[191]施之。

Comment: CZM treats this section as four fragments (#52.102–#52.105) corresponding respectively to filling in the moat, the use of caltrops, wooden spikes, and *gouzou* which are taken as stakes. RDSY/T, however, has this as a separate and complete fragment (his fragment 30) which he suggests might be a displaced fragment from a presumably lost chapter on 堙 or "mounding in the moat". In this, he links it with 52.11 above. WYJ has it as the second part of his penultimate paragraph (i.e. 52, para 23) which is the same placement as here.

52.28 子墨子曰：「守城之法，必數城中之木，十人之所舉為十挈[192]，五人之所舉為五挈，凡輕重以挈為人數。為薪樵[193]挈，壯者有

---

185. "闉池" is glossed as "填塞護城河" by LSL.
186. SYR has the following note on "水甬"：" 水甬，蓋漏水器 ". LSL writes："水甬——一種漏水器具。中間空，可使水通過。"
187. SYR's emendation to 中 is generally accepted.
188. There is some question about this character here and in the immediately subsequent two uses. 弋 is BY's proposal for what is also given as 杙 (e.g. WYJ and RDSY/T — see their notes 398, p. 835 and 12, p. 229 respectively), 代 or 戈 (e.g. Z&Q).
189. In this sentence, there is doubt about the initial character. LSL suggests 豕 for 涿. Z&Q have："涿弋；門丁".
190. CZM has the following for "狗走"："似屬鉤曲之器，故有蚤 (爪) 長。"
191. 耴 is read as 牙 following SYR.
192. There is some uncertainty about 挈. SYR takes it to be some kind of utensil for lifting or carrying wood whereas CZM takes it to be a variable unit of weight. I have followed the latter.
193. This character, written with radical #140 (i.e. ZWDCD #33316) is generally accepted as 樵.

52.27   When the enemy attacks by filling in the moat, make water jars (*shuiyong*) which are 4 *chi* deep, firmly sealed and buried in the ground, there being one every 10 *chi*. Cover them with an earthenware cover and await the order [for their use]. Use pieces of wood 1 *wei* in circumference and 2 *chi* 4 *fen* long and make a hollow in the centre. In this, place burning charcoal and cover it. Then, using a trebuchet, project it [at the enemy]. Make [bundles of] caltrops to cast [at the enemy], 2 *chi* 5 *cun* long and 2 *wei* or above in size. [Above the gates] fix wooden spikes, the spikes being 7 *cun* long with a gap of 6 *cun* between spikes. Their ends ·are sharpened. Have stakes (*gouzou*) which are 7 *cun* wide and 1 *chi* 8 *cun* long with a "claw" 4 *cun* long. Set them like dog's teeth (interdigitating).

52.28   Master Mo Zi said: "Among the methods of defending a city, there must be a calculation of the amount of wood within the city wall. That which ten men can carry is 10 *qie*. That which five men can carry is 5 *qie*. In general, the amount is determined by the number

挈，弱者有挈，皆稱其任。凡挈輕重所為，吏人[194] 各得其任。城
中無食則為大殺[195]。」

Comment: This is given as the penultimate section here but recent Chinese
editions combine it with the next section — for example, WYJ, MBJ, LSL and
Z&Q. In fact, the last two include it in the statement attributed to Mo Zi. CZM
has it separately as his #52.106 and this is the arrangement followed here.
RDSY/T, who has it as his fragment 14, writes: "It seems to me unlikely that this
66-graph fragment (possibly two strips of 33 graphs each) originally belonged
in the section 'Pei Ch'eng' (*Bei Cheng*). I suspect that it may have been in the
miscellaneous section 'Tsa Shou' (*Za Shou*). Since its location remains
obscure, however, I refrain from moving it."

52.29   去城門五步大塹之，高地三丈下地至[196]，施賊[197] 其中，上為發
梁，而機巧之，比傅[198] 薪上，使可道行，旁有溝壘，毋為踰越，
而出佻且比[199]，適人遂入，引機發梁，適人可禽[200]，適人恐懼而
有疑心，因而離。

Comment: In all the texts studied, this is the final component of chapter 52.
CZM has it as his #52.107 whilst for RDSY/T it is fragment 15. The latter does,
however, raise the possibility that it may be displaced from one of the lost
chapters.

----

194. 吏人 is understood as 使人 following SSX.
195. Read as 減 following BY.
196. Modern commentators accept WYZ's emendation of this sentence to read: "高地丈五
     尺，下地至泉，三尺而止。" based on chapter 62.
197. LSL takes 賊 as some kind of weapon ("指能傷害人的東西⋯"), although WYZ
     equates it with 棧, presumably in the sense of something to walk on. SYR takes it as 杙
     which RDSY/T follows, rendering it as "stakes". I have accepted this.
198. 傅 is read as 敷 following SSX.
199. According to WYZ this clause should read: "而出佻戰而北" with 佻 in the sense of 挑
     戰 and 北 in the sense of 敗逃 — see Z&Q.
200. Generally accepted by modern commentators as 擒.

of men. In respect to what constitutes a *qie* of firewood and fuel, those who are strong have their *qie* and those who are weak have their *qie*, this being designated as their responsibility. So, in each case, the actual weight of the *qie* determines what each person takes as their responsibility. If there is no food in the city, then the magnitude (of the *qie*) is reduced."

52.29   At a distance of 5 *bu* beyond the city gates, there should be a large trench. Where the ground is high, dig it 1 *zhang* 5 *chi* deep and where the ground is low, it should go down until there is water, or 3 *chi*, and then stop. Set up stakes in the middle. Above it, have a suspended bridge (drawbridge) with a concealed mechanism to control its movement. The upper surface (of the bridge) should be covered with brushwood and earth so that it looks like a path. On either side, there should be a ditch that cannot be jumped across. (The defenders) should go forth to challenge the enemy and feign defeat so the enemy pursues them to enter (the city). Then activate the bridge mechanism so the enemy can be seized. The enemy then becomes fearful and stricken with doubt, and so retreats.

53: 備高臨[1]

Comment: The text given for this chapter is that of the DZ (with the emendations indicated) and is the same as found in WYJ (in 2 paragraphs), CZM (in 4 sections) and the modern editions of MBJ, LSL and Z&Q. RDSY/T has what is here 53.1 as his fragment 23, then follows this with what in the present work is 71.1 and the opening sentence of 71.2 as his fragment 24, before proceeding to what is 53.2 below as his fragments 25 & 26. For the reasons behind this arrangement see his pp. 193–194.

53.1 禽子再拜再拜曰:「敢問適人積土為高,以臨吾城,薪土俱上,以為羊黔,蒙櫓俱前,遂屬之城,兵弩俱上,為之奈何?」子墨子曰:「子問〔羊黔之守邪?〕[2] 羊黔者將之拙者也,足以勞卒[3],不足以害城。守為臺城,以臨羊黔,左右出距[4],各二十尺,行城三十尺,強弩〔射〕[5]之,技機藉之,奇器〔 〕〔 〕[6]之,然則羊黔之攻敗矣。」

----

1. It is not altogether clear from the title, or indeed from the text, whether two methods of defence ("terrace walls", "joined crossbows") against one form of attack (the building of an earth bank against the wall) is being described in this chapter, or two methods of defence against two methods of attack (sheep's bank ramp and *lin* or "approacher"). It must also be possible that the section on the *yangqian* is misplaced here and what is being described is one method of defence (the "joined crossbow" or multiple-bolt arcuballista) against one method of attack (the *lin* or "approacher"). For a general discussion of the latter, taken to be a wheeled siege tower first recorded in the 《詩經》 (Mao #241, LCC, vol. 3, pp. 454–455), see RDSY/SC, pp. 437–441.
2. Added following WYZ — see WYJ, note 7, p. 839.
3. This is the generally accepted emendation of 本 found in the DZ — see WYJ, note 8, p. 839.
4. SYR's emendation of 拒.
5. Supplied by SYR to fill a presumed textual lacuna — see, particularly, WYJ, note 11, p. 840.
6. Commentators generally refrain from filling these lacunae. Z&Q have this note: "奇器:機巧的械器。〔 〕〔 〕:此為原文脫漏。"

53: Preparing against the High Approach

53.1   Master Qin made repeated obeisances and said: "May I ask what is to be done when the enemy piles up earth to make a height in order to approach our wall, placing firewood and earth on top to make a sheep's bank ramp (*yangqian*) and covering it with shields at the front, bringing it up against the wall with [soldiers carrying] weapons and crossbows on top of it?"

Master Mo Zi said: "Are you asking about the defence against the sheep's bank ramp? Those who use a sheep's bank ramp will be those who are stupid. [It is a device] which is sufficient to wear out the soldiers, but not sufficient to harm the city. In defence, make 'terrace walls' and bring them adjacent to the sheep's bank ramp. On the left and right, project rams, each being 20 *chi* in length. The 'movable walls' are 30 *chi* high and strong crossbows are fired from them, making use of these ingenious devices. If you do this, then the sheep's bank ramp attack can be defeated."

Comment: This first section, an exchange between Qin Guli and Mo Zi, is similar to that recorded in 71.1 ("Miscellaneous Defences"). That is, it is the question of how to defend against the *yangqian* or sheep's bank ramp. Mo Zi's response here is different insofar as the method recommended is the construction of "terrace walls" or "movable walls" rather than bombarding them with arrows and stones as suggested in 71.1. From these "terrace walls" crossbows can be used against the enemy. The penultimate sentence presents difficulties due to textual lacunae. It may be, as RDSY/T assumes, that *jiche* (trebuchets) are also to be used. RDSY/SC (pp. 189–190) appears to take this problematic sentence to be referring to the "joined crossbow" described in detail in the following section.

53.2　備高[7]臨以連弩之車，材[8]大方一方一[9]尺，長稱城之薄厚。兩軸四[10]輪，輪居筐中，重下上筐，左右旁二植，左右有衡植，衡植左右皆圜內[11]，內徑四寸。左右縛[12]弩皆於植，以弦鉤弦[13]，至於大弦。弩臂[14]前後與筐齊，筐高八尺，弩軸去下筐三尺五寸。連弩機郭同銅，一石三十斤[15]。引弦鹿長奴[16]，筐大三圍半，左右有鉤距，方三寸，輪厚尺二寸，鉤距臂博[17]尺四寸，厚七寸，長六尺。橫臂齊筐外，蚤[18]尺五寸，有距[19]，博[20]六寸，厚三寸，長如筐，有儀，有詘勝[21]，可上下。為武重一石，以材大圍五寸[22]。

7.　高 is the widely accepted emendation of 矢 — see WYJ, note 15, p. 841.

8.　CZM and modern general editions (MBJ, LSL, Z&Q) have this emendation of 杖 due to YY.

9.　方一 is taken to be erroneously duplicated (SSX).

10.　Emended from 三 following YY.

11.　There is general agreement that 闔 should be taken as 圓 and 內 (here and immediately following) as 枘 in the sense of 榫.

12.　On the emendation of 縛 to 縛 see WYJ, note 21, p. 842.

13.　LSL has the following note on this clause:"孫說上弦字當作距，即文的鉤距，也就是弩牙。《釋名‧釋兵》:"弩鉤弦者曰牙，似齒牙也。"" — note 8, p. 489.

14.　On 臂 the《釋名‧釋兵》has:"弩，其柄曰臂，似人臂也。"

15.　In this sentence, 同 is taken as 用 and in some modern editions there is 鈞 in place of 斤.

16.　Following SYR, 鹿長奴 is emended to 鹿盧收, 鹿盧 being taken as 轆轤.

17.　Read as 寬 here and subsequently — see, for example, Z&Q.

18.　蚤 is read as 爪.

19.　On 有距, Z&Q have:"指橫伸出兩旁。"

20.　Emended from 傅 — see WYJ, note 30, p. 842.

21.　Following Z&Q, I have taken 儀 as 瞄準的儀器 and 詘勝 as 屈伸.

22.　I have followed LSL's version of this sentence. 寸 is taken as superfluous by SYR.

53.2   Prepare against the high approach (?the *lin* or "approacher/ overlook cart") with the "joined crossbow" carriage (*liannuche*). [This is made of] timbers 1 *chi* square and is of a length corresponding to the wall's thickness. It has two axles and four wheels, the wheels being inside the frame. The inside itself is divided into upper and lower levels.[i] Both left and right sides have two vertical posts each, and left and right sides have a horizontal beam. The left and right ends of both horizontal beams all have a tenon which projects straight out for 4 *cun*. To the left and right the crossbows are all bound to the vertical posts. With a "tooth" all the strings are linked together right up to the main string. The crossbow "arm" (?stock) at the front and back is level with the frame [of the carriage] which is 8 *chi* high. The crossbow pivot extends below the frame 3 *chi* and 5 *cun*. The "joined crossbow" (*liannu*) control mechanism and its housing are made of bronze [requiring] 1 *dan* and 30 *jin*. The string is drawn around a windlass. The size of the frame is $3^{1}/_{2}$ *wei*. To the left and right there are "teeth" 3 *cun* square. The wheels [of the cart] are 1 *chi* 2 *cun* thick. The "arms" for the "teeth" are 1 *chi* 4 *cun* wide, 7 *cun* thick and 6 *chi* long. External to the "arms" and level with the frame there is a "claw" (*zhua*) which is 1 *chi* 5 *cun* long and extends transversely on both sides. It is 6 *cun* wide, 3 *cun* thick and of the same length as the frame. And there is an aiming mechanism which is able to rise or fall and can be directed upwards or downwards. The base of the crossbow weighs 120 *jin*

---

i.   Following CZM and Z&Q.

矢長十尺，以繩〔 〕〔 〕²³矢端，如如戈射²⁴，以磨鹿²⁵卷收。矢
高弩臂三尺。用²⁶弩無數。出入六十枚，用小矢無留²⁷。十人主
此車。遂具寇，為高樓以射道，城上以荅羅矢。²⁸

Comment: This second section provides a detailed description of the device
for firing multiple arrows, called by Needham and Yates the "multiple-bolt
arcuballista". The issue with regard to the present text is precisely how or
against what it is being deployed. For detailed descriptions of this type of
instrument see RDSY/SC, pp. 187–199 and RDSY/SC, pp. 440–441. Some
modern editions (e.g. LSL, Z&Q) include this section in quotation marks as
part of Mo Zi's reply.

54: 闕

55: 闕

- - - - - - - - - - - - - -

23. ZCY supplies 繫著.
24. Read as "如弋射" — see LSL for details of the *yishe* used by hunters.
25. 鹿 is WYZ's emendation of the unknown character that occurs here — see particularly
    WYJ, note 35, p. 843.
26. Z&Q suggest 用 is superfluous.
27. On this sentence, CZM has: "發矢曰出，收回曰入，所謂出入六十枚也。" 人 is
    taken as 入 (as used in the text above).
28. There are three emendations in this final sentence (which both CZM and RDSY/T have
    as a separate fragment): (i) 具 to 兒 (SYR). (ii) 道 to 適 read as 敵. (iii) 荅 to 答 or 筲
    (CZM).

and is made from timbers 1 *wei* 5 *cun* in size. The arrows are 10 *chi* long and have a cord attached to the end like an *yishe* which can be wound back by a windlass. The arrows extend above the crossbow "arms" by 3 *chi*. There is no limit to the number of crossbows. Sixty [large arrows] are fired and retrieved whereas small arrows are not retrieved. Ten men control this cart. When an attack is seen, then the enemy can be fired at from the high towers, whilst on the wall a protective screen is used against enemy fire.

54: Lost

55: Lost

56: 備梯

Comment: This chapter is as it appears in the DZ apart from the emendations indicated in the notes. WYJ has it as two paragraphs, the first on the cloud ladder corresponding to 56.1 & 56.2 and the second including the remainder of the chapter (56.3–5). CZM also has it as a single chapter but divided into 12 sections as indicated in the Comments to each section below. Likewise, in the modern editions of MBJ, LSL and Z&Q it appears as a single chapter as set out below. RDSY/T, however, isolates the first two sections below (56.1 & 56.2) as his fragment 28 on defence against cloud ladders which follows a fragment (27) interposed between the end of chapter 53 and the present chapter which is on defence against battering rams. This is material that does not appear in the *Mozi* itself (see his p. 211). He then has section 56.3 as his fragment 29 and the remaining two sections (56.4 & 56.5), which he takes to be misplaced in the present chapter, as part of his fragment 49 (see his pp. 223, 332).

56.1 禽滑釐子事子墨子三年，手足胼胝，面目黧黑，役身給使，不敢問欲。子墨子甚哀之，乃管酒塊脯，寄于大山，昧葇坐之，以樵禽子。[1] 禽子再拜而嘆。子墨子曰：「亦何欲乎？」禽子再拜再拜曰：「敢問守道？」子墨子曰：「姑亡，姑亡。[2] 古有其術者，內不親民，外不約[3] 治，以少間眾，以弱輕強，身死國亡，為天下笑。子其慎之，恐為身薑[4]。」禽子再拜頓首，願遂問守道。曰：「敢問客眾而勇，煙資吾池，軍卒並進，雲梯既施，攻備已具，武士又多，爭上[5] 吾城，為之奈何？」

---

1. There are several textual and interpretative issues in this sentence as follows: (i) 甚 for 其 (BY). (ii) 管 and 塊 as above (YTY). (iii) 大山 as 泰山. (iv) 昧葇 as 滅茅 (SYR). (v) 樵 as 醮 (WYZ) — see WYJ, notes 3–7, pp. 846–847.
2. On 姑 in this phrase, SYR has: "姑亡，言姑無問守道也。" — see also *Mozi* 48.
3. 約 is read as 飾 (SYR).
4. 薑 is read as 僵 — see, for example, MZQY.
5. The DZ has 上 here — see BY and WYJ, note 16, p. 848.

56: Preparing against Ladders

56.1　　Master Qin Guli had served Mo Zi for three years until his hands and feet were covered with calluses and his face was blackened by the sun. He had laboured to be of service and had not dared to express his own wishes. Master Mo Zi greatly pitied him, so, taking some purified wine and some dried meat, he went to Tai Shan, cleared a patch of grass to sit on, and made an offering to Qin Zi. Qin Zi bowed several times and sighed.

Master Mo Zi said: "What else do you wish?"

Qin Zi bowed repeatedly and said: "Dare I ask about the Way of defence?"

Master Mo Zi replied: "Put it aside for the moment! Put it aside for the moment! In ancient times, there were those who had this skill, but within, they did not become close to the people, and without, they did not manage the affairs of government. When few, they fought against many. When weak, they made light of the strong. The result was that they themselves died, their states were lost, and they became the laughing-stock of the world. You should be very careful about this. Otherwise, I fear you will end up a corpse yourself."

Qin Zi again made obeisance and bowed his head, wishing to ask further about the Way of defence. He said: "Dare I ask what is to be done when the enemy are many and brave, when they have filled in our moat, when the troops advance in a phalanx, when the cloud ladders are in position, when the equipment for attack is complete, when the warriors are increasingly many, and they are making a headlong rush to scale our walls?"

Comment: All commentators accept this opening exchange as the introduction to the brief consideration of the 雲梯 or "cloud ladder", a device said to have been invented by Mo Zi's rival Gongshu Pan (see *Mozi* 50.1), although it is only one of a number of aspects mentioned in Qin Guli's question. RDSY/T takes the long preamble as "suggesting that it is an early version of the text". In fact, he treats the first two sections here as a single fragment (fragment 28). CZM divides the opening exchange into four sections — his #56.1–#56.4. On this device, see also C&E B27 and RDSY/SC, pp. 446–455.

56.2 子墨子曰：「問雲梯之〔守〕⁶邪？雲梯者重器也，其動移甚難。守為行城，雜樓相見⁷，以環其中。以適廣狹為度，環中藉幕，毋廣其處。行城⁸之法，高城二十尺，上加堞，廣十尺，左右出巨⁹各二十尺，高廣如行城之法。為爵穴煇鼠¹⁰，施答其外。機、衝、錢、城¹¹，廣與隊等，雜其間以鎌、劍，持衝十人，執劍五人，皆以有力者。令案目者視適，以鼓發之，夾而射之，重而射，披機藉之，城上繁下矢、石、沙、炭，以雨之，薪火、水湯以濟之。審賞行罰，以靜為故，從之以急，毋使生慮。若此，則雲梯之攻敗矣。」

Comment: This list of measures which might be used to overcome the cloud ladders may represent the end of Mo Zi's response on this matter as RDSY/T assumes, although cloud ladders are again mentioned in 56.4 below. Certainly, it is the end of RDSY/T's fragment 28 on cloud ladders and the end of WYJ's 56, para 1. CZM divides this section into two parts — his #56.5 and #56.6.

— — — — — —

6. This character, absent from the DZ, is added following Qiu Shan, WNS and SSX.
7. Read as 相間 (YY).
8. SYR, and others following him, take 行城 to equate with the 臺城 spoken of in *Mozi* 53. For a description of these structures see RDSY/SC, pp. 443ff, 450.
9. The MZQY quotes SYR as follows on 出巨 in the *Mozi* 53: "巨當為距之假字，此行城編連大木，橫出兩旁，故以謂之距。" RDSY/SC speaks of "rams".
10. Written with the 人 radical.
11. On this list, CZM has: "…是四事並列：機，技機也 (見卅篇2)，衝，衝撞之器，棧，行棧 (見了篇49及西篇2)，城，行城 (見上節)，皆禦梯攻之器。" There is general acceptance of WYZ's reading of 錢 as 棧. On this Z&Q have: "從樓上伸出來的活動橋。" RDSY/T takes the "ingenious machines" as trebuchets.

56.2 Master Mo Zi said: "Are you asking about defence against cloud ladders? Cloud ladders are heavy pieces of equipment and moving them is very difficult. Defence consists of 'platform (movable) walls' with various towers placed at intervals as a means of encircling their centre. By taking the appropriate width or narrowness as the measure, surround the centre with rush screens, but do not widen its position. The pattern for 'platform (movable) walls' is that they are 20 *chi* higher than the city wall with a 10 *chi* wide parapet added on top. To the left and right project rams (*ju*), each 20 *chi* long. The [various towers][i] are tall and broad in the manner of the 'platform walls'. Holes are made as for smoking out rats and woven screens[ii] are set up on the outside. The 'ingenious machines', battering rams, (movable) bridges, and 'platform (movable) walls' are deployed over a width commensurate with that of the advancing line of enemy forces. Interspersed amongst these are 'chisels' and piercing implements, using ten men to manage a battering ram and five men to control a piercing implement, all being men of strength. Order those with unwavering gaze to keep watch for enemies, using the drum to give the signal to shoot at them from both sides and do so continuously. Set into action the crossbows against them and from the wall above harass them below with arrows, stones, sand and coals, falling like rain. Use blazing wood and boiling water to burn and scald them. Examine rewards and carry out punishments. Make plans in a calm way but follow them with swift action so you do not let anxieties arise. This is how attack by cloud ladders can be defeated."

---

i.   Added by YY.

ii.   According to CZM, these were screens woven of grasses made to obstruct arrows, although RDSY/SC speaks of "fire screens".

56.3 守為行堞，堞高六尺而一等，施劍其面，以機發之，衝至則去之，不至則施之。爵穴三尺而一一，蒺藜投必遂[12]而立，以車推引之。

Comment: There is a question whether this section, which makes no mention of cloud ladders, belongs here. RDSY/T, who has it as his fragment 29, suggests that it might come from one of the lost chapters (see his p. 223). He also says: "It is unclear where the 'movable parapets' are to be deployed." CZM treats the "movable parapets", the holes and the caltrops as three separate fragments — his #56.7–#56.9.

56.4 置[13]裾城外，去城十尺，裾厚十尺。伐裾，小大盡本斷之，以十尺為傳[14]，雜而深埋之，堅築，毋使可拔。二十步一殺，殺有一鬲，鬲厚十尺，殺有兩門，門廣五尺。裾門一施，[15]淺埋，弗[16]築，令易拔。城上希裾門而直桀。[17]

Comment: In terms of meaning, this section is relatively straightforward, describing first, the construction of a palisade fence with gates, and second, the use of the *sha* 殺. It is, however, not entirely clear what a *sha* is, but the probability is that it is some kind of protective structure divided by partitions which soldiers used to protect and conceal themselves before they went forth beyond the fence. I am not sure that "Death", as suggested by RDSY/SC, is an entirely appropriate term. CZM's suggested link with "scatter", in the sense of a place from which soldiers scatter, might be more relevant. For descriptions and consideration of these issues see RDSY/T, note 100, p. 334, RDSY/SC, p. 481 and CZM, MZJC, vol. 45, p. 62. CZM, in fact, divides the section into two parts (his #56.10 and #56.11) dealing with the fence and the *sha* respectively. Quite what these structures have to do with defence against cloud ladders is also not entirely clear. RDSY/T merges this and the next section below to form one fragment (his fragment 49) and suggests that this might more properly pertain to defence against the massed infantry assault ("ant approach") — see his p. 332. In fact, both this and the following section do appear in closely similar form in the chapter on that method of attack — see 63.11 and 63.12.

---

12. There is general acceptance of the reading of 隊 for 遂 (BY, SYR).
13. 置 is added following SYR.
14. Reading 傳 as 斷 following BY — but see also LSL who has: "傳，植也".
15. Punctuation following WYJ. Other modern editors have the comma after 一一.
16. Following modern editors, I have 弗 here rather than 勿.
17. There are several issues with this sentence: (i) The addition of 上 after 城 follows WYZ. (ii) 希 is read as 睎 in the sense of 望. (iii) 直桀 is taken as 置桀 (CZM).

56.3   In defence with "moving" parapets, the parapets are 6 *chi* high and at one level. Swords are set up on their faces and fired by a mechanism. If the battering rams come, then release them. If they do not come, then leave them set up. Cavities are made, one every 3 *chi*. Cylindrical caltrops are put in and must be used against troop lines.[iii] Pull them back and forth with a cart.

56.4   Arrange palisades outside the wall at a distance of 10 *chi* from it, the palisades being 10 *chi* thick. Collect timber for the palisades, both large and small pieces, and cut off the roots completely. Then cut the pieces into 10 *chi* lengths, mix them together and bury them deeply to make a strong construction that cannot be pulled up. Every 20 *bu*, there should be 1 *sha*, each *sha* having 1 *ge*, the *ge* being 10 *chi* thick.[iv] In a *sha* there are 2 gates, each gate being 5 *chi* wide. In each palisade there is 1 gate which is shallowly buried and not heavily built so it is easy to pull up. On the wall and facing towards the palisade gate, set up things to throw.

---

iii. For some description of these devices see RDSY/SC, p. 433 and elsewhere.

iv. For a description of the *sha* (which RDSY translates as "Death" and the *ge*, see RDSY/ SC, p. 481. For *sha* 殺, CZM has: "預備投擲敵人之所。" Following SYR, 鬲 is read as 隔 in the sense of 隔牆 or "partition wall" (MZQY).

56.5 縣火，四尺一鉤樴，五步一灶，灶門有鑪炭，令適人盡入，煇火燒門，縣火次之。出載而立，其廣終隊。兩載之間一火，皆立而待鼓而燃火[18]，即具發之。適人除火而復攻，縣火復下，適人甚病，故引兵而去。則令我死〔士〕[19]左右出穴門擊遺師，令貴士、主將皆聽城鼓之音而出，又聽城鼓之音而入。因素[20]出兵施伏，夜半城上四面鼓噪，適人必或[21]，有此必破軍殺將。以白衣為服，以號相得，若此[22]，則雲梯之攻敗矣。

Comment: As discussed in the Comment to the previous section, RDSY/T combines this with the previous section taking them both to be about defence against the massed infantry assault ("ant approach"). CZM has this section complete as his #56.12. The description is clear enough and, although the method would, in fact, seem to have a more general application than defence against cloud ladders alone, the section does end with a specific reference to that method of attack.

57: 闕

---

18. On the emendations to 待 and 燃 see WYJ, note 55, p. 852.
19. Added following BY.
20. Following WYZ, 因素 is read as 照舊 both here and in 63.12 where the same passage occurs.
21. 或 is read as 惑.
22. Emended from 也 following BY.

56.5 [In the case of] "hanging fires", every 4 *chi* there should be 1 stake with a hook on it and every 5 *bu* a furnace with a brazier of charcoal at the doors of the furnace.[v] The enemy soldiers are allowed to enter completely, upon which the gates are set ablaze with "hanging fires" to follow. Send out carriers and set them up, their width being equivalent to that of the enemy line. Between two carriers have one fire. When everything is set up, await the sound of the drum and set them alight, then release them all together. If the enemy troops extinguish the fire and attack again, the "hanging fires" are again released, bringing the enemy troops great distress and causing them to lead their forces away and flee. Then give the order for our crack troops to go out in all directions from the "sally ports"[vi] and attack the fleeing enemy. Order those brave soldiers and generals all to go forth when they hear the sound of the drum on the wall, and, when they hear the sound of the drum on the wall again, to re-enter. As before, when sending forth soldiers, create a diversion. In the middle of the night, create a clamour of drums on the wall on all sides so there is inevitably doubt within enemy ranks. By this, you will certainly rout the army and kill the general. Put on white garments as clothes and use shouts to communicate with each other. In this way, then, the attack by cloud ladders can be defeated.

57: Lost

---

v.   In this sentence there is general acceptance of 懸 for 縣 whilst many take 櫼 as 弋 — see, for example, MZQY. For a discussion of these "hanging fires" see RDSY/SC, p. 481.

vi. This is the term used by RDSY/SC to refer to the exit gates in the palisades.

58: 備水

Comment: This brief chapter is as it appears in the DZ apart from the minor changes indicated in the notes. WYJ has it as a single paragraph and CZM as four sections. In the modern editions of LSL and Z&Q it appears as two paragraphs as below. RDSY/T suggests that the first sentence above may be displaced from chapter 52 and treats it as a separate fragment (his fragment 32). He then groups the rest of the material together as a single fragment (his fragment 33).

58.1   城內塹外周道[1]，廣八步，備水謹度四旁高下。城地中[2]遍[3]下，令耳[4]其內，及下地，地深穿之令漏泉。置則瓦井中，視外水深丈以上，鑿城內水耳[5]。

Comment: This and the following short section are all that remain of the chapter detailing the defence against water (flooding). Two methods are described, one in each section. The first method is the digging of channels and wells to drain the water away. There is some variation in how this chapter is arranged as noted above. CZM has what is 58.1 above divided into three parts (#58.1–3) and treats 58.2 below as a single fragment (his #58.4).

58.2   並船以為十臨[6]，臨二十人人擿弩計四有方[7]，必善以船為轒輼[8]。
　　　　二十船為一隊，選材士有力者二十人共船，其二十人人擿有方，

---

1. 塹 is understood as 濠溝 (Z&Q). 周道 is taken to be the same as 州道 referred to in *Mozi* 52, and, as LSL notes, "指環城的道路。"
2. According to SYR, 地中 should be reversed in order.
3. Read as 偏.
4. Following the readings of SSX (氾 for 令) and SYR (渠 for 耳).
5. 水耳 is read as 水渠 — see previous note.
6. See RDSY/SC, p. 457 on these craft which he calls "approachers" or "overlookers".
7. There are issues with "計四有方". CZM (and others) take 計四 as 什四 (十四) and 方 as 鉬 ("hoe"). RDSY/SC, who takes the weapon to be called a *youfung*, provides a detailed discussion of the matter on pp. 457–458.
8. RDSY/SC terms this a "tank vessel". It is also the term for a form of hearse which is described in detail (with diagram) in the ZWDCD, vol. 8, p. 1768. See also *Mozi* 52 above.

58: Preparing against Water (Flooding)

58.1　Within the wall, but outside the trench, make an encircling road 8 *bu* wide. In preparing against water (flooding), make a careful estimation of the height of the ground at all points. Where the ground within the wall is sloping down (low), [create] a tile-lined channel within it extending to low ground. Wells should be dug at the deepest places in the ground and a measuring tile placed within each well. When the depth of the water outside exceeds 1 *zhang*, water channels are dug within the wall.

58.2　Boats are joined together [in pairs] to make 10 approachers (*lin*), each approacher having thirty men. Each man is in charge of a crossbow and four of every ten men have a *youfang*. It is necessary for those skilled in boats to make *fenwen* ("tank vessels"). Twenty such craft constitute a "squadron". Thirty men, capable and strong, are chosen for each craft. Of these, twelve men wield a

劍甲鞮瞀[9]，十人〔人〕[10] 擅苗。[11] 先養材上為異舍，食其父母妻子
以為質，視水可決，以臨輣輼，決外堤，城上為射機[12] 疾[13] 佐
之。

Comment: This is the second of the two methods and involves two kinds of
specially designed craft which are sent out to breach the enemy dikes, their
advance being covered by arrows fired from the wall. I have followed RDSY/
T's names for these. There is some variation in the reading of the distribution
of men on the craft. Modern editors (LSL, Z&Q) accept SYR's correction which
gives twelve men with *youfang* and eighteen with *miao* although RDSY/T
rejects this. The alternative is twenty and ten respectively. As for the weapons
themselves, it is not altogether clear what these are. On the *youfang*, RDSY/SC
writes: "The identity and shape of this instrument has perplexed a number of
scholars ..." (p. 457) A picture is provided on p. 458. *Miao* is possibly a spear.
CZM takes what above is the second sentence to be an ancient gloss, a
suggestion that RDSY/T also rejects.

59: 闕

60: 闕

---

9. I have followed Z&Q in the reading of this phrase.
10. Added to the DZ text by modern editors (including WYJ) in conformity with the similar
    prior statements.
11. The numbers (12/18) follow SYR. Most commentators emend 苗 to 矛. I have left the
    matter open, retaining *miao* — see RDSY/SC, pp. 458–459.
12. SYR's emendation for the rare character 羨 with the 手 radical — ZWDCD #13082.
13. Read as 急.

youfang and wear armour and leather helmets whilst the other eighteen men have a *miao*. Before training these capable soldiers, their parents, wives and children are held as hostages at a different place and provided for. When it is seen that the waters (dikes) can be breached, use the approachers and tank vessels to breach the outside (enemy) dikes, assisting them with rapid fire from the "shooting machines" on the wall.

59: Lost

60: Lost

61: 備突[1]

Comment: It is generally accepted that this is the remnant of a more substantial chapter on this aspect of defence. The text that follows is identical with that in the DZ as well as WYJ, CHANT and the modern editions of MBJ, LSL and Z&Q, apart from the emendation of 狀 to 伏 in the last group. RDSY/T treats this as two fragments (34 and 35) making a break after "吏主塞突門" and then repeating "城百步一突門‧突門". CZM includes what is here part of 62.12 as a second section in the present chapter — see CZM, MZJC, vol. 45, pp. 69–70. RDSY/T strongly opposes this.

61.1　城百步一突門，突門各為窯灶[2]，竇[3]入門四五尺，為其門上瓦屋，毋令水潦能入門中。吏主塞突門，用車兩輪，以木束之，塗其上，維置突門內，使度門廣狹、令之入門中四五尺。置窯灶，門旁為橐，充灶伏[4]柴艾。寇即入、下輪而塞之。鼓橐而熏之。

Comment: This one brief section is all that remains of the chapter on "surprise attack" if 突 is accepted as meaning that. The technique briefly described is clear enough. The enemy forces are lured through gates in the wall (presumably the outer wall) and then their possible retreat is blocked by the structure described. Smoke is released from the furnaces which then incapacitates them. I have used the term "sally port" for 突門 (Z&Q have 暗門) but RDSY/T's original term "irruption gate" might be preferable given that the idea was to let the enemy burst in so they could be trapped and smoked.

1. For an excellent discussion of this type of attack see RDSY/SC, pp. 461–463 where the issue of terminology relating to 突 is addressed.
2. On 窯灶, BY refers to the 《說文》 as follows: "窯，燒瓦灶也" — see also *Mozi* 62 below.
3. Some commentators (e.g. Z&Q) suggest 竇 should be taken as 灶.
4. BY originally suggested the emendation of 狀 to 伏 which is found in MBJ, LSL and Z&Q — see WYJ, note 11, p. 858. The meaning is taken as 狀 or 充實 (Z&Q).

61: Preparing against Sudden Attack

61.1 In the wall, every 100 *bu*, there should be one sally port (*tumen*). For each sally port there should be a kiln or furnace, and a *dou* (tube for blowing the fire of the furnace — *tuyère*) which enters the gate for 4 or 5 *chi*. Above the gate, construct a tiled roof which does not allow water or heavy rain to enter the gate. An officer controls the blocking of the sally port using two cart wheels bound together with wood and smeared with mud on the upper surface. Suspend [this structure] within the sally port letting it be commensurate in width with the sally port. Let [the *dou* — *tuyère*] enter the gate for 4 or 5 *chi*. Set up the kiln or furnace and place bellows (*tuo*) beside the gate. Fill the furnace full with firewood and artemisia. When the enemy enters [the gate], drop the wheels and block it. Activate the bellows and create smoke.

62: 備穴[1]

Comment: This is the second of the two composite chapters in terms of material from the DZ. The version given is that found in the modern editions of LSL and Z&Q and is based on the text of SYR. In relation to the DZ, 62.1 is a composite having the first 32 characters from DZ 62 and the remainder of the section from DZ 52. 62.2 below is also from DZ 52 and the two sections (62.1–2) comprise WYJ's paragraph 1. The following four sections (62.3–6) come from DZ 62 and are grouped by WYJ as his paragraph 2. From 62.7 to the end of the first three sentences of 62.13 comes from DZ 52 and makes up WYJ's paragraph 3. The remainder of the chapter, from the last part of 62.13 to 62.20, comes from DZ 62 and makes up WYJ's paragraph 4. The arrangements of CZM and RDSY/T are given in the Comment following each section.

62.1   禽子再拜再拜，曰：「敢問古人有善攻者，穴土而入，縛柱施火，以壞吾城，城壞，或中人為之奈何？」[2]子墨子曰：「問穴土之守邪？備穴者城內為高樓，以謹候望適人。適人為變，築垣聚土非常者，若彭有水濁非常者，此穴土也，急塹[3]城內穴其土直[4]之。穿井城內，五步一井，傅城足，高地，丈五尺，下地，得泉三尺而止。令陶者為罌，容四十斗以上，固順之以薄鞈*革[5]，置井中，使聰耳者伏罌而聽之，審之穴之所在，鑿穴迎之。」

1. The method in question is considered in detail by RDSY/SC (pp. 463–480). As the quotation which he gives from the *Tong Dian* indicates, it was to tunnel under the wall, supporting the tunnel with posts until a sufficient length of the wall had been undermined. The posts were then set on fire so the tunnel, and with it the undermined section of wall, collapsed, allowing attackers to enter.
2. With regard to the method tersely described as "縛柱施火" the《通典・兵門說》has: "鑿地為道，行於城下，攻城建柱，積薪於其柱，闞而燒之，柱折城摧。" According to Z&Q, 壞 should be understood as 倒塌. "或中人" is emended to "城中人".
3. Most texts have this character in a rare variant form — see ZWDCD #5659.
4. Both BY and SYR take 直 as 當.
5. In this clause, 固 is taken as "緊固", 順 is read as 幦 (SYR). The《說文》has this definition: "生革可以為縷束也。" — see Z&Q, note 11, pp. 852–853.

62: Preparing against Tunnelling

62.1 Qin Zi bowed repeatedly and said: "May I ask about the ancients who were skilled in attack and tunnelled through the ground to enter [the city], placing posts which they set fire to in order to damage our wall. When the wall was damaged, what did those within the city do?"

Master Mo Zi replied: "Are you asking about the defence against the tunnelling of earth? In preparing against tunnelling, erect a high tower within the wall to maintain a vigilant surveillance of the enemy. If the enemy brings about changes — for example, builds up walls of a lot of earth out of the ordinary, or causes the water in the moat to become unusually muddy — this indicates the tunnelling of earth. Urgently dig a channel within the wall and excavate tunnels to counter this. Dig wells within the wall, one well every 5 *bu*, sufficiently close to the wall. [If the wall is on] high ground [the wells should be] 1 *zhang* 5 *chi* deep and if on low ground reach to 3 *chi* below the water level and stop. Direct potters to make geophones (*ying*) with a capacity of 40 *dou* or more, cover them tightly with thin rawhide, and place them in the wells. Get those with sharp hearing to lie prostrate and listen to get detailed information about where the [enemy] tunnels are situated, then dig [counter-] tunnels to meet them."

Comment: Recent editions of the *Mozi* treat this as one discrete section (Z&Q), or as two sections, making a division between Qin Zi's question and Mo Zi's reply (LSL, MBJ), or as part of a single paragraph which also includes what is 62.2 below (WYJ). RDSY/T, however, argues against this arrangement claiming that there are breaks in the text. He has two short fragments (36, 37) which comprise the first 32 (from DZ 62) and the next 24 characters (from DZ 52) respectively, followed by a long fragment 38 which contains the rest of this section and all the following section (from DZ 52). The actual sense and meaning of the two sections is not significantly changed by the variations in arrangement. The essential components of a defence against tunnelling or mining, identified in this first section, are the above-ground surveillance using towers within the wall which give vantage points to look for the appearance of unusual mounds of earth or muddying of the waters of the moat, and below-ground detection using wells and geophones to pick up the sounds of enemy tunnelling. Counter-tunnels can then be dug.

62.2   令陶者為月明⁶，長二尺五寸〔大〕⁷六圍，中判之，合而施之穴中，偃一覆一。〔柱之外善周塗，其傅柱者勿燒，柱者勿燒柱善塗其寶際，勿令泄。〕⁸兩旁皆如此，與穴俱前。卜迫地，置康若灰⁹其中，勿滿。灰康長五¹⁰寶、左右俱雜相如也。穴內口為灶，令如窯，令容七八員艾¹¹，左右寶皆如此¹²，灶用四囊。穴且遇，以頡皋¹³衝之，疾鼓囊熏之，必令明習囊事者勿令離灶口。連版以穴高下，廣狹為度，令穴者與版俱前，鑿其版令容矛，參分其疏數¹⁴，令可以救寶，穴則遇，以版擋之，以矛救寶，勿令

---

6.   There is acceptance that 月明 should be emended, WYZ proposing 瓦罌 and CZM 瓦寶. I have followed the latter. For the constructional issues involved see RDSY/T's note 18, pp. 258–261.
7.   Suggested by WYZ.
8.   There is considerable doubt about this sentence. The version given is that of Z&Q based on CZM — see the former's notes 5 and 6, p. 854. For a detailed discussion of the textual and constructional issues involved see RDSY/T's note 25, pp. 261–262.
9.   These three characters are taken as "糠與炭" — see Z&Q.
10. There is general agreement that 五 should be read as 瓦 in the sense of 完 — see, for example, LSL, Z&Q.
11. Following SYR, 員艾 is read as 艾丸.
12. According to CZM, this and the previous clause beginning 左右 are likely to be later added notes.
13. On 頡皋, Z&Q have: "即桔皋，起重省力之具。"
14. In this clause, 參 is taken as 三 (SSX) and SYR has: "此言版上鑿空之數。"

62.2[i]   Direct potters to make tiled pipes 2 *chi* 5 *cun* in length with a diameter of 6 *wei*. Divide them in the centre so that one half is facing upwards and one half facing downwards. The outside of the posts should be skilfully covered all around with mud. If what supports the posts doesn't burn, the posts themselves won't burn. Skilfully cover with mud the joins in the drains so nothing can leak out. The two sides are both to be like this as the tunnel advances. Where the lower end reaches the ground, place charcoal and chaff in it but not so as to fill it completely. Charcoal and chaff are placed throughout the length of the pipes and are distributed equally to the left and right. At the internal openings of the tunnels there should be furnaces which should be like kilns. Let them contain seven or eight balls of artemisia. The left and right pipes should both be like this. The kilns use four bellows. When the tunnels meet, use well-sweeps (*jiegao*) to clear away the intervening earth and urgently stir up the bellows to provide smoke against the enemy. Be certain to issue clear orders to those attending the bellows not to leave the furnace openings. Make linked wooden planks of a height and width commensurate with that of the tunnel. Order the tunnellers with the planks to go forward together. Holes are cut in the planks to allow them to hold spears. There are variations in the density and number to allow them to be used to save the pipes. When the tunnels meet, the planks are used to resist the enemy and the spears are used to

---

i   As in the previous Chapter, it may be that the remainder of the Chapter is a continuation of Mo Zi's words. However, quotation marks have been omitted as discussed on the introduction (p. 733).

塞竇，竇則塞，引版而卻[15]，過一竇而塞之，鑿其竇，通其煙，煙通，疾鼓橐以熏之。從穴內聽穴之左右，急絕其前，勿令得行。若集客穴，塞之以柴塗，令無可燒版也。然則穴土之攻敗矣。

Comment: This section is a component of RDSY/T's fragment 38 and of WYJ's long opening paragraph. It is treated as a discrete section by CZM (#62.3) and in the modern editions of LSL, MBJ and Z&Q. As the notes indicate, there are significant textual and interpretative difficulties, especially concerning 月明 in the opening sentence and the whole of what is given above as the second sentence. The accounts of different commentators differ quite considerably. Those of CZM and RDSY/T should be consulted for further details. In essence, the construction seems to be one of pipes built on either side of the defensive tunnels which are used to transmit noxious fumes, created by burning artemisia, into the enemy tunnels when a breakthrough is made. Wooden barriers with holes to accommodate spears are made to protect the tunnellers at the points of connection of defensive and offensive tunnels.

62.3   寇至吾城，急非常也。謹備穴。穴疑有應寇，急穴。[16] 穴未得，慎毋追。[17]

Comment: Brief though this section is, there are significant problems with it and any translation must remain tentative. RDSY/T has argued that the first five characters are misplaced. If they are omitted this leaves an incomplete opening sentence. Z&Q's proposed rearrangement makes some sense of the second sentence and has been adopted. On the third sentence there are at least three distinct views. (i) BY's which is what is adopted above. That is, if the tunnels (or preparations more generally) are not ready, then don't pursue the enemy. (ii) SYR's which is that if the location of the enemy tunnels has not been determined, then the defenders should not leave the city in pursuit. (iii) CZM's which is that while the position of the enemy tunnels is not yet known, the defence tunnels should not be advanced. This section corresponds to RDSY/T's fragment 39 and CZM's #62.4.

---

15. This is the generally accepted emendation of the rare character 鄐 which appears here.
16. On the preceding 10 characters, Z&Q suggest the following rearrangement and emendation: "謹備寇，疑有穴，應急穴。" which I have followed.
17. On this sentence, BY has: "言己不謹其穴，且勿追寇。"

protect the pipes. Don't let the pipes become blocked. If the pipes are blocked, take up the planks and withdraw. If one blocked pipe is encountered, ream it out so smoke can pass. When smoke can pass, urgently work the bellows to produce smoke. If, from within the tunnel, the sounds of tunnelling are heard to the left or right, the tunnel is immediately blocked at the front and not allowed to proceed further. If there is a joining with the enemy's tunnel, the opening is blocked with brushwood and mud. Do not allow them to be able to burn the plants. In this way, then, the attack by tunnelling fails.

62.3   When the enemy reaches our city, it is a matter of great urgency. In carefully preparing [against] the enemy, if tunnels are thought to exist, respond to the enemy [tunnels] by urgently tunnelling. While [our] tunnels are not yet in place, we must be careful not to pursue [the enemy].

62.4   凡殺以穴攻者，二十步一置穴，穴高十尺，鑿[18]十尺，鑿如前，
步下三尺，十步擁穴[19]，左右橫行，高廣各十尺殺。

Comment: From this section to the end of the chapter, RDSY/T makes a major
rearrangement of the material. CZM also makes some changes but these are
much less radical. I shall summarise RDSY/T's changes briefly here before
considering this section specifically. From section 62.4 on, RDSY/T has four
fragments as follows:

(i)   Fragment 40 is the opening sentence of 52.4.

(ii)   Fragment 41 is the final sentence of 52.4.

(iii)   Fragment 42 comprises 62.7–62.12 plus the first part of 62.13.

(iv)   Fragment 43 comprises 62.4–62.6, the second part of 62.13, and 62.14–
62.20.

In the present section, there is a particular problem with 殺 in both instances
of its use. In the first sentence, a number of commentators, following SYR who
suggests inserting 為 immediately before it, take it as a technical term. It must
then be different from the 殺 elsewhere described. I have taken it in the sense
of "殺敗" (LSL) or "破滅" (Z&Q) rather than as a specific piece of defensive
military equipment. As the final character, CZM (and MBJ) place it at the start
of the next section (CZM's #62.5). I have taken it to be misplaced here and
omitted it from the translation. There is also a question about 擁穴. RDSY/T,
alone it would appear, takes 擁 as 壅 "to block" and argues that the blocking
is done to prevent enemy passage. On the face of it, it would seem an unlikely
thing to do. I have followed LSL, for example, in taking "擁穴" as a term for the
transverse tunnels.

62.5   俚[20]兩罌，深平城，置板其上，(冊[21]板以井聽。五步一密。用
桐若松為穴戶)[22]，戶穴有兩蔟藜，皆長極其戶，戶為環，壘石外

---

18. There is general acceptance of the reading of 鑿 as 廣.
19. I have followed LSL for example in taking "擁穴" as a term for the transverse tunnels.
RDSY/T takes 擁 as 壅 "to block", although it is hard to see why the defenders would
block their own tunnels.
20. There is general acceptance of the reading of 俚 as 埋.
21. 冊 in the sense of 覆蓋 is CZM's emendation of the unknown character which appears
here.
22. In the translation I have followed SSX's proposed rearrangement of the characters in
parentheses. His version reads: "冊板以聽，并五步一，密用桐若松為穴戶。" The
translation also includes SSX's proposed emendation of the unknown character
following 用 to 桐, the reading of 若 as 或, of 密 as 穴, and of 戶 as 門.

62.4 In general, to kill those who attack by tunnelling, excavate a [defensive] tunnel every 20 *bu*, each tunnel being 10 *chi* high and 10 *chi* wide. As the tunnel advances forward, there should be a fall of 3 *chi* for every 1 *bu*. Every 10 *bu* of advancement, excavate transverse tunnels to the left and right, the height and width of each one being 10 *chi*.

62.5 Bury two geophones (*ying*) so that the depth of the mouth of the geophones is level with the ground within the wall. Use joined planks to cover the geophones. Then, lying prostrate, listen. Every 5 *bu* have one well. For each tunnel, use *tong* or pine to make doors. Within the doors, place two caltrops making the length of each caltrops equal to that of the doors. The doors should have [iron] hoops. All around the doors of the tunnel there should be a

埻[23]，高七尺，加堞其上。勿為陛與石，以縣陛上下出入[24]。具鑪橐，橐以牛皮，鑪有兩缶[25]，以橋鼓之百十[26]，每亦熏四十什[27]，然炭杜之[28]，滿鑪而蓋之，毋令氣出，適人疾近五百[29]穴，穴高若下，不至吾穴，即以伯[30]鑿而求通之。

Comment: This is a problematic section. In trying to make sense of the first two sentences, I have followed SSX's proposed rearrangement given in the note. CZM, who divides this section into three parts, has the first part (#62.6), comprising the first sentence above, as being about the 殺 "*sha*" and ending at 聽. His #62.7 becomes "井，五步‥。" He then makes 密 (which is usually read as 穴) the first character of his #62.8 which includes the remainder of the section above. There is also uncertainty about the weights given as 斤 (assuming the emendations of 十 and 什 are accepted). I have followed SYR in taking them to refer to the well-sweeps but RDSY/T takes them to refer to the fuel — see his notes 161, 162, p. 294.

62.6   穴中與適人遇，則皆圍而毋遂，且戰北[31]，以須鑪火之然也，即去而入壅穴殺。有鼠竄[32]，為之戶及關籥獨順[33]，得往來行其中。穴壘之中各一狗，狗吠即有人也。

Comment: CZM has the first sentence of this section as the final sentence of his #62.8, transferring 殺 to the start of the next sentence and has this sentence as his #62.9. The translation above takes 遂 as 追遂 and follows Z&Q's interpretation of the problematic "且戰北".

- - - - - - - - - -

23. This is SYR's proposal for the unknown character which appears here.
24. In the translation of this sentence, I have followed CZM and Z&Q.
25. 缶 is usually given in the uncommon variant form with the addition of 瓦 (see ZWDCD #26750). RDSY/SC raises the possibility that two types of bellows are being referred to, i.e. 橐 and 缶 — see his p. 465 and particularly note a.
26. In this clause, BY takes 橋 as 桔橰. On 百十, SYR has: "百十，似言橋之重，'百'上疑脫'重'字，'十'當為'斤'。"
27. SYR proposes that this clause should read: "毋下重四十斤。"
28. In this clause, 然 is read as 燃 and 杜 as 填充 (Z&Q).
29. It is generally accepted that 五百 should be emended to 百.
30. 伯 is read as 倚 in the sense of 斜 (SYR).
31. On "且戰北", Z&Q have: "一面戰一面佯敗，誘敵入我穴。北：敗逃。"
32. Following BY and SYR, 鼠竄 is substituted for the two unknown characters which appear here.
33. For 關籥, Z&Q have: "即'管鑰'，門鎖與鑰匙。" There is general acceptance of SYR's reading of 繩幀 or 繩冪 for 獨順。

pile of stones 7 *chi* high. Add a parapet above it. Do not make steps but use a suspended ladder to go up or down, out or in. Prepare a furnace and bellows, the bellows being made of ox-hide. For the furnace have two bellows. Use well-sweeps weighing 100 *jin* with the very smallest not less than 40 *jin*. Use burning charcoal to put into it, fill the furnace and cover it so as not to allow smoke to escape. If the enemy is rapidly approaching our tunnel, if their tunnel is higher or lower than ours so it does not enter our tunnel, then excavate at an incline and seek to connect with it.

62.6   When within the tunnel there is a meeting with the enemy, in all cases oppose [them] but do not pursue [them]. There should be alternation between fighting and feigning defeat to draw the enemy into one's own tunnel. Then await the burning in the furnaces whilst hiding in concealed side tunnels like rats in their holes. Make a window with a locking cover through which one can observe the comings and goings within. Within the rampart of each tunnel have one dog. When the dog barks, it is an indication that there are people.

62.7 斬艾與柴[34]長尺，乃置窯灶中，先壘窯壁迎穴為連[35]。

Comment: This brief statement seems straightforward. CZM transposes it to follow what below is 62.8, combining it with 62.9 below to give his #62.11. For RDSY/T it is the start of the long fragment 42.

62.8 鑿井傅城足，三丈一，視外之廣陝而為鑿井，慎勿失。城卑穴高從穴難。[36] 鑿井城上[37]，為三四井，内新甀[38] 井中，伏而聽之，審之[39] 知穴之所在，穴而迎之，穴且遇，為頡皋[40]，必以堅材為夫[41]，以利斧施之，命有力者三人用頡皋衝之，灌以不潔十餘石。

Comment: This section, which corresponds to CZM's #62.10, outlines the method for detecting enemy tunnels so counter-tunnels can be dug, and also what to do when the tunnels meet. Here well-sweeps particularly are used.

62.9 趣伏此井中[42]，置艾其上，七分[43]，盆蓋井[44] 口，毋令煙上泄，旁其囊口，疾鼓之。

Comment: As this continues the instructions for the use of the furnaces, CZM combines it with section 62.7 above.

---

34. This is the generally accepted emendation of 此 following BY and SYR — see WYJ, note 80, p. 870.
35. Following WYZ, 版 is understood after 連, "連版" indicating "編連木板".
36. On this sentence, CZM has the following note: "從與蹤通，謂如果城牆太矮，鑿穴太高，則難以蹤跡或探測敵穴之所在。"
37. There is general agreement that 城上 here should read 城内.
38. 甀 is SYR's suggestion for the unknown character found here. Z&Q have: "甀，亦罌 一類的瓦器。"
39. 之 is generally accepted as being superfluous here.
40. Taken as 桔槔 or "well-sweep".
41. Here 夫 is taken as 趺. Z&Q have: "此指桔槔桿。"
42. All are agreed that significant changes are necessary to make this opening clause intelligible. The version I have followed, that of Z&Q which is based on proposals by BY, SYR and CZM, emends 趣 to 促, 伏 to 狀 as 裝, 此 to 柴, and 井 to 其 referring to 灶 — see Z&Q, note 10, p. 860 and WYJ, notes 90, 91, p. 871.
43. Following SYR, 七分 is read as 七八員 with the last understood as 丸.
44. 井 is again taken as 其 (CZM).

62.7 Cut artemisia and firewood, [preparing bundles] 1 *chi* in length. Place them in the kilns or furnaces. First, make a pile of stones to screen off the kiln [and then], where it faces the tunnel, have joined planks.

62.8 Dig wells close enough to the wall [having] one every 3 *zhang*. Survey the terrain outside [the wall] to establish where to place the wells, taking care not to make a mistake. If the wall is low and the tunnel high, it is difficult to detect the [enemy] tunnels. Within the wall, dig three or four wells and, within each, place newly made jars (*chui*) so it is possible to lie prostrate and listen to them, thus gaining a detailed knowledge of where the [enemy] tunnels are situated. Make [counter-] tunnels to meet them. If the tunnels do, in fact, meet, prepare well-sweeps which must have strong timber for the handles. Use sharp axes to make them. Give the order for three strong men to use the well-sweeps to rush against them (the enemy) and pour in more than 10 *dan* of foul material.

62.9 Hasten to fill the middle of the furnace with brushwood and place seven or eight balls of artemisia on top. Use a basin to cover the mouth of the furnace so as not to let the smoke leak out above. Bring the bellows next to the mouth and rapidly activate them.

62.10   以車輪輻[45]，一束樵、染麻索塗中以束之。鐵鎖，縣正當寇穴
口。鐵鎖長三丈，端環、一端鉤[46]。

Comment: The *wen* is taken to be a form of protective shield (see p. 745). RDSY/SC however writes: "Unfortunately, it is not possible to specify the nature of the *wen*, but it may have been some kind of giant pulley or winch." (see p. 471). This section corresponds to CZM's #62.12.

62.11   鼠穴高七尺，五寸廣、柱間也尺、二尺一柱，柱不傅爲，二柱共
一員十一。[47]兩柱同質[48]，橫員士、柱大二圍半，必固其員士[49]，
無柱與柱交者[50]。

Comment: There is considerable textual uncertainty in this passage. CZM provides a diagram of his interpretation of the structure being described here (p. 67). He also adds the contentious sentence from 62.2.

62.12   穴二窯，皆爲穴月屋[51]，爲置吏、舍人[52]，各一人，必置水。塞穴
門以車兩走[53]，爲輻[54]，塗其上，以穴高下廣狹爲度，令入穴中四

- - - - - - - - - - - - - - -

45. 輻 is usually written here with the 艸 radical but is presumably the same as 輻 found in *Mozi* 52 — see WYJ, note 93, p. 872 for a discussion. LSL has: "用作鎮壓杜塞之物。"
46. On these five characters, SYR has: "言鐵有兩端，一端爲環，一端爲鉤。"
47. There are several issues in this sentence as follows: (i) 鼠 is BY's suggestion for the unknown character which is found here. (ii) 五寸廣 seems too small hence the rearrangement — see CZM and Z&Q. (iii) 也尺 is taken as 七尺. (iv) 傅 is taken in the sense of 附 whilst 爲 is taken to include the 石 radical (ZWDCD #25048). (v) 員十一 is taken as 負士 (SYR, Z&Q).
48. 質 should be taken as 礩.
49. 員士 is taken as 負士 — see note 47 above.
50. There is uncertainty about this final clause, particularly concerning whether 無 should be retained or not — see Z&Q, note 8, p. 862.
51. WYZ rearranges this clause to read: "皆爲穴門上瓦屋。"
52. RDSY (i.e. RDSY/SC) takes both 置吏 and 舍人 to be titles (see p. 465). Hucker does list the latter (#5136) but with a quite different meaning. I think the matter is somewhat uncertain — see, particularly, WYJ, note 109, pp. 873–874.
53. On "車兩走", LSL has: "即車輪。車以兩輪跑，故稱輪爲'兩走'。" See also *Mozi* 63.
54. There is some uncertainty as to how the unusual character found here (ZWDCD #32166) should be read — see Comment. 輻 as above is the most common substitution.

62.10 Make a protective shield (*wen*) from cart wheels. Make one bundle of firewood using a hempen rope steeped in mud to bind it around the middle. Have an iron chain 30 *zhang* long with one end having a ring and the other end a hook.

62.11 [Make] "rat holes" (*shuxue*) 7 *chi* 5 *cun* high with a width between the pillars on either side equal to 7 *chi*. [On the side walls] have one pillar every 2 *chi* with a foundation stone placed beneath each pillar. Every two pillars should have a transverse piece of timber beneath them which connects them. The space under the timber should be filled with earth to support it. The circumference of each pillar should be $2\frac{1}{2}$ *wei*. The supporting earth must be packed firmly whilst the pillars themselves do not interconnect.

62.12 For every tunnel have two kilns (*yao*) and have tiles covering the doors of the tunnels. Have *zhili* and *sheren*, one of each. Water must be placed [there]. Block up the doors of the tunnels with a pair of carriage wheels making a protective shield which is coated with mud on its upper surface. The size of these is determined by

五尺，維置之。當穴者客爭伏門[55]，轉而塞之為窯[56]，容三員艾
者，令其突入伏尺[57]。伏傅突一旁，以二橐守之，勿離。穴矛以
鐵，長四尺半，大如鐵服說[58]，即刃之二矛[59]，內去竇尺[60]，邪鑿
之，上穴當心[61]，其矛長七尺。穴中為環利率[62]，穴二[63]。

Comment: This is another problematic section. CZM has the first sentence
alone as his #62.14. *Zhili* and *shiren* are taken to be personnel acting as
assistants (see RDSY/T, notes 106, 107, p. 282). The next three sentences are
not included in this chapter by CZM. Also, there is some uncertainty about
what a *wen* is here — that is, whether it is the same as the device previously
described (SYR) or the *lu-wen* used for blocking tunnels (RDSY/T). CZM has
the final two sentences as his #62.15.

62.13   鑿井城上[64]，俟其身[65]井且通，居版上，而鑿其一遍[66]，已而移
版，鑿一遍。頡皋為兩夫，而旁狸其植，而數鉤其兩端。[67] 諸
作穴者五十人，男女相半。五十人[68]。攻內為傅土之〔 〕[69]，受六

---

55. There is general acceptance of the reading of 鬥 for 門.
56. This clause is obscure in meaning. I have followed the interpretation given by LSL and
    MBJ.
57. There is doubt about 伏尺. BY notes that some texts do not have these two characters.
    ZCY suggests that 尺 should be read as 穴.
58. "鐵服說" is unclear. LSL takes it to be a weapon of some unspecified nature. CZM
    suggests 服說 should be read as 鈏鉞. Following the latter, I have translated it as
    "battleaxe".
59. According to Z&Q, the two 矛 are 酋矛 and 夷矛.
60. In this rather obscure clause, 內 is read as 穴 and 竇 as 穴口 (Z&Q).
61. In this clause, 上 is taken as 下 and 當心 as 地心 (Z&Q).
62. On "環利率", CZM has: "環利率即環利通索，簡言之為環索，類似近世鐵索纜
    車。"
63. Following Z&Q, I have taken "穴二" as "穴上下".
64. It is accepted that 上 should read 下 (SYR).
65. WNS has: "身者，穿之壞字也。"
66. There is general acceptance of 偏 for 遍 here and in the following use.
67. This is a particularly difficult sentence and the translation is quite tentative. Suggested
    changes include 兩端 for 兩夫, 埋 for 狸, 柱 for 植, 敷 in the sense of 附 for 數 — see,
    for example, Z&Q, notes 5–7, p. 864.
68. These three characters are regarded as superfluous.
69. There are several proposed emendations to make this sentence intelligible. They are as
    follows: (i) 內 to 穴 (SSX, SYR). (ii) "攻穴" should be read as "鑿穴" (Z&Q). (iii) 傅
    should be taken as 移 (CZM). (iv) 土 should be emended to 上 (e.g. Z&Q). (v) For the
    lacuna 具 should be supplied (CZM).

the height and width of the tunnel. Order that they be placed 4 or 5 *chi* into the tunnel and secured with rope. When the enemy is engaged in the tunnel, turn [the pulleys] to lower the protective shield to obstruct [the enemy] and light the kilns. Put three "balls" of artemisia into the kilns. Then let the enemy rush forward and enter the tunnel. From a concealed position to one side, work the bellows and do not leave the post. The lances used in the tunnels are made of iron and are $4\frac{1}{2}$ *chi* long. There are [also] large [weapons] like iron battleaxes, as well as two kinds of lance with sharpened blades. After the tunnel has progressed 1 *chi* from its opening, the digging should incline downwards so the tunnel descends down towards the centre of the earth. Use lances that are 7 *chi* long. Within the tunnel have encircling ropes for going up and down, two per tunnel.

62.13 Dig wells below the wall. Wait until the well is about to break through. Then, standing on a wooden plank, dig out one side. When that is complete, dig out the other side. Have two well-sweeps. At the sides, bury their posts and near the two ends have hooks. In all, have fifty people digging the tunnel with equal numbers of men and women. Within the tunnel have implements

參[70]，約枲繩以牛其下[71]，可提而與[72]投，已則穴七人守退，壘之中為大廡一[73]，藏穴具其中。

Comment: LSL, MBJ and Z&Q all treat this as a single section and, indeed, it does seem to deal with a single topic. However, both CZM and RDSY/T make divisions, the former into four sections (#62.16–#62.19) and the latter into two, these being the final part of fragment 42 and part of the body of fragment 43 following what above is 62.6. CZM summarises his four sections as follows: #62.16: The method of digging wells. #62.17: The method of using well-sweeps. #62.18: The numbers of people used. #62.19: The method of transporting earth when digging tunnels and what to do when the tunnel is complete.

62.14   難穴[74]，取城外池脣木月散之什[75]，斬其穴[76]，深到泉。難近穴為鐵鈇。金與扶林[77]長四尺，財自足。客即穴，亦穴而應之。

Comment: There is some question about "難穴". I have followed CZM and others in taking it to mean making things difficult for enemy tunnellers. RDSY/T, however, takes it as being "where it is difficult to tunnel". The interpretation of this phrase obviously influences the translation of the remainder of the section — see CZM #62.20.

62.15   為鐵鉤鉅[78]長四尺者，財自足，穴徹[79]，以鉤客穴者。為短矛，

---

70. Following SYR, 參 is read as 欙.
71. In this clause, 枲 is read as 大麻 and 牛 is taken as 絆 (SSX).
72. 與 here is read as 舉.
73. On 壘, CZM has: "疑是可供休息之壘。"
74. On "難穴", CZM has: "難穴即阻敵之穴攻。"
75. SYR suggests that this clause should read: "取城外池脣木屑木瓦散之外。"
76. Taken as "斬其內" (SYR).
77. Taken as "鈇與柄" (CZM).
78. There is general acceptance of 距 for 鉅 here.
79. Following SSX, 徹 is read as 通 here and in the following use.

for moving the earth, including six baskets bound around the bottom with hempen rope that can lift out the earth for distribution [around the opening of the tunnel]. When the tunnel is completed, seven men are left to defend it. Within the rampart create one large room within which the tunnelling equipment can be stored.

62.14 To make it difficult [for the enemy] to tunnel, collect up the wood and bricks scattered on the sides of the moat. [Inside the wall] dig a trench as deep as the water level. To make it difficult for tunnels near at hand make iron axes. An axe and its handle should be 4 *chi* long. Make enough for requirements. When enemies have tunnels, also have tunnels to oppose them.

62.15 Make iron hooks — enough to meet requirements — and when the tunnels communicate, use them to hook the enemy tunnellers.

短戟、短弩、虻⁸⁰ 矢，財自足，穴徹以鬥。以金劍為難⁸¹，長五尺，為鋑⁸²、木柄⁸³，柄有慮枚⁸⁴，以左⁸⁵ 客穴。

Comment: CZM treats this as three sections (#62.21–23) dealing respectively with iron hooks, the list of weapons, and the third and somewhat problematic implement.

62.16 戒持⁸⁶ 罌，容三十斗以上⁸⁷，狸穴中，〔三〕⁸⁸ 丈一，以聽穴者聲。

Comment: This is a further brief reference to the listening devices used for detecting the sounds of enemy tunneling. It is CZM's #62.24.

62.17 為穴，高八尺，廣〔八尺〕，善為傅堨。具爐牛皮囊，及瓦缶，衝穴二，益陳霍及艾，穴徹以熏之。

Comment: In this brief section, basically incomprehensible in its original form, I have incorporated the emendations and rearrangements in the text given. These are due mainly to SYR — see, for example, Z&Q, notes 10–16, p. 866. In summary, the changes are as follows: (i) The addition of 八尺 after 廣. This is LSL's suggestion. (ii) The emendation of 置 to 堨 (SYR). (iii) The emendation of the fifth clause from 具全牛交 plus the uncommon character ZWDCD #15556. (iv) The emendation of the sixth clause from 皮及 plus the rare character ZWDCD #5092. (v) In the penultimate clause the emendation of 蓋 to 益 and 靃 to 霍 (SYR). (vi) In the final clause the rearrangement of 熏之以 to 以熏之. In this form it is a further note on the construction of tunnels.

--- --- --- --- --- --- ---

80. There is variation in how this character is understood. Z&Q suggest emendation to 短 and I have accepted this. LSL takes "虻矢" as "飛箭" based on the《廣雅 · 釋器》— see his note 3, p. 508.
81. As they stand, these five characters are difficult to comprehend — as SYR initially observed. The proposed emendations are: 金 to 銅, 劍 to 鄗 and 難 to 拒 — see Z&Q, note 4, p. 865 which incorporates part of SYR's note.
82. BY has this note on 鋑: "《說文》云：'鋑，斤斧穿也'。案經典文，凡以穿為孔者，此字假音。"
83. There is general acceptance of 柄 for the unknown character which is found here and immediately following.
84. This is a somewhat perplexing clause, although most agree that 慮 should be read as 鑢. The translation follows MBJ but see LSL's note 7, p. 508.
85. On 左, CZM has: "左與挫音近。"
86. There is general acceptance of the reading of 備 for 戒. 持 is taken as 持有 (LSL).
87. On the emendation of 客 to 容 (BY) and 斤 to 斗 (WNS) see WYJ, note 150, p. 878.
88. According to SYR, 三 should be added here. Not all editors follow this (e.g. LSL).

Make short lances, short halberds, short crossbows and short arrows — enough to meet requirements — and when the tunnels communicate, use them for the fighting. For hacking the enemy, use a weapon with a bronze blade 5 *chi* in length. Make a hole in the head to fit a wooden handle and above the place where the hand grips the handle have a carved indentation (?). Use this to oppose the enemy tunnellers.

62.16 Prepare and have geophones with a capacity of 30 *dou* or above. Bury them in the tunnels, one (three) every *zhang*, to listen for the sounds of [enemy] tunnelling.

62.17 Make tunnels with a height of 8 *chi* and a width of 8 *chi*. Set up good supporting pillars. Prepare furnaces and ox-hide bellows as well as pipes [for the transmission of smoke]. Each tunnel should have two pipes. Add a supply of rapidly combustible material such as artemisia and, when the tunnels connect, use this to provide smoke [against the enemy].

62.18 斧以⁸⁹ 金為斫，柄⁹⁰ 長三尺，衛⁹¹ 穴四⁹²。為畾⁹³，衛穴四十，屬⁹⁴ 四。為斤、斧、鋸、鑿、鈇⁹⁵，財自足。為鐵校⁹⁶，衛穴四。

Comment: CZM treats this straightforward list of implements as four sections (#62.26–#62.29) — the axes, the baskets, miscellaneous implements, and the iron rails.

62.19 為中櫓，高十丈⁹⁷ 半，廣四尺。為橫穴八⁹⁸ 櫓，蓋具稿枲⁹⁹，財自足，以燭穴中。

Comment: Again CZM has a section for each of the items, describing medium-sized *lu* shields (#62.30), large *lu* shields (#62.31), and hemp stalks for use as illumination (#62.32).

---

89. The addition of 以 was proposed by SYR.
90. This is the generally accepted emendation for the uncommon character (ZWDCD #14785) which appears here.
91. Read as 每 (CZM).
92. WKY suggests this should read "每穴二斧".
93. There is general acceptance of the emendation of 畾 to 虆. For 虆, Z&Q have: "盛土的竹籠。"
94. LSL reads 屬 as 斸. Z&Q equate it with a kind of 鋤.
95. This is SYR's proposal for the unknown character which appears here. LSL has: "是一種類似於鑿的工具。" Z&Q take it to be a 大鋤 which is what I have followed.
96. Based on SYR's original note, Z&Q take 校 as 欄桿.
97. Modern editors accept SYR's emendation of 丈 to 尺 here.
98. There is general agreement following SYR that 八 should read 大.
99. In this clause, 蓋 is taken as 益 as in earlier instances (SYR). There is some doubt about the third character. I have followed LSL in taking it as 稿 in the sense of 乾枯.

62.18   Have axes made with metal blades and handles 3 *chi* in length. Provide four for each tunnel. Make baskets, forty per tunnel, and hoes, four per tunnel. Make axes of different kinds, saws, chisels and large hoes, sufficient for requirements. Make iron rails, four per tunnel.

62.19   Make medium-sized shields $10\,{}^1/_2$ *chi* high and 4 *chi* wide. Make large shields for placing across the tunnels. Have a large quantity of hemp stalks to provide illumination for the tunnels.

62.20   蓋持醋[100]，客即熏，以救目，救目分方鑿[101]穴，以益[102]盛醋置
穴中，文[103]盆毋少四斗。即熏，以自[104]臨醋上及以泄[105]目。

Comment: This is CZM's final section (#62.33) and completes RDSY/T's
fragment 43. On the use of vinegar to protect the eyes, RDSY/SC remarks:
"Just how effective this procedure was against the thick clouds of highly
irritating artemisia smoke in the deep and narrow tunnel is unclear, for no
descriptions of its use in actual battle have come down to us." (p. 469)

---

100. This is SYR's suggestion for the unknown character which appears here and twice more
     in this short section. Other suggestions include 酸, 醓 and 醯. It is clearly some kind of
     acidic liquid. LSL has: "當是一種酸性藥物。" RDSY/SC renders it "vinegar" which
     I have followed.
101. This is SSX's generally accepted suggestion for the unknown character which appears
     here.
102. Following SSX, 益 is read as 盆 here and in the following clause.
103. There is general agreement that 文 should be read as 大.
104. There is general agreement that 自 should be taken as 目 here.
105. There are differing suggestions for the emendation of 泄 — for example, to 油 (YY) or
     to 洒 (SYR). WYJ, noting the《説文》equates 洒 with 滌, has: "洒目即以救目也。"

62.20   Have a large quantity of vinegar so that, when the enemy creates smoke, the vinegar can be used to relieve the eyes. Once the eyes are relieved, attention can be directed [again] to digging out the tunnel. Use basins to hold the vinegar and place these within the tunnels. [They should be] large basins not less than 4 *dou* [in capacity]. When there is smoke, bring the eyes near to the upper surface of the vinegar or use it to wash the eyes.

63: 備蛾傅

Comment: This chapter is as found in the DZ apart from the emendations, of which there are many. Not all have been included in the notes — for further details see BY, WYJ and RDSY/T. WYJ has the same text as six paragraphs: para. 1 corresponds to 63.1, para. 2 to 63.2, para. 3 to part of 63.3, para. 4 to the remainder of 63.3, para. 5 to 63.5–9, and para. 6 to 63.10–12. CZM also has this material as a discrete chapter divided into 23 sections. In RDSY/T the material appears as a continuous series of fragments (44–49) apart from an additional sentence at the end of fragment 49 — see his discussion on pp. 308, 314, 324 and 332.

63.1   禽子再拜再拜曰：「敢問適人強弱，遂以傅城，後上先斷，以為法[1] 程，斬城為基，掘下為室，前上[2] 不止，後射既疾，為之奈何？」子墨子曰：「子問蛾傅之守邪？蛾傅者，將之忿[3] 者也。守為行臨射之，校機藉之，擢之，太氾迫之，燒苔覆之，沙石雨之，然則蛾傅之攻敗矣。」

Comment: There is some doubt about this opening section. Although most editors take it as a coherent section (some divide it into question and response — e.g. CZM #63.1 and #63.2, LSL, MBJ — and some do not — e.g. WYJ, Z&Q), RDSY/T takes there to be a discontinuity. As to precisely where the break is, he is uncertain, but he divides his fragments 44 and 45 after "行臨", considering "... several strips (to) have been lost between fragments 44 and 45" — see his pp. 308 and 311.

63.2   備蛾傅為縣脾[4]，以木板厚二寸，前後三尺，旁廣五尺，高五尺，而折為下磨車[5]，轉徑尺六寸。令一人操二丈四方[6]，刃其兩端，

---

1. This is WNS's emendation of the unusual character (ZWDCD #17792) found here.
2. The emendation from 止 due to BY is generally accepted.
3. Emended from 忽 — see WYJ, note 8, p. 884.
4. There is general agreement that 縣 should read 懸. On this construction CZM has: "縣脾是方形無底之木箱，前後各闊 三尺、兩旁五尺、高五尺，其中恰可容 一人。" A description in English based on the *Mozi* is given by RDSY/SC, p. 482.
5. 下磨車 is taken as equivalent to 轆轤 or the modern 滑車 — see Z&Q.
6. Following BY，方 is taken as 矛.

63: Preparing against the "Ant Approach"

63.1   Qin Zi bowed repeatedly and said: "May I ask about the situation where the enemy shows superior strength, and approaches and climbs the wall, with orders for those that lag behind in the scaling to be punished. They chisel into the wall to create steps and they excavate the wall to make shelters. Those at the front do not stop whilst those behind maintain a rapid fire of arrows. What can be done about this?"

Master Mo Zi replied: "Are you asking about the 'ant approach' (mass infantry assault)? In launching an 'ant approach', the general is being very aggressive. The defenders should make use of movable 'approachers' to fire on the attackers, using either mechanical firing devices or hand-drawn bows. [Use] boiling water to pour down on them, flaming screens to release over them, and sand and stones to rain down on them. In this way, then, the attack by 'ant approach' can be defeated."

63.2   In preparing for the "ant approach", make "hanging spleens" using wooden planks 2 *cun* thick. The width at the front and back should be 3 *chi* and at the sides 5 *chi*. The height should be 5 *chi*. To lower them construct pulleys, the wheels of which should have a diameter of 1 *chi* 6 *cun*. Direct one man to take hold of a lance 2 *zhang* 4 *chi* in length, sharp at both ends, and take up position in

居縣脾中,以鐵璪敷縣二脾上衡[7],為之機,令有力四人下上之,
弗離。施縣脾,大數[8]二十步一,攻隊所在六步一。

Comment: The majority treat this as a discrete section — e.g. WYJ as 63, para
2 and CZM as #63.3. It is about a single topic, the "hanging spleen" which
appears to have been a wooden box, presumably slatted and containing one
soldier, which was lowered over the side of the wall so the enclosed warrior
could use his double-ended lance to strike at enemy soldiers scaling the wall
— see RDSY/SC p. 482. RDSY/T combines this with all the next section (63.3)
and all but the final sentence of the following section (63.4) as his fragment 46.

63.3   為纍[9],苫廣從丈各二尺[10],以木為上衡,以麻索大遍之[11],染其
索塗中,為鐵鎖[12],鈎其兩端之縣。客則蛾傅城,燒苫以覆之,
連梃[13],抄大皆救之[14]。以車兩走[15],軸間廣大以圍[16],犯之[17]。
刺[18]其兩端。以束輪,遍遍塗其上。室[19]中以榆若[20]蒸,以棘為
旁,命曰火捽,一曰傳湯,以當隊。客則乘隊,燒傳湯,斬維而
下之,令勇士隨而擊之,以為勇士前行,城上輒塞壞城。[21]

----

7. There are several issues in this clause as follows: (i) 璪 is taken as 瑱 in the sense of 鎮.
   (ii) 敷 is taken as 附. (iii) 二 is regarded as superfluous. (iv) 上衡 is taken as equivalent
   to 上端的橫木.
8. Taken as 大概 — see Z&Q.
9. There is some debate about 纍 — whether it should be retained or read as 礧 (CZM) or
   壘 (BY). RDSY/T argues strongly for retaining it and I have followed this.
10. In this clause, 廣從 is taken as 廣縱 whilst 丈 and 各 are transposed.
11. According to SYR, these six characters should be rearranged to read "以大麻索編之".
12. Z&Q's emendation.
13. I have followed WYJ's emendation of the unusual character (ZWDCD #26837) which
    is found here in most texts. LSL makes the emendation to 匙. RSDY/SC terms 連梃
    "linked flails" — see p. 483.
14. Following SYR's emendations, these five characters read: "沙火皆止之。"
15. 走 is taken as 輪 following SYR.
16. 圍 is taken as 圍 following SYR.
17. It is difficult to know what "犯之" means here. LSL equates it with 抵觸.
18. This is the generally accepted reading of the unknown character appearing here. SYR
    equates it with the unusual character ZWDCD #24409.
19. There is general acceptance of the reading of 窒 for 室.
20. 若 is read as 或 — see, for example, Z&Q.
21. As can be seen from the preceding notes, a number of emendations are required to make
    this comprehensible. Detailed consideration of the several issues is given by Z&Q (notes
    13–28, p. 872) whilst the apparatus is described by RDSY/SC on p. 482.

the "hanging spleen". An iron chain is attached to the upper horizontal timber of the "hanging spleen" and this is suspended from the pulley above. Direct four strong men to lower and raise it and not to leave [their posts]. Set up "hanging spleens" at intervals of approximately 20 *bu* but, when the attacking forces are at hand, reduce this to 6 *bu*.

63.3   Make rope-bound screens (*da*) which, in both width and length, are 1 *zhang* 2 *chi* and which have a horizontal timber above. Use thick hempen rope to bind them up and smear them with a covering of mud. Use an iron chain hooked on to both ends to suspend them. When the enemy makes an "ant approach" to the wall, set fire to the screens to drop over them. Linked flails (*lianting*), sand and fire all stop them. Take two cart wheels and bind them to a large piece of wood, the distance between the axle-shafts being wide, and oppose them. Both ends of the large piece of wood are sharpened and both the wood and the wheels are everywhere coated with mud. The space between is filled with twigs of elm or hemp whilst at the sides there are brambles. This [apparatus] is called a "fire-thrower" (*huozu*). It is also called a "heat transferrer" (*zhuantang*).[i] It is placed facing the [enemy] troops. If the enemy scales [the wall] then set fire to the heat transferrer, cut its ropes and let it fall. [Then] give the order for brave warriors to follow it and rout them (the enemy), taking the heat transferrer as a forerunner for the brave warriors. Those on the wall should immediately repair the damage to the wall.

---

i.   The two English terms are those given by RDSY/T.

Comment: There is some variation in how this section is treated. Several editors have it as a discrete section (e.g. LSL, MBJ, Z&Q) whereas WYJ has it as two paragraphs 63, paras 3 & 4 (although para 4 also includes what, in the present text, is the first sentence of 63.4. RDSY/T has it as part of his long fragment 46 which comprises 63.2, the present section and all but the final sentence of 63.4 following. CZM divides the section into two components (#63.4 and #63.5) which correspond to the two main devices being described — the hanging screens (*da*) and what RDSY/T has called "fire-throwers" or "heat transferrers" which seem to be the same entity. There is some uncertainty about 縶 at the start and whether it should be read as 曩 (BY, YTY). I have followed the majority view in retaining it as "to bind".

63.4   城下足為下說鑱杙²²，長五尺，大圍²³ 半以上，皆剡其末，為五行，行間廣三尺，狸²⁴ 三尺，大耳²⁵ 樹之。為連殳²⁶，長五尺，大十尺²⁷。梃長二尺，大六寸，索長二尺。椎柄長六尺，首長尺五寸。斧柄長六尺，刃必利，皆築²⁸ 其一後²⁹。

Comment: This section, as constituted above, gives brief details of several implements. CZM treats it as four separate sections — his #63.6–9. In RDSY/T this section is the final part of fragment 46. Two issues are, first, whether the stakes are wood or iron (RDSY/T) and, second, whether the final five characters are misplaced here.

---

22. Both 說 and 鑱 are taken as 銳 and 杙 as 椿 — see Z&Q's detailed note 1, p. 874 and also WYJ, note 38, p. 887.
23. As elsewhere, 圍 is taken as 闈.
24. As elsewhere, 狸 is taken as 埋.
25. Following SYR, 大耳 is read as 犬牙.
26. On 連殳, Z&Q have: "一種軍器。即《備城門》篇中的大梃。" — see also RDSY/ SC's description (including diagram) on pp. 482–483 and LSL's reference to the *Odes* (his note 4, p. 514).
27. According to SYR, 大十 should read 大寸. Z&Q suggest 大十寸 with 大 being taken here as elsewhere in the sense of 粗. The alternative, exemplified by RDSY/T, is to take this as 10 *chi* large (in circumference).
28. This is SYR's suggestion for the unknown character which appears here.
29. According to LSL, this clause is incomprehensible and should be omitted which I have done in the translation — see his note 6, p. 514.

63.4   Below the wall put a sufficient number of sharpened wooden
stakes, each 5 *chi* long and greater than $^1/_2$ *wei* in circumference,
all sharp at the ends. Make five rows with a distance between the
rows of 3 *chi* and bury them to a depth of 3 *chi* set upright like
dog's teeth. Make linked maces (*lianshu*) 5 *chi* in length and
roughened over 1 *cun*. Flails are 2 *chi* in length and 6 *cun* in
circumference. The length of the rope is 2 *chi*. Hammers have
handles 6 *chi* in length and a "head" which is 1 *chi* 5 *cun* long.
Axes have handles which are 6 *chi* long and blades which must be
sharp.

63.5　　苔廣丈二尺，〔 〕〔 〕³⁰ 丈六尺，垂前衡四寸³¹。兩端接尺相覆，
　　　　　勿令魚鱗三³²。著其後行，中央木繩一³³，長二丈六尺。苔樓不會
　　　　　者以牒塞³⁴，數暴乾，苔為格，令風上下。

Comment: This section returns to the topic of (fire-) screens, starting with the
same basic dimensions as given in 63.3. There is some variation in the
punctuation of the third sentence but the meaning seems clear. The same
can't be said for the final sentence, the translation of which must be taken as
somewhat tentative. CZM treats this as a separate section (#63.11) whilst
RDSY/T combines it with the next section in his fragment 47. In WYJ it is part
of 63, para 5 which includes all the material from the second sentence of 63.
4 to the end of 63.9.

63.6　　牒惡疑壞者，先狸木十尺一枚一³⁵，節³⁶ 壞，鄧植以押慮盧薄於
　　　　　木³⁷，盧薄表³⁸ 八尺，廣七寸，經³⁹ 尺一，數施一擊⁴⁰ 而下之，
　　　　　為上下釘而斫之⁴¹。

Comment: There is some uncertainty about the precise details of the
description being given here although it does seem clear that it is about the
repair of a damaged parapet. CZM has it as his #63.11 whilst for RDSY/T it
completes his fragment 47.

---

30. Z&Q suggest "其長" as the missing characters which MBJ also has. LSL has "其縱".
31. There is some doubt about this clause. CZM thinks 寸 should read 尺. I have followed
    this.
32. 三 here is taken as 參.
33. In this clause, 中央 is taken to "…指後衡的中間" (Z&Q), whilst 木 is read as 大 (SYR).
34. In this clause, I have followed Z&Q who have this note: "苔樓：苔張開，形似城樓。
    不會：指不密合。牒：板木。"
35. There is a question here of whether the final 一 is superfluous — see RDSY/T, note 63,
    p. 326.
36. 節 is taken as 即.
37. There are several issues in this clause as follows: (i) 鄧 is taken as 斫 (BY). (ii) 植 is read
    as 木. (iii) One 慮 is regarded as superfluous (LSL, Z&Q). (iv) On "盧薄", Z&Q have:
    "柱上的橫木，俗稱壁柱。"
38. There is general acceptance of 表 as 長.
39. There is general acceptance of 經 as 徑.
40. On these four characters, Z&Q have: "指多次槌擊。"
41. In this clause, I have included the proposed emendations for the rare characters — 釘 for
    鈞 (CZM) and 斫 for ZWDCD #13952 respectively.

63.5   Screens (*da*) are to be 1 *zhang* 2 *chi* wide and 1 *zhang* 6 *chi* long. They are suspended by an anterior cross-member which projects 4 *chi*. The place of connection at either end must overhang by 1 *chi* to the right and left, but do not let them be unequal like fish scales. Attached to the centre of the posterior cross-member is a large rope, 2 *zhang* 6 *chi* long. The screen is exposed in an unconfined place and filled with pieces of wood which are kept dry. The screen should have a framework to allow the air to circulate above and below.

63.6   Where the parapet is damaged and thought likely to collapse, first bury pieces of wood, 10 *chi* long, one every *bu*. If the parapet does collapse, cut pieces of wood and attach cross-pieces onto the well buried posts. The attached pieces should be 8 *chi* long, 7 *cun* wide and have a diameter of 1 *chi*. They should be securely attached and lowered. Then nail them above and below and cut them.

63.7[42]   經一鈞、禾樓、羅石、縣荅、植內毋植外。

Comment: As indicated in note 42, this section is very problematic, particularly at the start. The translation is, therefore, only tentative. CZM treats it as two separate sections (#63.12 and #63.13) dealing with stones and screens, respectively. RDSY/T includes this and the following two sections (i.e. 63.7–9) in his fragment 48.

63.8   杜格[43]，狸四尺，高者十丈[44]，木長短相雜，兌[45] 其上，而外內厚塗之。

Comment: There is some doubt about the opening two characters of this brief statement which I have isolated as a section following CZM (#63.14). RDSY/T, who includes this as his fragment 48, speaks of a "wattle fence" and also retains 尺 as in the DZ and WYJ, for example, in relation to the height. Suffice it to say that it is some form of wooden barrier.

63.9   為前行行棧[46]，縣荅。隅為樓，樓必曲裡[47]，上五步一，毋其二十 畾[48]。爵穴十尺一，下堞三尺，廣其外。(轉傅[49] 城上樓及散與池 革盆。若轉，攻卒擊其後，煖失治，車革火。)[50]

Comment: This is a very problematic section, being, in effect, a disjointed series of statements with significant textual difficulties. CZM treats the section as five separate statements (#63.15–20) whilst RDSY/T indicates that several

---

42. This brief section is very problematic. CZM has: "此節必有脫誤，'經一'或上文'經尺一'之復出。" I have omitted the first three characters from the translation. Of the rest, 禾 is taken as 木, 罝 as 礧, and 植 as 杜 following various commentators.
43. The emendation of 杜格 to 柞格 proposed by SYR is generally accepted.
44. I have followed the modern editors LSL & Z&Q in having 丈 rather than 尺 (found in the DZ) here.
45. 兌 is read as 銳.
46. I have followed Z&Q's interpretation of this clause which involves regarding the first three characters as misplaced and taking 棧 as a walkway. They have: "行棧：指行城上的橋道，可伸可收。" — see note 7, p. 876. LSL takes 行棧 as a storehouse.
47. Following SYR, 曲裡 is read as 再重.
48. 畾 here is taken as 虆 or 籠 (SYR).
49. This is BY's proposal for the unknown character which appears here. By no means is there agreement on this. Thus, WKY has: "畾，纏也，所以穴上纏城上。"
50. It is very difficult to make any sense of these 24 characters. Z&Q omit them — see their note 12, p. 876 — as does RDSY/T. LSL does attempt a reading using emendations by SYR, YTY and WKY. I have included a translation of his version in parentheses.

63.7   [On the wall set up] wooden towers with piles of stones, and hang screens on the inside of the pillars but not on the outside.

63.8   Make an oak palisade buried to a depth of 4 *chi* and with a height of 10 *zhang*. [In it], long and short timbers are mixed together. The upper ends are sharpened and the outer surface thickly covered with mud.

63.9   [On the wall], have retractable walkways and suspend screens. At the corners, make towers. The towers must be of two storeys. Every 5 *bu* there should be a pile of earth, at the very least not less than 20 baskets. At a distance of 3 *chi* below the parapets excavate holes at intervals of 10 *chi* and widest towards the exterior. (With respect to changing direction on the wall, quickly prepare the moving towers, *sha*, pools of water and pitchers of hide. If the enemy scales the wall, and those soldiers undertaking the attack are not able to effect a timely retreat and leave behind military equipment, it should be dealt with according to military conventions. Also, there should be use of fire and smoke.)

of the statements appear to be incomplete. Several commentators take what are the final two sentences above as incomprehensible. Between this and the next section, RDSY/T interposes what, in the present text, are 56.4 and 56.5 — see the Comment to those sections and RDSY/T pp. 223, 332.

63.10   凡殺[51] 蛾傅而攻者之法，置薄[52] 城外，去城十尺，薄厚十尺。伐操[53] 之法，大小盡木斷之，以十尺為斷，離而深狸堅築之，毋使可拔。

Comment: The arrangement of the final three sections of this chapter follows CZM, 63.10–12 corresponding to his #63.21–23. RDSY/T groups these three sections together in his single fragment 50 whilst WYJ also treats them together in the final paragraph (63, para 6) of the chapter. RDSY/T calls the *bo* a "rough fence".

63.11   二十步一殺[54]，有鬲[55]，厚十尺。殺有兩門，門廣五步[56]，薄門板梯狸之，〔勿〕[57] 築，令易拔。城上希[58] 薄門而置搗[59]。

Comment: This is closely similar to part of 56.4 above. For reasons given in the Comment to that section, I have resisted calling a *sha* a "death" as RDSY does.

63.12   縣火，四尺一椅。五步一灶，灶門有爐炭。傳令敵人盡入，車火燒門，縣火次之，出載而立，其廣終隊，兩載之間一火，皆立而待鼓音而然，即俱發之。敵人辟火而復攻，縣火復下，敵人甚

---

51. Following CZM, I have equated 殺 with 破. RDSY/T retains the meaning of "to kill".
52. On the *bo* 薄, CZM has: "薄，柱也。亦得為障礙物。" RDSY/T speaks of "rough fences".
53. There is general acceptance of BY's emendation of 操 to 薄.
54. On *sha* here, LSL has: "殺 — 指柵籬左右橫出的圍子。" CZM has: "豫備投擲敵人之所，因名曰'殺'。" — see also RDSY/SC, p. 481 who uses the term "death".
55. On SYR's emendation from the unknown character found here, LSL has: "孫説當作'鬲'，通'隔'。從'殺'中間隔開，以藏人和器械。"
56. Of modern editors, both LSL and MBJ take 步 here to be a mistake for 尺 although Z&Q do retain the former.
57. Added following BY.
58. Read as 睎 (LSL) or 望 (Z&Q).
59. Z&Q take this to be a 裾 mentioned in 56.4 — see their detailed note 4, p. 878 which includes WYZ's earlier note.

63.10   In general, among the methods of repelling an "ant approach", there is the setting-up of barriers (*bo*) outside the wall at a distance of 10 *chi* from it. A barrier should be 10 *chi* thick. The method for cutting down [timber for] a barrier is to take everything large or small and cut it at the root, then cut it into 10 *chi* lengths. The pieces are gathered together and buried deeply in the ground to create a strong construction that cannot be pulled up.

63.11   Every 20 *bu*, there should be one *sha* (? "death") with an internal partition 10 *chi* thick. A *sha* has two gates [each] being 5 *chi* wide. A small part of the gate timbers is buried but not strongly, allowing them to be easily pulled up. Opposite the gates of the barrier, set up a palisade (*ju*).

63.12   [Have] "hanging fires" with a hook every 4 *chi*. Every 5 *bu* have one furnace. By the doors of the furnaces have braziers with charcoal. The enemy soldiers are allowed to enter completely, upon which smoke and fire are applied to the gates with "hanging fires" to follow. Send out carriers and set them up, their width being equivalent to that of the enemy line. Between two carriers there should be one fire. When everything is set up, the sound of the drum is awaited and, upon its occurrence, the fires are lit and all together thrown down. If the enemy should avoid the fire and attack again, the 'hanging fires' are again hurled down, bringing

病。敵引哭而楡⁶⁰，則令吾死士左右出穴門擊遺師，令貴士、主將皆聽城鼓之音而出，又聽城鼓之音而入。因素⁶¹出兵將施伏，夜半，而城上四面鼓噪，敵人必或，破軍殺將。以白衣為服，以號相得。

Comment: As noted earlier, this section is very similar to 56.5 in the chapter on cloud ladders — see the Comment to sections 56.4 and 56.5. There are several textual emendations, accepted since BY, and based on the earlier passages — for example, 火 for 人 as the second character and the addition of 白 in the penultimate clause.

64: 闕

65: 闕

66: 闕

67: 闕

---

60. In this clause, 哭 is taken as 師 (YY) and 楡 as 去 (BY) or as 逃 (SYR).
61. 因素 is taken as 照舊 — see, for example, Z&Q.

the enemy great distress. When the enemy army is led to withdraw, give the order for our crack troops on all sides to go forth from the sally ports and attack the fleeing army. Give the order to these brave men and their general all to go forth when they hear the drum sound on the wall and to return when they hear the drum sound again. As before, when the soldiers and general go forth, set up a diversion. In the middle of the night, create a clamour of drums from all sides on the walls. This must create doubt in the hearts of the enemy and you will rout their army and kill the general. Put on white garments as clothes and communicate with each other by calls.

64: Lost

65: Lost

66: Lost

67: Lost

68: 迎敵祠

Comment: This chapter is as it appears in the DZ apart from the emendations which become increasingly numerous as the chapter proceeds. Both WYJ and CZM also have it as a discrete chapter although the former does make a small addition (6 characters) to what is 68.2 below (see his note 15, p. 898). RDSY/T, who has the chapter as a continuous series of fragments (52–60), suggests that only the first and last sections of what is presently taken as chapter 68 (迎敵祠) actually belong to the original chapter (see his discussion pp. 351–352), although it may be, as Z&Q for example suggest, that the next section also belongs to this material.

68.1   敵以東方來，迎之東壇，壇高八尺，堂密[1]八。年八十者八人，主祭青旗。青神長八尺者八，弩八，八發而止。將服必青，其牲以雞。敵以南方來，迎之南壇，壇高七尺，堂密七。年七十者七人，主祭赤旗。赤神長七尺者七，弩七，七發而止。將服必赤，其牲以狗。敵以西方來，迎之西壇，壇高九尺，堂密九。年九十者九人，主祭白旗。素神長九尺者九，弩九，九發而止。將服必白，其牲以羊。敵以北方來，迎之北壇，壇高六尺，堂密六。年六十者六人，上祭黑旗。黑神長六尺者六，弩六，六發而止。將服必黑，其牲以彘。從外宅諸名大祠，靈巫或禱焉，給禱牲。[2]

Comment: This opening section is obviously a discrete section and all editors treat it as such (e.g. CZM, #68.1, RDSY/T, fragment 52, WYJ 68, para 1). There are three textual issues of note: (i) The meaning of "堂密" which is variously taken as referring to the depth of the hall, to stairs, or to a particular object. (ii) The punctuation following "年八十者八人" and the recurring phrase of similar

---

1.   From BY and SYR on, most commentators have taken 密 as 深 and I have followed this. Other suggestions are that steps are being referred to (see, for example, WYJ, note 2, p. 896) or that *tangmi* is a name (CZM) — see RDSY/T's detailed note 1, p. 354.

2.   There are some issues with this final statement. Whilst most commentators accept SYR's reading of 從 as 徙, CZM does not follow the reading based on this. His note in full is: "'從'孫改'徙'，非是，此言從外頭所有各大名祠起，均派巫致祭，且給以祭神牲品。" (p. 84).

68: Sacrifices for Meeting the Enemy

68.1   When enemies come from the east, meet them at an eastern altar. The altar should be 8 *chi* high and the depth of the hall 8 *chi*. Eight people of eighty years should lead the sacrifice to a green pennant and eight likenesses of a green god 8 *chi* high. There should be eight crossbows which fire eight arrows then stop. The general's clothing must be green and the sacrificial creature the chicken. When enemies come from the south, meet them at a southern altar. The altar should be 7 *chi* high and the depth of the hall 7 *chi*. Seven people of seventy years should lead the sacrifice to a red pennant and seven likenesses of a red god 7 *chi* high. There should be seven crossbows which fire seven arrows then stop. The general's clothing must be red and the sacrificial creature the dog. When enemies come from the west, meet them at a western altar. The altar should be 9 *chi* high and the depth of the hall 9 *chi*. Nine people of ninety years should lead the sacrifice to a white pennant and nine likenesses of a white god 9 *chi* high. There should be nine crossbows which fire nine arrows then stop. The general's clothing must be plain (white) and the sacrificial creature the sheep. When enemies come from the north, meet them at a northern altar. The altar should be 6 *chi* high and the depth of the hall 6 *chi*. Six people of sixty years should lead the sacrifice to a black pennant and six likenesses of a black god 6 *chi* high. There should be six crossbows which fire six arrows then stop. The general's clothing must be black and the sacrificial creature the pig. From all the large temples outside the city, priests and shamans are sent to say prayers and make the sacrificial offerings.

form which can vary to give the reading above, or that the sacrifices are made to flags with the likenesses on them (RDSY/T), or that such likenesses are made as a separate matter (Z&Q). (iii) There is some uncertainty about the final sentence. RDSY/T quotes SYR's suggestion that this means "… as for the houses and important sacrifices outside the wall, when the enemy arrives, one moves the people and the spirit tablets inside", only to reject it.

68.2   凡望氣³，有大將氣，有小將氣，有往氣，有來氣，〔有勝氣〕⁴，
有敗氣，能得明此者可知成敗、吉凶。舉巫醫卜有所，長具藥，
宮之，善為舍。巫必近公社，必敬神之。巫卜以請守，守獨智巫
卜望氣之請而已⁵。其出入為流言，驚駭恐吏民，謹微察之，斷，
罪不赦。望氣舍近守官⁶。牧⁷賢大夫及有方技者若工，弟之⁸。舉
屠，酤者置廚給事，弟之。

Comment: Whilst WYJ and the modern editions of LSL, MBJ and Z&Q have this section as a single paragraph, both CZM and RDSY/T divide it, albeit differently. Thus, CZM has the first sentence as #68.2, sentences 2–4 as #68.3 and the final sentence as #68.4 whilst RDSY/T, who has it as three fragments (53–55), transposes the questionable penultimate sentence to follow what is sentence two above. The latter is itself beset with interpretative difficulties evidenced in the varying punctuation in different editions. The somewhat free translation of this sentence follows particularly MBJ.

---

3.   RDSY/T draws attention to the articles by A. F. P. Hulsewé on "watching the vapours" (*Nachrichten der Gesellschaft für Natur- und Völkerkunde Ostasiens* 125, 1979, pp. 40–49) and D. Bodde on "watching the ether" (*Studia Serica Bernhard Karlgren dedicata*, Copenhagen, 1959, pp. 14–35). CZM equates 望氣 with the modern 氣象台.
4.   Added following CZM.
5.   On the rearrangement of this clause see WYJ, note 18, p. 898.
6.   RDSY/T suggests that this sentence be transposed to follow the second sentence of the section. CZM has it in the present position but in parentheses.
7.   Following SYR, 牧 is read as 收.
8.   On 弟之, BY has this note: "言次第居之、占次第字只作弟。"

68.2   In general, with the method of "watching the vapours" (*wang qi*), there is *dajiang* vapour, there is *xiaojiang* vapour; there is "going" vapour, and there is "coming" vapour. There is "success" vapour and there is "failure" vapour. If these things are clearly understood, it is possible to know whether there will be victory or defeat, good fortune or bad fortune. Bring forward those who are skilled in wizardry, medicine and divination, provide them with the necessary drugs and arrange good living conditions. The quarters for the shamans must be close to the altars for the gods of the soil and they must offer respect to the gods. The activities of the shamans and diviners are reported to the Defender and he is the only one to know the results of "watching the vapours". If they should come and go creating rumours, startling and terrifying officials and people, thoroughly and closely investigate them and put them to death, this being an unpardonable crime. The lodgings for those involved in "watching the vapours" must be close to the defence headquarters. In gathering worthy high officials as well as workmen with particular skills, rank them. In the case of butchers and wine-sellers, set up kitchens and give them duties, [then] rank them.

68.3 凡守城之法，縣師受事，出葆[9]，循溝防，築薦通塗，修城。[10] 百官共財，百工即事，司馬視城脩卒伍[11]。設守門，二人掌右閣，二人掌左閣，四人掌閉，百甲坐之。城上步一甲，一戟，其贊三人。五步有五長，十步有什長，百步有百長，旁有大率，中有大將，皆有司史卒長。[12] 城上當階，有司守之。移中中處，澤急而奏之。[13] 士皆有職。

Comment: This section is treated as such in modern editions (WYJ, LSL, MBJ, Z&Q). It has, however, three components as recognised in the divisions of CZM (#68.5–7) and RDSY/T (fragments 56–58). They are: (i) The duties of the *xianshi* and the *sima* for which I have given Hucker's titles applicable to the Zhou period (#2534 and #5713 respectively). (ii) The distribution and grouping of troops on the wall. (iii) The handling of documents.

68.4 城之外，矢之所逮，壞其牆，無以為客菌。[14] 三十里之內，薪、蒸、水[15] 皆入內，狗、彘、豚、雞食其肉[16]，斂其骸以為醢，腹[17] 病者以起。城之內薪蒸廬室，矢之所逮，皆為之塗菌。令命

---

9. On 出葆, Z&Q have: "視察堡壘。葆、通 '堡'。"

10. There are several points in this sentence as follows: (i) For 縣師 Hucker has "township preceptor" — see #2534. (ii) There is general agreement that "出葆" should be understood as "視察堡壘" (e.g. MBJ, Z&Q). (iii) 循 is taken as 巡. (iv) On "築薦通塗" Z&Q have "謂阻塞通道" which I have followed.

11. There is variation in the punctuation here. RDSY/T, for example, takes 卒伍 to be the subject of the following sentence with the meaning of "common soldiers".

12. For the first two of these five titles I have used Hucker's terms — see #7732, #5196 respectively. The last three I have Romanised. Hucker does have an entry for 百長 but it relates specifically to the Qing period.

13. There are some issues in this sentence, particularly concerning "移中中處". The version given follows CZM. There is general agreement among modern commentators that 澤 be taken as 擇 and 急 as 緊急.

14. The two important readings in this sentence are 逮 as 及 (see, for example, LSL) and 菌 as 梱 (SSX).

15. There is general acceptance of the reading of 木 for 水.

16. 肉 is found in most texts as the unusual variant ZWDCD #7254.

17. LSL places the comma after 腹. Most accept SYR's reading of 腹 as 復. I have translated 醢 as "broth". Modern editors such as LSL and Z&Q give 肉醬.

68.3   In general, in defending the city [is to have] township preceptors (*xianshi*) who have certain duties [such as] surveying the fortifications, inspecting ditches and dikes, blocking up roads beyond the wall, and maintaining the wall itself. The hundred officials provide materials. The hundred workmen carry out their various duties. The commander (*sima*) oversees the conditions of the wall and the troops. In setting up the defence of the gate, two men are assigned to manage the right leaf and two the left leaf. Four men are in charge of [opening and] closing the gate. One hundred armoured soldiers sit [by the gate] in defence. On the wall, every 1 *bu* there is an armoured soldier and a halberdier with three people to assist them. Every 5 *bu* have a squad leader, every 10 *bu* a file leader, and every 100 *bu* a leader of one hundred (centurion). To the sides there are grand marshals (*dashuai*) and in the middle there is a general-in-chief (*dajiang*). All these leaders have their particular responsibilities. Against the wall there is a flight of steps with one person to manage its defence. Military documents are moved to a conveniently central place where those that are urgent can be picked out and made known. All the officers have their duties.

68.4   Beyond the wall, as far as arrows can reach, anything resembling a wall should be destroyed so there is no way for the enemy to find shelter. Within a radius of 30 *li*, all firewood, twigs and wood generally is brought within [the wall]. With animals like dogs, pigs, sucking pigs and chickens, whose flesh is eaten, the bones are collected to make a broth which is used to help the sick recover their health. Within the wall, firewood, twigs, huts and houses as

昏緯狗纂馬，擊緯，靜夜聞鼓聲而譟[18]，所以閹[19] 客之氣也，所以固民之意也，故時譟[20] 則民不疾矣。

Comment: This collection of miscellaneous instructions is treated as a single fragment by RDSY/T (fragment 59) and as two sections by CZM (#68.8, #68.9), being divided under the headings "城之外" and "城之內". At this point, SYR has the comment: "凡守城之法以下至此，疑他篇之文，錯著於此。"

68.5   祝、史乃告於四望[21]、山川、社稷、先於戎[22]，乃退。公素服誓於太廟，曰：「其[23] 人為不道，不修義詳[24]，唯乃是王[25]，曰：『予必懷[26] 亡爾社稷，滅爾百姓。』二三子尚夜自廈[27]，以勤寡人，和心比力兼左右，各死而守。」即誓，公乃退食，舍於中太廟[28] 之右，祝、史舍於社。百官其御，乃斗[29] 鼓於門，右置旃，左置旄於隅

- - - - - - - - -

18. I have substituted BY's proposal for the rare character ZWDCD #36735 here and in the following use.
19. 閹 is taken as 遏 in the sense of 遏制 (Z&Q).
20. Generally found as an ancient variant (ZWDCD #36735).
21. Modern editors such as LSL and Z&Q take 祝 and 史 respectively as 太祝 and 太史 — presumably the Great Supplicator and the Grand Astrologer as listed by Hucker (#6152, #6212). On "四望", LSL refers to Zheng Xuan's 鄭玄 note on the *Rites of Zhou*《周禮 · 大宗伯》as follows: "四望：五嶽四鎮四瀆。"
22. Although I have taken this to indicate "before the battle" (as have Z&Q), it should be noted that LSL, for example, has a different view, regarding 先 as referring to the spirits of former warriors and quoting YTY who has: "先戎，謂始造兵為軍法者。其神蓋蚩尤，或云黃帝。"
23. I have followed LSL in taking 其 as 某.
24. There is general agreement that 詳 should be read as 祥. I have translated it as "virtue".
25. SYR proposes that this should read: "唯力是正。" YTY has: "是王，猶言自大。"
26. I have followed the general view that 懷 be taken in the sense of 思.
27. There are several issues with the preceding seven characters as follows: (i) 參 is read as 三. For "二三子" Z&Q have: "稱自己的部屬。" (ii) On 尚 I have followed SSX's reading of 夙. (iii) On 廈 I have followed BY's reading of 勵.
28. On 中太廟 SYR has: "侯國太祖之廟。"
29. There is general acceptance of 升 for 斗 (SYR).

far as an arrow can travel are all covered with mud. The order is given that, in the evening, dogs should be tied up and horses tethered. The tethering must be secure. In the still of the night, when the drum is heard, there should be a great shout. This is a way to dampen the enemy's spirits and to strengthen the people's resolve. Thus, if there are timely shouts, the people are not fearful.

68.5 The prayer-makers and chroniclers make an announcement to the four directions, the mountains and rivers, and the altars of soil and grain, prior to the conflict. Then they withdraw. The duke, dressed in plain garments, offers a pledge in the ancestral temple, saying: "Such people do not act in accord with the Way. They do not cultivate righteousness and virtue. They rely only on strength and arrogance, saying, 'We plan to destroy your altars of soil and grain. We will wipe out your people.' I urge all of you to strive day and night, and labour on my behalf. With singleness of purpose, we can strive together, risking our lives in defence [of our kingdom]." Having made the declaration, the duke then withdraws to eat, resting within the central ancestral temple on the right-hand side. The prayer-makers and chroniclers rest at the altar of soil. When the one hundred officials are all in attendance, then the drum is raised in the doorway whilst to the right is placed a banner

練名。射參[30]發，告勝，五兵[31]咸備，乃下，出挨[32]，升望我
郊。乃命鼓，俄升役，[33] 司馬射自門右，蓬矢射之，茅[34]參發，
弓弩繼之，校自門左，先以揮[35]，木石繼之。祝、史、宗人告
社，覆之以甑。

Comment: This final section is, like the first and possibly the second sections
above, taken to be part of the original material under the title "迎敵祠". CZM
(#68.10), RDSY/T (fragment 60) and WYJ (68, para 4) all treat it as a discrete
section. A detailed discussion of the procedures involved is given by
RDSY/T (see pp. 373–376). The translation of this section is very uncertain,
depending as it does on numerous emendations, interpretations and
additions. The more important of these are given in the preceding notes.

---

30. As elsewhere in this chapter, 參 is taken as 三.
31. The "five weapons" 五兵 are bow and arrow 弓矢, spear 殳, lance 矛, spear/lance 戈,
    and halberd 戟.
32. 挨 here is taken as 俟 (BY).
33. There is some doubt about this clause. In the translation, I have taken 俄 as 一會兒
    (Z&Q) and included 役 here rather than in the next clause, reading it as 旌 (YTY).
34. Read as 矛.
35. I have followed WKY in taking 揮 as 煇 indicating a flaming arrow.

and to the left a standard, one at each corner, and on the streamers are written the names of the commanders. Three arrows are released to announce [an impending] victory. The five weapons are prepared. Then [the troops] assemble below and await the command. The duke ascends [the temple platform] and surveys the space beyond [the wall]. Then he orders the drum [to be sounded] and, after a few moments, the banners are raised. The commander fires a stream of arrows from the doorway to the right. A spear is raised three times. Then all take up their bows and fire them. The commander first fires a flaming arrow from the doorway to the left, then all follow with wood and stones. The prayer-makers, chroniclers and the ancestral intendant make an announcement at the altar of soil and cover over the sacrificial vessel.

69: 旗幟

Comment: This chapter corresponds to the DZ chapter 69 apart from the emendations. WYJ has it as three paragraphs, the first two corresponding to 69.1 and 69.2 below and the third containing all the other sections (69.3–9). CZM also has the same material which is arranged very similarly to what appears below. The differences are that he divides 69.3 into two sections (his #3 & #4), 69.5 into two sections (his #6 second part and #7), and 69.6 into two sections (his #8 & #9). In addition, 69.7 below forms the first part of his #6. Although RDSY/T divides the material somewhat differently, it forms a continuous series of fragments (61–72).

69.1   守城之法，木為蒼旗，火為赤旗，薪樵為黃旗，石為白旗，水為黑旗，食為菌¹旗，死士為倉英²之旗，竟士³為雩⁴旗，多卒為雙兔之旗，五尺童子⁵為童旗，女子為梯末⁶之旗，弩為狗旗，戟為旌⁷旗，劍盾為羽旗，車為龍旗，騎為鳥旗。凡所求索旗名不在書者，皆以其形名為旗。城上舉旗，備具之官致財物，之⁸足而下旗。

Comment: This is treated as a discrete section by all editors (e.g. CZM #69.1, RDSY/T fragment 61). The first four characters are taken as a heading. RDSY/T suggests that 書 in the penultimate sentence indicates that "… the Mohists carried copies of these chapters when they were preparing their tasks of defence." (p. 383)

---- ----

1. On 菌, CZM has: "菌是食品，故食為菌旗。" I take it the flag shows an item of food, presumably the mushroom. SYR thinks 菌 should be taken as 茜 which the *Shuo Wen* equates with 茅蒐.
2. SSX takes "倉英" as "蒼鷹" which I have followed.
3. On 竟士, SSX has: "猶言勁卒。"
4. 雩 is read as 虎 following WNS.
5. Taken to indicate boys of fourteen and under — see, for example, Z&Q, note 5, p. 894.
6. I have followed CZM in reading "梯末" as "姊妹".
7. This is SYR's emendation of the unknown character which appears here. On 旌, Z&Q have: "用五色羽毛做裝飾的旗。"
8. Emended to 物 by CZM; for other views see WYJ, note 13, p. 907.

69: Flags and Pennons

69.1 Methods of defending a city. For wood, make a green flag. For fire, make a red flag. For firewood and fuel, make a yellow flag. For stones, make a white flag. For water, make a black flag. For food, make a *jun* flag. For "dare-to-die" soldiers, make a hawk flag. For vigorous soldiers, make a tiger flag. For many soldiers, make a flag of paired hares. For boys under fourteen, make a *tong* flag. For women, make a "sisters" flag. For crossbows, make a "dog" flag. For halberds, make a *jing* flag. For swords and shields, make a "feathers" flag. For carts, make a "dragon" flag. For mounts, make a "bird" flag. In general, if something is sought for which a flag is not [listed] in the book, then create a flag based on the form or name [of what is needed]. When a flag is raised on the wall, the officials responsible provide whatever materials or things are needed and when there is enough the flag is lowered.

69.2　凡守城之法：石有積，樵薪有積，菅茅有積，雚葦[9]有積，木有積，炭有積，沙有積，松柏有積，蓬艾有積，麻脂有積，金鐵[10]有積，粟米有積；井灶有處，重質[11]有居。五兵各有旗，節各有辨[12]，法令各有貞[13]，輕重分數各有請[14]，主慎道路者有經[15]。

Comment: This section comprises another list: first, of various important materials to be stored or piled up, and second, of various arrangements and rules. CZM has it as #69.2, RDSY/T as fragment 62 and WYJ as 69, para 2.

69.3　亭尉各為幟，竿長二丈五，帛長丈五，廣半幅者大[16]。寇傅攻前池外廉[17]，城上當隊鼓三，舉一幟；到水中周，鼓四，舉二幟；到藩，鼓五，舉三幟；到馮垣，鼓六，舉四幟；到女垣，鼓七，舉五幟；到大城，鼓八，舉六幟；乘大城半以上，鼓無休。夜以火，如此數。寇卻解，輒部幟如進數，而無鼓。

Comment: This section, which both CZM (#69.3 and #69.4) and RDSY/T (fragments 63, 64) separate into two parts with the division after the first sentence, deals with the provision of pennons or flags to the officers in charge of *ting* or posts along the wall, and with the use of these pennons in conjunction with drums to signal the stages of the enemy's advance or retreat. As described in 52.18, the *ting* (posts) were 100 *bu* apart along the wall.

----

9. In most texts, 雚 appears in a variant form. I have followed Z&Q in reading "雚葦" as "蘆荻".
10. WNS suggests that 鐵 should be emended to 錢. Z&Q accept this whereas LSL and MBJ have 銅鐵 which I have followed.
11. There is agreement amongst modern editors (LSL, MBJ, Z&Q) that "重質" indicates "重要的人質" — LSL has: "指敢死之士的父母妻子。"
12. 節 is read as 符節 and 辨 as 判 — see, for example, LSL.
13. 貞 is read as 定 following CZM.
14. Read as 情 (e.g. Z&Q) or 誠 (e.g. LSL).
15. There is uncertainty about this clause. SYR suggests 循 for 慎 whilst CZM suggests 行 for 經 — see, particularly, Z&Q, note 8, p. 895.
16. There is general acceptance of SYR's proposal to emend 大 to 六. His note reads in part as follows: "六即亭尉幟之數，蓋每亭為六幟，以備寇警緩急舉踣之用。"
17. 廉 is taken as 邊 — see, for example, LSL.

69.2   General methods of defending a city: Have stores of stones; have stores of fuel and firewood; have stores of rushes; have stores of reeds; have stores of wood; have stores of charcoal; have stores of sand; have stores of pine and cypress; have stores of fleabane and artemisia; have stores of hemp and oil; have stores of bronze and iron; have stores of rice and millet. Wells and furnaces should have their locations. Important hostages should have places to dwell. The five weapons each should have a flag. Tallies each should have two halves. Rules and orders each should be [clearly] established. The gradations of light and heavy each should have their basis. Those responsible for the inspection of roads each should have designated areas.

69.3   For each post captain (*tingwei*), have pennons with staffs of 2 *zhang* 5 *chi* in length and material (silk) 1 *zhang* 5 *chi* long, and half a strip wide, six in all. When the enemy attack reaches the outer side of the moat, those on the wall facing the enemy should strike the drum three times and raise one pennon. When the enemy is in the water of the moat, they should strike the drum four times and raise two pennons. When the enemy reaches the protecting palisade, they should strike the drum five times and raise three pennons. When the enemy reaches the subsidiary wall, they should strike the drum six times and raise four pennons. When the enemy reaches the parapets, they should strike the drum seven times and raise five pennons. When the enemy reaches the main wall, they should strike the drum eight times and raise six pennons. When the enemy is halfway up in their ascent of the wall, they should strike the drum continuously. During the night, fires take the place of the pennons but the numbers are the same. When the enemy is retreating, the pennons are used in the same sequence as for the advance but without the drum.

69.4   城為隆[18]，長五十尺。四面四門將長四十尺，其次三十尺，其次
二十五尺，其次二十尺，其次十五尺，高無下四[19]十五尺。

Comment: The version of this brief section (CZM #69.5, RDSY/T fragment 65)
given above depends on SYR's two proposed emendations, neither of which
RDSY/T accepts. In his alternative version the first general is the general of the
city, the flag is not crimson, and 四 is retained with the measurement (45 *chi*)
referring to the staff — see his pp. 398–399.

69.5   城上吏卒[20]置之背，卒於頭上，城下吏卒置之肩，左軍於左肩，
〔右軍於右肩〕[21]，中軍置之胸。各一鼓，中軍一[22]三。每鼓三，
十擊之，諸有鼓之吏，謹以次應之，當應鼓而不應，不當應而應
鼓，主者斬。

Comment: Although both CZM (#69.6 part two, #69.7) and RDSY/T
(fragments 66, 67) divide this section, treating the insignia and the drums
separately, modern editors (LSL, MBJ, Z&Q) do not. In WYJ it is part of his
third and final paragraph which includes all the sections in the present text
from 69.3 to 69.9. One issue of note is whether WYZ's proposed addition
should be accepted as above. For the contrary position see RDSY/T, note 37,
pp. 400–401.

69.6   道廣三十步，於城下夾階者，各二，其井置鐵薩[23]。於道之外為
屏，三十步而為之圜，高丈。為民圂，垣高十二尺以上。巷術周
道者，必為之門，門二人守之，非有信符，勿行，不從令者斬。

Comment: The arrangement of the final four sections varies somewhat. That
given follows Z&Q and MBJ. Both CZM (#69.8, #69.9) and RDSY/T (fragments
68, 69) treat the present section as two parts, making a division after what is
the third sentence above. There is variation in the reading of the second
sentence above, depending on whether 屏 is taken as a screening wall (e.g.
Z&Q) or as a latrine (e.g. RDSY/T, LSL).

---

18. According to SYR, this should read: "城將為絳幟。"
19. 四 is regarded as superfluous here (SYR).
20. Following WYZ, 卒 is regarded as misplaced here.
21. There is general agreement that this additional clause should be supplied (WYZ).
22. Here 一 is accepted as superfluous (SYR).
23. CZM's proposed emendation of 薩 is 罐. WYZ suggests 甕. In either case it is a
    receptacle of some sort.

69.4 For the general on the wall, there is a crimson flag 50 *chi* in length. For the generals in charge of the gates on the four sides, [the flag] is 40 *chi* long. [There is then a progressive decrease according to rank], the next being 30 *chi*, the one after that 25 *chi*, then 20 *chi*, then 15 *chi*, there being nothing less than 15 *chi*.

69.5 The officers on the wall [have an insignia] placed on their backs, the common soldiers on their heads, and the officers and soldiers below the wall on their shoulders. For the army on the left, it is on the left shoulder. For the army on the right, it is on the right shoulder. For the army in the middle, it is placed on the chest. Each (i.e. the left and right armies) has one drum whilst the middle army has three. The number of strikings of the drum ranges from three to ten. All those officers who have drums must be careful with respect to the number [of strikings] of their responses. Those who respond when they should not respond, or who do not respond when they should respond, are put to death.

69.6 The road [on the wall] is 30 *bu* wide with steps to ascend and descend. On both sides of these are wells with iron vessels [for water]. On the outer side of the road make screening walls, one every 30 *bu*. Make them round and 1 *zhang* high. Make latrines for the people with walls 12 *chi* or more high. Where streets and lanes join the road there must be gates with two men to guard them. Those without the correct identification do not pass. Those who don't comply with orders are executed.

69.7   城中吏卒民男女，皆辨[24]異衣章微[25]，令男女可知[26]。

> **Comment:** This brief section corresponds to RDSY's fragment 70. CZM has it earlier as the opening sentence of his #69.6.

69.8   諸守牲格者[27]，三出卻適，守以令召賜食前，予大旗，署百戶邑若他人財物[28]，建旗其署，令皆明白知之，曰某子旗。牲格內廣二十五步，外廣十步，表[29]以地形為度。

> **Comment:** This is treated as a single section by CZM (#69.10) whereas RDSY/T divides it, making the first sentence fragment 71 and joining the second sentence with what is here 69.9 in his fragment 72.

69.9   斬[30]卒，中教解前後左右，卒勞者更休之。

> **Comment:** On RDSY/T's interpretation, this final statement applies to troops training within a *shengge* as a kind of fenced enclosure. This is CZM's #69.11.

---

24. This is WYZ's generally accepted emendation of the rare character (ZWDCD #32253) which appears here — see, particularly, WYJ, note 55, p. 913.
25. According to WNS, "衣章微" should read "衣章微職".
26. CZM takes these last five characters to be a gloss.
27. The "牲格" is equated with the "杜格" and the "柞格". Z&Q have: "用上端削尖的木椿築成的障礙物，亦即木藩籬。"
28. On "署百戶邑", Z&Q have: "擁有管轄百戶人家的城邑。" 若 is taken as 或.
29. There is general acceptance of 袤 (i.e. 長) for 表.
30. 斬 is read as 勒 following SYR.

69.7 On the wall, the officers and soldiers, men and women, all should wear distinguishing clothes and emblems so men and women can be distinguished.

69.8 [In the case of] all those who defend the *shengge* (?fences) and are able to beat back three advances by the enemy, the Defender gives an order summoning them and bestows food on them in front [of others], provides them with a large flag, and gives them control over a town of one hundred households, or other materials and things. A flag to establish their official status lets everyone clearly know this. And this is called a *mouzi* flag. The internal width of the *shengge* is 25 *bu* and the external width is 10 *bu*. Its length is determined on the basis of the local topography.

69.9 In training troops, starting from the centre, teach those to the front and back, right and left [in sequence] so those who are tired can rest [in rotation].

70: 號令

Comment: The material in this chapter corresponds to the DZ 70 both in content and sequence apart from the numerous emendations. WYJ has the material divided into 15 paragraphs following the same order except for the insertion of what, in the present text, are 52.20 and 52.21 which make up the major part of his paragraph 6 in the present chapter.

70.1 安國之道，道[1] 任地始，地得其任則功成，地不得其任則勞而無功。人亦如此，備不先具者無以安主[2]，吏卒民多心不一者，皆在其將長。諸行賞罰及有治者，必出於王公。數使人行勞賜守邊城關塞、備蠻夷之勞苦者，舉其守率之財用有餘、不足，地形之當守邊者，其器備常多者。邊縣邑視其樹木惡[3] 則少用，田不辟，少食，無大屋草蓋，少用桑[4]，〔多財，民好食〕[5]。

Comment: All editors have this as the beginning of chapter 70 but there is some variation in the actual arrangement. I have followed modern editors LSL and Z&Q in taking it as the first section. Others, such as WYJ and MBJ, have a continuous opening paragraph to the end of what is here 70.2. RDSY/T, however, treats 70.1 as two separate fragments (73 and 74) making the break at the end of the third sentence above. CZM also makes a division between #70.1 and #70.2 at this point but includes what I have as 70.3 in his #70.2. There is also a textual issue at the proposed break concerning whether 王 is made the subject of the first sentence of the second part or is included with 公 in the last sentence of the first part. Two other issues are, first, whether RDSY/T, for example, is right in taking the opening sentence to be speaking of "…

---

1. On 道 here, LSL, for example, quotes Zheng Xuan's note on the《禮記 · 禮器》equating 道 with 從.
2. Z&Q have the following note on "安主": "使守城人安心。"
3. 惡 is taken as 缺乏 (Z&Q).
4. I have followed RDSY/T in regarding 桑 as an error which should read 燒. For an alternative reading see LSL, p. 529.
5. Based on CZM, these five characters are regarded as out of place here (perhaps a gloss) and are not included in the translation (see also SYR, Z&Q). RDSY/T has: "When there is too much materiel, however, the people will be overfond of eating."

70: Orders and Commands

70.1 The way of bringing peace to a state starts from the proper use of the land. If the land is properly used, then achievement can be completed. If the land is not properly used, then, regardless of labour, there is no achievement. People are also like this. If prior preparations are not made with respect to [military] equipment, then there is no way to bring peace to those who must defend the city. If the officers, soldiers and ordinary people are numerous but not of one mind, the responsibility invariably lies with their leaders. In all cases, the carrying out of rewards and punishments and the bringing about of order must come from the king or duke. [He] must frequently send people to reward those who defend the frontiers and passes, and those who prepare against barbarian invasion. He must ascertain whether the defensive leaders' materiel is more than enough or not enough, whether the topography is suitable for frontier defence, and whether their equipment and preparations are constantly adequate (many). If, in the border districts and regions, they see that trees and wood are lacking, there is little to use. If the fields are not opened up, there is little to eat. If there are no large houses with grass roofs, there will be little to use for burning.

a metaphysical relationship between the Tao and Earth *ti* 帝", referring to the *Guanzi* 24.[6] I have followed a more prosaic line. Second, there is the question of whether the five characters in brackets at the end of the section are part of the original text or not. I have followed CZM in taking the latter position.

70.2　為內堞[7]，內行棧[8]，置器備其上，城上吏、卒、養[9]，皆為舍道內，各當其隔部。養什二人，為符者曰養吏一人，辨護[10]諸門。門者及有守禁者，皆無令無事者得稽留止其旁，不從令者戮，敵人但[11]至，千丈之城，必郭迎之，主人利。不盡千丈者勿迎也，視敵之居曲，眾少而應之，此守城之大體也。其不在此中者，皆心[12]術與人事參之[13]。

Comment: In making this a section I have followed Z&Q. RDSY/T divides this passage into three fragments (his fragments 75–77), the first being a brief and possibly incomplete fragment comprising the first eleven characters only of the present section. His second fragment is then about servants or "food orderlies", although the surveillance of gates is also included. His final fragment he thinks "... suggests that there were two subsections, as yet unidentified in the extant text or now lost, called 'Mental Techniques' ... and 'Human Affairs' ..." (p. 413). CZM links this section with the second half of the previous section in his #70.2. WYJ includes all this and the next section in his 70, para 1. At this point a brief word seems apposite on the three characters 戮, 斬 and 斷 which are variously used throughout this chapter, in particular to indicate punishment. I have taken all three to be interchangeable in meaning "putting to death" or "executing", although this does seem to be a particularly harsh penalty for some of the offences described and also raises concerns about loss of manpower. On this, CZM has this comment: "王以 '斷' 為 '斬'，但從墨子各篇觀之，'斷' 字包含多種處罰方法，不盡是斬刑。" (p. 85) — see also RDSY/T, note 21, pp. 361–362.

---

6. See *Guanzi Duben*, vol. 1, p. 493 and Rickett, vol. 1, p. 115. Also, RDSY/T, p. 412.
7. There is general agreement that 堞 should be read as 堞.
8. I have followed Z&Q in reading 行棧 as 橋道.
9. Z&Q have this note on 養: "《公羊傳 · 宣公七年》何休注：'炊烹曰養'，軍隊中的炊事兵。"
10. On 辨護, LSL quotes SYR as follows: "猶言監治也。" Z&Q have: "辨識監護。"
11. I have taken 但 as 且 following, for example, LSL — but see RDSY/T.
12. 心 is taken as 以 following SYR.
13. The understanding of this sentence is somewhat difficult. Much depends on whether SYR's proposed emendation of 心 to 以 is accepted. For those who accept it (e.g. LSL, Z&Q), it becomes a matter of first principles or local conditions and affairs. For those who do not, a different reading is required — see, for example, RDSY/T and MBJ.

70.2   Make an inner battlement and an inner footbridge and put in place utensils that are prepared. On the wall, officers, soldiers and servants are all billeted inside the road, in each case appropriately divided according to their place of defence. Two servants are assigned to every ten men with one person to hold the tallies. This person is called the "servant officer" and is responsible for guarding every gate. Those who guard the gates and those responsible for the prohibitions of defence should not let anyone linger or remain beside them (i.e. the gates). Those who do not follow orders are put to death. Further, when the enemy forces reach [a city with] a 1000 *zhang* wall, they must be met at the outer wall, this being to the defender's benefit. In the case of a city with a wall less than 1000 *zhang*, do not go to meet them but look at the deployment of the enemy forces and their number, and [then] meet them. This is the principal point of defending a city wall. For any situation not covered within this, in all cases look at it in the light of basic principles and human affairs.

70.3   凡守城者以毆[14]傷敵為上，其延日持久以待救之至，明於守者
也，不能此，乃能守城。

Comment: CZM (#70.3) and RDSY/T (fragment 78) both treat this as a
separate fragment. For WYJ it is the start of his long paragraph 2 which ends
with the penultimate sentence of what is here 70.10. With regard to meaning,
there is variation as to whether waiting for help is a reasonable option or not.

70.4   守城之法，敵去邑百里以上，城將如今[15]，盡召五官及百長，以
富人重室之親，舍之官府，謹令信人守衛之，謹密為故。

Comment: This is also probably best treated as a specific section, as CZM,
for example, does (his #70.4). It certainly embodies a single, clear
recommendation. RDSY/T combines it with what is 70.5 below, creating his
fragment 79.

70.5   及傅城[16]，守將營無下三百人，四面四門之將，必選擇之有功勞
之臣及死事之後重者，從卒各百人。門將并守他門[17]，他門之上
必夾為高樓，使善射者居焉。女郭、馮垣一人，一人[18]守之。(使
重室子)。五十步一擊[19]。

Comment: This is a problematic section. The arrangement given basically
follows CZM, although he treats the final sentence as a separate fragment.
Thus he has the section apart from this as his #70.5, taking the final four
characters as a gloss. The last sentence above then becomes his #70.6. On
the contentious 擊, CZM has: "蘇云：'擊當作樓'。余疑'擊'為'隔'之音轉，
即寅篇11之鬲，參下戎篇21。" RDSY/T combines this section with the previous
section as his fragment 79 and also takes the final five characters as a
separate group. He leaves open the question of 擊.

---

14. There is general acceptance of the reading of 急 for 毆.
15. Following WYZ and BY, 如今 is read as 乃令.
16. There is wide acceptance of YY's suggestion that this refers to an "ant approach" by the
    enemy, although RDSY/T, for, one does not take this to be so.
17. SYR proposes the addition of 小 to give "他小門".
18. It is generally agreed that the duplication of "一人" is an error.
19. This final clause is very problematical both in text and in position. SSX proposes the
    emendation of 擊 to 樓 (see Comment above).

70.3   In general, in guarding a city, the best option is to quickly inflict damage on the enemy, but the advantage of waiting until relief arrives should also be recognised in defence.[i] Certainly, if these things can be done, then the defence can be successful.

70.4   In methods of defence of a city, if the enemy is 100 *li* or more away, the general in command then issues an order urgently summoning the [members of] the five offices and the leaders of a hundred men, as well as the kindred of rich men and important families to reside in official dwellings. He orders trustworthy men to defend and guard them for reasons of caution about secrecy.

70.5   When the enemy makes an "ant approach" against the city, the defending general [must have in his] camp not less than 300 men whilst the generals of the four sides and the four gates must choose officers of meritorious service and followers prepared to serve to the death, these numbering 100 men [for each general]. The gate generals collectively defend the other gates, above which must be built high towers to which skilled archers are sent to take up positions. The outer battlements and the earthen wall should have one man for defence. (Send the sons of important houses.) Every 50 *bu*, have one tower.

---

i.   There is some doubt about the second part of this statement involving where 不 should be placed (before 明 or following 能), and whether it should be emended to 必. In terms of meaning, the issue is, then, whether waiting for relief is a desirable option (Z&Q) or should be avoided (RDSY/T).

70.6　因城中里為八部，部一吏，吏各從四人，以行衝術[20] 及里中。里中父老小[21] 不舉守之事及會計者，分里以為四部，部一長，以苛[22] 往來，不以時行、行而有他異者，以得其姦。吏從卒四人以上有分〔守〕[23] 者，大將必與為信符，大將使人行，守操信符，信不合及號不相應者，伯長以上輒止之，以聞大將。當止不止及從吏卒縱之，皆斬。諸有罪自死罪以上，皆遝父母、妻子、同產。

Comment: The meaning in this section is quite clear and there is uniformity in arrangement. Both CZM (#70.7) and RDSY/T (fragment 81) have it as a discrete section.

70.7　諸男女[24] 有守於城上者，什六弩四兵。丁女子、老少，人一矛。

Comment: I have taken this as a discrete section following CZM, particularly (his #70.8). Some modern editors (LSL, Z&Q) do likewise. RDSY/T combines it with what below are the first three sentences of the next section (i.e. down to "…姦也") in his fragment 82.

70.8　卒有驚事[25]，中軍疾擊鼓者三，城上道路、里中巷街，皆無得行，行者斬。女子到大軍，令行者男子行左，女子行右，無並行，皆就其守，不從令者斬。離守者三日而一徇，而所以備姦也[26]。里正與皆守宿里門[27]，吏行其部，至里門，正與開門內[28] 吏。與行父老之守及窮巷幽間無人之處。

---

20. Z&Q take 衝術 as 道路, which is in accord with BY's proposal that 衝 should be read as the old form — ZWDCD #34904.
21. According to WYZ, 小 is misplaced here.
22. There is some doubt about this character. I have followed Z&Q's reading as 盤查.
23. Added following WYZ.
24. Based on what follows, 女 should be read as 子 (Z&Q).
25. In this opening clause, 卒 is read as 猝 and 驚事 as 警事 (LSL, Z&Q).
26. There are three points in this sentence: (i) 而‥ is probably superfluous (SYR). (ii) 徇 generally appears in a variant form (ZWDCD #10285). (iii) The second 而 is taken as 此 (SYR).
27. 正 is found here and in the final clause of the sentence in the ancient form. Also, according to SYR, "與皆守" should read "與有守者".
28. There is general agreement that 內 should be read as 納.

70.6   On the basis of the neighbourhoods within the city, eight divisions (wards) are created with one officer for each division. Each officer has four assistants with whom to patrol the streets and within the neighbourhood. The old and young people in the neighbourhoods do not take part in the business of defence, nor in planning. Four divisions are made in a neighbourhood, with one leader for each division to look into comings and goings which are at inappropriate times, or are for other strange or nefarious purposes. Officers from the four assistants upwards who have defensive responsibilities must be given reliable tallies by the Commander-in-Chief (Great General), and when he sends men out on defensive business, they should carry these reliable tallies. In the case of the reliable [tallies] not corresponding or calls not eliciting a matching response, military officers from leaders of a hundred men upward at once stop them and let the Commander-in-Chief hear of it. Those who should stop them but do not, and assistants to the officers who let them go are all put to death. In the case of all those who commit a crime meriting the death penalty or more, all their parents, wives, children and siblings are implicated.

70.7   Among the adult men who are defenders on the wall, in a file of ten, six should have crossbows and four [other] weapons. In the case of adult women, both old and both young, for each person there should be one spear.

70.8   If an urgent situation suddenly arises, the centre army rapidly strikes the drum three times. [Then] in the road on the wall and in the lanes and streets in the neighbourhoods, all people must refrain from moving about. Those who do move about are put to death. When [men] and women go towards the main army, the order is given to those moving for men to walk on the left and women to walk on the right, and that they do not walk together. [In this way] all go to their defensive [positions]. Anyone who does not follow the order is put to death. Those who leave their defensive positions have their corpses displayed for three days, this being used as a warning against treachery. The leaders of the neighbourhoods and all those with defensive responsibilities live [adjacent to] the neighbourhood gates. The leader personally opens the gate to

Comment: There are, in this section, some variations in arrangement and also some textual issues. As it stands above, it has three components. The first concerns the movement of people after the drum has sounded to declare an emergency situation. The second concerns the taking up of defensive positions and punishment for leaving these positions. The third is to do with surveillance of the gates and other areas within the wall. CZM treats the first two as separate fragments (#70.9 and #70.10). RDSY/T combines the two and adds them to what is 70.7 above as his fragment 82. Both CZM and RDSY/T combine the third component with what is 70.9 above to give #70.11 and fragment 83 respectively. I have followed Z&Q in separating 70.9 in that it deals with the issue of collaboration. Also, within the third component, there is the issue of *fulao* 父老, specifically, in the penultimate sentence, whether this is added after the first 與 (CZM) or both the first and second 與 (RDSY/T) and, related to this, whether 吏 should come before or after the full-stop. The matter is discussed by WYJ (note 58, p. 932). There is an issue with the placement of the last line which is also included in 70.11.

70.9   姦民之所謀為外心，罪車裂。正與父老及吏主部者，不得皆斬。得之，除，又賞之黃金，人二鎰。大將使使人[29]行守，長夜五循行，短夜三循行。四面之吏亦皆自行其守，如大將之行，不從令者斬。

Comment: As discussed in the previous Comment, this section is included with the last two sentences of the previous section by CZM (#70.11) and RDSY/T (fragment 83).

70.10   諸灶必為屏，火突高出屋四尺，慎無敢失火，失火者斬，其端失火以為事者[30]，車裂。伍人不得，斬；得之，除。救火者無敢讙譁，及離守絕巷救火者斬。其正及父老有守此巷中部吏，皆得救之，部吏亟令人謁之大將，大將使信人將左右救之，部吏失不言者斬。諸女子有死罪及坐失火皆無有所失，逮其以火為亂事者如法。圍城之重禁。

Comment: This is generally accepted as a discrete section. CZM has it as #70.12 and RDSY/T as fragment 84. The topic is, of course, fire control and the penalties for letting a fire get out of control or deliberately setting a fire. The

---

29. Following SYR, 使人 should read 信人 — i.e. 可靠的人.
30. There is some doubt about this clause. On "端失火", BY has: "因事端以害人。" SYR thinks 亂 should precede 事.

admit an officer. He then accompanies him in inspecting the areas of defensive responsibility of the elders right up to the narrow lanes and secluded places where no one lives.

70.9 What treacherous people plan is to collaborate [with the enemy] outside. It is a crime [that warrants] pulling apart by chariots. Leaders and elders, as well as officers in charge of divisions, who fail [to apprehend such people] are all put to death. If they apprehend them, they are free of guilt and are also rewarded with gold [to the amount of] 2 *yi* per person. The Commander-in-Chief sends trustworthy men to walk around the defensive areas. On long nights, there are five tours of inspection; on short nights, there are three tours of inspection. Also, the officers on the four sides all personally walk around their defensive areas like the walking around of the Commander-in-Chief. Those who do not comply with the order are executed.

70.10 Protective screens must be made for all furnaces. Chimneys should be high, extending 4 *chi* above the building. Care must be taken not to dare to lose [control of] a fire. Those who lose [control of] a fire are put to death. Those who deliberately lose [control of] a fire to create disorder are pulled apart by chariots. Five-man squads who do not apprehend [such people] are put to death. If they apprehend [them], they are free of guilt. Those who go to put out the fire dare not make a noise or clamour, whilst those who leave their defensive posts and obstruct the laneways for fire relief are put to death. The leaders, as well as elders and officers, who have defensive responsibilities for the division containing these laneways all involve themselves in putting out the fire. The officer for the division quickly orders men to inform the Commander-in-Chief. The Commander-in-Chief sends trustworthy men from the left and right to put it out. Division officers who fail to report it are put to death. In all cases, women who commit crimes warranting the death penalty, as well as those who lose [control of] a fire even if they cause no harm, right up to those who use fires to bring about disorder, are all treated according to the law. These are important prohibitions for a besieged city.

one issue of arrangement concerns the final five characters — whether they are the conclusion of this section (LSL, Z&Q) or a heading to start the next section (CZM, WYJ, MBJ, RDSY/T).

70.11 〔圍城之重禁。〕敵人卒[31]而至，嚴令吏民無敢讙囂、三最[32]、並行、相視、坐泣流涕、若視[33]、舉手相探、相指、相呼、相麾、相踵、相投、相擊、相靡[34]以身及衣、訟駮[35]言語及非令也而視敵動移者，斬。伍人不得，斬；得之，除。伍人蹳城歸敵，伍人不得，斬；與伯歸敵，隊吏斬；與吏歸敵，隊將斬。歸敵者父母、妻子、同產皆車裂。先覺之，除。當術需敵離地，斬。伍人不得，斬；得之，除。

Comment: In terms of context, it does seem more appropriate to have the first five characters as the start of this section in the form of a heading for what is a whole list of prohibited activities. As alluded to earlier, the triviality of some of these offences is in striking contrast to the severity of the recommended punishment. The punishment of the leaders of those who transgress, as well as their associates and family members, is notable, as is the encouragement to report the misdeeds of others. In most texts in which divisions are made (CZM, RDSY/T, LSL, MBJ, Z&Q), this is a discrete section. WYJ combines it with the next section in his 70, para 3.

70.12 其疾鬥卻敵於術，敵卜終不能復上，疾鬥者隊二人，賜上奉。[36]而[37]勝圍，城周里以上，封城將三十里地為關內侯[38]，輔將如令[39]賜上卿，丞及吏比於丞者，賜爵五大夫。官吏、豪傑與計堅守者，十人及城上吏比五官者，皆賜公乘。男子有守者，爵人二

---

31. As in other instances, 卒 is read as 猝.
32. Following WYZ, 最 is read as 聚 via its rare form ZWDCD #1618.
33. There is some doubt about "若視". Z&Q have "或相視" whilst LSL suggests 視 is superfluous and joins 若 to the following clause. I have followed the latter.
34. There is general acceptance of the reading of 摩 for 靡.
35. On 訟駮, Z&Q have: "相駁難。駮：駁字之誤。"
36. I have followed Z&Q's interpretation of this sentence — see their notes 1 and 2, p. 912. Also, 卒 is read as 倅.
37. There is general acceptance of the reading of 而 as 如.
38. On this title and the two following, see WYJ, notes 95–97, pp. 935–936.
39. There is some uncertainty about 令 here — see RDSY/T, p. 452 and WYJ, note 96, p. 936. CZM, who has 如今, specifically equates this with the English "then".

70.11 [Important prohibitions for a besieged city:] When the enemy suddenly arrives, strict orders are given to officers and people not to dare to make a noise or clamour, to gather in groups of three, to walk together, to watch each other, to sit silently weeping and let tears flow, to raise their hands and question each other, to point at each other, to call to each other, to signal to each other, to follow each other's footsteps, to throw things at each other, to strike each other, to touch each other's persons or clothing, to blame and refute, to argue and talk, as well as to watch the enemy's actions and movements without orders [to do so]. [Those who do these things] are put to death. If the five-man squad does not apprehend them, they are put to death. If they do apprehend them, they are free of guilt. If a five-man squad [member] scales the wall and goes over to the enemy and [the other members] of the squad don't apprehend him, they are put to death. And, if the leader of a hundred men goes over to the enemy, the regimental leader is put to death. If the regimental leader goes over to the enemy, the regimental general is put to death. In the case of those defecting to the enemy, parents, wives, children and siblings are all torn apart by chariots. Those who report on these matters before the event are free of guilt. Those who leave their positions at the time of facing the enemy are put to death. If the five-man squads do not apprehend them, they are put to death. If they do apprehend them, they are absolved from blame.

70.12 When a fierce battle has raged at the battleline and the enemy has been repulsed and driven down the wall, and is unable to scale it again, two men are chosen from every regiment and rewarded with an increased salary. If a siege is defeated, where the wall is greater than 1 *li* in circumference, the general in charge is enfeoffed with 30 *li* of land and made a *guannei hou*. Reward the deputy general with the title of *shangqing* and deputies and officers according to their roles, bestowing on them the rank of *wu dafu*. In the case of other officers who are brave and take part in the planning of a strong defence, knights-errant as well as officers on the wall and lesser officers of various ranks from the five

級，女子賜錢五千，男女老小先[40]分守者，人賜錢千，復之三
歲，無有所與，不租稅[41]。此所以勸吏民堅守勝圍也。

Comment: This section deals with the rewards of rank, money and tax relief
to be given to those who take part in a successful defence. It is treated as a
discrete section by those listed in the previous Comment (for CZM #70.14, for
RDSY/T fragment 86) whilst WYJ combines it with the previous section as his
paragraph 3. I have simply romanised the titles, although all are listed by
Hucker — 關內侯 as Marquis of Kuan-nei (#3321), 上卿 as Senior Minister
(#4987), and 五大夫 as Grandee of the Ninth Order (#7824). On these, see
also WYJ, notes 95–97, pp. 935–936 and RDSY/T, note 89, p. 452.

70.13   吏卒侍大門中者，曹[42]無過二人。勇敢為前行，伍坐[43]，令各知
其左右前後。擅離署，戮。門尉晝三閱之，莫，鼓擊門閉一閱，
守時令人參之，上逋者名。鋪[44]食皆於署，不得外食。守必謹微
察視謁者，執盾，中涓[45]及婦人侍前者，志意、顏色、使令、言
語之請。及上飲食，必令人嘗，皆非請也，擊而請故[46]。守有所
不說，謁者、執盾、中涓及婦人侍前者，守曰斷[47]之，衝[48]之，
若縛之，不如令及後縛者，皆斷。必時素誠之。諸門下朝夕立
若[49]坐，各令以年少長相次，旦夕就位，先佑有功有能，其餘皆
以次立。五日官各上喜戲，居處不莊，好侵侮人者一。

---

40. 先 is read as 无 (無) — (SYR).
41. CZM has the preceding seven characters in parentheses taking them to be a later added
    gloss.
42. There is some doubt about 曹. SYR reads it as 造. CZM has: " '曹' 猶今言 '處' 或
    '科' 。" Z&Q conclude: "此指曹官。" See also RDSY/T, note 96, p. 455 and Hucker
    #6916.
43. I have followed RDSY/T's reading of 坐 — see his note 97, p. 455. On 謁者 see also
    Hucker #7908.
44. 鋪 is generally accepted as 舖 — see, for example, Z&Q.
45. I have followed RDSY/T's translations of these titles.
46. In this sentence, there is general acceptance of SYR's reading of 若 for 皆. Also, the first
    請 is read as 情 and the second as 誥.
47. 斷 here and subsequently is read as 斬.
48. 衝 is read as 撞.
49. 若 is read as 或 here.

departments, are all rewarded with the title of *gongcheng*.[ii] In the case of men who took part in the defence, increase their rank by two grades. In the case of women [who took part in the defence], reward them with 5000 cash. In the case of men and women, old and young, who did not take part in the defence, give each person one thousand cash and remit their taxes for three years so they pay nothing, neither rent nor goods taxes. This is the way to encourage officers and people to be strong in the defence of a besieged city.

70.13   The officers and men responsible for the great gate are under the charge of no more than two men. The brave and daring are in the front line. The five-man squads are responsible for each other and each is ordered to know those on the left and right, and those to the front and rear. Those who leave their posts without permission are put to death. The commandant of the gate makes three inspections during the day and one at night, after the drum has sounded and the gate is closed. The Defender frequently deputes men to make an inspection and to inform those above of men who have left their posts. All meals are taken in the dwelling place and not outside. In respect to internuncios, shield-bearers, purifiers and women who serve at the front, the Defender must carefully and closely examine the nature of their intentions, expressions, assignments and talk. When superiors drink and eat, they must order people to taste [the food first]. If someone doesn't comply, he is bound and asked why. If there is something which displeases the Defender in respect to internuncios, shield-bearers, purifiers and women serving at the front, and the Defender says to beat and bind them, those who do not follow the order, or who bind them later, are put to death. He must frequently and plainly warn them. In the case of all those beneath the gate, morning or evening, sitting or standing, each is ordered to place himself according to age and seniority. In the morning and evening, when they take up positions, first place to the right those with merit and ability. All the rest are to stand according to rank. Every five days the officers each [report to] the superior any case of someone larking about, or not taking a serious attitude, or taking pleasure in ridiculing or harassing others.

---

ii.   There are several problems with this sentence. The translation follows LSL's interpretation which includes SSX's emendation of 千 to 壬.

Comment: Apart from WYJ who makes it the start of his 70, para 4 which ends with the penultimate sentence of 70.16, and Z&Q who make a division into two with a break at the end of the fifth sentence, all treat this as one section (CZM #70.15, RDSY/T fragment 87). I have followed the latter's terms for "謁者", "執盾", "中涓" and "婦人", but see also Hucker #7908 for the first.

70.14　諸人士外使者來，必令有以執將。出而還若行縣，必使信人先戒舍室，乃出迎，門守乃入舍。為人下者常司上之，隨而行，松上不隨下，必須〔 〕〔 〕隨。

Comment: This is a very problematic section and the translation given is rather free. Important emendations or issues include 令 to 必 (BY) and the position and meaning of 將 in the first sentence; who is making the apparent tour of inspection in the second sentence; and whether 門 should be emended to 問 (CZM). In the third sentence, the issues are whether 之 should be emended to 志 (SSX), 松 to 從 (generally accepted), and which characters should fill the lacunae. ZCY has suggested 命而. Some commentators don't accept lacunae here. For example, CZM takes the last three characters as a gloss on "隨而行", although RDSY/T disagrees with this — see his note 129, p. 462. I have largely followed LSL's version which includes some, but not all, of these proposals. In terms of arrangement, CZM has two sections (#70.16 and #70.17) with a break after "…入舍". RDSY/T also makes a break here and adds the remainder to his next fragment 89.

70.15　客[50]卒守主人，及其為守衛[51]，主人亦守客卒。城中戍卒，其邑或以下寇，謹備之，數錄其署[52]，同邑者，弗令共所守。與階門吏為符，符合入，勞；符不合，牧[53]，守言。若城上者，衣服，他不如令者。

Comment: There are several issues of arrangement with this section. I have followed the modern editors LSL, MBJ and Z&Q in treating it as a discrete section. Certainly, apart perhaps from the last sentence, there is uniformity of subject. CZM treats it as two sections (his #70.18 and #70.19). He also takes the five characters "及其為守衛" in the first sentence to be a gloss on 守 and

---

50. Following SYR, there is general acceptance of 客 as referring to a "guest" or "visitor" here rather than to the enemy, as is often the case elsewhere.
51. There is some doubt about this clause — see CZM, RDSY/T.
52. In this clause, I have followed Z&Q in reading 數 as 時常, 錄 as 記錄 and 署 as 名冊.
53. 牧 is read as 收 (e.g. Z&Q).

70.14   All men and officers who are sent out and return must be ordered
to present some form of identification when they go out and come
back. If a senior officer of the defence makes an inspection tour of
the district, he must send a reliable man beforehand to check that
the circumstances at the garrison are satisfactory. Subsequently,
his own man and the garrison commander can come out to meet
him, and when they have informed him of conditions, they can all
enter. Attendants must constantly observe the intentions of those
above them and follow them when they go forth — but only their
own superiors. They must not follow others unless ordered to do
so by their superior.

70.15   "Guest" troops [can assist] the defence of the "host" troops, but
when they are participating in defence, the "host" troops should
also defend the "guest" troops. In the case of troops within a city
whose own troops have already fallen to the enemy, great care
should be taken, frequently checking their register. Those from the
same town are not allowed to defend the same place together.
Those officers in charge of stairs and gates should examine their
[identification] tallies, and, if there is correspondence, they should
enter and be accepted. If their [identification] tallies don't
correspond, they are seized and the Defender informed. In the case
of those on the wall, if their attire arouses suspicion or they do not
follow orders, [then they too are seized and reported to the
Defender].

transfers the last sentence to the end of his 70.42. RDSY/T has this section in his fragment 89 which comprises the last sentence of 70.14, all this section and all but the final sentence of 70.16.

70.16　宿鼓在守大門中，莫，令騎若使者操節閉城者，皆以執圭[54]，昏鼓鼓十，諸門亭皆閉之。行者斷，必擊[55]問行故，乃行其罪。晨見掌文，鼓縱行者，諸城門吏各入請籥，開門已，輒覆上籥。有符節不用此令。寇至，樓鼓五，有周鼓[56]，雜小鼓乃應之。小鼓五後從軍，斷。命必足畏，賞必足利，令必行，令出輒人隨，省其可行、不行。

Comment: CZM treats this section as three fragments (#70.20–22). As mentioned above, RDSY/T includes all but the last sentence in his fragment 89. This last sentence is then combined with the first two sentences of the next section (70.17) as his fragment 90.

70.17　號[57]，夕有號，失號，斷。為守備程而署之曰某程，置署街[58]街衢階若門，令往來者皆視而放[59]。諸吏卒民有謀殺傷其將長者，與謀反同罪，有能捕告，賜黃金二十斤，謹罪。非其分職而擅取之，若非其所當治而擅治為之，斷。諸史卒民非其部界而擅入他部界，輒收，以屬都司空若候，候以聞守，不收而擅縱之，斷。

--- --- --- --- --- --- --- ---

54. There is some uncertainty about this clause. SYR has proposed 龜 for 圭. Z&Q suggest 主, writing: "主，是一種玉石，用來賞賜或祭祀的珍品，執主者必為有爵位有職守的人。"
55. 擊 is read as 繫 here.
56. In this clause, 有 is read as 又 and 周 as 遍 — see, for example, LSL.
57. I have taken 號 as a heading and in the sense of 口令 — see, for example, Z&Q.
58. Following SYR, this first 街 is read as 術.
59. There is general acceptance of 知 for 放.

70.16 The night drum is within the main gate of the Defender. In the evening, the order is given for a cavalryman or messenger carrying an identification tally to close the city gate. In either case it must be a person of rank. At dusk, the drum is struck ten times and the gates and pavilions are all closed. Those walking about are put to death [but first] they must be bound and questioned as to their reasons. Then the punishment is carried out. When daylight is seen the *fen* drum [is struck] and this allows people to move about. Each of the officers of all the city gates enters and requests the key to open the gate. Immediately this is done, he returns the key. Those who hold [identification] tallies do not use this order. When an enemy comes, the tower drums [are struck] five times and also drums are struck all around. Various small drums respond to this. Those who join the army after the small drums have sounded are punished. Commands must be sufficiently fear-inspiring and rewards must be sufficiently beneficial. Orders must be carried out. Once orders are issued, people must follow them at once. Be on the lookout for orders that can be carried out not being carried out.

70.17 Passwords: At night there are passwords. Omission of the password is punished. Create regulations pertaining to defence preparations and publish them, saying, "such and such a regulation". Display them publicly in offices, streets, lanes, stairways and gates, and order those going to and fro to look at them and know them. All officers, soldiers and ordinary people who make plans to kill or injure their general or leader, as well as those who have plans to rebel [are guilty of] the same crime. Those who are able to seize them and inform on them are rewarded with 20 *jin* of yellow gold and the perpetrators are punished severely. Those who take upon themselves activities which are not their responsibility, or those who take it upon themselves to control things which it is not their proper place to control are put to death. All officers, soldiers and ordinary people who take it upon themselves to enter other divisions that are not their own divisions are immediately detained and handed over to the *sikong* or *hou* of their division and the *hou* informs the Defender.[iii] Those who do not detain [such people] or who take it

---

iii. See LSL, note 9, p. 540 on these titles.

能捕得謀反、賣城、踰城敵[60]者·人，以令為除死罪二人，城旦四人。反城事父母去者，去者之父母妻子[61]。

Comment: There is variation in how this section is arranged and also some issues of interpretation. Probably the most accurate is CZM's arrangement which identifies three components (#70.23-25): A brief statement about passwords or watchwords (口號 — CZM, 口令 — LSL); a statement about the public display of regulations and the need for people to be familiar with them; and a large component about several crimes — planning to kill or injure leaders, doing things or going places that are outside the person's responsibility, and going over the wall so abandoning one's parents. All these crimes are to be punished by the execution of the perpetrator, or of the family members left behind in the last case. There are particular issues in the reading of the final sentence. I have followed CZM as well as MBJ and LSL. RDSY/T includes the first two components along with the last sentence of the previous section in his fragment 90 and makes the third component his fragment 91 in its entirety.

70.18 悉舉民室材木、瓦若蘭[62]石數，署長短小大，當舉不舉，吏有罪。諸卒民居城上者，各葆其左右，左右有罪而不智也，其次伍有罪。若能身捕罪人若告之吏，皆構[63]之。若非伍而先知他伍之罪，皆倍其構賞。

Comment: This section has two components: the bringing forth of materials from people's houses and the interrelated responses of adjacent five-man squads. This is recognised in CZM's division into #70.26 and #70.27. RDSY/T treats it as one fragment (92) which comprises this and the next section plus the first sentence of the following section — i.e. 70.18, 70.19 and the first sentence of 70.20. WYJ has a somewhat different arrangement. His paragraph 5 consists of the last sentence of 70.16, all 70.17 and the first sentence of 70.18.

---

60. BY suggests the addition of 歸 before 敵.
61. There are several issues with this sentence: (i) 反城 is taken as 翻城 (CZM). (ii) 事 is read as 棄 (SYR). (iii) It is agreed that the end of the sentence is deficient. CZM suggests "同產皆斷" which I have included in the translation.
62. On 蘭, Z&Q have: "即前文的'礌石'、大石塊。"
63. There is general agreement that 構 should be read as 購 in the sense of 賞求, both here and in the following instance — see, for example, Z&Q.

upon themselves to release them are put to death. In the case of
those who are able to seize one person who is planning to rebel,
betray the city, or scale the wall to go over to the enemy, use the
laws to commute the death penalty for two men or hard labour for
four men. In the case of those who go over the wall, abandoning
their parents, the parents, wives, children [and siblings of those
absconding are all put to death].

70.18   Completely bring out the materials from people's houses — tiles
or large stones — reckon up the quantity, and record the size. If
[material] that should be brought out is not brought out, the officer
is at fault. All the soldiers and people positioned on the wall in
each case protect those to their left and right. If those to the left or
right are guilty of a crime and they don't know about it, then the
next five-man squad is guilty of a crime. If someone is able
personally to apprehend a criminal or report him to an officer, in
all cases reward him. If someone is not in a five-man squad but
knows beforehand of another five-man squad's crime, in all cases
double his reward.

70.19   城外令[64]任,城內守任,令、丞、尉亡得入當,滿十人以上,
令、丞、尉奪爵各二級;百人以上,令、丞、尉免以卒戍。諸取
當者,必取寇虜,乃聽之[65]。

Comment: The only textual point of note in this section is whether CZM is right
in transferring 守 to the start of the section. He has this section as his #70.36.
RDSY/T includes it in his fragment 92 which comprises what, in the present
text, are 70.18, 70.19 and the first sentence of 70.20. In WYJ it is the opening
part of 70, para 7 which goes on to include 70.20 to 70.24.

70.20   募民欲財物,粟米以[66]貿易凡器者,卒以賈予[67]。邑人知識、昆
弟有罪,雖不在縣中而欲為贖,若以粟米、錢金、布帛、他財物
免出者,令許之。傳言者十步一人,稽留言及乏傳者[68],斷。諸
可以便事者,亟以疏傳言守。吏卒民欲言事者,亟為傳言請之
吏,稽留不言諸[69]者,斷。

Comment: The first sentence of this section raises issues both of
interpretation and of placement. On the former, I have adopted CZM's text (his
#70.37) for the translation as it gives a clear meaning. He treats it as an
individual section whilst RDSY/T includes it as the final sentence of his
fragment 92, making the rest of the section his fragment 94 after the
interposition of fragments 52.20 and 52.21 (part).

70.21   縣各上其縣中豪傑若謀士、居[70]大夫、重厚口數多少[71]。

Comment: CZM treats this brief section separately as his #70.40 although he
punctuates it slightly differently having the second comma after 厚. RDSY/T
combines it with what is 70.22 below as his fragment 95.

---

64. I have used Hucker's general term for this position — #3733.
65. In translating this sentence (rather freely), I have relied on CZM's note: "如亡去五人
    而俘虜得五人,則功罪可以抵銷。"
66. SYR suggests that 以 be transposed to follow 欲.
67. There is general acceptance of SYR's rearrangement of this clause to "以平賈予" with
    賈 taken as 價. The version of the sentence translated is that of CZM.
68. On this clause, SSX has the following note: "稽留,謂不以時上聞;乏傳,不為通
    也。"
69. Following BY and SYR, 諸 is read as 請 taken as 情 or 請.
70. There is widespread acceptance of YY's proposed emendation of 居 to 若 although
    RDSY/T suggests that 居 might be retained in the sense of "resident".
71. On 重厚, Z&Q have: "指富裕人家。"

70.19   Outside the wall is the Director's responsibility; inside the wall is the Defender's responsibility. If those under the Director, [his] assistants and the commandant abscond, they are held responsible. If the number of those absconding is a full ten men or more, then the punishment for each is to be downgraded two ranks. If the number is one hundred men or more, the Director, [his] assistants and the commandant are reduced to the ranks. In all cases they can atone for their crime, but to do so they must capture a number of the enemy equal to the number of men they have lost. Then they are pardoned.

70.20   In calling for people who wish to use materials, cloth or grain to trade or exchange for various utensils, they should be given a fair price. If townspeople who are friends, or older or younger brothers, commit a crime, even if it is not in the same district, and they wish to use husked or unhusked grain, gold or money, cloth or silk, or other materials to atone for it, order that they be allowed to do so. For transmitting messages, there should be one person every 10 *bu*. Those who delay a message or fail to transmit it are put to death. All matters that might be advantageous are quickly transmitted to the Defender as messages. Officers, soldiers and ordinary people who wish to convey something quickly should make a transmission of the message [by] asking an officer. Those who delay or do not request a message are put to death.

70.21   Each district reports [to those] above the number of its heroes, strategic advisers, senior officials and rich households.

70.22   官府城下吏卒民家，前後左右相傳保火。火發自燔，燔曼延燔
人，斷[72]。諸以眾強凌弱少及強姦人婦女，以讙嘩者，皆斷。

Comment: The two somewhat disparate components of this section —
protection from fire and the prohibition of oppression and rape — are treated
separately by CZM (#70.41 and #70.42). RDSY/T combines them with 70.21
as his fragment 95.

70.23   諸城門若亭，謹候視往來行者符，符傳疑，若無符，皆詣縣廷
言，請問其所使。其有符傳者，善舍官府。其有知識、兄弟欲見
之，為召，勿令里巷中。三老、守閭令屬繕夫為答。若他以事者
微者，不得入里中[73]。三老不得入家人。傳令里中有以羽，羽在
三所差[74]。家人各令其官[75]中，失令，若稽留令者，斷。家有守
者治食。吏卒民無符節，而擅入里巷官府、吏、三老，守閭者失
苛止[76]，皆斷。

Comment: Again, this section is something of a miscellany, although it deals
mainly with tallies. RDSY/T has it as a single fragment (96) whereas CZM treats
it as four fragments (#70.43 to #70.46) dealing respectively with tallies, the use
of feathers for messages, the individual in a household responsible for
provisions, and again tallies — or rather, the lack of them.

70.24   諸盜守器械、財物及相盜者，直[77]一錢以上，皆斷。吏卒民各自
大書於傑[78]，著之其署同[79]，守案其署，擅入者，斷。城上日壹發
席蓐，令相錯發[80]，有匿不言人所挾藏在禁中者，斷。

---

72. The translation of this sentence is based on LSL's notes 1 & 2, p. 543 which include
    SYR's note on 燔人 which reads: "謂延燒他人室".
73. The somewhat free translation of this sentence follows particularly Z&Q who base their
    interpretation on CZM. See also RDSY/T, note 220, p. 485.
74. In this sentence, I have followed SSX's proposals — first, to read 有 as 者 and, second,
    to rearrange the second clause to give: "羽在三老所".
75. 官 here is read as 宮 following SSX.
76. I have followed Z&Q in taking 苛止 as "詰問制止".
77. 直 here is read as 值.
78. There is general agreement that 傑 should be read as 揭.
79. Following SYR, 署同 is read 署隔.
80. On 錯發, Z&Q have: "交換發放".

70.22 Officers, soldiers and people in government offices below the wall protect those to the front and rear, and those to the left and right from fire. If a fire starts spontaneously, those who spread it to others are put to death. All those who use the many and strong to oppress the weak and few, as well as those who rape other men's wives or daughters, so creating a great clamour, are put to death.

70.23 At all city gates and posts, care is taken to examine the tallies of those coming and going. If a tally is doubtful, or there is no tally, then in all cases the person goes to the district court and is questioned about what he was sent for. Those who have satisfactory tallies are well lodged in government buildings. If they have friends or brothers whom they wish to see, they are sent for, but they (i.e. the tally holders) are not allowed within the streets and laneways. In the case of someone who has a question to ask of the *sanlao* or *shoulü*, then it is possible to allow the *sanlao's shanfu* to transmit it whereas, in the case of other matters, or people of lowly rank, they are not allowed to enter the streets or laneways. The *sanlao* are not allowed to go to the houses of the ordinary people. Messages and orders within the wards are by feathers, and the feathers are kept in the *sanlao's* office. The head of each household is responsible for orders within the dwelling. Those who fail to carry out, or who delay the orders are put to death. Households have a defender in charge of provisions. Officers, soldiers and ordinary people who are without tallies but take it upon themselves to enter the lanes and offices of a ward, and the officers, *sanlao* and *shoulü* who fail to stop and interrogate them are all put to death.

70.24 All those who steal defensive implements and weapons, or materials, or steal from others, if the value is one cash or above, are put to death. Officers, soldiers and ordinary people should each write their names in large writing on a placard within their offices (barracks). The Defender inspects their offices (barracks) and those who have entered on their own responsibility are put to death. On the wall, every day there is an issue of mats which allows them to be exchanged and reissued. If there is concealment of prohibited items, or failure to report such concealment, offenders are put to death.

Comment: CZM has this section as four fragments (#70.47 to #70.50). RDSY/
T has two fragments (97 & 98). In WYJ this is the conclusion of 70, para 7.
There is some uncertainty about the reading of the last sentence, whether the
reference is both to those who conceal prohibited items and those who fail to
report them, or only to the latter.

70.25 吏卒民死者，輒召其人，與次司空葬之，勿令得坐泣。傷甚者令
歸治病家善養，予醫給藥、賜酒日二升、肉二斤，令吏數行
閭[81]，視病有瘳，輒造事上。詐為自賊傷以辟事者，族之。事
已。守使吏身行死傷家，臨戶而悲哀之。

Comment: This section, which deals with the treatment of casualties, is taken
as a discrete fragment by both CZM (#70.51) and RDSY/T (fragment 99). WYJ
combines it with 70.26 below as his 70, para 8.

70.26 寇去事已，塞禱[82]。守以令益邑中豪傑力鬥諸有功者，必身行死
傷者家以弔哀之，身見死事之後[83]。城圍罷，主亟發使者往勞，
舉有功及死傷者數使爵祿，守身尊寵，明白貴之，令其怨結於
敵。

Comment: This section continues the consideration of the treatment of
casualties as well as other aspects of the aftermath of the battle. CZM has it
as his #70.52, RDSY/T as fragment 100, and WYJ as the second half of his 70,
para 8.

70.27 城上卒若吏各保其左右，若欲以城為外謀者，父母、妻子、同產
皆斷。左右知不捕告，皆與同罪。城下里中家人皆相葆，若城上
之數。有能捕告之者，封之以千家之邑；若非其左右及他伍捕告
者，封之二千家之邑。

---

81. On 行閭, Z&Q have: "赴閭巷，指傷者家。閭巷，古代稱街巷為閭。"
82. In translating this phrase I have followed Z&Q who have this note: "祭祀以報答神的
福佑。《史記·封禪書》'冬塞禱祠'，《索隱》云'塞與賽同。賽，今報神福也'。"
83. I have followed modern Chinese editors (LSL, Z&Q) in interpreting this phrase. Z&Q
have this note: "死於守城的人的遺屬。" RDSY/T takes it to mean that the chief
personally sees the corpse of the dead person.

70.25 In the case of an officer, soldier or ordinary person dying, immediately summon their relatives who, with the deputy *sikong*, bury them. Do not let [the family members] sit around weeping. In the case of those who are badly wounded, let them return home to heal the wound and be well looked after. Provide a doctor who gives medicines. Give them 2 *sheng* of wine and 2 *jin* of meat per day. Order an officer to go repeatedly to their village to see if the wound has healed. [If it has] he immediately notifies those above. In the case of those who falsely wound themselves to avoid their service, put the whole family to death. When the battle is over, the Defender sends officers to go in person to approach the families of the dead and wounded and to go to their houses to offer condolences and express sympathy.

70.26 When the enemy has withdrawn and the battle is over, offer a sacrifice repaying the spirits for their blessing and assistance. The Defender gives the order to reward heroes of the districts who fought valiantly and all those with merit. He must himself go to the families of the dead and wounded to offer condolences and express sympathy to them and personally see the surviving relatives of the dead. When the siege of the city has ended, the Chief quickly sends out messengers to give recognition to officers and men, picking out those with merit as well as those who have died or been wounded. He bestows on them rank and salary. The Defender himself honours and favours them, making it clear that he values them. This lets resentment be directed towards the enemy.

70.27 On the wall, soldiers and officers each protect those to their left and right. If there is someone who wishes to collude with [the enemy] outside the wall, his parents, wives, children and siblings are all put to death. Those to the left or right who know [of his plans] but do not seize and denounce him are all guilty of the same crime. Families in the wards below the wall are all to protect each other, just like those on the wall. Anyone who is able to seize or denounce [a traitor] should be enfeoffed with a district of one thousand households. If [the traitor] they seize is not to the left or right, but is in another five-man squad, enfeoff them with a district of two thousand households.

Comment: This section returns to the issue of the mutual responsibility people have for those near or adjacent to them, previously considered, for example, in 70.13 above, and also the penalties for failing to meet these responsibilities. In addition, there are to be rewards for those who identify transgressors. CZM divides this section into two parts (#70.53 and #70.54), the former containing sentences 1, 2 & 4, and the latter, sentence 3. RDSY/T has this section as fragment 101, and WYJ as the start of 70, para 9 which also includes 70.28 and 70.29.

70.28   城禁：使、卒、民不欲寇微職和旌者，斷[84]。不從令者，斷。非[85]擅出令者，斷。失令者，斷。倚戟縣下城，上下不與眾等者，斷[86]。無應而妄讙呼者，斷。總[87]失者，斷。譽客內毀者，斷。離署而聚語者，斷。聞城鼓聲而伍後上署者，斷[88]。人自大書版，著之其署隔，守必自謀[89]其先後，非其署而妄入之者，斷。離署左右，共入他署，左右不捕，挾私書，行請謁及為行書者，釋守事而治私家事，卒民相盜家室、嬰兒，皆斷無赦。人舉而藉之。無符節而橫行軍中者，斷。客在城下，因數易其署而無易其養。

Comment: In this and the following section the first two characters are taken as a heading. This section itself is almost entirely devoted to a somewhat random list of offences all of which attract the death penalty (assuming 斷 does mean this — see Comment to 70.2 above). The final sentence, however, repeats the instruction given in 52.20 which is one of the sections several editors move to the present chapter. Both CZM and RDSY/T combine this and the next section, in the first case as #70.55 and in the second case as fragment 102. WYJ also combines these two sections along with 70.27 as his 70, para 9.

---

84. In this sentence, 使 is read as 吏. In addition, 不 before 欲 is considered superfluous, whilst SYR suggests 欲 itself should be emended to 效.
85. It is generally agreed that 非 is superfluous.
86. As it stands, this sentence is by no means clear. I have followed what I take to be Z&Q's interpretation — see their notes 4 & 5, p. 928.
87. There is general acceptance of SYR's reading of 總 as 縱.
88. In this sentence, 伍 is taken as 五 and 上署 as 就位.
89. Following SYR, 謀 is taken as 課 in the sense of 查閱.

70.28   Wall Prohibitions: Officers, soldiers and ordinary people who copy the enemy's identification tallies and banners are executed. Those who don't follow orders are executed. Those who take it upon themselves to issue orders are executed. Those who neglect orders are executed. Those who prop up their halberds, lean against the wall, and do not go with the majority are executed. Those who do not answer or recklessly call are executed. Those who set free those who have committed a crime are executed. Those who praise the enemy and spread slander inside the wall are executed. Those who leave their posts and gather to talk are executed. Those who hear the city drum sound five times and are late going to their posts are executed. Everyone must write their own name in large writing on a placard which is hung at their post. The Defender must personally inspect the front and rear of his post and those who are not at that post or have recklessly entered it are executed. Those who leave their posts to the left or right and together enter other posts, and those to the left or right who do not seize [them], as well as those who carry private letters, make requests, or bear letters for others, or who set aside defensive matters to attend to private matters, or soldiers or ordinary people who steal [?from] each other's houses or children are all to be executed without [possibility of] pardon. People who bring reports are to be recorded [in a register]. Those who pass randomly within the army but have no tally are executed. When the enemy is beneath the wall, [those soldiers on the wall] must, at the appropriate times, change their posts but their support personnel should not change.

70.29   譽敵[90]：少以為眾，亂以為治，敵攻拙以為巧者，斷。客主人無
得相與言及相藉，客射以書，無得譽[91]，外示內以善，無得應，
不從令者，皆斷。禁無得舉矢書，若以書射寇，犯令者父母、妻
子皆斷。身梟城上。有能捕告之者，賞之黃金二十斤。非時而行
者，唯守及摻太守之節而使者。

Comment: This section continues the list of prohibitions, focusing on activities
that praise or over-estimate the enemy. As mentioned above, both CZM and
RDSY/T combine it with the previous section but I have followed Z&Q in
separating the sections on the grounds of taking "譽敵" as a heading.

70.30   守入臨城[92]，必謹問父老、吏大夫，請[93]有怨仇仇不相解者，召
其人，明白為之解之。守必自異其人而藉之[94]。孤之[95]，有以私怨
害城若吏事者，父母、妻子皆斷。其以城為外謀者，三族[96]。有
能得若捕告者，以其所守邑，小大封之[97]。守還授其印，尊寵官
之，令吏大夫及卒民皆明知之。豪傑之外多交諸侯者，常請之，
令上通知之，善屬之，所居之吏上數選具之，令無得擅出入，連
質之。術鄉長者、父老、豪傑之親戚父母、妻子，必尊寵之，若
貧人食不能自給食者，上食之。及勇士父母親戚妻子皆時酒肉，

---

90. I have followed Z&Q in taking this as a heading after the pattern of the previous section.
91. Following YY, 譽 is taken as 舉 in the sense of 拾.
92. I have followed CZM's interpretation of this clause. He has: "入臨城猶言擔任守城之
    事。"
93. SYR takes 請 as 諸.
94. In this sentence, "異其人" is understood as "辨認他們".
95. SYR has this note on 孤之: "謂不得與其曹伍相聚而處，皆防其為亂。"
96. On 三族, LSL has: "指夷三族。《儀禮‧士昏禮》注：'三族，謂父昆弟，己昆弟，
    子昆弟也'。"
97. CZM has the following note: "猶言邑之大小，等於犯罪者所在之邑。"

70.29 Praising the Enemy: [Those who] take few to be many, disorder to be order, or a clumsy enemy attack to be a clever attack are put to death. There should be no verbal exchanges between the enemy and the defenders. If the enemy shoots in letters, they should not be picked up. If [enemies] outside display themselves to [the defenders] within with skill, there should be no response. Those who don't follow these orders are all put to death. It is forbidden to pick up letters shot in by the enemy or to shoot letters at the enemy. In the case of those who transgress the orders, their parents, wives and children are all put to death and their own bodies exposed on the wall. Those who are able to seize and denounce them are rewarded with 20 *jin* of gold. Those who can move about at prohibited times are only the Defender, those carrying the tallies of the Grand Defender, and messengers.

70.30 When the Defender takes responsibility for the defence of the city, he must carefully question the *fulao*, the officers, and the great officers about all those who have unresolved grievances or enmities between one another. He should summon such people and definitively resolve [their disputes] for them. He must personally identify such people, make a record of them, and keep them apart. In the case of those whose personal grievances harm the affairs of the city or its officers, their parents, wives and children are all put to death. Those who collude with [the enemy] outside are to have all their family put to death. Those who are able to capture, seize or denounce such people are to be enfeoffed with a city the size of that which is being defended. The Defender gives them his seal, confers honours and favours on them, and gives them an official position, letting officers and great officers, as well as soldiers and people, all clearly know about it. In the case of local worthies who have frequent intercourse with feudal lords outside, [the Defender] should often visit them, order the local leader to get to know them well, and keep an eye on them. He should also frequently entertain them and invite them to dine [with him] so as not to let them come and go on their own responsibility. [He should also] bind them to him by holding hostages. In the case of leaders of the districts and wards, the *fulao* and local worthies, their relatives, parents, wives and children must be honoured and

必敬之，舍之必近太守。守樓臨質宮而善周⁹⁸，必密塗樓，令下無見上，上見下，下無知上有人無人。

Comment: This long section consists of a somewhat miscellaneous set of instructions to a Defender for when he takes charge of the defence of a city. The basic aim is to eliminate destructive differences among those in positions of authority, to foster harmony and well-being among them, and to keep abreast of events beyond the confines of the wall. Finally, there are recommendations about the construction of the Defender's tower. I have followed modern editors (LSL, MBJ, Z&Q) in making this one section. Both CZM and RDSY/T treat it separately — #70.56 and #70.57 in the first case and fragments 103 and 104 in the second case. WYJ has the major part of the section as his 70, para 10 with the final part about the tower being the start of his 70, para 11 which continues to include 70.31-33.

70.31 守之所親⁹⁹，舉吏貞廉、忠信、無害¹⁰⁰、可任事者，其飲食酒肉勿禁，錢金、布帛、財物各自守之，慎勿相盜。葆宮之牆必三重，牆之垣，守者皆累瓦釜牆上。門有吏，主者門里。篿閉，必須太守之節。葆衛必取戍卒有重厚者。請擇吏之忠信者¹⁰¹，無害可任事者。

Comment: This section continues the instructions to the Defender. I have not taken the first four characters as a heading as both CZM and RDSY/T do. CZM breaks this section into three fragments (#70.58–60) dealing respectively with the Defender's choice of close associates, the building of walls around the hostage building, and matters with regard to the gates. On the other hand, RDSY/T has this as part of a larger fragment (105) which also includes 70.32 and 70.33, similar to WYJ's arrangement of his 70, para 10.

70.32 令將衛，自築十尺之垣，周還牆。門闔者，非令衛司馬門¹⁰²。

---

98. RDSY/T, based on CZM, takes this to be a particular kind of encircling road — see his note 297, p. 508.
99. Both CZM and RDSY/T take this to be a heading. An alternative reading, and the one I have followed, involves taking the immediately following 舉 as 與 — see LSL.
100. On 無害, SYR has: "當以《漢書。音義》公平吏之義為是。"
101. In this clause, SYR takes 請 as 謹 and regards 者 as superfluous.
102. SYR takes 非 as 並. On the 司馬門 see Z&Q, note 13, p. 932.

favoured. If there are poor people who are unable to provide themselves with food, those above should give them food. In addition, at appropriate times, the parents, relatives, wives and children of brave knights are all to be given wine and meat. He (the Defender) must show them respect and they must be quartered near the Grand Defender. The Defender's tower should be adjacent to the hostage quarters and be skilfully encircled. It must be a thickly plastered tower which does not let those below see what is above, but does let those above see what is below. Those below do not then know whether there are people above or not.

70.31   For those to whom he is close, the Defender should pick officers who are honest and incorruptible, loyal and reliable, impartial and able to meet their responsibilities. There is no need to prohibit drink and food [such as] wine and meat. Each is to guard his own cash and gold, cloth and silk, and material things, taking care that there is no stealing from each other. The walls of the buildings housing the hostages must be three in number. On the tops of the walls, those defending all pile up broken fragments of pots. On the gates, there are officers who are in charge of all the gates of the wards. In closing and locking the gates, they must wait for the Grand Defender's tally. For the protecting guard, [the Defender] must select warlike soldiers who are particularly reliable. There must be careful selection of officers who are loyal and reliable, impartial and able to meet their responsibilities.

70.32   Order those guarding the general to themselves build surrounding walls 10 *chi* high. In the case of those on the large and small gates, in addition, order them to guard the *sima* gate.

Comment: There are differences of view on two points in this brief section (CZM #70.61). First, who is ordered to build the surrounding wall for the general, and second, whether those responsible for the large and small gates are also to be responsible for the *sima* gate (SYR) or not (RDSY/T).

70.33 望氣者[103] 舍必近太守，巫舍必近公社，必敬神之。巫祝史與望氣者，必以善言告民，以請上報守，守獨知其請而已。無與望氣妄為不善言驚恐民[104]，斷，弗赦。

Comment: The two key points in this section about the several types of prognosticator are that they be quartered in appropriate places and that they withhold any discouraging information from the general populace, informing the Defender alone. CZM has this as #70.62 whilst with RDSY/T and WYJ it completes fragment 105 and 70, para 11 respectively.

70.34 度食不足，食民各自占，家五種[105] 石升數。為期，其在薄害[106]，吏與雜訾[107]，期盡匿不占，占不悉，令吏卒微[108] 得[109]，皆斷。有能捕告，賜什三。收粟米、布帛、錢金，出內畜產，皆為平直其賈，與主券人書之。事已，皆各以其賈倍償之。又用其賈貴賤、多少賜爵，欲為吏者許之，其不欲為吏，而欲以受賜賞爵祿，若贖出親戚，所知罪人者，以令許之。其受構賞者令葆宮見，以與其親。欲以復佐上者，皆倍其爵賞。某縣某里某子家食口二人，積粟六百石，某里某子家食口十人，積粟百石。出粟米有期日，

---

103. This refers to a form of prognostication in keeping with the other omen-seekers mentioned in the passage. Z&Q have: "望氣者：負責觀察雲氣的人，古代巫師之術。" See 68.2, note 3 above. RDSY/T calls them "ether-watchers".
104. Two proposals regarding this statement are (i) 巫 for 無 (WYZ) and (ii) the addition of 者 after 望氣 (SSX).
105. 種 here is taken as 穀 (SSX).
106. SYR suggests emendation of 薄害 to 薄者.
107. 訾 is read as 資 following CZM who has this note: "猶言吏償以相當之值，但不限定一物。"
108. This is WYZ's proposal for the unknown character that appears here.
109. A very similar statement is to be found in the *Shi Ji* 30 (《史記・平準書》) — see vol. 4, p. 1430.

70.33 Those who "watch the vapours" must be quartered near the Grand Defender whilst the shamans must be quartered near the public altars of soil. They must be respected and treated as spirits. The shamans, prayer-intoners, recorders and those who "watch the vapours" must use favourable words to inform the people but must report the true situation to the Defender. The Defender alone should know the true state of affairs and that is all. Shamans and vapour-watchers, if they self-importantly spread bad news to startle and frighten the people, are executed without possibility of pardon.

70.34 If it is calculated that food will be insufficient, each person should make known how much they have, recording for a family the amount of the five grains in *dan* and *sheng*. A fixed time is set for this. Record [the results] in a register along with the various goods and materials which officers give in compensation. When the time limit is reached, in the case of those who have hidden [food] and have not made it known, or who have made it known but incompletely, order officers and soldiers to make observations and apprehend [them]. All are executed. Those who are able to seize and denounce [offenders] are rewarded with three tenths [of the grain]. Collect unhusked and husked grain, cloth and silk, cash and gold, and bring out and gather domestic animals. In all cases, value them at a fair price, give [the people] a contract with the Chief, and record it. When the siege is over, repay each person, rewarding them with double the price. Also use the price, value and amount to confer rank. In the case of those who wish to become officers, let them do so. In the case of those who do not wish to become officers, but wish to receive reward, rank, or emolument, or who wish to redeem relatives or acquaintances who have committed a crime, order that they be permitted to do so. In the case of those who have received rewards, let them visit the hostage quarters and hand over [to them] their relatives. In the case of all those who wish to assist their superiors again, double their ranks and rewards. [In the record there should be], for a certain district, or a certain ward, or a certain individual family with two mouths to feed, a pile of grain of 600 *dan*. For a certain district, or a certain ward, or a certain individual family with ten

過期不出者王公[110]有之，有能得若告之，賞之什三。慎無令民知
吾粟米多少。

Comment: This long section about the collection, documentation and
distribution of food supplies and other materials is clear in meaning. Both CZM
(#70.63) and RDSY/T (fragment 106) treat it as a discrete section. WYJ also
has it as a separate paragraph — his 70, para 12.

70.35   守入城，先以候[111]為始，得輒宮養之，勿令知吾守衛之備。候者
為異宮，父母、妻子皆同其宮，賜衣食酒肉，信[112]吏善待之。候
來若復，就問[113]，守宮三難，外環隅為之樓，內環為樓，樓入葆
宮丈五尺為復道。葆不得有室，三日一發席蓐，略視之，布茅宮
中，厚三尺以上。發候，必使鄉邑忠信，善重士，有親戚、妻
子，厚奉資之。必重發候，為養其親，若妻子，為異舍，無與員
同所，給食之酒肉。

Comment: This, and what are here the next two sections (70.36 and 70.37),
are about the employment and deployment of scouts or spies. Throughout, the
meaning is essentially clear (although see Comment to 70.37 below) but there
are variations in arrangement which might be summarised as below.

i.   Z&Q: Division into four sections — 70.35 and 70.36 as in the present text
      and 70.37 in two paragraphs.

ii.   CZM: All 70.35 and 70.36 apart from the last two sentences are included
      as #70.64. The last sentence of 70.35 is put in parentheses. The last two
      sentences of 70.36 are treated separately as #70.65. All of 70.37 is given
      as his #70.66.

iii. LSL and MBJ: 70.35 and 70.36 are combined as one paragraph. 70.37 is
      a single paragraph as below.

iv.   RDSY/T: All but the last two sentences of 70.35 are included in fragment
      107. He treats 發候 as a heading ("Sending out Scouts") and under this
      heading includes the last two sentences of 70.35 and all but the last two
      sentences of 70.36 as his fragment 108. The last two sentences of 70.36

---

110. RDSY/T has: "(CZM) believes that *wangkung* 王公 refers to the ruler of the state either
     a king or a duke: this phrasing suggests a Warring States date for the passage" — note
     340, p. 516.
111. On 候, SSX has: "謂訪知敵情者。" Z&Q have: "即今所説偵探或間諜。"
112. On 信吏, CZM has: "余按當作 '使吏'。" I have retained 信.
113. CZM's reading of 問 for 間 is accepted.

mouths to feed, a pile of grain of 100 *dan*.[iv] For bringing out the unhusked and husked grain have a time limit. When the time limit is passed, any grain that is not brought out is confiscated. Those who are able to seize or denounce [offenders] are rewarded with three tenths [of the grain]. Be careful not to let the people know the amount of unhusked and husked grain.

70.35 When the Defender enters the city, the first thing he does is to acquire scouts (spies). Having acquired them, he immediately quarters them and provides food for them. He does not let them know about the preparations for defence. The scouts (spies) are given different quarters and their parents, wives and children all share their same quarters. They are given clothing and food, wine and meat. A trustworthy officer [is sent] to look after them well. When the scouts (spies) have returned, they are questioned. The Defender's dwelling has three encircling walls. Towers are built at the corners of the outer encircling wall. [Also] towers are built on the inner encircling wall which are 1 *zhang* 5 *chi* [high] where they enter the hostage quarters. And make a double road. The hostage quarters should not have [separate] apartments. Every three days there should be an issue of mats. Closely inspect them and spread rushes in the dwelling to a thickness of 3 *chi* or greater. In sending out scouts (spies), knights of the districts and fiefs who are loyal and trustworthy, skilled and honest men, must be sent. Their close relatives, wives and children are to be substantially rewarded with money and property. It is certainly important, when sending out scouts (spies) and taking care of their parents or wives and children, to make separate quarters for them so they are not in the same place as [other] officers. Give them wine and meat as food.

---

iv. For the apparent anomaly in amounts see CZM, p. 128.

are moved to the end of the chapter as a separate fragment (120). All 70.37 is included as his fragment 109.

v. WYJ: 70.35 and 70.36, with the text as given here, comprise his 70, para 13. 70.37 is combined with what is here 70.38 as his 70, para 14 which ends with the first sentence of 70.39.

70.36 遣他候，奉資之如前候。反，相參審信，厚賜之，候三發三信，重賜之。不欲受賜而欲為史者，許之二百石之史。守珮[114] 授之印。其不欲為史而欲受構賞祿，皆如前。有能入深至主國者，問之審信，賞之倍他候。其不欲受賞，而欲為史者，許之三百石之史。扞上[115] 受賞賜者，守必身自致之其親之其親之[116] 所，見其見守之任。其欲復以佐上者，其構賞、爵祿、〔贖出〕[117] 罪人倍之。

Comment: For the various arrangements see the Comment to 70.35 above. CZM puts both the amounts following the two instances of 許之 in parentheses as possible glosses.

70.37 出[118] 候無過十里，居高便所樹表，表三人守之，比至城者三表，與城上烽燧相望，晝則舉烽[119]，夜則舉火。聞寇所從來，審知寇形必攻，論小城不自守通者，盡葆其老弱粟米畜產。遣卒候者無過五十人，客至堞去之。慎無厭建[120]。候者曹無過三百人，日暮出之，為微職。空隊、要塞之人所往來者，令可〔 〕[121] 跡者，無

---

114. There is some uncertainty about 珮. Both WYZ and YTY take it as qualifying 印. Z&Q suggest it should be read as 佩 equating 佩授 with 授與.

115. On 扞上, Z&Q have: "捍衛城池之上。扞：同'捍'。"

116. The duplication of 其親之 is taken to be an error.

117. Added following SYR.

118. There is some debate as to whether this initial character should read 出 or 士 — see RDSY, note 363, p. 526.

119. RDSY calls these "*feng* sail-signals". I have followed Z&Q in taking this to be a smoke signal from the beacon tower.

120. I have followed Z&Q in reading 厭建 as 淹滯 or 滯留 based on notes by SYR and CZM.

121. There is general acceptance of 以 in this lacuna; see also WYJ, note 346, pp. 964–965.

70.36   When [the Defender] sends out other scouts, they are rewarded materially as for the previous scouts. When they return, compare their reliability. If it is sound, reward them. If three lots of scouts are sent out and all three are reliable, double the reward. In the case of those who do not wish for rewards, but wish to become officers, promise them an official position of 200 *dan*. The Defender confers on them a seal. In the case of those who do not wish to become officers, but wish to receive rewards and salaries, treat them all as previously indicated. In the case of those who are able to penetrate deeply into the enemy's territory, once assured of the veracity of their reports, reward them twice as much as the other scouts. If they do not wish to receive rewards, but wish to become officers, promise them an official position of 300 *dan*. In the case of those knights who are rewarded for guarding the wall and the moat, the Defender must personally visit their parents to let it be seen how much he respects such men. In the case of those who wish to assist their superiors again, the rewards in terms of rank, emolument and the opportunity to redeem those who have transgressed are doubled.

70.37   The scouts are to set up flags on high and suitable places not more than 10 *li* [from the wall]. Each flag should have three men to guard it. Extending back to the wall, there should be three flags so there can be communication between the beacon towers on the wall and the positions of the flags. In the daytime, this is by smoke. At night, it is by fire. When it is heard where the enemy is coming from, and their formation and the inevitability of attack are known, give consideration to the small cities which cannot defend themselves. Completely protect the old and weak [people], the millet and rice, and the domestic animals [from them]. Send out not more than fifty soldiers and scouts, but, when the enemy reaches the parapet, withdraw them. Be careful that there is no delay. The group of scouts should not exceed three hundred men. In the evening, send them out carrying some identification. In the case of empty places, wild but strategically important places where people come and go, the scouts are to follow their tracks and establish their whereabouts. There should not be less than three men per ward. As soon as it is light, send them out to track. Each [scout] sets up his signal in the fields. The advance guard

下里三人，平而跡¹²²。各立其表，城上應之。候出越陳表，遮坐郭門之外內，立其表，令卒之半居門內，令其少多無可知也。即有驚，見寇越陳去，城上以麾指之，跡坐擊正期¹²³，以戰備從麾所指，望見寇，舉一垂¹²⁴；入竟¹²⁵，舉二垂；狎郭¹²⁶，舉三垂；入郭，舉四垂，狎城，舉五垂。夜以火，皆如此。

Comment: This completes the three sections on scouts or spies. Unlike the other two sections, this section must be regarded as somewhat uncertain in meaning, especially pertaining to the exact arrangement of signalling between the scouts and those on or by the wall, and also as to precisely how the latter are arranged.

70.38 去郭百步，牆垣、樹木小大盡伐除之。外空井¹²⁷，盡窒之，無令可得汲也。外空窒¹²⁸盡發之，木盡伐之。諸可以攻城者盡內¹²⁹城中，令其人各有以記之。事以¹³⁰，各以其記取之。事¹³¹為之券，書其枚數。當遂¹³²材木不能盡內，即燒之，無令客得而用之。

---

122. The translation of this difficult sentence depends on reading 隊 as 隧, acceptance of WYZ's suggestion of 以 for the lacuna, acceptance of YTY's comment on 跡 ("謂步其跡也") and WYZ's comment on 平而跡 ("平明而跡") — see WYZ's explanatory note, also Z&Q's note 12, pp. 939–940.
123. There are several issues with this clause: (i) On 跡坐擊 SSX has: "跡坐，當從上文作遮坐，擊下脫鼓字，謂坐而擊鼓也。" (ii) 正 is written in its ancient form. (iii) 正期 is taken as 整旗.
124. I have followed CZM in reading 垂 with 燧. YY thinks it should be read as 郵表 — see LSL's note 13, p. 554.
125. There is general acceptance of 境 for 竟 here.
126. On 狎郭, YY has this note: "狎郭，狎城，兩狎字並當作甲…甲者會也。" LSL simply equates 狎 with 近.
127. On this clause, WYZ has: "當作"外它井"謂城外人家之井也，恐寇取水，故塞之。"
128. On this clause, WYZ has: "當作"外它室"謂城外人家之室也。"
129. There is general acceptance of 納 for 內.
130. 已 is read for 以 here.
131. Following SSX, 吏 is read for 事.
132. WNS's note reads: "遂與隧同，道也。"

then sit both inside and outside the outer wall and also set up a signal. One half of the advance guard must be allowed to remain stationed within the outer wall so the enemy has no way of knowing their number. If there is an alarm, and the enemy is seen to have advanced beyond the signal in the field, those on the wall raise a flag to make known the enemy's movements. When the enemy is seen, one beacon is raised. When they enter the region, two beacons are raised. When they approach the outer wall, three beacons are raised. When they enter the outer wall, four beacons are raised. When they approach the inner wall, five beacons are raised. At night, fire is used, in all cases like this (i.e. the same numbers).

70.38 For a distance of 100 *bu* from the outer wall, high and low walls as well as trees and timber, both large and small, should be [knocked or] cut down and removed completely. The wells of private dwellings outside [the wall] should be filled in completely so that water cannot be drawn from them. Private dwellings outside the wall should be destroyed completely and trees completely cut down. Anything that might be used in attacking the city is completely taken inside the wall. Let each person have a record of what is theirs. When the matter (the attack) is over, each person can use the record to reclaim what is theirs. The officers making the bonds should write down the number of items. If there are trees and timber facing the road which cannot be completely brought within [the wall], then burn them so as not to let the enemy get hold of them and use them.

Comment: The subject now moves to the removal or destruction of anything outside the wall which the enemy could make use of. In terms of arrangement, RDSY/T here interposes between 70.37 and 70.38 what, in the present text, are 71.7–10. These are his fragments 110–112. The present section exactly corresponds to his fragment 113. Other editors do not make this change. CZM moves directly from 70.37 to 70.38 as does WYJ. The former has 70.38 as a single section (his #70.67) whilst the latter combines 70.38 with 70.37 and the first sentence of 70.39 as his 70, para 14.

70.39   人自大書版，著之其署忠[133]。有司出其所治，則從淫之法，其罪射[134]。務色謾正，淫囂不靜，當路尼眾，舍事後就，踰時不寧，其罪射。讙囂駴眾，其罪殺。非上不諫，次主兇言，其罪殺。無敢有樂器，弈棋[135]軍中，有則其罪射。非有司之令，無敢有車馳、人趨，有則其罪射。無敢散牛馬軍中，有則其罪射。飲食不時，其罪射。無敢歌哭於軍中，有則其罪射。令各執罰盡殺，有司見有罪而不誅，同罰。若或逃之，亦殺。凡將率鬥其眾失法，殺。凡有司不使去[136]卒、吏民聞誓令，代之服罪。凡戮人於市，死上目行[137]。

Comment: This section is predominantly a list of relatively trivial offences punishable by piercing the ears with an arrow, a punishment not hitherto mentioned. Some more serious offences calling for the death penalty complete the section. CZM has this as a two sections (#70.68 and #70.69) as does RDSY/T (fragment 114). In WYJ, this section minus the first sentence is his 70, para 15.

70.40   謁者侍令門外，為二曹，夾門坐，鋪食更，無空。門下謁者一長，守數令入中，視其亡者，以督門尉與其官長，及亡者入中報。四人夾令門內坐，二人夾散門外坐。客見，持兵立前，鋪食

---

133. There is general acceptance of the reading of 中 for 忠 (e.g. LSL, Z&Q).
134. There is some variation in the way this sentence is understood, in particular, whether the officials are the ones indulging in lewd behaviour (RDSY/T) or are responsible for the edict against it (LSL). On the punishment see RDSY/T's detailed note 447, p. 545.
135. These two characters are SYR's emendations and are generally accepted. LSL refers to the《說文》in identifying the game as *weiqi* 圍棋.
136. There is general acceptance of the emendation of 去 to 士.
137. Following SYR, this clause is read "死二日徇".

70.39   People should write [their names] in person in large writing on boards and display them at their posts (offices). The authorities should issue a proclamation in relation to military discipline that anyone who indulges in licentious behaviour will have their ears pierced with an arrow. Arrogant and self-important people who deceive the upright, make a continuous clamour, stop many people on the roads preventing them from going about their normal business or causing them to delay it to an inappropriate time without informing their superiors are to have their ears pierced with an arrow. Those who shout out and frighten the people are punished by death. Those who condemn their superiors without remonstrating with them or who unrestrainedly indulge in evil words are punishable by death. No one should dare to have musical instruments or [the game] *weiqi* in the army. Those who do are to have their ears pierced with an arrow. Without an order from an officer, no one should dare to gallop a cart or run on foot. Those who do are to have their ears pierced with an arrow. No one should dare to scatter oxen or horses in the army. Those who do are to have their ears pierced with an arrow. Those who drink or eat at inappropriate times are to have their ears pierced with an arrow. No one should dare to sing or wail in the army. Those who do are to have their ears pierced with an arrow. Let each person in charge of punishments complete the death penalty [where appropriate]. If there is an officer who sees a crime but does not report it, he should receive the same punishment. Or, if he lets [the perpetrator] escape, he should also be put to death. In all cases, generals and leaders who fight with the ordinary people in disregard of the laws are put to death. In all cases, supervisors who do not send knights, soldiers, officers, and people to hear the oath of command are to suffer the punishment in their stead. In all cases, people are put to death in the market place and their corpses exposed for three days.

70.40   The guards in attendance outside the gate of the defence headquarters should be in two groups sitting on either side of the gate. They are to take turns in eating so as not to leave [the gate] unattended. The guards at the gate are to select one leader who, at appropriate times, enters and informs the Defender of conditions. The Defender examines the list of those who have absconded and

更，上侍者名。守室卜高樓[138]，候者望見乘車若騎卒道外來者，
及城中非常者，輒言之守。守以須城上候城門及邑吏來告其事者
以驗之，樓下人受候者言，以報守。中涓[139] 二人，夾散門內坐，
門常閉，鋪食更，中涓一長者。

Comment: There is some doubt about the exact circumstances being
described in the opening sentences of this section. I understand the 謁者 to
be guards who are positioned outside the defence headquarters or the
Defender's quarters where they await orders. Both CZM and RDSY/T divide
this section into three parts. The divisions are the same – sentences 1–4 (CZM
#70.70, RDSY/T fragment 115); sentences 5 & 6 (CZM #70.71, RDSY/T
fragment 116); sentence 7 (CZM #70.72, RDSY/T fragment 117). WYJ
combines sections 70.40 and 70.41 in his final paragraph 70, para 16.

70.41   環守宮之術衢，置屯道[140]，各垣其兩旁，高丈，為埤倪[141]，立初
雞足置，夾挾視葆食[142]。而札書得必謹案視參食[143] 者，節[144] 不
法，正請之。屯陳垣外術衢街皆樓，高臨里中，樓一鼓聾灶[145]。

---

138. In this clause, SYR takes 室 as 堂 and inserts 為 before 高.
139. On 中涓, Z&Q have: "侍從的名稱。負責文書保管及傳達。" RDSY/T simply
     transliterates the term.
140. CZM takes 屯道 to equate with 夾道.
141. 倪 is BY's proposal for the unknown character which is found here. On 埤倪, Z&Q have
     the following: "同 '俾倪'，牆堞上鑿的孔，從內可觀外。"
142. SYR's proposal for these five characters is: "卒夾視葆舍". This is accepted by CZM,
     RDSY/T and Z&Q, for example, and is followed in the translation.
143. Following WNS, 參食 is read 參驗 in the sense of 驗證.
144. SYR suggests the emendation of 節 to 即.
145. 聾 is read as 襲. On "襲灶" Z&Q have: " 一種可以搬動的灶。"

makes the guard and their leader responsible for seeking out the absentees and reporting them.[v] Four men are to sit on either side of the defence headquarters gate within and two men are to sit on either side of the *san* gate without. When visitors are seen, they are to take hold of their weapons and stand in front [of the gate]. They are to take their meals in turns and are to announce the names [of the visitors] to their superiors. Below the Defender's hall is built a high tower. When those on watch look out and see carriages, or horsemen and foot-soldiers, approaching along the road outside, as well as anything out of the ordinary inside the wall, they immediately report this to the Defender. The Defender waits for those on lookout on the wall as well as the district officers to come and inform him of the circumstances in order to verify them. Those men below the tower are to receive the reports of the lookouts and announce them to the Defender. Two attendants (*zhongjuan*) sit on either side within the *san* gate. The gates are always closed. They take their meals in turn and there is one leader for the attendants.

70.41 For the connecting roads that surround the Defender's dwelling, build a narrow road with a wall on each of its two sides to a height of 1 *zhang* and make observation holes [so that those on the wall can look into the hostage quarters].[vi] And the wooden tablets that are written on and are obtained must be carefully examined and verified. If there are places where they are not satisfactory, then they are not, for the moment, passed on, pending correction. The walls on the narrow road outside the thoroughfares both have towers high enough to overlook the wards. On [each] tower there is one drum and a portable furnace. Then, if there is some reason,

---

v. I am uncertain about the exact meaning of the opening four sentences of this section. Much depends on who the 謁者 are. I have taken them to be guards at the gate of the defence headquarters — see LSL and Z&Q, note 1, p. 944. But see also RDSY/T who calls them "internuncios" and has a slightly different reading of the paragraph. For the terms 謁者 and 侍衛 (Z&Q's reading of 謁者) see Hucker #7908 and #5333 respectively.

vi. The text here is very uncertain. I have given Z&Q's version — see their notes 18 and 19, p. 944 as well as SYR and CZM for the difficulties. It is quite probable that the two clauses (from 立 to 食) are misplaced.

即有物故，鼓。史至而止。夜以火指鼓所[146]。城下五十步一廁，
廁與上同圂。請有罪過而可無斷者，令杍廁利[147]之。

Comment: This section is something of a miscellany. Both CZM and RDSY/T
subdivide it but differently. CZM has sentences 1 and 3-6 as his #70.73,
sentence 2 as his #70.74 and sentences 7-8 as his #70.75. RDSY/T retains the
order above but includes sentences 1–6 as his fragment 118 and makes
sentences 7–8 his fragment 119.

146. There is considerable doubt about this sentence. CZM suggests that the five characters
     from 立 to 罟 above might be displaced from here. I have simply offered a tentative
     translation of the sentence as it stands following LSL's reading.
147. CZM substitutes 罰 for 利, which I have followed in the translation.

the drum [is sounded]. When the officer arrives, this stops. At night, fire is used to indicate where the drum is. Below the wall there is one latrine every 50 *bu*. The latrines are the same on and below the wall. Those who have committed crimes but are not to be put to death are sent to clean out the latrines to punish them.

71: 雜守

Comment: This chapter corresponds to the DZ for *Mozi* 71 apart from three variations: (i) The transfer of 13 characters from before what is the penultimate sentence of 71.5 to the start of 71.8. (ii) The transfer of 4 characters from what would be the start of 71.14 to the start of 71.13. (iii) The omission of 43 characters that, in the DZ, follow what below is 71.14. WYJ has a closely similar arrangement apart from not making the transfer given in (i) above. Details of the arrangements of CZM and RDSY/T are given in the Comments following each section.

71.1 禽子問曰:「客眾而勇,輕意¹見威,以駭主人。薪土俱上,以為羊坽,積上為高〔壘〕²,以臨〔吾〕民,蒙櫓俱前,遂屬³之城,兵弩俱上,為之奈何?」子墨子曰:「子問羊坽之守邪?羊坽者攻之拙者也,足以勞卒,不足以害城。羊坽之政⁴,遠攻則遠害,近城則近害,不至城。矢石無休,左右趣射,蘭為柱後⁵,望以固⁶。厲吾銳卒,慎無使顧,守者重卜,攻者輕去。養勇高奮,民心百倍,多執數少,卒乃不怠。」⁷

Comment: The first issue with this section is placement. Whilst most editions have it here (e.g. SYR, CZM, WYJ, LSL, MBJ, Z&Q), RDSY/T places it in his section entitled "Defence against Overlooks" (i.e. *Mozi* 53) where it is his fragment 24. Secondly, there are problems in the reading of Mo Zi's reply to

----

1. Following ZCY, 輕意 is read as 肆意 ("recklessly and without restraint").
2. Both 壘 and the following 吾 are supplied on the basis of earlier passages — see LSL.
3. 屬 is taken as 會合 (LSL) or 連接 (Z&Q).
4. There is general acceptance of 攻 for 政 here.
5. CZM has the following note on this clause: "余以為蘭,蘭音形皆相近,即《號令》篇之蘭石及《備城門》篇之礜石,大石也;柱,即拄,撐持也,'柱後'猶今說'後盾',謂碎石之後,繼以大石也。" — p. 138.
6. Since BY, it has been suspected that there is a lacuna at the start of this clause which remains a problem. For example, RDSY/T takes it with the next sentence. Z&Q have this modern paraphrase which I have followed: "讓敵人看到防守的堅固。"
7. In the final clause, 卒 is added (BY) and 怠 replaces 殆 (WNS) — see WYJ, note 16, p. 979.

71: Miscellaneous Defences

71.1   Qin Zi asked, saying: "Suppose the enemy are many and brave, recklessly flaunting their courage to intimidate our leader. Suppose they bring up brushwood and earth to build a sheep's bank ramp (*yangling*), piling up earth to make a high [bank] in order to approach [our] people. Suppose they cover it with shields at the front and bring it adjacent to the wall, positioning swordsmen and archers on it. What is to be done then?"

Master Mo Zi said: "Are you asking about defence against the sheep's bank ramp? Attack by sheep's bank ramp is a clumsy form of attack. It is enough to tire out the soldiers but not enough to harm the city wall. In dealing with attack by sheep's bank ramp, if it is distant, then oppose it at a distance. If it is near, then oppose it near so the danger does not reach the city wall. Fire arrows and stones at it unceasingly and from both sides. Follow these with large stones thus demonstrating the resolve [of the defenders]. Send out crack troops who are not likely to retreat and who will ruthlessly strike so the attackers will readily flee. Cultivate a spirit of courage and the people's hearts will be strengthened one hundredfold. If those of your soldiers who seize many of the enemy are well rewarded, then they will maintain their resolve."[i]

---

i.   The rather free translation of this final sentence, which is based on WYZ's reading of 少 as 賞, follows LSL — see his note 7, p. 560.

Qin Guli, particularly what are, above, the final four sentences. I have largely followed CZM in translating these sentences. RDSY/T, however, takes a somewhat different view based, in part, on SYR. The problems are described in detail in his note 22, p. 200. He is also adamant that what CZM (and other modern Chinese editors) have as the first 16 characters of the next section actually belong with this section (his note 33, p. 201). This only really constitutes a problem if the present fragment is transferred. Adhering to the "majority" arrangement, I have left these characters in the next section. WYJ, in fact, has what are here sections 71.1–4 together as his 71, para 1.

71.2   作上[8]不休，不能禁御，遂屬之城，以御雲梯之法應之。凡待
煙[9]、衝、雲梯、臨之法，必應城[10]以御之曰[11]不足，則以木樶[12]
之。左百步，右百步，繁下矢，石、沙、炭以雨之，薪火、水湯
以濟之。選厲銳卒，慎無使顧，審賞行罰，以靜為故，從之以
急，無使生慮，養勇高奮[13]，民心百倍，多執數賞，卒乃不怠。
衝、臨、梯皆以衝衝之。

Comment: There are two main points to be made about this section. First, it does seem to continue the topic of how to respond to different types of attack, although it might be argued that these are not specifically raised in Qin Guli's question. Moreover, the second part of the section is noticeably similar to the second part of the previous section. Second, there are the problems presented by what are the second and third sentences of the version above. In the translation, I have basically followed LSL although most commentators take this to be about enlarging the wall. My impression is that the situations being considered are more pressing than would allow for further construction work on the wall so, in keeping with the previous section, the focus is taken to be on immediate measures. Related to this, there is the question of whether 100 *bu* to left and right refers to additions to the wall or to the distance over which the direct methods of hurling down different items are to be employed. This is CZM's #71.3 and RDSY/T's fragment 121 apart from the first sentence which he has in his fragment 24 — see previous Comment.

8. There is general acceptance of 上 for 士 here.
9. Following BY and SYR, 煙 is taken as 堙.
10. On 應城, LSL has this note: "指城上採取相應的措施。如備堙，備梯，備高臨之
    類。" — note 5, p. 561. The emendation of 廣 to 應 is due to BY.
11. There is doubt about 曰. WKY suggests emendation to 有.
12. See RDSY/T's detailed note on this character — note 4, p. 563.
13. This is SYR's proposed version of this clause and is followed by modern commentators
    such as RDSY/T, LSL and Z&Q.

71.2   If it is impossible to prevent the enemy piling up earth to a great height, and the earth pile has come near to the wall, respond to this by using the method of resisting cloud ladders. In general, when expecting [attack by] the filling in of moats, battering rams, cloud ladders, or "approachers" (*lin*), there must be the choice of the appropriate method of withstanding them. If the piled-up stones are inadequate, use wooden planks. To the left for 100 *bu* and to the right for 100 *bu*, throw down arrows, stones, sand and burning charcoal as thick as rain, and also pour down burning firewood and boiling water. Choose fierce and valiant soldiers, being careful not to send those with doubts. Examine rewards and carry out punishments, taking calmness as the basis. And if the advance must be swift, do not let the men waver. Cultivate a spirit of courage and the hearts of the people will be strengthened one hundredfold. If those of your soldiers who seize many of the enemy are well rewarded, then they will maintain their resolve. [If the enemy uses] battering rams, "approachers", or cloud ladders, all these can be opposed by striking them with battering rams.

71.3 渠長丈五尺，其埋者三尺，矢長[14]丈二尺。渠廣丈六尺，其弟丈二尺，渠之垂者四尺。樹渠無傅葉[15]五寸，梯渠十丈[16]一梯，渠荅大數，里二百五十八，渠荅百二十九。

Comment: This section corresponds to CZM's #71.4 and RDSY/T's fragment 122. It is predominantly about the *qu* shields previously described in 52.9 and 52.17. RDSY/T takes the "ladders" 梯, not mentioned in the previous accounts, to refer to the arms — see his note 24, p. 566.

71.4 諸外道可要塞以難寇，其甚害者為築三亭，亭三隅，織女之，令能相救。諸距阜、山林、溝瀆、丘陵、阡陌、郭門、若閭術，可要塞及為微職，可以跡知往來者少多及所伏藏之處。

Comment: This section is a relatively straightforward description of the need to establish difficulties to impede the enemy advance and to keep track of comings and goings generally. It is CZM's #71.5 and RDSY/T's fragment 123. WYJ has it as the concluding part of his 71, para 1.

71.5 葆民，先舉城中官府、民宅、室署，大小調處，葆者或欲從兄弟、知識者許之。外宅粟米、畜產、財物諸可以佐城者，送入城中，事即急，則使積門內。民獻粟米、布帛、金錢、牛馬、畜產，皆為置平賈[17]，與主券書之。

Comment: There are some variations in arrangement here. I have followed modern editors such as LSL, MBJ and Z&Q in making 71.5 and 71.6 separate sections. Both CZM and RDSY/T have 71.5 as two separate sections, the former as #71.6 and #71.7 and the latter as fragments 124 and 125. WYJ has a different arrangement with the first part of the present section (down to …門內) as his 71, para 2, then a short separate paragraph (3) which is here the first sentence in 71.8, with then a para 4 comprising the rest of 71.5 and all of 71.6.

---

14. On 矢長, Z&Q have: "當為 '夫長'。夫，通 '膚'，指渠露出地面的部分。"
15. 葉 is read here as 堞 — see, for example, Z&Q.
16. I have followed CZM in taking 十丈 as 七尺.
17. In this clause, 置 is read as 值 and 賈 as 價 — see, for example, CZM.

71.3   Shields (*qu*) are to be 1 *zhang* 5 *chi* long with a buried part of 3 *chi*. Their poles are to be 1 *zhang* 2 *chi* long. The width of the shields should be 1 *zhang* 6 *chi*. Their "ladders" should be 1 *zhang* 2 *chi* [long] and the shields should hang down 4 *cun*. In setting up the shields, the distance from the parapet should not exceed 5 *cun*, with one ladder every 7 *chi*. The overall number of shields and screens should be 258 per *li*, there being 129 of each.

71.4   All outside roads should have a fortification built to create difficulty for the enemy. On those that offer the greatest danger, build three posts (*ting*) in a triangular arrangement with one post at each corner like the "spinning damsel", so they are able to come to each other's aid.[ii] All large hills, mountains and forests, ditches and watercourses, hillocks and mounds, paths and fields, outer gates, and lanes and streets can have obstructions set up. Use identification signs so it is possible to trace and know the number of those coming and going, and also the places where they might conceal themselves.

71.5   In protecting the people, first consider the size of the government offices, people's houses and the various different dwelling places, then assign the ordinary people temporary quarters. If some of those being protected wish to go along with older and younger brothers, or with their friends, let them do so. All the grain, domestic animals and materials from houses lying outside the city that can be of assistance are sent into the city. When matters are pressing, then let [these things] be piled up within the gates. When the people contribute grain, cloth and silk, gold and money, oxen and horses, and domestic animals, in all cases a fair price is set and there is a contract with the leader which documents it.

---

ii.   RDSY/T takes both the *ting* and their arrangement to be triangular — see his note 27, p. 568.

71.6　使人各得其所長，天下事當，鈞其分職，天下事得，皆其所喜，天下事備，強弱有數，天下事具矣。[18]

Comment: The placement of this section is affected by the variations described in the Comment to 71.5. Both WYJ and RDSY/T consider it to be out of place here. CZM includes it in his #71.25.

71.7　築郵亭[19]者圉之，高三丈以上，令侍殺[20]。為辟[21]梯，梯兩臂長三丈[22]。連門三尺，報以繩連之[23]。輒再雜為縣梁。聾灶，亭一鼓。寇烽、驚烽、亂烽，傳火以次應之，至[24]主國止，其事急者引而上下之。烽火以舉，輒五鼓傳，又以火屬之，言寇所從來者少多，且奔還，去來屬次烽勿罷。望見寇，舉一烽；入境，舉二烽；射妻[25]，舉三烽一藍[26]；郭會，舉四烽二藍；城會，舉五烽五藍。夜以火[27]，如此數。守烽者事急。

Comment: This is the first of the two sections which RDSY/T transfers to the previous chapter. It corresponds to his fragment 110. Both CZM (#71.8) and WYJ (71, para 5 — combined with the next section) retain it and the following section in this chapter. On the subject matter, CZM has: "此言亭燧建築之制及其傳烽之法。"

---

18. There is general agreement that this fragment is out of context here. RDSY/T has suggested that WYJ's relocation may be correct, making it about the Defender. He also questions 皆 in the fifth clause, although modern commentators accept this. See RDSY/T, notes 35–36, p. 573 and WYJ, note 52, pp. 982–983.
19. It is not altogether clear what a 郵亭 was. According to Hucker (#8085), in Han times it was a postal relay station. Here it seems to have been some sort of beacon tower — see YTY, CZM.
20. On 侍殺, Z&Q quote SYR as follows: "'侍'當為'倚'、言邪殺為梯也" and add that "邪" is to be taken as 斜 and "倚殺，指圍亭上狹下寬，有坡度。"
21. 辟 is taken as 臂 as in the following clause.
22. 丈 is SYR's emendation of 尺.
23. In this sentence, 連門 is read as 連版 (SYR) and 報 as 迴繞 (Z&Q).
24. Emended from 正 by BY on the grounds of meaning and generally accepted.
25. There is general acceptance of SYR's emendation of 妻 to 要.
26. There is also general acceptance of WYZ's reading of 藍 as 鼓. I have followed Z&Q in changing 一 here to 三 and 二 to 四 in the next instance.
27. It may be that a different type of fire is being indicated for use at night — see LSL.

71.6   If you get each person to do what they are good at, the affairs of the world will be as they should be. If you equate their appointments with their responsibilities, the affairs of the world will be accomplished. If all people do what they like doing, the affairs of the world will come to completion. If the strong and the weak have their destiny, the affairs of the world are set out.

71.7   In making beacon towers (*youting*), they should be round and of a height greater than 3 *zhang*. They should be narrow at the top and broad at the base. Make ladders with arms, the two arms being 3 *zhang* in length. The connecting planks should be 3 *chi* (apart), making use of rope to bind them [to the arms]. Above the moat which surrounds the wall, there should be two suspended bridges. Prepare a portable furnace and have one drum in every beacon tower. [There are three situations in which a beacon fire is used] — when [the enemy] invades; when there is an emergency; when there is disorder. In transmitting these fires, respond in the proper sequence. When it reaches the leader of the country stop. When there are urgent conditions, then drag a well-sweep causing it to raise and disperse smoke [as a signal].[iii] When a beacon fire is already lit, immediately strike the drum five times and again use fire to signal [the enemy's] numbers and that they cannot be held back. When it is not known whether the enemy is coming or going, or their whereabouts are not known, there can be no stopping the lighting of fires. When the enemy is seen, light one beacon fire. When the enemy enters the region, light two beacon fires. When the enemy rapidly advances to a crucial point, light three beacon fires and strike the drum three times. When the enemy enters the outer wall, light four beacon fires and strike the drum four times. When the enemy advances close to the wall, light five beacon fires and strike the drum five times. In lighting fires at night, use the same numbers. Beacon fires in defence are a pressing matter.

---

iii.   The translation of this sentence follows Z&Q — see their note 13, p. 954.

71.8   候無過五十，寇至葉，隨去之，唯弇逮。[28] 日暮出之，令皆為微
職。距阜、山林，皆令可以跡，平明而跡。無跡，各立其表，下
城之應[29]。候出置田表，斥坐郭內外立旗幟，卒半在內，令多少
無可知。即有驚，舉孔表，見寇，舉牧表[30]。城上以麾指之，斥
步鼓整旗，旗以備戰從麾所指。田有男子以戰備從斥，女子亟走
入。即見放，到傳到城止。[31] 守表者三人，更立插表而望，守數
令騎若吏行旁視，有以知為所為。其曹一鼓。望見寇，鼓傳到城
止。

Comment: This is the second of the two sections which RDSY/T transfers to
to the previous chapter as his fragments 111 and 112 making a division after
the opening sentence in the section above. CZM retains the section in the
present sequence as his #71.9 whilst WYJ has it as the second part of his 71,
para 5. In subject matter it certainly does continue with the matter of scouts.
To quote CZM again: "此復言斥候之分配及工作，多為酉篇66之複出，但仍有
補充。"

71.9   斗[32] 食，終歲三十六石；參食，終歲二十四石；四食，終歲十
八石；五食，終歲十四石四斗；六食，終歲十二石。斗食食五
升[33]，參食食參升小半，四食食二升半，五食食二升，六食食一

---

28. This sentence occurs earlier in the DZ as what would be the penultimate sentence of
     71.5. SYR has it here (see his pp. 863–864) as do the modern editions of LSL and Z&Q.
29. On this sentence, see WYZ, who draws attention to a similar statement in the preceding
     chapter, and also Z&Q, notes 5 and 6, pp. 955–956.
30. There is a difference of view on what 孔表 and 牧表 are. Most follow SYR's suggestion
     which is what is adopted in the translation. The alternative, advocated for example by
     RDSY (see his note 422, pp. 539–540) is to regard 孔 and 牧 as the names of signal flags.
31. In this sentence, I have followed SYR in reading 放 as 寇, and WYZ in taking the first
     到 in the final clause as 鼓 and have emended 正 to 止 as the final character — see WYJ,
     note 84, p. 986.
32. There is general acceptance of 斗 for 升 here — for example, BY, YY, SSX.
33. Z&Q's gloss on this repeated construction is: "每日吃一斗糧的人，每頓要吃五升。"

71.8   [The number of] scouts should not exceed fifty. When the enemy reaches the parapet (outer wall), they should immediately withdraw without delay. Send them at night and order them all to have identification. Their orders are to look for the tracks [of the enemy] in all parts of the hills, mountains and forests where there can be tracks. At daybreak, they should look for tracks, there being not less than three men every *li*. Each one sets up a signal flag to inform those on the wall who, when they see the signal flag, set up a signal flag in response. When the scouts go beyond the signal flags in the fields, the advance defenders take up positions inside and outside the outer wall and set up flags and pennons. The advance guard must keep one half [of their number] inside the outer wall so [the enemy] has no way of knowing their number. If an urgent situation arises, [the scouts] raise an "outside" signal flag. If the enemy is seen, they set up a "second" signal flag. On the wall, a flag is used to indicate the direction of the enemy. When the advance guard see the flag, they take up their positions, strike the drum, raise the flag, and quickly send men equipped for battle to the place indicated. Men who are in the fields should be prepared for battle and follow [the commandant] in intercepting [the enemy]. Women should quickly go and enter [the city]. When the enemy is seen, strike the drum once through the city and stop. Three men are deputed to defend the signal flag, and further, to establish at the *chui* signal flag a lookout. The Defender frequently sends cavalrymen or officers to carry out a patrol and determine what the conditions are. At every point a drum is placed, and, when the enemy is seen, the drum is struck to transmit [the fact] around the city and then stopped.

71.9   [If the daily ration is] 1 *dou* of food, in the whole year 36 *dan* [will be used]. If each day, 2/3 of a *dou* is eaten, in the whole year 24 *dan* [will be used]. If each day 2/4 of a *dou* is eaten, in the whole year 18 *dan* [will be used]. If each day, 2/5 of a *dou* is eaten, in the whole year 14 *dan* and 4 *dou* [will be used]. If each day, 1/3 of a *dou* is eaten, in the whole year 12 *dan* [will be used]. On a ration of 1 *dou* per day, at each meal 5 *sheng* will be eaten. On a ration of 2/3 of a *dou* per day, at each meal 3 and 1/3 *sheng* will be eaten. On a ration of 2/4 of a *dou* per day, at each meal 2 and 1/2 *sheng* will be eaten. On a ration of 2/5 of a *dou* per day, at each

升大半，日再食。救死之時，日二升者二十日，日三升者三十日，日四升者四十日，如是，而民免於九十日之約矣。

Comment: This appears as a clear-cut calculation of rates of food consumption and distribution. RDSY/T has it as fragment 127, CZM as #71.10 and WYJ as 71, para 6. CZM adds the following eight characters "城中無食則為大殺", which are found at the end of 52.28 above, to the end of the present section. RDSY/T has these same characters as a separate fragment 22 and reads 殺 as "death" rather than "diminish" — see his note 392, p. 192.

71.10   寇近，亟收諸雜[34] 鄉金器，若銅鐵及他可以左守事者。先舉縣官室居、官府不急者，材之大小長短及凡數，即急先發。寇薄，發屋，伐木，雖有請謁，勿聽。入柴，勿積魚鱗簪[35]，當隊，令易取也。材木不能盡入者，燔之，無令寇得用之。積木，各以長短大小惡美形相從，城四面外各積其內，諸木大者皆以為關鼻[36]，乃積聚之。

Comment: This is a relatively straightforward account of the gathering of materials useful for defence, particularly metal and timber, from outlying areas, and their storage inside the city wall. The important point, apart from the obvious value for defence, is to leave nothing that can be made use of by the enemy. RDSY/T has this section as his fragment 128, CZM as #71.11 and WYJ as 71, para 7.

71.11   城守司馬[37] 以上，父母、昆弟、妻子，有質在主所，乃可以堅守。署都司空，大城四人，候二人，縣候面一，亭尉、次司空、亭一人。吏侍守所者財足，廉信，父母昆弟妻子有在葆宮中者，乃得為侍史。諸吏必有質，乃得任事。守大門者二人，夾門而

---

34. There is general acceptance of SYR's proposed reading of 雜 as 離.
35. There is some uncertainty about 簪. I have followed LSL and Z&Q in taking it as 參差. RDSY/T takes it to be a fish-trap — see his note 52, p. 578.
36. Modern commentators accept YTY's reading of 關鼻 as 貫孔, the idea being that a rope, for example, can be passed through the holes to join the timbers.
37. This represents a high official — see Hucker #5713 who uses the term "Commander" for Zhou times.

meal 2 *sheng* will be eaten. On a ration of 2/6 of a *dou* per day, at each meal 1 and 2/3 of a *sheng* will be eaten. Each day there are two meals. At a time of trying to save people from dying, 2 *sheng* are eaten per day for 20 days; 3 *sheng* are eaten per day for 30 days; 4 *sheng* are eaten per day for 40 days. In this way the people can escape from a 90-day period of privation.

71.10   When the enemy approaches, quickly collect from all the outlying districts any metal utensils, either copper or iron, as well as anything else that can be of assistance in defensive matters. First, take note of the dwellings of district officials and non-essential administrative buildings, making an inventory of the sum total of all timbers [in them], large and small, long and short so, when an emergency arises, these are the first to be taken away. When the enemy is right at hand, do away with the houses and cut down the trees. If there are requests [not to do this], do not heed them. In bringing in firewood, do not pile it up irregularly like fish-scales. Have [the piles] facing the road, allowing easy pick-up. If there is wood that cannot be completely brought in, burn it so as not to let the enemy make use of it. With the piles of wood, each must be uniform in terms of length, size, quality and form. [The wood from] outside the four sides of the city should, in each case, be piled up within [that particular side]. In the case of all large pieces of wood, make a hole through them and then pile them up together.

71.11   In defending a city, if those from the rank of Commander (*sima*) up have their parents, brothers, wives and children held as security in the chief's dwelling, then the city can be strongly defended. Appoint *du sikong* — four in the case of a large city — and two *hou* as well as a *xianhou* per side. Have a *tingwei* (post captain) and a deputy *tingwei* for each post. If the officials serving in the Defender's quarters are of sufficient quality [for the task], are incorruptible and trustworthy, and have their parents, brothers, wives and children under protection within the dwelling, then they can serve as officers. There must be a hostage for every officer, then they can be held responsible for affairs. There should be two men to guard the main gates. They should stand on either side of the gates and order those travelling to hasten their exit. Each should have four halberdiers standing on either side of the gates

立，令行者趣其外。各四戟，夾門立，而其人坐其下。吏日五閱之，上逋者名。

Comment: This section considers particularly the importance of holding hostages to ensure that important officials carry out their duties satisfactorily. Little can be said about the official titles. Modern commentators repeat SYR's point that they are, in each case, one of the "Five Offices" (五官). In the second sentence, "per side" is taken to refer to the four sides of the wall. In the third sentence, I have taken 財足 as the quality of the officials — Z&Q have: "其才幹足以任事。" This section corresponds to RDSY/T fragment 130, CZM #71. 12 and WYJ 71, para 8.

71.12 池外廉[38]，有要有害，必為疑人[39]，令往來行夜者射之，謀其疏者。牆外水中，為竹箭，箭尺[40]廣二步，箭下於水五寸，雜長短，前[41]外廉三行，外外鄉，內亦內鄉。三十步一弩廬[42]，廬廣十尺，袤丈二尺。

Comment: In this section, three separate things are described. First, there is the making of dummies or effigies outside the moat to draw enemy fire at night. Second, within the moat, there is the placement of stakes in three rows. Third, there is the provision of structures for crossbows. There is some variation in how these structures are understood. RDSY/T calls them "crossbow platform towers", Z&Q calls them 橐基, whilst LSL calls them 庫房 indicating places of storage. In fact, RDSY/T treats this final sentence as a separate fragment so the section above comprises his fragments 131 and 132. CZM also has this division (his #71.13 and #71.14). WYJ includes both in his 71, para 9 along with the following section (71.13).

---

38. LSL has this note on 廉："《儀禮·鄉飲酒》鄭注：'側邊曰廉'。"
39. YY has the following note on 疑人："蓋束草為人形，望之如人，故曰疑人。"
40. 尺 here is taken as superfluous — see, for example, Z&Q.
41. I have followed Z&Q in reading 前 as 箭.
42. On 弩廬, SYR has this note："弩廬即置連弩車之廬也。"

whilst the other men sit beneath the gates. An officer should inspect them five times a day and report to the superior the names of those not at their posts.

71.12 On the outer side of the moat, at points that are important or vulnerable, effigies must be made to let those going back and forth at night fire at them. Plan the distance between them. In waters that are outside the wall, place bamboo stakes over a width of 2 *bu*, the stakes being under the water a distance of 5 *cun* with a mixture of long and short ones. Stakes at the outer border [of the moat] should be in three rows, with the points of the outer row facing outwards and the points of the inner row facing inwards. Every 30 *bu* have one crossbow platform 10 *chi* wide and 1 *zhang* 2 *chi* long.

71.13 〔百步一隊〕[43]，隊有急，橛發其近者往佐，其次襲其處[44]。

Comment: The issue with this brief section is whether to follow WYJ's proposed transfer of the four characters from the body of what is here the next section to the head of the present section. Both CZM and RDSY/T have this arrangement (#71.15 and fragment 133 respectively), but modern editors such as LSL, MBJ and Z&Q do not. Whilst I have accepted WYJ's transfer, I have also included the fragment in the next section in parentheses. If the fragment is not placed at the start of the present section the meaning remains clear, as in the second sentence above.

71.14 守節出入[45]，使主節必疏書，署其情，令若其事，而須其還報以劍驗之。節出，使所出門者，輒言節出時摻者名。〔百步一隊〕[46]。閣通守舍，相錯穿室[47]。治復道，為築墉[48]，墉善其上[49]。[50]

Comment: As constituted above, and if the 4-character fragment is included, this section has three components. First, there is the use of tallies for messengers and the need to record their comings and goings and the nature of their business. Second, there is the 4-character fragment which certainly does seem out of context as SYR observed. Third, there is the statement about the need for precautions with regard to the Defender's quarters — a confusing passage of entry and a double walled road around them. RDSY/T has this as two separate fragments (134, 135) as does CZM (#71.16, #71.17). Both these commentators take "守節" as a heading. In WYJ the section is 71, paras 10 & 11.

---

43. Transposed from 71.14 below following WYJ — see his note 129, p. 991.
44. SSX has the following gloss on this final clause: "言軍有危急，則發其近者往助之，近者既發，則移其次者居之，以為接應也。" — see also SYR, p. 871.
45. There is some doubt about this opening clause. RDSY/T takes 守節 to be a heading. Z&Q transpose 使 from the following clause as they also do in the next sentence. I have followed this rearrangement.
46. These four characters are transposed to the previous section — see note 43 above.
47. On this clause, Z&Q have: "指旁門相互錯置，生人不易辨認。"
48. 牆 is read for 墉.
49. SYR rearranges this clause as follows: "善蓋其上。"
50. On the 43 characters that occur following 上 in the DZ and their possible rearrangement, see SYR, pp. 871–872.

71.13   Every 100 *bu* have one troop. If a troop has a pressing situation, those in the vicinity should quickly come to its assistance whilst the next in line take over their positions.

71.14   The Defender uses tallies as identification for messengers going out and entering. The officers responsible for tallies must keep a written record. The conditions recorded and the matter being undertaken must correspond. The return of the messenger is awaited to verify this. When a messenger goes out, the gate which he goes through, the time of his exit, and the name of the messenger must immediately be reported. [Every 100 *bu* have one troop.] The doors which give entry to the Defender's quarters are arranged to create a confusing passage. A double road is made around them (i.e. the Defender's quarters), for which walls are made and skilfully covered above.

71.15 取疏[51]，令民家有三年畜蔬食，以備湛旱，歲不為。常令邊縣豫
種畜芫、芸、烏喙、袾葉[52]，外它溝井可填[53]，塞不可，置此其
中。安則示以危，危示以安。

Comment: Both CZM (#71.18) and RDSY/T (fragment 136) take the opening
two characters to be a heading, as in the previous section. There is some
question about the precise meaning of the final nine characters.

71.16 寇至，諸門戶令皆鑿而類竇之，各為二類，一鑿而屬繩，繩長四
尺，大如指。寇至，先殺牛、羊、雞、狗、烏、雁收其皮革、
筋、角、脂、腦[54]、羽。彘[55]皆剝之。使櫃桐栗，為鐵錍，厚
簡為衡枉[56]。事急，卒不可遠，令掘外它林。謀多少，若治城
〔　〕[57]為擊，三隅之。重五斤已上[58]諸林木，渥水中，無過一
茷[59]。塗茅屋若積薪者，厚五寸已上。吏各舉其步界中財物可以
左守備者上。

Comment: This is a very problematic section. The arrangement given is that
found in WYJ, LSL, MBJ and Z&Q, although the first has four separate
paragraphs (his 71, paras 14–17). CZM makes a greater division, having six
separate statements #71.19–24. He also suggests two lacunae where only
one is shown in the text above. RDSY/T also has six fragments (his fragments
137–142) despite omitting what, in the text above, is the first sentence. The
result of all this is a translation which must remain very tentative.

---

51. There is general agreement that 疏 should read 蔬 as in the following clause.
52. See RDSY/T, notes 92–96, p. 592 for speculation on the exact nature of these plants. The
    point is that they are all poisonous.
53. There is general acceptance of 填 here for the rare character ZWDCD #26179.
54. This is the generally accepted emendation of the unknown graph normally found here
    — see, for example, SYR.
55. 彘 is taken to belong to the preceding list of animals and birds.
56. There are several issues in this sentence: (i) The emendations in the first clause follow
    SYR and CZM. (ii) 錍 is a kind of short axe. (iii) 厚 is read as 后 (SYR). (iv) 簡 is read
    as 蘭/闌 (SYR). (v) 枉 is read as 柱.
57. SYR suggests 上 for this lacuna.
58. There is a question as to whether the preceding eight characters are misplaced and should
    follow 錍 (CZM). In any event, it is agreed that 已 should be read as 以.
59. See RDSY/T, note 120, p. 599 on this term.

71.15   With regard to gathering vegetables, order the people and their families to have a three-year supply of vegetable and grain foods to prepare against flood or drought, or a bad harvest. Regularly order the border districts to prepare and cultivate the leaves of the *yuan, yun, wuhui* and *zhu*. In the case of houses outside [the walls], fill in the watercourses and wells that can be filled. Place these plants in those that can't be filled in. In times of peace, give thought to danger. In times of danger, give thought to peace.[iv]

71.16   When the enemy comes, give an order that, for all the leaves of the gates, holes are to be drilled and provided with covers. Each gate should have two holes. Through one of the holes pass a continuous rope 4 *chi* long and the thickness of a finger. When the enemy comes, first kill the oxen, sheep, chickens, dogs, ducks, geese, and pigs. Flay them all, taking their skins, hides, muscle, horns, fat, brains and feathers. Use catalpa, *tong* and chestnut wood and cut it with a short axe to make a stand for crossbow bolts.[v] When matters are pressing and the soldiers cannot go far, give an order to dig up the trees associated with houses outside [the wall] and determine their number. If the wall is in good repair, make a tower of a three-cornered shape. All timber that is heavier than 5 *jin* is immersed in water, but not more than 1 "raft" (*fa*). Cover thatched houses and piles of firewood with mud to a thickness of 5 *cun* or more. Each officer is to make known what material there is in his area and to assist his superior in preparing the defence.

---

iv.   It is unclear whether this last statement should be placed here and, indeed, what is meant exactly.

v.   The translation of this sentence is very tentative, involving several emendations and interpretations in which I have largely followed LSL (note 5, p. 571).

71.17 有讒人、有利人、有惡人、有善人、有長⁶⁰人、有謀士、有勇
士、有巧士、有使⁶¹士、有內人者、外人者⁶²、有善人者、有善
門⁶³人者。守必察其所以然者、應名乃內之。民相惡、若議吏、
吏所解、皆札書藏之、以須告之至以參驗之。睨者⁶⁴小五尺、不
可卒者、為署吏、令給事官府若舍。

Comment: There is also variation in arrangement of this section although,
apart from CZM's version, it forms a continuous sequence. What he does is to
divide it into three (#71.25–27) but ends #71.25 at "應名乃內之" where he
adds what above is 71.6. This does certainly seem in context here. RDSY/T
also subdivides the section (his fragments 143–145) but does not make the
addition. WYJ has this section as a single paragraph (71, para 18). There are
some uncertainties about the exact descriptions of the people listed. RDSY/T
takes "internal" and "external" to refer to messengers.

71.18 藺石⁶⁵、厲矢、諸材器用、皆謹部、各有積分數。為解⁶⁶車以
梓⁶⁷、城⁶⁸矣以軺車、輪軹⁶⁹、廣十尺、轅長丈、為三輻⁷⁰、廣六
尺。為板箱長與轅等高四尺、善蓋上治中令可載矢。

Comment: This short section deals with two quite different things. First, the
need to stockpile certain items in designated amounts, and, second, the
construction of open-sided, horse-drawn carts for carrying arrows (that is, if
SSX's emendation is accepted). Both RDSY/T and CZM treat these
descriptions separately, the former in fragments 146 and 147 and the latter in
#71.28 and #71.29. WYJ combines them in the penultimate paragraph of
chapter 71 (para 19).

---

60. I have followed YTY in reading 長 as 技.
61. There is wide acceptance of SYR's reading of 信 for 使.
62. YTY's comments on "內人" and "外人" are, respectively, "長於內政" and "優於外
    交".
63. I have followed SSX in reading 門 as 鬥.
64. Most accept SSX's reading of 睨者 as 兒童.
65. Following LSL, I have taken this as 藺石. Others (e.g. Z&Q, RDSY/T) read it as 礌石
    indicating a particular kind of stone which the latter calls "thunder stones".
66. There is general acceptance of SSX's suggestion that 解 should read 輗.
67. This is SYR's emendation of the rare character (ZWDCD #14987) which is found here.
68. I have followed CZM and others in reading 城 as 盛.
69. There is considerable uncertainty about this character (ZWDCD #39102) — see,
    particularly, RDSY/T, note 143, p. 609. His suggestion is 軹 as above.
70. I have followed CZM and RDSY/T in reading 輻 as 幅.

71.17 There are slanderous men and there are men who are beneficial. There are bad men and there are good men. There are skilled men and there are strategists. There are brave knights, there are clever knights and there are trustworthy knights. There are those who are "internal" and there are those who are "external". There are those who are skilled and those who are skilled in fighting. The Defender must examine what the case is for each man, give him the proper name, and then include him. When people detest each other, or are critical of an officer, the officer must resolve the dispute and record [the result] on wooden tablets which are stored to await a time when the matter can be laid open for consideration and verification.[vi] Youths who are shorter than 5 *chi* cannot be soldiers. Make them *zhili* and order them to perform duties in official buildings or barracks.

71.18 Piles of stones, sharp arrows, and the various materials and utensils that are used are carefully placed, each having its piles and allotted amounts. Make *yao* carts (open-sided carts) of catalpa wood and fill them with arrows. The solid wheels should be 10 *chi* wide and have a shaft of 1 *zhang*. Make three cloth coverings, [each] 6 *chi* wide. Make a wooden planked box the same length as the shaft and 4 *chi* high. Cover the top skilfully and arrange the interior to let it carry arrows.

---

vi. The rather free translation of this sentence follows Z&Q's reading of 須 as 等待 and 告 as 揭發 — see their modern language version on p. 965.

71.19   子墨子曰：「凡不守者有五：城大人少，一不守也；城小人眾，
二不守也；人眾食寡，三不守也；市去城遠，四不守也；畜[71] 積
在外，富人在虛[72]，五不守也。率萬家而城方三里。」

Comment: There is some variation in exactly how these five situations are
understood — as situations that are not readily defended (MBJ), as situations
that can't be defended (CZM, LSL, Z&Q), as situations that are not defended
(RDSY/T), or as grounds for not mounting a defence (AF). Of course, all
ultimately come down to the same thing. They are bad circumstances for
mounting a defence.

---

71. Read as 蓄 (LSL, RDSY/T).
72. There is general acceptance of SSX's reading of 虛 as 墟 which Z&Q equate with 村
落, writing: "此指富人在外，不在城邑。"

71.19   Master Mo Zi said: "In general, there are five situations that can't be defended. A large city with few people is the first. A small city with many people is the second. Many people but few provisions is the third. Markets being distant from the city is the fourth. Stores piled outside the city and rich men not in the city is the fifth. If there are approximately ten thousand families and the city is 3 *li* square [then it can be defended]."[vii]

---

vii.   This is Z&Q's proposal for a possible lacuna. The meaning may, however, just be that a city of ten thousand families should be 3 *li* square (e.g. LSL). CZM takes this last sentence as a later gloss.

Bibliography

The following bibliography is limited to works consulted in the preparation of the translation or cited in those consulted. For additional material, Yan Lingfeng's 1975 compilation (the *Mozi Jicheng*, MZJC) contains 91 titles on the *Mozi* and Mohism to that date whilst Qin Yanshi (2002), pp. 316–368 provides a comprehensive and up-to-date bibliography of Chinese writings on these topics. A comparable bibliography of Western writings on the subjects of Mohism and the School of Names (Mingjia) is given in Vittinghoff (2001), pp. 160–172.

I. Works in Chinese

Beijing Daxue *Xunzi* Zhushi Zu 北京大學《荀子》注釋組. *Xunzi Xinzhu* 荀子新注. Beijing: Zhonghua shuju, 1979.

Bi Yuan 畢沅. *Mozi Zhu* 墨子注. 1783, reprinted in MZJC 7 & 8.

Cao Yaoxiang 曹耀湘. *Mozi Jian* 墨子箋. Reprinted in MZJC 17.

Cen Zhongmian 岑仲勉. *Mozi Chengshou Gepian Jianzhu* 墨子城守各篇簡注. Beijing, 1958, reprinted in MZJC 45.

CHANT: Chinese Ancient Texts Database, CD-ROM. Hong Kong: Commercial Press, 2003.

Fan Gengyan 范耕研. *Mobian Shuzheng* 墨辯疏證. Beijing, 1934, reprinted in MZJC 28.

Fang Shouchu 方授楚. *Moxue Yuanliu* 墨學源流. Taiwan, 1957, reprinted in MZJC 39.

Fu Shan 傅山. *Mozi Daqupian Shi* 墨子大取篇釋. Reprinted in MZJC 6.

Fu Wuguang 傅武光 and Lai Yanyuan 賴炎元, trans. *Xinyi Han Feizi* 新譯韓非子. Taipei: Sanmin shuju, 1997.

Gao Heng 高亨. *Mojing Jiaoquan* 墨經校詮. Beijing, 1958, reprinted in MZJC 41.

———. *Mozi Xinjian* 墨子新箋. Reprinted in MZJC 41.

Guo Qingfan 郭慶藩. *Zhuangzi Jishi* 莊子集釋, 4 vols. Beijing: Zhonghua shuju, 1961.

Hanyu Da Cidian 漢語大辭典, 22 vols. Shanghai: Hanyu da cidian chubanshe, 2001.

Hong Yixuan 洪頤烜. *Mozi Conglu* 墨子叢錄. Reprinted in MZJC 9.

Hong Zhenhuan 洪震寰. "Mojing guangxue batiao lishuo" 墨經光學八條釐説. *Kexue shi jikan* 科學史集刊 4 (1962): 1–40.

———. "Mojing lixue zongshu" 墨經力學綜述. *Kexue shi jikan* 7 (1963): 28–44.

Hu Shi 胡適. *Mozi Xiaoqupian Xingu* 墨子小取篇新詁. Reprinted in MZJC 21.

Jiang Baochang 姜寶昌. *Mojing Xunshi* 墨經訓釋. Jinan: Qilu shushe, 1993.

Li Shenglong 李生龍. *Xinyi Mozi Duben* 新譯墨子讀本. Taipei: Sanmin shuju, 1996.

Li Yushu 李漁叔. *Mozi Jinzhu Jinyi* 墨子今註今譯. Taipei: Taiwan Shangwu yinshuguan, 1974.

Liang Qichao 梁啟超. *Mozi Xue'an* 墨子學案. Shanghai: Shangwu yinshuguan, 1921, reprinted in MZJC 18.

———. *Mojing Jiaoshi* 墨經校釋. Shanghai: Shangwu yinshuguan, 1922, reprinted in MZJC 19.

Liang Qixiong 梁啟雄. *Xunzi Jianshi* 荀子簡釋. Beijing: Zhonghua shuju, 1983.

Liu Chang 劉昶. *Xu Mozi Jiangu* 續墨子閒詁. Reprinted in MZJC 30.

Liu Cunren 柳存仁. "A New Interpretation of the Canon of the Moists (Parts I & II)." *New Asia Journal* (新亞學報), 6 (1964): 45–140 & 7 (1965): 1–134.

Luan Diaofu 欒調甫. *Mozi Yanjiu Lunwenji* 墨子研究論文集. Beijing, 1958, reprinted in MZJC 33.

Ma Zonghuo 馬宗霍. *Mozi Jiangu Canzheng* 墨子閒詁參正. Jinan: Qilu shushe, 1984.

Mo Di 墨翟. *Mozi* 墨子. *Dao Zang* 道藏 edition (1445), reprinted in MZJC 1; Tang 唐 edition (1553), reprinted in MZJC 2; Mao Kun 茅坤 edition (1581), reprinted in MZJC 3; Hōyaku edition (1757), reprinted in MZJC 4.

Mou Zongsan 牟宗三. *Mingjia yu Xunzi* 名家與荀子. Taipei: Taiwan xuesheng shuju, 1994.

Qian Mu 錢穆. *Mozi* 墨子. Shanghai: Shangwu yinshuguan, 1931.

Qin Yanshi 秦彥士. *Mozi Kaolun* 墨子考論. Chengdu: Bashu shushe, 2002.

Su Shixue 蘇時學. *Mozi Kanwu* 墨子刊誤. Zhonghua shuju, 1928, reprinted in MZJC 10.

Sun Yirang 孫詒讓. *Mozi Jiangu* 墨子閒詁. 1894, reprinted in MZJC 12–15.

Sun Zhongyuan 孫中原. *Moxue yu Xiandai Wenhua* 墨學與現代文化. Beijing: Zhongguo guangbo dianshi chubanshe, 1998.

——— ed. *Moxue yu Xinkeji Dianfan Tansuo* 墨學與新科技典範探索. *Zhexue Zazhi* 哲學雜誌 28 (1999), Taipei.

Tan Jiefu 譚戒甫. *Mojing Yijie* 墨經易解. Shanghai, 1935, reprinted in MZJC 34.

———. *Mobian Fawei* 墨辯發微. Beijing, 1964, reprinted in MZJC 35.

———. *Mojing Fenlei Yizhu* 墨經分類譯注. Beijing: Zhonghua shuju, 1981.

Tan Yuquan 譚宇權. *Mozi Sixiang Pinglun* 墨子思想評論. Taipei: Wenjin chubanshe, 1991.

Tang Junyi 唐君毅. "An Interpretation of 'Argument' (*pien*) in the 'Hsiao Ch'u' Chapter of the *Mo-tzu*." *New Asia Journal* (新亞學報) 4/2 (1960): 65–99.

Tang Xiaochun 湯孝純. *Xinyi Guanzi Duben* 新譯管子讀本 (2 vols.). Taibei: Sanmin Shuju, 1995.

Tao Hongqing 陶鴻慶. *Du Mozi Zhaji* 讀墨子札記. Peking, 1919, reprinted in MZJC 10.

Wang Huanbiao 王煥鑣. *Mozi Jiaoshi* 墨子校釋. Hangzhou: Zhejiang guji chubanshe, 1984.

———. *Mozi Jigu* 墨子集詁, 2 vols. Shanghai: Shanghai guji chubanshe, 2005.

Wang Kaiyun 王闓運. *Mozi Zhu* 墨子注. Reprinted in MZJC 16.

Wang Niansun 王念孫. *Mozi Zazhi* 墨子雜志. Reprinted in MZJC 9.

Wang Shunan 王樹枏. *Mozi Jiaozhu Buzheng* 墨子斠注補正. 1887, reprinted in MZJC 11.

Wang Yinzhi 王引之. *Jingyi Shuwen* 經義述聞. Shanghai, 1936 (SBBY 401–414).

———. *Jingzhuan Shici* 經傳釋詞. Taipei, 1968.

Wu Feibai 伍非百. *Zhongguo Gumingjia Yan* 中國古名家言. Beijing: Zhongguo shehui kexue chubanshe, 1983.

Wu Longhui 吳龍輝 et al. *Mozi Baihua Jinyi* 墨子白話今譯. Beijing: Zhongguo shudian, 1992.

Wu Rulun 吳汝綸. *Diankan Mozi Duben* 點勘墨子讀本. Reprinted in MZJC 11.

Wu Yujiang 吳毓江. *Mozi Jiaozhu* 墨子校注, 2 vols. Beijing, Zhonghua shuju, 1993 reprint.

Xiong Lihui 熊禮匯. *Xinyi Huainanzi* 新譯淮南子. Taipei: Sanmin shuju, 1997.

Xu Xiyan 徐希燕. *Moxue Yanjiu* 墨學研究. Beijing: Shangwu yinshuguan, 2001.

Yan Chongxin 閻崇信. *Mozi Daqupian Jiaoshi* 墨子大取篇校釋. Taipei: Wenshizhe chubanshe, 1983.

———. *Mozi Feirupian Huikao* 墨子非儒篇彙考. Taipei: Wenshizhe chubanshe, 1983.

Yan Lingfeng 嚴靈峰. *Wuqiubeizhai Mozi Jicheng* 無求備齋墨子集成, 46 vols. Taipei: Chengwen chubanshe, 1975.

Yang Baoyi 楊葆彝. *Mozi Jingshuo Jiaozhu* 墨子經説校注. Cited by Jiang Baochang, 1993.

Yin Tongyang 尹桐陽. *Mozi Xinshi* 墨子新釋. Reprinted in MZJC 20.

Yu Yue 俞樾. *Mozi Pingyi* 墨子平議. Reprinted in MZJC 10.

Zhang Chunyi 張純一. *Mozi Jijie* 墨子集解. 1936, reprinted in MZJC 23–26.

Zhang Huiyan 張惠言. *Mozi Jingshuo Jie* 墨子經説解. 1909, reprinted in MZJC 9.

Zhang Qihuang 張其鍠. *Mozi Tongjie* 墨子通解. Taipei, 1960, reprinted in MZJC 29.

Zhang Zhirui 張之銳. *Xin Kaozheng Mojing Zhu* 新考正墨經注. Cited by Li Shenglong, 1996.

Zhongwen Da Cidian 中文大辭典. Taipei: Zhonghua Xueshuyuan, 1973.

Zhou Caizhu 周才珠 and Qi Ruiduan 齊瑞端. *Mozi Quanyi* 墨子全譯. Guiyang: Guizhou renmin chubanshe, 1995.

———. *Mozi* 墨子. Taipei: Guji Publishing Co., 1998.

Zhou Yunzhi 周云之. *Mingbian Xuelun* 名辯學論. Shenyang: Liaoning jiaoyu chubanshe, 1995.

Zhuang Wanshou 莊萬壽. *Xinyi Liezi Duben* 新譯列子讀本. Taipei: Sanmin shuju, 1996.

II. Works in Other Languages

Ahern, Dennis M. "Is Mo Tzu a Utilitarian?" *Chinese Studies in Philosophy* 3 (1976): 185–194.

Ames, Roger T. *Sun-Tzu: The Art of Warfare*. New York: Ballantine Books, 1993.

Birdwhistell, Anne D. "An Approach to Verification Beyond Tradition in Early Chinese Philosophy: Mo Tzu's Concept of Sampling in a Community of Observers." *Philosophy East and West* 34 (1984): 175–183.

Chan, Wing-tsit. *A Source Book in Chinese Philosophy*. Princeton, 1963.

Chang, Li-wen. "A Short Comment on Mo-Tzu's Epistemology Based on 'Three Criteria'." *Chinese Studies in Philosophy* 10 (1979): 47–54.

Chao, Yuan Ren. "Notes on Chinese Grammar and Logic." *Philosophy East and West* 5 (1955): 31–41.

Chmielewski, Janusz. "Notes on Early Chinese Logic." *Rocznik Orientalistyczny*, 8 articles as follows: Part I, 26 (1962): 7–22; Part II, 26 (1963): 91–105; Part III, 27 (1963): 103–121; Part IV, 28 (1965): 87–111; Part V, 29 (1965): 117–138; Part VI, 30 (1966): 31–52; Part VII, 31 (1968): 117–136; Part VIII, 32 (1969): 83–103.

Chong, Chaehyun. "Moism: Despotic or Democratic?" *Journal of Chinese Philosophy* 35 (2008): 511–522.

———. "The Neo-Mohist Conception of *Bian* (Disputation)." *Journal of Chinese Philosophy* 26 (1999): 1–20.

Cook, Scott B. "The *Lü Shi Chunqiu* and the Resolution of Philosophical Dissonance." *Harvard Journal of Asiatic Studies* 62 (2002): 307–345.

Corswant, Willy. "Le philosophe chinois Me Ti et sa doctrine de l'amour mutuel." *Revue de Theologie et de Philosophie* 34.140 (1946): 97–124.

David-Neel, Alexandra. *Socialisme chinoise. Le philosophe Meh-ti et l'idée de solidarité*. Paris, 1907.

Defoort, Carine. "Caring for Whom? Moral Discussions between Early Confucians and Mohists." *Tijdschrift voor Filosofie* 57 (1995): 36–50.

Ding, Weixiang. "Mengzi's 孟子 Inheritance, Criticism, and Overcoming of Moist Thought." *Journal of Chinese Philosophy* 35 (2008): 403–420.

Duda, Kristopher. "Reconsidering Mo Tzu on the Foundations of Morality." *Asian Philosophy* 11 (2001): 23–31.

Durrant, Stephen W. "An Examination of Textual and Grammatical Problems in *Mo Tzu.*" Ph.D. diss., University of Washington, 1975.

———. "The Taoist Apotheosis of Mo Ti." *Journal of the American Oriental Society* 97 (1977): 540–545.

———. "A Consideration of Differences in the Grammar of the Mo tzu 'Essays' and 'Dialogues'." *Monumenta Serica* 33 (1977–1978): 248–267.

Faber, Ernst. *Die Grundgedanken des alten chinesischen Socialismus, oder die Lehre des Philosophen Micius, zum ersten Male vollständig aus den Quellen dargelegt.* Elberfeld, 1877.

Flanagan, Owen. "Moral Contagion and Logical Persuasion in the *Mozi* 墨子." *Journal of Chinese Philosophy* 35 (2008): 473–492.

Forke, Alfred. *Me Ti des Sozialethikers und seiner Schüler philosophische Werke.* Berlin, 1922.

Fraser, Chris. "Mohism." *The Stanford Encyclopedia of Philosophy (Winter 2002 Edition),* edited by Edward N. Zalta, URL=http://plato.stanford.edu/archives/win2002/entries/mohism/

———. "Moism and Self-Interest." *Journal of Chinese Philosophy* 35 (2008): 437–454.

Fung, Yu-lan. *History of Chinese Philosophy,* vol. 1. Translated by Derk Bodde. Princeton, 1952.

Geaney, Jane M. "A Critique of A. C. Graham's Reconstruction of the Neo-Mohist Canons." *Journal of the American Oriental Society* 119 (1999): 1–11.

Geisser, Franz. *Mo Ti: der Künder der allgemeinen Menschenliebe.* Berne, 1947.

Giles, Herbert A. *A Chinese Biographical Dictionary.* London: Bernard Quaritch; Shanghai: Kelly & Walsh, 1898.

Goodrich, L. Carrington and Chaoyang Fang, eds. *Dictionary of Ming Biography* 1368–1644, 2 vols. New York: Columbia University Press, 1976.

Graham, Angus C. "The Logic of the Mohist Hsiao-ch'ü." *T'oung Pao* 51 (1964): 1–54.

———. "Later Mohist Treatises on Ethics and Logic Reconstructed from the *Ta-ch'ü* Chapter of *Mo-tzu.*" *Asia Major* NS 17 (1972): 137–189.

———. *Later Mohist Logic Ethics and Science.* Hong Kong: The Chinese University Press, 1978.

———. *Divisions in Early Mohism Reflected in the Core Chapters of Motzu.*

Singapore, 1985.

———. *Disputers of the Tao.* La Salle, Illinois: Open Court, 1989.

———, and Nathan Sivin. "A Systematic Approach to the Mohist Optics (ca. 300BC)." In *Chinese Science, Exploration of an Ancient Tradition,* edited by Shigeru Nakayama and Nathan Sivin. Cambridge, Mass: MIT, 1973.

Hansen, Chad D. "Mo-Tzu: Language Utilitarianism." *Journal of Chinese Philosophy* 16 (1989): 355–380.

———. *A Daoist Theory of Chinese Thought: A Philosophical Interpretation.* New York: Oxford University Press, 1992.

Harbsmeier, Christoph. *Science and Civilisation in China* VII.1 (Language and Logic). Cambridge: Cambridge University Press, 1998.

Hsiao, Kung-chuan. *A History of Chinese Political Thought,* vol. 1. Translated by F. W. Mote. Princeton: Princeton University Press, 1979.

Hu, Shi. *The Development of the Logical Method in Ancient China.* New York, 1963 reprint.

Hummel, Arthur W., ed. *Eminent Chinese of the Ch'ing Period.* Washington, DC: Government Printing Office, 1943–1944.

Ivanhoe, Philip J. *Mozi.* In *Readings in Classical Chinese Philosophy,* edited by Bryan W. Van Norden and Philip J. Ivanhoe (pp. 55–110). New York: Seven Bridges Press, 2001.

Jenner, Donald. "Mo Tzu and Hobbes. Preliminary Remarks on the Relation of Chinese and Western Politics." *Bulletin of the School for Oriental and African Studies* 45 (1982): 501–524.

Jochim, Christian. "Ethical Analysis of an Ancient Debate: Moists versus Confucians." *Journal of Religious Ethics* 8 (1980): 135–147.

Johnston, Ian. "Choosing the Greater and Choosing the Lesser: A Translation and Analysis of the *Daqu* and *Xiaoqu* Chapters of the *Mozi.*" *Journal of Chinese Philosophy* 27 (2000): 375–407.

———. "The *Gongsun Longzi*: A Translation and an Analysis of Its Relationship to Later Mohist Writings." *Journal of Chinese Philosophy* 31 (2004): 271–295.

Knoblock, John. *Xunzi: A Translation and Study of the Complete Works,* 3 vols. Stanford: Stanford University Press, 1988–1994.

———, and Jeffrey K. Riegel. *The Annals of Lü Buwei.* Stanford: Stanford University Press, 2000.

Lai, Whalen W. "The Public Good That Does the Public Good: A New Reading of Mohism." *Asian Philosophy* 3 (1993): 147–160.

Lau, D. C. "Some Logical Problems in Ancient China." *Proceedings of the Aristotelian Society* 53 (1953): 189–204.

———. *Lao Tzu Tao Te Ching.* London: Penguin Books, 1963.

————. *Mencius*. London: Penguin Books, 1970.

————. *Mencius: A Bilingual Edition*. Hong Kong: The Chinese University Press, 2003.

Legge, James. *The Chinese Classics*, 5 vols. Hong Kong: Hong Kong University Press, 1960 reprint.

Leys, Simon. *The Analects of Confucius*. New York: W.W. Norton & Co., 1993.

Liao, W. K. *The Complete Works of Han Fei Tzu*, 2 vols. London: Arthur Probsthain, 1939 (vol. 1), 1959 (vol. 2).

Lowe, Scott. *Mo Tzu's Religious Blueprint for a Chinese Utopia*. Lewiston, NY: The Edwin Mellen Press, 1992.

Loy, Hui-Chieh. "Justification and Debate: Thoughts on Moist Moral Epistemology." *Journal of Chinese Philosophy* 35 (2008): 455–472.

Lucas, Thierry. "Later Mohist Logic, *Lei*, Classes and Sorts." *Journal of Chinese Philosophy* 32 (2005): 349–365.

Ly, Cyrus Y. C. "The Socio-Educational Thoughts of Motse." *Revue de l'Universite d'Ottowa* 33 (1963): 325–336.

Maeder, Erik W. "Some Observations on the Composition of the 'Core Chapters' of the *Mozi*." *Early China* 17 (1992): 27–82.

Maspero, Henri. "Notes sur la logique de Mo-tseu et de son école." *T'oung Pao* 25 (1928): 1–64.

Mei, Yipao. *The Ethical and Political Works of Motse*. London: Probsthain, 1929 (Hyperion reprint, 1993).

————. *Motse, The Neglected Rival of Confucius*. London: Probsthain, 1934 (Hyperion reprint, 1973).

Moritz, Ralf. "Die Ideologie des frühen Mohismus im alten China — das Ideal der allgemeinen Liebe." *Das Altertum* 3 (1988): 177–183.

Needham, Joseph and Robin D. S. Yates, eds. *Science and Civilisation in China*, vol. V:6 *Military Technology: Missiles and Sieges*. Cambridge: Cambridge University Press, 1994.

Perkins, Franklin. "Reconsidering the *Mozi* 墨子." *Journal of Chinese Philosophy* 35 (2008): 379–384.

————. "The Moist Criticism of the Confucian Use of Fate." *Journal of Chinese Philosophy* 35 (2008): 421–436.

Ralph, Philip L. "Mo Ti and English Utilitarians." *Far Eastern Quarterly* 9 (1949): 42–62.

Rickett, W. Allyn. *Kuan-tzu*. Hong Kong: Hong Kong University Press, 1965.

Rickett, W. Allyn. *Guanzi*, vol. 2. Princeton: Princeton University Press, 1998.

Robins, Dan. "The Moists and the Gentlemen of the World." *Journal of Chinese Philosophy* 35 (2008): 385–402.

Schmidt-Glintzer, Helwig. *Mo Ti — Schriften,* 2Bde. Dusseldorf/Köln, 1975.

Schwartz, Benjamin I. *The World of Thought in Ancient China.* Cambridge, MA: Harvard University Press, 1985.

Shun, Kwong-Loi. "Mencius' Criticism of Mohism: An Analysis of Meng Tzu 3A: 5." *Philosophy East and West* 41 (1991): 203–214.

Soles, David E. "Mo Tzu and the Foundations of Morality." *Journal of Chinese Philosophy* 26 (1999): 37–48.

Taylor, Rodney L. "Religion and Utilitarianism: Mo Tzu on Spirits and Funerals." *Philosophy East and West* 29 (1979): 337–346.

Tseu, Augustinus A. *The Moral Philosophy of Mo-tze.* Taipei, 1965.

Vittinghoff, Helmolt. "Recent Bibliography in Classical Chinese Philosophy." *Journal of Chinese Philosophy* 28 (2001): 160–164.

Vorenkamp, Dirck. "Strong Utilitarianism in Mo Tzu's Thought." *Journal of Chinese Philosophy* 19 (1992): 423–444.

Watson, Burton. *Mo Tzu. Basic Writings.* New York: Columbia University Press, 1963.

———. *Chuang Tzu.* New York: Columbia University Press, 1968.

Williamson, Henry R. *Mo Ti, A Chinese Heretic. A Short Sketch of His Life and Works.* Tsinan, 1927.

Winance, Eleuthère. "A Forgotten Chinese Thinker: Mo Tzu." *International Philosophical Quarterly* 1 (1961): 593–613.

Wong, Benjamin and Hui-chieh Loy. "War and Ghosts in *Mozi.*" *Philosophy East and West* 54 (2004): 343–364.

Wong, David B. "Universalism versus Love with Distinctions: An Ancient Debate Revived." *Journal of Chinese Philosophy* 16 (1989): 251–272.

Yates, Robin D. S. "The Mohists on Warfare: Technology, Technique, and Justification." *Journal of the American Academy of Religion* 47 (1979), no. 35, Thematic Issue: 549–603.

———. *The City under Siege: Technology and Organization as Seen in the Reconstructed Text of the Military Chapters of the Mo Tzu.* Ph.D. diss., Harvard University, 1980.

———. "New Light on Ancient Chinese Military Texts: Notes on Their Nature and Evolution and the Development of Military Specialization in Warring States China." *T'oung Pao* 74 (1988): 211–248.

———. "Early Poliorcetics: The Mohists to the Sung." In *Science and Civilisation in China,* vol. V:6, *Military Technology: Missiles and Sieges,* edited by Joseph Needham and Robin D. S. Yates. Cambridge: Cambridge University Press, 1994.

Zong, Desheng. "Studies of Intensional Contexts in Mohist Writings." *Philosophy East and West* 50 (2000): 208–228.

Personal Names Index

Places, Subjects & Writings Index